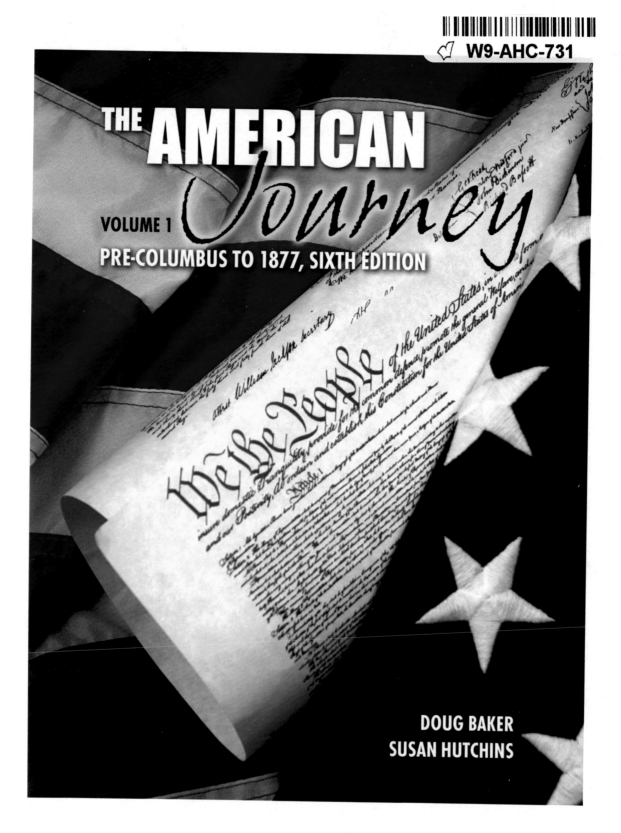

THE AMERICAN Journey

VOLUME 1

PRE-COLUMBUS TO 1877, SIXTH EDITION

DOUG BAKER
SUSAN HUTCHINS

rainmaker
education

Cover image © istockphoto.com

Images from clipart.com unless otherwise noted.

Send all inquiries to:
Rainmaker Education
College Division
PO Box 141
Oregon, WI 53575

ISBN 978-1935801-221

Printed in the United States of America
10 9 8 7 6 5 4 3 2 1

TABLE OF CONTENTS

Chapter 5

The Road to Revolution 82

The Winds of Change • The American Mindset • Indian Trouble • The Sugar and Currency Acts • The Stamp Act Crisis • The Townshend Duties Crisis • Trouble in Boston • Committees of Correspondence • The Gaspee Affair • The Tea Act • The Boston Tea Party • The Coercive or Intolerable Acts • The First Continental Congress • Breakdown of Government and the Failure of Compromise

Chapter 6

The American Revolution 102

Lexington and Concord • Second Continental Congress • Early Fighting in the War • Declaration of Independence • American Public Opinion • African-Americans and the Revolution • 1776-1777: The War in New York and New Jersey • The War in 1777 • Alliance with France • 1778-1780: The War in the South • The Treason of Benedict Arnold • The War at Sea • The War in the West • More Fighting in the Carolinas • Battle of Yorktown • Treaty of Paris • 1783 • Why the Americans Won their Independence • Nature of the American Revolution

Chapter 7

Launching the American Republic 124

The Continental Congress Serves as a Government • Colonies Became States • The First Federal Government • Articles of Confederation • The Dissatisfied • Disgruntled Soldiers March on Congress • The Fate of the Loyalists • A Republican Society • The Role of Women • Religion and the Founding Fathers • Settlement of the Northwest Territory • Crises Expose the Deficiencies of the National Government • Shays' Rebellion • The States Look for Solutions • The Constitutional Convention • The Ratification Debate • Election of George Washington

Chapter 8

Establishing a New Federal Pathway 144

Priorities for the New Government • Hamilton Establishes a Solid Economic Foundation • Jefferson-Hamilton Split Forms the First Political Parties • Securing the Northwest Territory • The Reelection of President Washington • Whiskey Rebellion • Foreign Policy • Washington's Farewell Address • Legacy of George Washington • The 1796 Presidential Election • Relations with France • Alien and Sedition Acts • Another Tax Rebellion • The 1800 Presidential Election

Chapter 9

Politics and War Under the Jeffersonians 164

A Judicial War • The Tripolitan War • The Louisiana Purchase • The Essex Junto and Aaron Burr • The 1804 Presidential Election • The War of 1812 • Declaring War • Preparing to Fight • The Attack on Canada: 1812 • Frigates and Victories at Sea: 1812 • Madison Wins Reelection • At Sea: 1813 and 1814 • Regaining the Northwest: 1813 • 1814 • The Creek War • The Hartford Convention • Battle of New Orleans • Treaty of Ghent • Results of the War

Chapter 15

Countdown to Civil War 274

Popular Sovereignty • The 1848 Presidential Election • The Compromise of 1850 • The Fugitive Slave Law: 1850 • Anti-Slavery Literature Fuels the Fire • The 1852 Presidential Election • Foreign Policy • The Kansas-Nebraska Act • Political Realignment • Early Developments in Kansas • "Bleeding Kansas" • The 1856 Presidential Election • The Dred Scott Case • The Panic of 1857 • The Lecompton Constitution • Harper's Ferry • The Rise of Abraham Lincoln • The 1860 Presidential Election • Southern Post-Election Viewpoints • Secession Begins • Formation of the Confederacy • The Failure of Compromise • The Battle Lines are Drawn

Chapter 16

The Civil War 302

Causes of the Civil War • North and South Compared • Organization of the Union Army • Draft Riots • Organization of the Confederate Army • Army Desertions • Women in the Civil War • POW Camps • The Home Front • Northern Opposition to the War • Southern Opposition to the War • Financing the War • Legal Approaches to Abolishing Slavery • War Diplomacy • General War Strategies • The First Battle of Bull Run • 1862: War in the East • 1862: War in the West • 1863: War in the East • 1863: War in the West • The War in 1864 • The War in 1865 • The Legacy of the Civil War

Chapter 17

Reconstruction: 1865-1877 334

President Lincoln's Plan • Andrew Johnson Becomes President • President Johnson's Reconstruction Plan • Congressional Reconstruction Policies • The 1866 Congressional Elections • Congressional Political Reconstruction • Andrew Johnson's Impeachment • Life in the South • Government in the Southern States • The Klu Klux Klan • The Supreme Court and Reconstruction • An Assessment of Reconstruction: Historians Debate the Times and the Legacies • The End of Reconstruction

FOREWORD

When I had the pleasure of teaching Doug Baker and Susan Hutchins, I knew they would go on to make important contributions to teaching and to the history profession. With the publication of this text, they have done just that. It is a clear presentation of the elements of American history from Reconstruction to the present.

While purposely listening to their students' cry for a no-nonsense presentation of the basics of American history this book is mostly pre-1865, they have not sacrificed interest. Indeed, by concentrating on the "why" of important events, they have provided a most interesting account that will both challenge and intrigue students.

In bemoaning the fact that students possess little knowledge of American history, Diane Ravitch has quoted a college professor who put the problem this way: "They have no furniture in their minds. You can assume nothing in the way of prior knowledge. Skills, yes, but not knowledge." Baker and Hutchins have provided students with the furniture in this text, and they have arranged it in an appealing setting.

James F. Baker, Ph.D.
Chair, Department of History/Geography
University of Central Oklahoma
Edmond, Oklahoma

PREFACE

Before beginning the task of actually organizing a textbook, we asked ourselves why colleges and universities needed another American history textbook. As teachers—and former students ourselves, of course—we have reviewed many textbooks and not found one that we were completely satisfied with. This is not to say that there are not many good textbooks on the market, but we felt that we could write a book that would more closely meet the needs of our students. We wanted a book that was more "student-friendly." We disliked the organization of many of the texts we had used, and there seemed to be too many questions left unanswered by most of them. It is true that the very nature of a survey course, which covers such a vast amount of material, demands that much detailed information be left out. It is also true that not everything that has happened through the years of our nation's existence since the Civil War is covered in this book. But we have tried to cover most events for a true understanding of not only what happened, but why it happened, what it led to, and how it fit in with other events of the time, all without leaving out some of the interesting personal stories of the leaders who helped make that history. To put as much information as possible in the students' hands, we have included extensive appendices and numerous maps.

We chose the title *The American Journey* because that is one of our perspectives on history. It is the story of man's and woman's journey from past to present with a building of memories that must be recorded and remembered, or the lessons learned along the way will be wasted. In other words, the metaphor of a journey conveys the appropriate idea that events and attitudes do not occur or exist in a vacuum. The present is linked with both the past and the future.

There are at least three reasons why it is absolutely vital to study and understand history:

(1) <u>To learn from our mistakes</u>: Nations, like individuals, can mature. And an important part of the maturation process is to experience failures and then learn from our mistakes. Of course, if you don't think the United States has ever made any serious mistakes, then there is no point in studying our history. Our favorite American diplomatic historian, Thomas A. Bailey, put it this way:

"Every generation of apes begins where the previous generation began, because apes can hand down no record of their experience. Man leaves a record; but how much better is he than the apes if he does not study it and heed its warnings?"—From *Woodrow Wilson and the Lost Peace*, p. v (Forward).

(2) <u>To understand the present</u>: Everyone is influenced in some degree by the past, whether he knows that past or not. Christianity, the Protestant Reformation, the Enlightenment, and other notable movements and events have had a profound impact on western civilization. Racism, slavery, the Civil War, and the Reconstruction period all played vital roles in determining the nature and extent of racial problems in the United States today. History gives us the perspective to judge the present. The present is full of the past. Or as the early twentieth century American poet, T.S. Eliot, wrote: "The historical sense involves a perception, not only of the pastness of the past, but of its presence."

(3) <u>To see where we are headed</u>: History is not deterministic, but a clear understanding of our past and present will give us the direction we are currently travelling. Then it is up to us collectively (which is the sum total of each citizen's contribution to thought) to determine whether we want to continue on that path or whether we wish to change the course of our American journey.

In order to learn from our past mistakes and to understand where we are presently and where we are headed, it is essential that the student be made aware of the facts, as well as differing viewpoints, of our past. In other words, a mere listing of events, names, dates, and places has little relevance, and it is no wonder that students are frequently turned off by that approach to history. Of course, paying attention to interpretations means making certain judgments, some of which are bound to conflict with some students' own personal views. But that is what the process of education is all about. The student should be aware that *The American Journey* introduces the student to an in-depth examination of American history, including varying interpretive viewpoints of our past.

Will an American history course or text help a student find a job? Maybe not, but it should increase his or her ability to question decisions that will affect the future of the nation with some knowledge of what questions to ask and why. Toward this goal, we humbly acknowledge our privilege to play a small part in imparting some of that necessary knowledge.

Doug Baker
Susan Hutchins

An engraving Frank E. Wright / H.W.zSmith & Co. Columbus notices for the first time the variation of the needle. Copyright 2010 iStockphoto.

Chapter 1 Contents

CHAPTER ONE

The American Journey Begins

Major Events

30,000-10,000 B.C.E.	The first inhabitants came to North America
8,000 B.C.E.-1500 C.E.	Tribes developed across North America (including the Maya, Aztec, and Inca)
1000	Vikings explored and established settlements on Greenland and Newfoundland
1095-1492	Europe prepared for overseas expansion
1488	Portuguese explorer Bartholomeu Dias (Diaz) sailed around tip of Africa
1492-1502	Christopher Columbus sailed west to trade for goods in Asia. Columbus made 4 voyages to the New World
1521	Hernán Cortés conquered the Aztec Empire. Spain conquered Central America, South America, and southern portions of North America
1533	Francisco Pizarro conquered the Inca Empire
1500s	The Portuguese, French, and English attempted to follow in the footsteps of the Spanish with little success

Introduction

The original inhabitants of the Americas came in small groups and thousands of years later in large waves. They came from the continents of Asia, Europe, and Africa. They reached out and conquered a continent. It was a journey with many pathways, but it became the American journey. The current generation is the most knowledgeable of generations. With centuries of knowledge and the latest technology, there is an understanding of many secrets of the universe unknown to those who came before. Yet a great many unanswered questions continue to puzzle historians, archaeologists, anthropologists, and scientists who make it their life's work to know the what, where, when, why, and how of the past. Where were the previous homelands of the first Americans? Who were they? What were their routes to the Americas?

At one time the earth was one contiguous continent. Through shifting and physical stresses on this super-continent, large areas drifted away millennia ago and developed the continents that exist today. Geology and climate shaped these bodies of land into their current forms. Most experts believe that one of the most important aspects of shaping the current continents, including North America, was the Great Ice Age, the Pleistocene Epoch, which they say began approximately 2 million years ago and ended about 10,000 years ago. Great glaciers covered approximately a quarter of the earth, and in North America most of present-day Canada and a good deal of the northern portion of what is the present-day United States. There were two large ice sheets or glaciers covering North America: the Laurentide Glacier was the largest and spread from the northern reaches of Canada, partway down the Atlantic coast and then west across the continent to the Cordilleran Glacier, which covered land from current-day Alaska down to what is now Seattle and east over the Rocky Mountains. There were gaps between these ice sheets, and it is through these gaps that many of the first Americans travelled during warming times or interglacial periods.

Archaeologists continue to debate the route the first Americans took to the Western Hemisphere. The most widely accepted theory brings them from Siberia 30,000-10,000 years ago across Beringia (the Bering Strait), a land bridge at the time between Asia and North America. As the ice sheets melted, the water released covered the land, and today the Bering Strait is a narrow waterway. The first groups of hunters and gatherers followed their food sources east from Asia, stepped onto another continent and unknowingly began the American journey. According to new artifacts uncovered in the last few decades, the first settlers might have reached the American continents in small water vessels landing on one of the western-most coastlines along North America. There is also speculation that the first Americans might have landed on the eastern shores and not the western. More accurate dating technology is bringing more evidence concerning when and from where these original groups of settlers came. During the 1930s, evidence with the technology available at the time dated fluted projectile points at 9,000 B.C.E. The archeologists labeled the artifacts and the group they belonged to Clovis Man. The Clovis-first theory became accepted as the beginnings of humans in North America. Other Clovis points were discovered in other areas of the continent, and the theory was that the Amerindians crossed Beringia and moved down North and South

Approximate Dates	Locations of Settlements or Encampments	Evidence
14,000 B.C.E.	Meadowcroft Rockshelter (near present-day Pittsburgh)	Bone, wood, fiber, artifacts
12,500 B.C.E.	Idaho (Cave in Southern portion of state)	Projectile point and blade
11,000 B.C.E.	Monte Verde (Southern Chile)	Wooden building foundations, plant remains, mastodon tusk, animal bones
9,500 B.C.E.	Clovis, New Mexico and North America	Tools from bones and stones, fluted spear points
9,000 B.C.E.	Folsom culture from Montana to south Texas	Tools from bone including needles

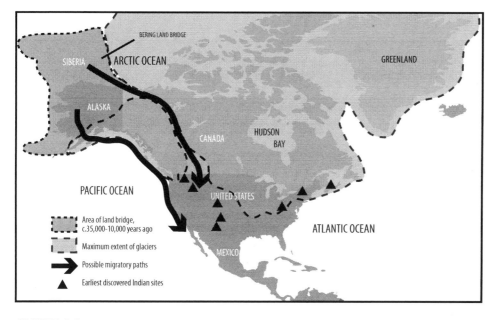

FIGURE 1.1 - The First Discoverers of America

America as well as spreading west to east across the Americas. However, more recent archaeological finds and improved dating techniques suggest men and women were at locations on the continents earlier than the Clovis artifacts.

Whether they came by land or sea, and whenever they came, the descendants of these original settlers spread throughout two vast continents, developed a diversity of cultures, and settled in various geographic locations from Alaska to Tierra del Fuego and throughout the Western Hemisphere.

How We Know

Without a written history, artifacts tell the story of ancient America. Archaeologists study bone, wood, plant fiber, fire-pit charcoal, projectile points from hunting spears, stone tools, and many other items previously belonging to ancient peoples to answer the many questions concerning their lives. As technology has improved, the accuracy of the tales of the past has improved, with old theories becoming obsolete and new theories coming under scrutiny. Radiocarbon dating, used since the 1950s, relied on counting the decay of the radioactive isotope carbon 14. AMS, a new method using an accelerator mass spectrometer to date radiocarbon,

counts the carbon-14 atoms in an artifact. It is one of the latest and most accurate of the dating techniques and allows the dating of much smaller pieces of material than the original procedure. Of course, radiocarbon and other dating techniques are all based on certain assumptions, although those assumptions are shared by the large majority of the scientific community. In addition to the various dating techniques, satellite imaging and airborne radar allow scientists to see the land with more precision by revealing such topographical elements as ancient canals in the jungles of Central America and roads in the deserts of the southwestern United States.

Ancient Paleo-Indians

The first Americans moved down and across the continents constantly searching for food. For these Paleo-Indians, food came from animals, fish, or plants they found edible. They were hunters and gatherers. Many species of large mammals were the quarry for the Indians, and on their roaming journeys they found mammoths, mastodons, camels, horses, saber-toothed tigers, bison, and more than two dozen other species of mammals. Estimates are that the large animals began dying out around 9,000 B.C.E., and by 7,000 B.C.E. more than 30 species were extinct. The two most likely reasons for the demise of these large mammals were climate change or overhunting. There was smaller game available when the large species died out, and the various tribes supplemented their diets with seeds, roots, berries, and other plants they gathered. When the glaciers melted and the waters covered Beringia, immigration to this new world ceased for thousands of years.

Most experts believe that from approximately 8,000-4,000 B.C.E., many of the wandering groups settled into more permanent encampments and developed primitive societies across the continent. Many researches believed that there was little interaction once the nomads settled into villages as tribes, but in fact there was quite a bit of interaction between tribes and sometimes over long distances. Flint, jasper, and obsidian have been found in a variety of areas far from their places of origin. In various areas in the Northeast and later in the Great Lakes area, they used a larger variety of materials to create their daily utensils. Some of the materials used for everyday storage or eating vessels were still made from bone, but they also began using copper, stone, and clay. In settlements south of the Great Lakes, the people began building permanent homes using wooden posts, logs, and clay.

After 2,500 B.C.E., travel and trade between the tribes increased, sometimes over long distances. Cultivation of foods, rather than total dependence on roaming animals and wild plants, allowed groups to thrive in various regions and create not only a more stationary lifestyle but also larger villages. Members of tribes in Mexico travelled into North America, bringing the seeds for domesticated corn and later peppers into the Southwest areas.

North American Indian Culture B.C.E.

Introduction

The native tribes of North America developed as the earliest newcomers crossed into the continent and journeyed south and east in small groups. Or perhaps each native tribe originated in the Americas as the Indian narratives have recounted. The Kiowa believed that they entered the world through a hollow log. However they came to the continents, all were hunters and gatherers for thousands of years, but ultimately transitioned from that lifestyle to a mix across the continents from the simple to the complicated. The earliest groups are in the Paleolithic Age, which experts date down to 8,000 B.C.E. In the age of the Archaic Culture from 8,000-1,500 B.C.E., most experts believe that the large mammals disappeared and the North American tribes moved further to the north. The Native Americans began to hunt smaller animals and gather more from the plant world to supplement their diets. The making of baskets allowed the people of

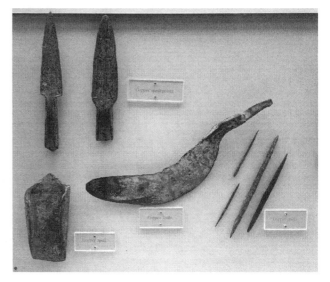

FIGURE 1.2 - Archaic Indian artifacts

the time to store food, which was crucial to transitioning from a strictly subsistence, or day-to-day, existence. Most of the native groups were similar in their way of life at this time. As the different groups developed dissimilar hunting techniques in various geographic environments, cultures diverged. The development of agriculture finally allowed many of the tribes to build their settlements and develop their cultures in a single location or maintain a winter camp but keep their nomadic ways in the spring and autumn months in some areas. Terrain, climate, contact with other tribes, war, and sheer ingenuity determined the many facets of tribal life until the Europeans intruded.

Similarities abound in the large number of tribes even when regional cultural differences existed. They were dependent on natural resources for food, clothing, and shelter. They had an affinity with the land. Elements of the natural world played an important part in their spiritual (religious) beliefs. Few had a system of writing, and history was passed down through the generations with oral storytelling. They were also clan-oriented and communal. Although some of the tribes lived in isolation, there was a good deal of trade between them. They sometimes traveled many miles to trade with other tribes. Warfare was a relatively common part of their existence. They enslaved their enemies or put them to death in cruel ways.

Estimates of the number of Native Americans living in North America when the Europeans began to settle are varied and hard to determine. No one was counting. In North America, the number is often put between 8 and 12 million. Mexico and Central America might have been as high as 20 million. There were many millions more in South America and the Caribbean islands. Altogether, a total of between 43 and 65 million might have lived in the Americas. The estimates have increased over the last few decades as more research has been conducted in this area of history. No matter what the exact numbers were, this was not an area of the world that was a vast wilderness empty of people and culture. They had developed cultures. The cultures were vastly different from those of the Europeans who came, but nonetheless they were vibrant and viable in the Classical Period from approximately 1,500 B.C.E to 1,500 C.E.

The Northwest Coastal Areas

The tribes that settled in this region lived in small settlements and developed a variety of languages and culture patterns. They adapted to their environments to live full lives with little deprivation. Those closest to the seas had the bounty from the Pacific, and those near the forest lands depended on the smaller animals for sustenance. There were also edible plants in abundance to supplement the animal resources. Trade became extensive in this region. The tribes of the Northwest Coast were known for not only their prowess as hunters of the sea, but their wood-carving skills and their art (from totem poles to their large canoes).

The Southwest Areas

The Southwest areas of North America were dry, and animals became scarce as a source of food. The introduction of agriculture between 2,000 B.C.E. and 500 C.E. from Central America led to the development of great cultures in this region. They could form larger villages once they had a stable source of food-corn. Later they added beans and squash plants to their diets. The seeds from these plants spread across the continent and changed the existence of many of the tribes. The Mogollon, the Hohokam, and the Anasazi (Navajo for "ancient ones") were three of the major tribes in what is today Arizona, New Mexico, large portions of northern central Mexico, and southern Utah and Colorado.

There were some similarities between these groups as they made their lives in this region. They lived in dry areas, grew corn, developed pottery, and built multi-unit dwelling places. All of the tribes declined because of newcomers and the climate. The Hohokam successfully built as much as 300 miles of irrigation canals to enable the cultivation of the desert. The artists of the Hohokam made sophisticated stone bowls, figurines, and painted vessels. It is also thought that the artists of the tribe used acid solutions to create etchings on jewelry centuries before the Europeans used the technique during the Renaissance. The Anasazi wove baskets, used the bow and arrow, grew and wove cotton into clothing and blankets, and built buildings with hundreds of rooms. What they did with the resources available in their area of the continent was quite remarkable.

Plains Areas

The flat fields of the plains in the middle section of North America led to a lifestyle for the natives that lasted for centuries. They were nomadic hunter-gatherers who hunted bison as their main source of sustenance. Many groups moved in and out of the areas because of its dryness. The Shoshonean people came from the Great Basin area to hunt bison and push the Athapaskan speakers, Kiowas and Apaches, farther south. Algonquian groups of the Blackfeet, Arapaho, and Cheyenne came from the east. From 1,500 B.C.E. to 1,500 C.E., the hunters killed bison with spears topped with atlatls (spear-throwers with a notch on one end to attach to the spear and a stone on the other) or drove them over cliffs. The bow and arrow later replaced the atlatl. When the Spanish horses wandered into the plains, or the Plains people stole them, hunting and life in general became easier for this group. From ancient times into the late 1800s, the Plains tribes hunted bison for food.

Eastern Woodland Areas

The wooded areas of this portion of North America from the Mississippi River east to the shores of the Atlantic had many geographical advantages that tribes in the West did not have, except for the coastal tribes along the Pacific coast. There were many sources of food from the forests and seas, and many tribes settled in this area of the continent that had consistent rainfall. Many tribes developed. There was a variety from small to large populations and simple to complex cultures. In the northern areas of what became New York, the great Iroquois Confederation developed a complex society. In the current Ohio region over to the Mississippi River and further south developed the mound builders of the Adena, Hopewell, and Mississippian and other small tribes.

Iroquois Confederation

One of the most powerful groups was the Iroquois, who formed the Five Nations with the Mohawks, Oneida, Cayuga, Onondaga, and Seneca in the 1500s. The Five Nations grew to six in the 1700s when the Tuscarora joined. This type of confederation was unusual for the Native Americans. They might form friendships or loose alliances with other tribes but seldom a formal confederation. They held council meetings once a year to decide matters of importance to all tribe members. Warfare was common among the various tribes of the Americas, but for the Five Nations, who were also very warlike, they required a unanimous vote from the council.

The Iroquois were also different from many other tribes in their respect for women. Women played an important role in decision-making and actually were the heads of the clans. As such, they chose the men who served on the tribal councils.

Mound Builders

Many tribes were mound builders from the Ohio area down to Louisiana. The Adena and later Hopewell tribes of the Ohio area built earthen mound centers from around 500 B.C.E. to 550 C.E. The mounds were often built in the shapes of snakes, sun, moon, sky, birds, and other designs. In the mounds, they buried their dead political and religious leaders with many items from this world. The Adena and Hopewell tribes were great trading nations. Building their settlements close to rivers allowed them to control goods, such as seashells from the South (very valuable as a bartering item) and minerals from the North. For the most part, the tribes of these trading centers lived on hunting and gathering. These groups vanished around 550 C.E., but the reasons are not clear. Perhaps it was a lack of food or radical changes in climate.

The Mississippian culture, often thought of as the third generation of mound builders, built their culture from about 1000-1400 C.E. They constructed Cahokia, the largest city north of Mexico, close to present-day East St. Louis, Illinois. The members of the tribe erected vast flat-topped mounds used for a foundation for the houses of the chiefs or religious leaders and burial mounds and perhaps also for boundary markers and defense. The city was a center for government and religious life, but the people also had game fields where they played a popular game, chunkey (chungke), in which the players threw lances at a rolling stone disc. At a time when many European cities were struggling, Cahokia had a higher population than any city in Europe and was thriving. The population of Cahokia and its outlying areas was perhaps as large as 30,000 inhabitants. They did not leave a written record, but there are a great many artifacts that record their history. Growing corn and trade allowed this city to reach its high numbers and high level of culture. Archaeologists are not sure why the area went into a decline. There could have been a number of factors: climate change, poor crop cycle, problems with surrounding tribes, or internal strife.

If interested, travelers may see mounds in Spiro, Oklahoma; Moundville, Alabama; Etowah Mounds in northern Georgia; and Cahokia Mounds near St. Louis.

Central and South American Indian Cultures

Finding and dating human artifacts in South America to a time preceding the appearance of Clovis Man has thrown the theories of the settlement of South America into disarray for archaeologists, anthropologists, and historians. Continuing to work from theories with some material to place a time frame on the artifacts discovered, more scientists are beginning to believe that perhaps there was a coastal landing on the Pacific side of South America. The reason that there is no conclusive proof of the event is the fact that the shoreline during the end of the last ice age was further west. When the ice melted, it pushed the coast further east, covering up landing sites. The old theory of the earliest settlers coming from one group of travelers from Asia into the Western Hemisphere and populating this immense amount of land in the Western Hemisphere does not satisfy as many as it once did.

In Central and South America, tribes frequently overran the territory of others as they did in North America and developed rudimentary civilizations. Three tribes in particular developed advanced civilizations: the Mayas, Aztecs, and Incas. These groups had many elements in their civilizations on par with many of the European groups who excused their conquests and brutality toward the natives with a claim of superiority. The cultures of Mesoamerica (current Central America) practiced religion, built impressive buildings from sports arenas to great steppe pyramids, and developed cities from the simple to the most complex. The Spanish took little note of these accomplishments with the gleam of gold blinding their perspective and hardening their hearts to all they called savage.

The Maya

The Maya civilization arose more than 3,000 years ago and reached its zenith from approximately 250 C.E. to 900 C.E. To see the steppe pyramids and other architectural sites they left behind is to know this was one of the great civilizations. They organized their territory into city-states to provide political and economic order for their total population of 2-3 million people. The rulers were both secular and religious figures. The Maya had a system of writing and studied mathematics as well as astronomy. From

FIGURE 1.3 - Mayan chromolithograph

Mayan hieroglyphics, those who study the past have a record of their lives, dynasties, political systems, wars, territorial expansion, and religious practices. The people of this empire also grew cotton along with other agricultural products and traded their goods with other groups in Central America from their sea worthy canoes.

From such great heights, the Maya empire experienced a rapid fall beginning about 900 C.E. The building of monuments and large-scale structures ceased, and the people left for other areas. Over time, the jungle encroached upon the large cities. There are many theories as to what happened to these people: severe drought, overpopulation, and environmental degradation are the most common suppositions, or perhaps a combination of all three.

The Aztecs

The Aztec people migrated from the north into the Basin of Mexico at the beginning of the 13th century. In 1325, they founded their great city of Tenochtitlan on an island in a lake and increased the size of the island by bringing in soil to raise the lake bed above the water. They built their buildings along canals that were used as transportation. There was the palace of the emperor, buildings, pyramids, and a large marketplace in this exquisite metropolis. The streets were kept sanitary with the work of more than a thousand street cleaners.

Once they constructed their capital and conquered the valley, the Aztecs built an empire by subjugating tribes to the east and south and demanded tribute, taxes, and victims for their blood sacrifices. By 1519, the Aztec empire spread over 500 miles.

Their culture was an amalgam of many of the previous cultures in the area. Their religion was filled with many gods that must be appeased, often with the blood of sacrificed victims. This was a practice that naturally disgusted the Spanish invaders and was another mark in their favor to rule the bloodthirsty, savage people. One of the positive elements of the cultures in the Central American region was their brilliant agricultural accomplishments. They cultivated maize (corn), sweet potatoes, beans, tomato, squash, and cacao beans (used for chocolate).

On November 9, 1519, Hernán Cortés (also spelled Cortez) and his army witnessed the grandeur of the Aztec capital. This Spanish invader arrived to take control of the Aztec empire and its wealth along with thousands of native allies who wanted to end Aztec control over their tribes. Little did these supporters of Cortés realize they were trading one despot for another.

The Inca

By 1300 C.E., the Inca tribe had settled in the high-altitude basins of the Andes Mountains of South America. They established their capital in Cuzco (in present-day Peru) and fed their expanding number by growing crops in terraces built up the steep hillsides. From their capital, the Incas dominated other tribes in the mountains and along the Pacific coast and built a well-integrated empire from present-day Colombia to Chile. They possessed many of the best qualities for ruling a large empire: competent administrators, great military strategists, and expert road builders. They kept tight control over their empire with a small ruling elite and a rigid class structure. A takeover at the top led to the fall of the empire.

First European Contact

The Native American cultures flourished in their isolation once most of the great ice sheets receded, but their reign did not last. Explorers and settlers came from across the Atlantic this time. For centuries, credit for discovering the Americas was given to Christopher Columbus, but evidence points to the possibility that the Norsemen were the first to come from Europe to North America and set up settlements for a brief time. The skilled seafarers of Scandinavia travelled far and wide in their small boats. We know much of this history from the Norse sagas. These tales of adventure told by the adventurer and orally passed down through the generations chronicle the accounts of discovery and exploration from the small island of Iceland to the Americas.

The sagas told the tale of Eric the Red's three-year banishment from Iceland and the land he found to the west. Rumors of this land enticed the veteran sailor to set his sails in that direction around 985 C.E. His boats landed on the uninhabited island of Greenland. The southwestern portion of the island was magnificent "green land." During a span of warming in the Northern Hemisphere, Eric brought new settlers to Greenland. There were enough settlers to build their longhouses in an eastern and western settlement in the southwestern portion of the island.

Rumors of land to the west enticed Eric's sons and others to load up their boats and travel west. Leif Ericson established a settlement in a land he named Vinland (Newfoundland, Canada), which was a short distance from Greenland. On the northern tip of Newfoundland, an archaeological dig found the remains of Norse work sheds and longhouses at L'Anse aux Meadows. It is thought to be the remains of Leif's settlement. The settlement lasted approximately 10 years. These settlers and others who tried to settle west or south of Greenland were not in uninhabited land. The natives, called the derogatory term Skraeling by the Norse, were hostile to the pioneers. The Norsemen may have been the first settlers, but nothing came from their time spent on the foreign lands, partially because too few knew of the discovery. However, even if many had known, few in Europe would have been in a position to take advantage of the discovery. It was the voyages of Columbus that brought the contact that ended the isolation of the Americas.

FIGURE 1.4 - L'Anse aux Meadows, recreated long house

Factors for Overseas Expansion

Holy Crusades

Pope Urban II in 1095 C.E. called Christians to organize into armies and travel to Palestine in the Middle East to retake the land of Jesus from the Saracens, Arabs of the Muslim faith. An increase in population and wealth in Europe helped supply the Crusades. There were four major Crusades and five minor ones from 1095 to 1291. One of them was even a misguided Children's Crusade. This was a disaster as most of the children were captured and forced into slavery. Of primary importance to the crusaders was the city of Jerusalem, a city of great holy significance for Christians. Thousands of Christian pilgrims traveled to the city to visit the Church of the Holy Sepulchre that commemorated the hill of crucifixion and the tomb of Christ's burial. Pilgrimages to such holy sites in Palestine were believed to gain the believer part of God's grace, thus reducing the soul's time in purgatory after death. In 1065, the Turks had conquered Jerusalem and massacred 3,000 Christians. The crusaders managed to take Jerusalem in 1099, but their brutality to the Muslim and Jewish inhabitants was anything but Christian. The Christians could not keep Jerusalem, and in the end lost all of the land gained by the Crusades.

There were positive changes in Europe from the Crusades that readied the major powers for their role in exploration and colonization. A sense of unity and the experience of mounting large military expeditions aided the growth of the continent of Europe. There was also the new understanding of establishing colonies in a foreign land for a brief period of time. There was new knowledge of trade and trade goods from the East. The crusaders found goods in the Middle East that Europeans wanted. There were silks and other beautiful textiles, and tapestries. Spices such as pepper, cinnamon, and cloves (which were important to hide the taste of bad meat during a time of no refrigeration), gems, china, dye, and many other goods came into Europe after a journey of thousands of miles across land and sea from Asia and the Spice Islands and then on ships of the Italians. This trade increased the wealth of the European nations as the population increased. It was these effects of the Crusades, along with the growing population and more viable economies, that helped lead Europe out of the Dark Ages.

Rise of National States

Other changes in Europe sped the nations toward overseas ventures. National states developed, which resulted in sufficiently powerful monarchies with governments of wealth and power able to bear some of the expenses and difficulties of exploration, conquest, and colonization. However, the monarchs often chose to claim the land and put the financial burdens upon private entities.

The Renaissance

The rise of the Renaissance in the 1400s led to a desire once again to search for knowledge and explore the works of scholars of the past and the present. While delving into this world of knowledge, there were those who began to rethink the geography of the known world and new possibilities for sailing that world. Most educated people for the last 2,000 years believed that the world was round, contrary to much that has been written. But the only way to prove or disprove existing theories was to sail forth.

The invention of the printing press by German printer Johan Gutenberg around 1450 brought about the dissemination of information and knowledge to many more Europeans because then written materials were affordable, and people had a great incentive to learn to read and write. The press was able to print dozens of books acquainting Europeans with the 20-year journey of Marco Polo, who traveled to Asia and returned in 1295. He claimed to have spent this time traveling through China, India, and Japan. Although many doubted some of his claims then and later because of little hard evidence, his writings describing the many wonders of Asia stimulated the imaginations of some in Europe to venture forth and attempt to bring back the amazing goods he described. The journeys of Marco Polo stirred an obsession in a young man, Christopher Columbus, to travel to Asia and follow in Polo's footsteps. Columbus carried the book with him on his voyages and looked for the landmarks described by Polo for proof that he had found Asia.

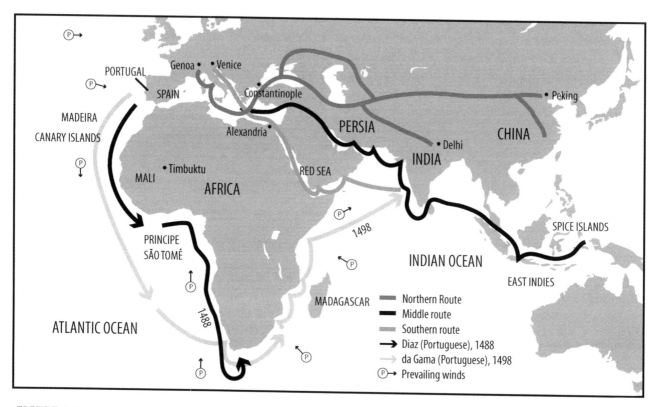

FIGURE 1.5 - Trade routes with the East

Improvements in Ship Designs and Navigation Instruments

The desire for new goods from distant lands combined with the technological advancements in sailing and navigation in the mid-1400s set the Europeans on a course of conquest that lasted for several centuries. European sailors before this time, because of limited geographic knowledge of the world, few navigation skills, and small cumbersome ships unable to maneuver in the blowing winds and strong currents of the Atlantic, stayed fairly close to European shores and the Mediterranean Sea. In the 1450s Portuguese seafarers changed the world of sailing for the Europeans. They developed the caravel, a ship that could sail into the wind more easily, and also discovered that if they sailed northwest to the Azores from the west coast of Africa that the calmer westward flowing wind would take them home. Having to sail close to a coastline because so little was known of the sea further out prevented the various countries and private adventurers from acquiring much knowledge about sailing to other locales. Better compasses and the use of an improved mariner's astrolabe (to determine a ship's location by calculating the position of the sun or stars) were instrumental in allowing ships to move further out to sea. The profits possible from the Asian goods in demand and advances in technology changed this small view of the world and its possibilities.

In the same 15th century, Portuguese Prince Henry the Navigator (died in 1460) initiated what became Europe's Age of Exploration by sea. Specifically, he encouraged Portuguese ships to travel down the west coast of the African continent, setting up trading posts along the shore to trade in gold and human beings. Arab merchants and various African tribes had traded for slaves over the centuries, but the Portuguese turned the slave trade into an immense and tragic business. As Portugal and Spain established sugar plantations on islands close to Africa — Madeira, the Azores, the Canaries, Sao Tome, and Principe — slave trading increased and continued to increase as these countries and later other European countries expanded their plantation interests to other parts of the world, including what they would label the New World in the Americas.

The adventurous Portuguese sailed further down the coast of West Africa. Emboldened by their successes, they searched for a water route to Asia through the continent of Africa. A water route would allow the Europeans to cut out the expense of the Arab merchant middlemen who brought the desired goods from Asia across a land route. They did not know that there was no such water route, but Bartholomeu Dias (sometimes spelled Bartholomew Diaz) edged around the southern tip of Africa in 1488. Vasco da Gama reached India in 1498. The Europeans labeled all the mysterious land of Asia and the islands close by the "Indies." Da Gama returned to his home with a cargo of jewels and spices. The European world soon underwent great changes.

Columbus Points the Way

While Portugal established successful trading posts on the western coast of Africa, began a lucrative trade for gold and African slaves, and claimed land in the Atlantic off the coast of northwest Africa, Spain, its neighbor on the Iberian Peninsula, finally came together as a united nation-state. The marriage of Ferdinand of Aragon and Isabella of Castile on October 19, 1469 unified most of Spain, which led to far-reaching consequences for the world. The monarchs, devout Christians, turned their attention to ridding Spain of the Moors, believers in the Muslim faith who had controlled areas of Spain since the early 700s.

While sailing as a young man aboard Portuguese ships— although he was from Genoa, Italy—and working in his brother's mapmaking shop in Lisbon, Columbus began to seriously consider the possibility of sailing across the Atlantic, or the Ocean Sea as it was called. He worked on voyages from Iceland to the Gold Coast of Africa, married a Portuguese woman, and made his home on the Portuguese colony of Madeira, a small Atlantic island off the coast of northwestern Africa. He was, however, captivated with the theories put forth by ancient and medieval scholars and geographers that the unexplored

FIGURE 1.6 - Christopher Columbus

Atlantic could be crossed because the distance between Europe and Asia was actually quite small. When he read the writings of Marco Polo with all of the tales of treasure, including gold, silver, silks and spices, Columbus was certain that he could sail west and in a short time reach the land of Cathay (China), Cipangu (Japan), and the Indies (India and the islands in the Indian Ocean).

Columbus began his efforts to find the funds to support his voyage to Asia in the 1480s. The Portuguese King John II, the Spanish monarchs Ferdinand and Isabella, and probably the English King Henry VII turned him down. Although Queen Isabella turned down Columbus, she thought there might be merit to his theories. She gave Columbus a small amount of money. A shorter trade route to the Indies would outmaneuver the Portuguese efforts to sail around Africa to reach the Indies, and cheaper goods would benefit Spain. She was also very interested in sending out missionaries to Christianize the Asians. Nothing could be done for Columbus until the Moors were out of Spain. Grenada, the last stronghold of the Moors, fell in 1492. They also expelled Jews who refused to convert to Christianity and persecuted others considered heretics to the Christian faith. The organized efforts necessary to rid Spain of its non-Christian enemies resulted in the coordination of economic, social, ideological, and military forces that enabled the nation to build an empire from the discoveries of a sailor committed to an idea. They agreed to support the dream of Christopher Columbus to sail west to Asia.

Columbus was not only interested in finding a faster route to Asia, also wanted to emerge from this undertaking a wealthy and powerful man. He asked for one-tenth of all the wealth that Spain received from the lands he discovered for himself and his heirs for all time. He requested the position of Viceroy and Governor of

FIGURE 1.7 - Painting of Christopher Columbus landing in the West Indies, on an island that the natives called Guanahani and he named San Salvador, on October 12, 1492

the lands and the title "Admiral of the Ocean Seas." The monarchs agreed and signed a contract with Columbus.

The First Voyage

The *Nina, Pinta,* and *Santa Maria* left Spain to cross the uncharted waters of the Atlantic on August 3, 1492. Although Columbus had read information and studied sea charts of what some believed lay west of Europe, there were no accounts from anyone who had actually sailed this route. With the crews close to mutiny, Columbus saw land on October 12, 1492, and named the island San Salvador, which means "Blessed Savior." The Indian (Columbus' name for the natives of the island as he thought he was in the East Indies) inhabitants called the island Guanahani. Columbus claimed the island as a possession of Spain. Columbus and other Europeans for more than a century repeated this claim hundreds of times over for Spain and other nations in the lands that belonged to others. Columbus wrote "I unfurled the royal banner and the captains brought the flags which displayed a large green cross with the letters F and Y at the left and right side of the cross. ... I was taking possession of this island for the King and Queen." The audacity of the Europeans then and later toward the land and possessions of others knew few bounds. He found the people attractive (even in their naked state), friendly, helpful, and stated that they could easily be converted to Christianity. He also found pieces of gold hanging from their noses. His excitement about the conditions he found was immense.

There are many aspects of the Columbus voyages that are unknown, including the exact location of Columbus' first landing, but the most widely accepted location of San Salvador is Watling Island in the Bahamas, although others insist that it is Samana Cay. Unfortunately, the matter might never be proved because there is no surviving map of the voyage and its landfalls. Without benefit of the official logs, history has been dependent on an account written by Bishop Bartolomé de Las Casas. Las Casas read and took notes from the logs compiled by Columbus before their disappearance. The bishop later traveled to the New World and wrote the first account of the Spanish conquest in the *History of the Indie*. One of Columbus' sons also compiled notes on his recollections of what his father had told him about his and also his brother's trip to the New World.

Columbus wrote in the ship's log that he believed he had arrived in the Indies and continued to sail in search of what he believed would be Asia. After his first landfall on San Salvador, he sailed to several small islands along the coast of a large landmass, convinced that this was the Asian continent. Actually, it was Cuba. He searched in vain for populous cities and the Great Khan of Cathay. He did not give up on his search even though he found little that resembled the Asian world as described by Marco Polo. During the latter days of this first voyage, the *Santa Maria* ran aground on a coral reef on December 24, 1492 off the coast of Hispaniola (Haiti/Dominican Republic). The men and supplies were put ashore with orders to build a fort and name it La Navidad. There was not enough space on the *Nina* to take on board all of the crew of the *Santa Maria*. This was the first attempt at a Spanish settlement in what became a New World for Europeans.

The Second Voyage

When Columbus returned to Spain with gold, kidnapped natives, and other items from the islands found on the first voyage, there were celebrations in every city he passed through on his route to an audience with the king and queen. Ferdinand and Isabella requested that he visit them personally to give his report and addressed the letter to "Don Christopher Columbus, Admiral of the Ocean Sea, Viceroy and Governor of the islands that

he discovered in the Indies." Because of his discoveries during the first voyage and his belief that the Indies were somewhere in the vicinity of the discovered land, the king and queen financed a return expedition to the New World. He prepared 17 ships with 1,500 men and the necessities to establish a Spanish colony in the islands: priests, soldiers, craftsmen, farmers, animals, supplies, and seeds for planting. He sailed on September 25, 1493. The monarchs specifically instructed Columbus to convert the indigenous populations to Christianity, expand the colony on Hispaniola, build a trading post, and continue the search for the route to Asia.

Once in the Caribbean, Columbus passed many new islands and landed on a few to visit with the natives or look for signs of gold. He returned to La Navidad, but after almost a year's absence, all the men were dead and the supplies had vanished. Columbus punished the Tainos, who had welcomed him on his first voyage and given so much aid and information about their area of the world. He destroyed villages and enslaved hundreds of the Indians. He demanded tribute in gold in such great amounts that many lost body parts when they could not deliver their assigned amount. The man who proclaimed the beauty of the islands and the beauty of the natives had lost his gentleness and awe. Before sailing back to Spain in 1496, he established the new colony east of La Navidad and named it La Isabella after the Spanish queen. As governor of the new colony, his problems were numerous. He was a failure as an administrator and was reluctant to face the king and queen. His strength and focus were sailing and finding Asia and gold. Fortunately for Columbus, the monarchs maintained their faith in Columbus and gave him ships for a third voyage.

The Third Voyage

In July 1498, Columbus returned again to the Caribbean but sailed much further south this time. He spotted an island to the north and named it Trinidad. Seeing land in the distance, the ship sailed further west. As the ships approached the land, there was yellowish water churning and swirling into the seawater, and it was not very salty. Columbus knew that this yellowish water was coming from a large river that could only come from a large body of land, a continent. He dismissed the idea that it might be Asia and believed that it was an unknown continent. He sent men ashore and found natives wearing items made from gold and pearls. Columbus could not stay and explore any longer, for he had supplies for the colony at Santo Domingo on Hispaniola. La Isabella had not been a good choice for the colony. The colony was in turmoil. Columbus had his brothers to help him, but this only made matters worse as many did not agree with the policies of any of the Columbus brothers. Some of the Spanish settlers and the Indians on the island of Hispaniola were rebelling. The Tainos were fighting against cruel treatment and attempts to make them into slaves. After many unfavorable accounts about Columbus and his mismanagement of the colony reached Spain, the king and queen sent a representative to investigate. After an investigation, Francisco de Bobadilla sent the Admiral of the Ocean Sea and his two brothers in chains back to Spain in November 1500. This treatment of Columbus and his brothers shocked Ferdinand and Isabella, and the charges were dropped. Columbus asked for ships and supplies for another voyage. He knew that others were sailing into the area from Portugal and England, and he needed to find Asia before they did.

The Fourth Voyage

In May 1502, Columbus set sail on his final voyage, the "high voyage." He still believed that the Indies were in the areas in which he had sailed. The voyage took 21 days from the Grand Canary Island off the coast of northwest Africa. The man who had found the route and the lands for Spain was denied shelter from a storm at Santo Domingo on Hispaniola. Columbus sailed on and landed on the coast of Central America. As he sailed down the eastern coastline, he found natives with more and more gold. After conflict with the natives and not finding an end to the land bridge, he decided to sail for home. He was very ill by this time. Because of the sorry state of his ships, he landed at Jamaica and stayed until a ship from Hispaniola rescued him and his crew. He returned to Spain in 1504 a few weeks before the death of Queen Isabella. In one of his last letters to King Ferdinand, Columbus made a final appeal for his privileges and titles and the passing on of these to his heirs. On May 20, 1506, Columbus died in Valladolid, Spain.

Consequences of Columbus Voyages

Soon after news of the Columbus voyage spread across Europe, monarchs or wealthy visionaries from Spain, Portugal, and England dispatched ships west to explore north and south from this newly discovered area. If Columbus could find populated islands to the west, perhaps there were other lands or discoveries to be made. Incredibly brave captains of the seas sailed west and then north and south from the Columbus finds. Some sailed to Greenland, others to the northern and eastern coast of South America. There was still the possibility of a western passage to the lands of Asia; there were stories from the natives of other lands in the area; and there were also the tales of other lands with treasures of silver and gold.

Another Italian navigator, Amerigo Vespucci, sailing to the New World first for Spain and then Portugal, made four voyages along the coast of South America to the newly discovered land. He claimed in his letters that this was a new land, a new continent, and he made himself out to be the great hero in most of his voyages. The German geographer Martin Waldseemüller proposed to honor the work and insight of Vespucci with a newly published world map in 1507 with the new land labeled as America, after Vespucci's first name. With each successful voyage, more knowledge spurred on more voyages and more discoveries.

The native populations of the New World did not stand a chance against the technology, numbers, and determination of the Old World invaders. Spanish exploration and settlement brought death to millions of natives from diseases for which the natives had no immunities, as well as from armed aggression. Researchers estimate that from 90-99 percent of the original native population were sent to their graves from the diseases and warfare of the Europeans, most of that by far from diseases. They brought smallpox along with their superior weapons of death. Disease also traveled from the New World to the Old when syphilis was carried back to Europe by the explorers. Because of the extreme drop in population and the problems getting the natives to work in the various enterprises of the Spanish masters, Africans were brought to the Americas in the early years of exploration as slaves.

Columbus failed to find a western route between Europe and Asia, but there was a great biological exchange, called the Columbian Exchange, between the Americas and Europe. The New World sent plants to Europe that would assist in feeding its rapidly growing population. Approximately three-fifths of today's food sources originated in the Americas. Plants such as tobacco, maize, beans, tomatoes, vanilla, chocolate, potatoes, squash, and peppers crossed the Atlantic to the Old World. From the Old World to the New, Columbus brought cattle, swine, horses, sheep, goats, sugar cane (brought into Spanish agriculture from the Canary Islands), wheat, rice, and coffee. Of course, diseases were also exchanged between the Old and New Worlds. Europeans brought smallpox, bubonic plague, typhus, influenza, measles, chicken pox, malaria, and diphtheria, while the Americas exported syphilis to the Old World.

Columbus also opened the way for many to eventually escape the Old World with its cruelty, purges, intolerance, and persecution due to ethnicity, nationality, or religious beliefs. However, that did not deter many of these from coming to the New World and using such evil practices on the natives and then the African slaves.

The Conquistadors

After the voyages of Columbus, the Spanish spread their empire in the "New Found World" onto the islands of the Caribbean Sea, west to the lands of current-day Central America, down into the eastern regions of South America in the Empire of the Incas, across northern and western portions of South America, and into the western and southern parts of North America. There were many conquistadors (Spanish conquerors) hoping to secure their fortune. They believed they had a right to the land of the various Indian groups they encountered. The Spanish believed their claims superseded that of the natives because of the authority of the Spanish monarchs Ferdinand and Isabella as well as that of the Pope of the Catholic Church. No matter that the land did not belong to this king or queen. Their rights as Christians and the might of their swords gave them power over non-Christians.

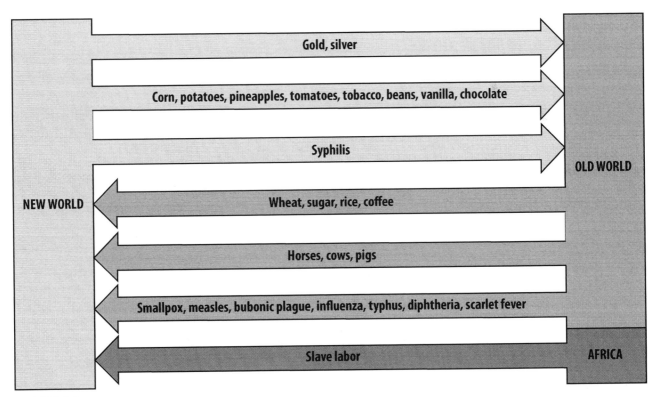

FIGURE 1.8 - The Columbian Exchange

The Spanish also had the authority of the Catholic Church behind their conquests. Pope Alexander VI issued a bill that divided the non-Christian world between Spain and Portugal in 1493. In 1494, Spain and Portugal formalized the Pope's declaration with the Treaty of Tordesillas. The treaty gave the land from a north/south line 1,100 miles west of the Canary Islands to Spain and the land east of the line to Portugal. As more discoveries uncovered more land to the west of the line, Spain claimed the land of the Americas, except that of Brazil, which was to the east of the line. The Portuguese claimed the land east of the line not owned by Christian princes, which included Africa and Asia. There were many in Europe who did not recognize the rights of ownership of these two nations. However, until those nations were ready to stake their own claims, the Spanish and the Portuguese gobbled up all they could.

Discovery and Conquest of the Islands and Nearby Coastlines

Columbus and those with him conquered the island of Hispaniola. This colony not only sent gold to Spain but also established a base from which to launch ships to explore the islands and coastline nearby. They did not know this territory, and the only way to discover what was beyond the sea was to explore. For the natives, loss, slavery, and death were the most common outcomes of the Spanish discoveries. One expedition discovered that Cuba was an island and another explored the coastline of Honduras and Yucatan. The conquest of Puerto Rico, Jamaica, and then Cuba was next on the agenda.

Juan Ponce de León sailed with Columbus on the second voyage. He stayed in the Caribbean and led the conquest of Puerto Rico in 1508 and discovered La Florida in 1513. He was the first European to explore a portion of North America. Contrary to popular belief, he was actually searching for natives to enslave and not searching for the fountain of youth. His attempt to build a Spanish settlement in 1521 in southwest Florida failed. The Native Americans drove the Spaniards out, and de León died from wounds inflicted by the Indians. Two other attempts by the Spanish to establish a colony on the Atlantic coast of North America also failed. Finally, the first permanent Spanish settlement in North America was established in 1565 by a Catholic mission at St. Augustine in La Florida.

Others established trading posts on the northern coast of South America and the eastern coastline of Central America. Vasco Núñez de Balboa took an expedition across the Isthmus of Panama connecting South and North America. This expedition discovered the Pacific Ocean on the western side of the Isthmus in 1513. This led to a claim by the Spanish for part of the Pacific Ocean according to the terms of the Treaty of Tordesillas and opened the west coast of Central and North America for Spanish settlement in the future. More explorers came and swarmed the area, constantly searching for new lands, hopefully with gold on or under that land.

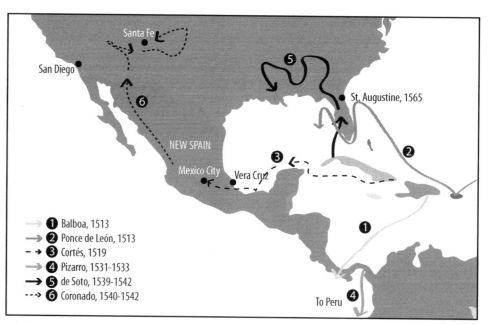

FIGURE 1.9 - Principal Early Explorations and Conquests

The Aztec Empire Falls

Hernán Cortés, the son of an unimportant nobleman in Spain, arrived in the Caribbean in 1504 to seek his fortune. In 1511, he took part in the conquest of Cuba before he led the expedition that conquered one of the wealthiest empires in the New World. Cortés served the governor of Cuba as his secretary and later mayor of the city of Santiago before he led an expedition to fame and fortune on the Mexican mainland. The governor put together a small convoy to search for a lost expedition with Cortés at the head. He then became suspicious that Cortés might use this as an excuse to search for his own treasure. The conquistador ignored the governor's orders to stay in Cuba as he prepared to disembark for his destination. With 11 ships, approximately 500 men, 16 horses, and about 20 guns, the expedition landed on the eastern coast of Mexico and began the march to the rumored wealthy empire of the Aztecs.

The Aztecs had many enemies from their conquest of neighboring tribes far and wide, and Cortés took advantage of this enmity to forge alliances as he marched toward the capital of Montezuma. The Tlaxcalans, an unconquered tribe, hostile to the Aztecs and the Spaniards, were broken by the Spanish forces and became invaluable in the conquest of Mexico.

Montezuma II, emperor of the Aztec empire, received word of the forces of Cortés landing on the coast. From the accounts of those who saw the Spanish leader and his forces, Montezuma surmised that Cortes could be the god Quetzalcoatl back to avenge his poor treatment in the past. The Aztecs believed that there had been four worlds destroyed before this one, and that this one could be destroyed as well. Hoping to assuage the anger of the supposed god and keep Cortés away, the emperor sent gifts of gold to the Spanish. Rather than bribe the Spanish to stay away, the gifts confirmed that the Spanish were getting closer to one of their goals in the New World.

FIGURE 1.10 - Hernan Cortes

The Spanish leader, as head of the government in Vera Cruz, sent off a messenger to gain the approval from the king of Spain for his venture. Cortés knew that he was in disobedience to the governor of Cuba and, as such, faced some sort of punishment, but if he could conquer the Aztec and bring a fortune to the king, then all could be forgiven. He then burned the ships to force the men to follow him on his quest.

The emperor of the Aztecs attempted to stop the march of the conquistadors with a plot to overcome the Spanish at Cholula, but the Spanish foiled his plans, destroyed the city, and continued on. Montezuma had no choice in the face of the invaders' strength but to welcome them into his capital, Tenochtitlan. It was a grand city, and many historians claim it was superior to the finest cities in Europe at the time. The host soon became the prisoner.

Just as Cortés gained control of the city of his dreams, events took a turn for the worse. A force sent by the governor of Cuba, Velasquez, arrived at Vera Cruz to arrest the conquistador and return him to face questions. Hearing this, Cortes returned to Vera Cruz, burned the ships, defeated the envoy, and convinced the men to follow him. When he returned to Tenochtitlan, the commander found his men under siege in their palace for daring to interrupt a religious celebration. The Aztecs turned on the commander and his men as well as Montezuma. Montezuma died either from a rock thrown by one of his people or at the hands of the Spanish. The Spanish attempted to sneak out of the capital with much of their treasure, but the Aztecs discovered them and attacked. This day—June 30, 1520—was called the "Sad Night" by the Spanish. Two-thirds of the conquistadors died as well as many of their horses. On August 13, 1521, they recaptured the city with assistance of warriors from neighboring tribes. In 1523, Cortés became governor of the city and in 1528 Captain-General of what the Spanish called New Spain. They built Mexico City on the grounds of the Aztec monuments and palaces.

The Incan Empire Falls

Francisco Pizarro took the greed and cruelty and the worst of the Spanish brutality into South America. Pizarro gained experience in New Spain serving Cortés and with Balboa in his expedition across Panama to the Pacific Ocean. As the conquistador served in other expeditions in Colombia and Peru in South America, he found more evidence of gold. He petitioned the Spanish governor of Panama to explore further inland, hoping to find more gold, but the governor denied his request. Pizarro then went over his head to request and receive permission directly from Spain to search the northwestern areas of South America.

His quest began with 168 men and about 30 horses. By 1532, Pizarro was in Incan territory and in contact with the Incan emperor Atahualpa. Feigning friendship with the emperor allowed Pizarro to capture the leader of the Incas and demand a large ransom. The Spaniard executed the emperor in August 1533 despite the payment of the ransom, another act of Spanish treachery and terror against the native tribes. The Spanish repeated the brutality when they conquered the Incan capital of Cuzco. The incredible treasures of the Incan empire were theirs, and Peru now belonged to Spain.

In the early days, the Spanish kept the Incan political structure intact. They even went to the extreme of crowning a new emperor, but of course one who was under their control. Soon the land was divided into large haciendas with the Indians as serfs and slaves. Lima, Peru became the headquarters for the Spanish and one of the wealthiest cities in the world. Peru became the headquarters for the second viceroyalty in the Americas.

The Spanish Empire in the Americas

As the empire of Spain grew through exploration, conquest, and settlements, it was necessary to increase the administrative elements and carry all elements of Spanish life into the new lands. There were two administrative units established in Spain to assure control and protect the interests of the Spanish monarchy. The House of Trade (Casa de Contratación), established in 1503, was organized to control the economic life of the colonies. Ships from the American colonies had to sail in convoys and land at designated ports in Spain. This allowed the collection of taxes from the commerce of the New World to proceed in an orderly manner. The Spanish government also tried to confine the trade of the New World colonies to Spain, but this was not feasible for long. As the ships of more countries stopped in these ports, the colonists purchased the lower-priced goods. By the 1600s, the Spanish navy could no longer enforce these rules rigorously, and Spain could not prevent the farmers and manufacturers from growing or producing enumerated items. As more settlers came and moved further out into the territories, the government of Spain had less control. Spanish settlers even eventually took exception to regulations from Spain, even when loosely enforced. As more North American colonies developed with settlers from other nations, the same rules and regulations brought the same resentment.

The second agency in Spain formed to handle the government of the Spanish portion of the New World was the Council of the Indies (Consejo de Indias). From 1524, the Council drafted laws, made government appointments, and heard judicial appeals. Because Spain was so distant, local government forces were necessary. In the early years, there were two viceroyalties to govern in the New World—New Spain and Peru.

Searching for Gold

In the early 1500s, Spanish colonization was mostly on the islands of Hispaniola, Puerto Rico, Cuba, and Jamaica. However, once the Spanish had control of the Aztec land, they explored other areas for treasure. Great wealth was found in some areas, but mostly the land was the treasure. Settlers eventually moved onto the mainland areas of North America, Central America, and South America. But first the search for gold pushed expeditions to explore the vast amounts of territory.

Francisco Vasquez de Coronado arrived in Mexico in 1535 with the newly appointed viceroy of New Spain. He rose quickly in the political ranks, but the stories of gold to the north captured his imagination. He is best known for his exploration north of Mexico in his search for the treasures of the legendary Seven Cities of Cibola.

The search for gold constantly pushed the exploration of the New World for the Spanish conquerors. Coronado traveled northeast of Mexico with 300 Spaniards and 700 Indians. He passed through the land that became Arizona, New Mexico, and Kansas. He encountered a variety of tribes, saw magnificent terrain, but did not find gold. He returned to Mexico in 1542, perhaps wiser but no richer. In fact, he went on trial for mismanaging the expedition, and the court found enough evidence that it assessed a fine.

Hernando de Soto attempted the same as Coronado, except in the southeastern portions of North America. De Soto returned to Spain after distinguishing himself as a brave conquistador during service with Pizarro. The king gave him the governorship of Cuba and permission to conquer land in North America. In 1539, with approximately 600 men, he landed in Florida. By 1542, the expedition had explored areas that eventually became 10 states of the United States, crossed the Mississippi River, and lost de Soto to a fever. They did not find gold as they had hoped. The survivors were the first Europeans to float down the Mississippi to the Gulf of Mexico. As much as the explorers continued to search for gold and silver outside of the land of the Aztecs and the Incas, they found little. It would be much later in the history of North America that gold once again dazzled the zeal for exploration and discovery. Settlement of the land and a chance for a good life was the pot of gold at the end of the rainbow for most settlers in the "New Found World."

The Conquistadors Settle the Land

The Spanish government established the House of Trade and the Council of the Indies to control the economic and political life of the new empire. However, it was the conquistadors who explored, discovered, conquered, and then controlled land in the New World with one thing in mind: profit. They claimed the land in the name of the monarch of Spain, but expected a share of any revenue. They usually received one-fifth of the plunder and authority over conquered land. They also sold the Indians into slavery for profit. The conquistadors received money from grants known as encomiendas. These grants gave a license to collect tribute, but not actually own the land, from the conquered Indian villages. In return, the grant held the holder responsible for the protection of the Indians and their conversion to Christianity by building a church and bringing in a priest.

The Spanish monarch desired revenue from its investments in the New World as well, but worried that the conquistadors could not assure the stability needed to bring in long-term profit and worried that they enslaved or mistreated too many Indians. The crown wanted the Indians to become Christians and taxpayers. In 1542, Spain passed the Laws of the Indies to protect the natives, especially from the encomienda system. The Spanish could not enslave the Indians, and the Indians were not to work in the mines unless absolutely necessary. Moreover, they must be treated well and taxed fairly. The law also stated that the encomienda grants ended at the deaths of the current encomendero.

The Spanish Catholic Church sent priests and missionary friars to convert the Indians to Christianity and make good citizens out of them. Although the conquistadors thought they had done enough by reading the requerimiento (in Spanish) requiring the Indians to accept Spanish rule and Christianity, much more was needed to bring about conversion and a good citizen for New Spain. In actuality, many of the Native Americans kept part or all of their previous beliefs.

FIGURE 1.11 - Landing of De Soto in Florida

In La Florida, even though the Spanish had built the town of St. Augustine (the first permanent European settlement in what was later the U.S.). In 1565, the Spanish built St. Augustine in La Florida (the first to keep the area from falling into French hands). This colony was close to failure until the Franciscan and Jesuit missionaries began building mission stations across the area and began converting the Native Americans. By 1606, missionaries controlled the coast as far north as the Carolinas and approximately 600 soldiers, priests, and settlers lived in the region. Similar methods secured New Mexico in the late 1500s to early 1600s, and by 1600 approximately 400 settlers lived in this area.

Effects of the Conquest

Wherever they settled, the Spanish changed the lives of most of the Amerindians significantly with Middle America (Mexico and Central America). There were cultural changes as the Indians were forced into towns in which they learned Spanish, became Catholics, and paid taxes; a decline in the population—perhaps as high as 90 percent—due to disease and enslavement; stress on the land with the introduction of wheat when the natives grew maize; deforestation because the Spaniards used wood for building, heating, and cooking; and Spanish animals competing with humans for food. In spite of all of these changes, some of the Indian villages survived, and the Indian culture and language still survive in some inland areas to this day.

Spanish Settlers

In the 1500s, approximately 240,000 settlers arrived from Spain. They came as future settlers from other countries to leave the problems of their country in the Old World and seek opportunity in the New World. For the first few decades, most of the settlers were young single men. They often married or had relationships with Indian women and created a mix of the races known as the mestizo. The racial structure became more complicated as more African slaves came into the empire to replace the Indian slaves. Many of the money-making efforts, such as growing sugar cane, required a great deal of labor.

The Spanish had a great liking for building urban areas. By 1574, there were approximately 120 towns in their empire in the Americas, and that number had almost doubled by 1628. They put into place a government much the same as the towns in Spain and laid out the towns in a grid pattern. There was a central plaza with the church and town hall and other public buildings around the plaza. The wealthier families lived close to the plaza, and the lower income families lived further away.

The Spanish government wanted control over every aspect of the new settlements, so it implemented a strict bureaucracy that was inefficient and slow in making decisions. Although the government in Spain wanted complete control, the distance allowed those in the New World many ways to circumvent that control. There were two large administrative units—the viceroyalties, controlled by viceroys. New Spain ruled Mexico, Central America, and the Caribbean, and the Viceroyalty of Peru ruled all of the Spanish possessions in South America. The audiencia was a council that performed legislative, advisory, and judicial functions. There was also an archbishop for each viceroyalty to administer the religious elements of the colonies. The portion of the Americas the Spanish controlled was wealthy beyond imagination at the time and sending tons of gold and silver into the coffers of Spain annually. Spain had to secure the empire to continue the flow of gold and silver that was making it the wealthiest country in Europe.

Other Nations Compete

In 1504, Norman fishing boats from France arrived off the coast south and east of Newfoundland to fish for cod along the Grand Bank. Soon ships from Portugal, England, and the Netherlands came to fish the same area. Sometimes as many as 500 ships were offshore, and the fishermen were sun-drying the cod to take back to Europe.

When other European countries decided to challenge the Spanish and Portuguese for foreign lands, the newcomers ignored the edict from the Pope and the two countries. More than 80 voyages were undertaken by explorers and colonizers between 1492 and 1504 into the Americas. The monarchs of Portugal, England, France, and the Netherlands sponsored these voyages, hoping to realize

FIGURE 1.12 - Jacques Cartier

Souza cleared the French ships from the Brazilian coast and began Portuguese settlement.

King John III of Portugal divided the land into 15 provinces, and the leaders of the provinces were responsible for bringing the natives to Christianity and settlers to Brazil. The Portuguese carved the country out of the wilderness with slave labor, both Indian and African. Most worked in the fields and mines under atrocious conditions. Portugal was invested heavily in the African slave trade for decades and brought in about 40,000 slaves a year through the 1600s. The reason for the high number of slave importation was the high death rate.

Although the Portuguese monarchs ruled Brazil with many of the same regulations established by the Spanish for their colonies, the Brazilian settlers basically ignored those rules. As was the case with all of the American colonies, distance provided a cushion from the strict oversight of the European rulers.

The French

Due to more pressing issues in Europe, France lagged behind Spain in the exploration of the Americas. French sailors fished the waters off Newfoundland, but no efforts to colonize came for quite some time. King Francis I did, however, send the Italian explorer Giovanni da Verrazano in search of the elusive Northwest Passage to Asia. Verrazano was unsuccessful in his mission, but he explored the Atlantic coast from the Carolinas to Nova Scotia. The king had no particular interest in further exploration of the Americas until others he respected convinced him to send Jacques Cartier in 1534 to the Americas to search for a Northwest Passage and gold.

Cartier set sail on April 20, 1534, and arrived on the northeastern shore of North America on May 10. He sailed up the St. Lawrence River as far as the first rapids. He met friendly native tribes and returned to France with exciting news that this land was fertile, overflowing with wildlife, and the people eager for trade. Cartier had claimed the land of eastern Canada for France. King Francis was eager to send Cartier on a second expedition once the king heard of the potential of the land and the accounts of the two Iroquois who returned with Cartier.

one or all of the following: a westward route to the East Indies, gold, advancement of the Christian religion, and additional lands to add to their kingdoms. One of the early money-making ventures for the European nations was returning with full holds of cod from the banks of Newfoundland.

The Portuguese

The Portuguese had a share of South America because of the division by the Pope of the unclaimed world between Spain and its neighbor in the Treaty of Tordesillas (1494), but they were slow to do anything with it. In 1500, Pedro Cabral, a Portuguese sea captain, reached the coast of South America but did not explore or stay in the area. The following year an expedition explored the same area of the coast. Amerigo Vespucci sailed with this expedition. The land was Brazil, and until 1530, only a few from Portugal came to explore and stayed. The Far Eastern trade was too lucrative for many to bother with finding anything of value in South America. However, if the owning nation ignored land in the time of discovery and exploration, the countrymen of another country would and did venture in. Therefore, in 1530, Martin de

On his next voyage, Cartier sailed as far as the site that would later become Montreal and founded a settlement that later became Quebec. The colonists abandoned New France, but others came later to establish an empire of woodsmen trading with the Indians for fur and establishing permanent settlements.

The French established Charlesfort on Parris Island, South Carolina in 1562, and when that settlement failed, another was established near the mouth of the St. Johns River in 1564.

The English

Hoping to compete with the Spanish and receive a share of any benefit the New World had to offer, English adventurers sanctioned by King Henry VIII and later his daughter Elizabeth I began their voyages west across the Atlantic. Even before that, Italian explorer John Cabot planted the English flag in 1497 during the reign of King Henry VII in what English tradition declares was Newfoundland.

There were several attempts to establish a presence in North America before the first permanent colony led to an established English presence. An important hindrance to English settlement was a lack of knowledge. The explorers were ignorant of the route, navigation, and the land to which they were traveling. They were further hindered by a lack of funding and competent leadership. It was not uncommon for ships to set sail from the shores of England only to have to return to shore for a variety of reasons, including not enough food and ships that were not seaworthy. In order to gain knowledge of the country and gain more support for future travels, the explorers brought captives from the Americas to England. For example, in 1535 William Hawkins brought a native king from Brazil to the court of Henry VIII.

A renowned English adventurer and soldier, Sir Humphrey Gilbert, received a patent in 1578 from Queen Elizabeth to discover and colonize "remote, heathen and barbarous landes [sic], countries, and territories not actually possessed of any Christian prince." Specifically, the patent gave him six years to establish one or more colonies in North America. After several failed attempts, Gilbert sailed for the New World in June 1583 with five vessels. When he arrived in St. Johns Bay, Newfoundland, he found ships from 36 different countries. Nevertheless, he reclaimed Newfoundland for England, confirming John Cabot's claim of 1497. Unfortunately, Gilbert went down with his ship on its return trip to England that same year. However, in 1584, Queen Elizabeth reissued his patent to his half-brother, Sir Walter Raleigh, who established Roanoke Colony in 1585 (see Chapter 2 for a discussion of Roanoke and its problems).

Conclusion

The voyages of Columbus, beginning in 1492, ultimately led to a clash of cultures between the Native Americans of the Western Hemisphere and the European invaders from the Old World. The Europeans, with their diseases and advanced weaponry, triumphed in the clash. Perhaps as much as 90 percent of the Native American population was decimated by the contact.

FIGURE 1.13 - Sir Humphrey Gilbert

The Americas were not a New World open for the taking as the Europeans claimed. The European settlers justified their taking of the land in their minds because of the differences between the cultures. The lands and the civilizations were an old world existing in isolation for thousands of years. It was not a paradise as so many have tried to claim. There were wars and brutality between the tribes that stagger the minds of civilized people. Some of the tribes, including the Caribs of the Caribbean, were cannibals. They ate body parts of their slain enemies to ingest the power of that enemy into themselves. The Aztec sacrificed humans to the gods to win their approval. The various tribes enslaved their enemies. It is clear, then, that cruelty was not unique to one side in this contact.

In the 1600s, the European takeover shifted to North America. The English came and stayed, and the culture clash shifted to new territory. Against all odds, thousands of the natives of the New World survived.

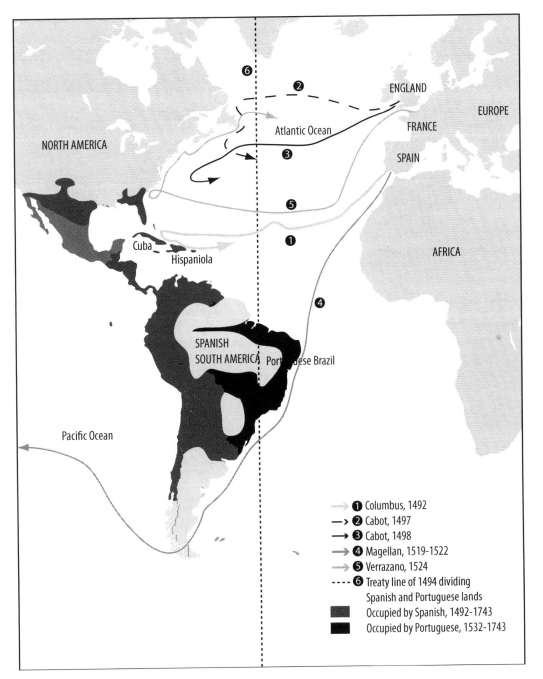

FIGURE 1.14 - Principal Voyages of Discovery

A replica cannon stands where a corner bastion once existed at the original Jamestown on Jamestown Island in Virginia. Copyright 2010 iStockphoto.

Chapter 2 Contents

CHAPTER TWO

England Colonizes the New World

Major Events

1580s	English established a colony at Roanoke Island
1588	The English navy defeated the Spanish Armada
1607	First permanent English colony in North America established at Jamestown, Virginia
1619	Roots of democracy and slavery planted in Jamestown
1620	Pilgrims established Plymouth Colony
1629	Puritans established Massachusetts Bay Colony
1630s	Colony of Maryland was established
1637	Pequot War
1639	Thomas Hooker wrote the Fundamental Orders of Connecticut
1660	King Charles II became King of England
1662	English settlements along the Connecticut River received a colonial charter
1663	Settlements in Rhode Island received a colonial charter. Land grants were given for the colonies of South and North Carolina
1664	English defeated the Dutch at New Amsterdam (New York City) and the former Dutch holdings became the colonies of New York and New Jersey
1675	King Philip's War
1781	King Charles II granted William Penn a charter for what became Pennsylvania and Delaware
1782	Trustees received a charter to establish the colony of Georgia

Introduction

Prior to the 1580s, English expeditions to North America were seasonal, short-lived, and focused on fishing the seas off the Newfoundland coast of Canada or plundering the Spanish treasure ships sailing to their homeland. By the 1580s, a small number of powerful English leaders determined that it was time for England to claim its share of the wealth of the New World as other European nations had. It is believed that John Cabot, an Italian navigator and explorer with English backing, was the first to set foot upon North America, when he claimed the island of Newfoundland in 1497. However, neither King Henry VII nor Henry VIII followed up on his claim because of internal issues. It fell to an English queen, Elizabeth I, and her successors, to profit from land claimed for England by John Cabot in 1497. The monarchs claimed the land, but they wanted others to take the financial risks entailed in finding that profit. Of course, the royals demanded a share of any wealth received from the resources of their land, which in the near future meant the wealth from permanent colonies.

Other countries claimed land for their monarchs, but very little was actually settled. The English moved into areas either not settled by other European nations or those nations were unable to keep the English out. The Spanish claimed and settled portions of the Caribbean, South America, Central America, and some southern portions of North America. The French claimed land to the north in Canada.

Ignored in all of these land grabs were the native inhabitants of the New World, the Indians, misnamed by Columbus because he mistakenly believed he had reached the East Indies in 1492. The various tribes along the Atlantic coastline planted their crops on land they cleared, hunted in unspoiled forests, raised their families, fought their enemies, and developed their own culture. There was an enemy coming to the New World, and this enemy would not only destroy the lives of millions of American Indians, but annihilate thousands of tribes as they took their homeland.

Explorers in the employment of queens, kings, corporations, and wealthy individuals in England, the Netherlands, and Sweden sailed to North America in the wake of the Spanish, and the French determined to compete with these nations in the Western Hemisphere in profitable ventures and trade as they did in Europe. For several of the nations, problems that they dealt with in Europe played out in the colonies and vice versa.

There were several reasons Englishmen went to the trouble and expense of permanent settlements or colonies. Although those involved denied it, one of the primary motives was to establish a base from which to launch raids on Spanish treasure and merchant ships that sailed from the New World. Privateering was an accepted and profitable venture for those who sailed and the government for which they sailed. There was also the hope to find a Northwest Passage to Asia, find gold or silver on the land as had the Spanish, or to find other resources that might benefit England. Sir Walter Raleigh, an aristocrat and explorer, had trouble with financing because of the high risk involved and the fact that there were no guarantees of any return on the investments. He funded much of the early attempts from his own pocket.

One of the barriers to English enthusiasm for the New World and colonization was that many in England lacked knowledge about the land, inhabitants, and possible assets. There were some writings available from those who had visited the distant land. The captains and crews of the ships sent by Raleigh for reconnaissance in the early 1580s returned with information about the land across the Atlantic and brought two Native Americans with them as well. A small group of enthusiastic propagandists gathered as much information as possible about the New World and wrote convincing tracts and reports on the resources of the area. Thomas Harriot wrote, "A Briefe and True Report of the New Found Land of Virginia" in 1588, publicizing the wonders, even if somewhat exaggerated, of North America. Harriot had made the voyage to Virginia and saw what he wrote of with his own eyes.

In the late 1500s and early 1600s England was a small, weak nation with many internal problems. Feudalism was breaking apart as a system of land ownership and tenancy. Landowners began selling their land or renting it rather than allowing tenants to work the land and give portions of crops or their time in service to live on the land. Property owners also enclosed large areas for the grazing of sheep rather than allowing tenants to farm the land. Those who had worked the land their entire lives were forced to move to the cities. The cities became overcrowded, and unemployment, crime, sewage and health problems soared. There was also persecution for many small religious sects that denied the teachings of the Church of England. The hope for a new chance to make a living and the right to religious freedom were the impetus for many to risk all in a land that was not settled.

England changed course from a weak second- rate nation in the 1500s to a strong world power in the 1600s with an international empire that began with colonies in Ireland and then North America and the Caribbean.

Ireland: A Training Ground

Ireland served as a training ground for future English colonization efforts. In the 1560s and 1570s, Queen Elizabeth sent her soldiers to regain control over the Irish in order to prevent the French or the Spanish from establishing a base on the island. If these adversaries gained control of Ireland, they would have another location from which to threaten an attack on England. The English justified their right to dominate Ireland with some of the same reasons later offered for the right to control the native tribes and take their land in North America. They claimed the Irish were pagans, savages, and nomads without a right to the land because they did not farm it to the fullest potential.

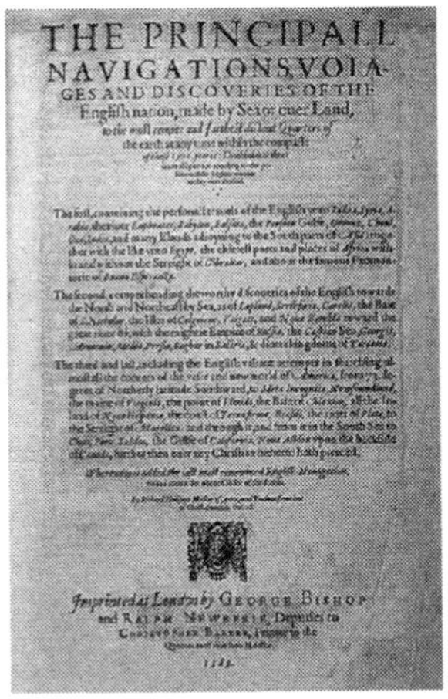
THE PRINCIPALL
NAVIGATIONS, VOIA-
GES AND DISCOVERIES OF THE
English nation, made by Sea or over Land,

FIGURE 2.1 - Principal Navigations by Richard Hakluyt

Once the English dubbed the Irish savage, the interlopers felt little need to treat the Irish with anything but brutality. Any violence doled out by the Irish was doubled by the English. Sir Humphrey Gilbert, half-brother of Walter Raleigh, fought a total war of terror in Ireland in 1569. He lined the pathway to his tent with severed heads.

Irish resistance led to the loss of their land. That land was then granted to English "gentlemen." The new landowners brought over settlers to colonize the land. The colonists were often inept at farming but used their status as Englishmen to exploit the native Irish. The Native Americans faced many of these same circumstances from their contact with the English in the New World.

Stating the Case for Colonies

The numbers and excitement grew in the 1580s for those who believed that colonies in North America could launch England into greatness. They also believed that England must act soon to counter the growth of French and Spanish interests in the area. The Hakluyt cousins, both named Richard, did what they could to increase the number of those who believed in the cause. Raleigh promoted and supported a colony in the New World on Roanoke Island.

The Hakluyts gathered information on trade, trade routes, and settlements in the Americas. They became not only experts on the subject of colonization but also voices of inspiration on the subject. Reverend Richard Hakluyt wrote *Divers Voyages to America*, which was a collection of accounts to North America. He wrote the *Discourse of Western Planting* to convince the queen and her secretary Walsingham of the importance of establishing colonies in the Americas. He knew that the success of colonization depended a great deal on government sponsorship and financing. Richard Hakluyt the elder wrote a small discourse, *Inducements to the Liking of the Voyage Intended Towards Virginia.* In 1589 Reverend Hakluyt wrote his greatest work, *The Principal Navigations, Voyages and Traffics of the English Nation.*

In their works *Discourse of Western Planting* and *Inducements for the Liking of the Voyage Intended for Virginia*, they explained their ideas on the purpose of colonies. Colonies would spread Protestantism to the native populations, provide resources and commodities for the home country, become a destination for the poor of the nation, and provide impetus for building a stronger navy. Moreover, there would be a base to search for the Northwest Passage, which in turn would bring more wealth to the nation with a shorter route to the wealth of the Pacific and Asia.

The writings of the Hakluyts brought more support for Raleigh and his proposed settlement of Roanoke by explaining the many benefits of a colony in North America. They opened the minds of many to the benefits awaiting colonial ventures. For those who failed to see any benefit to these expensive voyages and settlements into the unknown, the Hakluyts gave substance with explanations of the possibilities.

A "Lost Colony"

Sir Humphrey Gilbert and his half-brother Sir Walter Raleigh, holders of the first patents for English colonization in the New World, both served in the vile war to subjugate Ireland. The patent included permission to find "heathen and barbarous lands… not actually possessed of any Christian prince…to have, hold, occupy, & enjoy." Sir Humphrey Gilbert established the first English colony in the New World in Newfoundland, but the colony quickly folded due to the cold, harsh climate and the barren land. Gilbert's ship went down before he could establish the colony he was planning further to the south. The queen gave Raleigh, a favorite of hers, a patent along the Atlantic coastline, north of the Spanish land of Florida and south of the French-held land in Canada.

In 1584, Raleigh sent navigators Philip Amadas and Arthur Barlowe with two ships to explore the eastern coast, spy on Spanish fortifications in the Caribbean, and find a likely spot for a settlement from which to plunder Spanish ships. The small expedition found what they believed to be a perfect island, Roanoke, off the outer banks of current-day North Carolina. After his men returned to England with glowing reports and two Native Americans (Manteo and Wanchese), Raleigh and his fellow investors organized their first colonial venture.

Even Queen Elizabeth showed her support for the venture by investing her own funds, sending her ship the *Tiger* as the flagship, allowing the surrounding territory to be dubbed Virginia after her nickname (the "Virgin Queen"), and giving Raleigh the authority to seize men and ships.

Five ships and two small boats set sail with more than 600 men for their destination on April 9, 1585. The ships left only 107 men to begin the colony. It was evident that the other mission of the small fleet was privateering. Once the ships were in close proximity to the island of Roanoke, it was clear that the reports of the perfection of the island for the purpose of settlement were false. Navigation through the channels to the island was difficult, and the surrounding water was too shallow for the larger ships. The *Tiger* anchored several miles out to sea, which made it vulnerable to any passing Spanish ship. The small fleet could not stay, and it was now clear that the men left behind needed to find a more suitable location for the settlement. Problematic for the new settlement was the loss of the supplies aboard the *Tiger*. The leader of the fleet promised that supplies would come from England.

The men built a fort, jail, storehouses, and a small number of houses under the leadership of their governor Ralph Lane. Lane was called from duty in Ireland to serve as the governor of the new colony. Although the colonists set up their living arrangements and the security of a fort, they failed to find ways to supply food for the group. They had to depend on the Indians. This was the case time and again for the new colonies. They needed resupplying because they could not take care of their own needs. The Indians in the various areas were willing to give some food, often in trade for knives or other items and help them to survive in the new land. Eventually, the colonists demanded more than the neighboring tribes were willing to part with. Relations broke down between the men and their Indian neighbors, and the tribes refused to trade food with the Englishmen. The whites became very hostile and treacherous in their dealings with the native groups. This behavior can be partly explained by Lane's experience in Ireland and his views on how to deal with native groups that he believed were not to be trusted.

When Sir Francis Drake arrived with his fleet in June 1586, he offered the settlers passage home. Drake was in the area to strike at Spanish settlements and ships. He probably stopped at Roanoke to use the island as a temporary base as the colony's promoters planned. Drake did not realize that the water surrounding the island was too shallow to permit most of his ships to anchor close to shore. The men were certainly willing to row out to the ships to get away from the place of their failure.

FIGURE 2.2 -
Sir Francis Drake

In 1587 Raleigh sent another group to take up residence on Roanoke. John White, who travelled to the area with them, brought 107 men, women and children. Neither the island nor the natives were hospitable. White's daughter gave birth to the first English child born in what later became the United States. The parents named the child Virginia Dare. Because the colony was short on supplies and not faring well in providing for the inhabitants, White sailed for England to bring back supplies.

Delayed by the hostilities that eventually led to the Spanish Armada sailing to invade England, White did not return to Roanoke until August 17, 1590. He found the settlement deserted. The only sign of what happened was the word CROATOAN carved in a doorpost. This was the name of an Indian tribe on a neighboring island. Search parties combed the area with no success. To this day, the fate of the colonists is not known. Much conjecture abounded then and still does. Perhaps the surrounding tribes took the colonists hostage, or perhaps the colonists left the island because of hunger and settled with tribes elsewhere. In any case, it became known as the "Lost Colony" of Roanoke.

Defeat of the Spanish Armada

One of the most important factors that allowed England to successfully colonize the New World was the defeat of the Spanish Armada in 1588. In the second half of the sixteenth century, English pirates like Sir Francis Drake raided Spanish fleets in the Caribbean and Atlantic waters, attempting to slow down Spain's head start in gaining the gold, silver, and other wealth from the New World. Walking a political tightrope, English Queen Elizabeth I (ruled 1558-1603) officially condemned English pirates while doing little to stop them. King Philip II of Spain (ruled 1556-1598) grew increasingly agitated at Elizabeth for her apparent unwillingness to stop her countrymen from engaging in piracy against the Spanish. Piracy was not the only thing bothering the Spanish king. As a strong Catholic, he had never accepted the legitimacy of the Protestant Elizabeth as queen of England, and he had unsuccessfully plotted to replace her with Elizabeth's Catholic cousin, Mary, Queen of Scots. When Elizabeth had Mary executed in 1587, Philip's options were virtually exhausted.

Spain was the world's superpower in the sixteenth century, and England was not yet her military equal. This put Elizabeth in a dangerous situation. The Spanish king even attempted to arrange to marry Elizabeth in order to control England himself, but the Virgin Queen thwarted his advances and remained "married" only to England. Finally, Philip sent a fleet of some 130 ships to invade England in the summer of 1588. Fortunately for England, the queen's advisors had convinced her in the nick of time to authorize large expenditures on building up the British navy. This build-up was basically completed just in time to face the Spanish invasion force in July 1588.

While English ships outnumbered the Spanish approximately 200 to 130, the Spanish had more and heavier cannons. Nevertheless, the newly-built English ships featured the latest designs, making them smaller, faster, and more easily maneuverable. This advantage was multiplied by the fact of greater English sea experience on the unpredictable waters of the English Channel, where maneuverability was often crucial. When it had ended after a few weeks, the Spanish Armada had been badly beaten. Matters were then made worse for the Spanish when a sea storm pushed many of their ships onto the shores of Ireland on their journey back to Spain. Only about one-half of the Spanish ships returned home.

The great English victory here greatly helped England establish prosperous colonies in North America in at least two ways. First, the Spanish military threat was no longer an insurmountable obstacle to colonization in America. In fact, the defeat of the Spanish Armada represented a major turning point for England and against Spain. The latter began a long, slow period of military and economic decline on the world stage. Second, the fact that the English had won such a glorious victory over the world's superpower lifted their people's confidence to the point they believed there was nothing they could not accomplish. It is an historical lesson for all people to never underestimate the power of positive thinking.

The Plymouth and London Companies

In spite of the failure of Roanoke, there were those in England who believed that permanent English colonies were possible. One of the first challenges for a colonial venture was raising enough money. Joint stock was one of the solutions for the very expensive proposition of putting together a colony. Virginia, Plymouth, Massachusetts Bay, New Netherlands, and New Sweden were established through the money pooled by selling stock.

English merchants in Plymouth and London organized the Plymouth Company and the London Company, respectively, and applied in 1606 for patents to the king's land in Virginia. The investors hoped to find a western route to Asia and benefit from the bounty of the continent, whether it was gold, fish, furs, or other valuable resources. In 1606, King James I granted permission to the London group, also known as the Virginia Company of London, to settle the land from present-day North Carolina to New York and the Plymouth group from present-day Virginia to Canada. In the overlapping areas, the settlements must have at least 100 miles separation. Government of the colonies consisted of the joint stock companies or proprietors, a royal council of 13 in England, and a local governor and council in the colonies. The colonists were to follow the laws of England and to also retain all rights of Englishmen. All of this was decided without consideration of those Native American tribes who had the prior claim by living on the land for centuries. The English, as had

those of other European nations in the past, gave land that was not rightfully theirs to those who had no rights to the land either. This was only one of the elements of a Eurocentrist (European focus) view of the world.

In 1607, the Plymouth Company sent out men to settle their first and last colony. Approximately 100 men settled a colony in present-day Maine, but the venture was a miserable failure. There was not enough food, the weather was wintry, the native tribes were hostile, and there was conflict among the men. As a result, the colony only lasted about a year. In spite of this failure, the London Company was able to send men to establish a colony for the English in the New World.

Jamestown

After five months spent crossing the Atlantic Ocean, three ships arrived on the east coast of North America in May 1607 with 104 Englishmen and established the first permanent colony for England. They sailed into the Chesapeake Bay and 36 miles up a river they named "the James" after King James I of England. Additionally, he was the king who authorized the King James' Version of the Bible that was published in 1611. The new settlers chose the location of the first colony, Jamestown, for strategic purposes. Spain controlled the seas and areas of North America to the south of Jamestown, so the settlers needed a location that they could defend if discovered by the Spanish. The site they chose was a small strip of land connected to the mainland, with a water channel deep enough to allow the colonists' ships to tie up to trees along the shore. This site may have been a good choice for defense, but it was a disastrous choice for health and quality of life. The land was low and marshy, without fresh water for drinking. They drank from the salty James River, which led to health problems. The marshes were a breeding ground for dangerous mosquitoes. Of course at that time, they did not know the dangers of mosquitoes.

The first group of settlers consisted of 104 gentlemen, soldiers, and laborers. The new adventurers were there to look for gold, but the first order of business was to build a fort. These settlers were aware of the Roanoke difficulties with the Native Americans. Within a few days there was an attack. Luckily, the ships remained at anchor, and the sailors were able to frighten away the warriors with cannon fire. After a month, the raids ended and the chief of the local tribes sent food to Jamestown.

At Jamestown and most of the other colonies, the English ignored the fact that this was not unclaimed land on which they chose to settle. Setting a flag in the ground and calling it the property of the kings and queens of England did not make it so. Time and again the cycle of settling on other people's land brought death and destruction to both sides in the colonizing efforts. The English eventually prevailed at a tremendous cost to the Native American tribes.

The land around Jamestown belonged to an Indian tribe called the Paspaheghs. It was one of about 30 tribes known collectively as the Powhatan and led by the leader Powhatan. The English believed the land was unclaimed, but they were wrong. The Indians lived in villages and farmed corn, beans, and squash. Their methods of farming were primitive to the English, but they worked with nature and used digging sticks to open the earth for the seed and planted around the trees. They also hunted game, fished, and gathered berries to sustain themselves. When the settlers first arrived, Powhatan did not perceive them as the enemy. Instead, he believed that he could use them to fight his enemies and gain the axes, knives, and other implements made from metal. Tribes from the north and the west were raiding the villages in Powhatan's empire, and those from the north had metal hatchets from the French traders.

By January 1608 only 38 of the men were still alive. The first few years were known as the "Starving Time." Disease and famine killed most of them. Drinking from a salty, impure river caused many deaths from salt poisoning, dysentery, and typhoid fever. As for the food problem, too many were looking for gold and not interested in tilling the soil, fishing, hunting, or building proper shelter. They planned on receiving food from the tribes, but that was only a temporary gift as far as the tribes were concerned. The tribes often had only enough food for themselves to get them through the long cold winters. When the tribes stopped offering food, the colonists raided villages and took what was no longer offered.

John Smith, a former soldier, stepped into the position of leader and implemented a strict program of "work or do not

FIGURE 2.3 - Captain John Smith

eat." Times were extremely difficult, but a ship filled with timber sailed back to England, reassuring the stockholders in the company that the colony could bring in a profit. The company also continued to send new colonists, which kept the colony from disappearing entirely.

In these early years it was not unusual for the men to marry or cohabit with native women. One of the problems with these early colonies was that there were not enough women coming to North America. In 1619, the Virginia Company acted to resolve this problem and sent 147 women to the colony in the "Maids for Virginia" program. If a man wanted to marry one of these maids, he had to pay the company 150 pounds of tobacco.

Saving the Virginia Colony

The venture in Virginia was close to failure until tobacco saved it. The Indians in Virginia cultivated tobacco, but it was bitter and strong. John Rolfe brought a sweeter–tasting tobacco from the Caribbean island of Trinidad to Virginia, and the fortunes of the colony turned around. Pipe smokers in England craved Virginia tobacco, although King James I vehemently disliked tobacco himself. Rolfe also brought peace between the settlers and the Indians by marrying Pocahontas, one of Chief Powhatan's daughters, in 1614.

The settlers demanded a change in the land policies of the Virginia Company. The company owned the land, and the colonists were a source of labor. To keep the current population working and encourage more settlers to endure the hardships in the early years of the colony, the company instituted private ownership of some of the land. Those already there who were not indentured servants received 100 acres. Anyone who paid his own way or the passage price of another received 50 acres of land; this was known as the "head right." If you bought a share in the company, you received 100 acres of land. The tobacco plantations needed a large labor force, so indentured servants were brought over to provide much of the labor. Indenture meant to sell your services for 4-7 years in order to have your passage to North America paid.

The original charter was revised in 1609. The boundaries of the colony were 400 miles along the coast with the interior following the same boundaries to the Pacific Ocean. The stockholders elected the governing council in England, and the local council was replaced with a governor. Democracy began in 1619 in America with the establishment of an assembly of colonial representatives called the House of Burgesses, located in Jamestown. This was the first European-based representative assembly in the New World because all of England's competitor nations had no elements of representative democracy at all. The company allowed the colonists a say in their government in order to entice them to stay in Virginia. For many years the company made all of the strict rules for the colony. The House of Burgesses consisted of two members from each part of the colony who met with the governor and council to write the laws that governed the colony.

King James I wanted to have ultimate control of the colony and instituted a legal suit against the Virginia Company for mismanagement in 1624. He won, and Virginia became a royal colony. The king would now choose the governor and council, but the House of Burgesses continued its role as an elected body representing white men of property in Virginia.

The English and the Indians were living in relative peace, hunted together, lived with each other on the plantations or in the Indian villages, and traded with each other. Unfortunately, this was just the lull before the storm. Following the deaths of Pocahontas in 1617, while in England with her husband, and Powhatan in 1618, Opechancanough became the leader of the Powhatan. He wanted the English gone. On March 22, 1622, the warriors of Opechancanough attacked across the colony and killed 347 settlers, which was a quarter of the English population. Jamestown was prepared for the attack because of the warning from a warrior friendly to the English. Many left their plantations for the security of Jamestown. Food was in short supply again, and with so many people in close proximity, disease increased.

The relationship between the Indian tribes and the whites was a cycle of killing with periods of quiet and peace. This cycle was replayed countless times until the 1890s. In 1644 there was another attack from the Powhatan, and between 400 and 500 colonists lost their lives. This was the last. The tribes of North America gave way time and again to the overwhelming numbers of European newcomers in all of the colonies. By 1660 there were approximately 30,000 colonists settled in the Virginia colony. In 1677, the Powhatan signed a peace treaty that gave them land on a reservation in return for annual payments to Virginia's governor. The payments from the Native Americans continue today.

Bacon's Rebellion

There were often conflicts between colonists and local governments and between western-frontier colonists and the eastern coastal power centers in various colonies. These rebellions were directed not against British rule but against colonial policies or officials who many perceived as acting against the public good in North America. Often the rebels wanted the British government to step in and right the wrongs perpetrated against their rights as English subjects. In 1676, after his foreman was murdered with an Indian arrow, planter Nathaniel Bacon gathered a group of westerners to put down the Indian tribes who were ravaging the western settlements; he also attacked peaceful tribes at the same time. Virginia's governor, Sir William Berkeley, had implemented land policies that favored the Indians and his own inner circle. The rebels even managed to burn much of the capital of Jamestown. Nathaniel Bacon died of a fever, after which Bacon's Rebellion was put down by the colonial militia. More than 20 vigilantes were hanged.

Plymouth and the Pilgrims

Following the Protestant Reformation of the sixteenth century, conflicts between Roman Catholics and Protestants plagued Europe within and between countries. Both religious groups believed their interpretation of Christianity exemplified the true nature of the Bible's messages. Religious differences led to persecution, death, and war as well as the migration of thousands to the New World.

In England, King Henry VIII's desire for a male heir led him to attempt to annul his marriage in order to marry another woman. When the Pope refused to annul his marriage, Henry VIII broke his country's connection with the Catholic Church in the early 1530s. Instead, he organized the Church of England, also known as the Anglican Church, with himself as the head. Despite this action, the king considered himself a Catholic for the remainder of his life. Many Catholics in England remained loyal to the Roman Church, including the king's daughter Mary, who ascended to the throne in 1553. In spite of the king's separation from Catholic control, the Anglican Church essentially retained Catholic doctrine and ritual. Queen Elizabeth I followed her sister Mary to the throne in 1558, but not her religious beliefs. Under Elizabeth, England officially returned to Protestantism. Indeed, Elizabeth took England further away from Catholic doctrine and ritual, but not far enough for many Anglicans in England.

Separatists were devoutly religious Protestants who saw no hope for their souls if they remained in the Anglican Church. Facing persecution in many forms, including fines and imprisonment, a group from the congregation in the town of Scrooby left England in 1608 to settle in religiously tolerant Holland. The Separatists in Holland decided to move again, this time to an area in the New World. They were fearful that their children were becoming Dutch and that could result in horrific consequences if Catholic Spain took control of the Netherlands.

FIGURE 2.4 - Plymouth and the Pilgrims

Agents went to England to negotiate with the Virginia Company for a patent to settle in the new colony. A joint stock company formed with the Leyden, Holland Separatists and others who ventured to find their fortunes in North America. The group of 35 Separatists and 66 other settlers sailed from Plymouth, England aboard the *Mayflower* on September 16, 1620. Whether they were blown off course or decided to land outside of the Virginia Colony because there were perhaps questions about their patent, the passengers of the *Mayflower* landed outside of the legal limits of their proposed destination in November 1620. Their first landing point was at present-day Provincetown, located on the northeastern tip of what is now called Cape Cod. The next month they moved into Cape Cod Bay and settled in what they called Plymouth, after the English port that they had departed from.

Before leaving the ship at Provincetown, the Separatist leaders, now known as the Pilgrims, drew up the Mayflower Compact (November 1620), which established a preliminary plan of government with just and equal laws because they knew they did not have a patent to settle on this particular land. John Carver was elected as their first governor in late 1620, but he was replaced by William Bradford after Carver's death in the spring of 1621. Meanwhile, Myles Standish, an experienced military officer, was put in charge of protecting the little colony.

Indians Saved the Pilgrim Fathers

Almost half of the original Plymouth colonists died from diseases like scurvy and insufficient shelter during the winter of 1620-1621. As with Jamestown, the entire colony probably would have been lost had it not been for local Indians. In March 1621, an Indian named Samoset walked out of the wilderness and greeted the colonists with "Welcome, Englishmen!" He had learned a little English from some English fishermen working near the coast of what is now Maine. Samoset shared some information about the geography and history of the region around Plymouth and returned almost a week later with a small group representing the Wampanoag chief Massasoit, including Squanto (shortened version of Tisquantum). The name Massachusetts is derived from Massasoit.

Squanto had been kidnapped by an English explorer named Thomas Hunt in 1614, who took him along with other Indians to Spain. When a group of Spanish monks discovered that Hunt was attempting to sell Squanto and the other Indians into slavery, they took them in order to try to convert them to Christianity. However, Squanto convinced the monks to allow him to try to get back home. In doing so, he wound up in England first, where he learned the English language while working for a shipbuilder. In 1619, he returned home only to find that his own tribe had been wiped out by a European disease, probably smallpox. Squanto then adopted Massasoit's tribe and returned to his previous village site with Samoset in March 1621, which was the place the Pilgrims called Plymouth.

Chief Massasoit signed a treaty with Plymouth Colony, pledging friendship, protection, and the use of the land there. Squanto played a major role in teaching the Plymouth colonists how to plant maize (corn). He was also the prominent language translator, guide, and general assistant to Plymouth Colony until his death from some kind of fever in 1622.

The so-called First Thanksgiving of the Pilgrims was actually their participation in the annual fall harvest festival of the local Indians. In fact, there were far more Indians there (Massasoit and his tribe) than Pilgrims. This harvest festival lasted for three days and included wild turkey, waterfowl, fish, and venison. No mention is made in the records of cranberry sauce or mashed potatoes.

The Puritan Theocracy of Massachusetts Bay

Protestants in England worked for further reforms in the church. One such group was the Puritans. Their religious aim was to purify the church of any Popish tradition or ritual because they believed the Protestant Reformation had not gone far enough in the Anglican Church. James I disliked the Puritans and perceived them as a threat to the Church of England (Anglican) and to England itself. In 1625 the son of James I, Charles I, ascended the throne of England. Charles was not as tolerant of the Puritans or Parliament as his father. Charles I, married to a Roman Catholic, accepted that good works empowered by the Holy Spirit (received by participating in the sacraments of the church) would

FIGURE 2.5 - Sources of the Puritan "Great Migration" to New England

bring a Christian to salvation. The Puritans could not tolerate this doctrine because it was in opposition to their views of predestination. As Calvinists, followers of sixteenth-century French Reformer John Calvin, the Puritans taught that salvation was by God's grace alone, apart from good works. Moreover, they also emphasized God's sovereignty over everything, so much so that they taught that God had predestined who He would save and who He would damn even before they were born. Thus, human beings have absolutely no control over their own afterlife. Many Puritans believed that England was on a course that would bring its ruination. It was time to look for a new location to put into practice a society that functioned in accordance with God's will. That new location was a colony in North America.

A royal charter was issued to the Massachusetts Bay Company in 1629 with permission to establish what became known as the Massachusetts Bay Colony. The first group of Puritans arrived in America in October 1629 on board the *Arbella* to settle this colony dedicated to serving their religion and their moral code. This was the beginning of the "Great Migration" to Massachusetts Bay, which brought approximately 20,000 English Puritans to the region by 1640. In October 1629 the company chose John Winthrop to take charge of the colony in America as its governor; he had sailed aboard the *Arbella*. During one of his sermons while at sea, Winthrop gave a sermon that touched Americans for centuries and became a core ideology for the future of America. The sermon was "A Modell of Christian Charity," in which he claimed that this new colony was to be "a City on a Hill." This new venture would be an example to the world of the benefits of modeling a society around the Puritan perspective of perfection. Later Winthrop turned into a fanatic, losing sight of what human beings needed and dismissing the opinions of others.

The goal was to create a religious colony in thought, word, and deeds. In other words, the intent was to establish a theocracy, a society in which God allegedly is the ultimate Ruler. One of the first priorities was the organization of the colony to carry out these goals. The first decision was that each congregation would establish itself and have its own minister (congregationalism). Thus, the colonial church was known as the Congregational Puritan Church. In the beginning, Governor Winthrop was the head of the colonial government and ruled with a few assistants who sat as a general assembly. As such, the government was subject only to the English Crown. By 1634, the freemen of the colony were dissatisfied with Winthrop's dictatorial methods and strict controls, so they demanded to see the company charter. Winthrop had concealed the extent of the power of the colonists. The colonists then formed a representative assembly with men from each town and voted the governor out of office.

The situation in the colony deteriorated with a great deal of religious controversy. In spite of the prevailing view that the United States was created for religious toleration, the truth was that those who came first came to practice their religion only. One result of this was that even Puritans were persecuted for violating "Sabbath" (Sunday) laws, failing to attend church services, and other alleged spiritual deficiencies, all because some were not as "pure" as the Puritan leaders thought they should be. Over time there were many conflicts over the practice of various religious beliefs. Therefore, the colonial representatives voted Winthrop back into office in 1637 to bring order again. He was demoted to deputy-governor in 1644 and elected governor again from 1646 until his death in 1649.

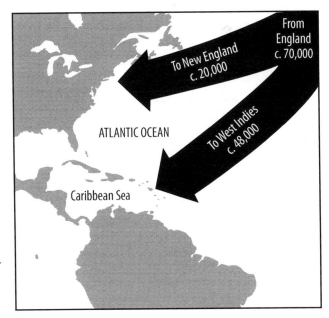

FIGURE 2.6 - The Great English Migration

New Hampshire

In 1622, Englishmen Captain John Mason and Sir Ferdinando Gorges were given a land patent from the Council for New England (based in Plymouth, England) for what was originally called the province of Maine, which then included all the land between the Merrimack and Kennebec Rivers. The first Englishmen there were fishermen, who settled at Odiorne's Point in present-day Rye, New Hampshire in 1623. In 1629, Mason and Gorges divided their land grant along the Piscataqua River, with Mason obtaining the land south of the river in what became known as New Hampshire. The land north of that river was called Maine and was under Gorges' dominion. The territory of New Hampshire originally included most of the southeastern portion of what is now the state of New Hampshire and part of present-day Massachusetts north of the Merrimack River.

Ironically, Captain Mason never set foot in New England, and Sir Gorges never set foot in any part of the New World. In fact, few Englishmen migrated to New Hampshire during the first several years of its patent until religious and political strife in Massachusetts Bay. Then in 1639, John Wheelwright led a group of persecuted Puritans northward into what became known as Exeter, New Hampshire. Others from Massachusetts Bay Colony soon followed, including many orthodox Puritans.

In 1641, the settlements in New Hampshire voluntarily merged with Massachusetts Bay, a relationship that ended when New Hampshire was given a royal charter in 1679, made effective on January 1, 1680. It was reunited with Massachusetts Bay in 1688, during the experiment known as the Dominion of New England (see Chapter 4). In 1691, New Hampshire was separated for the last time from the colony to its south and has enjoyed a separate existence thereafter. Maine, on the other hand, remained part of Massachusetts until 1820, when it came into the Union as part of the Missouri Compromise in

FIGURE 2.7 - Sir George Calvert, First Lord Baltimore

order to keep the balance between free states and slave states (see Chapter 10 for a discussion of the Missouri Compromise).

Maryland

In the earliest days of English attempts to settle colonies in the New World, Sir George Calvert played an active role. He was a member of the Virginia Company and of the Council for New England. His own enthusiasm for beginning a venture in North America was so great that he purchased land on Newfoundland for a settlement and named it Avalon. This area was cold and close to areas controlled by the hostile French, so the colony failed. Calvert's aspirations for colonization took a new direction when he converted to Catholicism. He resigned his position as a secretary of state to King James I in 1625. Surprisingly, his abandonment of the king brought rewards rather than enmity. James I conferred upon Calvert a title from the Irish peerage, Lord Baltimore. Following a visit to the colony of Virginia in 1628, he found a new location to establish a colony which he believed would build his fortune and at the same time provide a safe haven for his fellow Catholics who faced periodic persecution in England.

In 1632 King Charles I, the son of James I, granted a charter to Calvert to plant his colony along the northern border of Virginia. With this charter, Calvert held close to complete control over the land and the lives of the settlers of his new colony, Maryland, named by King Charles for his Queen Henrietta Maria. The only restrictions placed upon Calvert by the English government were to uphold the laws of England when making the laws for the colony, accept the advice and consent of the settlers of the colony with regard to law, and honor the established rights of Englishmen in the colonies as they were in England. The proprietary nature of the settlement was actually feudal in nature. The first Lord Baltimore died during the crafting of the charter, which left the settlement of the colony to his son Cecilius, the second Lord Baltimore and his brother Leonard Calvert, the first governor of the colony. In return for the proprietorship, Lord Baltimore was required to send two Indian arrows to the king annually and one-fifth of any gold or silver found in the colony.

In 1634, at least 200 mostly Protestant settlers arrived in America and established the town of St. Mary's at the southern tip of the colony in the Chesapeake Bay. Although Calvert had hoped for a Catholic sanctuary, the Protestants maintained a majority from the beginning. It was crucial for the success of the proprietor, Lord Baltimore, to bring more settlers to Maryland. Cheap land and some political say in their government was necessary to satisfy those who came. Settlers demanded an elected colonial legislature. In return for its creation, Lord Baltimore held on to the right to veto these laws. Selling land to colonists became his source of profit. He sold 1,000 acres at an annual charge, called quitrent, to settlers who brought five and later 20 adult males with them.

Contrary to what the Calverts had envisioned, more Protestants than Catholics came across the Atlantic from England. Events, conditions, and problems in England were often reflected in the colonies. Protestants were dominant in England, and persecution of Catholics occurred. In Maryland the Protestants were also a majority, and the Catholics needed the intervention and protection of Calvert. From 1645-1646, during the control of the Puritans over England, a Protestant group also ruled Maryland. They were powerful enough to force Governor Leonard Calvert into exile in Virginia. In 1647, in reaction to the Puritan rule in England, Lord Baltimore replaced his brother with a Protestant, placed a majority of Protestants on the colonial council, and recommended the passage of the Toleration Act to create a colony in which all who believed in the trinity of God the Father, Jesus Christ, and the Holy Spirit would have their religious beliefs tolerated. In 1649 the Maryland Assembly passed the Act of Toleration. It was not complete religious freedom for all, but it was an important step toward full liberty of conscience. Even so, tensions between Protestants and Catholics continued in Maryland. In the early 1650s, Protestants there actually repealed the Toleration Act, although that

proved to be only temporary. Trouble became so bad that a short-lived civil war erupted there in 1655 in order for the Protestant majority to maintain its hold on the government.

A rather severe labor shortage in Maryland resulted in changing the land-grant system to the so-called "Headright" system in 1640. That meant that each free adult man would receive 100 acres of land for himself, another 100 acres for his wife and for each of his servants, and 50 acres for each child in the family. This was the same system used in nearby Virginia.

The land of Maryland was as suited for tobacco crops as was the land in Virginia. Growing tobacco in the colony and selling it in England provided a good living for many planters. Indentured servants were first used by planters to cultivate their tobacco and other crops. But a labor shortage in England in the 1680s led to greater reliance on African slaves instead.

Founding Connecticut

The establishment of this colony was a mix of Dutch and English attempts, but the English overwhelmed the minimal Dutch efforts. In 1614, Adrian Block, a Dutch explorer, sailed up the Connecticut River from what is now called Long Island Sound. The land was fertile and trade with the Indians along the banks promising. His accounts of what he found brought a small number of settlers from the Netherlands to try their best at making a home in this wilderness. The settlement was near present-day Hartford and became part of the Dutch colony of New Netherland, which later fell into the hands of the English and became the colonies of Connecticut, New York, New Jersey, and Delaware. The Dutch settlers bought land from the Pequot tribe and established a beneficial trading arrangement. The Europeans traded guns and alcohol along with other items for seeds, food, lumber, and animal furs from the local tribe members.

As the small numbers of Dutch were settling into their areas, English settlers established the Massachusetts Bay Colony close by. In the years that followed, some of the Puritans of Massachusetts Bay moved south into the land claimed by the Dutch along the Connecticut River and began establishing settlements, either for better land or because of political and religious disagreements. There they established the towns of Windsor, Wethersfield, and Hartford, continuing to consider themselves British citizens and following British law and customs.

In 1636, Thomas Hooker, the prominent Puritan minister of Newton, Massachusetts Bay (now Cambridge, Massachusetts) took his congregation of roughly 100 people and founded the town of Hartford along the Connecticut River. For this he is known as the founder of Connecticut. Hooker disagreed with some of the practices and theories of the powers that be in the Massachusetts Bay Puritan leadership. Governor John Winthrop of Massachusetts Bay colony believed that the privileged few should govern the many. Freemen should gain their status slowly, and only members of the church should vote for elected officials to govern the colony. Hooker maintained that all should choose the governing council which would determine the settlement of matters that affected all. There were some who thought that Hooker was jealous of the power and influence of John Cotton, the minister of the Boston congregation, and left so as not to have to live in his shadow. But most

also agreed that the reputation of Hooker was spotless, and no matter the motive, his beliefs were sincere and above reproach. The congregation packed up their belongings, herded their cattle together, and started on another journey to found a community where they could practice their religious and political beliefs.

In 1638 a group of about 500 Puritans from Massachusetts Bay formed the colony of New Haven. The members of the new settlements lived peaceably with the Native Americans in the beginning. They traded with the groups close to them. The natives sold land to the colonists even though they did not think that anyone could own the land. The settlers wanted more land and the Indians to move further west. The Indians believed that even when they sold the land it was still theirs to use. As the white settlers encroached on Indian hunting and farming lands to a greater degree, tensions increased.

Fundamental Orders

By the middle of the 1600s there were more British citizens than Dutch in the colony. Therefore, the Dutch gave up control of the region. Although British law ruled the colony, the leaders of Connecticut, prominently including Thomas Hooker, wrote the Fundamental Orders of Connecticut in 1639. This is considered to be the first written constitution in North America. It was a plan for self-government, democracy, and adopted by the residents of Hartford, Windsor, and Wethersfield. These orders gave the people of these three settlements the right to elect a governor, six assistants, and a legislative assembly to make the laws.

In 1662 King Charles II gave a charter to the towns along the Connecticut River to establish the colony of Connecticut and included the New Haven Colony in the new official colony. There were now official boundaries for the colony and a new charter that replaced the Fundamental Orders.

Rhode Island

The despotism of the early leaders of Massachusetts Bay led some of its colonists to establish settlements elsewhere. Roger Williams, pastor of the Salem church,

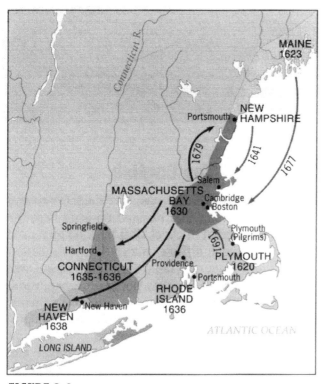

FIGURE 2.8 - Seventeenth-Century New England Settlements

publicly questioned the validity of the colony's charter and the right of the government to legislate the habits and opinions of its people. He urged the Salem church to separate itself from the other churches. The General Court reacted to this by expelling the deputies from Salem until they renounced Williams and banished the rebel minister from the colony in the spring of 1636. Fearing that those in control might decide to send him back to England, Williams voluntarily moved south of Massachusetts Bay and spent time with the Indians. He purchased land from the tribe, and he and other followers established a colony in present-day Providence, Rhode Island in the same year. Roger Williams began to implement his views of complete religious freedom and became the first known advocate of the separation of church and state, radical ideas anywhere in the seventeenth century.

FIGURE 2.9 - Anne Hutchinson on trial 1638

Anne Hutchinson was another radical thinker who challenged the authority of the Puritan leaders in Massachusetts Bay. Hutchinson and her husband moved from England to Boston in 1634 and quickly became an outspoken critic and charismatic figure there, declaring that nearly all of the Puritan ministers in the colony were not of the "elect" and therefore could not exercise spiritual authority. For this she was called an Antinomian, from two Greek words meaning "Anti-Law." Moreover, she openly declared that the Holy Spirit spoke directly to her, and she demanded a much more prominent role for women in the church.

The religious leaders became anxious to silence Hutchinson's influence as they observed that many women and other dissidents in the colony began to coalesce in their opposition around her. In 1637 and 1638, she was separately condemned by both a civil and religious court, convicted by both courts, and banished from the colony. She and other dissidents then moved south into the region now called Rhode Island, where they founded Pocasset (present-day Portsmouth).

Historians debate the real reasons Anne Hutchinson was persecuted by the powers-that-be in Massachusetts Bay. Was it because she deviated from the accepted theology that the Holy Spirit ceased to speak directly to believers with the close of the New Testament period? Was it because she represented a political threat to the established order of things? Or was it because, as a woman, she spoke with an authority that was completely contrary to seventeenth-century notions about women's place in society? It was probably a combination of all of these reasons. In any case, the exiles of Roger Williams and Anne Hutchinson benefitted the colony of Rhode Island, which promoted greater religious toleration and freedom than in any other colony during the entire colonial period in North America.

In 1663 the various towns making up several small colonies in the region, received a charter that combined them into one colony of Rhode Island. This charter gave the colony permission to establish a permanent government along the lines of Massachusetts Bay but did not require church membership to vote. This freedom brought many settlers from other parts of America and Europe.

Peril for the Native Americans of New England

Once Europeans decided to come and stay in the New World, the Native Americans faced grave dangers. The white man brought plagues that took the lives of millions because Native Americans had no immunity to their diseases. The worst killer disease was smallpox, but influenza, measles, chicken pox, dysentery, and others took a terrible toll on the native population. Those who survived the dreaded diseases had their lives threatened in other ways. The whites wanted the land that was held by the native tribes. In the early years of the Massachusetts Bay Colony, even Governor John Winthrop claimed that the land should not lay idle when Christians would put it to good use. Winthrop expressed a Eurocentric view that came to the New World with the settlers. What they saw as idle was to the Native American his land used for hunting and some for planting of crops.

This concept that Englishmen had a right to take Native American land because the latter were not using the land efficiently came from the attitudes and experiences of Englishmen in England itself. For centuries, the English had made the same argument against the Welsh, Scots, and Irish in the British Isles. Then when England would attack or otherwise attempt to gain control over those ethnic groups, the latter rebelled, prompting the English to brand them as wild savages. It was very easy to transfer these feelings toward Native Americans, especially because they looked so different from the Welsh, Scots, and Irish, and they were not even Christians. Therefore, a cultural English bias in the British Isles was compounded by racism and religious bigotry against the native peoples in America. Naturally, the result of such attitudes was increased conflict and war between the English colonists and Native American tribes.

Pequot War (1637)

The land was all-important to both whites and Native Americans in the English settlements. Hopes for finding gold were gone, but the promise of land ownership was another type of treasure for those who made their homes on the coasts and spread across the land. The lands in the Connecticut River valley drew Puritans and others into an area that was the homeland of the Pequot tribe. More contact between the two cultures led to incidents of violence on both sides and periodically to war. After the deaths of English settlers between 1634 and 1636 with no action against the guilty by the Pequot in spite of negotiations to resolve the issues, the English decided to take action. It is not certain if the deaths were caused by members of the tribes, but the British believed this to be the case. Men from the Massachusetts Bay militia under the leadership of John Endecott attacked the Indian settlements on Block Island and Pequot Harbor. The village was looted and burned, and there began a cycle

of retaliation on both sides. The Pequot attempted to form alliances with other tribes to force the whites from Connecticut and perhaps all of New England. Roger Williams intervened and kept the Narragansett from siding against the settlers.

The major fighting in the Pequot War came in 1637. By then, the colonists and their leaders believed that they must eliminate the threat of the Pequot permanently. The Pequot prepared to defend their territory. In May 1637, The Pequot Fort at Mystic was the main target for the men from Massachusetts Bay and Connecticut under the leadership of Captain John Mason. There were also Indian allies with the English from the Mohegan, Narragansett, and Eastern Niantic tribes. The troops surrounded a large Pequot village inside the fort at Mystic, attacked the fort and set fire to the wooden structures. Between 300 and 700 men, women, and children perished in the flames. Those attempting to flee were shot and killed. It was one of the worst massacres perpetrated by the English on the Native Americans. One reason for the quick and horrible attack was to avoid a large group of Pequot warriors only five miles away with the chief of the tribe, Sassacus.

In several engagements the colonial troops and their Indian allies hunted for and engaged the remaining warriors of the Pequot tribe until they were killed or surrendered. Women and children were sent as slaves to tribes fighting with the British. The Mohawks scored a great victory when they engaged Pequot warriors and killed Sassacus. They sent his head to the British in Hartford. The remaining leaders asked for peace. The Treaty of Hartford declared in 1638 that the Pequot nation no longer existed, although the Pequot did exist, but barely. In 1667 Connecticut established a reservation for the remaining members of the tribe, and in King Philip's War, they fought alongside the colonists.

King Philip's War (1675-1676)

Relations between the New England colonies and the Indian tribes were a mix of calm and tension following the Pequot War. Ministers began to reach out to the Native Americans for the purpose of converting them to the Christian faith, which was something that was mentioned time and again in the founding of the colonies. John Eliot translated the Christian Bible into the Algonquian language in 1663. Eliot also helped establish towns for "praying Indians", the nickname given to those who converted to Christianity. As was usual, the peace ended when both sides were caught up in actions and reactions that led to war.

By far the worst conflict between Native Americans and English colonists was known as King Philip's War, fought in New England. King Philip was a nickname given by the colonists to Metacomet or Metacom, chief of the Wampanoags, who ironically was the son of Massasoit, who had helped save Plymouth Colony from complete disaster in 1621.

King Philip bided his time as the English colonists committed a series of what he considered alarming offenses. His brother died under suspicious circumstances following an interrogation by authorities in Plymouth concerning the possibility of Indian attacks. The authorities hanged three Wampanoags for allegedly killing a "praying Indian" who related to the English the possibility of an attack from King Philip and his allies. His people were losing income as the fur trade declined. The colonists were moving onto more land that belonged to the tribes. In 1671 officials of Plymouth took King Philip into custody until he agreed to land sales and the turning over of weapons.

In 1675, the Wampanoags went to war to right all the wrongs done to their people and to stop the annihilation of their people and their way of life. The Narragansetts and the Nipmunks joined them. Their goal was to stop the encroaching settlers of Massachusetts Bay, Plymouth, New Hampshire, Maine, and Connecticut. In the beginning, the Native Americans were successful in the war. They destroyed 12 towns and came close to entering Boston. Ten percent of the men of fighting age in the colonies were killed and many others wounded or captured. The tribes, however, had major disadvantages: smaller populations, not enough food, and insufficient weapons and ammunition.

When a "praying Indian" killed King Philip in August 1676, the war basically came to an end, except for New Hampshire and Maine, where it lasted until 1678. The vengeance of the colonists was as extreme as the war. In Massachusetts and Connecticut, they executed warriors and sold many of the men, women, and children into slavery in the Caribbean islands. They placed King Philip's head on a pole in Plymouth for more than 20 years. Because the Puritans equated positive outcomes with God's approval, they equated negative outcomes with God's disapproval. They must have sinned mightily to have suffered so much during this war with the heathen natives.

The Dutch Came for Their Share

The Netherlands became a world naval power beginning in the late 1500s and continuing throughout the 1600s. Much of this power was due to the efforts of the Dutch East India Company. This Dutch trading company sent its ships to control as much of the world trade as it could manage. The company was interested in trade, not colonies. They established dominance in areas around the world with forts and trading posts, mostly along coastlines of the foreign countries. The Portuguese were ahead of the Dutch in many of the trade areas of the Indies and Asia, and the Dutch ousted them from several areas. They established commercial control in areas of Indonesia, Ceylon (modern-day Sri Lanka), Taiwan, Iran, South Africa, and others. Always looking for a quicker sea route to the Spice Islands and the Pacific, they hired Henry Hudson, an Englishman, to sail northeast from Europe. Hudson decided to sail west instead. In September 1609, while searching for a western route to Asia, Henry Hudson sailed his ship the *Half Moon* up what became known as the Hudson River (named after him) in North America and gave the Dutch a claim to land in North America along the Atlantic Coast.

The Dutch government gave a new joint-stock company, the Dutch West India Company, a monopoly in 1621 on the trade in the area Hudson explored and the right to settle the region, a right that included making alliances with the various Indian tribes. The company planted settlements at Fort Orange (1624) and Manhattan Island (1625), forming the colony of New Netherland. Peter Minuit reportedly purchased Manhattan Island from local Indians the next year (1626) for the equivalent of twenty-four dollars and changed the name to New Amsterdam (modern-day New York City), based on commercial interests that dated to as early as 1611. Some historians have compared the price of bread and other goods and estimate the price as closer to $1,000. Minuit then became the first governor of New Netherland, from 1626-1633.

The West India Company attempted to bring settlers to the area with a feudal system of land-holding. The company granted those who brought at least 50 settlers to the new colony 16 miles of land along the rivers. The owners of these huge estates were called patrons. The patrons could hold courts and were exempt from taxation for eight years. The colonists were divided into free colonists, who could own their own homesteads, and indentured farm workers, who were required to work on the company's farms or those of company officials. No trade was permitted with outsiders, and the company controlled the export trade.

In 1631, approximately 30 Dutch settlers formed a small settlement along the Delaware River and called it Zwaanendael because of the large number of swans swimming in the marshes. The Dutch settlers erected a large house and cleared land. They got along well with the local Lenape tribe and traded for furs to sell in Europe. Unfortunately, the theft of a metal coat of arms led to a massacre of the local tribe.

Several members of the Swedish government along with some merchants, sensing that profits from tobacco and the fur trade with the Native Americans could be a boon for Sweden, sent two ships of colonists under the leadership of Peter Minuit, the former governor of New Netherland. In 1638 the Swedish settlers bought land from the Lenape (sometimes called the Lenni-Lenape) and built Fort Christina, named for their young queen, in what was later northern Delaware. They called it New Sweden. The men of New Sweden planted tobacco and corn and traded for furs from the natives of the area. The colonists tended to live on isolated farms. The Swedes built the first log cabins in North America. These were the types of homes they built in the forests of their homeland.

Both the Dutch and the English settlers in neighboring areas wanted New Sweden. In 1641 English settlers from Connecticut built a settlement south of the Swedish settlement. The new Swedish governor, Johan Printz, built two forts to control the Delaware River. Realizing that the Swedish settlement might be too much

competition in the fur trade, the Dutch leader Peter Stuyvesant in New Amsterdam claimed New Sweden with warships at the ready. The Dutch did not attack the colony but did slowly gain control of the river. They established Fort Casimir along the neck of the Delaware Bay in 1651.

Meanwhile, a new governor, Johan Rising, arrived from Sweden with new settlers in 1654. This brought the population of the colony to more than 300. Rising expanded the number of farms and established more churches in the colony. He was planning a growing and permanent presence in North America. The Swedes had good relations with the Native Americans in the area and moved forward on pushing the Dutch out of the area. The Swedes demanded that the Dutch surrender Fort Casimir, and the lightly manned fort did.

The Dutch retaliated in August 1655. They took back Fort Casimir and attacked farms and houses of the Swedish settlers. On September 15, 1655, Governor Rising surrendered the colony. Many of the settlers stayed on under Dutch control.

King Charles II and Colonization

In 1660 Charles II returned to the throne as the king of England, an event which significantly impacted current and future English colonies in North America. There were six English colonies at that time. Charles II needed funds to run his nation and pay back his debts to those who had stood by him through his years of exile and assisted him in his return to the throne. He possessed land on the Atlantic Coast of North America that could serve both purposes. The king granted land along the eastern coast of North America to relatives, friends, and to those he was in debt to. He gave his brother James, the Duke of York and later King James II, land settled by the Dutch (New Netherland). Confronted by English warships in New Amsterdam Harbor, Governor Peter Stuyvesant signed a treaty without a fight in September 1664, signing over New Netherland to the English, who renamed the colony New York and its capital New York City.

Charles II also paid off a debt to an old friend by granting the largest land-holding proprietorship to William

Penn, land that the king named Pennsylvania. (See "Pennsylvania and Delaware" below for more details of this region.)

The land between the colony of Virginia and Spanish Florida—later named the Carolinas—went to eight proprietors who were on good terms with the English king and were owed favors. Charles II granted those friends a proprietorship to the land which gave them feudal power over its settlement and growth. (See "The Carolinas" below for more details of this region.)

The king had too many issues to deal with, so he turned the administration of the colonies over to a succession of councils, including the Council of Foreign Plantations, the Council of Trade, which was intended to oversee commercial and governmental issues, the Privy Council, and then the Lords of Trade. King Charles II needed money, and the colonies could perhaps supply this resource for his new government. The Lords of Trade paid close attention to British interests. One goal of the Lords of Trade was tighter control over the four royal colonies: Virginia, Jamaica, Barbados, and the Leeward Islands. As these and other colonies came under royal control, governors were sent under strict orders from England. The government in England wanted to assert more control, which resulted in limiting the colonial assemblies. In 1684 the charter of the Massachusetts Bay colony reverted to the crown when the colony did not pay enough attention to the Navigation Acts. The Dominion of New England was also implemented from 1686-1689 to gain more control of the colonies and centralize power (see Chapter 4 for a complete discussion of the Dominion of New England).

New Jersey

Following the defeat of New Netherland in 1664, England divided the land formerly controlled by the Dutch. The Duke of York granted land between the Delaware and Hudson Rivers to his friends, Sir George Carteret and Lord John Berkeley, to form the colony of New Jersey. The two proprietors believed that rental feels called quitrents and trade would provide them profits. In order to draw settlers to their colony, the proprietors issued their plans for the colony in a document called Concessions and Agreements. In exchange for a small fee on the land known as a quitrent (a fee that recognized that they did not completely own the land) and allegiance to the king as well as the proprietors, the settlers received cheap land, a representative assembly, and freedom of conscience. The proprietors maintained control of the colony, partially through selecting the governor.

Control of the land plagued this colony until the American Revolution. The Duke of York failed to notify Governor Nicolls of New York that the land of New Jersey was separate and in the possession of Carteret and Berkeley. Therefore, Nicolls granted the eastern half of the land between the rivers to Puritans in the area of New York. The western half of the land was granted to Quakers, following the sale of Berkley's share of the grant to a group of Quakers. The settlers naturally divided the land into East Jersey and West Jersey, which became official in 1676.

William Penn, the future proprietor of Pennsylvania, belonged to the company that established the Quaker presence in West Jersey. This first Quaker settlement had many of the freedoms and democratic ideas that Penn later put in place in Pennsylvania. The Laws,

FIGURE 2.10 - William Penn, holding paper, standing and facing King Charles II.

Concessions, and Agreements of 1677 provided freedom of conscience, a generous land policy, and a representative government that controlled taxation. Quitrents continued for this colony. West Jersey would naturally have a strong connection to Philadelphia because of the Quaker ties.

East Jersey formed economic ties to New York, but in many other ways the people in these settlements were closer to the Puritan towns of New England. They worked small farms surrounding a small village or town. William Penn and his associates bought East Jersey in 1681.

In 1702 the government of England reunited East and West Jersey into the royal colony of New Jersey. The proprietors of East and West Jersey determined that their system of government was not viable. Colonists refused to pay the quitrent. They were used to self-government, and a frontier life engendered that type of system in these independent newcomers. The proprietors gave up their right to govern but not their claims on the land. Litigation for those rights continued through the decades to the American Revolution.

The complications for the government of New Jersey continued as a royal colony. The governor of New York extended his governorship to New Jersey, but the problem colony retained its own General Assembly. New Jersey maintained two capitals, and the General Assembly met in Burlington and Perth Amboy. Finally, in 1738 Lewis Morris became the governor of New Jersey. By 1745 the colony was in a mass of confusion over land rights that at times erupted in riots and other acts of violence. Nevertheless, the colony prospered. With the growth of New York City and Philadelphia, the need for crops to feed these cities and others increased the profits of the farmers in New Jersey. Iron mining was another profitable industry. Iron ore was plentiful in the area.

For the Lenape, the American Indians of the area, the arrival of the whites meant devastation for their tribe. The whites had brought their diseases and killed them. The whites cut down their forests that were crucial for their hunting. The whites took their land and reduced them to a small reservation known as Brotherton. Those who could not stand this way of life left that land to find peace and their way of life outside of New Jersey.

Pennsylvania and Delaware

William Penn was a real estate developer in England who converted to the Quaker religion in 1667. The Quaker religion was founded as an offshoot of Protestantism by George Fox in England in the 1650s. Quakers, also known as the Religious Society of Friends, emphasize the individual spiritual enlightenment of Jesus as the Inner Light, without the need of clergy or other mediators. While the theology and worship practices differ widely, Quakers have been well-known for being peacemakers, pacifists (opposed to the use of violence), and people of integrity. Unfortunately, Quakers have suffered great persecution. For example, Charles II imprisoned approximately 3,000 Quakers during his reign. Even in the English colonies of North America, every colony except Rhode Island passed laws to prevent Quakers from worshipping according to their consciences.

Such persecution in England led William Penn to suggest a solution of allowing large numbers of English Quakers to settle land in America. King Charles II agreed, and Penn and other prominent Quakers purchased the province of West Jersey in 1676. Quakers also purchased East Jersey a few years later in 1681. When Penn asked the king for more land, he was surprisingly given what are essentially the modern states of Pennsylvania and Delaware in 1681, in lieu of a debt the king had owed Penn's late father, a wealthy English admiral. This made Penn the proprietor of the largest landholdings in North America at the time, a territory larger than England and Wales combined.

Calling his new land the "Holy Experiment," Penn issued a Frame of Government in 1682 that guaranteed freedom of religion, the normal rights of Englishmen, and created an elected General Assembly to help govern the colony. In that same year, he also personally oversaw the planning of a capital city along the Delaware River which he called Philadelphia (the city of "Brotherly Love").

With few of the hardships of the early colonial ventures to hamper the colony, Pennsylvania grew quickly. Within three years, 8,000 Baptists, French Huguenots, Lutherans, Catholics, and Quakers came to Pennsylvania. One reason for Penn's quick success was the work accomplished by the Swedes when the area had been New Sweden. Another reason was that Penn was well respected by the Indians living in his domain because he paid them for their land and treated them with respect as well. As a result, there were no major military conflicts with Indians for as long as Penn himself lived. Philadelphia became a cultural giant to rival Boston. By 1700 the city boasted a printing press, a newspaper, a fine hospital and school, and help for the disadvantaged.

Political tensions eventually arose between Penn's government and colonists far removed from Philadelphia. Penn's response was to issue the Charter of Liberties (sometimes called the Charter of Privileges) in 1701. Among other provisions, it allowed the "lower counties" (Delaware) to establish their own representative assembly. When the Delaware counties created their own assembly in 1703, Delaware effectively, but not officially, became a separate colony, although they shared the same governor with Pennsylvania.

When the colonies began their rebellion against the English government, Delaware sent representatives to the First and Second Continental Congress, and it became one of the first colonies to establish a government independent from the British government in 1776.

The Carolinas

The Spanish and French turned their attention to the southern portion of the North American Atlantic Coast north of Florida in the early 1500s. The Spanish conducted a few raids, capturing Native Americans to take to the island of Hispaniola beginning in the 1520s. Hernando de Soto, a Spanish explorer, landed in Florida in 1540, marched into the interior and then northward into land that later became the English colonies of South Carolina and North Carolina. There were some thoughts that the area could become a safe haven from pirates or storms for ships that sailed in the Spanish treasure fleet from the Caribbean to Spain. It was the French, however, who set up the first settlement. In 1562 a small group of settlers built a fort, Charlesfort, in Port Royal Sound, on what is now called Parris Island in present-day South Carolina. Without reinforcements or supplies from France, the settlers abandoned the location.

The Spanish, who frequented this coastline and did not want a French foothold in this area, planted a settlement in the same area in 1566. Pedro Menendez de Aviles built the fort of San Felipe, and Spanish settlers established the town of Santa Elena. The settlement boasted a mission, plowed fields, and even operated a pottery kiln. Hostile Indians and English privateers forced the settlers to abandon their efforts in 1587. This left Saint Augustine in Florida as the only Spanish settlement on the Atlantic Coast.

English interest in the coastal area between Virginia and the Spanish-held Florida was raised again under the rule of King Charles I. The lack of financial backing and the problems in England halted the plans of those granted a patent by the king on the land named Carolana until the reign of Charles II. In 1640 the English Civil War between the Roundheads and Cavaliers dominated the interests of the government, nobility, and wealthy of England. The Puritan victors beheaded Charles I, and with his life at stake, his son Charles II fled England. Until his return to the throne in 1660, events in a land 3,000 miles away held little interest for but a few.

In order to pay back eight loyal noblemen, King Charles II awarded them the patent to Carolana in 1663 and renamed it the Province of Carolina, after the Latin version of King Charles' name. Known as the proprietors of Carolina, the eight landlords divided the colony into three counties. The proprietors promised many things to entice settlers to come: an elected assembly with the sole right to tax, freedom of conscience, religious toleration, and land with a small quitrent (rent paid by a freeholder on land rather than pay in services to a landlord). This was not generous enough to bring many to the colony. There was an unsuccessful settlement at Cape Fear in 1665. In 1669 the proprietor Anthony Ashley Cooper, with the help of John Locke, his secretary and a political philosopher in his own right, put together the Fundamental Constitutions. This document promised hereditary nobility, religious toleration, and the inviolability of private property, including slaves. These promises along with more contributions from the proprietors brought approximately 100 settlers from

England to the land in 1670, when Charles Town (now Charleston, South Carolina) was established.

The new colony also brought settlers from England's West Indian island of Barbados. Many of the younger men on this wealthy sugar island turned to this southern land to make their fortunes, bringing their slaves with them from the island. By 1671 the population of the colony was approximately 30 percent slaves.

North Carolina

Geographic differences and distance naturally split the province of Carolina from its inception. North Carolina had an inhospitable shoreline with sandbars and dangerous currents. There wasn't a large port at a time when so much of the travel and trade was accomplished on the seas. The northern counties of Carolina were mostly ignored by the proprietors. Settlers from Virginia made up the bulk of the new Carolina settlers. They settled on small farms and raised corn and tobacco. Later naval stores became important. Small numbers of French Huguenots, German Palatines, and Quakers moved into the region. It was natural to pay more attention to the more profitable areas around Charleston, the major port area for the colony.

The proprietors appointed governors to Albemarle County that unofficially became North Carolina after 1712, but they did little else for the area. More settlers meant more problems for the Tuscarora Indians of the area. Not only were the whites taking land, but the British were kidnapping native men, women, and children to sell as slaves. The tribesmen began attacking the settlers. Soldiers from both North and South Carolina fought in the Tuscarora War (1711-1715) and defeated the tribe. Those Native Americans who survived moved away from the area. When seven of the proprietors sold their lands to the king in 1729, North and South Carolina were officially separated and each made a royal colony.

Pirates were another problem for the North Carolinians, at least for those who did not purchase stolen goods from these marauders of the oceans and seas. One of the most famous pirates to visit the area was Blackbeard. The pirates who used the Caribbean as well as the inlets of the outer banks of North Carolina to attack merchant ships

FIGURE 2.11 - Capture of Blackbeard the Pirate, 1718

and hide from capture or attack from the British navy or the navies of other countries were a real thorn in the side of the British Royal Navy. Ships of the British navy saw to the demise of Blackbeard and other pirates in the area.

Slavery came to North Carolina as it did to the other colonies because there was a general shortage of labor. As tobacco and rice plantations grew in size, the need for a larger number of workers increased.

Georgia

Georgia was the last English colony established in North America, and it was a venture to organize a colony for a grand purpose. The organizers wanted to help the poor to live a moral and useful life in North America. General James Edward Oglethorpe, a former soldier turned philanthropist, was the leader of 20 other trustees who were also philanthropists and received a charter to settle the land between the Carolinas and Spanish Florida in 1732. The purpose of the colony was to give self-sufficiency to poor Englishmen unable to support themselves and their families (those in debtor prisons in England), set up a buffer zone between the Carolinas and Spanish Florida, and provide products needed by the English. Oglethorpe was actively working to change conditions in prison for debtors who landed in jail because they could not pay their debts. Although he hoped that many of these unfortunate people could start anew in Georgia, few actually made it to the colony. It was the poor that Thomas Bray hoped to help that made up the bulk of the settlers. Bray was in charge of the Anglican Church's missionary efforts in North America. What better or more Christian way to assist those in economic hardship than a new homeland where they could start over and build a respectable life. This could also be a great service to England. To find a new place for the poor was indeed useful.

One of the most surprising characteristics of the Georgia Trusteeship was the promise of the trustees to sacrifice a profit and salaries from the venture. Instead, the charter provided for the trustees to oversee the colony for 21 years and then step aside as the colony became a royal colony. Funds to establish the colony came from churches, donations, pennies from schoolchildren, the trustees, and 130,000 pounds from Parliament. The possible benefits of Georgia impressed Parliament so much that they literally helped to support the project.

The trustees hoped to establish a moral environment for the colony. As is often the case in the colonies, rules established in England did not play out well in North America. The trustees banned strong liquor, farms or plantations over 500 acres, and slavery in hopes of creating a type of utopia. These restrictions, rather than enticing settlers to come, actually discouraged many who might have come and created dishonest people out of those who broke the restrictions that they disagreed with.

Oglethorpe arrived with the first boatload of 114 settlers in early 1733 and began laying out the city of Savannah. He threw himself into all elements of colonial life as the governor to build this community of morality and rebirth for the disadvantaged. There were some problems from the beginning. The plans for dividing the land were a problem. Each family on charity received only 50 acres which they could not sell, divide, or will to anyone but a male heir. The landholdings were too small and not truly the property of the family that worked the land.

However, he gained the trust of the local Creek tribe, which allowed a peaceful existence for his colonists. He built forts and was vigilant in keeping the colonists at the ready for any Spanish incursions. In 1739, when the War of Jenkin's Ear erupted mostly between the English in Georgia and the Spanish in Florida, Oglethorpe was at the forefront in leading the British into Florida with success and defeating a Spanish invasion of Georgia. The war in the remote area of North America spread to Europe and broke into a larger conflict, the War of Austrian Succession. In 1743 he returned to England to answer charges of mismanagement of the Georgian army, although the court found him innocent.

By the 1740s, the colony was still floundering. The policies were too restrictive, so the trustees decided to change the rules. They allowed slavery in 1750 and larger landholdings in 1752. Law enforcement ignored the policy of no strong drink, partially to participate in trade with the West Indies.

Certain products from Georgia fed the system of mercantilism. The colony provided England with timber, hemp, flax, and some silk. The trustees put a lot of hope and planning into a silk industry in Georgia that would provide jobs and replace the silk of other countries with British silk. However, the necessary elements did not fall into place for a successful silk industry. The silk worms that produced the strands for the cloth fed on white mulberry trees, but Georgia had black mulberry trees growing wild. The trustees ordered the colonists to plant white mulberry trees for a valid claim to the land. Once they organized a representative assembly, any who wished to serve must have planted at least 100 white mulberry trees per 50 acres. There were too few to train the Georgian farmers on how to care for the worms and wind the threads they produced. Worms died in some areas because the climate was not suitable. In spite of all of these problems, the trustees never surrendered to the unsuitability of a silk industry in Georgia.

The trustees gave back their charter to the Crown in June 1752, which was actually one year before it was set to expire. Georgia remained the least prosperous and populous of all the colonies. Once again the reach of the governments in London was too far and too out of touch with what was needed for success along the Atlantic Coast of North America.

Archeological site in Danvers, Massachusetts, showing the foundations for buildings that were at the center of the Salem witch trials in 1692.

Chapter 3 Contents

CHAPTER THREE

From Europeans to Americans

Major Events

1607-1776	Regional Development Systems of Labor Immigration Daily Life Colonial Women
1636	Harvard College was established as first college in the English colonies
1640	First book published in the colonies
1642	Massachusetts Bay law required that children and servants must be taught to read the Bible
1647	Massachusetts Bay passed a law for the establishment of schools
1650	Anne Bradstreet poetry was published anonymously
1692	Witchcraft hysteria and trials in Salem, Massachusetts
1720s	The Great Awakening began as a religious revival across the colonies

Introduction

After a small number of Europeans, mostly English, demonstrated that it was possible for settlers to not only live along the Atlantic coast but to thrive, increasingly larger numbers came for their chance at a better life. These were English colonies developed on land claimed by English kings and a queen but that actually belonged to the Native Americans. These English monarchs gave the land that was not rightfully theirs to companies, proprietors, or favored subjects who also had no right to the land. The land was settled for profit or religious sanctuary originally by the English, with a few pockets of citizens from other European countries. It was not enough. In order for the colonies to thrive, many more people were necessary from England and its European neighbors. The immigrants to the English portion of the New World brought their few belongings and the customs that made them English, French, Irish, Scots-Irish, German, Dutch, and Swedish. However, they needed more workers for the fertile land, so they brought black men and women to work the land as slaves. The English culture dominated the first tier of land along most of the Atlantic coast, but as more came from other lands and mixed with the inhabitants along the coast or moved further west to the frontier, their traditions became part of the fabric of life in the colonies as well. As the decades passed, the European cultures adopted elements from the lives of the Native Americans and the African slaves that evolved into an American culture.

Regional Development and Commerce

There were many differences between the colonies, but geography grouped them into three major regions. The northern colonies of New England were New Hampshire, Massachusetts, Rhode Island, and Connecticut. The Mid-Atlantic colonies, sometimes also called the Middle colonies, were New York, New Jersey, Pennsylvania and Delaware. The Southern colonies were Virginia, Maryland, North Carolina, South Carolina, and Georgia. The land and the climate in these three regions, along with culture, helped to determine the way of life in the various colonies.

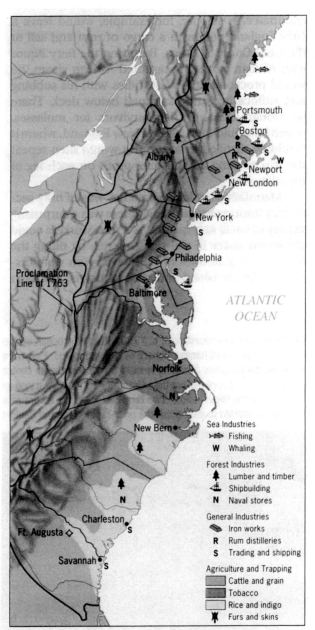

FIGURE 3.1 - The Colonial Economy

The New England Colonies

New England was a geographic area with thin, poor soil, a cold climate, and a short growing season, which forced the colonists there to turn to other industries for economic prosperity. The farmers in this region raised food for themselves and the locale in which they lived, so their farms remained small, and there was no large agricultural yield to export. The potential for economic strength in the area came from the thick forests and the ocean's bounty. Both provided raw resources for industries that in turn provided tens of thousands of jobs and products to trade. The Puritan capital of Boston, Massachusetts became an

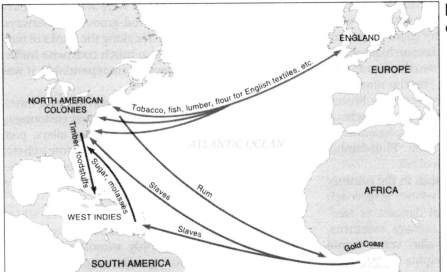

FIGURE 3.2 -
Colonial Trade Patterns

important seaport and another major colonial city. The lumber from the forests enabled the development of a strong shipbuilding industry, and the fish from the sea brought a multitude of fisherman to the fishing banks off the coasts of Maine and Newfoundland, casting their nets and developing a strong fishing industry. The fish were usually dried or pickled with salt and packed into barrels before export to Europe. Fishing for whales also provided important products for commerce in the colonies and overseas. Whales provided oil for lamps, ambergris for perfume, bone for the corsets of the women, and meat for the table.

There were a multitude of trade opportunities for the merchants of New England. They sold dried fish and furs in the markets of Europe. They also bought manufactured goods such as cloth, furniture, and china to sell in the colonies. The triangular trade was also important to the merchants of New England. Molasses made from sugar cane grown in the Caribbean islands was brought to New England and distilled into rum. The rum was shipped to Africa and exchanged for slaves, who were then brought to the Caribbean and sold and the profits used for more molasses so that the triangle continued.

The Mid-Atlantic (or Middle) Colonies

In the Mid-Atlantic colonies, especially Pennsylvania, there was good soil for agriculture to play an important role in the economic life, but the climate was much cooler than in the South. Large farms in Pennsylvania, particular those of the German settlers, raised an abundance of wheat and corn for all of the colonies.

Two of the largest cities of the colonies were in this mid-Atlantic region. Philadelphia, Pennsylvania and New York, New York developed into large harbors and trade centers because of their locations on deep ports off the Atlantic. Many of the crops came to these cities for export to other colonies or overseas.

The Southern Colonies

The Southern colonies had rich soil, a warm climate, and many rivers that flowed deep into the interior. Because of the geography of the region, the Southern colonies developed into major agricultural powerhouses with export crops of tobacco, indigo, rice, and much later cotton. Large farms or plantations developed in these colonies along with the small farms of the poor. Because of the large scale of export agriculture, slavery became more entrenched in the South as a labor system, especially by the 1680s and 1690s. The plantations and farms were scattered because of the amount of land necessary to grow the cash crops for exports.

With the rivers providing ships access to the plantations far inland and the scattering of the people, few good-sized cities developed in the South. The port cities of Charleston, South Carolina, and Savannah, Georgia were small, yet the largest cities of the region. Because the Southern colonies sold so much of their agricultural products in England and bought so many of the English manufactured products, they were closely tied to England by trade.

Systems of Labor

In the 17th century the need for labor grew, particularly in the Middle Colonies and the tobacco areas of Virginia and Maryland, as the settlers increased the size and scope of their plantations, farms, and other types of businesses. So many colonists were landowners that few found it necessary to hire out their labor to others. The Native Americans were extremely resistant to servitude, so another source of labor was necessary. Voluntary or involuntary servitude filled that need. Indentured servants, convicts, and slaves were brought to the colonies. Indentured service had existed in England for some time, so it was natural that the system should follow the English across the Atlantic when the labor shortage became a problem.

Indentured servitude in the colonies was a labor system in which a man or woman sold their labor to an employer for a particular period of time to pay for their passage to the colonies. In the early days in Virginia, the London Company paid the passage of those who would work in the new colony for the company for seven years. Soon colonial land owners or business proprietors were following the same practice. Skilled workers generally signed over their labor for three years and others from four, five, or even seven years, which was the usual maximum length for an indentured labor contract. At the end of their time served, the males were to receive clothing, tools, and sometimes money or land. Often times they left years of service with nothing. Females were also indentured and usually worked as household servants. They could usually expect marriage after their terms of indenture because of the shortage of women in many areas in the 1600s.

Involuntary Servitude

There were those who came to the colonies against their will. In the early years the English government sent a few shiploads of convicts to the colonies. That increased in later years. English ships delivered the convicts mostly to the West Indies, Maryland, and Virginia. By 1775 approximately 50,000 had been sent. An act of Parliament in 1718 set the term of service at seven years for lesser crimes and 14 for felonies, which in reality sometimes turned into lifetime indentures. After the Revolutionary War, the British continued to unload convicts illegally on American shores until 1787. After that, Australia replaced the North American coast as a dumping ground for English criminals.

Other undesirables were also sent over the decades as well as some who were kidnapped or impressed so that money could be made by selling their labor to purchasers in the colonies. Scots and Irish prisoners of war were sent to the colonies. The London Common Council sent 100 poor children to Virginia as "bound apprentices" in 1619. Apprentices were young men who lived with and were trained by skilled artisans or experts in a variety of positions in the trades. The apprentice learned a skill, and the artisan had a source of labor for a number of years.

	17th Century	18th Century	Total	Percent
Spanish America	292,500	578,600	871,100	11.7
Brazil	560,000	1,891,400	2,451,400	33
British Caribbean	263,700	1,401,000	1,664,700	22.5
Dutch Caribbean	40,000	460,000	500,000	6.7
French Caribbean	155,800	1,348,400	1,504,200	20.3
Danish Caribbean	4,000	24,000	28,000	20.3
British North America and future United States	10,000	390,000	400,000	5.4
TOTAL			7,419,400	100

This table clearly shows the huge concentration of the slave system in the Caribbean and South America. British North America's southern colonies constituted the extreme northern periphery of this system. {Source: Philip D. Curtin, The Atlantic Slave Trade (Madison: University of Wisconsin Press, 1969)}

FIGURE 3.3 - Estimated Slave Imports to the New World 1601-1810

Slavery in the Colonies

It is estimated that as many as 10 million Africans were transported against their will to the Western Hemisphere by the major European powers. The demand for labor in the sugar fields on the islands controlled by the European powers in the West Indies and the Spanish plantations in Central and South America, along with the Portuguese plantations of Brazil, led to a slave trade of massive proportions. Portugal dominated the slave trade from Africa in the 1500s. Slavery was traditional on the African continent as it had been in many civilizations over the centuries. With the need for more labor in the Americas, African rulers of the coastal nations realized that they had a resource that others wanted and supplied that market with a seemingly endless number of captives from the interior of the continent. The Europeans established forts along the west coast of Africa for the exchange of people and goods. The African captives were purchased with cash, but more often they were traded for tools, cloth, guns, or liquor. The Dutch took control of the slave trade from Africa for most of the 1600s. England was the next European nation to control the slave trade in the late 1600s and became the largest slave-trading nation of all. Spain granted England the right to bring slaves into Spanish America until 1743.

The captured African men and women faced inhuman conditions on the voyages across the Atlantic Ocean, a voyage known as the Middle Passage. They were completely disoriented and afraid of what was to become of them. Their quarters below decks were dark, hot, wet, and generally miserable and unhealthy. They were packed together so closely that they were often elbow-to-elbow for weeks or months. They might or might not be taken on deck for exercise, fresh air, and a quick wash with sea water. Thousands died during this Middle Passage from Africa to the West Indies. Many died from disease but also from starving themselves,

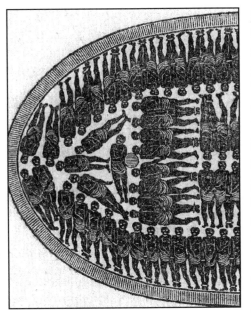

FIGURE 3.4 - Middle Passage slave ship conditions.

jumping overboard, or attempting to take over the ships. It was difficult for many of the slaves to adjust to their loss of freedom. To make them into acceptable slaves, they had to be "seasoned." This "seasoning" or training was intended to break their spirit of independence and often took place in the West Indies. Potential slave owners eventually preferred a slave who had not come directly from Africa.

A Dutch trading vessel brought the first group of 20 black laborers to Jamestown in 1619. This first group was treated as bound servants. By 1649, there were 300 Africans in Virginia. Some were bound servants and some were free men. The system of slavery developed over the next century through accepted practices, laws, and eventually slave codes in the various colonies. Virginia and Maryland led the way in bringing about the legalization of slavery in the English colonies. These tobacco colonies needed a stable source of labor for the tobacco plantations and farms. A Virginia Act of 1661 and a Maryland Act of 1663 assumed that some black servants served for life. One obstacle to slavery was the belief that only non-Christians could be enslaved. If a black man or woman were or became a Christian, they should not be held in bondage. In 1667, Virginia declared that "the conferring of baptisme doth not alter the condition of the person as to his bondage or freedome." The other colonies followed with laws that conformed to this justification. When lack of religion was no longer a rationale for slavery, the supposed savagery of the black race took its place. Virginia was the first to adopt a slave code which reduced the slaves to the level of chattel in 1682. By 1712, South Carolina had passed the harshest of the slave codes. As more slaves were brought into the various rural areas or cities, the white population wanted more laws to restrict the freedom of the slaves in order to protect the whites.

By the 1700s, slavery was legal and accepted in the colonies. New England traders became active in the

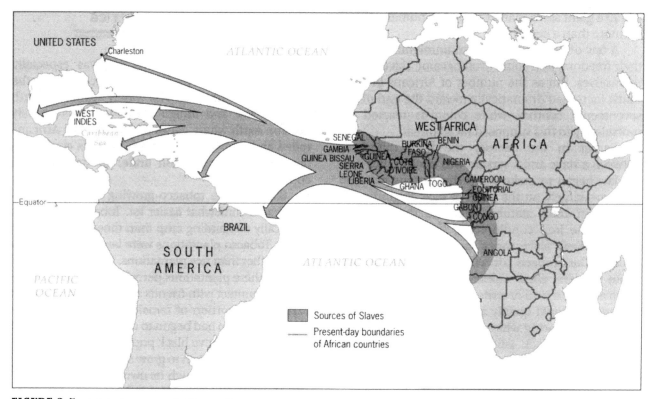

FIGURE 3.5 - Main Sources of African Slaves, c. 1500-1800.

slave trade and Newport, Rhode Island was a principal port of entry for the many slaves brought to North America. The number of slaves brought into the colonies increased dramatically. In 1700, slaves were approximately 11 percent of the colonial population. By 1770, the percentage had doubled to approximately 22 percent. The distribution of slaves was not even across the colonies. By that time, there were very few slaves in the colonies of New England or the Middle Colonies. By the mid-1700s, 60 percent of the slaves worked the tobacco fields of Maryland and Virginia and 30 percent worked the rice and indigo fields of North Carolina, South Carolina, and Georgia. Most of those brought from Africa worked as field hands, but there were also house servants, artisans, and free blacks.

For many of the slaves, resistance to white control remained throughout the generations. There were ways to thwart the will of the masters. One could claim illness, break equipment, slack off on the job, or attempt to run away. Some went to the extreme and participated in insurrections and rebellions. In April 1712, there was an insurrection by the black servants or slaves in New York City. The militia put down the insurrection,

and 21 blacks were executed. In 1739 there were three uprisings in South Carolina. The most serious was the Cato Conspiracy or Stono Rebellion. There were 30 white and 44 black fatalities before the rebellion was put down. A plot by black servants was uncovered in Charleston in January 1740. The whites in Charleston hanged 50 black slaves.

There were not many who spoke against slavery during colonial times; however, in Germantown, Pennsylvania, Francis Pastorius and the German Friends (Quaker religion) declared that slavery was contrary to Christian principles. In 1696 the leaders of the Friends warned against importing slaves and by 1755, they went so far as to exclude anyone from the denomination who imported slaves.

Many have noted that in the Declaration of Independence Thomas Jefferson and those who signed the document declared that "all men are created equal" even though he and many others signing the document were slaveholders. Jefferson attempted to add into the section of the document that listed the grievances against the King of England that he had negated every attempt by the colonies to stop the slave trade. The Southern delegates did not want anything to change with the slave labor system and demanded that the Continental Congress not include this statement. In the transition from English colonies to an American nation, there was a growing split between North and South on the issue of slavery.

Criticism of the slave trade increased throughout the colonies and then the states after the American Revolution. The new Federal Constitution had provisions to end the slave trade in America.

The next major blow to slavery in the country resulted from legal steps taken to abolish slavery in the northern sates: Pennsylvania, 1780; Massachusetts, 1783; Connecticut, 1784; Rhode Island, 1784; New York, 1785; New Jersey, 1786; the Northwest Territory, 1787. Most of the northern states passed laws that gradually ended slavery, although Massachusetts, Vermont, and New Hampshire adopted state constitutions that were interpreted by their state courts as making slavery unconstitutional. Petitions for emancipation of the slaves were also submitted to the national Congress. The South was very resistant to the elimination of slavery even though there were many emancipation societies in that portion of the country. Once the dependence on cotton for the Southern economy was firmly established (by about 1830), the South in general held more tightly to the slave system. After the breakdown of compromise after compromise on the issue, the South seceded from a nation that they believed was trying to take away their freedom. The result was the Civil War (1861-1865) which was to decide the issue.

Immigration

During the 1600s and 1700s Europeans were influenced by many factors to leave their homeland and find a better life. Some left to escape war, poverty, or religious persecution. Others left to take advantage of opportunity in the Americas for free or cheap land, a way to make a better living, or political freedom. As the colonies matured, there was a need for more laborers. Landowners and shipping interests hired agents to spread the word of the opportunities in the colonies.

Huguenots

The Huguenots, French Protestants, were the first of the non-English immigrants to arrive in significant numbers. Louis XIV, king of France, rescinded the Edict of Nantes in 1685, which had granted religious toleration to the group. Without this protection many of the Huguenots decided that they would be safer away from France. The king sent troops out to the villages to demand conversion to Catholicism or emigration. Some converted, and others left for the sanctuary of Protestant countries, specifically the various German principalities, the Netherlands, and England. Life was hard for these immigrants. Facing difficulties and prejudice, many left England for the colonies. Many settled in the larger towns of Boston, New York City, and Charleston, becoming prosperous merchants or skilled artisans. The advertisements of the Carolina proprietors were especially compelling as an inducement to come to the South. The ability to establish their churches in the colonies was especially pleasing to the Huguenots. This group assimilated well into colonial life. By the time of the Revolution, there were few, if any, differences between them and the English in the colonies.

Scots-Irish

The Scots-Irish were descendants of Scots living in Ireland. As Protestant Christians, the Scots-Irish were often harassed or otherwise persecuted by the Irish Catholic majority. Therefore, a desire for religious freedom, along with greater economic opportunities, motivated most of the Scots-Irish to come to America.

The major wave of Scots-Irish immigration to America came in the 18th century, with perhaps nearly 300,000 arriving in the English colonies before the American Revolution (1775-1783), making them the single largest non-English immigrant group during the colonial era. They tended to settle in Pennsylvania and further south, drawn to frontier river valleys, which suited their highly individualistic nature. Living in frontier river valleys led them into more frequent clashes with American Indian tribes, a reality that tended to harden their hostility to Indians even beyond that of the average colonist.

FIGURE 3.6 - Immigrant Groups in 1775.

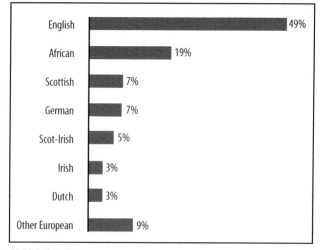

FIGURE 3.7 - Ethnic and Racial Composition of the Amerian People.

Germans

Perhaps as many as 225,000 German immigrants came to colonial America before the American Revolution, by far the largest number during the 18th century. Although economic opportunity remained a strong motivation for their decision to come, most of them had lived in areas closer to France and were often displaced by the frequent wars between Germans and the French.

Close to 50 percent of the German immigrants settled in Pennsylvania, with the remaining settling in New York, New Jersey, and the South. When German immigrants told the English-speaking colonists in Pennsylvania that they were "Deutsch" (German word for "German"), it was mistakenly interpreted as "Dutch" instead. The result was that the German immigrants were given the nickname of the "Pennsylvania Dutch."

German immigrants were usually hardworking farmers or skilled artisans and thus a boost to the colonial economy. They also represented a wide variety of Christian groups, including Roman Catholic, Lutheran, and several other smaller Protestant sects. In this way, German immigrants probably brought a greater cultural diversity to colonial America than any other single ethnic group.

Religion

Religion has been a dominant influence in civilizations for thousands of years. In order to understand the universe in which they lived, mankind developed or had revealed to them religious beliefs and practices to bring order and reason to their lives and the world around them. Within groups and later nations, conflict over religious beliefs and practices brought persecution and even death. When Europeans began to explore the world and discover new lands, uppermost in the minds of many was to bring their Christian religion to the non-Christians and save their souls, even if it meant using coercion to convert the so-called heathens. In the New World, settlement quickly followed discovery, and the Europeans who came to the Americas brought their religious views along with their families and few possessions. Many actually left their lives in England to establish colonies with the dream of practicing their religions their way without persecution. It was ironic that those who came to freely practice their religions in the New World were often intolerant of the religious beliefs of others. Puritans in Massachusetts branded and even hanged those of the Quaker religion. There was toleration in many areas, however. It was impossible to enforce a religion in a large area as more came to settle with a variety of religious beliefs. Even though it was not the intention of many to establish freedom of religion for all, it was the eventual outcome.

The Church of England (or Anglican Church) was the official creed in Virginia, Maryland (even though this colony was originally established as a safe haven for Catholics from England), New York, the Carolinas, and Georgia. Puritan Congregationalism was the official religion of Massachusetts.

The first settlers of Jamestown belonged to the Church of England, the Anglican Church. In the 1530s, King Henry VIII broke away from Papal authority over the pope's refusal to annul his marriage and became the Supreme Head of the Church of England, although he still viewed himself as a Catholic for the rest of his life. Before the end of that century, the Church of England was officially a Protestant church. Church attendance was mandatory in the early Virginia settlements. In those days, not only did the settlers attend church for most of the day on Sunday, but they also attended a church every day. This situation was relaxed as more settlers came over the years, but in Virginia the church remained a dominant force in the lives of the colonists.

Catholics and Jews

Catholics and Jews were the least accepted of the large number of religious groups in the colonies. Catholics never numbered more than about 2 percent of the colonial population, and Jews represented an even smaller portion of the population. The hostility between Catholics and Protestants can be traced to the 1500s in Europe, when Catholics who disagreed with the practices of the Church split into a Protestant understanding of the Bible and Christianity. That hostility and discrimination

Estimated Religious Census, 1775

Name	Number	Chief Locale
Congregationalists	575,000	New England
Anglicans	500,000	N.Y., South
Presbyterians	410,000	Frontier
German churches (incl. Lutheran)	200,000	Pa.
Dutch Reformed	75,000	N.Y., N.J.
Quakers	40,000	Pa., N.J., Del.
Baptists	25,000	R.I., Pa., N.J., Del.
Roman Catholics	25,000	Md., Pa.
Methodists	5,000	Scattered
Jews	2,000	N.Y., R.I.
EST. TOTAL MEMBERSHIP	1,857,000	
EST. TOTAL POPULATON	2,493,000	
PERCENTAGE CHURCH MEMBERS	74%	

FIGURE 3.8 - Estimated Religious Census, 1775

Established (Tax-Supported) Churches in the Colonies, 1775*

Colonies	Churches	Year Disestablished
Mass. (incl. Me.)	Congregational	1833
Connecticut	Congregational	1818
New Hampshire	Congregational	1819
New York	Anglican (in N.Y. City and three neighboring counties)	1777
Maryland	Anglican	1777
Virginia	Anglican	1786
North Carolina	Anglican	1776
South Carolina	Anglican	1778
Georgia	Anglican	1777
Rhode Island	None	
New Jersey	None	
Delaware	None	
Pennsylvania	None	

*Note the persistence of the Congregational establishment in New England.

FIGURE 3.9 - Established (Tax-Supported) Churches in the Colonies, 1775*

followed the Catholics who emigrated from Europe to the colonies. In 1740, the English Parliament forbade the colonies to naturalize Catholics. No colony allowed a Catholic to vote or hold office, even in Maryland, which was originally organized as a refuge for Catholics. Both Protestants and Catholics in Europe hated the Jews. Both Catholics and Jews faced great disadvantages and prejudice, but they were allowed to worship as they pleased.

The first record of Jews in North America was in the settlement of New Netherland in 1654. Jews had faced discrimination and persecution for hundreds of years before the establishment of the English colonies. The Jewish settlers continued to face discrimination and suspicion in the colonies, but they were allowed to come and worship as they pleased in most areas. The first colony to provide legally for religious toleration and include the Jews was South Carolina with the Fundamental Constitutions of 1669. The colony hoped to draw settlers from Barbados, including Jewish merchants. The Jews trickled into South Carolina, Rhode Island, and New York in the 1700s. In 1730 the Jews in New York City built the first synagogue in North America. An organized migration arrived in Georgia in 1733. Neither James Oglethorpe nor the Georgia trustees wanted Jews, but the charter establishing the colony did not exclude them. All of the colonies sought immigrants, and those with skills were especially welcomed.

The Society of Friends, known as the Quakers, settled in the colony of Pennsylvania. George Fox had been the founder of the group in England. They received the name Quakers because they often shook when praying. In Pennsylvania, all religions were accepted.

Witchcraft

Unable to explain evil, affliction, misfortune, or bad luck, Europeans and the colonists in North America turned to Satan and his servants on earth, witches, as an explanation. Magical power was supposedly given to those who sold their eternal souls to Satan. There were those in the towns or villages who cured with herbs, predicted the future, told fortunes, or even found lost items for a small price. It was not unusual when circumstances went awry for the townspeople that those who proclaimed such gifts and

FIGURE 3.10 - Salem witch trial.

were viewed as loners or odd in some way were accused of causing the misfortunes with witchcraft. The majority of those accused were female.

The Puritans in New England were particularly diligent in their watch for the use of witchcraft. By 1650, Virginia had convicted only one witch out of nine suspects. The guilty party was sentenced to a whipping and banishment. By 1650 in England, the trials of suspected witches had in effect stopped. Between the beginnings of the Puritan colony of Massachusetts and 1692, 93 persons were prosecuted as witches, and 16 were executed. It was not easy to prove witchcraft, so the trials were thorough in collecting evidence and examining witnesses.

A final hysteria and series of executions in Salem, Massachusetts in 1692 ended the practice of trying and executing anyone for witchcraft in the colonies. The rural Salem Village and the neighboring seaport Salem Town were beset with problems. There were problems between the two sections of Salem, Indian attacks, and disease. Within the midst of these misfortunes, several girls in the town became ill and began having seizures. They had been listening to the tales of witchcraft and voodoo from a West Indian slave and claimed they were bewitched. They began to accuse women around the village of bewitching them with the use of witchcraft. As the girls spread their tales of what they saw and experienced, mostly women were arrested, put in jail, put on trial, and some executed on the words of these young women. Eventually, more than 100 people were accused of worshipping the devil and carrying out his will with witchcraft. Fifty "confessed" that they were witches to escape further punishment, and 19 were eventually hanged. An older man was crushed to death with stones for refusing to make a plea. The people of the towns and those involved in judging the accused guilty soon realized their mistake when the accusations spread from the usual poor suspects and began targeting those in prestigious families, including the governor's wife.

The Great Awakening

The Puritans in New England had worried about a decreasing religious faithfulness from the 1660s, but the concern in the other colonies grew in the 1700s. In spite of the importance of religion to the settlement of new lands and the lives of many settlers, church membership was not high in the colonies. Further decline was fought by many ministers. Numerous factors led to an apathy that threatened to diminish the place of religion in the colonies. New ideas on science and the Enlightenment, with the explanation of natural laws applying to society, had an effect on the colonists as it had on their European cousins. Doubt concerning long-held traditional beliefs grew. The colonies became more secular in their interests as commercial prosperity increased. The older generation that had held so firmly to a world centered on traditional religious faith and practices had passed on. More colonists were moving into a wilderness with little contact with organized religion.

In response to this apathy toward religion, ministers searched for ways to ignite faith and piety across the colonies. The result was a great religious revival movement called the Great Awakening that began in the 1720s. Some ministers used enthusiasm and appealed to the emotions of their listeners, and others preached sermons that attempted to scare members into changing their ways. Pastor Theodore Frelinghuysen, preaching in the Dutch Reformed Church in New Jersey, appealed to listeners to perform penance for their misdeeds and perform more good deeds. Gilbert, John, and William Tennent Jr. preached from the Presbyterian Church that everyone could win salvation by repentance and living upright lives. Jonathan Edwards, an outstanding Puritan Congregational minister in Northampton, Massachusetts, railed against the new enthusiasm and instant conversions. He disagreed with the teaching that salvation was quick and easy or in the hands of an emotional sinner. He reiterated the Puritan ideas of the sovereignty of God, along with predestination and salvation through God's grace, from his pulpit. He wanted to touch their hearts and convert all. In his favorite sermon, "Sinners in the Hands of an Angry God," Edwards explained the horrible fate that awaited unrepentant sinners in such graphic terms that he came close to stopping a few hearts from fear. He later died of smallpox as a missionary to Indians.

Evangelists came from England to spread the message of Christianity from the viewpoint that all can be saved and that religion must touch the heart of the person. John and Charles Wesley, founders of the Methodists, came and preached in many of the colonies. George Whitefield came and preached a message of repentance on the part of the sinner and forgiveness on the part of God to crowds up and down the Atlantic coast. Some of his sermons held in large open areas attracted thousands of colonists. It was said that people standing in the back of crowds as large as about 35,000 people could hear every word he preached. Whitefield made seven trips to America. The colonists were caught up in the enthusiasm of the speakers, and thousands claimed they were now converted and saved. At the revivals, the listeners showed they were moved by the words of the ministers through weeping, clapping, and even fainting as they listened to the impassioned sermons.

Just as the ministers were split, so were congregations and their members. In the Congregational Churches, the split was between the "Old Lights,"—who were the traditionalists—and the "New Lights,"—who were the revivalists. In the Presbyterian Church the split was between "Old Sides" and "New Sides." Those who were the traditionalists were not comfortable with such a prominent place that emotion held in the Great Awakening.

After 1745 the enthusiasm began to die down, but there were long-lasting results from the Great Awakening. The division in the Congregational Churches and in the Presbyterian Church reaped some change in these denominations. The "Old Lights" accepted more rationalism in their theology and the "New Lights" continued to support evangelism. The Congregational Church remained split, but the Presbyterian Church healed the split. The Presbyterians, Baptists, and Methodists continued to gain members. By the time of the American Revolution, the Baptists had risen to third in the colonies in the number of churches. The "New Lights" created new colleges to train ministers in their view of religion, including Princeton, Brown, Rutgers, and Dartmouth.

The common people gained more control over their churches as they questioned the authority of the ministers. This questioning of authority leaped to other areas of authority and advanced democratic ideology in important segments of American life. Moreover, even though some preachers came from England to help fuel the Great Awakening, Americans generally viewed this revival and their own churches as uniquely American churches. This helped prepare the very next generation to take the next step and view themselves as Americans rather than merely transplanted Englishmen who happened to be living in America.

The Enlightenment or the "Age of Reason"

For several thousand years mankind turned to their religions and ruling classes for answers to the major questions in life: Who are we? Where do we come from? How does the universe function? For centuries the Catholic Church, kings, princes, and other ranks of aristocracy filled that role for the Christians of Europe. When the Protestant Reformation split the Christian world in the 16th century, the various churches and religious leaders that emerged fulfilled that role for this new group of Christians. Life was hard, and the reward

would come in the afterlife was the general consensus of the ordinary man and woman. A small number of philosophers, enlightened by the discoveries of a small number of scientists, reasoned that men who could unravel the laws that ruled nature could unravel the injustices and falsehoods that prevented the ordinary individual from true liberty. God was still in his heaven, but mankind could understand the world God had made; this was the focus of the Enlightenment.

In the 1500s, 1600s, and 1700s a few scientists, through observation and reason, challenged the supposed infallibility of the Church and aristocracy with new scientific theories and proof of their validity. In the 1540s, Nikolaus Copernicus, a Polish astronomer, put forth the theory that the sun was the center of the universe, and the earth rotated around this center. This theory contradicted the Catholic Church. Its position was that all of the planets revolved around the earth. Copernicus discussed his observations and proof with other scientists but did not publish his theory until shortly before his death. Galileo, an Italian scientist, in the 1600s built the first high-powered telescope, proved that the weight of falling objects did not proportionately affect the rate of their fall, and that the earth did revolve around the sun. The Church and the Inquisition declared him a heretic, and he recanted his conclusions on the sun as the center of the universe, although legend says that he declared on his death bed, "It [the earth] still moves." Isaac Newton, an English scientist, in the late 1600s published his work that defined and explained the laws of gravity and the motion of the planets.

Enlightened by the discoveries of these geniuses that humans could discover the truth concerning the laws of nature through observation, experimentation, and reason, philosophers in England and France challenged the status quo in religion, politics, economics, and psychology. Such philosophers became known as the philosophes. In other words, it was increasingly believed by the philosophes that everything in the universe was governed by natural law, and that man's duty was to discover that law and to correct anything that was out of harmony with it. Individuals had the power to understand their world and improve it if they could end the complete control over their lives by the Church, long-standing falsehoods, and powerful but unjust rulers.

In England in the late 1600s, John Locke, inspired by the conclusions of Newton, published his newly-realized thoughts on psychology, economics, and political theory. In his *Two Treatises on Government,* the *Second Treatise of Civil Government* proposed that men naturally possess the right to "life, health, liberty and property" and that "rulers derive their power from their subjects." A legitimate government protected the rights of its subjects, and illegitimate governments did not. The people should rebel against an illegitimate government, but only when the provocation is extreme. The French philosopher Marquis de Montesquieu wrote that in government there should be checks and balances to defend liberty against tyranny. Jean-Jacques Rousseau believed in the principles of the Enlightenment and in his work *The Social Contract,* written in 1762, wrote that "Man is born free, but today he is everywhere in chains." He disputed the divine right of kings, the idea that to rebel against a king was to automatically rebel against God.

When these ideas from the scientists and philosophes reached the English colonies, there were those who were very open to the ideas of the Enlightenment. Benjamin Franklin, the greatest of the colonial scientists, demonstrated that lightning did not exist to display the wrath of God but as a natural phenomenon of weather conditions. He organized the American Philosophical Society in 1743 to increase inquiry by scientists in the English colonies. Others in the political realm, such as George Washington, Thomas Jefferson, Thomas Paine, and again Benjamin Franklin, adopted the ideas of the Enlightenment philosophers on the rights of subjects and the true role of government. In other words, if a specific government itself were contrary to political natural law, then it was the people's moral duty to overthrow it and replace it with a government that was consistent with natural law. This political aspect of the Enlightenment played a major role in leading to the American Revolution when it was widely perceived that the English government threatened the liberties of their American colonists.

Deism

The religious element within much of the Enlightenment was called Deism. This belief system maintained that the monotheistic God created the universe and all the natural law to govern it. Then He stepped back to allow man, to whom he gave the ability to think and reason, to rule that universe. Deists often used the analogy of "The Great Watchmaker" for God as their creator. The universe was the watch that God had wound up, and it would tick away while man discovered and maneuvered all of its mechanics into either good or bad positions. After all, it was reasoned, God made man with sufficient intelligence to discover and apply natural law. Thus, why did God have to spend His own time governing the universe?

Deism did not appeal to the masses of colonists, who maintained some version of traditional Christianity as their religious belief. However, many American intellectuals, the influential leaders in society, were indeed influenced in various degrees by the teachings of Deism. Among other things, this meant a rejection of the traditional Christian teachings of the inherent sinfulness of mankind, the divinity and savior-status of Jesus Christ, and the divine inspiration of the Christian Bible as God's word to mankind. Deism, by contrast, emphasized the inherent goodness and intelligence of man and his ability to solve his own problems without divine intervention or advice.

Education

The education of youngsters in the colonies expanded as the colonial societies matured. There were regional differences in the methods of founding schools, but accessibility increased across the colonies. Families were mainly responsible for teaching youngsters the alphabet, some of the basics of reading, and elementary math skills in the earliest days. Such "schools" were called Dame Schools because they were usually taught by women in the home. This rudimentary system of primary education continued for many in the outlying or frontier areas, but for the areas with a higher concentration of families or a strong purpose for education, schools became more necessary and desired.

New England Schools

For the Puritans in Massachusetts in the early days of settlement, a general system of education was more important than for the early settlers of the other colonies. The government oversaw the establishment of public schools. The General Court, the provincial government of the colony, considered education a key to maintaining their goal as a community following the commandments of the Bible. Individual salvation was at the core of the Puritan religion, and in order to know the necessities for salvation and a Godly life, it was important for individuals to read the Bible. The wealthy could afford tutors or private schools, but the remainder needed assistance with this goal. The Law of 1642 required that parents teach their children and masters teach their apprentices and servants to read the Bible. The government imposed a fine for those who did not. The "Old Deluder Satan" law of 1647 strengthened the goal of a general system of education with the demand that towns of 50 or more families establish a primary or common school to teach reading and writing, and towns of 100 families or more must establish a Latin grammar school (a secondary school) to prepare young men for college. Once again the government imposed a fine if this law was not followed.

The larger towns established more schools as they had more residents to provide for buildings and teachers. There were five public schools in Boston. The students only needed to bring firewood to attend. The students received lessons in the basics in the common schools. The buildings were one room, usually with no supplies—including textbooks—and the discipline meted out by the teacher was quick and stern. The *New England Primer* was first printed in 1690 and became the standard text for a hundred years. For more than two centuries, most females did not advance beyond home schooling, the "Dame Schools," or the common school. Connecticut, Plymouth, and New Hampshire followed the lead of Massachusetts. Rhode Island did not mandate a system of education, fearing the dominance of a particular religion. Because of the influence of religion upon education, in a religiously tolerant colony as Rhode Island, this type of dominance was unacceptable.

Middle Colonies' Schools

Education in the Middle Colonies was not usually free. Private benefactors and churches established a parochial program of education in this region. The churches played a major role in opening schools in New York, New Jersey, Pennsylvania, Delaware, and Maryland (the latter was a southern colony). In the New England and Middle colonies, apprenticeship usually required the masters to provide for the education of the apprentices. Because of this requirement, some of the larger cities established classes in night schools.

Southern Schools

The South was the region with the fewest schools and the least interest in educating the general population. As in the other colonies, many of the wealthy planters and merchants hired private tutors for their sons and daughters. There was, however, much less emphasis on education for those of lesser means. One reason for few schools was that the scattered population of the South meant that not many areas had enough students to begin a school. Some communities did have "Old Field Schools." These were small one-room schools, usually built in abandoned tobacco fields, which accepted students for a small fee. George Washington attended an "Old Field School" for most of his formal education. Another factor in the lack of interest in a general system of education was that an educated person would be less interested in taking a common job in the fields of the wealthy.

Colonial Colleges

There were few colleges in the colonies. Most of the wealthy sent their sons to England for their college degrees. As more settlers came and cities increased in sophistication, colleges in America became necessary. Initially, the primary role of the colleges was to train ministers for the colonial churches. There were nine colleges established by the time of the American Revolution. Harvard was the first college, established in Massachusetts in 1636, partially from a bequest and the library of John Harvard as well as a grant from the General Court. Cotton Mather, the youngest student to attend Harvard College, began his studies at the college in 1675 at the age of 12. The college of William and Mary was established in Virginia in 1693 and Yale in New Haven, Connecticut in 1701. In the 1700s the colleges added more liberal and secular elements to their curriculum. King's College (later named Columbia) was founded in New York in 1754 and had no theological faculty. Training for doctors was first provided by the College of Philadelphia in 1765. The College of William and Mary offered the first lectures in law by 1779.

Summary of Colonial Education

The story of education in the colonies was truly remarkable. Only a small number of children advanced beyond the primary level in school, but the American colonies had the most literate population in the British Empire. In New England by 1754, 90 percent of the adult white males and 40 percent of the female population could read and write. In the other regions, the literacy rate for men was from 35 percent to 50 percent. The colonies began the establishment of a system of education that grew to a completely free system of pre-college education for all economic classes. Distance or

other factors prevented all from attending schools, but it was a remarkable accomplishment nonetheless. This access to education increased the intellectual level of the American colonies and played a role in preparing an educated society to contemplate a democratic future when the forces for rebellion began to gather.

Health and Medicine

There were many dangers for the early settlers of the colonies, but one danger that they had in common with their European cousins was susceptibility to disease and primitive medical treatments for health problems. Oftentimes if the disease did not kill you, the treatment would. The immigrants brought European diseases with them and also had to deal with diseases in the Americas caused by mosquitoes or other conditions. The major killers were smallpox, typhoid fever, diphtheria, cholera, whooping cough, scarlet fever, measles, influenza, yellow fever, dysentery, and malaria.

The prevailing theories of physicians educated in the medical schools of 17th and 18th century Europe

Name	Original Name (If Different)	Location	Opened or Founded	Denomination
1. Harvard		Cambridge, Mass.	1636	Congregational
2. William and Mary		Williamsburg, Va.	1693	Anglican
3. Yale		New Haven, Conn.	1701	Congregational
4. Princeton	College of New Jersey	Princeton, N.J.	1746	Presbyterian
5. Pennsylvania	The Academy	Philadelphia, Pa.	1751	Nonsectarian
6. Columbia	King's College	New York, N.Y.	1754	Anglican
7. Brown	Rhode Island College	Providence, R.I.	1764	Baptist
8. Rutgers	Queen's College	New Brunswick, N.J.	1766	Dutch Reformed
9. Dartmouth (begun as an Indian missionary school)		Hanover, N.H.	1769	Congregational

FIGURE 3.11 - Colonial Colleges.

concerning disease were that illness came from an imbalance of the humors, a disturbance in the body's tension, or other crude doctrinaire theories. The humors were heat, cold, dryness, and moisture. Doctors took action to put all of these in balance in their cures. One dangerous treatment for a body that was not balanced was to bleed the patient. This led to the death of many patients who lost too much blood, including George Washington, after his presidency. Moreover, medications often contained lead, urine, or other dangerous substances.

Almost anyone could practice medicine in the colonial period. There were very few college-educated physicians in the colonies. Few could afford to study in the medical colleges of Europe, but when they did travel to Europe to study, it tended to be in Edinburgh, Scotland. There were no medical schools in the colonies until the College of Philadelphia opened its doors in 1765. This was followed by Harvard in 1783 and King's College in 1798. By the time of the Revolution, about 5 percent of the physicians in the colonies had a medical degree. Most of the doctors in the colonies taught themselves from medical books or served as an apprentice to a physician. Many of the colonists taught themselves the rudiments of medical care because there was often no doctor in the vicinity. On the plantations, the master or the mistress had to act as the physician. Midwives or female neighbors most often delivered babies. Childbirth was dangerous, and many died.

An important contribution of the English colonies to health care was the eventual acceptance of inoculation to prevent diseases or diminish the harm. Smallpox was a particularly deadly disease at the time in Europe and the colonies, which left far too many dead from periodic epidemics. Cotton Mather, a clergyman in Massachusetts, learned from his slave that in Africa people were inoculated against smallpox by infecting them with a small amount of the disease.

Literature in the Colonies

One of the most important gauges of what is important to a society is the literature written by a few and read by many. Although there were talented authors writing in all of the colonies, the written works of the New England authors dominated the literary world of the colonies. The New World authors wrote sermons, histories, diaries, poetry, Indian captivity narratives, and newspaper stories that expressed the thoughts of those trying to build a complete society far from England.

The earliest works in English were published in England and promoted the colonies to those who might consider settling along the East coast of North America by recording the experiences of the earliest explorers. In 1588 Thomas Harriot published *A Briefe and True Report of the New Found Land of Virginia*. Harriot was a surveyor on Sir Richard Grenville's 1585 expedition to Virginia. This book was extremely popular in England. Many craved information about the New World. Captain John Smith, one of the earliest settlers, wrote several books on his adventures and travels through Virginia and on a later trip along the coast of New England. In his account, *A True Relation of Occurrences in Virginia*, published in 1608, he described the settlement of Virginia. In his account of the exploration of the northern area that he named New England, *A Description of New England in 1616*, Smith gave a geography lesson among other lessons to those who came later. In his later book, *The Generall Historie of Virginia*, published in 1624, he gave the world the romantic account of the Indian Princess Pocahontas saving his life. The truth of this account and a few others that placed Smith in a heroic light has been questioned.

From the Puritan flock, religious feeling compelled some to put pen to paper and produce a fine literature for posterity. Inspired by their religion and in the belief that they were carrying out the will of God, Increase Mather, his son Cotton Mather, and others produced moving sermons and other writings that showed the Puritan way of life as the fulfillment of God's plan for mankind on earth and the negative consequences for those who did not comply with the will of God. Cotton Mather wrote mostly pamphlets, but his 444 publications make him one of America's most published authors. His *Magnalia Christi Americana*, published in 1702, was a mix of biographies, church history, and warnings to those who fell away from the teachings of the earlier Puritans of Massachusetts Bay. Histories of the struggles and triumphs of God's people gave future generations a sense of what the Puritan settlers accomplished with their religious emphasis in colonization. *William Bradford's History of Plymouth Plantation*, written in 1646 by the governor, gave insight into the struggles and triumphs of the Pilgrims. John Winthrop, the first governor of Massachusetts Bay, wrote the *History of New England* in 1649. Edward Johnson wrote the *Wonder-Working Providences of Sion's Saviour in New England* in 1654 to counter criticism of the Puritan colony.

Because of the early printing establishments in Cambridge, poets in New England published their work more frequently than those in other areas. The first book published in the colonies was *The Whole Booke of Psalmes* in 1640, which eventually went through 27 editions by 1750. The first book of poems written by a woman and published anonymously in 1650 England was Anne Bradstreet's *The Tenth Muse Lately Sprung up in America.* Bradstreet covered many subjects in her verse, including love in her tribute in "To my Dear and Loving Husband." She also wrote philosophical and religious verse. The best-selling poet and author of the time was Michael Wigglesworth, a clergyman who wrote *The Day of Doom* in 1662 and *Meat Out of the Eater* in 1670. Both of these books were published in several editions. His works were also sermons put into verse.

The Puritans held a narrow view of what was acceptable for publication and entertainment, but they did allow the publication of what is known as captivity narratives. These were accounts of the experiences of colonists taken captive by Native Americans. These were accepted because they were factual accounts and played out the idea of good versus evil, a favorite theme for the Puritans.

By the 1700s, literary taste was moving away from so much emphasis on religion and becoming more secular. Literary works from England were well received in the colonies and dominated this type of literature. Almanacs increased in popularity, and only the Bible outsold this type of writing. Almanacs were a collection of information that included weather, recipes, tides, farming, poems, and witty sayings along with many other types of information. *Poor Richard's Almanak*, published by Benjamin Franklin, was familiar to many, but his was not the only or the best selling. Travel accounts across the various colonies became very popular as well.

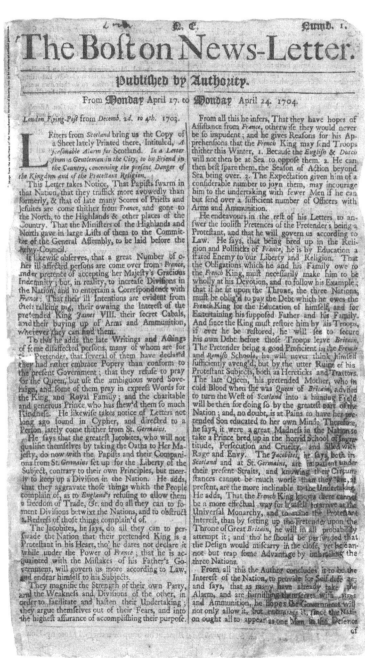

First issue of the Boston News-Letter, regarded as the first continuously published newspaper in British North America. Published April 24, 1704

Boston brought forth the first newspapers. To support a newspaper, the population has to be large enough to provide for the necessary financing and intellectual enough to want a regular newspaper. The first multi-page newspaper in the colonies was *Publick Occurrences*, which published one issue in 1690 and was shut down by the colonial authorities. The first newspaper to stay in business was *The Boston News-Letter*, which was first published in 1704. By 1763 there were 23 newspapers circulating in the colonies. The news covered included accounts of events in Europe, government pronouncements in the local areas, notices of departure and arrival of ships for coastal cities, advertisements for goods and services, as well as notices of runaway slaves and wives, essays and poems, but not illustrations or cartoons. Readership was quite large and, therefore, the newspapers assisted in developing a unity among the colonists.

Oral Traditions of the Native Americans and African-Americans

The Native Americans did not have a system of writing, but that did not mean that they were devoid of literature. It was merely in an oral form passed from generation to generation through stories. The stories recounted the beliefs of the various tribes, their history and their fictional accounts for entertainment. The Jesuit missionaries in New France included these oral accounts in their reports back to their French superiors. Some of the missionaries translated into French stories performed by the tribes. The beauty of the stories was often lost in translation. The English tended to disparage the value of the Native American oral tradition.

The first Africans brought to Virginia also had a heritage of orally transmitting stories and folk tales. The first African-Americans to write in English and pass on their poetry and stories were poets Jupiter Hammon and Phillis Wheatley. Hammon's first poem was published in 1760 and Wheatley's in 1767, written at the age of 13. By this time other African-Americans were writing autobiographies of their experiences.

Daily Life

Initially, the few settlements had small populations, but some grew quickly into cities along the Atlantic coast. Inhabitants lived much as they had in Europe once the settlements were out of the initial phase of extreme hardship. Boston was the first city of any size, but by 1760 Philadelphia had approximately 23,000 inhabitants and New York approximately 18,000. The population in Boston had grown to approximately 16,000, but in the South the only city of any size was Charleston, with around 8,000 residents. There was generally no nobility, but there was still separation of social classes and income levels once the colonists had firmly established their cities and towns. In New England there was less social stratification, but the leaders in the churches and government became the new nobility.

By 1750, 90 percent of the colonists continued to reside outside of the cities and towns, mostly on the seacoasts and rivers, where they farmed the land. This meant anything from farming land a mile away to setting up a farm on a frontier a considerable distance from the nearest town. The average farm was about 100 acres, but ranged in size from a southern plantation with hundreds of acres to very small landholdings of a few acres. By the 1700s, 50 percent of the white population consisted of subsistence farmers who worked their land without servants or slaves. Thomas Jefferson, one of America's most notable Founding Fathers, thought that farming the land was an ideal life and the best basis for an economy that would enhance and protect a democracy.

Colonial Women

In the 17th and 18th centuries, women were viewed in all parts of the world as inferior to men because they were allegedly the weaker sex. The English colonies in North America were not an exception to this prevailing view. However, there was a perennial shortage of women during most of the colonial period that helped give women a slightly higher status than elsewhere, including England. Most colonists married young and raised large families due to hardships and the need for many hands

A New England Dame school in old colonial times, 1713.

to work to sustain the family. Because of the shortage of women and the need for large families, married women tended to be treated almost as equal partners in the business affairs of the family. This seemed to be true whether the family business was a shop, a warehouse, or a farm. Therefore, married women in the English colonies of North America were probably better off than women anywhere else in the world at that time.

Outside the home context, women did not usually fare very well. Girls were usually denied access to education beyond primary school, effectively eliminating professional careers. Even most teachers outside of the so-called "Dame Schools" were men, not women. Moreover, even when a married woman managed to work outside the family context, her wages legally belonged to her husband. With the exception of Maryland, where malaria from low marshlands killed off so many men in the early colonial period, women could not own property in their own name. Moreover, women could not vote or hold public office.

Conclusion

Because of distance and difficulties in travel, the colonies had not developed into a unified area. However, they had enough in common to join together and rebel against the government of England. By 1750 an American culture had formed. This American culture included the establishment of a complex economy based mostly on agriculture and small shops, the creation of schools, varied and often vibrant religious traditions, and the rise of a body of truly American literature. Moreover, this developing American culture was enriched by the influx of different European immigrants and African-American slaves and by the new ideas generated by European scientists and Enlightenment thinkers.

French explorer Robert De La Salle (1643 - 1687) is pictured here on the banks of the lower Mississippi River, in what is now Louisiana, claiming the entire Mississippi basin for France on April 9, 1682. Engraved by an unknown artist, edited by John O'Kane Murray and published in 1879, it is now in the public domain.

Chapter 4 Contents

CHAPTER FOUR

Imperial Rule and Conflict in North America

Major Events

1608	Samuel de Champlain founded Quebec for France
1651	First Navigation Act passed to control colonial trade by requiring goods to and from the colonies travel on British ships
1682	Robert de LaSalle sailed down the Mississippi River to the Gulf of Mexico and claimed the land west of the river for France
1685	James II succeeded Charles II to the English throne
1686	Dominion of New England was created as a super colony to tighten British government control
1688-89	Glorious Revolution in England ended the rule of James II and brought William and Mary to the throne…it also ended the Dominion of New England
1689	King William's War began
1701	Queen Anne's War began
1739	War of Jenkins' Ear began
1744	King George's War began
1754	French and Indian War began
1763	Treaty of Paris ended the French and Indian War

Political Institutions and American Democracy

There was no real central authority in the British Empire dedicated to colonial supervision, and thus there were no comprehensive, coherent colonial policies in place. Instead, the colonists, aided by weak British administration and relative isolation of some 3,000 miles across the North Atlantic that required roughly six weeks travel (one-way) to cross, maneuvered their way in the political chaos to gain increasing political power fashioned out of their own American experiences.

The closest thing to a central authority was the Board of Trade and Plantations, created in 1696, but it was only an advisory board that really did not make actual decisions. The Privy Council was the administrative unit for the entire British Empire. The Council, along with the navy (admiralty) and the Treasury departments, were the supervisory elements of the British government for England and all of her colonies. Confusion among these agencies and lack of first-hand experience about the American colonies added up to weak administrative authority. For example, most officials had never been to America.

British officials in America included governors, though some of them were actually Americans, tax or customs collectors, and army and navy officers. Many of them were either incompetent or corrupt. They were usually appointed to their positions because they knew someone important and wanted an easy job; some had used bribery to win their positions. Some officials even stayed home in England and sublet their American jobs to others, who naturally received very small salaries. This, in turn, led to those British officials being easily bribed by Americans.

By 1775, eight colonies were royal colonies, where the king appointed the governor. Maryland, Pennsylvania, and Delaware were proprietary colonies, which meant that they were under the overall authority of the proprietors (owners) who appointed the governor. The other two colonies, Connecticut and Rhode Island, possessed self-governing charters that allowed the governor to be elected. This scenario had not been the case from the beginning, but various kings periodically changed the status of some of the colonies. Nevertheless, this was the situation among the thirteen colonies on the eve of the American Revolution in 1775.

In addition to a governor, almost all of the colonies had a two-house legislative body. The upper house, most often called the Council, was usually appointed by the king on recommendations from the governor in the royal colonies and by the proprietor in the proprietary colonies. They were elected by voters in the self-governing colonies. The Council served as the official advisory board to the governor and as the highest court of appeals in each colony. The lower house was always elected by voters.

Even in the royal colonies, the governor's salary was paid by the legislature. This enabled legislatures to use their power of the purse strings to wield greater influence. During a political stalemate, American politicians simply reminded the governor where his salary came from, and this would often force the governor to yield to their demands or to at least compromise an end to the crisis. This was a leading factor that gave Americans their most significant experience with democracy through the colonial assemblies. In 1767, the Townshend Act removed this power of the purse strings by paying governors' salaries from part of the revenue collected from the Townshend import duties (see Chapter 5). By then, however, it was too late to prevent Americans from having the experience of exercising political clout.

By 1720, the colonial legislatures could tax their citizens, appropriate funds, and pass laws applicable to their own colony. While the governor and the Privy Council (in London) each had veto power over their actions, the power of the purse strings and the colonial practice of passing vetoed laws in slightly different form substantially got around most vetoes. In any case, relatively few vetoes were issued. Each assembly tended to view itself as its own Parliament and to ignore the London Parliament as much as possible. Colonial legislatures gained even more practical power because the average term of appointed governors was only about five years, whereas incumbent legislators were fairly consistently reelected at each election. This continuity gap of time in office favored legislatures over governors.

The form of local governments varied from region to region. In New England, a type of direct democracy via town meetings was the norm. Men would gather at appointed times in a local church, tavern, or public building and debate the issues of the day. In the South, on the other hand, county government dominated local politics. In the Middle Colonies, there was a combination of the two types of local government.

Voting privileges were reserved for white men. Even then, there were property qualifications in all the colonies, and some had religious qualifications also; belonging to the official colonial church never hurt anyone, especially those seeking public office. Wealthier Americans feared the masses of people and often exhibited snobbery toward them, believing that governance was the rightful privilege of the elite. Therefore, property qualifications were even higher for officeholders in all the colonies than it was for the right to vote. Property was not that difficult to obtain in colonial America, and the more industrious citizens could gain enough to at least be able to vote. Nevertheless, some historians think that as many as about half of the white adult male population was not eligible to vote. Even among those who could vote, many often failed to exercise their right, yielding to the upper classes unless especially riled up at some political official. On the eve of the American Revolution in 1775, America was not the representative democracy that it is today. However, it was more democratic than England or anywhere else in the world at that time.

The Dominion of New England and the Glorious Revolution

The Dominion of New England

Since the time of the Magna Carta (Latin for "Great Charter"), which limited King John's power in 1215, England had been evolving a tradition of natural rights that placed it on the path of representative democracy. At the same time, England continued the monarchy. Parliament, its legislative body, naturally attempted to gain more power at the expense of the crown, which led to periodic clashes between those allied with Parliament and those allied with the monarchy. In this context,

the kings often sought to maintain more control over Britain's colonies as a foreign policy prerogative. For example, in 1679, King Charles II separated a region north of Massachusetts Bay that the latter had claimed and created the royal colony of New Hampshire. When it became clear that Massachusetts Bay was not going to enforce the Navigation Acts (see "Economic Colonial Policy" below), he revoked that colony's charter in 1684 and made it a royal colony as well.

James II succeeded his brother Charles II to the throne in 1685. He sought even more control over the colonies but was also worried about future Indian wars in the New England region in light of King Philip's War in 1675-76 (see Chapter 2). Partly to facilitate better coordination of the area's military, then, James II combined all of the New England colonies into a kind of super colony called the Dominion of New England in 1686, to which New York, East Jersey, and West Jersey were added in 1688. The Dominion was essentially ruled by the royally-appointed governor because it had no colonial assembly. Headquartered in Boston, Governor Sir Edmund Andros was a capable and intelligent man, but he was also politically inept in his public relations with colonists. He came across to most people as high-

FIGURE 4.1 - Andros' Dominion of New England.

handed and bold about it. His flaunting of his own connection to the Church of England angered the city which had a long Puritan tradition. Andros took other steps that bred resentment in the Dominion. He restricted town meetings, newspapers, and the local courts. Furthermore, he revoked all land titles, thus jeopardizing land ownership rights.

The Glorious Revolution

England experienced the Glorious Revolution, sometimes also called the Bloodless Revolution, from 1688 to 1689. This civil war resulted from King James II's exercise of autocratic authority over Parliament and the courts. Not only did his actions potentially threaten progress toward more representative democracy, but there was widespread fear that he might attempt to reestablish the Roman Catholic Church as the official church in England. The king's allies lost the revolution, and James II was forced into exile in France. In February 1689, he was replaced by his Protestant daughter Mary and her husband, William of Orange (William III), who ruled Britain jointly as William and Mary, and for whom the College of William and Mary in Virginia was later named.

In April 1689, when news arrived that James II had fallen, a Boston mob marched against Governor Andros. Andros was captured trying to flee in women's clothes; his boots underneath his dress betrayed him. He was shortly thereafter sent packing on a ship to England, and each of the individual colonies composing the Dominion returned to its former status. Massachusetts Bay did not get all that it wanted though, for in 1691 a new charter combined Plymouth and other small regions with Massachusetts Bay, making it a royal colony and removing religious qualifications for voting and office-holding. Needless to say, the Puritans were not happy with that decision.

Other repercussions from the Glorious Revolution were felt in New York and Maryland. In New York, a German immigrant and wealthy merchant named Jacob Leisler, who held deep resentment for never being accepted by the upper elite in that colony, organized a private militia in May 1689 that sent Lieutenant Governor Captain Francis Nicholson, a surrogate for Andros, into

exile. Leisler then claimed himself to be the head of New York. In 1691, William and Mary appointed a new governor there. When Leisler hesitated to yield to the new governor (although only briefly), his enemies used the occasion to charge him with treason. He was convicted and hanged, along with one of his sons-in-law. In Maryland, news of the Glorious Revolution led many there to assume, incorrectly as it turned out, that their Catholic proprietor, Lord Charles Baltimore, had been allied with James II. So under the leadership of John Coode, who led what is usually called the Protestant Association, Baltimore's officials were forced out of their offices. An elected commission chose a committee to temporarily govern Maryland while it formally asked the new monarchs for a royal charter, which was granted in 1691. Under the new charter, Maryland's colonial assembly made the Church of England the official colonial church and prohibited Catholics from voting, holding public office, or practicing their religion in public. In 1715, Maryland became a proprietary colony again when the fifth Lord Baltimore became a member of the Anglican Church.

Economic Colonial Policy

Mercantilism

By the time of Jamestown, Virginia's founding in 1607, the British government had adopted the economic philosophy called mercantilism, to which the words merchant and mercantile are related. The other powerful nation-states in Western Europe, chiefly Spain, Portugal, and France, had likewise based their colonial policy on mercantilism. The idea was that nations needed to acquire colonies in order to increase their national wealth, which was then measured by the amount of gold and silver in circulation within an economy. Colonies would provide raw materials to the mother country, whose manufacturers could then make finished goods out of them. By not having to purchase raw materials from a foreign source, manufacturers could keep their costs of production down, thereby making them more competitive in world trade. Specifically, the mother country could then hope to export more than it imported. Because gold and silver were the mediums of exchange used in international trade, if a country's exports exceeded its imports, then the net result was more gold and silver within the nation. Therefore, a country could increase its national wealth and thus its prestige and power. At the same time, the mother country's colonies would also constitute guaranteed markets for the finished goods, thus boosting its own exports. Modern nations no longer measure their national wealth this way, but rather in the total output of goods and services.

The Navigation Acts

Britain's economic emphasis in the seventeenth century was to establish a trade monopoly in which her colonies could only engage in trade within the empire. To do this, Parliament passed a series of Navigation Acts in the second half of that century. The first major one, enacted in 1651, aimed at reducing Dutch influence in the New World by requiring all goods to and from the colonies to be shipped on British ships. Colonial ships were considered British ships also, because the colonies belonged to the empire. The 1651 act was declared void after the restitution of Charles II to the throne in 1660. All other parliamentary laws passed under Oliver Cromwell's rule, a brief historical period in which the monarchy itself was abolished, were void. Therefore, the Navigation Act in 1660 included this 1651 provision. It also required that certain products, called "enumerated" goods, must be sold to merchants in England or other British colonies, whether or not it was the best price that could be obtained for them. At first, enumerated goods included principally tobacco, indigo, wool, and sugar. Later, rice and naval stores like masts, pitch, and tar were added to the list. The Navigation Act in 1663, also called the Staple Act, required that all foreign goods headed for the colonies must first be shipped to England, where import taxes would be collected and English middlemen could get their share of profits. The Act in 1673 created a system of customs officials to enforce the Navigation Acts. Finally, the Navigation Act in 1696 established a series of vice-admiralty courts to try cases involving disputes between merchants and shippers. These courts did not use the jury system; instead, judges appointed from among the local populations heard and ruled on cases brought to them. These courts did not bother most colonists until their jurisdiction was expanded in 1764 to try cases of alleged smugglers (see Chapter 5).

Manufacturing and Export Restrictions

In the eighteenth century, the British government expanded its emphasis to include certain manufacturing and export restrictions in a more concerted effort to protect British industries in England itself. It was also hoped that such restrictions would economically benefit the entire empire by fine-tuning a balance of trade among its many colonies. At the end of the seventeenth century, the Woolen Act (1699) prohibited the colonial export of woolen products in order to protect the English wool textile industry. In 1732, the Hat Act was designed to do the same for the English hat manufacturers. The Molasses Act of 1733 imposed import duties on sugar, molasses, and rum from the non-British West Indies. Finally, the Iron Act (1750) forbade the production of iron-finishing equipment.

Conclusion

Despite the Navigation Acts and the manufacturing and export restrictions, the American colonies enjoyed some positive advantages from mercantilism. Southern tobacco planters had a monopoly in the British market, killing the English tobacco industry. Most colonial products were neither restricted nor banned. For those products they exported, the colonies had guaranteed markets for their goods somewhere in the British Empire. In any case, widespread smuggling, despite the Navigation Acts, allowed colonists to get around some of those restrictions. Finally, the colonists enjoyed the protection of the mighty British navy as a part of the British Empire. The acid test was that overall colonial economic prosperity continued to grow throughout the eighteenth century.

Salutary Neglect

The relative geographical isolation from England and the lack of any sophisticated communications technology gave the North American colonies the advantage of developing their own specific economic and political practices within the larger context of British imperial rule. This trend was intensified by certain foreign policy crises faced by Britain, to the point that historians refer to a period of salutary (beneficial) neglect. Some historians mark it from 1689-1763, for it was in 1689 that the first of four major wars were fought between Britain and France, most often with other allies on both sides. Other historians prefer to identify this period as running from 1715-1763, for in 1715, the so-called Hanover kings, from the small German state of Hanover, were placed on the British throne. This resulted in Britain spending valuable time and resources in defending her German allies in Europe against France, principally. The point is that the preoccupation of England with fighting a series of wars against France and others caused England to involuntarily neglect her colonies. This neglect was beneficial (salutary) to the American colonies because it enabled them to develop a great deal of practical independence, economically through widespread smuggling, politically through the colonial assemblies, and culturally, by at least subconsciously viewing themselves as Americans rather than Englishmen who just happened to be living in the New World.

New France

The Protestant Reformation had formally begun in 1517, when a German Catholic monk nailed his 95 Theses to the door of the church in Wittenberg to challenge other church scholars to a debate on matters of doctrine and practice. The end result was to split Western Christianity in half and pit the emerging Protestants against Roman Catholics and vice versa. The Catholic Church had a powerful ally in the government of France, which attempted to completely wipe out Protestantism within its borders. The Reformed Church, founded by French Protestant Reformer John Calvin in the sixteenth century, was by far the largest Protestant group in the country. Its members were called Huguenots, although the origin of that term is still debated by scholars today. French troops and others allied with the Catholic Church were responsible for the St. Bartholomew's Day Massacre, the worst of the many religious massacres in the sixteenth century. Begun in August 1572 on the feast day of St. Bartholomew, and lasting for several months, more than 10,000 Huguenot men, women, and children were slaughtered just for being Protestants.

After France's internal religious wars finally ended with the Edict of Nantes (1598), granting religious toleration

to her Protestants, that nation began looking outward at the dawn of the seventeenth century. A series of outstanding ministers (political leaders operating under the king's authority) helped France look to the New World for exploration and colonization. In 1608, just one year after the English founding of Jamestown, the settlement of Quebec, overlooking the St. Lawrence River in what is eastern Canada today, was founded by Samuel de Champlain. Champlain was a soldier-explorer who later became known as the "Father of New France." Then in 1642, Montreal was established upriver from Quebec, to its southwest. These two settlements became the central core of New France.

After a series of different French companies failed to make high profits in New France, it came under the more direct political control of the French king. Unlike England, France had no tradition of representative democracy yet, for the king was still considered the absolute monarchial ruler of the country. Therefore, there were no representative assemblies and no jury trials in New France. Moreover, the Catholic Church was established as the official religion.

FIGURE 4.2 - France's American Empire at its Greatest Extent, 1700.

By 1750, the population of New France had grown to only about 60,000, compared to more than 2 ½ million in the English colonies to the south. There were at least two important reasons for this slow growth in population. First, the peasants in France did not experience what their counterparts did in England. During the sixteenth century in England, wealthy landowners forced the tenant farmers off the land because they wanted to make more room to raise sheep (especially for the wool) during the Enclosure Movement. When those peasants moved into the cities, the overcrowded conditions led to numerous social problems. A popular sentiment was that anyone who wished to go to the New World should be encouraged to do so. Unlike the English peasants, the poor in France usually owned the land they lived on, so that left little motivation to move to New France, especially since the agricultural season was so short. Second, the Huguenots were legally prohibited from migrating to New France, where they might have enjoyed a little more religious freedom despite the official status of the Catholic Church.

French Exploration of the Continent

Because of the conditions in New France, those who did choose to live there were of a hardier, adventurous nature. Many of them branched out southward and westward into parts of what is now the United States. For example, free-spirited Frenchmen took advantage of the fashion trend in Europe toward beaver hats and other items made with beaver fur by wandering far and wide to trap beaver. Called coureurs de bois ("runners of the woods"), these trappers soon invited Indians to be their partners for the obvious advantages that Indian knowledge of the land, languages, and customs of other tribes would be extremely helpful to them. In exchange for their help, Indians received French goods like metal cooking utensils and tools, things to which they quickly became accustomed. French trappers established fur trading posts in numerous places around the Great Lakes and along the Ohio, Missouri, Platte, Arkansas, Red, and Mississippi Rivers. Unfortunately, the fur business eventually resulted in the mass slaughter of beaver in much of North America, which in turn, harmed the land and many natural habitats of other animals as well.

In their zeal to convert Indians to Christianity, Catholic missionaries also fanned out over much of the continent.

Jesuit priests led the way in this great effort. Although they were largely unsuccessful in this endeavor, these missionaries made valuable contributions to the knowledge of geography, languages, and customs of many Indian peoples.

In addition to seeking profits in the fur trade and converting Indians to Christianity, others were drawn into the wilderness of the continent to counter British influence and thus enlarge French imperial influence. The settlement of Detroit was founded in 1701 by Antoine Cadillac in an attempt to discourage English settlers from moving into the Ohio valley in large numbers. To counter Spain's movement into the lower Mississippi River valley, Robert de La Salle went down the Mississippi in 1682 all the way to the Gulf of Mexico, naming the huge land mass to the river's west Louisiana, in honor of French King Louis XIV, and officially claiming it for France. This was the origin of French claims to the Louisiana Territory. After La Salle's voyage, the French built several outposts in present-day Louisiana and Mississippi, the most important one being New Orleans in 1718. New Orleans was of vital economic importance because it controlled access to and from the Gulf of Mexico and the Mississippi valley and further stimulated and facilitated both the beaver fur trade and grain farming. Grain production was particularly large and successful in what is now the state of Illinois. The expansion into the lower Mississippi valley also led to the rise of a French plantation system and the use of black slaves, just as in the English colonies. Other famous French explorers included men like Louis Joliet and Father Jacques Marquette, both of whom traveled in the 1670s and early 1680s by canoe from Green Bay (on Lake Michigan) south to the site where the Arkansas River flows into the Mississippi. Pierre Gaultier de Varennes left the Lake Superior region in 1743 to get within sight of the Rocky Mountains.

Relations among the French, English, and Indians

There were also English settlers and traders who ventured far west of the Atlantic coastal region of the official English colonies, although they were relatively few in number. Both the French and English recognized that the battle to eventually dominate North America would probably be won by the side who could win over the most important Indian tribes. The English had the advantage of being able to trade with greater supplies of manufactured goods, such as pots, pans, tools, blankets, guns, and gunpowder, because the British imperial economy was significantly superior to the French economy. However, the French usually enjoyed better relationships with most Indian tribes because they were far more willing to tolerate and even to assimilate Indian customs and culture than the English. The English almost always tried to change Indians and bend them to their thinking and ways of doing things, which was highly resented by most Indians. By contrast, French fur traders often married Indian women and adopted Indian culture. Despite the fact that Catholic missionaries were not successful in converting most Indians, when they did so, they allowed them to keep their own customs and tried to "Christianize" those customs if they could.

For their part, Indian tribes were concerned with their own independence and way of life. Therefore, they made alliances when convenient to do so, sometimes shifting allegiances when necessary, but not fully trusting any European group permanently. On balance, however, most Indians were friendlier with the French more often than with the English. The most important exception was the Iroquois Confederacy of tribes, consisting of the Mohawk, Seneca, Cayuga, Onondaga, and Oneida tribes. They had formed an alliance among themselves before contact was made with Europeans, although the historical evidence is not clear whether the alliance only went back to the fifteenth century or as early as the twelfth century. In the early seventeenth century, Quebec founder Samuel de Champlain made an alliance with the Huron Indians, which led him into battle with their enemies, the Iroquois tribes. After just a few shots were fired from French muskets, the Iroquois fled the battlefield, thereafter to become the enemies of the French, and usually (but not always) allies of the British in later wars. At the same time, the Iroquois continued to trade with the French as a way of playing the French and British against each other.

The First Three Colonial Wars

French expansion on the North American continent gave rise to growing tensions between French fur traders and English traders and settlers. At the same time, French King Louis XIV was aggressively expanding his reach as the most powerful monarch on the continent of Europe. These conditions led to a series of four different wars between England and France, along with different allies for both nations, which did not come to a decisive conclusion until the Treaty of Paris in 1763.

King William's War

In 1688, the Grand Alliance of European nations, which included England, the Netherlands, Spain, and the Holy Roman Empire, fought a war against France known as the War of the League of Augsburg. One of the main leaders against France was William III (also known as William of Orange), the chief magistrate of the Netherlands (Holland) at the time, who was put on the English throne the next year (1689) as a replacement for James II (see "The Glorious Revolution" above). The war spilled over into North America in 1689, where Americans called it King Williams' War. However, England and France did not send large numbers of troops to North America. Instead, the war there was fought mostly between French fur traders and English traders and settlers, along with Indian allies for both sides, in a kind of guerilla warfare. Most of the fighting occurred in northern New England and upper New York, with the worst clash coming at Schenectady, New York, which was burned to the ground in a 1690 raid by Indians allied with the French. The war was ended by the Treaty of Ryswick (a town in the Netherlands) in September 1697. This war really did not change the basic picture much in either Europe or North America.

Queen Anne's War

The second war began in 1701 as a major European war to prevent the French from controlling the Spanish throne. The Spanish King Charles II had died the year before without an heir and given all of his possessions to Philip, his great-nephew and a grandson of French King Louis XIV. Charles II had ruled over Spain, most of Italy, and the southern portion of the Low Countries on the continent of Europe. Therefore, Philip became King Philip V of Spain upon the death of Charles II. Fearing a union between France and Spain, and given Louis XIV's aggressive stance in Europe, eventually England,

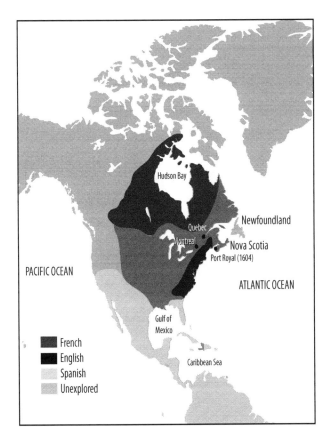

FIGURE 4.3 - British Territory After Two Wars, 1713

the Netherlands, and Portugal joined the Holy Roman Empire in this war that became known as the War of Spanish Succession (1701-1713).

Meanwhile, when William III, the king of England, died in 1702, he was succeeded to the throne by Queen Anne, a daughter of former King James II. Thus, the war in North America was called Queen Anne's War (1702-1713). Like King William's War, this war in America was fought principally between French fur traders and English traders and settlers, although there was fighting in South Carolina, where Spanish raids based in Florida were made. British colonists also attacked in New France to the north, temporarily taking the important town of Port Royal in Acadia, but being defeated in attempts to conquer the cities of Quebec and Montreal. The worst American disaster, however, occurred at the small town of Deerfield, in western Massachusetts, where Indian allies of the French killed about 50 settlers and forced more than 100 of them to flee in the winter of 1704.

After being decisively defeated in Europe, France and Spain signed a series of agreements known collectively as

the Treaty of Utrecht (a city in the Netherlands) in the spring of 1713, thus officially ending the war. Philip V retained the Spanish throne, but he was removed from the French line of succession. Spain also lost most of its territory in Italy and in the southern portion of the Low Countries, thus greatly diminishing French influence in Europe. England was the great beneficiary of the war in North America, where she was given Acadia, renamed as Nova Scotia (New Scotland), Newfoundland, and a large part of Canada on all sides of the Hudson Bay. This left Quebec, Montreal, and the many smaller settlements along the St. Lawrence River caught between English territory to the northwest and the southeast.

The War of Jenkins' Ear and King George's War

A third military conflict broke out in late 1739, when England declared war on Spain as the result of several tensions between those two nations, tensions that included Spanish resentment of English loggers operating on the coast of Honduras, an unsettled border dispute between Spanish Florida and the English colony of Georgia, and Spanish claims of frequent English smuggling in the Spanish West Indies. The war was called the War of Jenkins' Ear (1739-1742), so named because English Captain Robert Jenkins allegedly had an ear cut off by a Spanish sword after being accused of smuggling in the West Indies back in 1731. He displayed the ear in the British Parliament on more than one occasion, and it came to symbolize the growing animosity between England and Spain that finally led to war in 1739.

In North America, Georgia Governor James Oglethorpe led an invasion of Spanish Florida early in the war, where in 1740 he was eventually forced to retreat after making small gains. The Spanish in turn attacked Georgia, but they were rebuffed in the 1742 Battle of Bloody Marsh on St. Simons Island off the southeast coast of the colony. This proved to be the decisive battle of the war, so that 1742 usually marks the end of the War of Jenkins' Ear.

Meanwhile, a much larger conflict called the War of Austrian Succession had begun in 1740, theoretically to prevent a woman, Maria Theresa, archduchess of Austria, from officially ascending to the Austrian throne. More significantly, Prussia and Austria were disputing the region of Silesia, which lay between them. The major powers that eventually became involved in this war were Prussia, Spain, and France on one side against Austria, England, and the Netherlands on the other. During a part of the War of Austrian Succession (1740-1748), the North American English colonists called this King George's War (1744-1748), after George II of England, when France joined the larger war in 1744.

In June 1745, during King George's War, New England colonists, assisted by the British Navy, captured Louisbourg on Cape Breton Island, which guards the entrance to the St. Lawrence River and, in effect, to all of New France. Later that same year, a combined force of French and Indian allies destroyed the town of Saratoga, New York. Then in 1748, the last year of the war, Indians attacked the town of Schenectady, New York, which had been rebuilt after its previous destruction by Indians during King William's War. The war was officially ended by the Treaty of Aix-la-Chapelle in late 1748. It mostly restored the status quo, including Maria Theresa's reign in Austria and the return of Louisbourg to France, although Prussia did win the economically rich region of Silesia.

The French and Indian War

War Begins

The first three colonial wars, beginning in 1689 and ending in 1748, had cumulatively made a dent in French power in North America, but they had certainly not

destroyed it. However, continuing tensions there finally led to a decisive war in the 1750s that changed the course of the future on the continent. In North America, that war was known as the French and Indian War, which officially ran from 1754-1763. In 1756, it became part of a much larger European conflict known as the Seven Years' War (1756-1763), which began partly over colonial conflicts between England and France in both North America and India and partly as another segment of the previous War of Austrian Succession. This was world history's first truly world war, eventually pitting England, Prussia, and Portugal against France, Spain, Austria, Russia, and Sweden. For our purposes, we are more interested in the American version of the war, that is, the French and Indian War.

Both the British and the French claimed the vast region between the Appalachian Mountains and the Mississippi River, from Canada to the Gulf of Mexico, known as the Ohio Country because of the prominence of the Ohio River, which flowed into the Mississippi. Control of this region was crucial to the fortunes of New France, if it were going to keep the lower Mississippi valley united with it. The immediate focal point of conflict concerned the upper Ohio valley, territory that is today western Pennsylvania and eastern Ohio. English colonial traders won new trading privileges from several of the Indian tribes in that region in the late 1740s and began to undersell their French competitors. This was also considered prime real estate for the next major wave of English settlements. In fact, a group of wealthy Virginians, including George Washington's two half-brothers, formed the Ohio Company in 1747 and obtained a large land grant in the Ohio valley. Within six

Dates	In Europe	In America
1688-1697	War of the League of Augsburg	King William's War, 1689-1697
1701-1713	War of Spanish Succession	Queen Anne's War, 1702-1713
1740-1748	War of Austrian Succession	King George's War, 1744-1748
1756-1763	Seven Years' War	French and Indian War, 1754-1763
1778-1783	War of the American Revolution	American Revolution, 1775-1783
1793-1802	Wars of the French Revolution	Undeclared French War, 1798-1800
1803-1815	Napoleonic Wars	War of 1812, 1812-1814
1914-1918	World War I	World War I, 1917-1918
1939-1945	World War II	World War II, 1941-1945

FIGURE 4.4 - The Nine World Wars

years, the Ohio Company had established a trading post near present-day Pittsburgh. In addition to economic conflicts, there were also grave concerns of a religious nature. The government of New France was heavily influenced by Roman Catholic priests, and English colonists, who were overwhelmingly Protestant, were fearful that their religious freedom would be threatened by Catholic French expansion in the region. From the French perspective, they feared the anti-Catholicism among the English and were well aware of the fact that Catholics were still being persecuted in England.

Meanwhile, the French had begun to construct a series of forts linking Lake Erie to the Ohio River. Tensions were mounting, and armed conflict was not far off, when in 1753, Virginia Governor Robert Dinwiddie sent an envoy to a French outpost near Lake Erie, warning them that they were trespassing on land belonging to Virginia. A young lieutenant-colonel named George Washington, then twenty-one years old, persuaded Governor Dinwiddie to send him on this mission. Young Washington, along with six other Virginians, delivered the message to the French and returned with the stern French reply that they did not recognize it as Virginia's land.

The next year, Washington was sent back into the disputed territory as the head of a militia of more than 150 troops and some Indian allies. In late May 1754, about 40 of his troops attacked a contingent of about three dozen French soldiers approximately 40 miles south of Fort Duquesne—the most important of the French forts in the Ohio valley—and situated where the Allegheny and Monongahela Rivers unite to create the Ohio River (at present-day Pittsburgh). Washington's Indian allies massacred the wounded French soldiers after the battle, prompting Washington to hastily build a fort to defend against the retaliating French. This outpost was aptly nicknamed Fort Necessity. During the next month, several hundred reinforcements arrived at the fort. Nevertheless, on July 4, more than 600 French troops attacked Fort Necessity. After approximately one-third of his men had been killed or wounded, Colonel Washington surrendered. He and his men were permitted to return to Virginia with the loud and clear message that the French were not going to abandon the Ohio valley. War had begun.

The Albany Congress

The situation in 1754 did not look very good from the point of view of the English colonists. The French occupied a series of forts that formed a military wall from Lake Erie to the Ohio River. This wall not only blocked English expansion into the Ohio valley, but it also cut off English trading in that region. In the previous three colonial wars against the French and their Indian allies, the colonists had not been united in their own defense. The British government recognized the need for better colonial cooperation with its own redcoats if they were to be successful in this war. Therefore, it called for an intercolonial conference to be held at Albany, New York. Seven colonies sent a total of more than 20 delegates to what history calls the Albany Congress, which met from June 19 to July 11, 1754. The delegates were also joined by representatives of the Iroquois Confederation, by this time also called the Six Nations. The seven colonies consisted of Massachusetts, New Hampshire, Connecticut, Rhode Island, New York, Pennsylvania, and Maryland.

Benjamin Franklin, of Philadelphia, Pennsylvania, played the most important role at the Congress when he proposed the Albany Plan of Union. The month before this Congress, Franklin had published a cartoon of a disjointed snake with the caption of "Join, or Die." Franklin's proposal called for a permanent union of the English colonies, except Delaware and Georgia, in order to coordinate the defense of the colonies and Indian relations. Thomas Hutchinson, of Massachusetts, amended the proposal to weaken it a bit and to get it passed. Specifically, it provided for an executive called a president-general appointed by the king of England and a Grand Council elected by the colonial legislatures. The Grand Council would have the authority to tax the colonists for purposes of common defense.

Although the Plan was unanimously approved by the delegates at the Albany Congress, all of the colonial legislatures rejected it, as did the British government. The British government feared that it gave the colonists too much independence. From the colonial perspective, fear of a Grand Council's right to tax and historic disunity among the various colonies sabotaged the proposal. The colonies failed to unite, and once again a colonial war

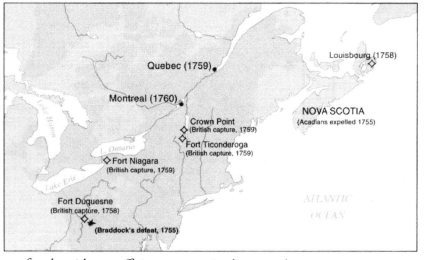

FIGURE 4.5 - Events of 1755-1760

else can." He immediately fired government ministers and replaced them with competent men. He also strengthened the British Navy and sent more redcoats to North America. A series of British victories ensued. In late July 1758, British General Jeffrey Amherst's forces captured Louisbourg on Cape Breton Island, giving the British control of the access to the St. Lawrence River. The next month the British also captured Fort Frontenac on Lake Ontario. This latter defeat by the French greatly weakened the communication and resupply route to Fort Duquesne, which the French abandoned in late November 1758. General John Forbes captured it the next day. Shortly thereafter, the fort was renamed Fort Pitt in honor of Secretary of State William Pitt.

was fought without sufficient cooperation between them and the British government.

The Actual War

The early part of the French and Indian War resulted in a series of British disasters. In July 1755, General Edward Braddock's combined force of 2,000 British redcoats and Virginia militiamen were ambushed by French and Indian allies just ten miles from their target of Fort Duquesne in western Pennsylvania. They lost about half of their men in the ambush, including the death of Braddock himself. It would have been worse if George Washington had not bravely used the militiamen to fight Indian-style from behind trees. Although personally unscathed, Washington did have two horses shot out from underneath him, and four bullets passed through his coat during this battle. His courage under fire led to his promotion as commander of the Virginia militia.

More disasters followed Braddock's defeat near Fort Duquesne. Nearly all of the major Indian tribes openly sided with the French after this British defeat, believing that France would win this war. Even the Iroquois, who had been pressured to nominally declare war against the French in 1755, rarely engaged the enemy in major fighting and refused to enter Canada for that purpose.

British fortunes in the war were remarkably turned around with the rise of William Pitt, who became British Secretary of State in late 1756. Pitt was a determined and optimistic man who allegedly declared, "I know that I can save England, and that nobody

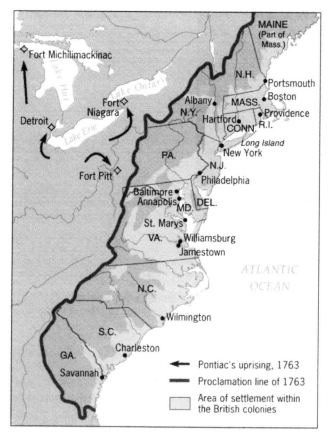

FIGURE 4.6 - British Colonies at End of French and Indian War, 1763

More important victories followed in 1759, including at Fort Ticonderoga and Fort Niagara, both in July of that year. But the most decisive British victory in the French and Indian War came at the fortress city of Quebec that same year. Quebec had long been considered an impregnable fortress because it stood on rocky heights overlooking the St. Lawrence River. British General James Wolfe came up the St. Lawrence to attack the city, but made slow progress until he courageously sent a small group of troops one September night up a part of the rocky cliff that was not well guarded. Other redcoats followed, and by morning, the French commander, the Marquis de Montcalm, found himself face to face with a British army. Both commanders, Wolfe and Montcalm, died in the battle, but the victory belonged to the British. One year later, in September 1760, General Jeffery Amherst captured the city of Montreal, and was then named the military governor of Canada until the peace treaty ended the war in 1763.

The Treaty of Paris

In February 1763, the Treaty of Paris formally ended the French and Indian War as well as the entire Seven Years' War. Britain won most of India and all of North America from the Atlantic to the Mississippi River, with the exception of the city of New Orleans. Spain gave up Florida to Britain, but in compensation, France gave New Orleans and the entire Louisiana Territory (land between the Mississippi River and the Rocky Mountains) to Spain. France was allowed to keep four islands in the New World, two fishing bases off the coast of Newfoundland and two sugar islands in the Caribbean. For American history, the most significant result of the war and the Treaty of Paris was that France lost virtually every possession in North America. The importance of this was to free Britain from worrying about France so that she could focus attention on her colonies. When she did that in the coming years, increased friction eventually led to the American Revolution.

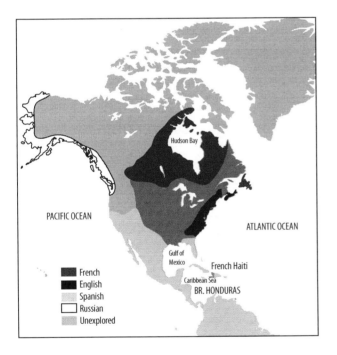

FIGURE 4.7 - North America before 1754

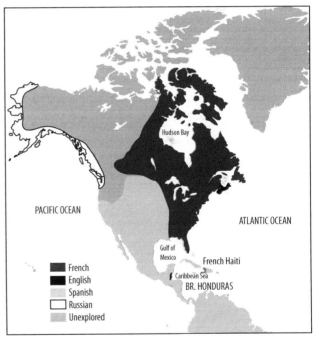

FIGURE 4.8 - North America After 1763 (after French losses)

Stamp commemorating the bicentennial of American independence (Boston Tea Party).
Copyright 2010 iStockphoto.

Chapter 5 Contents

CHAPTER FIVE

The Road to Revolution

Major Events

1763	Pontiac's War began Proclamation of 1763 ordered no settlement west of Appalachian Mountains
1764	Sugar Act (Revenue Act) passed to raise revenue in the colonies Currency Act was passed by the British Parliament
1765	Stamp Act put the first direct tax on all printed materials Patrick Henry wrote the Virginia Resolves to protest the Stamp Act Stamp Act Congress convened to discuss and protest the Stamp Act
1766	Parliament repealed the Stamp Act
1767	Townshend duties were placed on the colonies by the Parliament Daughters of Liberty organized a boycott of British goods to protest the Townshend duties
1770	Boston Massacre
1773	Boston Tea Party
1774	Parliament passed the Coercive Acts to bring Boston under control First Continental Congress convened to protest Coercive Acts and other problems
1775	Parliament declared Massachusetts in a state of rebellion

The Winds of Change

With the end of the French and Indian War in early 1763 came the end of the French threat in North America. This was a crucial turning point in American history because it allowed Britain to give far greater attention to her thirteen colonies there. When that attention brought with it very different policies, the British learned too late that the Americans had drifted apart from Mother England and were not willing to yield to the demands of the British Empire. The resulting series of conflicts led both sides down the road to revolution.

Other results of what was called the Seven Years' War outside of North America also impacted British policies toward her American colonies. The war had nearly doubled Britain's national debt, from almost 73 million pounds in 1754 to about 140 million pounds by 1763. The country's annual budget before the war only ran about 8 million pounds; after it, the annual interest on the debt alone was about 5 million pounds. British politicians knew they needed to raise large sums of new revenue. Many of them reasoned that since the American colonies greatly benefitted from the French defeat in the region, and their analysis showed that the colonies were paying only about one-fourth of the British costs of governing them, it seemed natural that those colonies pay their fair share of the taxes required to offset the debt. Besides, Americans should not protest because only the citizens of Poland paid fewer taxes than they did at the time.

Not only had the war produced a huge national debt for Britain, but her empire was now double its previous size before the war. This meant that more revenue would be needed to defend that additional territory, including the cost of about 10,000 redcoats to protect the American colonial frontier during any future Indian wars. Many colonists had traded with the French during the war, because the American attitude was that "all's fair in love and war" and business has nothing to do with foreign policy considerations. Therefore, the British calculated that they could not count on much American cooperation in future Indian conflicts, and they again would have to bail out the Americans in case another such conflict should arise.

At the very time that Britain was facing the enormous challenges of an expanded empire, it also experienced significant political changes. Most of these changes resulted from the accession to the throne of a new king, George III, after the death of his grandfather, George II, in 1760. George III stubbornly wanted to restore some of the authority that the crown had lost over the years, so he appointed a number of incompetent men to government positions and made more extensive use of bribery in order to develop some control over Parliament and the various ministries (government agencies). This created political instability, however, as one minister (head of a ministry) after another followed each other in fairly quick succession.

The new political instability was compounded by the personal shortcomings of the new king. Ascending to the throne at the young age of twenty-two, George III was insecure and immature. He often took on more than he could adequately handle on the political stage.

FIGURE 5.1 - George III

Moreover, he suffered from an unknown malady that manifested itself in periodic fits of insanity. These grew worse with age and interfered with his official duties during the 1760s and 1770s, the time when tensions between Britain and her North American colonies flared up and led to the American Revolution.

In April 1763, shortly after the end of the Seven Years' War, the king appointed George Grenville as the new Finance Minister. Although a variety of titles were used for Grenville's position in the eighteenth century, this office became known as prime minister during the next century. It was the highest political position in Britain next to the crown. Grenville shared the majority view at the time that the American colonists needed to help pay down the national debt. As a result, he became the architect of a new colonial policy that sought to gain increased revenue from the Americans.

The American Mindset

Not only were the winds of change blowing in the British government after the end of the Seven Years' War, but by 1763 there was a new American mindset firmly in place. This mindset, which clashed with the new aims of British officials, had evolved throughout the eighteenth century. Part of the reason for American resistance to the new colonial policy direction was sheer geographical separation from Britain. Separated from England by about 3,000 miles of Atlantic Ocean, the colonies naturally were able to develop their own brand of economic and political practice. Then after a new line of German kings on the throne of England helped lead to the period of salutary neglect (see Chapter 4), the quasi-independent spirit of the Americans was only intensified. In addition to geographic isolation and British foreign policy toward the continent of Europe, at least three movements accounted for the American unwillingness to simply go along with efforts to raise more revenue in the colonies.

Political Impact of the Great Awakening

The first movement that contributed to the eventual new mindset among Americans was the Great Awakening of the first half of the eighteenth century (see Chapter 3).

Although it was a religious revival movement, ironically, the most important impact that the Great Awakening had on colonial society was political. Americans who experienced that movement observed that it had been an American revival, not a transplanted one from England or elsewhere. This meant that the colonial churches were, in a very real sense, distinctly American churches. That idea acted like yeast in a lump of dough, for many members of the very next generation took the next logical step and concluded that they were Americans. Even though Americans argued during the ensuing conflicts for their rights as Englishmen, the cultural mindset told them that they were actually Americans. For many, this was probably a subconscious thought, but subsequent events demonstrated that it was nevertheless a real concept. As such, it helped make revolution possible, although by no means did it make it inevitable.

The Enlightenment

The second movement that contributed to new attitudes among Americans was the Enlightenment. This new worldview emerged in the seventeenth century, especially in England through the influence of men like Francis Bacon, Sir Isaac Newton, John Locke, and others. Essentially, it arose simultaneously with the scientific revolution and viewed the universe as operating on a series of fixed, mathematically-precise natural laws. It became dominant in much of Western Europe by the eighteenth century, when it flourished and crossed the Atlantic to the New World. Man's moral duty, it declared, was to discover as much natural law as possible by means of observation, experimentation, and reason. Then, if he found something that was out of harmony with its natural law, it was also his moral obligation to correct the situation, if it were humanly possible. Not only were material things in the universe governed by natural law, but so were things like human behavior and institutions. It was believed that through his reason, man's discovery and use of natural law would lead to great progress and even possibly human perfection.

This elevation of human reason and its resulting optimistic view of human nature were at odds with the traditional Christian worldview, as was its tendency to attribute natural causes for things in opposition to supernatural causes. Those who took Enlightenment thinking to its natural conclusion were, in fact, not Christians but Deists. Deism is the belief that a Supreme Being (God) created the universe and all the natural laws to govern the universe. Then, precisely because He created natural law to govern the universe, God never or rarely intervenes in His creation. This is sometimes called the "watchmaker" concept of God, that He wound up the universe as a person winds up a watch (in the days before battery-powered watches), and when He was done, He laid the watch down and went off somewhere to the far reaches of the universe. Meanwhile, the clock is ticking along nicely without His intervention. Deism denies the divinity of Jesus and the doctrine of the Trinity, and views the Judeo-Christian Scriptures as little more than a fascinating collection of ancient literature, but certainly not as the inspired Word of God. Thomas Jefferson, one of America's Founding Fathers and a leading Deist, once went through the Christian gospels, literally cutting out all references to the deity of Jesus and miracles. What he had left, he said, he could accept as historical fact and rational ethical teachings. Thus, Deism is definitely not a Christian religion; rather, it is a religion of reason and science and is also called Rationalism.

Deism never attracted much support among the general colonial population, but many intellectuals adopted it. However, most Americans were influenced by the non-religious aspects of the Enlightenment. The greatest impact that it made on American thinking was political in nature. Enlightenment political thinkers had taught that if a government were contrary to the natural law for political institutions, then it was not only the people's right but their moral duty to overthrow that government and replace it with one that was in harmony with political natural law. Most influential on Americans among the political thinkers of the Enlightenment was John Locke, an English philosopher who had published his *Two Treatises of Government* in 1690 at the close of the Glorious Revolution (see Chapters 3 and 4). In his famous political work, Locke had argued that natural law revealed that men have certain natural rights that cannot be taken away, even by government. Moreover, Lock had said that all governments were part of an implied social contract between the people of a society and its government. Therefore, he wrote, the authority of government rests upon the consent of the governed. Although he did not care what type of government people created,

Locke declared that they always had the right to fire the government, which is the right of revolution. Ironically, Locke's political ideas enjoyed a far greater acceptance among Americans than they did among Englishmen in his own country. Not only did it contribute to American attitudes of resistance to new British colonial policies, but it also laid the philosophical foundation for the later Declaration of Independence in 1776.

Government versus Liberty

Finally, American resistance to any new colonial policies aimed at increasing revenue was emboldened by the ideas expressed in the writings of the Real Whigs in England. Whigs were those British politicians who sought to expand the authority of the Parliament at the expense of the monarchy. But a literary group of radical Whigs, calling themselves the Real Whigs, wrote incessantly in the eighteenth century about the need to diligently preserve the natural rights of man from the power of government. They drew their ideas chiefly from John Locke, who had argued that the most important natural rights were life, liberty, and property. The Real Whigs were influenced by the traditional Christian view of human nature and by the experience of history to conclude that man is naturally subject to corruption. As the nineteenth century British Lord Acton would later put it, "power corrupts and absolute power corrupts absolutely." Therefore, the Real Whigs concluded that power must be restrained in order to prevent it from encroaching upon the natural rights of man.

These ideas had a profound impact on American thinking as the writings of the Real Whigs became widely read in the colonies, especially among the intellectuals. Government itself was considered the most serious potential threat to liberty, especially because of its power to tax. By definition, taxes took something away from the financial profits or incomes of people and were thus interpreted to be an infringement upon people's property rights. Therefore, while both the Real Whigs and Americans recognized the need for taxes, they wished to limit them in scope and amount for fear that an intrusive government might attempt to take away too much of their property rights (and thus their liberty). The influence of this movement was not limited to the eighteenth century among Americans, but it also played a role in the widespread anti-tax and anti-government attitudes held by Americans ever since that century.

Indian Trouble

With the fall of New France in the French and Indian War, the eastern Indian tribes had lost their political leverage. Most of the tribes had practiced the political art of playing one European power against the other to their own advantage. Realizing that those days were gone, most Indian leaders feared widespread encroachment on their lands by American settlers. Indeed, Americans did begin settling west of the Appalachian Mountains in larger numbers once the war ended. Moreover, the British did not continue the traditional French practice of giving gifts to the Indian tribes. In fact, General Jeffrey Amherst, commander of the British redcoats in the colonies from 1760-1763, seemed to deliberately antagonize numerous tribal leaders in the belief that they were incapable of mounting any kind of meaningful military effort. Trouble was certainly brewing.

Even before the French and Indian War ended, the Creeks and Cherokees in the South realized their precarious situation. After Cherokee raids along the Virginia and Carolina frontier ended in their defeat in 1761, both tribes were forced to accept the construction of a series of British forts on the lands they occupied. This reality was not lost on tribal leaders in the Ohio Country, for they feared a similar fate awaited them. In this context, a religious leader named Neolin, also called the Delaware Prophet, encouraged unity among the eastern tribes against English colonial expansion onto their lands. Neolin also warned against the evil influences of European goods, especially alcohol, and predicted that Indian unity would result in both military victory and a miraculous resupply of deer and other game on Indian lands.

FIGURE 5.2 - Pontiac

Pontiac's War

One Indian leader who fully supported Neolin's call for united action against the English colonists and tried to implement it was Pontiac, an Ottawa chief whose local tribe lived in the Ohio Country not far from Fort Detroit. Beginning in May 1763, Pontiac began an armed resistance against British redcoats and colonial settlers by laying siege of Fort Detroit. Eventually, more than a dozen tribes participated in this uprising known as Pontiac's War, including the Ottawa, Delaware, Seneca, Chippewa, Huron, Shawnee, Miami, Mingo, Kickapoo, Potawatomi, Wea, and Mascouten. Although this uprising was called Pontiac's War, historians are divided as to how much inter-tribal coordination was actually present. North American Indians did not have a strong tradition of working together during military campaigns, and it is unclear whether this uprising was an exception to that tradition or not. Certainly, the participating tribes shared the same goal, however, and to that extent it was a general Indian war. Militarily, all British forts in the West were captured or destroyed by July 1763, with the exceptions of Fort Detroit, Fort Niagara, and Fort Pitt. Thereafter, western settlements were attacked almost at will, resulting in roughly 2,000 settlers being killed or taken as captives.

Meanwhile, a group of Scots-Irish in central and western Pennsylvania used Pontiac's War as an excuse to take their security into their own hands. This armed group called themselves the Paxton Boys, named after a nearby village called Paxton. Having already developed hostile attitudes toward all Indians because of periodic Indian conflicts over the years, about fifty of the Paxton Boys attacked the village of Conestoga in December 1763 and killed several peaceful Indians there.

After attracting more support among other Scots-Irish settlers, a group of about 500 marched to Philadelphia in January 1764 to demand protection from the colonial government. Government leaders, including Benjamin Franklin, negotiated an end to the Paxton Boys' raids by granting them immunity from prosecution on murder charges stemming from their attack on Conestoga.

Pontiac's War was already winding down in 1764, when Colonel Henry Bouquet began a systematic burning of several Indian villages. The resulting widespread loss of food stores for the coming winter finally helped force Pontiac and other tribal leaders to agree to a truce. For all practical purposes, then, the war was over by the end of 1764.

The Proclamation of 1763

To prevent further escalation of Pontiac's War, as well as future Indian wars, the British government issued the Proclamation of 1763 in October of that year. It prohibited all settlements west of the Appalachian Mountains, including those that already existed. This measure was designed to buy the government sufficient time in which to negotiate purchase treaties with the various tribes for land west of those mountains and thus avoid future violent clashes between settlers and Indians.

Most of the tribal leaders accepted the Proclamation as the best deal they could expect. Americans, on the other hand, felt entitled to that Indian land, especially after "winning" it as the spoils of war in the French and Indian War. Feeling betrayed by their own government, settlers ignored the new restriction in large numbers, and even the 10,000 British soldiers in the colonies could not effectively enforce the ban. The Proclamation Line, west of which was off limits, was incrementally moved further west over the next several years as British authorities negotiated agreements with various tribes, proving that the restriction had been designed to be temporary all along. Nevertheless, the issue proved contentious and soured colonial-British relations, helping to set the negative tone for the next two decades.

The Sugar and Currency Acts

The Sugar Act

By 1764, Finance Minister George Grenville was ready to work with Parliament to find ways to raise revenue in the colonies, since each colony averaged only about one-fourth of the British costs of governing them. The first of these measures was passed in April of that year. The American Revenue Act, better known as the Sugar Act, cut the import duty on foreign molasses in half,

from six pence to three pence per gallon. The former Sugar and Molasses Act of 1733 had placed the high tax on foreign molasses in order to reduce or prevent the colonies from trading with the French sugar islands in the Caribbean. However, the British West Indies only produced about one-eighth of the amount of molasses required for the New England rum industry. (Rum is distilled from molasses.) Therefore, it had been necessary for the colonies to obtain molasses from foreign sources, especially the French sugar islands, which were only too happy to sell it because the French much preferred wine over rum. Because of the prohibitively high import duty on foreign molasses, Americans simply smuggled it into the colonies, thus frustrating British efforts to cut off trade with the French West Indies.

Grenville realized that the high import duty had been a failure for more than thirty years. Desperately in need of raising revenue in the colonies, he switched policies with the Sugar Act. The new law was designed to make smuggling less profitable and thus persuade Americans to discontinue that practice. Moreover, by reducing or eliminating the smuggling of foreign molasses, it would come through legal customs, where the duty on it would be collected. Unlike all previous British tax measures, the Sugar Act represented the first time that British tax policies were explicitly designed to raise revenue rather than to merely regulate trade. The Sugar Act also levied new import duties on certain foreign products, including sugar, wine, indigo, coffee, and textiles.

In an effort to strengthen the enforcement of all trade laws, the Sugar Act extended the jurisdiction of the vice-admiralty courts to include smuggling cases. Vice-Admiralty courts (naval courts) existed throughout the British Empire, having been created by the Navigation Act of 1696 to settle cases between merchants and shippers. These courts did not use a jury system, but judges appointed from the local area heard the arguments and made the rulings. In addition, accused persons were generally considered guilty unless they could prove their innocence, which contradicted the longstanding English notion of being legally regarded as innocent until proven guilty. Most juries had been sympathetic to those accused of smuggling and usually failed to convict. Clearly, the intent of the new law was to stop smugglers by actually convicting them. Therefore, while most Americans had not been concerned about the vice-admiralty courts before passage of the Sugar Act, afterwards it raised great alarm, for these courts would involve larger numbers of colonists. Moreover, Parliament had created a kind of super vice-admiralty court in Halifax, Nova Scotia, in the Act for the Encouragement of Officers Making Seizures the year before (1763). This particular court had jurisdiction over all the North American colonies, and its judge was sent directly from England to Halifax. Now British officials could opt to send a case to the Halifax court if they thought a local vice-admiralty court might rule in favor of a defendant.

For awhile, the smuggling of foreign molasses continued despite the Sugar Act. However, when the import duty was further lowered from three pence to one pence per gallon in 1766, all incentive to smuggle molasses disappeared, and the illegal practice ended.

The Currency Act

The Currency Act was another controversial law pushed by Grenville and adopted by Parliament in April 1764. The colonies experienced an almost perpetual shortage of gold and silver coins, for they imported more than they exported each year, and gold and silver were the medium of exchange for international trade. This shortage was particularly acute during the French and Indian War, resulting in the colonies printing paper money to help finance wartime expenses. British merchants, however, argued that the colonial currency was inflated and thus not worth as much as the equivalent in gold or silver. So they complained when Americans paid their debts to them with this currency. The Currency Act of 1764 prohibited the colonies from issuing any more paper money. Unfortunately, the colonies were already experiencing an economic slowdown in the aftermath of the French and Indian War. This new measure devalued the worth of the colonial currency further because no one wanted to accept it, making the economy worse.

Americans were not happy with the Sugar and Currency Acts. For the first time, some began to articulate the principle of "no taxation without representation," although that slogan would not become a rallying cry until the Stamp Act crisis the next year. The truth was that colonists had become so used to smuggling to avoid trade regulations that many seemed to believe it was one of their natural rights. After all, what does politics have to do with making money? Therefore, they were angry that the Sugar Act was obviously designed to interfere with major smuggling operations. Then too, its increased import duties on other foreign goods and the Currency Act's ban on paper money hit them financially hard at the very time that the economy was already sluggish. Despite their anger, the colonists did not coordinate their protests, and matters smoldered until erupting more virulently the next year.

The Stamp Act Crisis

The Stamp Act

Even if the Sugar Act had immediately succeeded in raising large sums of money from the colonies, it would have been insufficient even to cover the costs of the additional 10,000 troops kept in America to keep peace with the Indians. Therefore, George Grenville persuaded Parliament to enact two additional measures, the Stamp Act and the Quartering Act. In March 1765, the Quartering (or Mutiny) Act required the colonies to provide British redcoats with food and housing, either by paying for barracks or allowing them to use existing inns and empty public buildings as barracks. But it was the Stamp Act that aroused the most intense opposition in the colonies.

The Stamp Act, enacted in March 1765, required that a stamp tax be paid on almost all printed materials, including newspapers, playing cards, wills, diplomas, land deeds, licenses, pamphlets, bonds, and almanacs. Special revenue stamps affixed to an item was proof that the stamp tax had been paid. Unlike the Sugar Act, the stamp tax would affect most colonists and would therefore raise more revenue. The old system of obtaining revenue from the colonies was a kind of requisition system, in which the British government formally requested a specific sum from each colony annually. Each colony could raise the money in its own way. Obviously, this requisition method had not worked well, for the colonies averaged paying only about one-fourth of their required sums each year.

The significance of the Stamp Act was that for the first time ever, the British Parliament had legislated a direct, or internal, tax on the Americans. Prior to this, all British-imposed taxes were import duties, which the colonists paid only indirectly in the form of higher prices for foreign goods. But the stamp tax was a direct, or internal, tax because the tax was placed on a product only after it had entered a colony, and individual customers paid it directly, as in today's sales and excise taxes. Although the stamp tax was not excessively high, it was a principle that largely motivated American reaction. The colonies had always, albeit grudgingly at times, accepted the notion that Parliament had the right to impose import duties because it was a method of regulating trade. But only the colonial assemblies had imposed direct taxes on the people up to now. Americans now believed this standard practice was in jeopardy and that the Stamp Act might lead to a number of excessive direct taxes that would replace the right of the colonial assemblies to directly tax their own citizens. An additional concern was that alleged violators of the new tax law would be tried in vice-admiralty courts, where there was no jury system.

The Virginia Resolves

Although passed in March 1765, the Americans first learned of the Stamp Act in April. With the new law set to go into effect on November 1 of the same year, it gave the colonies about seven months to organize a protest movement. A young, fiery lawyer from Virginia, named Patrick Henry, seemed to fire the first very public shot against the tax. In May, when most of his fellow members of the House of Burgesses had left to return to their homes, Henry introduced seven resolutions to protest the stamp tax. Known collectively as the Virginia Resolves, two of the most radical were defeated, and one other that passed was rescinded the next day, leaving four of them intact. However, many colonial newspapers printed all seven of the Virginia Resolves and thus made Virginia lawmakers look more radical than they were.

The most important principle in the Virginia Resolves was "no taxation without representation," the concept that as Englishman, the colonists were entitled to taxation by their own consent. This principle echoed the writings of James Otis, a rising Massachusetts lawyer, who wrote *The Rights of the British Colonies Asserted and*

Proved in 1764 in protest of the Sugar Act. He basically argued that Parliament had no authority to tax the colonies because the latter were not represented in that legislative body. This argument reflected John Locke's view of property as a natural right of free men, and that it could not be infringed upon except by the consent of the people themselves through their political representatives. Ironically, the colonists had long agreed that the London Parliament did represent them for purposes of normal legislation, for that was considered part of keeping the British Empire functioning smoothly. This attitude had usually included the acceptance of import taxes. But property rights were viewed as a special natural right because it was too easy for a tyrant to come along and confiscate all of someone's property. In this way, liberty and property were considered inseparable. Therefore, the direct taxation of property, including goods, was almost universally believed to be the sole prerogative of the people's representatives.

Even though this philosophy was widely accepted in Britain as well, the difference was that Americans denied that the British Parliament actually represented them. The American experience with political representation, called Actual Representation, was based on the colonial practice of legislators being directly elected by specific groups of voters within each colony. The British practice, called Virtual Representation, accepted the tradition

FIGURE 5.3 - Patrick Henry in the House of Burgesses

that many members of Parliament had not been elected directly by voters. Based on this system, the British countered the colonial argument by declaring that every member of Parliament represented every subject within the entire British Empire. In other words, the British told the Americans that they were indeed politically represented in Parliament and, that as such, that body had every right to tax them. This difference in perceiving political representation reflected the different political traditions between Britain and the colonies. Because of these different traditions, neither side in the debate really understood the other.

While Otis had argued for the principle of "no taxation without representation," he also acknowledged what had become true after the Glorious Revolution (1688-89), that Parliament was the supreme authority in the British Empire, and it must be obeyed. Virginia's House of Burgesses followed suit from Otis in refusing to pass the more radical proposals of Patrick Henry, one of which claimed that taxes adopted by any body other than the colonial assemblies could be ignored. Another rejected resolve had declared that anyone who disagreed with this principle was "an Enemy to this his Majesty's Colony."

Mob Violence

Despite the relative moderation of the Virginia House of Burgesses, feelings against the Stamp Act ran deeper than most people on both sides of the Atlantic had anticipated. The first major steps of actual resistance against the new tax occurred in August 1765 in Boston, Massachusetts, where a coalition of artisans and small businessmen, known as the Loyal Nine, united with the city's two common laborers' associations. Usually at odds with each other, these groups joined forces to show that colonists from all walks of life opposed the tax. One of the significant figures who helped organize this resistance was Sam Adams, second cousin to John Adams and an activist in Boston's town meetings. In that month, protestors hung an effigy of Andrew Oliver, a stamp agent (or distributor), and broke most of the windows in his private home. This prompted Oliver to resign his post the next day. Later that month, a mob of common laborers completely destroyed the home of Lieutenant Governor Thomas Hutchinson, who was Oliver's brother-in-law.

For the first time, a British tax policy galvanized opposition in the colonies from people of all social classes. After the events in Boston, demonstrations followed during the summer in major towns all across the North American colonies. They often became ugly mobs, destroying the stamps where they were stored, burning effigies of stamp agents and other governmental authorities, and otherwise threatening officials. For example, one stamp agent in Connecticut was placed in a wooden coffin and lowered into the ground. When he heard dirt being thrown on top of his coffin, he finally shouted his resignation and was released. By November 1, when the new tax was to go into effect, not a single stamp tax agent was in place to enforce the law.

Americans who resisted the Stamp Act began calling themselves Sons of Liberty, a name first coined by Isaac Barre, a sympathetic member of Parliament. He applied his name to American tax protesters in his speech against the Stamp Act when it was first proposed in early 1765. By early 1766, there were chapters existing in nearly every colony. These chapters were usually led by lawyers, artisans, or merchants, men such as Sam Adams and Paul Revere in Boston. The chapter in Boston was essentially a renamed version of the previous Loyal Nine. Although not highly organized, the Sons of Liberty was the first step to creating greater unity among the colonists. Additional steps would soon be taken.

The Stamp Act Congress

In June, James Otis, a member of the Massachusetts colonial assembly, successfully urged that body to call for a special intercolonial congress to protest the Stamp Act in a more united fashion. Delegates from nine colonies met for about two weeks in New York City in October 1765. Only New Hampshire, Virginia, North Carolina, and Georgia were not represented in what became known as the Stamp Act Congress. This Congress adopted a series of resolutions similar to the more moderate Virginia Resolves and known as the Declaration of Rights and Grievances. Essentially, it utilized the "no taxation without representation" principle to affirm that only the people through its legislative representatives had the right to tax themselves. Actual Representation was also affirmed in what was simultaneously a denial of the British practice called Virtual Representation. At the same time, however, the delegates carefully expressed their loyalty and subjection to both the Parliament and the Crown. The Stamp Act Congress met in secret, and its resolutions were not even made public until they were leaked to a Boston newspaper about six months later.

Non-Importation Agreements

The most effective American response to the Stamp Act was a series of non-importation agreements circulated among the merchants and manufacturers in major colonial towns and cities. By the time of the Stamp Act, about one-fourth of all British exports were sold in the American colonies. The colonial business community understood the significance of this fact and calculated that a freeze on the purchase of goods made in Britain would exert sufficient pressure on British merchants and manufacturers that they would, in turn, force Parliament to repeal the hated Stamp Act. Therefore, colonial businessmen drew up these non-importation agreements and encouraged their fellow businessmen to sign them, pledging not to import any more British goods until the Stamp Act was repealed.

The economic pressure had its intended effect. In March 1766, Parliament repealed the Stamp Act, but at the same time passed a Declaratory Act that insisted Parliament had the right to "bind" the colonies "in all cases whatsoever." This repeal and the Declaratory Act were urged by Lord Charles Rockingham, whom King George III had replaced George Grenville with as the new Finance Minister in July 1765. Rockingham had opposed the Stamp Act in the first place because of practical, not philosophical, considerations. He very much believed that Parliament had the right to tax the colonies.

The Townshend Duties Crisis

Lord Rockingham's government in Britain lasted only about one year. In July 1766, King George III dismissed him as Finance Minister and asked William Pitt to form a new government on his own terms. Pitt, who had been the Secretary of State during the French and Indian War, appointed Charles Townshend the new Finance Minister

the next month. Townshend was a poor choice, however, for his reputation for drinking and partying led to his nickname, Champagne Charlie.

The Townshend Duties

Still looking for a way to raise increased revenue in the wake of the Stamp Act's repeal, Charles Townshend persuaded Parliament to enact the Revenue Act of 1767 in June of that year. This new law instituted a series of so-called Townshend duties on certain items imported from Britain. These included painters' paints, glass, paper, lead, and tea. To enforce the new import duties, the Revenue Act created the American Board of Customs Commissioners, headquartered in Boston. The selection of Boston was undoubtedly because it was the center of most colonial smuggling operations. However, it was also the most radical city in colonial America by this time, and the Board's location there was certain to lead to trouble.

This act of Parliament also explicitly authorized the use of writs of assistance to help enforce the collection of the new import duties. Writs of assistance were basically blanket search warrants that authorized British officials to search for smuggled goods. Unlike the later United States Constitution, which required that law enforcement officials show reasonable cause to a judge that a specific person may be involved in a crime, British officials armed with these writs could use them to search any person or place at any time.

They had been in use from time to time since the 1670s during the reign of King Charles II, although the general salutary neglect of the colonies by the British government had meant that most colonists had not paid much attention to them. That all changed in 1761, when Massachusetts Governor Francis Bernard reauthorized their use in an effort to crack down on smuggling in that colony. That same year, James Otis represented a group of Boston merchants to challenge the legality of all writs of assistance in the courts. He argued before the court that such writs were "against the fundamental principles of law" and should be thrown out of the empire. He lost the legal challenge. The writs continued to be used until the political climate became so hot in the 1770s that most authorized officials refused to use them.

Initial Colonial Reaction

Townshend believed that since the new import duties were, by definition, external or indirect taxes, the Americans would accept them. It was direct taxes that they hated, he said, in an obvious reference to the harsh reaction against the Stamp Act. But subsequent events proved him wrong. Because the Townshend duties were levied on British imports, not foreign goods, it was obvious to the Americans that this was intended merely to raise revenue and not to regulate trade. The result cemented colonial anger against taxes and confirmed the belief of "no taxation without representation"—heard with a great roar in the Stamp Act crisis—now applied to all taxes (defined as intended to raise revenue) imposed by the London Parliament, whether they were direct or indirect taxes.

John Dickinson, a prominent Philadelphia lawyer, wrote a series of essays published as *Letters from a Farmer in Pennsylvania* in 1767, in which he eloquently argued that Parliament had the right to regulate trade but not to tax the colonies for the purpose of raising revenue. Dickinson's essays and his earlier dominant influence in the writing of the Declaration of Rights and Grievances at the Stamp Act Congress resulted in his being later called the Penman of the American Revolution.

American anger against British authorities was intensified by the fact that the Revenue Act had specified that the colonial governors' salaries would be paid out of the revenue generated by the Townshend duties. Heretofore, those salaries had been paid by the colonial assemblies, and American politicians had become quite skilled in pressuring governors to at least meet them halfway on controversial matters. Now that leverage was gone, and Americans were suspicious of a complete imperial takeover of their local governments.

That suspicion seemed to be confirmed by two additional British actions. First, there was the New York Suspending Act, passed about a week after the Revenue Act. The New York Suspending Act dissolved the New York colonial assembly for refusing to adequately comply with the Quartering Act of 1765. British troops sent to the colonies to protect them from further Indian wars were stationed in cities along the Atlantic coast because it was easier to supply them there. New York City was the headquarters for those troops in North America, so naturally there were more troops stationed there than anywhere else. Other colonies, such as Massachusetts, had also failed to comply, but Townshend wanted to make an example out of New York because it was the biggest culprit on this issue.

Second, the Massachusetts assembly officially called upon other colonial assemblies to sign a joint petition to protest the Townshend duties. The new British Secretary of State for North America, Lord Wills Hillsborough, demanded that Massachusetts Governor Francis Bernard get the assembly to withdraw its letter to the other colonies or else dissolve the assembly. When the Massachusetts assembly voted 92-17 in late 1768 to refuse to withdraw its letter, Governor Bernard promptly dissolved the assembly.

The Daughters of Liberty

While the Stamp Act crisis had seen the emergence of the Sons of Liberty to protest a hated tax, the Townshend Duties crisis gave colonial women the opportunity to show that they could play a prominent political role in protesting unpopular British policies. Various chapters of the Daughters of Liberty arose in response to the call for a boycott of all British goods, begun by the Boston town meeting in 1767. Many other towns across colonial America followed suit. Called non-consumption agreements, the various resolutions called for boycotts of British food, tea, cloth, and sometimes even toys. This worked a hardship on many colonial families, but it also gave birth to a home manufacturing boom. Of particular importance was the rise of homespun cloth. The Daughters of Liberty often organized public demonstrations of women spinning their own cloth in order to dramatize the role that they were beginning to play in the growing political crisis.

Colonial merchants were hard-pressed to support the boycott because it cut into their sales and thus their profits. It was even more difficult for them to support the idea of non-importation agreements that had been so successful in repealing the Stamp Act. But merchants who refused to go along often found their businesses blacklisted in the colonial newspapers. It was not until late 1768 that a significant group of Boston merchants finally signed a non-importation agreement in that city. Leading merchants in New York City, Philadelphia, and Charleston followed Boston's example.

Repeal of the Townshend Duties

Meanwhile, political turmoil reigned in Britain. First, Charles Townshend had died unexpectedly in September 1767 and was replaced by Augustus FitzRoy, better known as Lord Grafton. But when Lord Grafton resigned in January 1770, Lord Frederick North became the new Finance Minister of the British Empire. Lord North occupied this office until his resignation late in the American Revolution.

By early 1770, American economic pressure was taking its toll on the economy in England, and merchants were crying for relief. Lord North acknowledged that it was not politically wise to levy import taxes on British goods entering other parts of the empire. Therefore, with his support in March 1770, Parliament repealed all of the Townshend duties except the duty on tea. The tax on tea was intentionally kept in force as a reminder to the colonies that Parliament still maintained its right to tax them.

Trouble in Boston

Background

The American Board of Customs Commissioners was unpopular right from the start. The radicals in Boston harassed the Commissioners the moment they arrived in November 1767. In June 1768, tensions mounted further when British authorities seized the *Liberty*, radical leader John Hancock's ship, on suspicion of its use in smuggling. Mobs reacted by destroying much of the property of customs officials. This violent reaction convinced the British government that soldiers were needed to protect the customs officials and control any further mob activity. Therefore, about 3,000 troops were sent to the city in September of that year.

Unfortunately, British occupation in the city continued to breed hostility between redcoats and civilians.

General Thomas Gage had replaced Jeffrey Amherst in August 1763 as the commanding officer of all British troops in North America. However, he had married an American woman from New Jersey and maintained his headquarters in New York City. The immediate commander on the ground in Boston was Lieutenant Colonel William Dalrymple. The military occupation was hard to ignore at best, with the presence of one soldier for roughly every seven civilians. British army discipline was harsh, and desertion was sufficiently serious that troops blocked the only road outside the city and questioned everyone going past their checkpoint. This was aggravating enough, but deserters either faced a firing squad or were hanged, often in full view of passers-by. Additionally, some military offenses merited public lashings. Dalrymple foolishly made things even worse by selecting Sunday as the army parade day, marching past shops and churches with its noisy band music. Bostonians objected to such obnoxious interruptions to their lives, but the truth was that relatively few citizens in the old Puritan city were still regular churchgoers. Nevertheless, the army practice needlessly antagonized the people.

Matters were made worse by the fact that soldiers often interrelated negatively with civilians in other ways. Due to poor army pay, many of them took part-time jobs, although only the lowest-paid, dirtiest jobs were usually offered to them. This placed them in direct competition with the uneducated laborers in the city, who desperately needed jobs, especially during the economic slowdown. Furthermore, whenever you have male soldiers mixing with a civilian population, you also have dating relationships with the local single women. This often led single men in the city to charge soldiers with stealing their girlfriends and other such social misbehavior.

The nature of the British presence and interaction in the city, coupled with the harsh winter of 1769-70, put everyone in a foul mood. Fights between soldiers and civilians were not uncommon occurrences. After one such fight on Friday, March 2, 1770, the city was flying with rumors about more trouble to follow the next Monday, March 5. Ironically, that was the very day that Parliament repealed all of the Townshend duties except the duty on tea. Of course, no one could know that then, as all communications had to travel by ship. When the rumored trouble came on March 5, it would lead to a celebrated tragedy that is still remembered in American history today.

The Boston Massacre

A verbal scuffle between a male civilian and the lone sentry in front of the Customs House broke out on Monday night, March 5, 1770, at about 9:00 o'clock in the evening. A crowd of some 60 people quickly gathered and immediately took the side of the civilian, shouting angry insults at the soldier. Finally, so much commotion was raised that it attracted the attention of a guardhouse

FIGURE 5.4 - Paul Revere.

about a block away. A Captain Thomas Preston and seven other soldiers arrived on the scene. But their presence only aggravated the crowd even more, so that they began to add snowballs and rocks to their arsenal, pelting the troops from a distance. Eventually, both sides grew physically closer to each other, and in the resulting skirmish, one of the soldiers was knocked down to the ground. Later testimony established that some of the troops thought they heard an order to fire upon the crowd, although such an order had not actually been given. When it was over, five civilians lay dead or dying, and at least six others were injured. One of the dead was Crispus Attucks, a runaway slave, later memorialized as the first black martyr of the American Revolution.

Attorney John Adams approached his older second cousin Sam Adams and urged him to use his influence to keep a lid on protests of what the more radical groups in the city were calling the Boston Massacre. In fact, it was one of those radicals, Paul Revere, who memorialized this phrase by engraving "massacre" on a pewter plate. Sam Adams agreed to keep things relatively quiet. Meanwhile, realizing that the tragedy had not been an actual massacre, John Adams volunteered to become the soldiers' chief defense attorney. In that capacity, he managed to convince local authorities to postpone the trial of the soldiers until that fall in order for cooler heads to prevail. He also persuaded them to

charge the soldiers with first-degree murder, because he reasoned that it would be easier to persuade a jury that it clearly had not been a premeditated crime. Although most of the defendants were acquitted, two of them were convicted of manslaughter. Those two exercised their right to plead that they were clergy in civilian life, a defense requiring the competent reading of a portion of the Christian Bible in court. This defense, called the Benefit of Clergy, could only be used once in a lifetime, and it always resulted in being branded on the left thumb. That way, if someone attempted to use this defense again, his thumb would be checked first. These two defendants were thus branded and released.

By this time, Sam Adams had become the most prominent and influential of all the radicals in Boston. As a result of the so-called Boston Massacre, the reputation of Sam Adams as the preeminent leader of the radical movement throughout colonial America was etched in history.

FIGURE 5.5 - Boston Massacre.

Committees of Correspondence

For awhile after the Boston Massacre, calm prevailed in the colonies, even in Massachusetts. But just beneath the surface, a movement was beginning to pick up steam. This movement would no longer attempt to split hairs between Parliament's right to pass general, or regulatory, legislation for the empire and its alleged power to tax. Instead, the very notion of imperial control over its colonies was being challenged. Such a notion would make it possible for a revolution to occur in the near future.

This movement became quasi-organized with the creation of committees of correspondence. Sam Adams envisioned such committees to expand the geographical reach of revolutionary ideas to more than just the major colonial cities. He saw a need to embrace the smaller towns in the interior of colonial America and to keep them in touch with leaders of the movement elsewhere. Therefore, at his request, the Boston town meeting established the very first committee of correspondence in November 1772 and named him as its head. Some 80 smaller towns in Massachusetts followed Boston's example by establishing their own committees. Committees of correspondence soon arose throughout the 13 colonies. In 1773, Virginia created one as a standing committee to its House of Burgesses, so that it could serve as the center for radical communications among all the local committees in that colony. Other colonies followed Virginia's example, thus creating a loose intercolonial network for radical thought and action. In this way, the committees of correspondence formed the basis for later colonial unity.

The Gaspée Affair

While the committees of correspondence were keeping revolutionary ideas alive, occasional acts of violence punctuated colonial resentment against British thinking and actions. The most glaring of these incidents occurred just off the shore of Providence, Rhode Island in June 1772, when Americans burned and sank the *Gaspée*, a British navy ship that ran aground in shallow water while chasing a colonial vessel suspected of carrying smuggled goods. The authorities further alienated the colonists

when they announced that suspects would be taken to England to stand trial for treason. However, no witnesses could be found, and no arrests were made.

The Tea Act

In May 1773, Finance Minister Lord North persuaded Parliament to pass the Tea Act as a measure to bail out the East India Company and prevent it from going financially under. The company had a monopoly on British trade in the East Indies, but it had also been saddled with the responsibility for keeping the peace in the relatively new and large colony of India. The American boycott of British tea as a means of protesting the Townshend duty on it, although waning in intensity, nevertheless was sufficient to cause a rather large surplus of the company's tea. (Americans continued purchasing more Dutch tea smuggled into the colonies than they were British tea, even though Dutch tea was inferior to the British tea.) These factors meant that by early 1773, the East India Company was nearing bankruptcy. There was a purely political motivation in passing the Tea Act; many leading British politicians were major financial investors in the company. Therefore, if the company went bankrupt, so would several major politicians.

Among its provisions, the Tea Act gave the East India Company a monopoly on tea sold in the American colonies and allowed direct sales of tea to those colonies. Previous to this act, all British tea was required to be shipped to England, where it was sold to English middlemen and where the Townshend duty on the tea was paid. British authorities once again misjudged American public opinion. They believed that Americans would be happy because the elimination of English middlemen would lower the price of tea—even below the price of smuggled Dutch tea. However, colonists realized that this was Parliament's subtle way to get them to accept the tax. This plan was especially apparent since the new law exempted the East India Company from the Townshend duty on tea that entered England itself. Principle was more important than price for most Americans. There were also cries of monopoly, with many colonial leaders fearing that this might simply be the first step to granting the company a complete monopoly on all trade with the colonies. Moreover,

FIGURE 5.6 - The Boston Tea Party.

the company soon angered Americans by its refusal to sell tea to any colonial wholesalers who had supported either of the previous two rounds of non-importation agreements. In other words, the East India Company was mixing politics with business, a concept that was completely foreign to American thinking.

The Boston Tea Party

In late fall of 1773, East India Company tea began arriving in the major colonial ports. By this time, Americans had built up a full head of steam and were determined that no tea would be unloaded. In New York City and Philadelphia, mass demonstrations forced the governors of those two colonies to order the tea back to England. In Charleston, South Carolina, the tea was eventually unloaded and stored in a public warehouse for nonpayment of the Townshend duty. Ironically, the tea was later sold to help finance Patriot soldiers during the American Revolution.

It was a very different story in Boston. Tea arrived in Boston Harbor aboard three ships in late November 1773. Thomas Hutchinson, an American politician whose private home had been destroyed during the Stamp Act crisis in 1765 when he was the lieutenant governor, was now the governor of Massachusetts, having replaced Francis Bernard in the summer of 1769 (first as Acting Governor and then, in March 1771, as regular governor). Although Hutchinson himself opposed the Townshend duty on tea, he insisted that the rule of law required obedience even to unjust laws. Given the earlier destruction of his home, Hutchinson was in no mood to compromise. Rather, he was determined to unload the tea and at least auction it off in order to pay for the import duties. A Boston port law required that action if goods sitting on ships in the harbor were not unloaded within 20 days of their arrival.

On the night of December 16, just before the tea would have to be unloaded and auctioned off, Sam Adams spoke at the Old South Church to more than 5,000 Bostonians (more than one-fourth of the city) and urged his fellow compatriots to destroy the tea. "This meeting can do nothing more to save the country," he declared. Immediately after that meeting, a large group of them marched to the docks and thereby physically prevented officials from stopping the impending incident. Then perhaps as many as 150 Sons of Liberty, loosely disguised as Mohawk Indians, boarded the three ships and dumped 342 chests of tea into the harbor. This so-called Boston Tea Party represented the key point of no return toward revolution. Although other subsequent events in which both sides reacted badly to the other, also played a part. An act of destruction that took three hours indirectly led to a revolution that would last eight years.

The Coercive, or Intolerable, Acts

With the massive destruction of private property in the so-called Boston Tea Party, Americans lost most of the sympathy from its former supporters in the Parliament in London. Lord North, in consultation with King George III, moved decisively to win approval from Parliament for a series of four measures the British called the Coercive Acts. When Americans learned of these laws, they called them Intolerable Acts instead.

The first of the Coercive Acts was the Boston Port Act, passed in March 1774. It closed the entire port of Boston, effective June 1, until three conditions were met. First, full restitution for the market price of the destroyed tea would have to be made to the East India Company. Second, the Townshend duty on tea would also have to be paid. Finally, some kind of assurance, perhaps an official apology, would have to be made that nothing like this would occur in Massachusetts again. This law really took dead aim at the heart of Boston's economy, to say nothing of the entire colony.

The second Coercive Act was adopted in May, when Parliament approved the Massachusetts Government Act. This law greatly revised the colonial charter. The council, the upper house of the colonial legislature, had previously been an elected body. Now the king was given authority to appoint all of its members, as well as many other government officials. Towns all over the colony were permitted only one town meeting annually, unless permission for additional meetings was granted by the governor. In other words, all of Massachusetts was being punished for the sins of Boston. In a related move, General Thomas Gage, the commander-in-chief of all British redcoats in North America, replaced Thomas Hutchinson as governor of Massachusetts in May. Now that a prominent colony had a military governor, many Americans suspected that this might be the beginning of a plot to destroy all vestiges of self-government in the colonies.

Another Coercive Act was the Administration of Justice Act, also passed in May 1774. This law allowed for British officials charged with crimes in connection with their official colonial duties to be transferred to another colony or to England itself for trial. This was obviously intended to avoid juries which might be prejudicial toward those officials. Americans interpreted it as an intention to allow officials to get away with murder. It was also deemed unnecessary because the trial of the redcoats after the Boston Massacre had certainly been fair to those troops.

The last of the official Coercive Acts, passed in early June 1774, was the Quartering Act. Actually an amendment to the original Quartering Act of 1765, this new measure empowered a colonial governor to order the use of barns and unoccupied houses and other buildings if adequate barracks were not provided by the colonial legislature.

Although there is controversy over whether or not this act allowed for the quartering of British troops in occupied private homes, the language of the act does not specifically state.

Americans interpreted a fifth act of Parliament, passed in October 1774, as another Intolerable Act, although it only directly concerned British Canada. There was some fear that the overwhelming French population might be influenced by events in the colonies to their south. In order to prevent rebellion and make British rule more manageable in Canada, Parliament enacted the Quebec Act. The new law granted complete religious freedom to the inhabitants, who were overwhelmingly Roman Catholic. It reestablished French civil law, which had been suspended when Britain had won Canada in 1763, and extended the territory of Quebec to include the region between the 13 colonies and the Mississippi River north of the Ohio River.

The Quebec Act angered Americans on two primary fronts. First, they feared that an expansion of Catholicism on the North American continent might eventually endanger their own religious freedom as Protestants. Second, some of the 13 colonies had laid claim to western lands all the way to the Mississippi River. Those colonies and land speculators who were eyeing the Ohio Country felt betrayed that their interests were being sacrificed to their former enemies, the French.

Other American Reaction

The British authorities had designed the Coercive Acts, not just to punish Boston in particular and Massachusetts in general, but also to send a message to the other twelve colonies that they should fall in line, for the same things that were happening to Massachusetts could happen to them also. This message was received loud and clear. However, rather than humbly bow to British authority in fear, colonial leaders outside of Massachusetts reasoned that because similar things could happen to them, all the colonies should stick together and support the New England colony. This was hardly what the British expected, but it is what they received.

Thomas Jefferson, an important Virginia planter, wrote and circulated a pamphlet entitled *A Summary View of the Rights of British America*, defending American rights and arguing that each colony was a separate part of the empire, like England, and thus subject to the crown but not to Parliament. Other leaders sent food to Boston in a show of support. In Virginia, the House of Burgesses called for June 1, the day that Boston Harbor would be closed, to be a "day of fasting, humiliation, and prayer" on behalf of that city. On June 1, many shops closed and flags were flown at half-mast all over the colonies. Americans were ready to actively resist imperial rule, but they were not yet ready to make a complete break with Britain.

The First Continental Congress

In the spring of 1774, Sam Adams and his Committee of Correspondence in Boston called for an immediate boycott of all British goods. However, leaders in other colonies preferred that another intercolonial congress like the Stamp Act Congress of 1765 come together to discuss options first. When legislatures in Virginia and elsewhere formally called for such a gathering, Boston finally agreed.

FIGURE 5.7 - Samuel Adams

From September 5 through October 26, 1774, 55 delegates from every colony but Georgia met in Philadelphia's Carpenter Hall in what history calls the First Continental Congress. The process for electing the delegates was illegal in most colonies because the colonial governors had prohibited meetings for the purpose of electing delegates to this body. Thus, even before they started with business on the opening day, the First Continental Congress was in open defiance of British authority.

The list of delegates at this Congress read like a "who's who" of current and future American leaders. They included George Washington, Patrick Henry, and Richard Henry Lee from Virginia, John and Sam Adams from Massachusetts, and John Dickinson and Joseph Galloway from Pennsylvania. Peyton Randolph, an experienced politician from Virginia, was selected as the president of the Congress.

The Galloway Plan and the Declaration of Rights and Grievances

Delegates to the Continental Congress had two basic goals. First, they wanted to clearly define the colonies' relationship to the British government. Closely related to that question, of course, was the matter of what natural rights they were willing to stand for. Second, they wanted to create an organized strategy to protest the Intolerable Acts in order to force their repeal by Parliament. Some of the delegates, like Patrick Henry, Richard Henry Lee, and Sam Adams, were eager to denounce all Parliamentary authority over the colonies and to regard it as a legislature only for England itself. Most of the delegates, however, were not willing to go that far. Joseph Galloway, a more conservative delegate from Pennsylvania, proposed that a permanent intercolonial legislature be established. Called the Grand Council, its members would be appointed by the colonial assemblies, except for a President-General to be appointed by the king. Agreement of both the London Parliament and the Grand Council would be required in order to pass laws that applied to the colonies.

John Adams played the leading role in helping to defeat the Galloway Plan by a narrow margin. In its place, Adams proposed a compromise between the more conservative and the radical positions held by the delegates. This compromise was spelled out in the Declaration of Rights and Grievances adopted by the Congress. It accepted the proposition that Parliament had the authority to regulate trade in the empire, as long as it wasn't disguised as an attempt to raise revenue in the colonies. Parliament had no authority to tax the Americans because the latter was not represented in that legislative body, and taxes could only be levied by the consent of the people. In this Declaration, the delegates asserted the following: "We ask only for peace, liberty and security. We wish no diminution of royal prerogatives, we demand no new rights." In one sense, this was true, because their fundamental position was based on the English tradition that taxes were voluntary gifts of the people to their government and could not, therefore, be given without the people's consent through their legislative representatives. On the other hand, the American interpretation of just who their legislative representatives were, and were not, constituted a radical departure from British practice in England itself. The American legislative experience, based on Actual Representation, had led them to a fundamental split with the British government. It seems that 3,000 miles of ocean separating the colonies from England were finally, albeit indirectly, about to result in a revolution.

The Continental Association

The delegates agreed that economic pressure should be the principle means of winning repeal of the Intolerable Acts. But there were differences of opinion on exactly how to proceed along this line. Many delegates favored a total ban on trade, including the import and consumption of British goods and the export of goods to England. Southern delegates, however, balked at that suggestion, for such a radical step would harm the southern economy, which was substantially dependent upon tobacco and rice exports for their prosperity. An ingenious compromise was crafted that time-staggered the various components of economic pressure and made almost everyone happy. A ban on the importation of British goods would take effect on December 1, 1774. Prohibition of the consumption of British goods would become effective on March 1, 1775, and a ban on the export of colonial goods to England and the British West

Indies would become effective on September 10, 1775, with rice being exempted to appease South Carolina. A three-month delay in the start of the non-consumption agreement would give merchants sufficient time to sell goods they had already imported from England before the ban on such goods was adopted. The delay in the non-exportation agreement was partly designed to give the other measures time to work.

To enforce the economic sanctions, the Congress created the Continental Association. Unlike the two previous non-importation agreements, an enforcement organization gave real clout to the boycott. Local chapters of the Continental Association were variously named committees of inspection, observation, or public safety. Such committees were elected by voters who were eligible to elect members of the colonial assembly. They were instructed to monitor the boycott in their local area and to expose violators by publishing their names in the local newspaper. Often these committees went much farther than that, however, hanging and then burning effigies of uncooperative Americans and otherwise harassing them. The worst form of harassment was tar and feathering, the practice of literally applying hot tar to a person's skin (after being stripped of some or all clothing) and sticking chicken (or other fowl) feathers to the tar. It was a painful and humiliating experience, but no one died from this treatment. The British magnified the frequency of tar and feathering for the obvious propaganda purpose of showing that American radicals were monstrous terrorists. However, probably no more than a few dozen cases of tar and feathering occurred in the colonies from 1765 through 1775. Most of those occasions were in 1775 itself, before the practice then gradually died out.

Other Steps

The First Continental Congress also passed a series of other resolutions, including a recommendation that colonists prepare to defend themselves militarily against a possible attack by British redcoats, especially in Massachusetts. Finally, if their grievances were not remedied, they voted to convene a Second Continental Congress the next May (1775).

Breakdown of Government and the Failure of Compromise

By the end of 1774, in most colonies radical American leaders were abandoning their colonial assemblies and being elected to what were called provincial conventions (or congresses); in this way they could completely ignore the governor. Governors, who had little enforcement machinery, were powerless to stop this trend. Some of them reorganized new colonial assemblies, but others did not bother to do that. In any case, popular support allowed the provincial conventions to actually function as the real colonial governments in most colonies. These conventions oversaw the creation of new militia units and the collection of guns, ammunition, and gun powder. At the local level, the numerous committees of correspondence and committees of inspection, observation, or safety expanded their original purpose and became de facto governments. Major activities included identifying and harassing colonists who failed to support the cause. In effect, colonial America was already moving toward independence, although even most of the radical leaders still proclaimed their allegiance to the British crown.

With rebellion in the air, British leaders in London debated how to avert an all-out war against her own colonists. Former Finance Minister William Pitt (also known as Lord Chatham) pleaded for reconciliation by urging the removal of all British troops from the colonies, but his proposal was overwhelmingly voted down in January 1775. British merchants were unhappy at the American boycott, which was quite effective in reducing trade between the two sides. But Parliament and King George III were in no mood to compromise. In February, Parliament declared Massachusetts to be in a state of rebellion, and in March, New England fishermen were banned from fishing in the Grand Banks off the coast of Newfoundland.

Also in March, Edmund Burke, a friend of the Americans, urged his fellow members of Parliament to repeal the Coercive Acts and to give up its right to tax the colonies. Burke's proposal was soundly defeated. In response, Lord North offered the so-called Conciliatory Propositions, which Parliament did adopt. These propositions would have returned the Americans to the old requisition system under which the colonies had taxed themselves, but only if they met their requisite sums each year. North's offer explicitly ignored the issue of the right to tax, although it did imply that Parliament would return to taxing the Americans if they failed to meet their annual quotas. In the political climate of early 1775, this was sure to be rejected by American leaders. However, it became a mute point, because the proposal did not reach the colonies until the American Revolution had already begun.

This engraving depicts the portrait of the first President of the United States, George Washington, when he was a General in the Continental Army. Copyright 2010 iStockphoto.

Chapter 6 Contents

CHAPTER SIX

The American Revolution

Major Events

1775	Shots fired at Lexington and Concord
	Second Continental Congress convened in Philadelphia
	Congress voted to create the Continental Army and selected George Washington as its commander-in-chief
	Battle of Bunker Hill
	American forces invaded Canada
1776	Thomas Paine published his pamphlet Common Sense
	Declaration of Independence was adopted by Continental Congress
	Washington and his army escaped from Long Island and evacuated New York City
	Crossing of the Delaware River and Washington's victory at Battle of Trenton
1777	Battle of Princeton
	British victory at Brandywine Creek
	British began an occupation of Philadelphia
	British victory at Germantown
	Washington and his troops face the winter at Valley Forge
	American victory at Saratoga
1778	France became an ally of the American Patriots
	British began new strategy aimed at subduing the South
1780	British General Cornwallis gained control of much of South Carolina
1781	Cornwallis surrounded at Yorktown, Virginia
1783	Treaty of Paris formally ended the American Revolution

Introduction

Following the path that changed a rebellion into a revolution, the colonists exercised reason, threats, and entreaties with the hope that the British government would stop repressing the rights of its citizens. King and Parliament refused the efforts of the Americans and judged that the government's actions were just, as they were the ultimate authority. After all, the British government established the colonies for the benefit of the homeland. The colonists considered that they were justified, as English citizens, to dispute unlawful actions taken by their government. When violence and death entered into the clash of opinions, the course was set for dissolution of the relationship. Against all odds, a minority of American colonists went to war against the British colossus and achieved a victory that few would have considered possible.

Lexington and Concord

In late 1774, radicals in Massachusetts organized themselves into a militia and called themselves minutemen, because theoretically, they could be called upon in a minute's notice to lay down their work, pick up their muskets, and head out to a rendezvous designated by the Massachusetts Committee of Safety.

Tensions were still high in the spring of 1775 when Massachusetts Governor Thomas Gage learned from a spy that the minutemen in the colony had a cache of gunpowder and shot (round "bullets") hidden since February at Concord, a small town about 18 miles west of Boston. Both sides recognized that armed conflict seemed all but certain, and Gage had been instructed by officials in London to make the first move to thwart any real organized revolt. Thus he wanted to seize those military supplies before the minutemen could use them against British soldiers. If possible, he aimed to do this before the minutemen realized what had happened. Therefore, in order to avoid arousing suspicion, Gage sent Major John Pitcairn and about 700 redcoats under the cover of darkness on the night of April 18 for the purpose of taking the supplies at Concord the next day.

Radicals in Boston were alert for any such move and spotted the British troops moving west out of the city. William Dawes, Paul Revere, and Dr. Samuel Prescott all rode on horseback through the countryside shouting, "The British are coming! The British are coming!" Church bells rang out in the middle of the night to rouse minutemen and other citizens of impending trouble. Revere reached Lexington and warned the minutemen there, but the British captured and detained him shortly thereafter, before releasing him. Incidentally, Paul Revere was never famous in his lifetime for his "midnight ride." He was a well-known silversmith and associate of Sam Adams at the time, whose engraved plate describing the Boston Massacre had kept radical fervor alive. But it was not until the famed American poet, Henry Wadsworth Longfellow, published his poem "The Midnight Ride of Paul Revere" in 1863, during the middle of the Civil War, that Revere became famous for this adventure.

The Fighting Begins

Near dawn on April 19, when British troops arrived in Lexington, just five miles east of Concord, they found about 70 minutemen waiting for them on the common green. Seeing that they were badly outnumbered, the American commander ordered a withdrawal. When the withdrawal did not proceed as quickly as the British desired, an unknown soldier fired a shot, resulting in several redcoats firing their weapons. When the gunfire ended, eight Americans lay dead and another ten wounded. One British soldier was slightly wounded.

With the arrival of daylight, the cover of darkness was blown, and the redcoats proceeded to Concord without the element of surprise. At least a few hundred minutemen from nearby towns had arrived before the British did and occupied the common area near the center of town. At first, they did not challenge the British, but simply watched as the latter searched for the hidden supplies. But at the Old North Bridge, shots were fired, resulting in British casualties of three dead and nine wounded, while two Americans died. According to American literary giant, Ralph Waldo Emerson, who watched the brief battle from his own house, a British soldier fired the first shot at Concord. This shot was immortalized in his "Concord Hymn" as "the shot heard 'round the world."

The Battle of Concord forced the British back to Boston without having found the military supplies. But as they retreated, Americans attacked them along the road from behind trees and shrubs. This produced the fiercest fighting of the day, which ended with more than 270 British casualties and nearly 95 casualties for the Americans. The fighting had definitely begun.

Second Continental Congress

The Second Continental Congress convened in Philadelphia on May 10, 1775, less than a month after the battles at Lexington and Concord. It had no legal authority because its delegates were elected by colonial legislatures that had been dissolved by royal governors during late 1774 and early 1775. Nevertheless, with the absence of reliable militia and an insufficient number of regular army troops, most of the governors had fled to England by the end of 1774, leaving the officially dissolved colonial legislatures to constitute what little government there was in the colonies. Despite this murky legal foundation, the Second Continental Congress found itself assuming the role of a national government.

The most positive aspect of this Congress was that all 13 colonies had agreed to united action. Each colony sent a delegate to the Second Continental Congress. Beyond that, the delegates were politically divided, with most opposing independence and vainly hoping for some kind of reconciliation with Britain. Most hoped for American autonomy under the umbrella of the British Empire. There was fear that an independent America could not adequately defend itself from foreign attack, especially by their traditional enemies of France or Spain. Moreover, American protests had been principally aimed at an encroachment of power by the British Parliament over the colonies. Few had questioned the authority of the monarchy in England. One of the best known moderates was Pennsylvania delegate John Dickinson. He had shown revolutionary fervor with his *Letters from a Pennsylvania Farmer* (1767) protesting the Townshend duties. Among the minority who favored ultimate independence were delegates from

FIGURE 6.1 - George Washington

Massachusetts, including cousins John and Sam Adams, George Washington and Thomas Jefferson of Virginia. Most of them realized that immediate independence was an unattainable goal that would have to wait for better military organization and events that would propel more Americans to favor independence.

Creating the Continental Army

Early in the American Revolution, most of the fighting involved militiamen, so-called citizen soldiers who were protecting their homes and country. Militias were well suited for combating Indian raids or putting down slave revolts, but they were not effective in facing a threat from a well-trained European army. Therefore, in June 1775, Congress voted to create the Continental Army. Although at the time, it amounted to a declaration that the militiamen around Boston constituted the official American army (see "Early Fighting in the War" below). But this action envisioned a more disciplined armed force that would be necessary to defend against any offensive British military actions. Even moderates like John Dickinson admitted that military organization was required under the circumstances.

At first, Congress set a soldier's enlistment period at one year. But that soon proved to be an insufficient amount of time to properly train and then effectively use soldiers. To encourage volunteers to sign up for longer time periods, Congress gave a bonus of 20 dollars to those who signed up for three years, payable at the time of enlistment. For those who signed up for the duration of the war, no matter how long that proved to be, 100 acres of free government land was promised, to be received after the war ended. It eventually became clear that completely voluntary enlistments were going to be woefully inadequate to wage this war. Therefore, Congress later gave each state a quota of troops to be filled, in effect, establishing a military draft. In reality, however, the situation can best be described as coerced enlistments. In most towns, the Committee of Safety functioned almost like a local draft board. This system of truly voluntary enlistments and coerced enlistments led to more than 235,000 men serving at one time or another in the Continental Army.

Financing the War

To finance the troops and military supplies, Congress initially authorized the design and printing of about $2 million of paper money, called Continental dollars. These dollars were not backed up by gold or silver because Congress had none of these things. But it was still hoped that Americans would accept and use them as legitimate currency. The longer the war continued, however, the more Continental dollars were issued. By 1780, about $242 million were in circulation, resulting in high inflation and virtually no trust in the paper money. So terrible was the inflation that by 1781, it cost more to print the money than what that money could purchase.

Congress utilized three other means to help finance the Revolutionary War. It used the requisition system, in which official requests of specific amounts were made to each state (colonies were declaring themselves states during the war). Unfortunately, states tended to ignore the requisitions just as the colonies had done to Parliament before the Revolution. Thus, the Continental Congress only collected a total of approximately $6 million in coins from the states. Another means of financing the war, especially after 1781, was to borrow money from various European nations, including

Holland and France. A total of about $8 million was obtained in this way. Finally, Congress also issued certificates similar to modern government bonds, which was actually a form of borrowing from the bondholders. Of course bondholders were promised their principal with interest at a future date. Late in the war, under the Articles of Confederation government (see Chapter 7), Robert Morris was named Superintendent of Finance. A wealthy merchant from Philadelphia, Morris did an outstanding job of coordinating the finances with what he had to work with.

George Washington and a Declaration of War

Soon after creating the Continental Army, the delegates then chose George Washington to be its commander-in-chief. A wealthy Virginia planter, Washington did have some military experience as an officer in the French and Indian War (1754-1763), although he had not particularly distinguished himself. His highest rank in the militia had been colonel, but now the Continental Congress turned to him to lead their ragtag army as their commanding general. Actually, his appointment was largely a political one, for the most natural choice was Artemas Ward, who was leading the militia in the Boston area. However, it was widely considered that appointing Ward or another New Englander would leave Americans in the middle and southern colonies without any connection to what they would probably term New England's war. Furthermore, the British government might well then assume that intense opposition to its policies was limited to that region, rather than being a broad-based opposition. So when John Adams, a well-respected leader from New England, suggested George Washington, the delegates unanimously elected him.

Not long after Washington's selection as commander-in-chief, Congress officially declared war against Britain when it drafted and then approved a document entitled "A Declaration of the Causes and Necessity of Taking Up Arms." Thomas Jefferson, a Virginia planter, wrote the original draft of this document, although the moderate John Dickinson revised Jefferson's work to soften the language a bit, in hopes of leaving room for eventual reconciliation. Pressure was already building from merchants in the middle colonies. Their prosperity depended upon trade with Britain, and they wished to seek a negotiated settlement with the empire. Within a few days of declaring war against Britain, Congress adopted what history labeled the Olive Branch Petition. Again, John Dickinson played a major role in getting this document drafted. It reaffirmed loyalty to the Crown, blamed the current crisis on Parliament and ill-informed advisors to the king, and petitioned that each colonial legislature be recognized as its own independent parliament, subject only to the king. In other words, the petition sought to remove the British Parliament in London from having any jurisdiction over the American colonies. By fall 1775, King George III had rejected the Olive Branch Petition, officially declared the colonies to be in a state of rebellion, angrily denounced the Americans as traitors, and hired thousands of German soldiers (Hessians) as mercenaries to supplement British redcoats. (Hessians quickly became known for their ferocious fighting, even requiring the British at times to intervene to prevent mass slaughters.) The English king's actions in 1775 ended all realistic hope of reconciliation, and the war would continue to its end.

Early Fighting in the War

After beginning in Lexington and Concord, the Revolutionary War's next area of battle was Boston. In fact, by nightfall the day after Lexington and Concord, April 20, nearly 20,000 minutemen from all over Massachusetts (and some militia from Connecticut) had gathered around the city to box in the outnumbered British troops. Although most of them soon left for spring planting back at their farms, those who remained dug in for a siege. For almost one year, both sides stared at each other from their respective lines.

The Battle of Bunker Hill

On June 17, 1775, during their only attack in the Boston area, General Thomas Gage authorized an attempt to take Breed's Hill north of the city on the narrow Charlestown Peninsula. Led by newly arrived General William Howe, British redcoats made three different frontal assaults up the hill, mistakenly believed to be Bunker's Hill. Howe could have cut off the Americans, who had occupied the hill only the night before, by closing the peninsula to their rear. Instead, he foolishly insisted on teaching what he thought were cowardly Americans the lesson of not tangling with the mighty British Army. In the end, the British took the hill, but only after Americans there ran out of ammunition. Howe's strategy led to a slaughter of British troops. Although outnumbered nearly two to one, Americans inflicted more than 1,000 casualties on the British while suffering less than half that number themselves. Technically a British victory, the Battle of Bunker Hill was viewed as a moral victory for the Americans who had faced the powerful enemy and inflicted much greater damage than they received.

Lake Champlain and the Fight for Canada

Meanwhile, during the previous month of May 1775, Americans under the command of Ethan Allen and Benedict Arnold captured the British military strongholds at Fort Ticonderoga and Crown Point on Lake Champlain. There they confiscated large numbers of cannon and much gunpowder that were then given to troops in Boston.

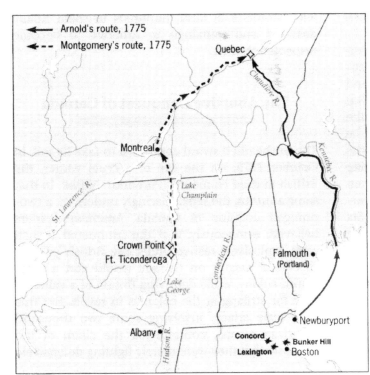

FIGURE 6.2 - Revolution in the North, 1775-1776.

That same fall, Americans began a two-pronged invasion of Canada. It was estimated that the British had about 700 redcoats in Canada, mostly in Montreal and Quebec (the city), and it would be the next spring before the St. Lawrence River thawed sufficiently to send in British reinforcements. Americans also believed, erroneously as it turned out, that French inhabitants in Canada were anxious to overthrow British rule. Therefore, it appeared relatively easy to bring Canada into the war on the American side and prevent the British from using it as a land base from which to attack Americans to the south. Not only was this assumption wrong, but also the invasion of Canada served to undermine the Americans' claim that they were fighting a defensive war against the British.

Even so, the American invasion of Canada, involving about 2,000 American troops, almost proved successful. Americans divided their forces into two parts, with one group headed for Montreal and the other for Quebec. The Montreal-bound group was led by General Richard Montgomery and moved northward by way of Lake Champlain toward their destination. General Benedict Arnold led his group toward Quebec, first by moving by water from Newburyport, Massachusetts, and then by land through the desolate region of Maine, mostly following the Kennebec River before entering Canada. Arnold's men suffered greatly from hunger and freezing weather. They resorted to eating shoe leather and dogs in order to survive. Nevertheless, many of his men died before reaching Quebec.

General Montgomery took Montreal rather easily in September 1775 and rendezvoused with General Arnold's forces outside Quebec in late November. The battle for Quebec began on December 31, but ended in defeat early on January 1, 1776, in blinding blizzard conditions. In a further blow to the American cause, General Montgomery was killed in the fighting at Quebec, and General Arnold was wounded in one leg. Americans retreated from Canada by way of the Lake Champlain route. Meanwhile, the British had burned the town of Falmouth (present-day Portland), Maine, in October 1775, and Norfolk, Virginia, in January 1776. The only military significance of the fight in Canada was that British-Canadian actions against the colonies were delayed until the spring of 1777, mostly due to the heroic actions of General Benedict Arnold. After the American defeat at Quebec, Arnold took his troops south to Lake Champlain, where they gathered and repaired every boat they could find to stop the British. Without roads in the area, the British needed to control the lake in order to keep their supplies moving by water, supplies that their soldiers traveling by land needed. After the British built a fleet of ships for this purpose, the smaller American fleet was destroyed. But by then, the winter of 1776-1777 was fast approaching, and the British retreated back to Montreal until the next spring.

The British Evacuate Boston

After the Battle of Bunker Hill, General Thomas Gage left Boston for England, leaving General William Howe as the commander of all British troops in North America. Ironically, Howe was the very commander who tactically blundered that battle. The situation remained relatively calm in the region for the next nine months. Then, during one night in March 1776, General Washington's Continental troops amazingly managed to haul up several heavy cannon (obtained from Ft. Ticonderoga and Crown Point the year before) onto the Dorchester Heights south of Boston. Looking upward at enemy artillery, Howe evacuated the city of Boston by ship, temporarily moving his troops to Halifax on the eastern coast of Canada.

In other early war fighting, Americans defeated a Loyalist army at Moore's Creek Bridge in North Carolina in February 1776. Then in June 1776, Americans repulsed the British invasion at Charleston Harbor in South Carolina. By the end of June 1776, the American military situation was not a bad one. Although their invasion of Canada had been rebuffed, they had forced the British evacuation of Boston and won victories at Concord and in North and South Carolina.

Declaration of Independence

Since April 19, 1775, Americans had been fighting a war to change British colonial policies. Few Americans supported independence from Britain as either desirable or practical. But events propelled the Second Continental Congress toward declaring that independence in July 1776, more than 14 months after the war had begun.

The British burning of Falmouth (now Portland, Maine) and Norfolk, Virginia, and the hiring of thousands of Hessian soldiers to fight for the British had embittered many against British rule. Such harsh British actions seemed fitting only for a bitter, traditional enemy, but not for one's own citizens who were seeking a redress of grievances. Foreign policy played an important role also, for France was willing to provide military supplies only if Americans separated themselves from Britain.

Then in January 1776, the publication of a pamphlet called *Common Sense* created the kind of political agitation that pushed members of the Second Continental Congress over the top for independence. Its author was Thomas Paine, an Englishman who had met Benjamin Franklin in London and had come to America in late 1774, where he obtained a job as a journalist with the *Pennsylvania Magazine*, based in Philadelphia. After the Second Continental Congress began meeting in May 1775, Paine became acquainted with most of the delegates. Some of them appreciated his radical political ideas and encouraged him to publish his views.

In his *Common Sense*, Paine called it absurd and contrary to natural law that a small country should rule a much larger one. By that rationale alone, he asserted that Americans should be free of the relatively small country of Britain. Paine also rejected the British political model of a mixture of monarchy and representative democracy, insisting that a republic was the best form of government because its authority rested with the people. Ironically, Paine liberally used language from the Christian Bible because he knew it would appeal to most Americans. He himself, though, would become a famous critic of Christianity, publishing *The Age of Reason* in 1794, a scathing denunciation of Christianity and the Christian Bible. *Common Sense* became the most widely-read and discussed written work other than the Bible in early American history, selling somewhere between 120,000 and 150,000 copies within months after its initial publication. It was reprinted in newspapers and read aloud in public gatherings all over the colonies.

FIGURE 6.3 - Thomas Paine.

Strategically, Paine made the goal of independence easier to swallow by attacking King George III, calling him "the Royal Brute of Great Britain." Since the mid-1760s, Americans had rejected Parliament's right to tax or otherwise rule over them. This left only the king, whom Americans had been carefully trying to woo into recognizing their concerns about Parliament's policies. However, by early January 1776, harsh British actions (like the burning of towns and the hiring of Hessian mercenaries) made it increasingly difficult to blame Parliament alone for America's woes. Paine made it possible for others to also blame the king for many of their problems. With little hope that any part of the British government would listen to their grievances, it was inevitable that a movement for independence would eventually gain sufficient momentum for concrete action to take place.

On June 7, 1776, delegate Richard Henry Lee of Virginia made a motion in the Second Continental Congress that "these United Colonies are, and of right ought to be, free and independent States, that they are absolved of all allegiance to the British Crown, and that all political connection between them and the State of Great Britain is, and ought to be, totally dissolved." Moderates in Congress prevailed in postponing a vote on the motion until July, giving them time to go home and consult with fellow citizens. In the meantime, Congress named a five-member committee, including Thomas Jefferson, John Adams, and Benjamin Franklin, to draft a document that would explain and defend any decision to completely break from the British Empire. Thomas Jefferson, then in his early thirties, was chosen by the committee to write a first draft of what was called the Declaration of Independence. In it, he eloquently wrote about concepts that Americans and many others take for granted today, declaring: "We hold these truths to be self-evident: That all men are created equal; that they are endowed by their Creator with certain unalienable rights; that among these are life, liberty, and the pursuit of happiness; that, to secure these rights, governments are instituted among men, deriving their just powers from the consent of the governed; that whenever any form of government becomes destructive of these ends, it is the right of the people to alter or to abolish it, and to institute new government."

Debate on Lee's motion resumed, and it was subsequently adopted on July 2, 1776. The day before, Pennsylvania and South Carolina voted against the motion, Delaware's two-man delegation was deadlocked, and New York abstained. But after continued discussions, Pennsylvania and South Carolina shifted their positions to support the motion, and the newest delegate from Delaware rode all night long to cast the tie-breaking vote in his state's delegation in favor of independence. Like the First Continental Congress, this one also voted on a one-state, one-vote basis, meaning that the majority within a state's caucus would determine how that state's one vote would be cast. Therefore, on July 2, the vote for independence was unanimous, with only New York abstaining. But then on July 15, New York officially changed its mind and officially added its support to the motion as well.

Meanwhile, Congress turned its attention to Jefferson's proposed document. Besides its lofty political idealism, the declaration listed more than two dozen complaints against King George III, including the accusation that he had forced the evil institution of slavery upon the colonies. Although Jefferson himself was a slaveholder, he was never comfortable with that institution, recognizing it as essentially evil, but never managing to allow himself to free his own slaves. Delegates from other slave states, however, succeeded in removing this language from the document because they had no desire to declare slavery an evil system. Other debates focused on whether certain rights were *inalienable* or *unalienable*, although curiously, little to no attention was paid to Jefferson's loftier political ideals, undoubtedly because they were viewed as "self-evident," just as Jefferson had written in his declaration. Jefferson made the changes that Congress asked him to, and the revised Declaration of Independence was formally adopted on July 4, 1776. A month later, on August 2, members of Congress signed the document, although four of them refused to do so, including Pennsylvania moderate John Dickinson. Despite the fact that Congress had voted for independence on July 2, Independence Day is celebrated every 4th of July in honor of the actual Declaration of Independence.

Copies of the Declaration of Independence were widely distributed throughout the colonies, though without the names of the signers. They were all well aware that their actions constituted treason, and the death penalty awaited them if they were caught. In fact, they acknowledged that in the last clause of the Declaration itself with these words: "…we mutually pledge to each other our lives, our fortunes, and our sacred honor." As Benjamin Franklin put it, "Indeed we must all hang together. Otherwise we shall most assuredly hang separately."

American Public Opinion

American public opinion was badly divided during the American Revolution. Those calling themselves Patriots supported the war from the outset and the goal of independence at least by the middle of 1776. On average, Loyalists probably were just as upset about British colonial policies as the Patriots, but for a variety of reasons, they opposed violent revolution and independence. Patriots preferred the name Tories for their American opponents, for Tories in England were those who generally sided with the king in disputes with Parliament. Calling them Tories was akin to accusing Loyalists of preferring monarchial and tyrannical rule to representative government. Although not true, such propaganda often succeeded in putting Loyalists on the defensive. Then there were Americans who were neutral, preferring to be left alone and not caring which side won. Long after the American Revolution, John Adams had referred to the divisions at that time by declaring that one-third had been Patriots, one-third Loyalists, and one-third Neutrals. However, historians today discount Adams' estimate, with most of them identifying two-fifths as Patriots, one-fifth as Loyalists, and another two-fifths as Neutrals. The actual breakdown might be somewhat different, but those fractions are generally accepted today.

Not surprisingly, the Patriots were particularly strong in New England, where the focal point of British anger had been aimed since the so-called Boston Tea Party (1773). Loyalists were particularly strong in the southern colonies and in New York, where the Anglican Church was stronger. Members in that church had long been taught submission to the king, who was the official head of the Church of England (Anglican). Even so, Virginia was an exception to that rule. Elsewhere, a majority of the Quakers (as pacifists) and Germans in Pennsylvania and the Scots in the Carolinas were also Loyalists. There was no clear-cut socio-economic breakdown that could identify anyone as a Patriot or a Loyalist. Aristocrats in Virginia tended toward the Patriot position, while aristocrats elsewhere were more often Loyalists. Many Americans who thought very little of the established political elites leaned toward the Loyalist side, often believing that Patriots were simply using revolution to increase their own political power. Loyalists probably embodied a higher percentage of older Americans, while Patriots probably attracted a higher number of younger Americans. Beyond these observed tendencies, it is impossible to speak more precisely about what groups of Americans were Patriots or Loyalists.

Patriots Take the Upper Hand

Two facts about the relationship between Patriots and Loyalists are most important. First, it is almost certain that Patriots outnumbered Loyalists in every single colony. Second, the Patriots on the whole were far better organized. Neutrals, of course, played no significant role in the court of public opinion because they refused to take sides. Therefore, the Patriots were able to get the upper hand. Even before the revolution began, Patriots had organized committees of safety or committees of correspondence. These committees became the de facto governments in many local communities, especially where the absence of British troops left Loyalists unprotected, which was the case in the large majority of places. At the encouragement of the Second Continental Congress, Patriot leaders in several colonies began to organize and convert their colonies into states, even writing and adopting state constitutions early in the war. And, of course, there was the Second Continental Congress at a kind of national level.

Patriots adopted the position that allegiance to the colonies was of primary importance. Therefore, those Americans who sided with Britain were considered traitors. Congress formalized that thinking in June 1775, when it formally declared that all Loyalists were traitors. As they became organized, states took steps to more precisely define treason and to provide penalties for it. Thus began a systematic persecution of Loyalists, which became stronger after the adoption of the Declaration of Independence in July 1776. Nevertheless, no bloodbath occurred in America as would be the case in France during the French Revolution. Few Loyalists were executed, and most of those who were had been caught spying or otherwise actively working for the British. Instead, Loyalists who were especially vocal in their support of Britain were frequently chased from their homes, which were then confiscated and sold to Patriots as a way to raise revenue for the revolution. Other forms of punishment included the loss of voting rights, imprisonment, and deportation to England or Canada. Unofficially, some zealous Patriots took matters into their own hands by tarring and feathering Loyalists or vandalizing their property.

Persecution took its toll on the Loyalists. It is estimated that about 80,000 fled, most to Canada and some to England, still leaving a few hundred thousand remaining in America. Among those, perhaps 30,000 or so took up arms and fought for the British. But British officials failed to fully trust Loyalists, which led to their ineffective use and frequent abandonment. The result was that the large majority of Loyalists learned to protect themselves by remaining quiet and unnoticed. In effect, then, the combination of Patriot and British actions turned most Loyalists into virtual Neutrals, and the British suffered the loss of many potentially important allies.

African-Americans and the Revolution

African-American Military Service

One of George Washington's first decisions as commander-in-chief of the Continental Army was to prohibit African-Americans from serving in the army. However, as the need for more troops continued to escalate and states had increasing difficulty in meeting their enlistment quotas (see "Creating the Continental Army" under "Second Continental Congress" above), this rule was rescinded. Most African-Americans who enlisted came from northern states, where there were more free blacks and slavery was diminishing in importance to the economy.

Southerners offered greater resistance to the idea, in part because they had fewer free blacks and in part because the southern economy was quite dependent upon slave labor. There was also great fear in the South that armed African-American soldiers would desert their units for freedom in the North or perhaps even lead out in massive armed slave revolts. Nevertheless, southern Patriots eventually bowed to the pressure of trying to meet their enlistment quotas by signing up limited numbers of African-Americans. In some states, even slaves were permitted to serve as long as they had the permission of their owners. In most cases, slaves were given their personal freedom in exchange for their military service. However, in Georgia and South Carolina, where more than half of the population were slaves, African-Americans were never permitted to serve in the American military.

It is estimated that about 5,000 African-Americans, both free and slave, served in the Continental Army during the revolution. They were sometimes placed in segregated units, but more often they were included in units with white soldiers. When integrated with white soldiers, African-Americans were usually given the more menial tasks of cooking and driving wagons that white soldiers wanted to avoid.

The British also used African-Americans in their army. The royal governor of Virginia, Lord Murray Dunmore, started this British trend when he proclaimed freedom to any slaves who escaped and joined a newly formed Loyalist army in November 1775. At other times, British commanders in the South simply encouraged slaves to escape as a way to hurt the economy there. British control of all the major southern ports allowed them to offer transportation on naval vessels to runaway slaves. The numbers of slaves who served in the British Army during the revolution is not known, but most historians believe that it was less than those who served the American Patriot cause.

Effects of the Revolution on Slavery

The effect of the American Revolution on slavery in America was very different in the North from what it was in the South. Even white southern Patriots had not been anxious to use slaves in their military cause.

As noted earlier, Georgia and South Carolina did not permit any African-Americans from serving in the Continental Army. The natural fear that the war would reduce the number of slaves was magnified by British actions in encouraging slaves to escape from their masters. The result was that almost one-third of all slaves in South Carolina had escaped slavery by the end of the war. Added to this was the concern that the spread of democratic ideals through the revolution might find fruitful ground in slaves' minds and thus lead to massive slave rebellions, even after the revolution had ended. These concerns were translated into new state laws all over the South designed to increase the slaveholders' control over their slaves, such as stricter curfews and the enforcement of illiteracy among the slaves.

To most northerners, fighting a war for freedom and independence seemed terribly inconsistent with the claims of ownership of some people over other people. Northerners could see this inconsistency easilier than their southern counterparts because slavery was no longer a vital part of the North's economy. Therefore, the effect of the American Revolution on slavery in the North was the adoption of legal steps to end the practice of slavery there. Most northern states passed laws that gave freedom to slaves when they reached a certain, arbitrary age, thus providing for a gradual end to slavery. Pennsylvania, New York, New Jersey, Connecticut, and Rhode Island adopted this approach.

By contrast, Vermont, Massachusetts, and New Hampshire adopted state constitutions that were interpreted by their courts as making slavery unconstitutional. The most famous example of such a court case occurred in Massachusetts in 1781. In that year, Elizabeth Freeman (Mum Bett was her original slave name) sued for her freedom on the basis that the Massachusetts Constitution stated that "all men are born free and equal." A lower court agreed with her. Then in 1783, the Massachusetts Supreme Judicial Court confirmed the lower court's decision in the *Quock Walker Case*, thereby immediately abolishing slavery in that state. Elizabeth Freeman's determination in taking her case to court foreshadowed the boldness of a later famous civil rights leader, W. E. B. DuBois, who was Ms. Freeman's great grandson.

1776-1777: The War in New York and New Jersey

The Battle for New York City

General William Howe had evacuated his troops from Boston in March 1776 and temporarily regrouped in Halifax, on the east coast of Canada. Within a few months, he settled on a strategy of winning Loyalist areas and cutting off New England from the rest of colonial America. To accomplish this goal, Howe decided that he needed to seize control of New York City. Its harbor and other waterways were well suited for the British navy, its greatest military strength and still the most powerful one in the world. Moreover, the city was located not far from the center of the colonies, and its population numbered many Loyalists.

General Washington knew the obvious value of New York City to the British war cause and correctly guessed that Howe's next move would be to take the city. So Washington marched his troops south from Boston to meet the expected enemy, establishing a fortified position at Brooklyn Heights on Long Island. Having no more than about 18,000 men, Washington calculated that he could not hold the city against a superior number of British redcoats, who would have British naval support. However, he also knew that to give up New York City without a fight would likely destroy Patriot morale. In early July 1776, British troops began arriving in New York City, and by August, there were more than 35,000, not counting some 10,000 sailors under the command of Admiral Richard Howe, Sir William's brother.

In late August 1776, the British attacked Washington's Continental Army in the Battle of Long Island, inflicting heavy casualties and forcing the Americans to seek refuge elsewhere on the island. When Howe failed to pursue and defeat them, the Americans were able to retreat across the East River to Manhattan Island under the cover of darkness and a dense fog. The war could have been over had Howe pursued his enemy. But his ineptness allowed the Americans to survive and fight another day.

After his narrow escape from Long Island, Washington evacuated Manhattan because he knew that he could not hold it. Then both sides fought limited engagements in the New York City area until the British captured two forts along the Hudson River, Fort Washington on November 16 and Fort Lee on November 18. New York City remained in British hands for the remainder of the revolution, but it did them little good.

American Victories at Trenton and Princeton

Meanwhile, the Continental Army retreated across the Delaware River to Philadelphia in Pennsylvania, allowing the British to occupy most of New Jersey. Had General Howe attacked the Americans in Philadelphia, he probably would have destroyed them and ended the war. But for a second time, he inexplicably failed to attack and finish off the enemy. Meanwhile, Patriot morale was at a low point. Thomas Paine lamented in his pamphlet called *The Crisis*, that "These are the times that try men's souls."

Then in a daring move on Christmas night 1776, General Washington and about 2,200 of his troops crossed the icy Delaware River. The next morning they attacked a group of about 1,000 Hessian soldiers at Trenton, New Jersey. A spy in Washington's army had alerted the Hessian colonel in Trenton that an attack was imminent. But when a group of New Jersey militiamen attacked them in the middle of Christmas night, the Hessian commander assumed that it was the predicted attack. Then when blizzard conditions produced very poor visibility the next morning, the sentries were pulled way in. When Washington's troops finally arrived in Trenton the next morning (on December 26), nearly all the Hessian soldiers were seeking shelter from the weather inside buildings. Although one Hessian sentry thought he spotted American soldiers and sent a note to the colonel, the commanding officer simply put it in his pocket (without reading it) in order to not have his card game interrupted. Therefore, caught by surprise, the Hessians surrendered after brief fighting, and more than 900 were captured as prisoners of war. So one-sided was the battle that Washington's army lost no one. Just more than a week later, on January 3, 1777, Washington surprised and won a battle against British troops at Princeton, New Jersey. The Continental Army then settled down for the winter in Morristown in northern New Jersey.

The two American victories in New Jersey were not of great military significance, and territorial control did not change hands. However, they were of enormous psychological significance as Patriot morale was given a major boost. What made these battles amazing is that the enlistment period for many of Washington's troops was about to expire on December 31, and those cold, hungry soldiers would then be able to return to their own homes and families. Most historians agree that the genius of General George Washington lay in the fact that he was able to get the most out of his troops despite poor conditions. That ability reflected the respect, admiration, and even love that the large majority of his troops had for him.

The War in 1777

British authorities in London devised a military scheme over the winter of 1776-1777 that was intended to fulfill the strategy of cutting off the more radical New England from the rest of the colonies. The plan involved the convergence of three different British armies at Albany, New York, a feat that would consolidate British control along the Hudson River down to New York City and thus isolate New England. General John Burgoyne would lead an army south out of Montreal, Canada along Lake Champlain and the Hudson River. Another force led by Colonel Barry St. Leger would also leave Montreal but move along the St. Lawrence River and across eastern Lake Ontario and then east along the Mohawk River toward Albany. Meanwhile, General William Howe was supposed to lead an army up the Hudson River from New York City to Albany.

General Burgoyne, nicknamed "gentleman Johnny," was more of a playboy than a professional soldier. His army of between 7,000 and 8,000 redcoats, a few hundred Indians, and roughly 1,000 cooks, musicians, and women (many were wives of officers) left Montreal in June 1777. Once inside New York, they first traveled by ship down Lake Champlain. In July, the British easily took Fort Ticonderoga at the south end of the lake, when a force of about 3,000 Americans abandoned it due to low food and military supplies. The British then headed by land toward the Hudson River. The large party of approximately 9,000 people and their heavy load of supplies did not travel swiftly. They were further slowed down on land by the numerous trees that Americans had cut down and laid on the only viable path the British would have to use.

Bad news for the British came in August, when Colonel St. Leger's combined British and Indian force traveling along the Mohawk River to the west met unexpected resistance from Americans under the command of Benedict Arnold in Fort Stanwix and a group of Oneida Indians. On August 6, the British and their Seneca Indian allies inflicted heavy casualties in the Battle of Oriskany. But on August 23, the British were beaten back at Fort Stanwix, resulting in most of their Indian allies abandoning the campaign.

Fighting Around Philadelphia

Instead of moving north from New York City to rendezvous with Burgoyne, General Howe headed south to take Philadelphia. He hoped to meet Washington's Continental Army in open warfare and decisively defeat them in order to allow Burgoyne's mission to be unimpeded. For his part, Washington was surprised to learn that Howe was moving south. In reaction, Washington moved out of the area near New York City, where he had been keeping an eye on Howe, and prepared to defend Philadelphia. Howe inexplicably gave Washington time to prepare his defenses by first delaying and then by taking six weeks to move his troops by sea rather than to march them overland. Meeting the British troops south of the city at Brandywine Creek, the British defeated the Continental troops on September 11, after which they occupied the city of Philadelphia. In another engagement, the British again defeated the Americans at Germantown, north of Philadelphia, on October 4. General Howe apparently believed that the capture of Philadelphia was more important than the objective of Albany, New York, for he never made a move toward Albany. Instead, he settled down to enjoy the high living that was available in Philadelphia.

Valley Forge

With winter approaching, Washington moved his troops to Valley Forge, Pennsylvania, more than 20 miles northwest of Philadelphia, and spent the winter of 1777-1778 there. Conditions at Valley Forge were

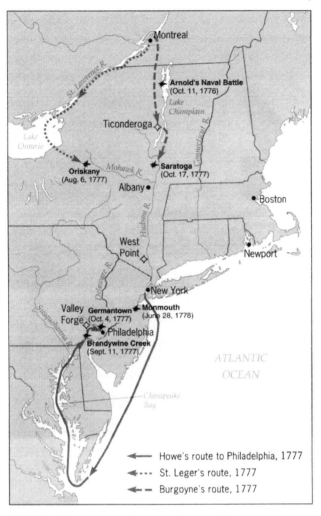

FIGURE 6.4 - New York-Pennsylvania Theater, 1777-1778

American Victory at Saratoga

Without the hope of additional troops, General John Burgoyne's British army camped north of Albany near the small town of Saratoga. Discouraged and running low on food, desertion became a serious problem for the British. In July, Burgoyne sent out a large Hessian hunting and foraging party to acquire much needed food. But on August 16, they were defeated at the Battle of Bennington in Vermont. Sensing that victory was at hand, militiamen and an American army of about 7,000 soldiers commanded by General Horatio Gates moved in for the "kill." Two battles were fought near Saratoga, one in September and the other one in early October 1777. Although the British won both battles, they lost more than 1,000 troops, and morale suffered. Finally, having been surrounded, Burgoyne formally surrendered to General Horatio Gates on October 17, 1777.

Not only did the American victory at Saratoga, New York, result in the largest single capture of British redcoats (about 5,700), but it also bolstered Patriot morale everywhere. It was the turning point of the entire American Revolution, for Benjamin Franklin used this glorious victory to finally persuade France to officially enter the war against Britain.

Alliance with France

France was eager to get revenge against Britain for its defeat in the Seven Years' War (called the French and Indian War in North America) back in 1763. Britain's American colonies were the most important oversees part of the entire British Empire. Trouble for Britain there presented France with an opportunity to weaken that empire and perhaps eventually take possession of the British West Indies. Almost from the beginning of the revolution, the French government had been secretly supplying about 90 percent of the gunpowder to the American Patriots, in addition to other military supplies. This was especially true after the Declaration of Independence, for if the Americans could actually break off from the British Empire, France could drive a wedge between them by establishing an important alliance with an independent American nation. In 1777, French nobleman, the Marquis de Lafayette,

horrific, with food and blankets in short supply, cold winter temperatures, and holes in many soldiers' boots, for those who still had boots. Despite these conditions, there was some optimism after hearing the news of Burgoyne's surrender in October of that year.

More importantly, the Continental Army obtained the voluntary services of a German officer, Friedrich von Steuben, better known as Baron von Steuben, in February 1778. Stationed with Washington's army at Valley Forge, von Steuben introduced tougher military discipline through his extensive drilling of the troops. In fact, in 1780 he wrote what became the standard drill manual for the American army. After the war, von Steuben became an American citizen and moved to upstate New York, where he died in Steubenville (named after him) in 1794.

offered his military services to the Continental Army for the duration of the war.

Shortly after the Declaration of Independence was adopted, the Second Continental Congress sent Benjamin Franklin to Paris as minister (ambassador) to France. His most important mission was to exploit the French desire to seek revenge by encouraging that government to openly enter the war on the Patriots' side. But two factors delayed the French decision to declare war on Britain. First, King Louis XVI represented monarchial despotism and was not anxious to openly support a group of democratic revolutionaries who were the antithesis of his own political theories. Second, before Saratoga, Americans had not won a major decisive victory, so there was no need to stick the French neck out in order to help a cause that did not look promising. News of the huge American victory at Saratoga changed minds of officials in both Britain and France. In London, Lord North proposed that Parliament give up its right to tax the Americans and withdraw British troops from the colonies. In effect, it was an offer to give the American Patriots everything they wanted except independence. But members of Parliament were more concerned about the upcoming Christmas recess and thus refused to consider the measure until early 1778. Meanwhile, Benjamin Franklin learned about Lord North's proposal from a spy and redoubled his efforts to persuade the French to declare war. He offered the American success at Saratoga as an effective exhibit to the viability of the independence movement. Although still reluctant, Louis XVI's advisors finally convinced him that the time was now ripe to take revenge on the British. On February 6, 1778, France signed two separate treaties with the United States, ironically on the very day that the London Parliament passed Lord North's proposal. In the Treaty of Amity and Commerce, France became the first nation to officially recognize the independence of the United States of America and to establish an economic trading relationship with it. In the Treaty of Alliance, France promised to fight an open-ended war against Britain until the Americans won their independence or otherwise agreed to negotiate an end to the conflict.

The alliance with France was a major help to the American movement for independence. The French began to openly send weapons, gunpowder, troops, and ships to the American war front. More importantly in the long run, British focus on the rebelling colonies was partially diverted to Europe and the Caribbean. No longer would the British have the luxury of using its more experienced soldiers and officers against the rebels. The British situation went from bad to worse when Spain allied with France, but not with the Americans, in June 1779, transforming the conflict into a world war. Holland also joined the anti-British alliance in 1779. In this major war, Britain had absolutely no allies; furthermore, at least six neutral European nations expressed official disdain for Britain by forming the so-called Armed Neutrality alliance (though they remained officially neutral).

The most immediate effect of France's entry into the war was the British decision to evacuate Philadelphia and reinforce New York City, which was already their main base of operations in North America. This decision was made because the French Navy threatened the British blockade of the American coast as well as its supply lines from England. General Sir Henry Clinton, who replaced William Howe as commander-in-chief of all British troops in North America in early 1778, ordered the evacuation from Philadelphia in June of the same year. On June 28, General Washington's army attacked the withdrawing British redcoats at Monmouth, in northern New Jersey. Thereafter, except for his role in forcing the British surrender at Yorktown, Virginia, in late 1781, Washington and the bulk of his army remained just outside the New York City area, where they kept an eye on Clinton's forces.

1778-1780: The War in the South

In early 1778, after their humiliating defeat at Saratoga, British officials in London devised a brand new strategy. Rather than attempting to isolate New England from the rest of colonial America, the new thinking focused on the South, where thousands of Loyalists were expected to not only cheer invading redcoats, but to join them in the fight against the Patriots. Beginning in Georgia and then moving through the Carolinas, the plan was to continue northward until the rebels were completely defeated.

Late in 1778, British troops arriving by sea attacked at Savannah, on the coast of Georgia, and began occupying the town on December 29. A short time later, the British also occupied Augusta, Georgia, on the border with South Carolina. While they organized several separate Loyalist militia units, the British also appointed a new royal governor and seated a Loyalist legislature.

The Struggle for South Carolina

Feeling good about things in Georgia, General Henry Clinton sailed with troops from New York City toward Charleston, South Carolina, in late 1779. Americans in Charleston were then trapped and suffering from a smallpox epidemic. Nevertheless, the Continental troops dispatched there under the command of General Benjamin Lincoln held the city as long as possible. When he finally surrendered on May 12, 1780, the British captured about 5,500 prisoners of war, the worst Patriot disaster of the Revolutionary War.

Shortly after the capture of Charleston, General Clinton returned to New York City and left General Lord Charles Cornwallis as commander of the redcoats in the South. By mid-summer 1780, Cornwallis had pushed out the regular Continental Army troops and theoretically had military control in South Carolina. He even gained the assistance of several thousand slaves who fled their Patriot masters to fight or otherwise serve the British military in the Carolinas. Many, though not all, were given their freedom in exchange for their help. In any case, the loss of slave labor clearly undercut the financial well-being of Patriot slaveholders.

Then in August, more bad news came for the independence movement. General Horatio Gates, the hero of Saratoga, had reestablished a Continental Army in the South. On August 16, at Camden, South Carolina, Cornwallis inflicted a serious blow to Gates' army, many of whom panicked and fled the battlefield (including Gates himself).

During these dark days for the Patriots of South Carolina, Francis Marion led an officially-sponsored resistance movement in order to keep hope alive for the revolution. He and his men knew the swamplands well and used them to launch quick hit-and-run raids against the British before quickly and mysteriously disappearing back into the swamps. Nicknamed the "swamp fox," Marion unnerved the British by making it difficult for

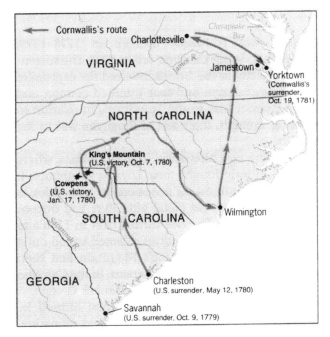

FIGURE 6.5 · War in the South, 1780-1781

them to consolidate their hold on the region and by tying them down in the interior. Meanwhile, Americans there turned on one another in particularly savage ways, with groups of Patriots and Loyalists using guerilla warfare tactics to frequently raid and plunder each other. It seemed that civilization itself was being threatened by increasingly barbaric behavior.

After the American defeat at Camden, General Washington replaced Gates in the South with General Nathaniel Greene, though he did not take actual control of the southern army until December 1780. By then, things were already looking a little brighter for the American cause. On October 7, a militia force of about 1,400 men defeated an army of mostly Loyalists, but including British redcoats, in the Battle of King's Mountain, just inside South Carolina near the North Carolina line.

The Treason of Benedict Arnold

Benedict Arnold had given valuable military service to the Continental Army, helping to capture British cannons in the Lake Champlain area and almost capturing Quebec early in the Revolutionary War. In fact, he had been wounded twice in service to his country, first at Quebec and then at Saratoga. Despite his obvious brilliance, Arnold was a troubled man who was never satisfied with the recognition afforded to him. He was also greedy, using the cover of war to line his own financial pockets in underhanded business enterprises. Tragically, these character defects would lead him to commit treason against the American cause and make his very name synonymous with treason.

In June 1778, shortly after the British evacuation of Philadelphia, Arnold was appointed as that city's military commandant. It was essentially a non-combat position given to allow the wound he received at Saratoga (1777) time to heal. While there, Arnold took every opportunity to live very well, including marrying a young woman from a wealthy Loyalist family. He eventually faced a court-martial for his shady business dealings and received an official reprimand for his conduct. But what particularly irked Arnold was his failure to be promoted. Therefore, in 1779, he initiated secret, long-distance communications with General Henry Clinton, the British commander-in-chief based in New York City, offering information for money. Clinton did not really trust Arnold, so he kept putting off the negotiations.

In the meantime, Arnold repeatedly asked General Washington to give him command of West Point. Its position on the Hudson River made it very appealing to the British, whose control of it would probably enable them to cut off New England from the rest of the colonies and, perhaps, to win the war. In the spring of 1780, Washington granted Arnold's request for the command at West Point. Almost at once, he offered to sell out the garrison there to the British for a price. After repeated demands for Clinton to send him a representative with whom he could personally negotiate the price, Major John Andre finally made it through enemy lines to meet with Arnold. Andre was caught attempting to return to New York City in September 1780 and eventually hanged as a spy. In the same month, Benedict Arnold succeeded in fleeing to Clinton in New York City. He was given a command in the British Army as a general and harassed Americans in Virginia shortly before the British surrender at Yorktown in late 1781. Arnold survived the war and later died in England.

News of Benedict Arnold's betrayal shocked the Patriots all over America. It could not have come at a worse time, for things were going very badly for the movement in the South. Nevertheless, American Patriots redeemed the terrible situation by vilifying Arnold in a kind of collective psychological release. As a result, the shock and anger at Arnold's treason became a catalyst for new energy and determination to win the independence that he had so shamefully betrayed.

The War at Sea

During the American Revolution, the American Navy, if it could be called that, consisted of a handful or so of variously sized ships. It therefore posed no real threat to the mighty British Navy. Nevertheless, it was the beginning of the American Navy, and several captains distinguished themselves in the war. The most famous American naval commander was Captain John Paul Jones, of Scottish ancestry. He won a battle in the English Channel on September 23, 1779, when he captured and boarded the British ship *Serapis* just before his own ship sank. When asked to surrender, Jones was alleged to have said, "I have not yet begun to fight." He probably never spoke those words, however, for they first appeared in an 1825 book outlining the history of the American Navy by Richard Dale. Nevertheless, for his daring and valor, John Paul Jones became later known as the Father of the American Navy.

More harassment of the British Navy came from the much larger group of privateers. The Second Continental Congress had authorized privateers to raid and otherwise hassle British shipping. During the revolution, more than 1,000 privateers became "captains" of their vessels, "employing" about 70,000 men in the cause of independence. They captured approximately 600 British merchant ships and became such a threat that merchant vessels were forced to travel by convoy in order to better defend themselves and keep insurance rates from skyrocketing.

The War in the West

At the time of the American Revolution, no more than 200,000 Indians lived in the region west of the Appalachian Mountains and east of the Mississippi River. Despite the Proclamation of 1763, issued by King George III to prevent conflicts between settlers and Indians, perhaps as many as 50,000 colonists had moved into the same area by 1778. In order to stop the colonial incursion onto their lands, most tribal Indians joined the British in this war.

Chief among the pro-British tribes were most of the great Iroquois Confederacy. Mohawk leader Joseph Brant, along with his sister Mary, had persuaded most of the Iroquois to side with the British, including the Mohawks, the Cayugas, the Senecas, and some of the Onondagas. These Iroquois raided colonial settlements in western New York and Pennsylvania until Continental troops under the command of General John Sullivan conducted a systematic military campaign against them in August and September of 1779. Whole Indian villages were completely destroyed and food supplies burned.

The Revolutionary War split the Iroquois Confederacy. Two of its tribes sided with the Americans, the Tuscaroras and the Oneidas, the latter perhaps because Protestant missionaries had converted them to Christianity. The Iroquois never reunited, and after Americans won their independence, they were forced to sign the Treaty of Fort Stanwix in 1784, yielding their claims to most of their land. (The Treaty of Fort Stanwix was the first treaty the United States ever signed with an Indian nation.) Many Iroquois then moved north into British Canada, where they permanently settled.

Most of the Shawnee and the Delaware tribes attempted to remain at peace with Americans. But often, American troops and militiamen did not distinguish between hostile and peaceful Indians. Even after Delaware Chief White Eyes signed a treaty in 1778, pledging support for the American war effort, Americans did not keep their end of the bargain by providing his tribe with basic supplies. Militiamen burned down the town of Choshocton in 1781, a town of at least 2,000 Shawnee and Delaware Indians. These and other similar events turned neutral tribes into hostile ones, including most of the Shawnee and Delaware. Even those tribes who realized that western expansion was inevitable, and therefore ought to align themselves with the Americans by joining their side, had little hope of a brighter future for their people.

British forces were especially vulnerable in the West because they were few in number and scattered among a vast wilderness. They occupied forts at Niagara, Detroit, and in other parts of the northwest. (Remember that the Mississippi River was the western edge of British-claimed land south of Canada. Therefore, the northwest lay in the Great Lakes region southward to the Ohio River.) If their Indian allies could be avoided, the more distant British forts might easily be taken. To prove this, General George Rogers Clark and a force of about 175 men left Fort Pitt (present-day Pittsburgh) in 1778 and headed for present-day Illinois. By early 1779, Clark's men had captured the British fortifications at Kaskaskia, Cahokia, and Vincennes (in Indiana).

More Fighting in the Carolinas

The year 1780 had ended on a more positive note for the Patriots in South Carolina because of the victory at King's Mountain (see "1778-1780: The War in the South" above). Not long before that battle, General Cornwallis had moved into North Carolina in a vain attempt to prevent rebels and supplies from entering South Carolina. But news of the Patriot victory at King's Mountain forced Cornwallis to return to South Carolina. The American winning streak continued on January 17, 1781, when General Daniel Morgan won a decisive victory over the highly rated British troops under General Sir Banister Tarleton at the Battle of Cowpens, also near the North Carolina line.

Moving back into North Carolina, Cornwallis's main army fought a hard battle against General Nathaniel Greene at Guilford Court House on March 15. With most of his army devastated, Cornwallis was forced to retreat to the coastal town of Wilmington, to await the arrival of more troops and supplies from New York City by way of the Atlantic Ocean. While Cornwallis was waiting for those reinforcements and supplies, General Greene turned back to South Carolina. Now having the numerical advantage, as well as momentum on his side, Greene pushed the redcoats out of their outposts and back to Charleston.

Battle of Yorktown

In the spring of 1781, the British southern strategy appeared to be a lost cause, for they managed to occupy and control primarily the port cities like Charleston and Savannah and little else. Furthermore, Loyalists had not come out to fight for the British in the huge numbers that were expected. Therefore, in May 1781, shortly after receiving reinforcements and supplies at Wilmington, Cornwallis moved northward into Virginia. After several successful raids there, Cornwallis proceeded to dig in near the Chesapeake Bay on the peninsula between the James and York Rivers. He selected Yorktown, along the York River, which offered a water route for new supplies and fresh troops, or in the worst-case scenario, an escape route for his army of more than 7,200 men.

Meanwhile, General Washington's army outside New York City had been significantly enlarged by the arrival in mid-1780 of a French army under the leadership of the Count Jean Baptiste de Rochambeau. Then news that a large French naval fleet had left France for North America in the spring of 1781 gave Washington a plan to defeat Cornwallis at Yorktown. In August, the combined armies of Washington and de Rochambeau began marching the 300-mile journey southward toward Virginia, using a multitude of mostly back roads to confuse Clinton into remaining in New York City. About the same time, Admiral Francois Joseph Paul de Grasse, whose fleet had first arrived in the West Indies, began moving up toward the Atlantic entrance of the Chesapeake Bay. The idea was to cut off Cornwallis from using the water route and thus to box him in at Yorktown. Timing was impeccable as the French fleet arrived at their destination about the same time as a British fleet. On September 5, 1781, in the Battle of the Virginia Capes, the French navy beat back the British ships, thus giving the French control of the Chesapeake Bay.

When the armies of Generals Washington and de Rochambeau arrived just outside Yorktown to join a French army already in the area under the command of the Marquis de Lafayette, their combined forces consisted of at least 16,000 troops. Outnumbering Cornwallis' army by more than two to one, the Americans and French began a siege of the British position at the end of September. During the siege, American and French troops dug trenches at night and remained in them during the day. For nearly three weeks, they increasingly tightened the noose around Cornwallis' neck by using the darkness to dig trench lines still closer to the British position. Finally, realizing that his situation was hopeless, General Cornwallis agreed to surrender his army on October 17, exactly four years after Burgoyne had surrendered to Gates at Saratoga, New York. The British formally surrendered at Yorktown two days later, on October 19, 1781, while the British military band appropriately played a popular tune, "The World Turned Upside Down." Without French assistance, Americans could not have defeated Cornwallis at Yorktown. The French naval blockade prevented reinforcements and supplies from reaching Cornwallis, and nearly half of all the ground troops in the land battle were French.

The Battle of Yorktown proved to be the last major battle of the Revolutionary War. There were several skirmishes for more than a year afterwards, with most of the fighting involving conflicts between Loyalists and Patriots in the South. Nevertheless, the war had still not been won. The British continued to occupy the ports of Charleston, Savannah, Wilmington, and New York. Moreover, Admiral de Grasse's fleet was later defeated in the West Indies, leaving the Americans without substantial French naval support for any future fighting. On the other hand, the war was not going well for the British in other parts of the empire, including India and the Mediterranean. Because it had dragged on for so long, the British people had grown tired of the war and demanded that it stop. Subsequent political events in England and France would produce an official end to the war on terms quite favorable to the American Patriots.

Treaty of Paris, 1783

Anti-war sentiment in England forced Finance Minister Lord North to resign in March 1782, thus toppling the Tory government. The Whigs, who were friendlier to the Americans and more suspicious of royal power, took control of Parliament, and Lord Shelburne was named the new finance minister. Despite his desire to continue the war, King George III had lost most of his allies in Parliament and after a few months, he finally realized that it was time to negotiate a peace.

The chief American diplomats in Paris were Benjamin Franklin, John Adams, and John Jay. Congress gave them strict instructions to fully cooperate with France in the peace talks and to sign no separate peace treaty with England. But the complexity and intrigue of the multi-lateral relationships led the American diplomats to negotiate directly with England. For one thing, the French showed little interest in settling the war because they had promised Spain that it would regain control of Gibraltar (on the south coast of Spain) from England. Yet the British continued to militarily hold that rock fortress, and the Americans worried that their alliance with France would force them to continue the war beyond the time of their best interests. For its part, Spain wanted to expand its territory in North America by acquiring the region between the Appalachian Mountains and the Mississippi River, a desire that directly conflicted with American claims. When the American officials in Paris believed that France was about to help negotiate that area for Spain, they initiated separate peace talks with the British.

A preliminary peace treaty between the United States and England was signed on November 30, 1782. In theory, it was a violation of the Treaty of Alliance (1778), although in reality, the French government reluctantly but officially approved its terms. Its implementation, however, was conditional upon France and Spain formally coming to terms with England. For this reason, British and American armies remained in their places watching each other, in the event that the preliminary peace fell through.

France and Spain did settle with England, and the Treaty of Paris, officially ending the American Revolution, was signed on September 3, 1783. Congress ratified it on January 14 of the next year. The British had been anxious to prevent the French from any future domination of the Americans, so they had offered the Americans quite generous terms. Specifically, England recognized the independence of the United States of America and agreed that its borders extended west to the Mississippi River, north to the border with Canada, and south to the border with Florida. Spain had won Florida back from England. Furthermore, Americans were given a part of the fishing rights around the island of Newfoundland, off the east coast of Canada.

For its part, the United States agreed to end its persecution of the Loyalists and to restore all property that had been previously confiscated from them. It also promised not to interfere with attempts to collect financial debt that individual American citizens owed to various British creditors. The failure of the United States to fully live up to these agreements would sour relationships with England for many years to come.

Why the Americans Won their Independence

Many reasons factored into the Patriots' successful fight for independence. Foremost among them was the assistance of foreign intervention. By the summer of 1779, France, Spain, and Holland had entered the conflict against Britain, and the British found themselves in a world war with absolutely no allies on the continent of Europe. This threat to homeland security and its other imperial outposts meant that the British could no longer afford to have her best military officers fighting the Americans. The alliance with France (1778) was especially significant because it promised to wage war against Britain until the Americans won their independence. Moreover, France also added to the troop numbers on the ground in America and threatened British shipping in the Atlantic. Of greatest importance was the French naval victory in the Battle of the Virginia Capes in September 1781 which directly contributed to the British surrender at Yorktown late in the war.

Another reason why Americans won their independence was the complicated logistics involved in this war. The British had to cross the Atlantic Ocean and subdue their colonies 3,000 miles away. Two-way communications usually took about three months, for information traveled the same way that people and supplies did, by ship. Many supplies and even some troops were lost at sea due to violent storms. When British troops arrived in America, they did not know the land as well as the Americans. Furthermore, poor roads made the transportation of military troops and supplies extremely difficult, often giving the Patriots sufficient time to react to changing troop movements. Even when naval vessels were used instead, British commanders were often clumsy in their deployment of troops. Finally, in terms of logistics, there was no "one" strategic place that the British could take control and declare victory—as in the capture of the king in a chess game. As it was, British troops held every major city at one time or another during the war, but it did them little good in the long run. By contrast, all the Americans had to do was survive until the British gave up.

Poor decision-making on the part of British political and military leaders also contributed to the American Patriots' success in winning independence. It has been said that the British Empire was a great empire ruled by little minds. King George III himself eventually showed signs of some mental instability, and Lord North was not a very effective finance minister. Perhaps more important was the fact that the British Secretary of War, Lord George Germain, failed to adequately coordinate the complex war. The irony was that during the French and Indian War, a military court had declared Germain to be "unfit" to serve the British in any military capacity. Then in the very next major war, he was one of the top civilian officials in charge of coordinating the war effort. British planners also made poor decisions with regard to the Loyalists. They continually overestimated their numbers and then failed to use them effectively because they did not completely trust them. At the same time, the British underestimated the number of rebels and, therefore, the number of troops that were required to subdue them.

The British were also handicapped by certain political considerations. For example, in the early portion of the war, they might have used the full power of their military muscle to crush the rebellion. But they calculated that such an overwhelming show of force would have made ruling the colonies much more difficult than they already were, if not impossible. With a few exceptions, the British tempered their use of military force during the war for fear of making more Patriots out of Loyalists

and Neutrals. By the time they found themselves in a world war, it was too late to do otherwise.

Finally, the American Patriots won the war for independence because they eventually won the war of political will. The Patriots were fiercely determined to win the struggle for independence, for they really believed in the concept of liberty that they were fighting for. By contrast, the longer the war lasted, the more British citizens in England grew weary. More soldiers, more dead and wounded bodies, and more taxes seemed too high a price to pay in order to keep the 13 colonies, and many began thinking the American Patriots might be right after all. In the end, American Patriot perseverance paid off, and the United States of America was born.

Nature of the American Revolution

Political Ideals or Economic Self-Interest?

Historians have long debated the nature of the American Revolution. The older, and traditional, view is that Americans fought the revolution for the principles and ideals of the Enlightenment. These included belief in the natural rights of man that are derived from natural law and that no government may deny to its citizens, and in self-government through a representative democratic political system. A newer view arose to prominence in the early twentieth century, when the influence of the Progressive Era led many historians to conclude that economic and social class issues were the driving motivational forces behind the American Revolution. Since the end of World War II, it has been more common for historians to see that both sets of factors— Enlightenment principles and socioeconomic issues— played an important role in the revolution, although the old debate between the traditional and Progressive Era views still continues.

It is difficult to ignore the role of democratic principles in the revolution, for both the words and actions of the Founding Fathers clearly reflect the influence of the Enlightenment. One cannot read such historical documents as the Declaration of Independence, the Constitution, or *The Federalist Papers* without seeing democratic principles actuate nearly every line. Moreover, newspapers of the Revolutionary War era reflected similar ideology. To dismiss all of this evidence as merely Patriot propaganda, during or after the fact of the revolution, is surely to stretch the truth beyond recognizable limits.

At the same time, there is also evidence that many Americans of the period sometimes used democratic ideology to hide mere economic self-interest. The most notable example of this concerns the slogan, "No taxation without representation." Undoubtedly, many Americans believed in this principle and therefore denied that the British Parliament had the right to tax them. However, it is also true that the first national government of the United States, under the Articles of Confederation, failed to give Congress the authority to tax Americans. It is not unfair to see at least a little hypocrisy in that failure, and to conclude that many Americans before the revolution simply objected more to paying taxes than to Parliament's belief that it had the authority to tax them.

Another example of economic self-interest was the widespread practice of smuggling in order to avoid paying import duties. Some have argued, not entirely without merit, that Americans were spoiled in their ability to get away with smuggling (and other things), and they simply rebelled when Mother England attempted to tighten the reins. However, if this or any other self-interest motivation was the main factor in causing the American Revolution, then why did approximately 60 percent of the colonial population refuse to support that revolution? It seems more appropriate, therefore, to conclude that both self-interest and democratic principles were important factors in the American Revolution.

Was the American Revolution Radical?

Was the American Revolution radical or not? It certainly cannot be regarded as radical when contrasted with the French Revolution less than a decade later (1789-1799). There was no real class war and no social meltdown of society, as happened in France. Indeed, one can even argue that the American Revolution was conservative in the sense that it was, in part, an attempt to conserve the rights and freedom of action that they had experienced before British colonial policies sharply changed in 1763. Some historians argue that our revolution was radical in the sense that it established a society based on the "money" principle, that unlike previous and then-existing societies, the United States was the first in world history to measure the status of persons by their cash flow.

However, the most radical aspect of the American Revolution was its actual attempt to apply the principles and ideals of the natural rights of man in the context of a full-blown representative democracy, a democracy without the trappings of royalty. To be sure, these ideals were implemented hypocritically and unequally. American Indians were completely beneath the radar screen of these principles until recent years. Property qualifications for voting and holding public office prevented significant numbers of white males from inclusion in the democratic process until the 1830s. Slavery existed until the nation eventually fought a civil war in the 1860s. Then it was a hundred years later before the country faced the matter of full citizenship rights for its African-Americans. And women did not get the right to vote nationally until 1920. Despite these and other blind spots and shortcomings, America has always been its best when it takes positive steps toward the democratic ideal. It is these steps, in fact, that constitute the American journey toward a society whose citizens enjoy, in the words of Jefferson's Declaration of Independence, "the right to life, liberty, and the pursuit of happiness."

1789: The inauguration of George Washington as the first President of the United States. Also present are (from left) Alexander Hamilton, Robert R. Livingston, Roger Sherman, Mr. Otis, Vice President John Adams, Baron Von Steuben and General Henry Knox. Original Artwork: Printed by Currier & Ives. (Photo by MPI/Getty Images) Copyright 2010 iStockphoto.

Chapter 7 Contents

CHAPTER SEVEN

Launching the American Republic

Major Events

1774	First Continental Congress met in Philadelphia
1781	Articles of Confederation ratified as first fundamental law of the United States
1783	Economic depression hit the new nation
1786-87	Shays' Rebellion in Massachusetts
1787	Northwest Ordinance clarified rights of the people in the Northwest Territory and banned slavery there. Constitutional Convention established a new fundamental law of the nation
1787-1790	Ratification debate on the Constitution and eventually all 13 states ratified it
1789	George Washington unanimously elected as the first President John Adams elected as the first Vice President

Introduction

"Government, even in its best state, is but a necessary evil; in its worst state, an intolerable one." This statement from Thomas Paine, author of *Common Sense,* summed up for many in the colonies the British government in 1776. Government was necessary, but the governmental restrictions of the British Parliament were unacceptable. As the colonies took the steps that broke the ties with one government, they realized they must replace the old system with a new one. Americans proved that they could win a war against one of the strongest powers in the world. Could they build a government that would last and protect the rights they had fought for, including life, liberty, and the pursuit of happiness? Thomas Paine also wrote, "In framing a government which is to be administered by men over men the great difficulty lies in this: You must first enable the government to control the governed, and in the next place, oblige it to control itself."

In building a new American government, leaders were on guard against a central government that was so strong that it was a threat to the rights of the people. From those fears, they developed a government that was too weak to serve the needs of a nation of united states, although they were wise enough to correct their course.

Americans had played an important role from the beginning in the colonial governments established by Great Britain. The colonies functioned under a system of shared governance between local legislative bodies and government officials sent by the mother country. This relationship satisfied for the most part both parties until the 1760s. As the government in Britain became more restrictive of colonists' rights, these British citizens, who had enjoyed a great degree of independence under the most enlightened government in the world at the time, grew more insistent that their government was wrong. In 1774, Parliament's response to the actions of the Bostonians was the passage of the Coercive Acts, known as the Intolerable Acts by the Americans. The Coercive Acts were among the last in a long line of intolerable actions and led to the organization of the First Continental Congress. The colonies sent representatives to the Congress to determine the next step in the clash for their rights as Englishmen. If the colonies had any

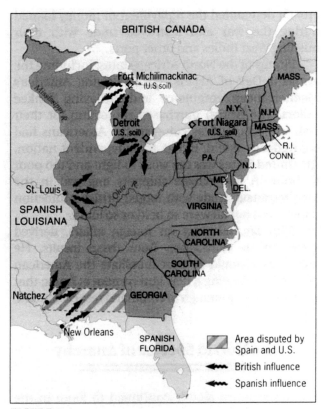

FIGURE 7.1 - Main Centers of Spanish and British Influence After 1783

chance of stopping the erosion of their rights by the actions of the British Parliament, strength and unity were necessary. "Join together or die" became the motto for many.

The Continental Congress Serves as a Government

Twelve colonies selected 55 delegates to attend the First Continental Congress in Philadelphia from September 5 to October 26, 1774. Georgia declined to send delegates. There were conservative and radical delegates, which reflected the division of opinion within the colonies toward Parliament's policies. The conservative delegates hoped to find the means to continue the relationship with Britain. The radicals wanted extreme change, and for a minority that meant ending the relationship.

The bond loosened further in a cycle of action and reaction that hardened the resolve of both sides to stand their ground. Paul Revere arrived in Philadelphia to advise the delegates of the most recent actions of Massachusetts.

The colony supported the new "Suffolk Resolves," which recommended resistance to the Coercive Acts. The Congress advised Massachusetts to form an independent government and prepare for British retaliation. It also passed 10 resolutions establishing what they believed were the rights of the colonists, including the rights to "life, liberty and property." The delegates officially declared that 13 acts of Parliament passed since 1763 violated American rights.

In this forum of unity, Americans began to build their case for independence, although most were not prepared to take this action yet. However, they were prepared to take a stronger stand against what they considered the abuses of Parliament. Congress believed that it was time to take action as a united group against the British government. The delegates called for a Continental Association to implement economic sanctions. The purpose of the Association was to form local committees throughout the colonies that would deny the entry of British goods and deny the exportation of American goods to Britain. This tactic had worked in the past, notably during the Stamp Act and Townshend Act crises. Local groups, intent on enforcing this unified action, searched out those not following the policies and frequently punished the uncooperative. Ironically, the assembly of representatives continued to declare loyalty to the king and sent a summary of the proceedings to King George III as well as the American and British public. One of the final acts of the Congress was to pass an agreement to meet again in May 1775 if Parliament refused to address the grievances of the colonies.

King George and Parliament refused to alter their stand on colonial policies. In fact, they increased the rift by sending troops to Lexington and Concord, Massachusetts, in April 1775. The two sides exchanged gunfire, resulting in the deaths of British colonial citizens. On May 10, 1775, the Second Continental Congress convened in Philadelphia. This time delegates from Georgia arrived in September. In the summer of 1775, the delegates reconfirmed their loyalty to King George III with the Olive Branch Petition and requested the dismissal of his ministers and a reevaluation of the policies of Parliament that were mistreating his subjects. While claiming their loyalty, Congress prepared for King George III to ignore the pleas of his citizens and issued a statement of the Causes and Necessities of Taking Up Arms. It was a

convoluted road the colonists traveled, but most wanted to exhaust every chance for a peaceable solution. There was no satisfactory accommodation by the British, and rebellion turned to war. Without a government in place, the Second Continental Congress filled that function and became the governing body during the Revolutionary War. They created the Continental Army, selected George Washington as commander, issued paper money to pay expenses, formed committees to negotiate assistance from foreign countries, and finally, created a new system of government.

Colonies Became States

The colonies became states, and eleven of them needed a new system of government when they refused British rule. Rhode Island and Connecticut continued the use of their colonial charters, but deleted all references to British control. New Hampshire, New Jersey, Pennsylvania, Delaware, Maryland, Virginia, North Carolina, and South Carolina adopted state constitutions in 1776. New York and Georgia followed in 1777. Massachusetts developed their constitution through the work of a convention called for this purpose, and submitted the finished document to the people for ratification in 1780.

The constitutions had much in common. They attempted to correct all of the problems created by the disproportionate authority vested in the monarch, or authoritarian system. After all, the British had a constitution, even if it was not a formal written document, and the government continued to ignore the rights of the citizens when they wished. The new American governments would be republican in nature, meaning that political power originated from the people rather than from a powerful authority figure or group. They organized strong, bicameral legislatures, with the exception of Pennsylvania, which decided on a unicameral body. The chief executives for the states were weak and most were limited to serving one year. Exceptions were Pennsylvania and New Hampshire, which established plural executive councils. They also conducted frequent elections for office. Most required those holding office and voting in elections to meet certain property qualifications. There were also innovative measures in the constitutions, with many passing Bills of Rights.

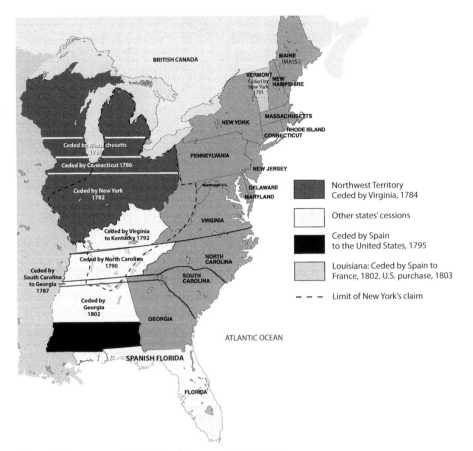

FIGURE 7.2 - Western Land Cessions to the United States, 1782-1802.

The enumeration of specific rights of the citizens placed limits on the ability of the government to interfere with certain rights.

The First Federal Government

It was clear to many in the Continental Congress during the summer of 1776 that independence was the next logical step. The citizens of the colonies were divided in their views. There were those who wanted to remain British subjects, those who did not care, and those who wanted to form an independent America. Richard Henry Lee of Virginia proposed a resolution to the Continental Congress on June 7, 1776, for independence and a new system for the central government. It was time to make the break with Britain official, according to the Patriots. Nothing was changing between the government and its colonies except that the relationship was spiraling further into an untenable situation. An important reason to define the status of the conflict was that a rebellion

would bring little or no help from the European enemies of Great Britain, but if it were a war for independence, some of the European powers might give assistance to a struggling new country.

Once the delegates voted to accept the actual Declaration of Independence on July 4, 1776, it was necessary to put in place a federal government to handle national issues, including fighting and funding the war, commerce, and foreign policy. Fearful of any strong system of government that could repress liberties, as Americans perceived the British king and Parliament had done, Lee recommended a loose confederation of states. John Dickinson of Pennsylvania headed the committee charged with organizing a formal plan of government. The committee presented Congress on July 12, 1776, with a list of "Articles of Confederation and Perpetual Union." Congress debated the articles and came to an agreement on 13 of them. On November 15, 1777, the new system went to the states for ratification, with the stipulation that they would not take effect unless and until all 13 states had ratified them.

Ratification was not complete until 1781. Disputes over representation in the Congress (the small states wanted equal representation, and the large states proportional according to population) and the future of the western lands of several states delayed the ratification process. There were several states with unsettled frontier areas along their western borders, including Georgia, South Carolina, North Carolina, Virginia, New York, Connecticut, and Massachusetts. Some of them claimed the Mississippi River as their western borders; Virginia even claimed what would later be almost the entire Northwest Territory. Many Americans in the smaller states were alarmed by such extravagant land claims. Maryland in particular insisted that these states relinquish their western lands to the national government. After Virginia agreed to eventually cede its huge claims to the West (though it did not officially cede those claims until 1784), Maryland ratified the Articles of Confederation on March 1, 1781, thus officially putting the Articles into effect.

Articles of Confederation

The first constitution of the United States was a brief document with only 13 articles. The federal government was now a "firm league of friendship" between the states, with the states holding the power in this relationship. This was clear from Article II, which declared, "Each state retains its sovereignty, freedom, and independence, and every power, jurisdiction, and right, which is not by this Confederation expressly delegated to the United States, in Congress assembled."

The government consisted of a unicameral Congress with one vote per state on all issues. Congress had the power to set up a postal department, raise an army and navy, declare war, enter into alliances and treaties with foreign powers, control the development of the western territories, regulate Indian affairs, and coin, borrow, or request money from the states. Congress could not levy any taxes. The national government was to pay its financial obligations with money requisitioned from the states. For the passage of important pieces of legislation, a yea vote from nine of the 13 states was necessary. There were no executive or judicial branches of government. Article IX provided for the appointment by Congress

of a president of the Congress, but the president was primarily the chairman of the meetings and could not veto legislation. The first president was John Hanson of Maryland. Any amendment to the Articles required the unanimous vote of all states. They wanted a weak national government, and that is certainly what they created.

The Dissatisfied

In the summer of 1783, the country and the Continental Army awaited the signing of the peace treaty to end the war. Congress chose to furlough most soldiers but not completely disband the army until all documents were official and the British evacuated New York. During the spring and summer of that final year of a state of war between the United States and Britain, some in the military turned against the national government.

The Newburgh Conspiracy

Throughout the war, Congress had difficulty meeting financial obligations, a situation that did not end when the soldiers laid down their guns. The coffers of Congress remained bare. In 1781, there was a request to the states to approve a change in the Articles of Confederation and allow Congress to initiate a duty of five percent on foreign imports. There was to be no duty, as Rhode Island, motivated by local interest over national, refused to give its support for the amendment. Frustrated by the failure of a measure that might have resulted in compensation for back pay and payment to replace the promised pensions, a group of officers put Congress on notice. In December 1782, Congress received a letter that warned the patience of many men with constant deprivation and lack of consideration by Congress and the public was at an end. The threat of military action against the government was obvious. The officers did not carry out their threats of a military solution. However, they were not finished with this course of action, and neither were members of Congress who wanted the soldiers to take action in the hope that this might force the states to cooperate in the attempts to strengthen the national government. Some, including Alexander Hamilton, his former military aid, even mentioned the situation to General George Washington, hoping for his cooperation with these plans. He refused, as he firmly believed that the military must remain under the control of civilian authority to guarantee freedom in the new republic.

Washington moved about 11,000 troops into the vicinity of Newburgh, New York. The officers remained dissatisfied, as their financial grievances were not resolved. General Gates, second in command to Washington, entered into the conspiracy, giving his approval for the circulation of two anonymous letters known as the Newburgh Addresses. The first letter, written and distributed on March 10, 1783, called for a meeting to draw up a list of grievances for Congress to address. Washington learned of the plan and forbade the meeting. Instead, he called his own meeting of the officers to discuss the situation. Washington counseled his men to have patience and not resort to violence. He also advised his fellow soldiers to do nothing that would sully their glorious service to the nation. Washington's words did not appear to influence the soldiers' feelings until he placed his spectacles on his nose to read a letter. He then stated, "Gentlemen, you must pardon me. I have grown gray in your service and now find myself growing blind." This statement moved these battle-hardened veterans to back down from their positions that might have lead to mutinies or even a military coup. Instead, the officers adopted resolutions of loyalty and confidence in Congress and criticized the previous addresses. Washington then followed through on his promise to help alleviate the problems and sent his own circulating letter to the states begging for more power to be given to Congress.

Disgruntled Soldiers March on Congress

On May 26, 1783, Congress furloughed many of the Continental Army's troops, and in June, both Washington and Congress agreed to grant more soldiers leave until the ratification of the peace treaty with Britain allowed their actual discharge. However, a group of approximately 300 disgruntled soldiers marched to Philadelphia to demand justice from Congress and Pennsylvania for their service. When Pennsylvania failed to send assistance to disperse these angry men demanding their pay, Congress adjourned rather than face the mutineers. The representatives decided to move

their meeting place to Princeton, New Jersey, and then to Annapolis, Maryland. On November 3, 1783, most of the troops received their formal discharge. A small force remained with General Washington as he awaited the evacuation of the British from New York City.

The Fate of the Loyalists

One group of Americans decided to depart rather than stay in a country without British rule. During the Revolution, Americans divided into three groups. Loyalists remained true to the mother country, neutrals declined to support either side, and Patriots supported a break with Great Britain. When circumstances made their lives intolerable, Loyalists departed for Canada or Europe. As the Revolution moved from the battlefields into the halls of government of state after state, Americans loyal to George III faced exile, disenfranchisement, expulsion from political positions, higher taxes, and confiscation of their property. By 1782, all states had passed confiscation acts. New York received over $3 million and Maryland over $2 million when they sold Loyalist property. When the British Army departed, so did approximately 7,000 Loyalists. These were the last of approximately 80,000 loyal supporters of the king and parliament to emigrate from the new United States.

The Loyalists turned to the British government for compensation of their losses because of the Revolution. A commission examined 4,118 claims and authorized payments of more than 3 million pounds to these loyal subjects.

A Republican Society

To understand the ideology of republicanism is to understand the American mind during and after the Revolution. Many of the political leaders in the 1770s and 1780s, who were leading the revolution and then establishing a new American government, held to the belief that the society that represented the best examples of government and a good life was that of the ancient Roman Republic. A republic embraced rustic simplicity, a virtuous community serving the public good, and a military devoted to the nation. This ideology played a role in ending the tolerance of so many in the colonies toward what they perceived as a corrupt British government. A denial of colonial rights was part of the corruption that led to rebellion and then revolution. Along with the growing mistrust in monarchy, there was also distaste for patriarchy, luxury, and inheritance of property and position. The ideals of the ancient Roman Republic rang true for this generation of Americans. In order to reach this utopian state, Americans must have a government based on the sovereignty of the people, independence, ownership of their own property, the willingness to sacrifice private interest for the good of society, otherwise known as virtue, and establish equality of opportunity.

The Founding Fathers were idealists, but they were also realists. They realized that self-interest played a role in all areas of a society, but they believed that if they developed a republic, the competition of so many interests would neutralize any harm to the public good, including its government and economy. George Washington was a devout believer in republicanism and referred often to the necessity for virtue and service to the nation as both a military leader and the first president of the United States under the Constitution. The leaders of the nation in the 1780s formed a democratic federal republic under the Articles of Confederation. When that flawed system failed, they did not dispense with their philosophical underpinnings, but set up a new constitutional system to carry out their ideals.

The Role of Women

The many changes wrought by the Revolution bypassed women. Abigail Adams in 1776 reminded her husband John Adams, a powerful force in politics then and later the president of the United States, "remember the ladies, and be more generous and favorable to them than your ancestors." Independence, liberty, equality, all terms held dear by men, were reserved for men. Women assisted in the war effort, and yet this did not earn for them the full respect and rights that later generations believed they deserved. They were in many instances just another form of property. Their role in life was to serve the needs of husband and family and at times their country. The Founding Fathers forgot the women. Through a fluke

in the wording of the New Jersey law on suffrage, women had the right to vote for a short time in that state. However, New Jersey soon realized its "error" and abolished that right.

Despite the lack of full respect and rights, women did receive more respect and honor under the philosophy of republicanism than before. Civic and personal virtue was at the core of republicanism. The republic could not last without virtuous citizens. It was the role of mothers to instill these values in their children. Increasing the education level of future republican mothers led to the increased ability to produce good republican children. This led to an increased acceptance in upper and middle class families of a formal education for their daughters as well as their sons. For example, Massachusetts passed legislation in 1789 that provided for the education of females in the elementary schools. Despite these few changes, there was little improvement in the lives of American women. Women have had to fight for their rights every step of the way along their American journey.

Religion and the Founding Fathers

Part of the republican form of government included the notion that church and state should not be entangled with each other. Many had originally fled England or other European nations, where the union of church and state had led to religious persecution, in order to seek religious freedom. It was true that some in America sought to use their newly found religious majority status to persecute others, notably the Puritans in Massachusetts Bay Colony before 1691. It was also true that most of the American colonies had official colonial churches, whose ministers' salaries and/or church buildings were at least partly financed by tax money.

But the Founding Fathers, under the later Constitution, were responsible for another kind of revolution, one in which church and state were kept relatively separate. Thomas Aquinas, the renowned Catholic theologian and philosopher of the 13th century, had established the basic philosophical defense for uniting church and state. He declared that natural law was God's eternal moral law that can be derived from reason. However, because natural law was God's law, the church was in the best position to interpret and apply it. This provided a major part of the rationale for the church exercising moral authority over political governments. The Enlightenment, whose height of influence came in the 18th century, took a different approach. Because natural law can be deduced by human reason based on observation and study, every free person was capable of understanding it. Therefore, natural law could be deduced by individual reason alone, without mediation and control by the church or any other institution known to man. Influenced by Enlightenment thinking, America's Founding Fathers sought a system of government in which church and state were separate, and where religious freedom could flourish. This was a revolutionary concept that had never before been implemented anywhere in the world, which made America's pioneering of it just as radical as its implementation of democratic republicanism in the political sphere.

Some argue today that America was founded on Judeo-Christian values, especially including the Ten Commandments. However, it is one thing to state that America was established as a nation of mostly Christian citizens, and quite another to declare that it was created as a Christian nation. Many, though by no means all, of our Founding Fathers were Deists or Unitarians, and while both religious schools of thought believed in a monotheistic God, neither could be classified as Christian in the 18th or 19th centuries. Examples of these religious professions include famous Americans like Thomas Paine, George Washington, Ethan Allen, Thomas Jefferson, Benjamin Franklin, John Adams, and John Quincy Adams.

While examples of inconsistencies regarding the relationship of church and state can be found among the Founding Fathers, there is sufficient evidence to conclude that they never thought they had created a Christian nation. First, the references to God in the Declaration of Independence were made in the context of Enlightenment language, suggesting the Deistic concept of God rather than the Judeo-Christian God. Second, the evidence concerning the Constitution also points away from the creation of a Christian nation. For example, the Founding Fathers soundly rejected an attempt at the Constitutional Convention to rewrite the preamble to the Constitution to read that the United States was dependent upon God. Indeed, there are absolutely no references to God or Jesus in that official document. Moreover, the only reference to religion in that document's original form is to prohibit religious tests for holding public office (Article VI, Section 3). And the First Amendment includes the "establishment clause," which prohibits Congress from enacting any laws "respecting an establishment of religion." According to Thomas Jefferson's understanding, that amendment erected "a wall of separation between Church and State." Finally, John Adams was even more blunt in denying that they had created a Christian nation. In his "A Defense of the Constitutions of Government of the United States of America" (1787-1788), Adams wrote, "It will never be pretended that any persons employed in that service [of the U.S. government] had interviews with the gods, or were in any degree under the influence of Heaven, more than those at work upon ships or houses, or laboring in merchandise or agriculture; it will forever be acknowledged that these governments were contrived merely by the use of reason and the senses." Then the Treaty of Tripoli, ratified by the Senate and signed by President John Adams in 1797, emphatically stated, "the government of the United States of America is not in any sense founded on the Christian religion…."

Perhaps the famous early 19th century Christian evangelist Timothy Dwight provides the most persuasive testimony. Dwight bemoaned the fact that "We formed our Constitution without any acknowledgment of God. The Convention, by which it was formed, never asked, even once, his direction, or his blessing upon their labors. Thus we commenced our national existence under the present system, without God." Indeed, when it was proposed at the Philadelphia convention to pray for God's blessing during the debate, it was voted down, with Alexander Hamilton declaring that they did not need "foreign aid."

As stated earlier, republicanism depended upon civic and personal virtue among its citizens, a virtue that the Founding Fathers believed was best bestowed by mothers to their own children. Without such virtue, defined as a personal and voluntary willingness to sacrifice private interests for the public good, the republic could not long endure. The use of religious legislation or other government religious action to instill such virtue contradicts the very spirit of republicanism. That is perhaps the most fundamental reason that the Founding Fathers believed that government should be neutral in matters of religion.

Settlement of the Northwest Territory

After the American Revolution, Congress encouraged the settlement of the territory north of the Ohio River, despite the fact that the British continued to occupy forts in the region, which was a violation of the 1783 Treaty of Paris. There was also a serious threat from the Indian tribes in the region. Moreover, Congress wanted the revenue from land sales in the area and the settled territories to grow a nation. The 1784 Ordinance provided for a governor, secretary, and three judges selected by Congress. Learning from their past experiences as colonies, Congress also guaranteed inclusion into the Union as states equal to the other states as soon as the territories met certain conditions. When the population was sufficient, later set at 60,000, the inhabitants could write a constitution. State boundaries would be set with statehood to follow soon after. In the 1785 Ordinance, Congress called for a survey of the area. The survey established townships and laid out physical patterns for settlement. Each township consisted of 36 one-square mile sections of 640 acres. Funds from the

sale of Section 16 went to public schools. Most of the other sections were sold at public auction for at least $1 per acre. The result was that speculators bought most of the land and then sold it for huge profits.

The Northwest Ordinance of 1787 provided more clarification. In that law, Congress included freedom of religion, trial by jury, and public support of education as specific rights of the inhabitants of this territory, reflecting the philosophy of republicanism. Significantly, Congress also banned slavery in the Northwest Territory, which was the first time that the national government had limited the expansion of slavery. The Northwest Ordinance of 1787 set the pattern for the development of the entire West in American history, with the exception of California in 1850. The Northwest Land policy was easily the greatest area of success for the Articles of Confederation government.

Crises Expose the Deficiencies of the National Government

Facing Economic Challenges

Following the Revolution, the new government faced the daunting task of untangling a morass of financial

Surveying the Old Northwest   Sections of a township under the Land Ordinance of 1785.

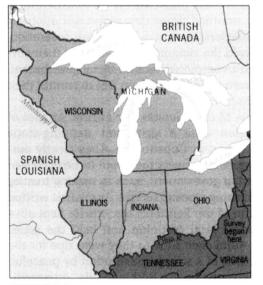

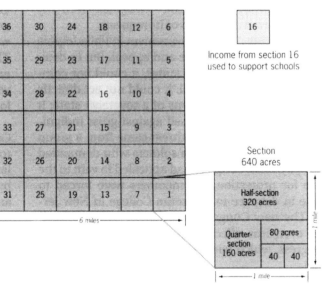

FIGURE 7.3 - Surveying the Old Northwest.

problems. The Articles of Confederation denied Congress the authority to tax, so the options to help solve national financial problems were few. This significant weakness was one of the deciding factors in ending the first system of government. Congress requisitioned money from the states to retire loans, pay depreciated bills of credit, and take care of other unpaid obligations. The states sent small amounts of money to the national treasury, but this was not a priority for them, and thus they usually did not meet their full requisitioned amounts.

Robert Morris, superintendent of finance from 1781-1784, estimated the national debt at $30 million, but he actually underestimated the total. Morris took action to improve the stability of the nation's finances by chartering the Bank of North America in Philadelphia in 1781. He hoped that this would ease the problem of the circulation of currency and the lack of credit. This was the first national commercial bank. The government was the principal stockholder, and the bank loaned money back to the nation. Congress also attempted to set up tariffs on imports to finance the business of government, but the states withheld their approval. The states were unwilling to give up their revenue from imports for the sake of the nation.

Debts remained from the Revolutionary War. Soldiers had not received all of the compensation promised, and without the ability to raise revenue, Congress could not meet this obligation. Congress did have access to land, however, and paid some of the soldiers with western land grants. Bills of credit were another debt problem of the public treasury. The Continental Congress and the states issued bills of credit to pay for expenses during the war. These bills (known as Continentals) became a circulating paper currency with the understanding that at some point in the future the governments would redeem them for specie—gold and silver coins. During the war, the value of the bills decreased, which led to issuing more and creating a problem with inflation. In 1785, the country defaulted on its debt to France. However, John Adams was able to maintain the country's credit with the Dutch.

Trade problems affected many areas of the country. In parts of the South, the loss of slaves (many taken by the British) affected the ability to increase crop production for export, especially tobacco in Virginia. Britain now closed most ports previously open to American products when the colonies were part of the British Empire. Seventy-five percent of American exports went to England, Ireland, and the West Indies before the war. After the war, only 10 percent of American exports found their way to British markets. Indigo and rice from South Carolina, naval stores (principally tar and pitch used in maintaining wooden ships) from North Carolina, ships built in Massachusetts, and the fishing industry in several New England states, along with the goods of other states had difficulty finding markets. Benjamin Franklin, John Adams, and Thomas Jefferson appealed to Britain and other governments to offer trade concessions to the United States. They failed to get such agreements, in part due to the weakness of the central government. Congress appealed to the states for a fifteen-year grant to regulate foreign commerce. An amendment to the Articles of Confederation prepared by a committee under the leadership of James Monroe went to the states. Article IX of the Articles declared that Congress not enter any treaty of commerce that deprived any state of its individual right to impose duties. The states let the proposal die. There were some promising trade markets in France, Holland, Sweden, and a few in the Mediterranean. American ships were vulnerable in the Mediterranean to attacks by the Barbary pirates from North African ports. The American ships no longer were under the protection of Britain. The pirates took ships and held sailors for ransom. The country would deal with this situation in the near future. In the meantime, it had a negative impact on the nation's economy.

Imports were also a problem for the fragile economy. American ports remained open to products from Britain, particularly manufactured products. Indeed, when the colonies had been part of the British Empire, it had guaranteed markets for its exports and enjoyed protection from cheap foreign imports. But with independence, Americans lost their special status, and the new country was flooded with cheap foreign imports from other nations as well. Compounding the problem was the fact that American factories were slow to step up to the challenge of providing finished products for the home market, having also experienced some restrictions on manufactured products during the colonial era. Furthermore, British companies that imported goods to the United States extended favorable terms to American merchants, who in turn extended lenient credit to their consumers. However, when customers, especially many soldiers and farmers, could not pay their debts, some merchants were forced into bankruptcy. Moreover, the lack of sufficient exports resulted in a net reduction in specie (gold and silver coins) and also damaged the economy, for exporting more than you import was the major way to increase the circulation of specie in any economy of that time period. Therefore, an imbalance in foreign trade caused loss of income, bankruptcies, and too little specie. The result was that the United States experienced an economic depression by the fall of 1783, a depression that did not end until late 1786.

The national government was impotent to handle the economic crisis and its root causes. The Articles of Confederation not only denied Congress the right to tax, but it also denied it the authority to regulate interstate commerce. Instead, such regulation came under the jurisdiction of the states. Therefore, the states were in economic competition with each other. The power to impose tariffs on goods entering each state from another state was a source of revenue and a tool to protect the products of each state. For example, New York taxed goods from New Jersey and Connecticut. Americans had also not given up on smuggling goods into areas to avoid paying tariffs. This was a tactic often used during colonial times to circumvent the Navigation Acts of Parliament.

Shays' Rebellion

In August 1786, rebellion broke out again, and though it was on a local level and was contained quickly, it still alarmed state and national leaders. When rebellion of American citizens was added to the country's financial difficulties, many believed it was time to strengthen the Articles of Confederation. Others contemplated an entirely new system of government. It was interesting that Thomas Jefferson perceived the rebellion in a very different light. He wrote to James Madison, "I hold it that a little rebellion now and then is a good thing, and as necessary in the political world as storms in the physical." Perhaps the fact that he was in France at the time as the American minister (ambassador) affected his view, for he certainly did not maintain that view when he later became the president of the United States.

The economic depression that hit the new republic by the fall of 1783 affected both manufacturers and farmers. In Massachusetts, where business interests had surpassed the influence of farmers very early in its colonial history, the legislature shifted the major share of the state tax burden, to pay off their Revolutionary War debts, from businesses to farmers. In this way, farmers in that state may have been the most hurt by the depression and its ripple effects among all Americans. The result was an increasing number of farm foreclosures and even farmers serving time in debtors' prison. Farmers there wondered if they had simply replaced with one tyrannical government for another. Furthermore, many of them concluded that if Americans overthrew one government which had violated their rights, they believed they had the right to do the same again if necessary. When the state leaders refused to listen to the farmers' pleas to lower taxes, issue paper money, and stop the foreclosures, a rebellion broke out.

The rebellion was called Shays' Rebellion because Daniel Shays, who had been a captain in the Revolutionary War, emerged as its leader. When state leaders ignored farmers' efforts to change things within the system, Shays' group began to shut down the county courts to prevent them from issuing foreclosure orders. When the insurgents appeared in Springfield and forced the state Supreme Court to adjourn, this gained the attention of the federal government because this was the site of a federal arsenal. Congress authorized General Knox to raise a force of approximately 1,340 men from Massachusetts and Connecticut for service. The official reason for the authorization was the possibility of action against Indian tribes, but the primary reason for the troops was to protect the arsenal if necessary. The federal forces proved unnecessary because Massachusetts raised its own army with public donations to put down the rebellion.

The insurrection in the eastern portion of the state crumpled, but in the west, it actually grew in size and danger. In January 1787, Shays returned to Springfield with his force of about 1,200 men to attack the arsenal. He expected the support of Luke Day and his forces, but they were delayed. On January 25, 1787, the troops at the arsenal aimed their artillery at the rebels, opened fire, and sent them running. Four insurgents died. Shays' men were decisively defeated a short time later in early February, and the rebellion was over by the end of that month. Shays himself fled to Vermont before moving to New York later. A newly elected governor of Massachusetts eventually pardoned most of the insurgents, including Daniel Shays, because he feared an all-out revolution if they hanged too many. A new state legislature also agreed to some tax relief for farmers, helping to calm things down.

The States Look for Solutions

Shays' Rebellion was a wake-up call for many Americans across the nation. Its significance was to persuade many wealthier citizens, who had more to lose if such a rebellion spread further, that urgent action was needed to strengthen the national government. Even before Shays' Rebellion, the economic crisis caused by the depression had led a small group from Maryland and Virginia to meet at George Washington's home in 1785 to discuss trade problems in the Potomac and Chesapeake areas. Washington recognized from the early days of the new country that the federal government was too weak. In June 1783, Washington was head of the Continental Army, and yet he involved himself in politics when he sent a letter to the states urging them to strengthen the central government. The group that met with Washington in 1785 called for a conference with more representatives from states in the region to discuss trade and other economic problems. Changes were necessary on a larger scale.

Nine states appointed delegates to the proposed regional conference although the gathering in Annapolis, Maryland, in September 1786 included delegates from only five states (Virgina, Delaware, Pennsylvania, New Jersey, and New York). After conferring for a short time, the delegates concluded that the economic problems did not rest with the states alone, but were also the result of a weak United States government. The solution was to change the Articles of Confederation and strengthen the national government. The representatives in Annapolis called on Congress to call for a general convention of delegates from all of the states to meet in Philadelphia in May 1787. The current state of affairs was unacceptable to the delegates in Annapolis, and they endorsed the statements of Alexander Hamilton that claimed there were "embarrassments which characterize the present state of our national affairs, foreign and domestic."

The Constitutional Convention

The Articles Congress, headquartered in New York City, did not seem eager to call for a general convention. But

Under Articles of Confederation	Under Federal Constitution
A loose confederation of states	A firm union of people
1 vote in Congress for each state	2 votes in Senate for each state; representation by population in House (see Art. I, Secs. II, III)
Vote of 9 states in Congress for all important measures	Simple majority vote in Congress, subject to presidential veto (see Art. I, Sec. VII, para. 2)
Laws administered loosely by committees of Congress	Laws executed by powerful president (see Art. II, Secs. II, III)
No congressional power over commerce	Congress to regulate both foreign and interstate commerce (see Art. I, Sec. VIII, para. 3)
No congressional power to levy taxes	Extensive power in Congress to levy taxes (see Art. I, Sec. VIII, para. 1)
Limited federal courts	Federal courts, capped by Supreme Court (see Art. III)
Unanimity of states for amendment	Amendment less difficult (see Art. V)
No authority to act directly upon individuals and no power to coerce states	Ample power to enforce laws by coercion of individuals and to some extent of states

FIGURE 7.4 - Strengthening the Central Government

in February 1787, after six states had already selected delegates to attend it, Congress accepted the petition and officially called for the states to send delegates to Philadelphia "for the sole and express purpose of revising" the Articles of Confederation. Better known later as the Constitutional Convention, it met from May 25 through September 17, 1787. Seventy-four delegates were chosen altogether, but the maximum number of 55 delegates from 12 states actually attended the convention. Only Rhode Island refused to send any delegates, because it feared a loss of power to a stronger national government. Delegates frequently came, went home to conduct personal business, and then returned, all at different times.

The Actual Delegates

Who were the delegates at the convention? Often known collectively as the Founding Fathers, the delegates were all white men. As a whole, these men owned more property than the average American, and they were better educated as well, more than half of them having attended college. There were more lawyers among them than any other profession. As to their ages, most of them were in their 20s and 30s, which is quite young for Founding Fathers of a new nation. While the average age was in the early 40s, the youngest was 26 and the oldest, Benjamin Franklin, was 81 years old. In fact, only four of the delegates were over 60 years of age. Fortunately, Philadelphia was Franklin's hometown, so he could go to his own home to eat and sleep each night.

Fortunately, for the nation then and in the future, some of the nation's sharpest minds and most experienced individuals in government made their way to this convention. They had served their states and their nation as soldiers, state governors, members of Congress, and members of state legislative bodies, including those who had experience with drafting state constitutions. The presence of both George Washington and Benjamin Franklin certainly gave the convention a stronger sense of legitimacy.

Nearly all of the delegates agreed that the current national government was too weak to resolve the problems facing the United States as a country. Many of the states were actually functioning well, but the delegates knew that individual state success was not enough to guarantee the success and security of the nation. The delegates also agreed that they did not wish to create any system of government that might promote tyranny, of which they recognized three forms. First, they wanted to avoid the tyranny of one-man rule, which in that era meant a monarchy. Second, they also wanted to prevent the tyranny of oligarchy, the rule by a small elite group of some kind. Finally, and perhaps most significantly, they also feared the tyranny of the majority. This latter fear resulted largely from a suspicion that the common man might be willing to hand power to a demagogue during a time of crisis, a leader who would persecute those chosen as scapegoats for the crisis. The result of wanting to avoid the tyranny of the majority was to create a complex and difficult process for a new national government, so that it would be very difficult for the masses, in a time of perceived crisis, to find scapegoats and trample on their natural rights.

No one better understood this principle than James Madison of Virginia, who arrived in Philadelphia with many firm ideas on the form of government best suited to the ideals of the Revolution and republicanism. One of the great minds of the time, Madison studied governments of the past to determine what system would best serve this new nation. He determined that the republican system of Rome was the best one to protect liberty and promote a strong federal system. Along with his fellow delegates from Virginia, he spent the time waiting for representatives from other states to arrive polishing his plans and convincing the others of the suitability of his plan.

With delegations from nine states present, the Convention opened on May 25. One of the first orders of business was the election of a presiding officer. George Washington accepted the unanimous support of his fellow delegates for that position. In addition, the members decided on a few other simple procedural matters, including keeping the proceedings secret. They wanted no pressure or influence from the public or the press, believing that delegates would be much freer to express or float new ideas without such public scrutiny during the proceedings. Although official minutes were taken for posterity, it was James Madison's personal notes that later provided the most thorough and detailed account of what transpired at the convention. The official minutes of the meetings were released publicly in 1818, while Madison's notes were not published until after his death in 1836.

The Virginia Plan

Early at the convention, Edmond Randolph, the governor of Virginia, presented Madison's plan to the delegates. Known as the Virginia Plan, it shocked many in the hall. This was not a plan for a revision of the central government under the authority of the Articles of Confederation. Instead, this was a plan for a new constitution establishing an entirely new system of government. The Virginia Plan proposed a more powerful national government with a bicameral national legislature. The people of the states would elect the lower house, the House of Representatives. The House of Representatives would elect the members of the upper house, the Senate. The population of a state determined the size of their delegation to both the House and the Senate. The two houses of Congress would elect a chief executive to a seven-year term, federal judges, and a Council of Revision with the power to change the laws of Congress.

Once the delegates recovered from the shock of a proposal to eliminate the current central government, the delegations began to split into mostly large versus small state positions on the plan. With the plan to award seats in both houses based on state populations, the large states with larger populations would have a decided advantage in this new system. The large states could control Congress, the executive branch, and the federal courts. Virginia, Pennsylvania, and Massachusetts naturally were in favor of this plan. Georgia, South Carolina, and North Carolina hoped to become large states and favored the plan in general, but sided with the small states on some of their points. The small states of Delaware, New Jersey, Connecticut, and Maryland opposed the Virginia Plan. They could lose their influence in the national government with this plan. The New York delegation split, with some members siding with the small states and some, chiefly Alexander Hamilton, aligning with the large states on this matter. The delegates agreed to debate the issue as a "committee of the whole." With this procedure, discussion was more relaxed because there was not a vote to hold a member to a particular position.

The New Jersey Plan

On June 15, William Paterson of New Jersey presented an alternative plan to that proposed by Virginia. This plan, known as the New Jersey Plan, proposed a unicameral Congress with equal representation of the states (regardless of population), elected by popular vote, and conducting its business on a one-state, one-vote basis, all features of the Articles government. It also proposed that Congress appoint a committee of three as the head of the executive branch, and it called for a weaker judicial branch than the Virginia Plan. This plan essentially kept the government as it was under the Articles of Confederation with a few alterations. Among its differences with the Articles of Confederation was that Congress would be given explicit authority to tax and regulate interstate commerce. Paterson pointed out that the purpose of the convention, after all, was to revise the Articles, not eliminate the current government. James Wilson of Pennsylvania, sometimes referred to as "the unsung hero of the Convention," and James Madison eloquently challenged Paterson's plan. In a vote on the New Jersey Plan, only New Jersey and New York voted aye.

The Connecticut or Great Compromise

Debate between the two major plans raged for about one month. Although the delegates made progress on most issues, the question of how to divide representation in the Senate remained a heated issue. The large states posited that they represented the majority of the population; therefore, their claim for more seats was only fair in a representative government. The small states countered that they would be at the mercy of the power of the large states if representation in the Senate were not equal.

When delegates from some of the small states threatened to walk out of the convention in protest, cooler heads prevailed in an effort to reach a compromise. Roger Sherman of Connecticut had a previous compromise measure rejected. But in mid-July, it was officially approved. This Connecticut Compromise, also called the Great Compromise because it was the most significant one at the convention, divided state representation in the House of Representatives according to population and provided for equal representation of the states in the Senate—specifically two senators per state. The convention accepted this proposal and expanded the duties of the House, which represented the people directly. For example, all bills that dealt with taxation and the appropriation of funds must originate in the House.

Debating Other Issues

Although there were areas of disagreement between the small and the large states, there were also important principles on which the members of the convention agreed. It was this spirit of agreement on fundamental principles for a just and effective system that allowed the Constitutional Convention to work out disagreements and emerge with a new government. The convention agreed to a government of three branches with checks and balances on each. They rejected the "council of revision." The three branches of government—legislative, executive, and judicial—reflected the principle of "separation of powers." Also reflecting the principle of "checks and balances," Congress would set the shape and size of the judicial branch, with the president nominating federal judges, in addition to justices to the Supreme Court, and the Senate having the authority to confirm them. Underscoring the need to protect individual rights from too much governmental power, the delegates also understood the vital importance of creating the judicial branch as independent from too much influence by the other two branches of government. To that end, all federal judges and Supreme Court justices would be appointed for life. In short, the delegates to the Philadelphia convention agreed to implement a republican form of government. The principles of "checks and balances" and "separation of powers" were so integral to James Madison's ideas that he later became renowned as the Father of the Constitution.

Another subject for debate was the chief executive. Under the Articles, there was a president of the Congress, but not a national executive. A chief executive was necessary, but the main question was whether this should be one person or a committee arrangement. One man might have too much power. They certainly did not want a king. One man might also favor his home state or region. On the other hand, a committee of executives might not work well together. The convention finally agreed to one chief executive and then limited terms to four years, but without limitation on the number of terms that may be served.

There would be no direct election of the president. As much as most of the Founding Fathers feared a government that was too strong, they also feared too much power in the hands of ordinary citizens. Voters did not and still do not directly elect the president of the United States. Instead, each state is entitled to the number of presidential electors equal to its total members in Congress (House and Senate combined), to be selected as the state determines. Originally, virtually all the states authorized their legislatures to choose the electors. By the 1824 presidential election, however, the large majority of states changed this procedure to have their voters elect the electors, which is the reason that popular vote totals are not given in most tables detailing the results of presidential elections until the 1824 election. These electors then meet in their respective state capitals and cast their votes, which are then delivered in a sealed condition to the president of the United States Senate, who oversees the counting of the votes in front of both houses of Congress.

A majority of the electoral votes are required for a candidate to be elected as president of the country, with the original Constitution stating that the runner-up would be the vice president. If no candidate received a majority of the country's electoral votes, the House of Representatives must decide the outcome, on a one-state one-vote basis, from a maximum of the top five original candidates. The 12th Amendment to the Constitution, ratified in 1804, changed some of these details. Most of the Founding Fathers expected that most states would nominate a so-called favorite son from their own state and that no candidate would receive a majority of the electoral votes. In this way, they hoped that the House of Representatives would elect the president (and vice president), thus serving to further isolate this important decision from the popular whims of the people.

As part of the system of "checks and balances," the president was given authority to veto legislation, but Congress could override that veto by a minimum two-thirds majority in both houses of Congress. The president was commander-in-chief of the armed forces, but only Congress could declare war.

The motion to award seats in the House of Representatives according to a state's population passed. This was the group directly elected by the people, and to insure their service to their constituents, they faced reelection every two years. The election of senators posed a problem, but the delegates finally agreed that the state legislatures would elect the members of the upper house. The change to require the direct election of senators by popular vote was not made until the 17th Amendment was ratified in 1913. A new, stronger federal government was taking shape.

Southern States and the Issue of Slavery

Slavery existed in nearly all of the states and had from the time of their colonial foundations. However, by this time states in the North were turning away from this system. The majority of the slaves were in the southern states, and their representatives at the convention fought to protect their slave system. Many would walk away if there were not an accommodation for slavery in the Constitution. Even the revered George Washington owned slaves. How would the members of the convention calculate slaves into the population of each state? After some debate, the delegates decided that the total population of a state consisted of the total white population but only "three-fifths of all other persons." In other words, this so-called Three-Fifths Compromise actually declared that a slave counted as three-fifths of a person. Interestingly, the Constitution does not use the word "slavery." This decision satisfied one issue for the South.

The other issue was the banishing of the slave trade. Many delegates hoped to end the practice of bringing new slaves into America. A compromise with the South was to delay banning this trade for about 20 years, or specifically not before January 1, 1808. These compromises prevented the southerners from abandoning the convention and perhaps ending the development of a new government. However, these would not be the last compromises between the North and South on the issue of slavery.

Finally, a New Constitution Emerged

The convention proceeded to draw up a rough draft of a constitution with 23 resolutions. The debates continued to work out the remaining specifics. Then on September 17, 1787, 39 of the 42 delegates present on that day signed the document that outlined a new constitution for the United States. Elbridge Gerry of Massachusetts and Edmond Randolph and George Mason of Virginia refused to sign it. The primary reason these delegates refused to sign was that the Constitution, in their opinion, created a government that was too strong. During the ratification debate in the country, Randolph changed his mind and endorsed the Constitution.

The delegates sent the finished document to the Articles Congress. When Congress read the proposal of the delegates, there were members who wanted the convention censured for exceeding its authority. However, Congress resolved to send the document to the state legislatures and recommended electing delegates to state ratifying conventions. It was the job of these conventions to decide if the new Constitution would fade into obscurity or change the course of American government. Congress also declared that the Constitution would not go into effect unless and until nine states ratified it. The battle over who governed and how continued.

The Ratification Debate

Supporters of the new Constitution (Federalists) and opponents (Anti-Federalists) quickly organized their forces. Both used the press to present their cases to the public in each state. Seventy-seven essays, together known as *The Federalist Papers,* appeared in New York newspapers under the anonymous signature of "Publius." The essays brilliantly laid out the case for the new Constitution and system of government. They reminded the public of the unsatisfactory performance of the federal government under the Articles of Confederation. Intentional weakness built into the Articles prevented the United States from solving its internal and external problems that should be under the purview of a central government. They also publicized the features of the Constitution that advanced the principles of republican government. Alexander Hamilton, James Madison, and John Jay were "Publius," and these three co-authors had been staunch supporters of a stronger constitution for some time. Today, *The Federalist Papers* are among the most respected and revered documents of early American history.

State	Date	Vote in Convention	Rank in Population	1790 Population
1. Delaware	Dec. 7, 1787	Unanimous	13	59,096
2. Pennsylvania	Dec. 12, 1787	46–23	3	433,611
3. New Jersey	Dec. 18, 1787	Unanimous	9	184,139
4. Georgia	Jan. 2, 1788	Unanimous	11	82,548
5. Connecticut	Jan. 9, 1788	128–40	8	237,655
6. Massachusetts (inc. Maine)	Feb. 7, 1788	187–168	2	475,199
7. Maryland	Apr. 28, 1788	63–11	6	319,728
8. South Carolina	May 23, 1788	149–73	7	249,073
9. New Hampshire	June 21, 1788	57–46	10	141,899
10. Virginia	June 26, 1788	89–79	1	747,610
11. New York	July 26, 1788	30–27	5	340,241
12. North Carolina	Nov. 21, 1789	195–77	4	395,005
13. Rhode Island	May 29, 1790	34–32	12	69,112

FIGURE 7.5 - Ratification of the Constitution.

Federalist Support

The Federalist side in the debate for ratification of the Constitution was far more efficiently organized than the Anti-Federalists as both sides launched their campaigns. Some of the finest minds of the times represented the Federalist view, including James Madison, Alexander Hamilton, and John Jay. The Federalist view attracted a larger percentage of elite members of society. Merchants, lawyers, and planters viewed the new Constitution as the best hope for the future of the new United States. Artisans, shopkeepers, farmers and others of the middle class also realized the benefits that a strong national government would bring to the struggling national economy.

Anti-Federalist Opposition

The Anti-Federalists found most of their support in the ranks of small farmers and Americans of modest incomes. This side in the national debate did not attract many nationally prominent men, was not an organized coalition, and opposed the new Constitution for several reasons. Anti-Federalists maintained that Congress should not have the power to tax. This had been a main point of contention with the British Parliament.

Some claimed that the new office of president was too powerful. Still others criticized the new Constitution for not including a Bill of Rights to protect individual liberties. They also feared the domination of government by the elite to the detriment of the common man. The Federalists smoothly negated a major issue for the Anti-Federalists when they agreed during the ratification debate to use their influence to add a Bill of Rights when the new government began functioning.

Americans Decide

Better organization, the rational and dispassionate arguments of *The Federalist Papers*, and the public endorsement of the Constitution by most newspapers and by George Washington and Benjamin Franklin, the two most respected Americans, all contributed to the Federalist victory. The Constitution was officially ratified and adopted when New Hampshire became the ninth state to ratify it on June 21, 1788. There was still some apprehension over the fact that the two most populous states, Virginia and New York, had not yet ratified the document by the time of its formal adoption. Would the Constitution actually work without the support of those important states? This fear dissipated when Virginia ratified it just four days after New Hampshire, and New York followed suit about a month later, although the votes in both states' special conventions were close (89-79 in Virginia and 30-27 in New York). Rhode Island, the only state that refused to send any delegates to the convention, eventually conceded that it might as well go along too, and ratified the document in late May 1790, a good 13 months after George Washington had been inaugurated as the country's first president under the Constitution.

ORDER OF RATIFICATION BY STATE	
Delaware	December 7, 1787
Maryland	April 28, 1788
Pennsylvania	December 12, 1787
South Carolina	May 23, 1788
New Jersey	December 18, 1787
*New Hampshire	June 21, 1788
Georgia	January 2, 1788
Virginia	June 25, 1788
Connecticut	January 9, 1788
New York	July 26, 1788
Massachusetts	February 6, 1788
North Carolina	November 21, 1789
Rhode Island	May 29, 1790

*New Hampshire was the ninth state to ratify the Constitution.

Election of George Washington

In January and February of 1789, the citizens of the United States took the first steps toward forming a new government as set forth in the United States Constitution. The states elected their national representatives to Congress, and the presidential electors met in the various states to cast their ballots for a president. On April 6, 1789, the Senate counted the ballots, and to the surprise of none, George Washington received unanimous support as the first president with all 69 votes. The Constitutional Convention had Washington in mind as the first president, and many believed he was the only leader with enough stature to measure up to the position as head of a new system of government. Most also believed that he would smooth out any difficulties created by the compromises or any other problems that were certain to arise. The electors chose John Adams of Massachusetts as the first vice president. The American Revolution had led to the launching of the American republic. Now it would begin its journey under the Constitution.

FIGURE 7.6 - Inauguration of George Washington.

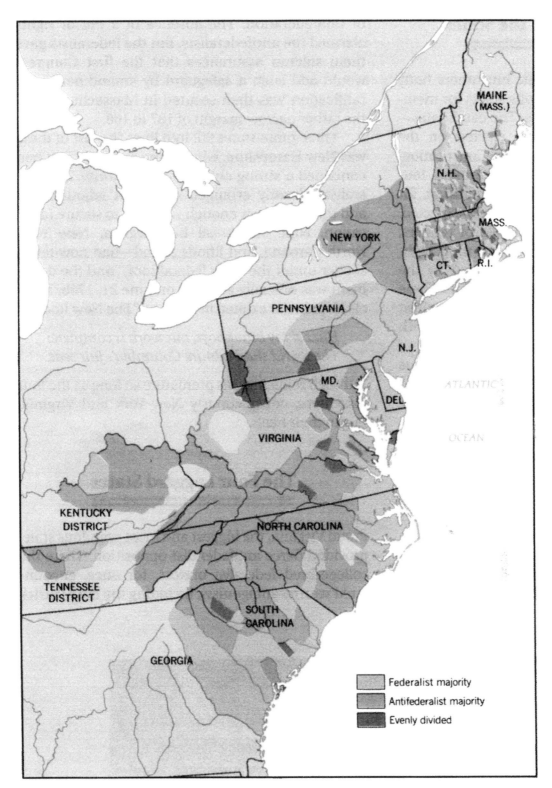

FIGURE 7.7 - The Struggle Over Ratification.

A copy of the original Bill of Rights document, outlining the 10 amendments to the United States Constitution. Note this replica of the original proposed 12 amendments, the first two of which were not ratified. So the third article is actually the first amendment right to freedom of speech. Copyright 2010 iStockphoto.

Chapter 8 Contents

CHAPTER EIGHT

Establishing a New Federal Pathway

Major Events

1789	Washington inaugurated president in New York City Congress established a schedule of tariffs to pay for the bills for the new country Judiciary Act established the judicial branch of government
1790	Congress funded the national debt and assumed the debts of the states
1791	Bill of Rights ratified to the Constitution Bank of the United States created Political parties began to form War with Indians in the Northwest Territory
1792	Washington and Adams reelected
1793	Washington proclaimed neutrality in the Napoleonic War
1794	Battle of Fallen Timbers Whiskey Rebellion collapsed Jay's Treaty with Britain Congress voted to fund a navy
1795	Treaty of Greenville Pinckney's Treaty U.S. government paid tribute to pirates in the Mediterranean Sea
1796	President George Washington wrote his Farewell Address
1797	John Adams became president XYZ Affair
1798	Alien and Sedition Acts Quasi-war with France
1799	Virginia and Kentucky Resolutions
1800	Thomas Jefferson elected as the third president Aaron Burr elected vice president

Introduction

On July 2, 1788, the president of the Congress, Cyrus Griffin of Virginia, proclaimed the demise of the former federal government under the management of the Articles of Confederation and the birth of the new federal government organized by the Constitution. However, at this point the government was just a theoretical plan—an entity that existed on paper only. The next step was to take the outline of government in the Constitution and form it into a functioning system of governance. On February 4, 1789, the nation held its first presidential election, when the electors of the states cast their ballots. The states were also in the process of electing senators and representatives to stand for their interests in the national Congress. On April 6, the temporary presiding officer of the Senate counted the electoral votes. A reluctant George Washington, already known as the "Father of our Country," received a unanimous 69 votes as expected and became the first president under the Constitutional system. He was the definitive hero of the Revolutionary War and the embodiment of integrity and republican virtue. In 1785, John Adams connected Washington to 4 million Americans when Adams wrote, "I glory in the character of Washington because I know him to be an exemplification of the American character." In the election of 1789, John Adams received 34 votes, and as the runner-up, he was thus elected to the position of vice president. (In 1804, the 12th Amendment changed part of this procedure so that the first balloting would be for president, and the second balloting would be for vice president, rather than have the runner-up being named as vice president.)

The new president's eight-day journey from his Mount Vernon, Virginia plantation to the current capital of the nation, New York City (for 1789 only), was a grand procession that allowed the jubilant citizens in the cities along the route to express their elation with cheers, floral offerings, and celebrations. Vice President John Adams arrived in the capital before the president and took his oath of office on April 21. Washington took his oath of office on the balcony of Federal Hall at the corner of Wall and Broad Streets on April 30, 1789. He was visibly nervous as he took the oath of office. The new president then proceeded into the Senate chamber and delivered the first inaugural address to the senators, which was the first of many precedent-setting actions. In his first address as president, Washington urged the country to continue in the "preservation of the sacred fire of liberty." Although this was the second system for the federal government, the ideals burned in the fires of revolution remained essential. One of the important aspects of Washington's two administrations was to establish numerous firsts in the execution of presidential duties that became rules of conduct for future heads of the executive branch. The first president was fully aware of the importance of setting precedent and later explained to James Madison, "It is devoutly wished on my part that these precedents may be fixed on true principles."

Once the festivities of the inauguration concluded with the first inaugural ball, it was time to commence the business of governing. One of the major failures of the federal government under the Articles of Confederation was the inability to form a strong connection with the general public. Local ties were much stronger than national ties. To this end, President Washington accepted and then promoted his role as the symbol of the nation and its central government. In order to reinforce national loyalty, he chose his officials from many states. In the fall of 1789, to strengthen this allegiance, but also to see how the country and its people fared, Washington, accompanied by two secretaries and six servants, toured the New England states. The president took special note of the work performed as he visited places of employment in city after city. In Boston, he visited a sail manufacturing plant and commented on the good character of the young female workers. In Hartford, Connecticut, he commented on the equality of the people in the state. Vermont and Rhode Island were not included in the tour because the former was not yet a state and the latter had not yet ratified the Constitution. A tour across the South in the spring of 1791 continued the president's goal to forge a united nation politically, socially, and geographically. Washington noted that the South lagged behind the Northeast and the middle Atlantic region in industry and prosperity, conditions that continued far into the future as dividing points for the country.

Priorities for the New Government

The Articles of Confederation had left the country in desperate financial circumstances because it had not given Congress any authority to tax. This weakness had been corrected in the Constitution. It was therefore necessary to establish a source of revenue immediately. Income raised on foreign trade with the United States was constitutional and acceptable to most, so in 1789 Congress quickly established a schedule of tariffs on approximately 30 foreign imports to pay for the business of government. The average tariff rate was 8 percent. Import items that arrived on American ships paid a tariff 10 percent lower than those that arrived on foreign ships. Congress also passed the Tonnage Act, which assessed a levy of 50 cents per ton on foreign ships docking at American seaports.

Congress established the structure of the third branch of government with the Judiciary Act of 1789, passed on September 24 of that year. This law created a six-man Supreme Court with a chief justice and five associate justices. The law also provided for an attorney general and for a federal judicial system of 13 district courts and three circuit courts. The judicial branch was the weakest branch for quite some time. It gained strength with the acceptance by the other two branches that the Supreme Court encompassed the right to declare laws of Congress unconstitutional. John Jay, of New York, was the first Chief Justice of the Supreme Court.

The President's Cabinet

Crucial to the development of an effective executive branch was the establishment of the executive departments of State, War, and Treasury by Congress. Just as vital for the president's successful initiation of the executive division of government was his selection of two of the most gifted men of the times to head the State and Treasury departments. Add into this stellar inner circle the advice of Virginia Congressman James Madison, and all of the necessary elements for an auspicious beginning were in place. Washington was strong in his leadership style, but he also depended heavily on his cabinet's and Madison's views on many subjects. In fact, he often presented the views of his advisors as his own.

The president invited Thomas Jefferson to head the State Department. Alexander Hamilton, Washington's aide during the Revolutionary War, supervised the Treasury Department, and Henry Knox stepped in as head of the War Department. Edmond Randolph accepted the position of Attorney General. The secretaries of the departments managed several areas of the federal government during these early days. For example, Jefferson not only controlled the diplomatic offices of the country but also the federal court system, the marshals, patents, copyright, and an official library. Hamilton managed the nation's finances, credit, banking, accounting, and the collection of taxes; but he also presided over the customs department, the coast guard, lighthouses, and the post office. Knox, not one of the president's wisest appointments, supervised the United States Army of 1,000 troops, the navy, shipbuilding, the national arsenal, and Indian affairs.

Washington was a very able administrator, one of his strengths as the commander of the American forces during the Revolution, and an exacting taskmaster with regard to regular reports from his departments. But it

FIGURE 8.1 - Thomas Jefferson.

was not always efficient to have separate papers on every issue. He began calling his department secretaries together as an advisory council, and when they met in this capacity they were called the presidential cabinet.

Bill of Rights

The Federalists, supporters of a strong federal system and a new Constitution to replace the Articles of Confederation, had a promise to keep. The Anti-Federalists had opposed the Constitution in part because of the omission in the document of protections for individual rights from governmental power. During the ratification debate, the Federalists had assured the opposition that this oversight would be corrected once a new government was in place. Indeed, they kept their word, as adding a Bill of Rights was a priority for both Congress and President Washington.

James Madison, a member of the House of Representatives from Virginia and later considered the "Father of the Constitution," spearheaded the movement to write a proposed Bill of Rights. Some House members who had earlier opposed ratification of the Constitution sought to use this process as a way to weaken the authority of the national government by stripping that government of much power and giving it back to the states. In other words, they were attempting to undo much of the work of the Founding Fathers, who had intentionally created a strong national government in the Constitution. As a result, the House committee with jurisdiction over this process sifted through approximately 210 proposed amendments. James Madison, who chaired the committee, strongly resisted the effort to weaken the national government and initiated recommendations for 12 amendments to the Constitution that maintained federal power while protecting citizens from abuse by the government. Ultimately, Madison was successful in getting Congress to pass these 12 amendments on to the states for ratification, and 10 of them were ratified.

FIGURE 8.2 - James Madison

Known as the Bill of Rights, the first ten amendments to the Constitution were ratified on December 15, 1791. The significance of most of these amendments is that they emphasize individual rights rather than states' rights. They deal with issues such as freedom of speech, religion, and the press, as well as the right to bear arms, protection against cruel and unusual punishment, and illegal seizures of property by the government. The Ninth Amendment makes it clear that the Bill of Rights did not itemize every individual right entitled to American citizens. The 10th Amendment gave ease to those who feared the excessive power of a central government when it stated that all rights not specifically declared in or specifically prohibited by the Constitution were reserved to the "States respectively, or to the people."

Washington's Relations with Congress

Washington adamantly opposed, in the early days, exceeding the power the Constitution gave the office of president. However, the vague language of that document often blurred the lines of power. Washington conferred with his cabinet frequently concerning the constitutionality of decisions and policies. He respected the separation of powers but at the same time believed that a forceful executive was important to a strong, effective government. As time passed, Washington increased the power of the executive branch to the alarm of many. Jefferson and Madison questioned whether he still held dear the principles of republicanism, liberty, and limited government. He remained cordial with Congress throughout his terms, in spite of an initial negative experience in the summer of 1789 with the Senate when seeking its "advice and consent" on a treaty with the Creek Indians. The president disliked the tone of the questions from the senators and the lack of a true debate of the issue, and he swore to never appear before that body again for "advice and consent." Respectful of the separation of powers between the executive and legislative branches, Washington used his veto power only for bills he considered unconstitutional.

Hamilton Establishes a Solid Economic Foundation

Economic problems inherited from the Revolutionary War and not resolved by the federal government under the Articles of Confederation threatened the future of the United States. Although the Constitution gave power over fiscal and commercial matters to Congress, Secretary of the Treasury Alexander Hamilton took the lead in steering the country toward economic security when Congress asked that he report his fiscal plans. In his economic strategies, Hamilton planned to pay the national debt, establish the United States as a financially responsible nation, and tie the financial affairs of the wealthy to the new government and vice versa for the success of both. The criticism that Hamilton was an elitist was accurate, but the brilliance of his program put the nation on a firm fiscal footing. Jefferson was especially critical of Hamilton's strategies, but once President Washington supported the plans of the secretary of the treasury, Congress accepted Hamilton's financial proposals.

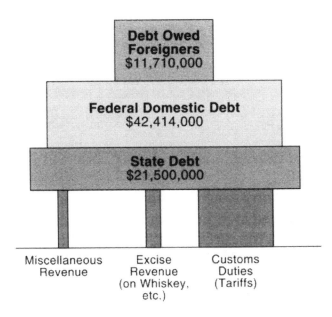

FIGURE 8.3 - Hamilton's Financial Structure Supported by Revenue.

Funding the Debt

The government owed $42,414,000 in domestic debt and $11,710,000 in foreign debt. In order to ensure future credit and economic credibility, America's loans to the people of the nation in the form of government bonds and all foreign loans must be repaid "at par." Funding "at par" meant to pay off debts at face value, including all interest. During the Revolutionary War, Americans purchased government bonds (called Continental bonds) to assist in shouldering the monetary burden, and soldiers were also sometimes paid with these bonds. The value of those bonds had greatly depreciated to 10 or 15 cents on the dollar. Speculators had bought up large amounts of the bonds for pennies on the dollar and made a great profit on them. There was criticism that the original owners of the certificates of debt would not benefit as had originally been the intent because many had sold their original certificates for far below value. Repayment of foreign loans also included repayment of the entire loan with the interest accumulated.

The Federal Government Assumes State Debt

Hamilton was not finished with his plans for the "assumption" of debt. He also proposed that the federal government assume the $21,500,000 in state debts acquired during the war for independence as part of the national debt. Debts incurred from the concerted efforts of the states in the Revolutionary War were an appropriate national obligation, according to Hamilton. The most important reason for this "assumption" was the expectation of binding the states more firmly to the success of the federal government. Hamilton faced strong opposition as well as support with this portion of his plan. Some states like Virginia had eliminated most of their debt, but others like Massachusetts had not.

Hamilton asked Jefferson for his assistance in squashing the resistance to "funding and assumption." Hamilton and Jefferson were on opposite sides on this issue. Jefferson approached Madison, who also opposed Hamilton's "funding and assumption" design, in order to determine their reaction to Hamilton's request. In the end, Jefferson and Madison agreed to support Hamilton in exchange for his support in moving the capital of the

United States to a permanent site on the Potomac River between the southern states of Maryland and Virginia. (From 1790 to 1800, Philadelphia was the nation's capital.) Congress approved the plan in August 1790.

Meanwhile, architects were hired and construction began on the creation of a brand new capital city to be carved out of parts of Maryland and Virginia in the South. It was eventually named Washington in honor of George Washington and the District of Columbia in honor of Christopher Columbus (the name Columbia was an alternate for Columbus). In 1800, the federal government moved to Washington, D.C., and John Adams became the first president to live in the presidential mansion (not named the White House until the War of 1812).

Bank of the United States

The next step toward financial stability, according to Hamilton, was to organize a national bank. The proposal for the Bank of the United States recommended that Congress charter the Bank, the treasury secretary supervise its records, and the government hold a fifth of the capital and appoint a fifth of the directors. This meant that the Bank would operate as a combination of government and private banking interests. The Bank would only handle major transfers of money, service the national debt, assist in collecting taxes, extend loans to major private enterprises and to the government itself, and the Bank's certificates would circulate as a supplementary currency to replace the old Continental dollars. In these ways, the Bank would be both a safe place for federal revenues to be deposited and a means to provide credit for an expanding economy.

Strong opposition to the Bank proposal initially came from Congressman James Madison, who was particularly concerned that such a national bank would give too much influence on national economic policies to an elite group of wealthy private investors, who would make up 80 percent of the board of directors. But there was also criticism of the proposal on the grounds that it was unconstitutional. Reacting to this opposition, President Washington asked the members of his cabinet to submit written opinions. Jefferson argued that Congress did not have the authority to

organize a bank because the Constitution did not specifically grant this power. Jefferson's position was the view of a "strict constructionist" with regard to the Constitution, namely that Congress cannot take a given action unless the Constitution gives explicit authorization for it. Hamilton, by contrast, maintained a "loose constructionist" view. In this view, Congress had "implied powers" that emerged from the specific powers listed in the Constitution. Hamilton argued that because Congress had specific constitutional authority to collect taxes and regulate trade, its "implied powers" allowed the establishment of a national bank within that same scope of power. Moreover, he argued that Article I, Section 8 of the Constitution authorized Congress to pass whatever laws it believed were "necessary and proper" in the course of fulfilling its explicit responsibilities. This "necessary and proper" clause is also often called the "elastic clause" because it stretches the power of Congress beyond the specific powers listed in the Constitution.

President Washington supported Hamilton's proposal, as he usually did, even though he was not convinced totally that either side was completely correct, at least partly because he tended to support the views of the department head most closely involved with a particular issue. Hamilton also persuaded a majority in Congress to pass his Bank bill, which officially created the Bank of the United States when President Washington signed the bill in February 1791. It was located in Philadelphia, the nation's capital, and was chartered for 20 years with an initial capitalization of $10 million, $2 million coming from the federal government and the remainder from the sale of Bank stock to the general public.

The Bank connected the government and the moneyed interests of the North and the East even more closely, which brought a great deal of criticism toward the government then and later from agricultural interests in the South and the West. Despite the controversy over its constitutionality and its policies favorable to manufacturing interests, the Bank was a successful part of Hamilton's plan to strengthen the financial viability of the national government and promote economic growth and stability.

Jefferson-Hamilton Split Forms the First Political Parties

The Constitution said nothing about political parties because the Founding Fathers viewed them as "factions," a term then used to refer to groups that would only tear the country apart. However, in any representative democracy, groups will emerge in order to elect candidates of a similar political philosophy, whether they are called political parties or not. In other words, they are unavoidable in a representative democracy.

The first political parties in American history arose gradually during George Washington's first presidential term in office, and they involved major differences between Thomas Jefferson and Alexander Hamilton. The first indication of important differences between those two men concerned the nation's fiscal policy and powers of the branches of the government under the Constitution. However, there were actually fundamental differences between the two men concerning the most desirable nature of society and government for a democratic nation. The Jeffersonians became known as the Democratic-Republican Party, often simply referred to as the Republicans. Their party reflected the libertarian philosophy of 18th and 19th century classical liberalism. At its core, classical liberalism taught that a general state of economic equality would produce the best results for society, including the safest environment for maintaining a healthy democracy. Believing in the fundamental goodness of people, libertarians like the Jeffersonians advocated maximum individual freedom and limited government so that enlightened citizens could fulfill their lives while still doing the right thing in their effect on others in society. They therefore feared Hamilton's vision of a strong activist federal government and opposed high tariff rates and a national bank, preferring that the federal government pursue a laissez-faire policy of "hands off" the economy. In the context of 18th and 19th century America, Jeffersonians then sought a society based on the agrarian interests of individual freeholders, a broad distribution of wealth, less influence from industrialism, urbanism, and organized finance, and the decentralization of government by vesting in the states the greatest extent of power. At the national level, Jeffersonians generally followed the motto that government that governs least governs best.

By contrast, the Hamiltonians, as followers of Alexander Hamilton came to be known, reflected a conservative political philosophy, in which the rise of the "natural aristocracy" (Hamilton's term) to the socio-economic top of society is praised, partly because they work harder and make wiser choices. Moreover, if free to pursue their own interests, the "natural aristocracy" will create an economically more diverse society, thus providing greater opportunities and jobs for others. Taking the name Federalists, the Hamiltonians believed that it was the responsibility of the federal government to play an activist role in promoting and strengthening this "natural aristocracy," based on merit rather than birth, so that the greatest good for the greatest number could be accomplished sooner rather than later.

Evolution of Major Parties*

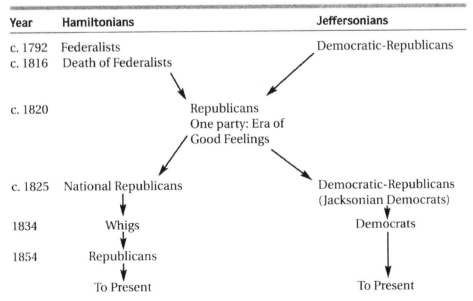

FIGURE 8.4 - Evolution of Major Parties.

Federalist Features	Democratic-Republican (Jeffersonian) Features
Rule by the "best people"	Rule by the informed masses
Hostility to extension of democracy	Friendliness toward extension of democracy
A powerful central government at the expense of states' rights	A weak central government so as to preserve states' rights
Loose interpretation of Constitution	Strict interpretation of Constitution
Government to foster business; concentration of wealth in interests of capitalistic enterprise	No special favors for business; agriculture preferred
A protective tariff	No special favors for manufacturers
Pro-British (conservative Tory tradition)	Pro-French (radical Revolutionary tradition)
National debt a blessing, if properly funded	National debt a bane; rigid economy
An expanding bureaucracy	Reduction of federal officeholders
A powerful central bank	Encouragement to state banks
Restrictions on free speech and press	Relatively free speech and press
Concentration in seacoast area	Concentration in South and Southwest; in agricultural areas and backcountry
A strong navy to protect shippers	A minimal navy for coastal defense

FIGURE 8.5 - The Two Political Parties, 1793-1800

Therefore, the Federalist Party favored support from the federal government for finance, industry, commerce, and shipping, especially through high tariff rates and a national bank. Federalists also doubted the general public's capacity to govern effectively, so they held the conviction that government officials must be chosen from the elite class of Americans.

Jefferson and James Madison toured New York and New England from May through June of 1791 attempting to gauge the support they could raise from others of like minds, particularly from Anti-Federalists who had criticized the new Constitution. Their goal was to form a national political alliance. Jefferson, Madison and others came to doubt the president's commitment to unity and the ideals of the Revolution as he sided more consistently with Hamilton on issues.

The differences between Hamilton and Jefferson developed into a personal as well as a political feud. Each fired salvos at the other in the press and in letters to President Washington. The *Gazette of the United States* circulated the views of the Federalists, and the *National Gazette* was the news resource for the Democratic-Republicans. One of Washington's firm convictions was that the president and the government had to rise above factions or divisions that led to the

development of political parties. Yet, as events unfolded and practicalities emerged, the president leaned more toward the Federalist views. He was a Federalist in many of his political positions and had held those beliefs from his leadership of the Constitutional Convention, particularly with regard to a strong federal government. However, many of Washington's personal interests were those of a Virginia landowner and in accord with the Jeffersonians. He attempted to keep both of his brilliant secretaries working with him on effective governance. The differences with Hamilton and his supporters and then with Washington concerning the nation's friendship with France led to Jefferson's resignation as Secretary of State in 1793.

Securing the Northwest Territory

With independence from Britain, Americans were now theoretically free to expand westward to the Mississippi River. However, the United States did not immediately have the military power necessary to subjugate the Indians there or to force the British to abandon their forts in the Northwest Territory, which they had promised to do in the 1783 Treaty of Paris. Furthermore, the British were also supplying Native American tribes with weapons in their hostilities against Americans moving into the Ohio Valley. President Washington did not want to go to war with the British over the situation, but he was unwavering in his stand that the United States must eliminate the threat of the British and the rebellious tribes.

Indian tribes in this region had formed the Ohio Valley Confederacy (often called the Miami Confederacy), which had existed since the French colonial days. The tribes revived the confederacy's existence during the American Revolution and again in 1785, when the Americans began moving into the Northwest Territory. When action on the part of the Confederacy was necessary, various villages or individuals from the tribes, not the entire tribe, fought as a unit. Little Turtle, a chief of the Miamis, and others claimed the Ohio River as the southeastern border of the confederacy tribes, but this was not recognized by the United States. In 1790, President Washington first sent a personal envoy into the region for the purpose of seeking a peaceful settlement that would enable more American citizens to move there. But the mission failed, and the Miamis even burned one captured American. So in late 1790, the president ordered General Josiah Harmar to enter the territory and destroy the ability of the tribes to wage war against the thousands of Americans moving into the territory. But General Harmar turned back his army after losing about 200 troops. General Arthur St. Clair next took his army of at least 2,000 men into the region in 1791. On November 4, under the leadership of Chief Little Turtle, the Miami Confederacy ambushed and killed more than 600 of St. Clair's forces; many of the wounded died soon after the battle, putting the American death total at more than 900. This was easily the worst military defeat for American troops in the entire history of the Indian wars.

Finally, after Canada's governor urged Indians in February 1794 to destroy every American settlement in the Northwest Territory, President Washington made one last effort to negotiate a treaty in the Ohio Valley. He sent General Anthony Wayne, who had earned the nickname of "Mad Anthony" in the American Revolution, with instructions that if his peaceful mission were rejected, he was to use his force of about 3,500 regular army troops and Kentucky militiamen to systematically destroy Indian villages in the territory.

General Wayne trained his troops for months in forest warfare and the fighting style of the tribes before marching them into battle. The key battle was fought on August 20, 1794, near present-day Toledo, Ohio. In this Battle of Fallen Timbers, so named because one or more tornadoes had recently left many fallen trees there, Wayne's troops defeated a group of Indian warriors numbering between 1,000 and 2,000. Just two miles from the battle site, the British held Fort Miami, though they refused to fight with the Indians for fear of risking a war with the United States that they did not want. Moreover, following this battle, the British refused aid and shelter to the fleeing Indians. Curiously, the Indians blamed their defeat on Tecumseh's sister (Tecumseh was a Shawnee chief), who was in her monthly cycle and therefore unclean, resulting in the failure of the "magic" corn to make the warriors invisible to their enemies.

The tribes' only option after this betrayal by their former allies was the peace table, and the Treaty of Greenville was signed in August 1795 as the result. Twelve tribes agreed to give up land in their southern territory, which included most of present-day Ohio and small pockets in parts of what are now Indiana, Michigan, and Illinois. The Indians received $20,000 in goods, an annual payment of $9,000 in goods, the right to continue to hunt in the region, and what appeared to be acceptance by the American government of tribal sovereignty on lands that Indians did not cede to the United States. With the tribes subdued, Americans flooded into the area and peace existed in the region until the War of 1812. An important Indian veteran of Fallen Timbers who did not sign the treaty was Tecumseh. Never accepting the treaty, Tecumseh attempted to build another confederacy, led Indian resistance in the future, and participated in the War of 1812 on the British side.

The Reelection of President Washington

George Washington intended to serve one term as president. He had longed for his plantation life at Mount Vernon since the end of the Revolutionary War, but stepped out of retirement when his country needed his services in 1789. The nation faced serious problems once again in 1792. Americans were splitting into political factions, there were issues dividing the

North and South, and the rivalry between Britain and France affected the trade of the United States. Associates convinced Washington that his leadership was crucial to the security of the federal government and the nation.

On December 5, 1792, presidential electors cast their ballots, and George Washington and John Adams were reelected to the presidency and vice presidency, respectively. This was Washington's last term in office. There were many who attempted to persuade him to run for a third term in 1796, but he declined. He set a two-term precedent of presidential service, which lasted until the presidency of Franklin D. Roosevelt, who won an unprecedented third consecutive term in the election of 1940 and a fourth term four years later.

NO POPULAR VOTE	
George Washington	132 electoral votes
John Adams	77 electoral votes
George Clinton	50 electoral votes

Whiskey Rebellion

Hamilton's second report on the public credit recommended an excise tax on the manufacture of distilled liquors to supplement the federal income received from tariffs and federal land sales. A 25 percent whiskey tax, approved by Congress on March 3, 1791, adversely affected farmers in back country areas who converted rye and corn crops into whiskey. It was more cost-effective to transport barrels of whiskey rather than the bulky grain because of the high cost of transportation and the poor quality of the roads. The farmers increased the production of whiskey in the 1790s and often used this commodity in lieu of cash in their local areas.

Opposition to this tax developed into a serious problem for Washington during his second administration. Many perceived the excise tax as an income tax and compared it to the Stamp Act of 1765 that roused colonial Americans into action against the British. This was a poor area of the country, and they perceived this federal action as proof that the new government was not more responsive to their problems than had been the British government. More than 20 counties in Pennsylvania, Maryland,

Virginia, Kentucky, Ohio, and North Carolina resisted the implementation of this law. From September 1791 to November 1794, displeasure concerning the levy led to attacks upon tax collectors and their farms or homes. In July 1794, a federal revenue officer's home was burned to the ground in western Pennsylvania by a mob of about 500 people. Then in August 1794, about 7,000 armed insurgents met outside Pittsburgh, Pennsylvania to demonstrate their defiance of the law and flew a flag with six stripes representing six counties in Pennsylvania and Virginia.

This disregard for federal law was especially alarming to Washington and others who were constantly on guard for any signs of discontent that could lead to overturning the current system. The president declared western Pennsylvania to be in a state of rebellion and called up the militia from several states and led the troops for their first mile in the advance into the rebellious area. Henry Lee commanded the force of approximately 13,000 men and was accompanied by Alexander Hamilton himself (as second in command), ironically the man most responsible for creating the whiskey tax in the first place. The rebellion had collapsed before the troops arrived in the area, although the militia did arrest 20 people. Two men, though not ringleaders, were convicted of treason for their inconsequential role in the insurrection. But not wanting to create any martyrs, President Washington pardoned both of them, calling one a "simpleton" and the other one "insane."

Washington had exercised his authority as commander-in-chief, reassuring some that the government was strong enough to withstand any threat but also alarming others that the federal government was exerting too much power. Later, the Democratic-Republican Congress under President Thomas Jefferson repealed the whiskey tax. Nevertheless, the greatest significance of the Whiskey Rebellion was that the Washington administration sent a loud and clear message to the entire nation that the old ways of reacting to unpopular laws, especially taxes, were gone. Instead, peaceful, legal means would have to be employed in the future.

Foreign Policy

Effects of the French Revolution in the United States

Foreign policy dominated Washington's second term in office. In this area, Washington depended less on the advice of his cabinet and trusted advisors and more on his own convictions. In 1789 a revolution began in France and resulted in the establishment of the French Republic in 1792 and the execution of King Louis XVI in 1793. In the first years of the revolution, the American public generally sided with the revolutionaries' desire to end the monarchy. After all, the United States began as colonies under the rule of a monarch and later overthrew that power. However, when the mob beheaded the king, and the revolution turned extremely bloody via its Reign of Terror, public opinion divided sharply in its support of the new republic. When France declared war on Britain, Spain, and Holland in 1793, Americans divided even more sharply over which side to support. Hamilton and Jefferson took opposing sides on this issue. Hamilton's support went to the British. He thought this situation presented an opportunity to end America's treaties of 1778 with France, and ensure the important British trade with the United States. Jefferson's sympathies were with the new French Republic. Nevertheless, both men agreed that the United States was in no position, militarily or economically, to actually enter the war. President Washington agreed and issued a Neutrality Proclamation in May 1793, although in deference to Jefferson's pro-French sympathies, the word "neutrality" was never used in the proclamation.

Meanwhile, a thorny problem arose with the arrival in April 1793 of the minister (ambassador) of the French Republic to the United States, Citizen Edmond Genet. The minister's mission was to win the friendship of the Americans and negotiate a new commercial treaty. But after arriving in Charleston, South Carolina, and before presenting his credentials to President Washington, Genet busily engaged himself in commissioning privateers and sending them off to interfere with British

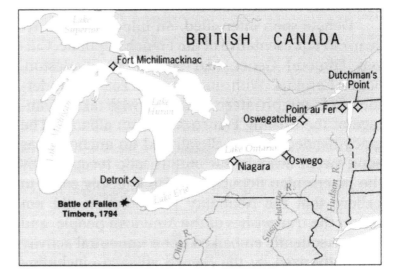

FIGURE 8.6 - American Posts Held by the British After 1783.

shipping. He also set out to organize expeditions against Spanish and British territories in North America.

By the time Genet made his formal call on the president, he had garnered a great deal of support from Americans and the president's ire. Washington gave the representative from France a very chilly reception and sent a communication via Jefferson that the Frenchman had violated the national sovereignty of the United States with his military commissions. Any privateers commissioned by Genet were to leave American waters, and the United States refused their ports to any prizes from these privateers. When Genet broke his promise and armed a prize brought into an American port, Washington warned him against dispatching the vessel. Genet threatened to lay his case before the people of America and sent the French privateer out to sea. The thwarting of his authority was too much for Washington to take, and he called for the dismissal of Genet. Before the president or Congress could take action, however, the power in France had switched to the Jacobin party, and a new minister from France arrived with orders for the arrest of Genet. But Washington refused to extradite the Frenchman, who remained in the United States, became an American citizen, and married a daughter of New York Governor George Clinton.

Jay's Treaty

Despite sharply divided public opinion over the French Revolution, there were several grievances, both long-standing and current, between the United States and Great Britain that needed attention. First, the British continued to occupy military posts in the Northwest Territory despite the agreement in the 1783 Treaty of Paris to evacuate these forts. The British government continued to assert that pre-Revolutionary War debts to British merchants and Loyalist property seized by the states during the Revolution must be resolved before the evacuation of these forts. Second, the British seizure of at least 300 American merchant ships doing business in the French West Indies and impressing or imprisoning American sailors because of its war with France was the most current problem between the two nations. Third, most Americans living in the Northwest Territory believed that the British were stirring up the Indians against them. Finally, the United States was still seeking compensation for the loss of the slaves whom the British had taken with them at the close of the American Revolution. It was imperative to resolve most of these issues for peace to continue between the two countries and for the United States treasury to benefit from the tariffs that British goods brought.

In 1794, President Washington sent Supreme Court Chief Justice John Jay to England as the American special envoy to resolve these issues. What became known as Jay's Treaty was signed in November 1794. Jay's Treaty included the British agreement to withdraw from the military posts on American soil in 1796, to establish two different commissions to deal with the issues of pre-Revolutionary War debts owed to Britain and compensation for illegal seizures at sea, and to place British trade with the United States on a most-favored-nation basis. At the same time, the treaty failed to answer the grievances about impressment, inciting Native Americans against white American settlers, slaves removed by the British during the American Revolution, and Loyalist claims.

Many in the United States howled against the treaty. Southern planters did not want to repay pre-war debts, especially because there was not a resolution on the issue of lost slaves. Northern shipping interests railed against the failure to answer the grievance against impressments or even obtain a British promise to cease its seizure of American ships in the future. Most Democratic-Republicans were especially hostile to the treaty, accusing Jay of selling out to the British. Even President Washington was not very satisfied with the treaty. Nevertheless, the president did send Jay's Treaty to the Senate, which finally ratified it in June 1795, by a vote of 20 to 10.

The fight continued in the House of Representatives in early 1796, however, for appropriations were required to implement some parts of the treaty, and the Constitution mandates that all funding bills originate in the House. Viewing this appropriations process as a back-door way to effectively defeat the treaty, opponents successfully got the House of Representatives to request from the Washington Administration all the papers detailing the treaty negotiations. The president refused to turn them over, asserting the principle of executive privilege for the first time in American history and thus setting a very important precedent. Eventually, pressure from western Americans fearing another British delay in evacuating the forts in the Northwest Territory and from merchants and others who would profit from improved trade relations with Britain caused the House to narrowly approve the appropriations necessary to implement the treaty.

Pinckney's Treaty

Although most boundaries of the United States were in place, there were still questions concerning the exact lines of demarcation between the states and Spanish territory abutting the southern and western-most frontier areas. Thomas Pinckney, the minister to Britain from South Carolina, negotiated a treaty with Spain in October 1795, the Treaty of San Lorenzo. In what was better known as Pinckney's Treaty, Spain formally recognized the western boundary of the United States at the Mississippi River and the southern boundary at the 31st parallel. The treaty also gave Americans free navigation of the Mississippi River and the right to deposit goods at the port of New Orleans for three years and thereafter at a location to be determined.

The Pirate Problem

Barbary pirates, from territories along the coast of North Africa, preyed upon American commercial shipping in the Mediterranean Sea. The United States did not have a navy to stop this violation of freedom of the seas. In

1794, Congress voted to finance a navy with money for six frigates. On September 5, 1795, Washington and the Senate agreed to the terms of tribute set by the Dey of Algiers in a treaty of peace and amity. This agreement gained the release of American seamen held hostage and an agreement to stop the attacks on American shipping. The payment was set at $1 million, with annual payments to follow. This brought the release of 115 Americans but did nothing to stop other groups of Barbary pirates in other areas along the coast of North Africa from taking hostages and ships in the future. The United States later revisited the problem but with a very different outcome, as the new nation constructed a navy and a more secure federal system.

Washington's Farewell Address

Washington refused to consider a third term. He was exhausted physically and mentally, not only because of the rigors of the job, but also because of the increasing criticism of him and his policies. Some of the articles in the opposition press were brutal attacks on his character. It was clear that the president sided more closely with the Federalists in his views on the scope of the federal government and its power.

But the president could not leave his people without warning the nation of pitfalls he believed could emerge and undo the progress made under the new Constitutional system of government. In 1796, Washington wrote his Farewell Address with the assistance of Hamilton and Madison and had it published in a newspaper in September. Some of his advice was followed, and other areas were ignored even during his own presidency. He admonished Americans to be righteous, remain obedient to the government, and stay united. He spoke against "the baneful spirit of faction," and yet the Federalist and Democratic-Republican parties existed in their formative stages. He warned against "foreign entanglements" and "permanent alliances," and future presidents and diplomats often kept the words of Washington in mind when formulating foreign policy. Indeed, future alliances often proved the warnings against these entanglements to be wise words from the past.

Legacy of George Washington

The federal government was now a functioning system. Washington took the bare bones outline of the executive branch in the Constitution and turned it into a functioning organization with precedents that reached far into the future. It was true that he had many contributions from his advisors and department secretaries that he often claimed as his own ideas, but without the vision and commitment of Washington to good government, the republican experiment might not have succeeded. His legacy was multi-faceted. He set the job of the chief executive and kept faithful to the division of power with the other two branches. He kept the nation out of war. Through treaty, the Mississippi River opened to Americans in the West and increased the commercial viability of that region.

He established precedents in the presidency that future leaders of the nation followed as if they were part of the Constitution. Some of the precedents included: respecting the authority of Congress; using the veto sparingly; the president's leadership role in foreign policy and treaty-making; establishing the secretaries of the departments into an advisory cabinet; firing officials in the executive branch previously confirmed by the Senate without the Senate's approval; nominating a Chief Justice of the Supreme Court outside of the justices currently sitting on the bench; and serving as president for only two terms.

It can be argued that a failure of President George Washington was the continuation of slavery. In 1786 he privately vowed to never purchase another slave and expressed the sentiment that slavery should be "abolished by slow, sure and imperceptible degrees." He kept his public silence on the issue as the debate on slavery in the constitutional convention was fought to a conclusion that kept slavery legal. He was aware, as were others holding the same views against slavery, that the southern states would not accept the Constitution or the new system of government without the inclusion of the legality of slavery. When the time came for the Bill of Rights to make the ratification rounds in the states, an anti-slavery amendment was not included. Washington felt that his views on slavery could only emerge safely after his death, so he included a provision in his will to free his own slaves after the death of his wife Martha. Some historians question whether emancipation without a civil war would have been more possible at this time before the development of "King Cotton" bound slavery to the South so securely. However, the painful reality was that the country might not have survived at all with emancipation at that early stage in its history.

President George Washington died on December 14, 1799, at his Mount Vernon home after a brief illness. In his eulogy before Congress, Henry Lee expressed the sentiments of most in the nation. Washington was "first in war, first in peace, first in the hearts of his countrymen." This assessment remains valid today, more than 200 years after his death.

The 1796 Presidential Election

When Washington kept to his decision to retire from office, the logical candidate for the Federalist Party was Vice President John Adams, for the influential Alexander Hamilton (who had resigned as secretary of the treasury in 1795) had made too many enemies with his pro-business policies. Adams was a strong Federalist with a brilliant mind. A Patriot before and during the American Revolution, Adams served as a delegate from Massachusetts to the Continental Congress between 1774 and 1777; he also served as a diplomat to France and Britain from 1778 to 1788. Hoping to attract southern support, Thomas Pinckney of South Carolina was the choice for the position of vice president. Because of his dislike for Adams, Hamilton worked behind the scenes to bring Pinckney to the presidency. The Federalists criticized the Democratic-Republicans for their support of France, generally supported Jay's Treaty as a solution to peace with Great Britain, and supported increasing development of commerce and industry.

Thomas Jefferson, the former secretary of state, was the standard-bearer for the Democratic-Republican Party. Jefferson also had a long, distinguished career in politics prior to joining the Washington Administration. He served in the Virginia House of Burgesses and the Continental Congress during the Revolution. He was one of the committee members charged with writing an explanation of why the colonies had the

right to break away from Great Britain. It was mostly his analysis and words that formed the Declaration of Independence. Jefferson was also responsible for writing a bill that established religious freedom in Virginia. His foreign policy experience came from serving as minister (ambassador) to France beginning in 1785. Aaron Burr of New York was Jefferson's choice for vice president. The Democratic-Republicans criticized Jay's Treaty, favored more power for the states than the federal government, and championed the interests of farmers.

When the electoral votes were counted, John Adams was elected president with 71 votes, and Thomas Jefferson was elected vice president with 68 votes. Because the Constitution stated that the electors would cast two votes, and the candidate with the most votes, if it were also a majority, would be the next president and the candidate with the second-largest number of votes would be the vice president, the nation now had a team leading the government from opposing parties with opposing views on many issues.

1796 PRESIDENTIAL ELECTION	
JOHN ADAMS Federalist	71 electoral votes
THOMAS JEFFERSON Democratic-Republican	68 electoral votes
THOMAS PINCKNEY Federalist	59 electoral votes
AARON BURR Democratic-Republican	30 electoral votes

Relations with France

The relationship between the United States and France was close to a crisis situation when Adams took office. He called the first special session of Congress in May 1797 to discuss the increased tension between the two nations. President Adams and the Federalists were critical of the extreme radicalism and violence of the French Revolution. For its part, France interpreted Jay's Treaty as a decided shift toward a pro-British policy by the American government. Because of its war with Britain, the French government was very sensitive to any action that seemed to favor its archenemy. As a result, the French had seized about 300 American merchant ships on their voyages to British ports in the Caribbean, Atlantic, and Mediterranean by the time Adams had delivered his inaugural address in early March 1797. Matters were made even worse when Charles Cotesworth Pinckney left France after the French foreign minister hurled insults at him and refused to recognize him as America's new minister to France. By this time, Hamilton was leading a group of so-called "High Federalists," who were already calling for war against France.

XYZ Affair

Although many Federalists desired to settle the problems between the two countries through war, President Adams decided to appoint a three-man commission to hopefully settle the differences by negotiating a treaty of commerce and peace. The commission consisted of Charles C. Pinckney and John Marshall (both Federalists) along with Elbridge Gerry (a Democratic-Republican). In October 1797, the three-man commission met informally with the French foreign minister, Charles Maurice de Talleyrand. Talleyrand delayed an official meeting with the commission, hoping to secure monetary promises from the United States before an official meeting. To those ends, Talleyrand sent three French agents to the commissioners with demands that the United States pay a cash bribe of about $250,000, guarantee a loan to France, and that the president apologize for his anti-French comments in order to secure an official meeting with the foreign minister. "Not a sixpence," was the response of the commission, which soon translated into "Millions for defense, but not one cent for tribute!" in the American press. The Americans refused to comply with the demands of Talleyrand. Pinckney and Marshall set sail for the United States, while Gerry remained in France with the hope of avoiding a French declaration of war.

The demands of Talleyrand outraged the nation. However, the Democratic-Republicans in Congress wanted to know if the commission had in any way twisted the events to coincide with the Federalist view on the situation with France. In response, President Adams released the commission's documents and reports in total, but substituted the letters XYZ for the names of Talleyrand's agents. Outrage now reached a firestorm.

The Quasi-War with France

By 1798, the United States was involved in the so-called Quasi-War with France, a term historians use because there was no formal declaration of war by either nation. Most Federalists demanded a declaration of war, but Adams was not ready to commit the country to this course even though American and French warships and merchant ships were exchanging fire and capturing ships in the Caribbean and off the American coast. Before any formal declaration of war could be feasible, the defenses of the nation required strengthening. Therefore, the Federalist-dominated Congress passed 20 acts to consolidate the national defenses and created the Navy Department on May 3, 1798. Although enjoying his retirement, Washington came to the aid of the nation he loved and helped create by accepting the position of commanding general of the army. Hamilton accepted the position of second in command, as the inspector general. Finally, Congress also officially repealed the 1778 Treaty of Alliance with France, a treaty that had pledged each nation to an alliance "forever."

In early 1799, Talleyrand initiated an end to the hostilities with a letter to President Adams assuring him that a minister from the United States would be received with respect. The foreign minister wanted the grain that the United States could supply; he also wanted to avoid adding to the list of his country's enemies. For his part, despite taking steps toward military preparedness, President Adams agreed with the former president in wanting to remain neutral in major powers' wars while the country was still young and relatively militarily weak. So Adams alarmed most of his own party members in Congress when he asked for the confirmation of a new minister to France in early 1799. By late that year, the Quasi-War was essentially over, although not officially until a formal agreement was signed. Meanwhile, the president also sent another three-member commission to France to negotiate such an agreement. When they arrived in Paris in early 1800, Napoleon Bonaparte, who had recently come to power as a self-proclaimed emperor, was eager to rid himself of problems with America. He had grandiose plans for the entire continent of Europe. The Convention of 1800, also known as the Treaty of Morfontaine, was signed in September 1800, ending what had been officially about 2½ years of the

Quasi-War. This treaty, which superseded the treaties of 1778 and formally ended the defensive alliance between the two nations, was ratified by the Senate on December 21, 1801.

Alien and Sedition Acts

In the summer of 1798, during the first year of the Quasi-War with France, the Federalist Congress and president passed a series of four laws known collectively as the Alien and Sedition Acts. They took dead aim at the Democratic-Republican opposition, whom the Federalists deemed as traitors for their continued sympathies for France. But in the absence of a formal declaration of war, it was obviously impossible to legally muzzle the war's opponents.

Fearing that most recent immigrants were likely pro-French and Democratic-Republican, Congress passed the Naturalization Act as part of these Alien and Sedition Acts. The Naturalization Act changed the period of residency prior to American citizenship from five years to 14 years. The Alien Act further transgressed against recent immigrants by authorizing the president to order all aliens regarded as dangerous to the public peace and safety, or suspected of "treasonable or secret" inclinations, out of the country, even during peacetime. Finally, the Alien Enemies Act authorized the president in time of declared war to arrest, imprison, or banish aliens subject to an enemy nation. The Alien Act expired in 1802, while a Democratic-Republican Congress repealed the Naturalization Act the same year.

It was the Sedition Act that specifically aimed at silencing Democratic-Republican citizens who dared speak against the Federalists and especially in sympathy for the French. The law not only made it illegal to conspire or revolt against the federal government, but it also outlawed "speaking, writing, or publishing any false, scandalous, or malicious statement, with the intent to defame or bring into contempt or disrepute the President, the Congress, or the Government." Punishment by a maximum of two years in prison and a fine of $2,000 could be imposed upon violators of the latter provision. Although clearly a gross violation of the First Amendment guarantees of free speech, the passage of the Sedition Act proves that the Bill of Rights is only worth the paper it is written on when, and if, Americans as a whole insist upon it being enforced. Unfortunately, in times of great fear and panic, such insistence has not always been present. What made the Sedition Act of 1798 even more sinister was the fact that the Federalist members of Congress set the law to automatically expire on March 3, 1801, the day before the next presidential inauguration, just in case the Democratic-Republicans won the 1800 presidential election.

Twenty-five persons, nearly all Democratic-Republican newspaper editors and publishers, were charged with violating the Sedition Act. Ten of them were convicted, including Democratic-Republican Congressman Matthew Lyons of Vermont, whose only crime was declaring that President Adams had "an unbounded thirst for ridiculous pomp, foolish adulation, and selfish avarice." Nicknamed "Spitting Lion" for having spit in the face of a Federalist, Lyon won easy reelection to his House seat while serving his four-month jail sentence. In 1801, after assuming the presidency, Democratic-Republican President Thomas Jefferson pardoned all 10 persons convicted under the Sedition Act.

Virginia and Kentucky Resolutions

Jeffersonians raised an outcry against the Alien and Sedition Acts as autocratic and unconstitutional federal laws. They feared that the Federalists might even attempt to suppress the entire organized opposition of the Democratic-Republican Party and establish some form of dictatorship. Not wanting to be prosecuted under the Sedition Act himself, Jefferson secretly wrote a series of resolutions adopted by the Kentucky state legislature in 1798 and 1799. James Madison also secretly wrote a resolution that the Virginia state legislature formally approved in 1798, although it was not as strong as some of Jefferson's statements.

The Virginia and Kentucky Resolutions, as they came to be called, were based on the compact theory of the Constitution. This concept maintained that the states had created the federal government when they had entered into a "compact" (or agreement) of shared power. Therefore, the states held more power in the relationship because they were the originators of the national government. When the states decided that the federal government had overstepped its authority, the states had the right to correct the transgression. The Kentucky resolutions maintained that each state had the right to judge when the national government had exercised powers not delegated to it and to nullify those acts. The Virginia resolutions claimed that the states "have the right and are duty bound to interpose for arresting the progress of evil." Thus was born the related doctrine of nullification, the alleged right of a state, acting through its legislature, to declare a federal law nullified or unconstitutional, that is, unenforceable within its jurisdiction.

Jefferson and Madison hoped that other states realized the dangers the Federalists were to the nation and would follow the examples of Virginia and Kentucky, but that was not the case. In fact, several northern Federalist states repudiated the resolutions and declared that the Federal judiciary was the exclusive arbiter of the Constitution, a position later claimed by the Supreme Court in 1803. Lacking political support from other states, the legislatures of both Virginia and Kentucky declared that they were loyal to the Union, and neither took any further steps to impede enforcement of the Alien and Sedition Acts.

In their opposition to the Alien and Sedition Acts, Jefferson and Madison had drafted documents based on a controversial Constitutional theory that was later used by the South to justify not only nullification, but also secession of states from the Union. These two Founding Fathers did not intend to promote disunity in the nation; they were merely responding to a specific situation in which they could find no other remedy, because the Federalist judges and Supreme Court justices refused to hear legal challenges to the Alien and Sedition Acts. Nevertheless, they set a precedent for another generation of Americans opposed to certain acts of federal power to take steps that would lead to a civil war.

Another Tax Rebellion

In July 1798, Congress passed and the president signed a law creating a federal tax on property. Once again, taxation ignited a rebellion. In 1799, John Fries led an armed group in an attack against tax assessors and collectors in Pennsylvania. Fries' rebellion was small and put down quickly. The rebel leader and his cohorts were arrested. Fries was convicted of treason and sentenced to be hanged. But President Adams followed the precedent of George Washington and pardoned him and others involved in the incident. Once again, the message was loud and clear that the federal government did not allow violent rebellion to challenge its authority.

The 1800 Presidential Election

In many respects, the presidential election of 1800 was similar to the one in 1796, though the outcome was different. The partisan press on both sides waged a campaign that was ruthless and personal. President John Adams stood for the Federalists again. Charles C. Pinckney of South Carolina was the choice of the party for vice president. Thomas Jefferson, the only vice president to run against the president he served with, represented the Democratic-Republicans as their presidential candidate. Aaron Burr was again the party's choice for vice president. Federal authority versus states' rights and the extent of the states' power was the primary issue in the campaign.

The Federalists supported a strong federal government with the states in a subordinate position. The campaign was much more focused on states' rights than foreign policy. Democratic-Republicans, according to the Federalists, were radicals who would resort to violence and destroy the country. And the Federalists claimed that Jefferson was not a Christian but a Deist. In fact, what could be considered a slogan in the campaign was a vote for Adams was a vote for "God, and a Religious President" and a vote for Jefferson was a vote for "Jefferson, and no God." The Federalists continued to prosecute opposition editors under the Sedition Act.

The Democratic-Republicans held the view that federal authority should be subordinate unless specifically allowed a primary position by the Constitution. Jefferson and most in his party opposed the Alien and Sedition Acts. They also criticized the president for deficit spending, increasing direct taxes to pay for defense, and promoting a troubling foreign policy. There was actually a growing anti-British reaction concerning the impressments of American seamen that Democratic-Republicans attempted to tap into.

When the Democratic-Republicans won control of the legislature in New York, Burr's home state, Adams' candidacy was in danger, for that state's legislature chose the presidential electors. Indeed, New York's 12 electors were able to tilt the election to the Democratic-Republicans. However, when all the electoral votes were counted, Jefferson and Burr each had 73 votes, compared with 65 for Adams and 64 for Pinckney. The original electoral system was still in place, which meant that the electors balloted twice, with the runner-up becoming the vice president. But something had gone very wrong. Democratic-Republican electors had inadvertently failed to predetermine that one of them would vote for a third person instead of Burr in order to ensure that Jefferson would receive one more vote than Burr and thus be elected president.

When Burr then refused to concede to Jefferson, the issue was sent to the House of Representatives in accordance with the Constitution. Under this scenario, each state in the House had just one vote for a presidential candidate. With 16 states, the winner needed nine votes to be elected president. What further complicated matters was the fact that the new Congress, dominated by Democratic-Republicans as a result of the Congressional election, would not be seated until after the inauguration of the new president. Therefore, the Federalist Congress found itself in the ironic position of having to select one of two Democratic-Republican candidates to be president. For 35 ballots, neither candidate received a majority of the states' votes in the House. Finally, Alexander Hamilton threw his support to Jefferson because he feared Burr even more than Jefferson, and on the 36th ballot, the House of Representatives voted 10 to 4 to elect Thomas Jefferson as the third president of the United States. Two states, Delaware and South Carolina, abstained on the thirty-sixth balloting round.

The remedy to prevent a repeat of these circumstances in the future was the ratification of the Twelfth Amendment in 1804, before the presidential election of that year. Among other provisions, this amendment to the Constitution stated that electoral votes would be specifically cast, one for president and one for vice president.

The election of Thomas Jefferson is often referred to as the "Revolution of 1800," a concept first declared by Jefferson himself. It was hardly a revolution in any ordinary sense of that word. Jefferson barely won the election, and would not have except that Aaron Burr's tireless political work in New York City gave Democratic-Republican candidates for the New York state legislature a majority there. The true nature of the "Revolution of 1800" lay in the fact that political power was transferred from one political party to another without violence or other challenges. This had never happened in Britain. It was truly remarkable for such a young country already torn by rather severe partisan animosity. Moreover, the party that was swept into power held it for a generation. No one was certain of the impact of the new political control. Only time would tell if the system would work as disagreement became more entrenched and the parties grew even stronger.

1800 PRESIDENTIAL ELECTION

THOMAS JEFFERSON		
Democratic-Republican		73 electoral votes
AARON BURR		
Democratic-Republican		73 electoral votes
JOHN ADAMS		
Federalist		65 electoral votes
CHARLES C. PINCKNEY		
Federalist		64 electoral votes
JOHN JAY		
Federalist		1 electoral vote

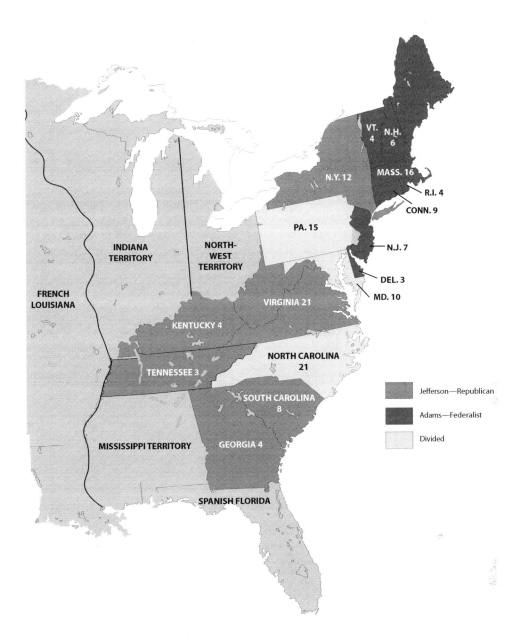

FIGURE 8.7 - Presidential Election of 1800 (with electoral vote by state).

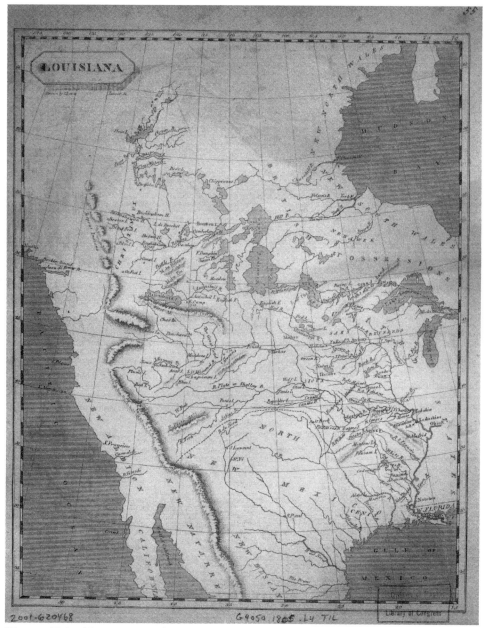

Historical Map | Louisiana Purchase. Copyright 2010 iStockphoto.

Chapter 9 Contents

CHAPTER NINE

Politics and War Under the Jeffersonians

Major Events

1801	Sedition Act of 1798 expired
	Judiciary Act and the "midnight judges"
	Undeclared Tripolitan War began
1802	Alien Act of 1798 expired
1803	*Marbury v. Madison*
	Louisiana Purchase
1804	Alexander Hamilton killed in duel with Aaron Burr
1804-1806	Lewis and Clark Expedition
1807	*U.S.S. Chesapeake* Incident
	Embargo Act
1810	"War Hawks" elected to Congress from the South and the West
1812	The War of 1812 began against Britain
1813	Battle of Lake Erie
	Tecumseh killed in Battle of the Thames
1814	British invaded Washington, D.C.
	Francis Scott Key wrote "The Star-Spangled Banner"
	Treaty of Ghent signed
1814-1815	Hartford Convention
1815	Battle of New Orleans

Introduction

Thomas Jefferson was the first president to be sworn into office in the new capital of Washington, D.C., which at that time was a small town of about 3,000 inhabitants. In keeping with his democratic ideals, Jefferson dressed in everyday casual clothes for his inauguration. He even forsook the horse-drawn carriage and instead walked to the Capitol for the ceremony, which was held on March 4, 1801.

Changes and Continuity

Federalists had feared this day, believing that Jefferson's presidency would undo most of what they had put in place. Outgoing President John Adams even left the city before Jefferson's inauguration. The two men had once been good friends, but strong philosophical differences and years of political bickering had made them bitter personal foes. Yet in his inaugural address, Thomas Jefferson struck a conciliatory tone, saying, "We are all Republicans; we are all Federalists." In his address, Jefferson outlined his view of limited government, asserting that a "wise and frugal government, which shall restrain men from injuring one another, which shall leave them free to regulate their pursuits of industry and improvement, and shall not take from their mouth of labor the bread it has earned. This is the sum of good government."

Indeed, the Jefferson Administration did make several changes from the earlier Federalist years of domination, changes made possible by the fact that Democratic-Republicans had also taken control of Congress as a result of the elections in 1800. American colonial experience had left Jefferson and his party with a fear of large standing armies, preferring to rely on local militia. The result was that the military budget was slashed. The army budget was cut in half, and the navy budget by about two-thirds. Led by Albert Gallatin, the very capable Secretary of the Treasury, the national debt was substantially reduced by the end of Jefferson's first term in office. Other changes included the abolition of all federal internal taxes, including the hated whiskey excise tax, which had been aimed at grain farmers, who were part of Jefferson's agrarian ideal. These changes left only

FIGURE 9.1 - Thomas Jefferson, 1800

two sources of revenue for the federal government, tariffs collected on foreign imports and the sale of western lands.

At the same time, the new administration kept much of the Federalist financial policies in place. The policy of the federal government assuming the debts that the states incurred during the American Revolution was left untouched, as was the tariff on foreign imports and even the hated Bank of the United States (national bank). Keeping these measures in place reflected President Jefferson's realization that politics in the real world was sometimes very different from political theory discussed among gentlemen who were not in power. The fact that some of the president's actions were inconsistent with his earlier well-known views did not seem to unduly bother him. To his credit, Jefferson bowed to reality when he knew it was necessary, which was fairly often.

One area in which Jefferson and his political allies did not budge involved their intense opposition to the Alien and Sedition Acts, originally passed by the Federalist Congress under President John Adams in 1798, partly in an effort to silence Democratic-Republican criticism of Adams. President Jefferson quickly pardoned everyone who was serving a sentence under the Sedition Act. Then the Democratic-Republicans allowed the Sedition Act to expire in 1801 and the Alien Act in 1802. Congress outright repealed the Naturalization Act of 1798, which had required a period of 14 years as a resident of the United States before eligibility for citizenship. In its place, Congress passed another Naturalization Act in 1802 that required a residency of only five years.

A Judicial War

Part of the great philosophical divide between the Federalists' desire for a strong national government and the Democratic-Republicans' favor of states' rights was reflected in their opposing views on the role of the judicial branch of government. Naturally, the Federalists supported a strong, independent judiciary, while Democratic-Republicans viewed the prospect of the encroachment of the federal courts on states' rights with alarm.

The Controversial Judiciary Act of 1801

This debate was intensified into a veritable war when the Federalist Congress passed the Judiciary Act of 1801 in February of that year, the month before the new president was inaugurated. This law created sixteen new federal judge positions, freeing up each Supreme Court justice from having to preside over a federal circuit court. Although the change was a justifiable reform to keep up with the growing number of legal cases, the timing, coming between President Adams' defeat and Thomas Jefferson's inauguration, was obviously designed to pack the judicial branch with Federalist judges as a check on Democratic-Republican power in the legislative and executive branches of government. Having lost the election in late 1800, the Federalists were determined to maintain some kind of influence during Democratic-Republican times. The new Judiciary Act also reduced the number of Supreme Court justices from six to five (after the first vacancy would occur). President Adams had recently appointed John Marshall, a Federalist, as Chief Justice and the sixth member of the Court. Therefore, when the Judiciary Act became law, President

Jefferson could not appoint anyone to the Court until a second vacancy occurred.

President Adams and his close advisors were very busy in the month before Jefferson's inauguration, finding and appointing the new federal judges. A few of them were not appointed until the night before Adams was set to leave office. Democratic-Republicans saw this as a power grab, denounced it, and dubbed the new judges as "midnight judges." In 1802, Congress repealed the Judiciary Act of 1801, thereby removing the sixteen "midnight judges" by deleting their positions.

Impeachment Efforts

In another attack on the Federalist judiciary, Democratic-Republicans in Congress attempted to impeach Federalist judges who had refused to act to stop prosecutions under the earlier, and much-hated, Sedition Act. One such judge, John Pickering of New Hampshire, was impeached. Pickering was an easy choice because of his alcoholism and bizarre conduct, and the Senate convicted and removed him from office in 1805.

FIGURE 9.2 - Chief Justice John Marshall

In early 1804, the House of Representatives voted to impeach Supreme Court Justice Samuel Chase, largely on alleged grounds of judicial misconduct. Justice Chase had been particularly vocal in his support of the Sedition Act, and while serving on the Supreme Court, he had frequently and publicly denounced President Jefferson. Although he was guilty of bad manners and extreme partisanship, Chase had done nothing of an impeachable offense. Instead, this was an attempt to get rid of a mouthy political opponent.

After his impeachment by the House, his case went to the Senate for eventual trial. In early 1805, the attempt to oust Chase from the Supreme Court failed when Democratic-Republicans in the Senate could not garner the required two-thirds majority necessary for conviction. Chase's acquittal by the Senate helped to establish the important precedent that the impeachment process was not to be used to settle political differences. Although that would later be violated in the impeachment cases of Presidents Andrew Johnson (1868) and Bill Clinton (1998), those were exceptions rather than the rule in American political life.

Marbury v. Madison

John Marshall, the new Chief Justice, used his force of personality to help fashion a strong, independent judicial branch of government. His first good opportunity to do so resulted from a case involving the "midnight appointment" of William Marbury, who had been named as one of the justices of the peace in Washington, D.C. just before John Adams had left office. John Marshall, who had worked closely with President Adams to deliver the commission paperwork to the appointed individuals, inadvertently failed to deliver a few of them, including the paperwork for Marbury. When he took office, Jefferson's Secretary of State, James Madison, refused to deliver the commission to Marbury so that Jefferson could appoint a Democratic-Republican to that position. Marbury sued the Secretary of State, requesting that the Supreme Court order Madison to deliver the commission to him.

Marbury's lawsuit placed the Supreme Court in a difficult political position. If the Court ordered Madison to deliver the commission to him, it was very likely that

the order would be disobeyed, and the Court had no way of enforcing its orders. According to the Constitution, the judicial branch must rely on the executive branch to enforce its decrees. On the other hand, if the Court ruled against Marbury, then it would be supporting the Jefferson Administration. In a brilliant stroke, Chief Justice Marshall found a way to avoid a defiance of its ruling and extend judicial power at the same time. In the 1803 Marbury v. Madison case, Marshall wrote on behalf of the Federalist majority on the Court, declaring that while Marbury had a right to the position that President Adams had appointed him to, the Supreme Court did not have the authority to order the government to give him the commission that would finalize his placement in that position. In making this judgment, the Court declared that the portion of the Judiciary Act of 1789 that authorized the Court to issue such orders was unconstitutional.

This decision set a precedent for the eventual acceptance of the principle of judicial review. That is, because the Constitution was the fundamental law of the nation, and the Supreme Court had an obligation to uphold the law, the Supreme Court could determine if a given law violated the Constitution or not. Judicial review stood in direct opposition to the concept of nullification, the idea that state legislatures had that authority, an argument used by Democratic-Republicans in the Kentucky and Virginia Resolutions against the Alien and Sedition Acts. The Constitution does not directly answer the question about who has the authority to declare laws Constitutional or unconstitutional. Eventually, however, judicial review was accepted, although one could argue that the U.S. Civil War indirectly settled the issue once and for all, as it did the question about secession.

The Tripolitan War

The first foreign policy crisis faced by the Jefferson Administration involved the issue of paying tribute to the Barbary pirates. The term "Barbary coast" is named after the ethnic group of people often called Berbers and consists of the most northern portion of North Africa just north of the Sahara Desert and west of the Nile River, encompassing the small nations of Morocco, Algeria, Tunisia, and Tripoli (present-day Libya). Pirates along the Barbary coast, particularly in Tripoli, had been harassing shipping in the western Mediterranean Sea since the days of the Crusades. Nations had long paid tribute to these pirate states in order to prevent their ships from being molested. Even the United States, under Presidents Washington and Adams, had paid tribute. The Treaty of Tripoli, negotiated in 1796 and ratified in 1797, was supposed to end the practice, but Barbary pirates continued their practice of extortion as if there had been no treaty.

The crisis deepened in early 1801, when the pasha (ruler) of Tripoli demanded a greater share of tribute and then challenged the United States by cutting down the flagpole of the American consulate office in Tripoli in May of that year. This action amounted to an unofficial declaration of war. Despite his aversion to war, President Jefferson could not ignore this threat to the young republic, and he ordered the navy to exact a punishment on Tripoli. This undeclared Tripolitan War continued off and on until a peace treaty was signed in June 1805. In exchange for $60,000, which was basically ransom money to win the release of some American prisoners, the government of Tripoli ended its harassment of shipping. The other Barbary nations, though weakened by Tripoli's defeat, continued to exact tribute until 1816, when the total threat to Mediterranean shipping finally ended.

As a result of the Tripolitan War, the size of the U.S. Navy increased somewhat. President Jefferson believed that a fleet consisting of mostly small gunboats, the type that had been used in the war against Tripoli, could protect the American coastline without risking major conflict on the high seas. Nicknamed the "mosquito fleet," some 200 gunboats were built and put into service.

The Louisiana Purchase

In the middle of the Tripolitan War, another crisis threatened to draw the United States into a potentially much more serious armed conflict, this time with France. It concerned the port city of New Orleans and the much larger area of Louisiana, of which New Orleans was only a small part. Louisiana consisted of about 828,000 square miles and stretched from the

Gulf of Mexico in the south to British Canada in the north. The Mississippi River formed the eastern edge of Louisiana and the western boundary of the United States. By the turn of the nineteenth century, several hundred thousand Americans had moved into the Ohio and Mississippi River valleys, some 250,000 in Kentucky alone. Mostly farmers, they relied on those major rivers to ship their agricultural products to the eastern part of the nation. As of yet, adequate roads had not been built across the Appalachian Mountains, which formed a natural barrier dividing Americans on either side of it. Therefore, "road" travel across those mountains was too dangerous and thus too expensive, not only for getting western agricultural products to the East, but also in sending eastern manufactured goods to the West.

New Orleans was located next to the Mississippi River not far from where that river flowed southward into the Gulf of Mexico, making it an important port city. American farmers had to depend upon their ability to float their agricultural products down the river to New Orleans, where they could warehouse them until larger ships came to take them to the East coast.

When France lost the Seven Years' War (North Americans called it the French and Indian War), Spain acquired Louisiana in the 1763 Treaty of Paris. But in the Napoleonic Wars, begun in 1799, French Emperor Napoleon Bonaparte dreamed of reasserting French power and influence in North America. Spain was one nation among many in Europe that was at war with France at that time. In October 1800, a weakened Spain was forced to cede its claim to Louisiana back to France in the secret Treaty of Ildefonso. The treaty was not kept secret forever, however, and the Jefferson Administration learned of the plan to transfer Louisiana back to France in 1802. Jefferson knew that a militarily weak Spain was not a serious threat to Americans, as we could bide time until it became necessary to use force to seize New Orleans. But the prospect of that city being controlled by the French was a different matter altogether. France was a major power, and under Napoleon, it was also a major menace. American concern grew to alarming status when Spanish officials suddenly closed New Orleans to American use in October of 1802, just before the French were to actually take possession of Louisiana, and in violation of Pinckney's Treaty (1795).

Americans reacted angrily and talk of war was in the air. President Jefferson wanted no part in what he knew would be a major war. Moreover, he understood that America's only chance in a war with France was to make an alliance with Britain, and like Washington, the president hated the idea of entangling alliances. Yet Jefferson knew that he must act. Therefore, in early 1803, he sent Virginia Governor James Monroe as a personal envoy to Paris, France. He was sent to assist Robert R. Livingston, the American minister (ambassador) to France, who had been instructed to purchase New Orleans and as much territory to its east as possible. (The precise border between Louisiana and West Florida had not been established in the Treaty of Ildefonso.) They were officially authorized to spend a maximum of $2 million, but Jefferson privately told them to spend up to $10 million if necessary.

Even before Monroe arrived in Paris in April (1803), the French negotiator asked Livingston what the United States would be willing to pay for all of Louisiana. Napoleon had grown frustrated because of recent setbacks to his plans to reestablish French power in the western hemisphere. He had hoped to retake the Caribbean island that now includes Haiti and the Dominican Republic because it was a rich source of sugar cane. Louisiana would then serve as the source for most of the island's inhabitants' other food. However, a major revolt of that island's ex-slaves, led by Toussaint L'Ouverture, and a wave of mosquitoes carrying yellow fever discouraged Napoleon and drove him to focus on his grandiose schemes in Europe. At the same time, he was short on cash to resume his Napoleonic Wars, which he had suspended in 1801. Fearing that British naval supremacy might someday force him to grant Louisiana to the British, and knowing that New Orleans itself was virtually indefensible, Napoleon offered all of Louisiana to the Americans, in the hope that the United States would eventually become a major power to counter British influence in the western hemisphere.

On April 30, 1803, Livingston and Monroe signed three related treaties with France, pledging about $15 million for the entire Louisiana Territory, in exchange for certain French commercial privileges at the port of New Orleans. The significance of the Louisiana Purchase is that it doubled the size of the United States without war and for only about 3 cents an acre. Although only authorized to spend up to $10 million for the city of New Orleans, Livingston and Monroe had committed the nation to its largest land purchase ever.

When President Jefferson learned what Livingston and Monroe had done, he had mixed feelings. As a scientist and lover of nature, Jefferson had always been obsessed with the West and had dreamed of an "empire of liberty" extending all the way to the Pacific coast. He also knew that the low price was a "steal." However, as a strict constructionist, the president doubted that he had the Constitutional authority to make such a large land purchase because the Constitution said nothing about it. Purchasing a port city was one thing, but a major part of a large continent was something else. For a time, Jefferson leaned toward asking for a constitutional amendment that would give specific authorization for such a purchase. But his advisors finally persuaded him to scrap that idea as one which would take far too long, thus giving the untrustworthy Napoleon time to change his mind. So Jefferson submitted the treaties to the Senate, which quickly ratified them. The president allowed reality to change his thinking, and he would never again publicly voice support for strict constructionism.

Lewis and Clark Expedition

Even before the Louisiana Purchase, President Jefferson was eager to know more about the West. Of special interest was his desire to find a water route all the way to the Pacific Ocean, the famous Northwest Passage that the Spanish, French, and British had been trying to find ever since Columbus rediscovered the New World in 1492. The president believed that the Northwest Passage would bring prosperity to the nation that controlled it, so he also wanted to establish trading relationships with various Indian tribes and to thwart any potential domination of that region by the British who were based in Canada. To undertake this effort, in early 1803, Jefferson appointed Meriweather Lewis, a former army officer and his current personal secretary, to head up a major expedition to the northern portion of the Louisiana Territory and on to the Pacific. At Lewis' request, the president agreed that William Clark, the younger brother of Revolutionary War hero General George Rogers Clark, would be co-leader with Lewis.

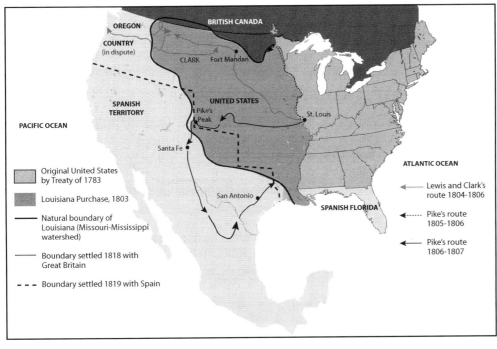

FIGURE 9.3 - Exploring the Louisiana Purchase and the West.

Clark was also a former soldier and had had experience with Indians. Lewis was in his late 20s at the time, and Clark was just a few years older than Lewis, making both of them physically capable of conducting the expedition.

News of the Louisiana Purchase only served to increase the meaningfulness of the planned expedition. The Lewis and Clark Expedition officially began in May 1804, when a party of nearly four dozen men left the St. Louis area. This group of experienced frontiersmen, which Jefferson nicknamed the Corps of Discovery, also included William Clark's slave York. The Corps journeyed by water up the Missouri River, collecting samples of soil, plant life, even a few live animals (including a prairie dog), and creating a better map of the regions they entered. In October of the same year, they arrived among the Mandan Indians and spent the winter with them near present-day Bismarck, North Dakota, in a place they built and called Fort Mandan. There they hired a French-Canadian man as a guide because his young teenage Shoshone Indian wife Sacajawea knew the languages and the terrain of the mountain tribes to the west, from which she had been originally stolen. Sacajawea proved to be an enormous help to the Corps of Discovery, although she, along with the slave York, was never officially acknowledged for service to the expedition.

At Fort Mandan, Lewis and Clark sent more than a dozen men back to St. Louis with the big keelboat loaded with their collected samples and other goods to eventually be presented to President Jefferson. This left a party of 33 people, including Sacajawea's young son who had been born that winter, to continue the journey in April 1806, crossing the Rocky Mountains, going down the Snake and Columbia Rivers (beyond the Louisiana Territory), and heading to the Pacific coast, which they reached in November 1805 in what is now Oregon. Crossing the Rockies was the toughest part of the entire voyage, for the expedition suffered great cold and hunger, once killing a horse in order to avoid starvation. They spent that winter near the Pacific coast and began their journey home the next March. By late September 1806, the party arrived back in St. Louis, officially ending their nearly 2½ year expedition.

As might be expected, the members of the Corps of Discovery were welcomed back as national heroes. The expedition seemed to boost William Clark's career, but curiously, it did not seem to do Meriwether Lewis any good. He died under somewhat mysterious circumstances a short time later, although his death was ruled a suicide. It probably was, for Lewis would be classified today as a manic-depressive, and he never recovered emotionally from the trip.

Although the Lewis and Clark Expedition was the first official exploration of new lands in the history of the nation, other explorers soon followed into the West. Foremost among them was Zebulon Pike, who "discovered" the mountain peak that bears his name (Pike's Peak) in what is now Colorado in 1807. As for statehood, Louisiana became the first state to be carved out of the Louisiana Territory when it officially entered

FIGURE 9.4 - Meriwether Lewis and William Clark

the Union on April 30, 1812, exactly nine years after Robert Livingston and James Monroe had formally pledged that the United States would make the Louisiana Purchase.

The Essex Junto and Aaron Burr

Not every American was happy with the acquisition of the Louisiana Territory. Most Federalists feared that New England, the center of their influence, would eventually lose any meaningful political clout as the nation moved further west into the Territory. The West did not hold much promise for manufacturing interests. Therefore, it was widely believed that a majority of citizens who moved there, as family farmers and small-business merchants, would be typical Democratic-Republican voters. It seemed, then, that the Federalist Party was facing the proverbial handwriting on the wall.

While not representing a majority of Federalists, a group of extremists within that party organized the Essex Junto. The word *Essex* is the name of the county in Massachusetts that many of the group came from; the word *Junto* simply refers to a group of people with a common purpose. Led by Massachusetts Senator Timothy Pickering, the Essex Junto concluded that secession from the United States was their only hope for retaining political power and influence. The Junto conspired to create a northern confederacy out of the five New England states and New York.

New York was deemed to be the key state, both financially and politically. So the Essex Junto needed a governor who would be part of their conspiracy, someone who would be in the best position to help lead that state to secede from the Union and become part of a new nation. State elections were scheduled in New York for June 1804, and a new governor would be elected then. The Essex Junto approached Alexander Hamilton, the most famous Federalist of his era, and asked him to run for governor and support their goal. But Hamilton rejected their offer, not because he was a great patriot, but because he sincerely believed that the French Revolution (1789-1799), with its social meltdown, would soon be exported to the United States, and he envisioned himself as the American "Napoleon" who would pick up the pieces afterwards.

Rejected by Hamilton, the leaders of the conspiracy next focused their attention on Vice President Aaron Burr. Although he was a Democratic-Republican, Burr was also well known for his radical, maverick style. Furthermore, by 1804, he had so embarrassed the Jefferson Administration because of repeatedly and publicly sticking his foot in his mouth that he knew Jefferson would not accept him as a running mate later in that year's presidential election. Whatever Burr actually knew about the Essex Junto conspiracy has never been precisely determined. However, he did run as the Federalist candidate for governor of New York in the spring of 1804. During the campaign, Alexander Hamilton let it be known publicly that Burr was part of a secession plot. Hamilton's comments ruined his chances and guaranteed his defeat. Burr blamed Hamilton for his defeat and eventually challenged him to a duel. Even though his own son Philip had been killed in a duel in 1801, Hamilton accepted the challenge because he believed his honor was at stake. Besides, if his refusal to fight Burr in a duel were ever made public, it would ruin Hamilton's image as an American "Napoleon." Because dueling was illegal in New York, the two men met across the Hudson River from New York City in Weehawken, New Jersey, on July 11, 1804. Ironically, it was at the same site where Hamilton's son had been killed in his duel. And in another amazing twist, the pistols used in the Hamilton-Burr duel were the same ones used in Philip Hamilton's duel, having been borrowed each time from Alexander Hamilton's brother-in-law. When Burr and Hamilton took the necessary number of steps and turned to fire, Hamilton never fired on purpose (the hair trigger on his pistol did accidentally fire high in the air), apparently believing that the vice president would not do so either. That was Hamilton's last mistake, for Burr did fire, hitting the former Secretary of the Treasury, who died the next day. Burr was then indicted for murder in New Jersey, while New York officials indicted him for issuing a challenge to a duel, a misdemeanor in New York. A lack of extradition procedures in those days meant that Burr would not be arrested as long as he remained outside of those two states. Instead, he stayed with friends in South Carolina, until he returned to Washington, D.C. in November 1804 to resume his duties as the presiding officer of the U.S. Senate. Meanwhile, all charges against him were dropped in New Jersey and New York.

Soon after he left the vice presidency in March 1805, Burr became embroiled in a plot with General James Wilkinson, the governor of the Louisiana Territory. Their ultimate goal is a bit sketchy to this day, but it definitely involved the raising of a private army and establishing some kind of independent country in the southwest part of the continent. Some evidence suggests that Burr had dreams of glory as an emperor of this new country. In the fall of 1806, Burr and about 60 other men started down the Ohio River headed for the Mississippi River and ultimately, to meet General Wilkinson at Natchez, in present-day Mississippi. Meanwhile, however, Wilkinson had changed his mind and turned against Burr, even writing a letter to President Jefferson confessing his role in the plot, before fleeing to New Orleans. Eventually, Vice President Burr was arrested, and in 1807 he was tried on the charge of federal treason in Richmond, Virginia, with Chief Justice John Marshall presiding over the trial. When all the testimony had been heard, the evidence only proved that Burr had taken part in conversations where he had spoken approvingly of a vague plot. Marshall interpreted the Constitution strictly, and because it requires evidence from at least two witnesses to an overt act, he instructed the jury to return a "not proved" verdict. The jury did so, and Burr was released.

With his political career and reputation now ruined, Aaron Burr fled the country and ended up in Paris, France. There he tried to persuade Napoleon to make peace with his arch-enemy Great Britain and to help create a French-Anglo armed force to attack the United States (and possibly Mexico) and install him as the emperor there. But while Napoleon was many things, being stupid was not one of them, so he completely ignored Burr's suggestions.

Then in 1812, Burr returned to the United States and resumed his law practice in New York. However, Burr's character led him to father two illegitimate children in his 70s, was divorced for adultery at the age of 80, and finally died of natural causes in 1836. What a life! And what makes it even stranger is the fact that Aaron Burr was the grandson of the famous Great Awakening preacher, Jonathan Edwards; Burr's mother was Edwards' daughter. Moreover, Burr's own father was a Protestant minister who became just the second president of what later became known as Princeton University.

The 1804 Presidential Election

Having dumped Aaron Burr, President Jefferson's running mate in 1804 was George Clinton of New York. Jefferson's Federalist opponent that year was Charles C. Pinckney of South Carolina. During the campaign, Jefferson reminded voters that his administration had repealed the hated Alien and Sedition Acts, acquired the Louisiana Territory, and reduced the national debt. Federalists made a weak attempt to accuse Jefferson of overreaching his presidential authority in making the Louisiana Purchase, but their campaign never gained much traction. Jefferson won a landslide election, sweeping fifteen of the seventeen states with an electoral margin of 162 to 14.

THE WAR OF 1812

Background

For the new nation, there was a short time span between its first war with Great Britain for independence and its second war with Britain to actually secure that independence. Following the American Revolution, the United States existed in an uneasy truce with Britain. Both countries claimed land in Maine, the British were slow to give up their seven forts south of the Great Lakes (the 1796 Jay's Treaty resolved this issue), and British alliances with Native Americans threatened Americans moving west. This uneasy truce would eventually be interrupted, largely by the United States becoming caught in the middle of a war between Britain and France.

The French Revolution (1789-1799) had resulted in Napoleon Bonaparte, a military strongman, taking over France as a self-proclaimed emperor. Napoleon, of course, was not content to be the emperor of France. Because emperors must have empires, Napoleon proceeded to start a series of wars with other nations in Europe and especially with Britain. The Napoleonic Wars against Britain were fought in two major stages, from 1793-1801 and again from 1803-1814. Beginning in 1806, the British issued a series of Orders in Council that barred foreign shipping from entering ports under French control. The French also announced with several decrees that Britain was under a blockade. These "paper blockades" technically violated international law, but a nation like Britain, who held naval supremacy on the high seas, often ignores legal niceties when they believe they can get away with it. These British and French actions put the United States in a most difficult position because both sides were attempting to cut off American trade with the other side, an attempt that both violated our rights of neutrality and endangered the American economy because of our extensive trade relations with both nations. Despite those violations, large numbers of American merchants experienced huge profits until late in the Napoleonic Wars. In fact, American trade with

FIGURE 9.5 - Crewmen of Chesapeake prepare cannon, 1807.

foreign countries more than doubled from 1791-1807.

Freedom of the Seas

Although both sides were guilty of violating American neutrality, British violations were felt more negatively than French violations, principally because the British navy was still the most powerful navy in the world at that time. One major example of British violations included British warships waiting off the United States coast and then seizing whole cargo (or merchant) ships as they entered international waters, stealing the cargo and not returning the ships. However, the British violation that angered Americans even more was the policy of impressment. The British navy had a major desertion problem because of its harsh discipline. To compensate for that, the British would often stop American merchant ships in international waters, board them, forcibly remove anyone they accused of being a British naval deserter, and impress them into serving in their navy. Such impressments were sometimes even practiced when an American vessel was in one of its own harbors. Some of those whom the British impressed were indeed British deserters carrying fraudulent papers. However, many were also American citizens. Approximately 6,000 Americans were impressed into the British Royal Navy from 1803 to 1812.

The most serious incident occurred in June 1807, when, for the first time, a British warship attacked an American naval vessel. When the *HMS Leopard* attempted to stop the *USS Chesapeake* off the coast of Virginia, the American commander initially refused. The British then fired upon the *Chesapeake*, killing three Americans and wounding 18 others. Four sailors were then impressed into the British navy.

The Hated Embargo Act

In growing frustration at both British and French harassment, Congress enacted the Embargo Act in December 1807, about six months after the *Chesapeake* incident. The Embargo Act was an extreme measure, prohibiting all exports from the United States, in both American and foreign ships. President Jefferson knew that both sides depended on the United States for a significant portion of their food and raw materials during the Napoleonic Wars. He hoped that by depriving them of these things, such "peaceful coercion" (Jefferson's term) would cause both nations to agree to allow America to trade freely again. However, this law had no positive impact on British or French policies toward Americans. Instead, several Latin American nations increased their trade with Britain, thereby helping to compensate for the reduction in trade with the United States. Britain also experienced several years of bumper grain harvests during this time. Finally, Napoleon compensated by taking what France needed from other parts of Europe under his control.

Rather than affect British and French policies toward Americans, the embargo succeeded in significantly reducing America's foreign trade, thus hurting the economy in the short term, especially in New England. The embargo was hated in that region, where many did a brisk illegal trade along the Canadian border, converting the word *embargo* into protest words like "Mobrage" and "Dambargo." Hatred for President Jefferson increased as well, helping to galvanize the Federalist Party. Although Jefferson's Secretary of State, James Madison, was elected president in 1808, the Federalist Party candidate, Charles C. Pinckney, won more than three times as many electoral votes as he had garnered in 1804.

Frustrated by the failure of the embargo to change British or French policies, Congress repealed the Embargo Act on March 1, 1809, just three days before the inauguration of James Madison. The policy of using economic coercion did not end, however, for the Embargo Act was replaced by the Non-Intercourse Act of 1809, which allowed American trade with every nation except Britain and France, who were our two most important trading partners.

A long-term benefit of the embargoes was to provide great incentive for more American manufacturing, in order to compensate for the significant lack of imports from other nations. Thomas Jefferson and his Democratic-Republican Party were the political champions of farmers and feared an economy dominated by manufacturing interests. Ironically, however, President Jefferson and his fellow Democratic-Republicans probably did more to promote industrialization in America than even the Federalist leader, Alexander Hamilton, had done. The embargoes and the War of 1812 combined to help give rise to the factory system in the years after the war.

Declaring War

Macon's Bill No. 2

When the Non-Intercourse Act expired in 1810, Congress replaced it with Macon's Bill No. 2. This new law opened economic trade with Britain and France, but if either nation ended its harassment of American shipping, the president was authorized to restore the embargo against the other one. Although President Madison had not favored this bill, this was Congress' way of using the proverbial carrot rather than the stick to coax one or both nations to respect the freedom of the seas. Hoping to prompt the United States into restoring its embargo against Britain, Napoleon sent vaguely-written word in August 1810 that France might stop its harassment of American shipping. President Madison, while not trusting Napoleon, hoped that the mere prospect of America trading with France and not Britain would lead the British to end its harassment. But his hope quickly evaporated, as French harassment continued. Moreover, by formally accepting Napoleon's message as a promise to end harassment, the provision in Macon's Bill No. 2 giving Britain three months to ends its harassment became effective. Britain ignored the deadline, and finally in the spring of 1811, President Madison reestablished the embargo against Britain.

War Hawks Help Lead the Nation to War

In the 1810 Congressional elections, a group of young firebrands, mostly from the South and the West, were elected on promises to secure America from all threats. Known as the War Hawks, they dominated the House of Representatives. Henry Clay from Kentucky, one of the leaders of the War Hawks, became Speaker of the House and a dominant force in politics for years to come. John

C. Calhoun of South Carolina was another firebrand. While these War Hawks were definitely concerned about the threat on the high seas, they were also very concerned about the threat from the Native Americans, as white Americans moved further west. The Native Americans were viewed as a menace to settlers, and many thought that the British were stirring the Indian tribes into an anti-American mindset. Therefore, eliminating the British presence in Canada would eliminate that threat. Moreover, the idea of acquiring Canada as American territory was an enticement for some Americans to want to eliminate British control to the north.

The motto of "Free Trade and Sailors' Rights" along with the anti-British sentiments of the western and southern states sealed the fate of the nation toward a path of war. President James Madison sent a war message to Congress on June 1, 1812. Madison gave Congress five reasons for going to war against Great Britain in 1812: (1) impressment of American sailors, (2) blockades of the American coast, (3) blockades preventing American ships from docking on European coasts, (4) confiscation of American ships at sea, and (5) the incitement of Indian hostility in the Northwest. The United States Congress declared war on June 18, 1812, with a vote of 79-49 in the House and 19-13 in the Senate. The vote for passage was close and indicated the division in the country. The parties were also divided, with the Federalists not supportive of the war (not a single Federalist member of Congress voted for the war) and the Republicans supportive of the war. In fact, the Federalists mockingly referred to it as "Mr. Madison's War." New England and the Mid-Atlantic states were unenthusiastic about the war at best, but fervent support came from the western and southern states.

Causes of the War

Historians have long debated the true causes of the War of 1812. Was it for American rights on the seas, putting the British in their place on the continent, protecting American pride and independence, or a war of expansion against the British in Canada and the Indians in the West? For many it was a combination of factors. Americans were certainly angered over the impressment of many of their fellow citizens. Yet ironically, most Americans in New England, the region most affected by impressment and other violations of American neutrality, opposed the war

throughout its entirety. Instead, the war was promoted more by the agrarian interests of the West and South, which were not as affected by what was happening at sea. It is also clear that American pride, or national honor, was a contributing factor, as many Americans believed that Britain had never really accepted American independence. This factor is reflected in the alternate name for this war, the Second War for Independence. It is equally clear that many Westerners also saw war with Britain as an excuse to take more land from tribal Indians, because it was assumed that they would ally themselves with the British, a factor that historians usually call the Western Cause. While historians debate which one of these causes was the single most important one, it cannot be doubted that each of these factors played a role in taking the nation into war.

This war could have been avoided if the United States had had just a little more patience. Ironically, the British government agreed to relax the Orders in Council on June 16, 1812, just two days before the American declaration of war. However, that news did not reach the United States until after the declaration of war, because the telegraph had not yet been invented. There simply was no way to know, given the state of communications technology in 1812. The country was emotionally ready for war except for New England, and this was the section most affected by the actions of the British because of its overseas commercial trade interests. The course was set for war even though the nation was divided on the issue.

Preparing to Fight

The United States faced economic challenges as it commenced the War of 1812. The economy had been weakened by 4½ years of varying degrees of embargoes. Also, when the Bank of the United States was not rechartered in 1811, the financial system was left without a unifying force. Furthermore, federal funds for a military venture were short because of years of tightening the budget by the Democratic-Republicans.

The Army

Militarily, the country was no better off. The regular army was extremely small, with approximately 11,700 officers and men, due to budget cuts and a traditional suspicion of a standing army. The war effort had to rely heavily on the poorly trained state militias, which raised approximately 35,000 troops. Undoubtedly, more recruits would have enlisted if supplies for the soldiers had been at least adequate and if the War Department had not fallen behind in paying the soldiers. At the beginning of the war, British land forces from Canada stood at approximately 5,000 regular soldiers and 3,000 militiamen. The British also used Indian allies to boost their forces. The bulk of British forces, luckily for the Americans, were involved with the war in Europe.

In the early stages of the war, the American senior officers were not the best and the brightest. They had their training in the field during the American Revolution and were generally too old and timid to lead effectively. There were a few competent officers, but Winfield Scott, one of the talented few, labeled the rest as "imbeciles and ignoramuses." It would take two years for President Madison to improve the overall leadership of the military forces.

The Navy

On the seas, the Americans were greatly outnumbered but did well during the first year of the war. The British navy had spared approximately 79 ocean-going ships out of over a thousand to the 16 of the United States. The British in the early years of the conflict focused on defeating France and keeping it bottled up. Once Britain defeated France, America bore the brunt of the full force of British attention. A tight blockade of the American coast was the result. American privateers, however, were quite successful at devastating British commercial shipping in the war. About 1,350 British merchant ships fell to the privateers. The injured commercial interests of the British merchant class became such a problem that the merchants began to clamor for peace.

The Attack on Canada: 1812

The Americans perceived Canada as an easy target from the early days when war was only a consideration. On July 5, 1812, General William Hull, governor of the Michigan Territory and a former officer in the American

Revolution, arrived at Fort Detroit to take command of the forces that were to invade Canada in that area. Most of the enemy in this part of Canada was at Fort Malden, which was about 20 miles south of Detroit. Instead of taking advantage of the small number of British troops, Canadian militiamen, and Indians led by the great Shawnee Chief Tecumseh, Hull stayed just across the river in Canada and sent out several raiding detachments to engage the enemy. After the fall of the American Fort Michilimackinac (July 12, 1812), guarding the Upper Great Lakes, Hull retreated back to Fort Detroit. When the British General Sir Isaac Brock arrived at Fort Detroit, General Hull surrendered on August 16. In the meantime, Fort Dearborn (present-day Chicago) was abandoned (also in August) when the small contingent there marched toward Fort Detroit in an effort to reinforce it. Unfortunately, however, those troops were massacred on their journey, not knowing of Fort Detroit's surrender. This left the entire area north and west of Ohio in enemy hands. It was a very inauspicious beginning for the Americans. After serving time as a prisoner of war, Hull returned to face a court-martial. The general was found guilty of cowardice and sentenced to be shot, but President Madison pardoned him because of his service to the country in the Revolutionary War.

Invading Canada from the Fort Detroit area had been part of a three-pronged American strategy aimed at Canada. The Niagara and Lake Champlain areas were also scheduled as bases from which to invade that region

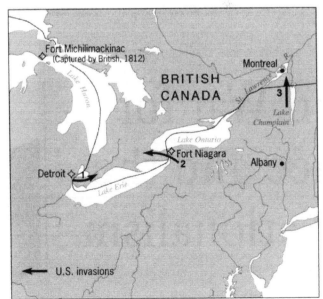

FIGURE 9.6 - The Three U.S. Invasions of 1812.

in the second half of 1812. Those invasions also failed miserably, due to the fact that New York militiamen refused to cross the border into Canada. Americans were defeated in the Niagara area at the Battle of Queenstown in October 1812, and failure to enter Canada thwarted an attempt to take the city of Montreal.

The only bright spot for the Americans in 1812 was the land victory of Captain Zachary Taylor, whose forces successfully defended Fort Harrison in Indiana Territory in September. Despite that victory, this was one of the bleakest times in history for the American military. By the winter of 1812-1813, the British controlled about half of the entire Northwest region.

Frigates and Victories at Sea: 1812

Almost the only American victories in 1812 occurred at sea. The small American navy was more eager and prepared for war than the army. The officers were also more capable. As soon as word spread concerning the declaration of war, ships cleared New York harbor and missed the forthcoming British blockade. The general strategy of the navy was to disrupt British maritime trade and avoid British warships. On August 19, the American ship *Constitution* defeated the British *Guerrier* in the Atlantic. The *Constitution* gained its nickname of "Old Ironsides" in this battle when shots bounced off its thick oak hull. The American navy defeated or captured three more ships in quick order. The American victories at sea in 1812 barely made a dent in the British supremacy of the sea. But they did prompt *The Times* newspaper in London to ask, "What is wrong with British sea power?"

Madison Wins Reelection

The year 1812 was a presidential election year, and the Democratic-Republicans nominated President James Madison for reelection to another term. Despite the dismal failures in the land war that year, the Federalists knew it would be almost impossible to win a presidential election during wartime. Therefore, they tried to appeal to Democratic-Republicans discontented with the war by nominating the Democratic-Republican mayor of

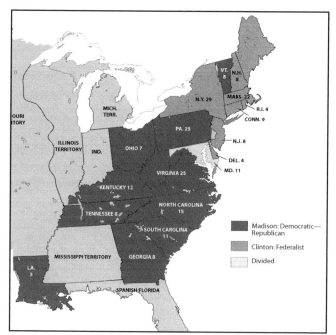

FIGURE 9.7 - Presidential Election of 1812 (with electoral vote by state).

New York City, DeWitt Clinton, to run against Madison. The Federalist strategy failed, however, as Madison won reelection by a margin of 128 to 89 electoral votes, much closer than his first victory four years earlier. While these results did reflect uncertainty about the war, most historians believe that the success of the American navy that year boosted morale in the country and helped Madison in his bid for a second term.

At Sea: 1813 and 1814

By 1813 the American frigates were effectively stymied either by the blockade along the American coast or the strength of the British navy at sea. By the end of 1813, only the *Constitution* and the *Essex* were at sea. At the end of 1814, even the *Constitution* was bottled up in port. Destroying British commerce was now up to the American privateers and their ships. Their favorite hunting grounds were in the Caribbean, but they also ranged into the North Sea and the Indian Ocean, attacking British merchant ships as well as military transports. The British lost 1,345 vessels to the privateers with a great loss to the merchants, as well as causing the price of their insurance to skyrocket.

In 1814, the British blockade was damaging the American economy by greatly interrupting the flow

FIGURE 9.8 - Drawing of Tecumseh and W.H. Harrison

of imports and exports. This particularly damaged the economy of New England and led to Americans there trading with the enemy. This was not only illegal, but it was also an act of treason.

Regaining the Northwest: 1813

Victory on the Great Lakes

By mid-August 1813, Commandant Oliver Hazard Perry was ready to challenge the British gunboats on Lake Erie, thanks largely to Noah Brown, a shipbuilder who built several ships on the shores of Lake Erie. Approximately one-fourth of Perry's 400 men were free blacks. At the west end of Lake Erie, Perry took out his nine ships of various sizes and engaged the British commander, Robert Barclay, and his six ships at Put-in-Bay, near present-day Sandusky, Ohio. Perry's command ship, the *Lawrence*, was destroyed, but he left the ship in spite of the flag flying over the ship with the motto, "Don't give up the ship." Perry boarded the *Niagara* and won the engagement on September 10. His message to General Harrison at the end of the battle was encouraging to all troops, "We have met the enemy and they are ours."

On to Canada

In April 1813, several months before Perry's victory at Put-in-Bay, a 1,600-man brigade under General Zebulon Pike had landed at York (present-day Toronto), the capital of Upper Canada. His troops drove off the Canadian defenders, looted houses, and burned government buildings. The British later repaid this insult in kind in the capital city of the United States.

Perry's victory in the Battle of Lake Erie gave the Americans control of that lake, boosted American morale, and forced the British to evacuate Fort Detroit and Fort Malden. Meanwhile, General William Henry Harrison, the victor at the battle against the Shawnee at Tippecanoe in 1811, was sent to the Northwest to secure the area. In 1813, Harrison built a fortified camp 60 miles south of Detroit and named it Fort Meigs. From there, he was ready to launch a major attack on Canada.

Perry then used his small force of ships to take Harrison's troops across Lake Erie, and on October 5, 1813, Harrison caught up with the British at the Thames River in southern Canada. Indians under Tecumseh formed the left flank in the battle. The Americans were fierce in this battle, for many wanted revenge for the massacre of fellow Americans at Raisin River. The battle went to the Americans. It was during this battle that the great Indian leader Tecumseh was killed.

There were several important results from the Battle of the Thames. First, the Indians lost the cohesive force of Tecumseh, and with him, the last best chance to ever stop American expansionism. Second, the United States now had control of western Canada. Third, the Northwest region was secure, with Lake Erie no longer accessible to the British. Finally, the country could now celebrate a major victory.

Now that the western portions of Canada were secure, General James Wilkinson was brought up north to coordinate an attack on Montreal and attempt to secure the eastern portions of Canada. At Chrysler's Point on November 11, 1813, Wilkinson's forces were routed and he retreated back across the border into New York. The British then invaded New York. Other American forces retreated from Canada, burning the Canadian towns of Newark and Queenston along the way. The British retaliated by attacking Fort Niagara, Black Rock, and Buffalo. Their Indian allies also were sent across the border, spreading terror across upper New York.

1814

In April 1814, Napoleon surrendered to the British in France and was exiled to the Mediterranean island of Elba. The United States had used the Napoleonic Wars as a kind of shield behind which to go to war against Britain. Now the Americans were destined to face thousands of new British troops, a reality which threatened to change the course of the war. Approximately 15,000 British troops were soon on their way to Canada.

War in Eastern Canada

Americans attacked again along the Niagara frontier before the British could reinforce their troops in Canada. They captured Fort Erie and won the Battle of the Chippewa on July 5, 1814. The Americans then met an enlarged force of troops, and the Battle of Lundy's Lane was a standoff on July 25. The Americans retreated back to New York. The British then planned a three-pronged attack to secure victory. There would be a naval invasion along the Chesapeake Bay (1814), a land invasion from Canada along the Hudson River to cut off New England (1814), and an attack on New Orleans (1815) at the mouth of the Mississippi River, which was a key to the West.

The British Invasion up the Chesapeake Bay

On August 19, 1814, a British force under the command of General Robert Ross landed on the coast of Maryland 30 miles southeast of Washington, D.C. They defeated the green American troops at the Battle of Bladensburg. President Madison and his cabinet members had ridden horses to the battle site, vainly trying to rally the militiamen there, who fled in chaos. This was the worst performance of American troops up to this time. Now nothing stood between the capital city and the British army. The British entered Washington and proceeded on August 24 to set fire to the Capitol building, the

presidential mansion, and other public buildings, in retaliation against the American burning of York the previous year. First Lady Dolley Madison was in the city as the British were closing in. She stayed as late as possible, hoping the president would come and also to pack as many state papers as she could. Mrs. Madison saved the portrait of George Washington. When British troops entered the mansion, they found warm dinner plates on the dining table, indicating a very close call for the First Lady. A short time later, the British army moved out and headed for nearby Baltimore, Maryland, an important industrial and financial center.

The people of Baltimore prepared to fight the British this time, even though the British attacked on land and sea (by way of the Chesapeake Bay). The Americans fought two skirmishes before retreating into the city itself. British ships tried to force Fort McHenry, near the coastal edge, into surrendering. For 25 hours, they bombarded the fort. At dawn on September 14, the American flag still waved. This inspired an American witness to the bombardment, Francis Scott Key, who had been detained on a British warship during a humanitarian mission, to write a poem commemorating the event. This poem, entitled "The Star-Spangled Banner," was one of two or three unofficial national anthems until Congress passed a resolution officially naming it as the national anthem in 1931. After the British failed to capture Baltimore, they withdrew from the Chesapeake Bay.

The Battle of Plattsburgh

At the same time the people of Baltimore were defending their city, the British began an invasion of upper New York from Canada in an effort to cut off New England from the rest of the war. Approximately 10,000 British troops were involved in this campaign. However, because of the lack of roads, all of their supplies had to be shipped across Lake Champlain and down the Hudson River, which flowed from that lake. A smaller American fleet, commanded by Thomas Macdonough, bravely met the British supply boats on the lake near Plattsburgh, New York, on September 11, 1814. Macdonough won an unexpected victory, forcing the British to retreat back into Canada and saving New York. The war was stalled in the North and East but became active in the South.

The Creek War

Before turning our attention to the British invasion at New Orleans, it is important to address the southern situation in the context of the Creek War. The situation in the Creek nation brought the attention of the government to the Southeast. Many young members of the Creek tribe rallied to Tecumseh's cause of a united Indian confederation; Tecumseh's mother had been a Creek. The Creek tribe divided into the Upper Creek towns (Red Sticks), who wanted to return to the traditional way of life, and the Lower Creek towns, who were more assimilated into the American way of life. A civil war broke out when the Lower Creek chiefs executed several Red Stick members for their massacre of two white families. The Red Sticks then attempted to destroy all things associated with the white man. On August 30, 1813, the Red Sticks attacked Fort Mims in Mississippi Territory. Out of 575 Americans, only 17 escaped death or enslavement.

With the regular army occupied by the War of 1812, southern states called up their militias to put down the Creek threat. As early as December 1812, Andrew Jackson's Tennessee militia was ready to fight the Creeks. But a lack of supplies had demoralized his men and halted his operations by late 1813. But after Jackson executed John Woods for insubordination and mutiny in March 1814, his militia was ready to fight the Creeks again. Approximately 600 Cherokee warriors joined Jackson in the fight against the Red Sticks. The decisive battle in the war occurred at a fortified Red Stick position at Horseshoe Bend on the Tallapoosa River in March 1814. The Creeks refused terms of surrender, so Jackson defeated them soundly after allowing the women and children to leave the battle site. After this Battle of Horseshoe Bend, the Creeks signed the Treaty of Fort Jackson, ceding 23 million acres of land in Alabama and Georgia to the United States and moving to the most western part of the Mississippi Territory. Shortly after this, Andrew Jackson became a major-general in the regular army.

After his victory at Horseshoe Bend, Jackson was instructed to disband his troops. He later claimed that he did not receive the letter until after he had sent troops into Spanish Florida. His aim in Florida was to prevent a British invasion of Pensacola as a staging ground for further mischief by the British, which he did by seizing it in November 1814. The Spanish were neutral in the war, and the American government did not want to do anything to alienate the Spanish. However, allowing the British to use Florida was intolerable to Jackson.

The Hartford Convention

In October 1814, finally fed up with what they perceived as an unnecessary and detrimental war, the Massachusetts legislature sent out a call for delegates to attend a conference to discuss the war and the position of New England. Meeting at Hartford, Connecticut, from December 15, 1814 to January 5, 1815, delegates came from Connecticut, Massachusetts, Rhode Island, New Hampshire, and Vermont. Some members at the Hartford Convention wanted to secede from the Union, but this was rejected by most of the delegates, although a resolution justifying secession as a last resort was passed. They finally managed to write several proposed amendments to the Constitution that they felt would counteract the power of the South. Among these were proposals to require a two-thirds majority vote in Congress for any future declaration of war and to prohibit the election of two consecutive presidents from the same state. These proposals were all ignored by the nation as a whole and never adopted. Soon after the Hartford Convention ended, news reached the nation of the glorious American victory at New Orleans. The timing could not have been worse for the Federalists, whose debate and resolutions at the convention resulted in a widespread public perception that they were treasonous. The Federalist Party never recovered after that, and it soon disappeared except in the history books.

Battle of New Orleans

General Jackson received word from spies that New Orleans faced attack soon. So he left his position in Mobile (now in Alabama) on the Gulf Coast and headed for New Orleans to take charge of defending the important port city. After arriving on December 1, 1814, Jackson began work immediately on improving the defenses of the city and organizing the people. The

British found an unguarded bayou outside of New Orleans that they could use to bring in land forces and attack the city. Jackson discovered the British and mounted a night attack with regular army troops, militia, two battalions of free blacks, a group of Choctaw Indians, and a group of pirates led by Jean Lafitte, whose men Jackson had promised pardons in return for their help at New Orleans. The Americans retreated from the skirmish, but took up positions a few miles west of the enemy and dug in. By December 27, the British, under the command of General Sir Edward Pakenham, had amassed about 6,000 troops, and on December 28, they advanced toward the American line. Jackson managed to fortify his line with a strong defensive rampart. In front of the rampart was a ditch four feet deep and 10 feet wide. The British attacked the line without success and sent men back to the fleet for more artillery and a request for more troops. The final British attack occurred on January 8, 1815. The British charged repeatedly but lost the battle. British casualties numbered 2,036 men. About one-third of that number were killed, including Pakenham. Approximately 500 British were captured as prisoners of war. American casualties were eight killed and 13 wounded, although these American numbers vary among different sources. This was the greatest American victory since the Battle of Yorktown during the Revolutionary War.

Treaty of Ghent

In 1812, the Russian government had offered to try to mediate an end to the war. In 1813, President Madison formally accepted this offer, but the British rejected it. Peace talks between the United States and Britain finally began in August 1814 in Ghent, Belgium. But the British delayed serious peace negotiations for some time, hoping to win the war outright and gain territory as well. Before the British defeat at New Orleans, the Americans offered peace on the terms of *status quo ante bellum*, everything as it was before the war. But not until news reached Great Britain of the retreat from New York and the loss at Baltimore, along with pressure from the English people to stop subjecting them to such a costly war, was Britain ready to seriously consider ending the war without victory. The negotiators agreed to peace and signed the Treaty of Ghent on December 24, 1814. In another strange twist of fate, the state of communications in the early 19th century meant that the Battle of New Orleans was fought just over two weeks after the peace treaty had been signed in Europe.

The Treaty of Ghent resolved none of the issues that had led to the War of 1812, for neither neutral rights nor impressment were even mentioned in that document. So many claimed later that the war was not actually about these two issues. All territorial possessions remained as they had been before the war.

Results of the War

If the Treaty of Ghent was essentially a return to the *status quo*, then what had the war accomplished? Actually, there were several major and minor results of this war, as outlined below.

Major Results of the War

The War of 1812 restored American pride and national honor, and a wave of nationalism swept the nation, even in New England. It also gave America a national identity among other nations and announced that the United States had arrived on the world stage, although not yet as a world power.

The war also helped create two important national heroes, William Henry Harrison and Andrew Jackson, both of whom would become later presidents of the country. In another political result, Federalist opposition to the war caused that party's extinction soon after.

Along with the embargoes of the prewar era, the War of 1812 gave rise to a powerful new incentive to increase manufacturing in the nation. This helped contribute to the development of the factory system after the war, a development that in turn proved to be a prerequisite to the Industrial Revolution after the country's Civil War.

Finally, the power of American Indians to prevent further Western American expansion was forever broken. The key reason for this result was that never again would any Indian tribe have a European ally to arm them or to fight with them.

Minor Results of the War

The presidential mansion received its current name of the White House as a result of the remodeling and repainting made necessary by British fire and smoke damage in August 1814. Someone asking for the location of the presidential mansion was told that it was that white house down Pennsylvania Avenue. The name of White House has stuck ever since.

Our national anthem, "The Star-Spangled Banner," came out of this war when Francis Scott Key penned its words aboard a British warship in September 1814, although Congress did not get around to making it the official national anthem until 1931.

Finally, the name "Uncle Sam" to designate the United States government was a result of the War of 1812. Sam Wilson was a Troy, New York meat-packer who sold meat to the U.S. Army during the war. When government officials made a surprise visit to his place of business one day during the war, Sam was absent. However, his employees gave the officials a tour of the workplace. Noticing the letters *U.S.* stamped on several meat barrels, one of the officials asked if they represented the United States. He was told that instead, they referred to Uncle Sam, an affectionate nickname they had given to their boss, Sam Wilson. Someone picked up on the "play on letters," and Uncle Sam became associated with the United States government. Nevertheless, it was not until about 100 years later, during World War I, that the term Uncle Sam was made most famous by its appearance on military recruiting posters containing the message, "Uncle Sam Wants You!"

FIGURE 9.9 - Uncle Sam.

Image of an antique steam locomotive in the American West. Copyright 2010 iStockphoto.

Chapter 10 Contents

CHAPTER TEN

A Growing National Identity

Major Events

1817-1825	The Era of Good Feelings
1817-1818	First Seminole War
1818	Convention of 1818
1819	Adams-Onis Treaty Panic of 1819 *McCulloch v. Maryland*
1820	Missouri Compromise
1823	Monroe Doctrine proclaimed
1825	Erie Canal completed

Introduction

Peace reigned once again in the United States, and it was time to put together a strong, unified nation. The country had been divided during the course of the War of 1812, but following the war, Americans felt pride in their nation and a stronger unity of purpose. The country was ready for another step in its journey. A sense of nationalism, which may be defined as a strong sense of national consciousness, manifested itself on several fronts. The country expanded its areas of settlement. Progress in technology led to growth in a national transportation system, which increased the ability to further expand the nation as well as increase economic prosperity. A national bank was revived in the organization of the Second Bank of the United States. The federal government attempted to protect the American business community through the Tariff Act of 1816. Along with these areas of progress, the United States also expanded its cultural identity. An American school of literature and art were now popular. Politically, President James Madison oversaw the first year of peace, and then President James Monroe stepped into his place, continuing many of his plans to increase the strength and greatness of the nation.

Introduction to the Monroe Administration

President James Monroe oversaw the expansion of this nationalistic fervor during his two terms in office from 1817 to 1825. In the election of 1816 he had been the standard-bearer for the Republican (or Democratic-Republican) Party and had easily defeated the Federalist candidate, Rufus King of New York. The Federalist Party was only a shadow of its former self, and this was the last presidential election that it would field a presidential candidate. Indeed, many of those who had Federalist leanings had abandoned the party name and informally endorsed King. Monroe carried 16 states to King's three, with a total electoral vote of 183 for Monroe and 34 for King.

On March 4, 1817, James Monroe, the last of the Virginia Dynasty of presidents, and his Vice President Daniel D. Tompkins, the governor of New York, swore

FIGURE 10.1 - James Monroe White House Portrait

to uphold the Constitution before a record number of Americans assembled in Washington, D.C. In the first inaugural address held outdoors, Monroe focused on the unity of the nation following the War of 1812. He spoke on issues that would increase this unity, such as the protection of domestic manufacturing, the construction of roads and canals to facilitate American commerce, and the need to improve the country's defenses along with a larger peacetime army. When the new president retired for the evening, it would not be at the White House, for it had been burned by the British during the war. A refurbished Washington, D.C. was another national legacy of the War of 1812.

The president came into office with a wealth of experience in government. Monroe had an extensive history of public service, a lengthy list of qualifications for the office, and many connections to the highest leadership in the nation's history. All of this influenced his presidency. He was an officer to George Washington during the American Revolution and became a member of the Continental Congress in 1783. He was a U.S. Senator from his home state of Virginia. In fact, Virginia called him into service as a member of the assembly, a U.S. Senator, and later as its governor. Monroe also served as Secretary of State and, for a short time during the War of 1812, as Secretary of War under President Madison.

The Era of Good Feelings

The two terms of President Monroe were labeled the "Era of Good Feelings" because of a decided lack of partisan strife across the nation. The Federalist Party had greatly damaged its viability as a national party with its less than enthusiastic support and sometimes its complete lack of support for the War of 1812, which left the Democratic-Republican Party with little opposition for a short time. Indeed, the Federalist Party had virtually collapsed shortly after Monroe first took office, and nearly everyone in Congress called himself a Republican.

Following the example of George Washington, in his first few months of his presidency, Monroe traveled the country on a 15-week goodwill tour of the northern states from the East Coast to Detroit in 1817. The purpose of the tour was to inspect military fortifications as well as to foster a better relationship with the Americans in the former Federalist-dominated area of the nation. Monroe was met with such supportive enthusiasm, even in the Federalist stronghold of Boston in the Northeast, that on the surface it did indeed seem that there was a new feeling of togetherness across the nation. In fact, the label "Era of Good Feelings" originated from a Bostonian newspaper, the *Colombian Centinel*.

However, the so-called "Era of Good Feelings" was an oversimplification of the true state of affairs of the nation. There was calm and prosperity during the early years of the Monroe administration, but there were also several major differences among the sections of the nation. Tariffs, the Second Bank of the United States, the issue of what part of government was responsible to pay for internal improvements, and eventually slavery all became divisive issues. Monroe was so cognizant of the divisions in the nation that he purposely put together a cabinet with members from the various sections.

Territorial Expansionism

The United States experienced a great internal migration during the years from 1815 to 1828. Americans moved further into the Northwest areas of northern Indiana and Illinois and southern Michigan. At the same time, there was greater movement into the southwestern portion of Georgia and further westward in the Deep South, as cotton land was sought in the ever-expanding cotton kingdom in that region. (See Chapter 14 for the story of cotton's expansion.) Mississippi achieved statehood in 1817, and Alabama became a state in 1819.

The possibility of owning their own land pulled Americans further west. Following the War of 1812, more land was accessible. The federal government had land to sell, and the banks made credit easily available. During the war, most Indian tribes had sided with the British, and their obstacle to mass settlement had been removed by the war in the western and southern portions of the nation. Improved transportation allowed American farmers to move west and take their products to market at a reasonable price. An improved economic prosperity assisted the movement west as well.

Canadian Boundaries Settled: Negotiations with Great Britain

Territorial expansion and foreign policy crossed paths during the Monroe presidency. Settlement of boundary disputes with foreign governments also expanded the nation and settled problems the United States had with Great Britain and Spain.

In 1817 and 1818, the United States and Great Britain resolved armament and boundary issues on the Canadian-United States border. With the Rush-Bagot Agreement, the two countries agreed to naval disarmament of the Great Lakes and established the principle of unfortified borders, leading to the longest undefended border between two countries. The number of ships allowed on the Great Lakes was one or two from each country, depending on the specific lake. This ended the possibility of a naval armaments race between the two nations and helped to increase peaceful relations. This was just the beginning of the disarmament agreements involving the United States and Great Britain. Complete mutual disarmament was not reached until the Treaty of Washington in 1871.

The two nations also signed the Convention of 1818, which finalized an agreement to set the Canadian-United States boundary at the 49th parallel from the Lake of the

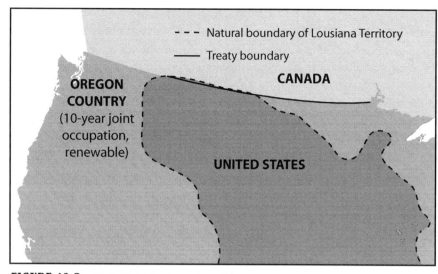

Natural boundary of Lousiana Territory

Treaty boundary

OREGON COUNTRY (10-year joint occupation, renewable)

CANADA

UNITED STATES

FIGURE 10.2 - U.S.-British Boundary Settlement, 1818.

Woods (in Minnesota) to the Rocky Mountains. It was also agreed that both countries would jointly occupy the Oregon Territory for 10 years. Today this region includes the states of Washington, Oregon, Idaho, and parts of Montana, Wyoming, and roughly half of the Canadian province of British Columbia.

Florida Secured: Negotiations with Spain

Florida had long been a political football among the European powers. Having first been claimed by Spain as a result of Christopher Columbus' voyages, Britain was given jurisdiction there by Spain in the Treaty of Paris (1763) that ended the French and Indian War (called the Seven Years' War in Europe). The British government then divided Florida into the two different provinces of East Florida and West Florida. The problem was that the region known as West Florida had originally been part of the French colony of Louisiana. But when Britain ceded both Florida provinces back to Spain in the 1783 Treaty of Paris, which ended the American Revolution and a major war in Europe, the exact borders were not specified. Complicating the border situation was the fact that in the secret Treaty of San Ildefonso (1800), Spain returned the Louisiana Territory to France, again without specifying the border between it and West Florida. Finally, the United States inherited the border dispute when it made the Louisiana Purchase from France in 1803. Nevertheless, a growing American presence in West Florida and a weakened Spain led the United States

to annex West Florida in stages, first in 1810 and then in 1812. Although Spain protested, there was nothing militarily that it could do about the situation.

Meanwhile, Seminole Indians were harassing American border settlements near East Florida during the First Seminole War (1817-18). The Spanish could not prevent the Indians from threatening Americans in that region. Moreover, under the Spanish, East Florida had become a haven for runaway slaves as well as hostile Indians. Therefore, General Andrew Jackson, the national hero since the Battle of New Orleans in the War of 1812, was sent to secure the border. Jackson's orders were to respect the Spanish controlled areas of East Florida, but to end the ability of the Seminole tribe to raid American settlements. Exceeding the authority of his orders, Jackson invaded East Florida and briefly captured two Spanish forts before leaving. He also executed two British traders in the area on charges of aiding the enemy. For a time, both Spain and England were angry at the United States for the actions of Jackson. However, feelings were soothed, and Jackson was not punished for his actions. In fact, most Americans were pleased that Jackson had brought East Florida under American military control.

After difficult negotiations with Spain, Secretary of State John Quincy Adams and the Spanish Minister Luis de Onis signed the Adams-Onis Treaty in 1819. In this treaty, Spain agreed to abandon its claims to all of Florida and to set the boundary between the United States and Mexico all the way to the Pacific Ocean. Spain also agreed to give up its claims on the Pacific Northwest. In return, the United States government agreed to assume responsibility for paying claims up to $5 million that American citizens had made against Spain over damage to U.S. shipping in the Napoleonic Wars. Moreover, the United States agreed to abandon any claims that Texas was part of the Louisiana Territory.

A Transportation Revolution

Westward expansion continued to grow as the availability of cheap land, pressure from population growth, and the removal of Indian opposition made it more attractive to Americans. But as more Americans moved further west and the national market economy evolved, it became necessary to improve various modes of transportation for personal travel as well as to provide more efficient and cheaper ways to move agricultural products to Eastern markets and manufactured goods to Western markets. Roads, steamboats, canals, and railroads all played major roles in tying the nation together in what can only be called a transportation revolution in the early 19th century.

Construction of Roads

In 1815, stagecoaches provided the fastest transportation for persons to travel overland and for mail delivery. For those who needed to travel by wagon over rural roads, it was a grueling task. There were a few turnpikes and toll roads with solid stone foundations and gravel topdressing. For example, the Philadelphia and Lancaster Turnpike, built in 1794, had begun the effort to make passable roads. Private companies, often with state aid, built local and interstate roads at a profit. By the War of 1812, turnpikes had connected the major commercial cities north of the Potomac and east of the Allegheny Mountains. The most important federal road project was the construction of the National Road, also called the Cumberland Road, which began in 1811. It was to be 66 feet wide with a surface of stone covered with gravel, and the bridges were

to be of stone. The original line from—Cumberland, Maryland on the Potomac River to Wheeling, Virginia (now in West Virginia) on the Ohio River—opened for traffic in 1818. Plans called for the National Road to extend all the way to St. Louis on the Mississippi River, but funding ran out, terminating this important road in Vandalia, Illinois in 1839, a total of 591 miles from its eastern origin.

The improvement of the road system was one of the areas of disagreement across the nation. Should the states or the federal government finance the construction of the new roads? With the nation growing in many

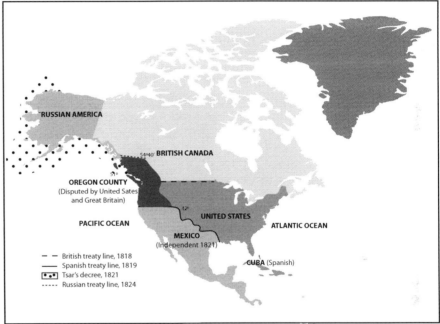

FIGURE 10.3 - The West and Northwest, 1819-1824.

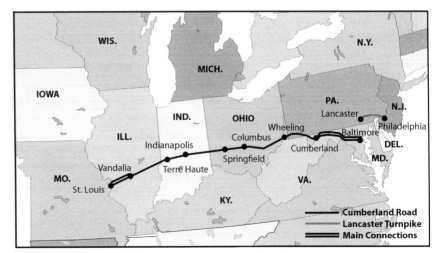

FIGURE 10.4 - Cumberland (National) Road and Main Connections.

directions, modes of transportation needed to expand and improve to support this growth. However, President Monroe vetoed the Cumberland Road Bill authorizing repair of that road and the establishment of tollgates in 1822 because of his view that the federal government lacked constitutional authority to pay for internal improvements. He did propose a constitutional amendment to explicitly grant the federal government such authority, but Congress did not follow up on his proposal. Costs for this type of infrastructure were left mostly to the states.

The Rise of Steamboats

Water transportation modes increased as well. An engineer by the name of Robert Fulton perfected a steam engine and put it in the first successful steamboat called the *Clermont*. In 1807, the *Clermont* steamed up the Hudson River from New York City to Albany, New York, a distance of approximately 150 miles. The ship completed the journey in 32 hours, averaging nearly 5 miles per hour. While the public had widely criticized it as "Fulton's Folly," the *Clermont* proved that steamboats were a vast improvement over keelboats, whose crews used poles to push their way up rivers at less than one mile per hour. The result was that steamboats replaced the slower keelboats and were widely used on the Mississippi River and its tributaries. By 1860, more than 1,000 steamboats were in service on America's major river highways.

FIGURE 10.5 - Robert Fulton.

A Canal-Building Craze

At the same time that roads and steamboats were connecting Americans from the East to the West, a canal boom was taking place. Relatively short canals, or man-made rivers dug out of the ground, had been built in isolated regions during the colonial period. Barges, or flatboats, were pulled by horses or mules walking on a path next to the canal and guided by a helmsman at the stern of the barge. However, it was the ambitious

plans of New Yorkers to build the Erie Canal that really opened the doors to a much wider use of canals as a means of transporting goods in the early 19th century.

The Erie Canal was built to connect the Great Lakes to the Atlantic Ocean. Specifically, the canal connected Buffalo, New York, on the shore of Lake Erie, to Albany, New York on the banks of the Hudson River. From there, barges could travel on the Hudson River to and from New York City, which lay on the Atlantic coast. New York Governor DeWitt Clinton championed the idea, although critics dubbed the canal "Clinton's Big Ditch" or "the Governor's Gutter" because the longest canal at the time was only 27 miles long, and this proposal seemed highly improbable. Nevertheless, the New York state legislature authorized the construction of the 346-mile canal linking Buffalo and Albany. The canal also extended from Albany to nearby Troy, New York, thus making a grand total of 363 miles. The project began at Rome, New York on July 4, 1817, and it was completed in October 1825. The most famous of all American canals, the Erie Canal was a monumental engineering achievement, 363 miles long, 40 feet wide, and 4 feet deep. Its construction was praised around the world as the "longest canal in the least time ... with the least experience ... for the least money ... and of the greatest public utility of any other in the world."

The Erie Canal impacted both New York and the nation. It opened up a route for Western goods to flow into the harbor of New York. Lumber, grain, and flour flowed from the New York harbor to world markets. Manufactured goods flowed from east to west. New York became the busiest of America's ports. Prior to the canal, the cost to move goods from Buffalo to New York City was $100 per ton. After the canal was completed, the cost was $8 per ton. More farmers moved closer to the canal, which in turn increased production of grains. Cities also grew up along the canal as well. Some of the negative aspects indirectly resulting from the canal were the diseases that came down the canal as well as the rowdy culture that seemed to come with the workers along the

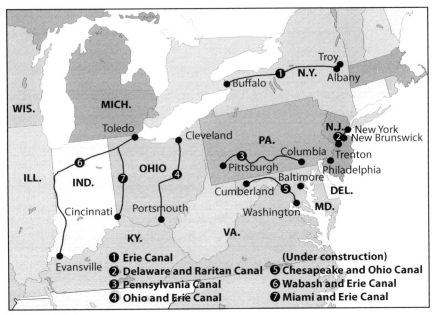

FIGURE 10.6 - Principal Canals in 1840.

Erie Canal
Delaware and Raritan Canal
Pennsylvania Canal
Ohio and Erie Canal

(Under construction)
Chesapeake and Ohio Canal
Wabash and Erie Canal
Miami and Erie Canal

canal system. Reformers in the Second Great Awakening were particularly critical of the canal workers, liquor on the canal, and the breaking of the "Sabbath" by running boats on Sundays.

The positive economic impact of the Erie Canal on the New York and national economy was not lost on others. Between 1815 and 1840, state governments and private investors built more than 3,000 miles of canals all over the nation.

The Railroad Revolution

The development of railroads, often called the "Iron Horse," ultimately became the most important means of transportation in the nation in the 19th century because railroad tracks can be laid on top of the ground and connect almost any two desired points of destination. Other railroads may claim to have been the first in America, but it was the Baltimore and Ohio (B&O) that became the first real major railroad system in the nation. The Baltimore and Ohio Railroad Company was formed in 1827 by a group of Baltimore merchants and bankers who were anxious to connect the port city of Baltimore to the growing population in the Ohio River valley. Construction began the next year and eventually the terminus for the B&O Railroad was completed at Wheeling, Virginia (now in West Virginia) in 1853. The first train on this railroad was the *Tom Thumb*, built

by Peter Cooper of New York in 1830 as the first steam-powered locomotive in American history. It had a top speed of 10 miles per hour.

Other port cities rivaled each other after the B&O success and created a railroad-building craze from the 1830s to 1860. By 1860, there were roughly 30,000 miles of railroad track in use in the United States, about three-fourths of it in the North. This was more than the rest of the world. Railroads were made safer and thus more successful after Samuel F. B. Morse's invention of the electric telegraph in 1837. By 1860, there were more than 50,000 miles of telegraph lines across the nation. It was, of course, the railroads that played a major role in making the United States a great industrial nation. At the same time, railroads brought an end to the canal-building era.

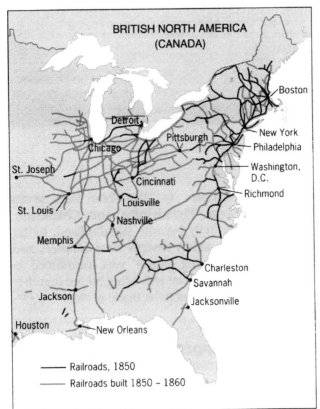

FIGURE 10.7 - The Railroad Revolution.

A Factory System Developed

Great Britain developed the first factory system in the 1750s and dominated industrialism for decades. This industrial revolution developed machines to replace the muscle of man in the manufacture of products.

The machine method of making products on a grand scale did not take hold in the United States for quite some time. In America, land was cheap, and most workers were not eager to work in an indoor environment under a master. Neither capital nor raw materials were readily available. The British also kept secret how to manufacture the machines necessary to make the products, particularly in the textile industry. It was also against British law to export the machines or for mechanics to leave the country. And finally, America did not have a large number of consumers willing to purchase the output of the factories on a large scale.

But industrial secrets cannot be kept forever. In 1791, Samuel Slater gave life to the factory system in the United States when he escaped from England with the plans for spinning machinery in his head. Slater settled in Rhode Island, and with the backing of a Quaker capitalist, Moses Brown, he put into operation the first American machinery for spinning cotton thread. However, he needed a cheap source of cotton fiber for his thread. Another mechanical genius, Eli Whitney, gave Slater's factory cheap cotton and in turn made the growing of cotton a thriving enterprise for the southern United States, when Whitney perfected the cotton gin (short for "engine") in 1793. Cotton was raised in the South, but the process of separating the seeds from the cotton lint was so expensive that cotton cloth was costly and rare. The new cotton gin could quickly separate the seeds from the lint and turn out cotton much more efficiently and cheaply. The result was that King Cotton spread across the South, as cotton became the chief source of fiber to make thread and thus cloth.

During the life of the Embargo Act, from late 1807 to early 1809, and again during the War of 1812, it became obvious that more manufacturing plants were needed to provide goods that were previously bought from England. However, before 1815, America was a nation of self-sufficient farmers and small businesses, and manufacturing stayed on a small and limited scale. New and more efficient transportation and the move into a market economy with new available markets changed the system into a national market economy. Once a national economy developed where farmers could sell their crops for profit, there was money available to purchase the goods that rolled out of the factories.

New England became the center for manufacturing in these early decades. Its stony soil was not conducive to large-scale farming, so workers were more available. Coastal ports provided capital from shipping as well as arrival points for raw materials and departure points for goods. Numerous rapid rivers also provided the power for the machines that manufactured the products.

The small manufacturing boom during the War of 1812 was damaged following the war by the dumping of cheap English surplus products. Mills in Rhode Island were forced to close their doors. However, Congress provided some relief for industry in the United States by passing the protective Tariff Act of 1816. The tariff placed a duty of approximately 25 percent on imports into the country.

The Lowell System

Francis Cabot Lowell established another system of manufacturing at the time on the Charles River in Waltham, Massachusetts, in 1813. The factories were placed on rivers because their rapid currents were necessary to turn large paddle wheels, which in turn were connected to a system of interconnected shafts that powered the machines doing the work. Lowell used power looms and combined the spinning of yarn and the weaving of cloth. His new factory system became known as the Lowell System. The elements of the Lowell System were to reduce costs to compete with British imports, use the newest innovations in mechanization, concentrate all processes of textile production in one factory, and hire young women to perform the work. In 1826, the town of Lowell was founded and six firms were established there.

The Lowell System was perceived as a model of the positive aspects of the factory system. It was very different from the factories of England because of its use of and concern for the welfare of the young women working the machinery in the factory. Boarding houses were built for the young, single daughters of the New England farmers who came to turn out the cloth. There were cultural and economic advantages for the young ladies. Their parents let them come to Lowell because the owners of the factory promised to look after the welfare of the young women. For many, it did not seem proper for single women of good reputation to be on their own. Reading groups, sewing circles, and church were part of their leisure time activities. In fact, attendance at church was mandatory. Most only stayed one to three years, but it gave them an independence that they sorely desired. The pay was half that of what men would make, but factory work paid more than the other dominant occupations for single women, such as domestic service and seamstress.

As the textile market became more competitive, conditions worsened for the young women of Lowell. Wages declined, hours increased, overcrowding was common, and even the boarding houses which were such a source of pride began to deteriorate.

Workers Push for Change

The labor movement in the United States had been weak, but as a result of worsening conditions, the New England textile mill girls organized a union, the Factory Girls' Association, and joined the small but growing number of labor unions. In 1834, they struck against wage reductions, and in 1836 they struck again against rent increases in the boarding houses. Lack of organization prior to this can be explained by the fact that the unskilled workers in the mills had been relatively satisfied with wages, women were too apprehensive to strike, and the children in the mills were too young to even consider such action.

In the 1790s, skilled craftsmen and journeymen organized America's first associations that can be equated to unions. Philadelphia was the cradle of American unionism. Shoemakers (cordwainers) formed a short-lived union in Philadelphia in 1792 and then a more lasting union, the Federal Society of Journeymen Cordwainers. The union conducted the first organized strike in 1799. Shoemakers, printers, carpenters, tailors, shipbuilders, and other craftsmen organized strikes and unions on the city level in most large cities in the Northeast. The unions formed to protest against the new conditions of expanding markets. Workers were pressured to produce more for less pay, longer hours, and less control over the work environment. The first strike for the 10-hour day occurred when house carpenters in 1791 in Philadelphia put down their tools in a spontaneous strike.

Strikes are necessary tools for the labor movement, but a strike in Philadelphia of journeymen shoemakers to protest a cut in boot prices led to criminal prosecution. Eight journeymen shoemakers were found guilty of criminal conspiracy in their joint efforts to raise their wages. Nineteen court cases ended with the verdict of criminal conspiracy after strikes of skilled workers in various American cities. These convictions slowed down the development of unions in the United States, but the workers would not be denied their say for long. A recession at the end of the War of 1812, and then the economic downturn following the Panic of 1819, left few unions surviving. Those that were left functioned as benevolent societies. The upturn of the economy in the 1820s had the opposite effect. The number of workers' associations increased, and this time the unskilled workers in the mills joined the fray. They were actually the first to use the term union for their organizations. The workers struck for higher wages, although an even more important issue of that era was the demand for a 10-hour day. Even though the activities of these first unions were local, they established many of the practices that the national labor unions of the post-Civil War era came to use.

The Panic of 1819

The Panic of 1819 interrupted the prosperous times following the War of 1812. One of the contributing factors for the prosperity had been the inflation brought about by state banks issuing paper currency in excess of their reserves. Much of this money was loaned to speculators purchasing government land in the frontier areas. About one-third of those buying land in the West bought land on credit allowed by the Land Act of 1800. Over-speculation in land purchases was risky and put many banks and borrowers on an unstable economic footing.

Causes of the economic Panic of 1819 included speculation in the sale of Western lands, overextending investments in manufacturing, collapsing foreign markets, a slumping cotton market, an influx of foreign goods, and the contraction of credit by the Bank of the United States to state banks in debt to the national Bank. The state banks in turn called in their loans to debtors. Although the practices of the Bank of the United States were not the only cause of the Panic of 1819, many, especially in the West, blamed the Bank for the entire problem, and hostility against the Bank would give Andrew Jackson a cause in the future that rallied many to him and his Jacksonian Democracy. The Bank would gain the label the "Monster" for many.

As a result of the above factors, banks closed, businesses failed, farmers lost their land, and prices collapsed. The situation hit the southern and western states the hardest. Several state legislatures, including in Missouri, Illinois, and Kentucky, passed legislation to give relief to debtors. It was not an uncommon practice at the time to send debtors to work houses or prison. Because of the problems with land purchases during the Panic, Congress passed the Land Act of 1820, which abolished the practice of purchasing land on credit, lowered the price of federal land to $1.25 per acre, and reduced the minimum amount for purchase to 80 acres. The Relief Act of 1821 allowed farmers to actually return land that had not been paid for to the government.

During the Panic, it was time for another presidential election. Proof of the weakness of the party system came in that 1820 election. James Monroe's candidacy for a second term went unopposed. Out of 235 electoral votes, Monroe received 231. There were three abstentions and one vote by a New Hampshire elector for John Quincy Adams. It was the feeling of most, and particularly of the New Hampshire elector, that only Washington deserved the distinction of a unanimous victory.

The Supreme Court and Nationalism

In the ongoing contest over political power between states' rights and federal authority, the Supreme Court heard several cases and expanded the rights and powers of the federal government in its contribution to the growing nationalism. In the 1803 case of *Marbury v. Madison,* the Supreme Court had established the power of judicial review, which allowed the Court to rule on the constitutionality of state laws. The state of Maryland tested the power of state versus federal authority when it passed a law to place a tax on the Maryland branch of the Bank of the United States, claiming that the Bank was unconstitutional. When the case reached the U.S. Supreme Court, the Court ruled in *McCulloch v. Maryland* (1819) that the Bank was constitutional under the general welfare clause of the Constitution and through the doctrine of implied powers of Congress. Therefore, Maryland could not tax a federally chartered bank. Chief Justice John Marshall wrote in the ruling, "The power to tax involves the power to destroy." The states could not be allowed this power over an institution chartered by Congress.

In 1821, in the case of *Cohens v. Virginia*, the Marshall Court again advanced the powers of the federal government over the states by limiting the authority of the state courts. Cohens was found guilty of illegally selling lottery tickets in Virginia. He had appealed to the Supreme Court, but the Court sustained the state verdict. Marshall was not satisfied with upholding the Virginia court ruling alone, however. He went so far as to rule that the Supreme Court had the right to review the decisions of all state supreme courts in cases involving the powers of the federal government.

One more blow was aimed at the power of the states in the case of *Gibbons v. Ogden* (1824). The state of New York granted a monopoly to the steamboat company of Aaron Ogden for the water commerce between New York and New Jersey. Thomas Gibbons, a former partner of Ogden, secured his own license to ferry items across the river under the Federal Coasting Act of 1793 and went into competition with Ogden. Ogden sued Gibbons, and the New York state court upheld Ogden's monopoly. But Gibbons appealed to the Supreme Court, and the Court ruled that Gibbons' license was valid and that only Congress had the right to regulate interstate commerce, that is, commerce that crosses state lines.

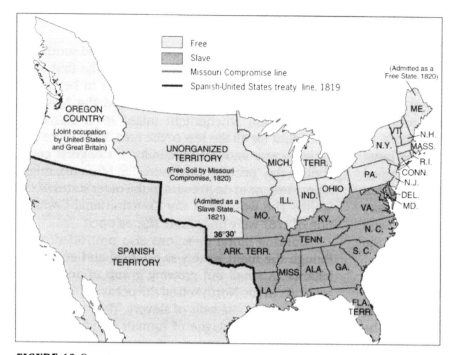

FIGURE 10.8 - The Missouri Compromise and Slavery, 1820-1821.

The Missouri Compromise

Before 1819, slavery had not been the major source of sectional conflict. Instead, such sources had been the Federalist economic programs, Jay's Treaty, the Louisiana Purchase, and the War of 1812. However, Eli Whitney's new cotton gin and the resulting spread of both cotton and slavery in the South were raising the stakes and heating up the slavery question on both sides. Then when Missouri Territory applied for statehood as a slave state in 1819, the divisive issue of slavery was revitalized among American citizens as well as in Congress.

After Alabama joined the Union as a slave state in December 1819, the nation was evenly divided, with 11 free states and 11 slave states. That meant that representation in the Senate was also evenly divided between 22 members from free states and 22 from slave states. However, in other ways the South felt it was losing ground in its battle to maintain its slavery system. If the North became too powerful, the South believed its system would be threatened. The House of Representatives is based on population, of course, and in 1819, the northern free states held 105 seats to the slave states' 81 seats. More importantly, the population of the North was continuing to grow at a more rapid

rate than that of the South. The South also felt vulnerable when the issue for Missouri statehood came before Congress. Their fears were confirmed when Representative James Tallmadge, of New York, introduced an amendment that would prohibit the introduction of new slaves into Missouri and provided that the present slaves' future children born after statehood would become free at age 25. Although the House did pass the Tallmadge amendment, the Senate rejected it.

From the anti-slavery North's perspective, Missouri's application for statehood as a slave state threatened to upset the delicate balance in that it would give the slave states an edge in the number of slave states versus free states. Moreover, Missouri's status as a slave state might well set a precedent for other states that were to come out of the Louisiana Territory.

A firestorm of debate and several rejected amendments on the question ensued over the next year. Finally, a compromise was reached in 1820 that allowed Missouri into the Union as a slave state while Maine was admitted as a free state. Maine had long been claimed as a part of Massachusetts. But Massachusetts reflected itself as the most anti-slavery state in the Union when it dropped its claim to Maine in the interests of maintaining the balance between free states and slave states. Now the balance would be 12 to 12. In addition, slavery would be barred in the remaining Louisiana Purchase territory north and west of Missouri above the 36° 30' parallel line of latitude. Representative Henry Clay of Kentucky played the major role in engineering the Missouri Compromise (1820). For his accomplishment, he became forever known as the "Great Compromiser." Perhaps the greatest significance of the Missouri Compromise was that for the second time in American history, Congress had limited the expansion of slavery somewhere in the United States. (The first time had been its prohibition against slavery in the Northwest Territory, passed as part of the Northwest Ordinance of 1787 by the Articles of Confederation Congress.)

Maine was formally admitted into the Union as the 23rd state in March 1820. Meanwhile, Missouri's formal admittance was delayed by a debate over its state's constitutional exclusion of free blacks. Congress eventually pressured Missouri to remove that measure and replace it with a statement prohibiting discrimination against other states' citizens, but without specifically defining free blacks as citizens. Missouri was then admitted into the Union as the 24th state in August 1821.

Foreign Policy Matters

Russian Claims

In September 1821, Czar Alexander I of Russia claimed the territory along the Pacific Coast of North America all the way south to San Francisco Bay and stated that all surrounding waters were closed to commercial shipping of other nations. Secretary of State Adams informed the Russians that any new attempts at colonization in the Americas by a European nation were unacceptable. Following negotiations, the Russians pulled their claim north of the line 54° 42', which gave up all claim to the Oregon Territory but secured their claim to Alaska. This episode was an indication of Adams' desire to shut down any future colonization of the Western Hemisphere.

The Monroe Doctrine

Between 1807 and 1821, Spanish colonies to the south of the United States were throwing off the colonial yoke that Spain had imposed on them for centuries. These revolutions alarmed the monarchs of Europe, and these powers withheld formal recognition of the new nations, as did the United States initially. For its part, the United States did not wish to alienate Spain in its negotiations on the Florida territory, so it waited until Spain had ratified the Adams-Onis Treaty before extending diplomatic relations with several of Spain's former colonies. Revolutions that threatened one colonial power were perceived as a threat to all colonial powers. Even though the European monarchs did not take any action to maintain Spain's control over its colonies in the Western Hemisphere, the United States was uneasy about this possibility because several nations advocated the "principle of intervention." This doctrine stated the right of all monarchs to suppress revolutions wherever they occurred.

In this setting, George Canning, the British Foreign Secretary, wanted commercial trade with these new nations without recognizing them as sovereign nations and thereby insulting all monarchs, including his own, King George IV. Canning also wanted additional support for his position from the United States in order to prevent France or any other European nation from interfering in matters as they stood in South America, Central America, and the Caribbean. The joint resolution he offered stated that Great Britain and the United States did not want territory for themselves, but neither would they allow others to intervene in Latin America. The British navy was strong enough to impose its will on any European powers that might send expeditions to Latin America.

President Monroe favored the joint agreement with Great Britain. He believed that the two nations working together

FIGURE 10.9 - Monroe Doctrine.

would have more power to advance their aims. However, Secretary of State John Q. Adams prevailed upon Monroe to take a stand on the issue solely from the American position. According to Adams, it was not necessary to join the British in this instance, and the United States did not wish to destroy the possibility of further expansion, perhaps to Mexico and Cuba, in the future. Adams' view prevailed, and President Monroe stated the position of the United States on this issue before Congress on December 2, 1823. The Monroe Doctrine stated that the Western Hemisphere was not open to colonization by any European power; that the political system in the Americas was different and separate from that of Europe, and the United States would consider any attempt on the part of European powers to extend their system to any point in the Western Hemisphere as a danger to its own peace and safety; and finally, that the United States would in turn not interfere in the internal affairs of European nations, nor take part in European wars of solely foreign interest.

When the terms of the Monroe Doctrine reached the great powers of Europe, it received little attention.

From a realistic perspective, it was a unilateral doctrine that the United States was in no military position to effectively enforce. Nevertheless, the British swallowed their pride and, in effect, heeded the Monroe Doctrine for most of the remainder of the century because it was in their self-interest to do so. At the same time, no major power seemed either interested enough or strong enough to take on the settlement of new colonies, or to retake old ones, in the Western Hemisphere. The Doctrine's major significance would come in later years as the United States continued to hold fast as its power increased and circumstances demanded a stand against future European intervention in America's backyard.

The Monroe Doctrine was President Monroe's final action in the promotion of a nationalist agenda. The country had emerged from war strengthened and determined to put the nation on strong footing. Although there were issues that would continue to divide the nation and shortly after 1824 bring back a strong two-party system, the nation stood stronger and more committed to one America for all.

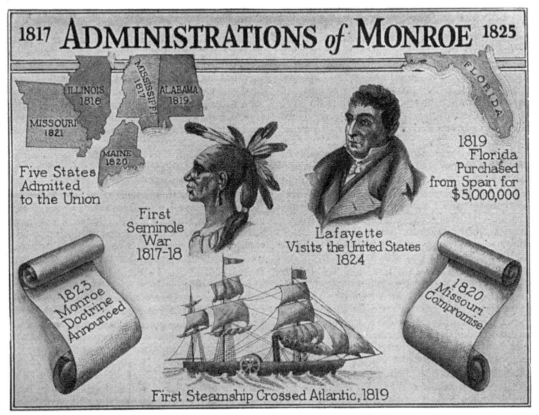

FIGURE 10.10 - Monroe Presidency.

Andrew Jackson on his horse. Statue in Lafayette Park across from the White House Rose Garden, Washington, D.C. Copyright 2010 iStockphoto.

Chapter 11 Contents

CHAPTER ELEVEN

The Jacksonian Shadow

Major Events

1825	House of Representatives elected John Quincy Adams president
1826	Founding Fathers Adams and Jefferson died on the same day
1828	"Tariff of Abominations" passed Andrew Jackson elected president *The South Carolina Exposition and Protest* was published
1830	Webster-Hayne Debate Indian Removal Act was passed
1832	"Bank War" began Black Hawk War *Worcester v. Georgia* Jackson defeated Henry Clay to begin his second term
1833	Vice President John C. Calhoun resigned
1836	Specie Circular issued Texas won independence from Mexico Martin Van Buren elected president
1837	Panic of 1837
1838-39	"Trail of Tears"
1840	William Henry Harrison elected president
1841	President Harrison became first president to die in office
1842	Webster-Ashburton Treaty

Introduction

Driven by market influences, westward relocations, and political changes between 1815 and 1846, a more dynamic democracy emerged in the United States. Major change led to divisions in the nation concerning the role of the federal government and how to meet the needs of various groups of Americans. Farming in the 1820s began changing from subsistence levels in local economies toward a market economy in a national arena, which necessitated a much more sophisticated national transportation system. Finding funds for a national transportation network of roads, canals, and railroads was an important question. Who would pay and who would benefit? The economic developments of a "market revolution," transportation projects, and government seeming to focus on the needs of the wealthy businessmen in the Northeast clashed with the values of the American Revolution for many. The common ideology of the American Revolution was known as "republicanism." This was the belief that the liberty of the people depended on the maintenance of "virtue," supporting the common good over private interests and a constant vigilance against the concentration of political or economic power. Reaction against the power and control of a sector of the United States led to a movement across the new nation dedicated to increasing democracy in the Republic called the "Age of the Common Man."

Andrew Jackson rose to power during this period of change because of his dedication to and agreement with the values of "republicanism" and his bond to the lives and ideals of the "common man." Jackson was a child of the American Revolution, both literally and figuratively. He joined the American forces at the age of 13 when the British invaded his home state of South Carolina. For a short time, he was a prisoner of war. He understood the stakes of the war and developed his own beliefs of liberty and the role of government from this point forward. Jackson was also tied to the westward movement of the nation when he, as a young man, moved west along

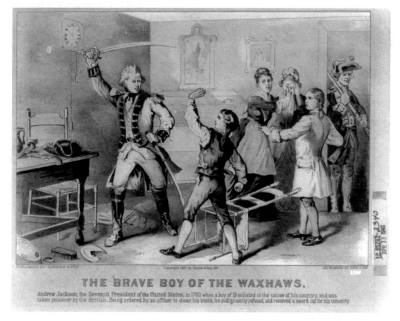

THE BRAVE BOY OF THE WAXHAWS.

Andrew Jackson, the Seventh President of the United States, in 1780 when a boy of 13 enlisted in the cause of his country, and was taken prisoner by the British. Being ordered by an officer to clean his boots, he indignantly refused, and received a sword cut for his temerity.

FIGURE 11.1 - Depicts incident in the childhood of Andrew Jackson, showing him standing up to British soldier

with thousands of others. The government encouraged westward expansion during these years with easy credit to purchase public land and even by giving 1.6 million acres of western land to enlistees in the War of 1812. He was a Westerner when he chose to make Tennessee his home after the new territory split from North Carolina. However, he was not a "common man" for long with the growth of his home, the Hermitage, from a small farm to a large plantation with many slaves. Nevertheless, Jackson continued to think as a common man. For many, Jackson symbolized the culmination of the American dream from its inception, which explains why his name was given to an age.

The move to broaden the influence of ordinary citizens and thus democracy began in New Jersey (1807) and Maryland (1810) with the abolition of property and taxpaying qualifications for white male suffrage. Between 1810 and 1821, seven other states eliminated their suffrage restrictions. Changes in the state constitution of Maryland eliminated religious qualifications for voting and holding public office. There was an increase in popular elective offices. The voters of 22 states took the selection of the presidential electors away from the state legislatures. By 1828, only the legislative bodies of South Carolina and Delaware chose the presidential electors. The influence of Andrew Jackson stretched like a shadow

Presidential Election Results in 1824			
CANDIDATES	POPULAR VOTE	ELECTORAL VOTE	POPULAR PERCENTAGE
Jackson	153,544	99	42.16
Adams	108,740	84	31.89
Crawford	46,618	41	12.95
Clay	47,136	37	12.99

FIGURE 11.2 - Election of 1824

into the past and forward for years from his victory in the 1828 presidential election.

The 1824 Presidential Election

The Candidates

The presidential election of 1824 was one of the most unusual in the nation's history. The candidate who came in second in both the popular vote and electoral vote became president. Congressional caucuses selected presidential candidates traditionally, but state legislatures took over this year because this was still during the so-called Era of Good Feelings, when nearly everyone called himself a Republican after the Federalist Party had disappeared shortly after its vigorous opposition to the War of 1812. Even though the Congressional caucus did meet, only 66 of the 216 members were present. The caucus nominated William H. Crawford, the Secretary of the Treasury. State legislatures chose three of the four candidates for president.

Four candidates competed for the presidency under the same party mantle of "Republican" John Quincy Adams of Massachusetts, Secretary of State under President Monroe; Henry Clay of Kentucky, Speaker of the U.S. House of Representatives; William H. Crawford of Georgia, Secretary of the Treasury, even though he suffered from a debilitating stroke; and Andrew Jackson of Tennessee, U.S. Senator. John C. Calhoun, of South Carolina and former Secretary of War under President Monroe, withdrew his candidacy for president and chose to run for vice president on both the Adams and Jackson tickets. The major issues

FIGURE 11.3 - Andrew Jackson.

supported by the candidates were protective tariffs and internal improvements. Jackson also attacked the "King Caucus" as a nominating body, declaring that the people had the right to choose their candidate.

The Results

In the 1820s, Andrew Jackson answered the call to national politics because he was afraid for the liberty of the nation. Honing his political skills in Tennessee, he served as a member of the state constitutional convention, U.S. Representative, U.S. Senator, and a

Superior Court judge. He was a leader of men before serving in any of his political positions, but those seemingly natural leadership skills improved greatly with his military service. He became a national legend, serving as a general in the Tennessee militia, a major-general in the U.S. Army, defeating the Creek tribe and the British in the War of 1812, and commanding troops in the Seminole War in Florida. He also served as the provisional governor of Florida. Jackson lost his first attempt at the presidency in 1824. Although he won more popular and electoral votes than any of the other candidates, his electoral votes did not constitute a majority, as the election chart illustrates.

A "Corrupt Bargain" for the Presidency?

According to the 12th Amendment to the Constitution, if there were not a candidate with a majority of the electoral vote, the House of Representatives would choose the victor from the top three candidates of the general election. Personal grudges and power politics came to play in the House decision for the sixth president of the United States. Clay was out of the running for the presidency because he finished in fourth place. However, he continued to have a role in the election due to his position as Speaker of the House. Crawford was no longer a viable candidate because of his stroke. Therefore, Clay promised his support to Adams. Although Adams and Clay were from different sections of the country and had little in common personally, they had much in common politically with their commitment to a protective tariff, a national bank, and a partly federally funded national system of internal improvements to expand the domestic market. Although Jackson garnered the most votes with overwhelming support from the western section of the country, Clay refused to give his support to a man he considered a rival for the affections of the West. Besides, Jackson strongly opposed most of Clay's political principles. The result was that Clay was able to convince some state delegations in the House of Representatives to vote for Adams even though their state legislatures supported Jackson.

The House of Representatives met on February 9, 1825 for the momentous vote. On the first ballot, John Quincy Adams won the presidency. Adams received the votes from 13 states, Jackson 7, and Crawford 4. A few days later it appeared that Henry Clay received his reward for

supporting Adams when the president-elect announced his nomination of Clay for Secretary of State. This was a very important appointment for Clay because three of the four previous presidents had held this position before moving into the highest office.

There was and is no proof that Adams and Clay struck a bargain per se, and if they had, this was certainly not a unique or new political maneuver and not necessarily an example of corruption. However, with the changing mood of the country toward politics as usual and corruption, the appearance of a "corrupt bargain" that robbed the people of a favored candidate for president led to an outcry for years from Jackson and his supporters. The so-called "corrupt bargain" led to many problems for John Quincy Adams and damaged his chances for success before his presidency even began.

Introduction to the John Quincy Adams Administration

John Quincy Adams had many of the qualifications necessary to produce a strong and effective presidency. He was well educated (spoke seven languages) and an intellectual with a vision for a strong United States that included increasing the intellectual capital of the nation with a stronger higher education system. He came from an important American political family; he was the son of former President John Adams. His political experience was vast: U.S. Senator from Massachusetts, minister (ambassador) to the Netherlands, the first U.S. minister to Russia, a negotiator for the Treaty of Ghent ending the War of 1812, minister to England, and Secretary of State under Monroe. In fact, he was the author of the Monroe Doctrine and negotiated the Adams-Onis Treaty with Spain that was signed in 1819 and gave the United States East Florida and defined the western limits of the Louisiana Purchase. Yet, he could not triumph over his weaknesses, a questionable election result, a hostile group of Jackson's supporters in Congress, and the lack of an appealing personality. Most important, he was not the choice of a majority of Americans, and he was out of touch with the changes sweeping the nation.

Opposition forces organized against the president following his first annual message to Congress in early

1825. President Adams recommended more support from the federal government for roads and canals, a national university, an astronomical observatory, standardization of weights and measures, and exploration of various parts of the United States, among other proposals. Adams also encouraged more support for the arts, science, and literature. These proposals advocated more government support for seemingly elitist interests rather than issues of primary concern to the common person, and they brought opposition from many, including southern proponents of states' rights. Southerners did not want intervention from the federal government in general because they thought that any added attention to their local affairs could possibly open the door on the slavery issue on a national level again or increase the hated tariffs. Vice President Calhoun, a states' rights Southerner from South Carolina, used his power in the Senate to fill important posts in this body with other states' rights senators, and in effect worked against Adams. The president might have built more support for himself and strengthened his party, but he would not use the power of patronage to keep men in his camp with government jobs.

The Nation Mourns

On a sad note for both the president and the nation, the president's father, former President John Adams, and Thomas Jefferson died. These two Founding Fathers and former adversaries died within hours of each other on July 4, 1826. Not only was it a bit unusual that they both died on the same day, that date was precisely the 50th anniversary of the signing of the Declaration of Independence. It was reported that Adams stated shortly before his death that "Thomas Jefferson still survives." Apparently, the former president believed that the country would still have the wisdom of Jefferson to guide and protect the ideals of the Revolution. Actually, Jefferson had already died before Adams did. In any case, on many issues the country was growing into a new phase of democracy.

Foreign Affairs

With regard to foreign relations, President Adams and Secretary of State Clay hoped to create stronger ties with

FIGURE 11.4 - John Quincy Adams

Latin America. With this in mind, Adams decided to send two American delegates to the Panama Congress, an organization dedicated to forging a union of Latin American nations to stop any foreign intervention in the area. This proposal met with general criticism in Congress on the grounds that this assembly of Latin American countries had the force of a government, a fact that could impact the neutral foreign policy position of the United States, as well as southern Congressmen fearing the issue of slavery coming up during a meeting that included the presence of black representatives. Congress finally agreed to the delegates' attendance, but one died before reaching the meeting and the other arrived too late for any important participation. During the congressional debate on whether to participate in any capacity with the Panama Congress, Clay received another insult on the supposed "corrupt bargain" from Senator John Randolph. Smarting from numerous slanderous comments, Clay challenged Randolph to a duel, which ended in no injuries to either man.

The "Tariff of Abominations"

An important issue for the country was the question of tariff rates. Whether the tariff, import taxes, should be high or low was often a sectional issue of division. The Northeast, some states in the Middle Atlantic region, and the West supported high tariffs on some imports to protect manufacturing or other enterprises from foreign competition. This was especially true of New Englanders, who wished to protect their textile and wool industries. The supporters of protectionism assembled a convention at Harrisburg, Pennsylvania in the summer of 1827 with delegates from 13 states in attendance. They wanted protection duties on textiles, hemp, flax, hammered bar iron, steel, and other goods. They presented their position to Congress, which was considering tariff rates in 1828.

Supporters of Jackson were looking toward the next election and planned a scenario certain to embarrass Adams. President Adams generally favored higher tariff rates and asked Congress to pass a new tariff bill. But the Jacksonians dominated the House Committee on Manufactures and used their influence to frame a tariff bill with much higher tariff rates than could be expected to pass Congress. As a result, they could deny President Adams a tariff bill during the last full year of his first term in office and blame him for the failure. So the committee incorporated extremely high tariffs on raw materials, such as iron, hemp, and flax, and eliminated some of the protective elements for woolen goods, a primary interest for protection in New England. However, the bill passed to the surprise of many, with several New England members of Congress voting for it in the belief that protection was worth a higher price for raw materials. The president signed the Tariff Act of 1828 in May of that year.

In general, the South rejected higher tariffs for the fundamental reason that while its agricultural products competed in a world market devoid of agricultural tariffs, it had to purchase manufactured goods, which it largely did not produce, in a very protected environment. That meant the South paid more for manufactured goods due to a protectionist tariff that did not benefit their region, leading to an outcry that high tariff legislation was sectional in that it was designed to benefit some sections of the country at the expense of others. South Carolina took the lead in attempting to stop what New England shippers and southern planters labeled the "Tariff of Abominations," and it continued this leadership role up to the opening of the Civil War. Speaking for a small minority at the time, a speech given on the

issue stated that the "question is fast approaching the alternative of submission or separation." The southern state adopted a set of eight resolutions, labeling the tariff unconstitutional and oppressive. Georgia, Mississippi, and Virginia also protested the high tariff proposal.

Vice President Calhoun anonymously wrote a pamphlet entitled *The South Carolina Exposition and Protest* in 1828 in response to the high tariff. This paper outlined a theory of state sovereignty and the right to nullify acts of Congress. Specifically, it supported what was called the Compact Theory of the Constitution, that the Union under the Constitution had been created by an agreement among the states. The result was the belief that any state could withdraw from this agreement, and thus from the Union, whenever it wanted to, a doctrine known as secession. Calhoun was not yet ready to publicly announce his split with nationalism, but President Andrew Jackson would later deal with the tariff issue as well as the views of Vice President Calhoun and South Carolina.

The Two-Party System Returns

During the presidency of John Quincy Adams, intense debate over several political issues eventually resulted in the development of two rival political parties once again. The National Republicans, led by President John Quincy Adams and Henry Clay, echoed much of the platform of the defunct Federalist Party of the late Alexander Hamilton. Its real brainchild was Henry Clay, whose political philosophy was summed up in what he called the American System. The American System called for high, protective tariffs, a national bank, and the use of federal funds to help finance a set of internal improvements, which was a national transportation network of roads and canals that would keep the westward-expanding nation economically connected. The National Republicans believed that the national government had a prominent role to play in keeping the nation moving forward economically. Thus, they took the name *National* Republicans.

The Democratic-Republicans were led by Andrew Jackson and opposed all three major elements of the American System. This party essentially represented the philosophy of the first Democratic-Republican Party of Thomas Jefferson and James Madison, believing that the national government was best when it governed least and allowed individuals to rise according to their own ability. Fearful of too much central control, Democratic-Republicans argued for states' rights, although the party eventually suffered somewhat from a division between those. Some Democratic-Republicans like John C. Calhoun interpreted states' rights to include the right of nullification and even secession, while others believed the nation must always be kept intact.

The 1828 Presidential Election

The Campaign

The Jackson camp eagerly awaited the presidential election of 1828. In fact, it had been four years in the making. There were once again two parties with distinct political differences. The Democratic-Republicans nominated Andrew Jackson, or "Old Hickory," as his supporters called him. For their part, the National Republicans identified their nominee, President John Quincy Adams, with the oak tree for his solid credentials and his unwavering support for the things he believed in.

The issues of the election campaign were clear according to the followers of each candidate. Jackson's followers proclaimed their candidate as a true self-made man, a Westerner, the champion of the common man, a low-tariff man, and a states' rights supporter. The Democratic-Republicans also denounced Adams for his aristocratic character, a high tariff, and of course, the "corrupt bargain" that had denied the voters their chosen candidate in the 1824 election.

Mudslinging was widespread in this race. Adams chose to keep to the high ground personally during the election, but his followers were not so distinguished. They claimed that Jackson's mother was a prostitute and his wife an adulteress. Jackson and his wife had married unknowingly before her divorce from her first husband was final, although they had rectified the situation as soon as they discovered the mistake. They seemed unable to bury this hurtful personal attack. The Adams camp also recounted the duels, brawls, and executions ordered by the opposition candidate. Jackson had killed a man in a duel, which came close to costing the general his life as well, and he had participated in a shootout that resulted in a bullet in his arm that was not removed until he was in the White House. Dueling was not uncommon in this age. A quote that claimed the race was between "one who can write and one who can fight" was accurate, even though this did not cover all of the candidates' qualifications.

Not to be outdone, the Jackson camp launched an attack on the morals of the president as well. They accused Adams of providing a servant girl for the sexual lust of the Czar of Russia while he was minister to Russia, using taxpayer money to furnish the White House with furniture used for gambling, and supporting the idea of monarchy.

At the end of the race, it was clear that the country's center of political geography had moved westward. That reality, along with the voters' tiring of the lackluster Adams, spelled a significant electoral victory for the first western president of the United States.

Introduction to the Jackson Administration

Jackson arrived in Washington to take his place as the seventh president shortly after the death of his beloved

Presidential Election Results in 1828		
CANDIDATES	**POPULAR VOTE**	**ELECTORAL VOTE**
Andrew Jackson	647,286	178
John Quincy Adams	508,064	83

FIGURE 11.5 - Election of 1828

wife Rachel. He mourned her until his own death and held a grudge against many of his critics and opponents in the 1828 election, which he believed had a hand in her death because of the scandalous accusations against Rachel. But on his inaugural day, March 4, 1829, his broken heart was somewhat mended. The people had their hero in control of their destiny, and the hero was finally in his proper place. This special bond manifested itself in the desire to touch Jackson after his inaugural speech and with a reception for the public at the White House following his speech. This was a departure from normal inaugural celebrations. The reception turned into mass chaos, as hundreds of "guests," or the "mob" as many critics called them, poured through the doors and damaged the White House to the extent of thousands of dollars. The damage would have been worse if the staff had not thought to lure the crowds out of the White House by setting up tubs of punch and pails of liquor on the lawns. The new president even had to leave the White House in order to avoid injury from the crush.

Jackson came into office full of fire and on a crusade to protect liberty, virtue, and morality, the cornerstones of "republicanism." These fundamental ideals drove much of the Jackson program of "reform, retrenchment, and economy" in government. He hoped to reduce the size and expense of the national government, pay off the national debt, which he accomplished primarily through the sale of public lands in the West (thus being the only president to pay off the national debt), end the monopoly of the Bank of the United States (the national bank), adjust the tariff to satisfy all sections of the nation, improve relations with England, increase trade in the West Indies, settle claims with France, make sure that the will of the people was not denied in future elections, and move the Indian tribes west of the Mississippi River. The inaugural address outlined his plans on March 4, 1829, and included his position concerning the rights of the states.

Putting the federal government's house in order was a priority. He put together his cabinet and then went about the business of cleaning up the corruption by removing officials who had held their positions for too long. Jackson did not choose a strong and effective cabinet, other than Secretary of State Martin Van Buren, but he remedied this mistake by forming a small group of unofficial advisors known as the "Kitchen Cabinet." It was to this small

group that he turned most often for advice and support. Next he took on what he perceived as the corrupt federal bureaucracy with his "policy of rotation." Jackson's opponents accused the new president of beginning the "spoils system" in government. This was the practice of keeping the party faithful committed with rewards of government positions, but the practice was as old as politics itself. The label for party patronage came from a speech delivered by Senator William Learned Marcy of New York, who claimed "to the victor belongs the spoils." Opponents expected wholesale firings, but Jackson removed only 919 jobholders out of 10,093 in 18 months, and not more than 20 percent of office-holders were removed on political grounds during his eight years in office.

The "Petticoat Affair"

With so many weighty decisions on his agenda, it was amazing that Jackson lost time and political capital because of his decision to champion the wife of his Secretary of War and close friend John Eaton. And yet, personal affronts affecting his decisions were not uncommon for the president before and during his presidency, although it was a definite weakness in his leadership. The situation with the Eatons brought back painful memories of the slander against Jackson and his wife Rachel. The wives of the cabinet secretaries, led by Vice President Calhoun's wife, and some of the cabinet members ostracized Mrs. Margaret (Peggy) Eaton because of rumors that her first husband killed himself over the relationship of Peggy and Eaton while she was married to another man. President Jackson ordered the cabinet to accept Mrs. Eaton and to order their wives to do the same. Even Emily Donelson, the president's niece and official hostess, refused to call on Mrs. Eaton in her home, although she agreed to receive the lady in the White House. The wives refused to socialize with Peggy Eaton, and the cabinet split on the issue.

Eaton, of course, and Van Buren were allies to the president on this issue. Van Buren and Calhoun used the issue to hopefully further their political futures. Calhoun was not supportive of Mrs. Eaton and did nothing to improve her situation, but he believed that others would appreciate his stand for morality. For his part, Van Buren reaped the future rewards from Jackson's appreciation of his support with the vice presidency and eventually the presidency. Jackson asked the Cabinet members who refused to support Mrs. Eaton to resign. They refused, but Van Buren and Eaton later resigned their Cabinet positions to break this deadlock. Jackson then demanded the resignation of the three Calhoun supporters. The president appointed five new Cabinet secretaries in 1831. The "petticoat affair" then finally ended.

States' Rights versus the Union

The debate over the power of the states versus the power of the federal government was not a new issue. The South continued its grumbling over the "Tariff of Abominations." President Jackson supported states' rights as appropriate for control over local issues. However, he maintained that a strong Union was necessary for the safety of the nation, and it was the purpose of the federal government to ensure that nothing threatened the Union. Calhoun and South Carolina misread the president's views on this issue. In January 1830, Robert Hayne, Senator from South Carolina and Daniel Webster, Senator from Massachusetts, clashed in the Senate over the rights of the states and the nature of the Union. In this famous Webster-Hayne Debate, Senator Hayne demanded respect for the rights of the South, and argued that if federal laws violated state sovereignty, then nullification of federal law and eventually secession were legitimate actions. Webster took two days to refute the position of Hayne and Vice President Calhoun concerning acceptable actions by the states and the Union of the United States, which according to Webster was a union of people not states. "It is, Sir, the people's Constitution, the people's government, made for the people, made by the people, and answerable to the people." Webster closed his speech with these eloquent words: "Liberty *and* Union, now and forever, one and inseparable!"

Jackson needed to make his position on the Union and states' rights more clear. He agreed with many of the elements of a states' rights position, but not nullification, secession, or insecurity of the Union. Calhoun and Hayne went too far. At a dinner to celebrate the birthday of Thomas Jefferson on April 13, 1830, and to reaffirm the Democratic-Republican Party's connection to Jeffersonian principles, Jackson and Calhoun clarified their opposing views. In his toast Jackson claimed, "Our Union: It must be preserved." Calhoun responded, "The Union, next to our liberty, most dear. May we always remember that it can only be preserved by distributing equally the benefits and burdens of the Union."

In his second inaugural address Jackson attempted to clarify his views on the issue of states' rights and the Union:

> In the domestic policy of this Government there are two objects which especially deserve the attention of the people and their representatives, ... They are the preservation of the rights of the several States and the integrity of the Union. ...Without union our independence and liberty would never have been achieved; without union they can never be maintained.

Not convinced of the benign intentions of the government toward the South, after the election of 1832, the legislature of South Carolina voted to nullify federal tariff laws and secede from the Union if the federal government attempted to collect tariffs in the state after February 1, 1833. Jackson prepared for a showdown with the state. In December 1832, he issued a Proclamation on Nullification stating that "Disunion by armed force is treason."

Calhoun then resigned in 1833 as vice president in order to take his place for South Carolina in the U.S. Senate, believing that the issue would be settled in Congress. Jackson mobilized troops and supposedly claimed that he would hang Calhoun if South Carolina continued on this course of action. South Carolina postponed its secession deadline. Meanwhile, Congress passed the Force Bill, authorizing the president to use troops, if necessary, to collect the tariff. The bill also included a plan to gradually reduce the tariffs, which helped to mollify this fractious southern state. Moreover, when South Carolina sent representatives to other slave states to discover if any of them would join her in secession, the replies were all sympathetic but without commitment for secession at that time. The reduction in the tariff rate and the lack of concrete support from other slave states led South Carolina to back down and rescind its nullification law.

Moving the Native Americans West

Indian policy brought the most severe criticisms of the Jackson presidency. Personally, President Jackson believed that the Native Americans were in the way of white expansion. Of course, he was known as an Indian fighter. During the War of 1812, Jackson defeated the Creek tribe at the Battle of Horseshoe Bend. Several of the Native American tribes supported the British in the War of 1812. Showing his contradictory nature on some issues, Jackson saved, brought home, and raised an Indian baby orphaned by the battle. At the same time, Jackson also maintained that it was to save the Indian tribes that they must move west.

In 1830, Congress, with the urgent support of President Jackson, passed the Indian Removal Act. Congress demanded the tribes move west of the Mississippi River into the "Great American Desert," which was thought suitable for Indians only. They could move under their own volition or by government force. The government would exchange land in the West for the Indian land in the Southeast.

The Cherokee nation was one of the tribes opposed to moving. This tribe was very similar to the whites by this time. They farmed, had their own alphabet and newspaper, often dressed as the whites, and lived in much the same way as white society. They also understood white law and attempted to keep their lands protected from the whites in Georgia who wanted it by working through the white system of justice. In the case *Cherokee Nation vs. Georgia*, the Cherokee petitioned the U.S. Supreme Court to intervene against a state law that declared the laws of the Cherokee Nation null and void after June 1, 1830. The Court denied an injunction against the actions of Georgia. Georgia then insisted that white residents in the Cherokee nation must secure a license from the governor and take an oath of allegiance

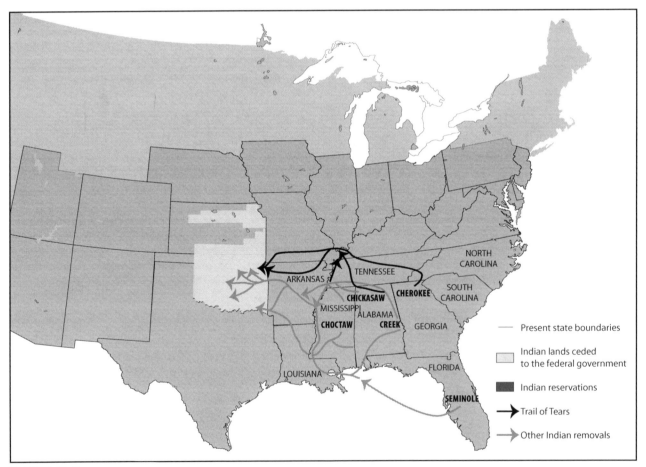

FIGURE 11.6 - The removal of the southern tribes to the West.

to Georgia. The Supreme Court, under the leadership of Chief Justice John Marshall, in *Worcester vs. Georgia*, ruled in 1832 that only federal law affected the tribal governments, and that the Cherokees were a "domestic dependent nation" and thus entitled to federal protection. The Supreme Court relied on the Executive branch to enforce its decision, and still does, so the Court was powerless to ensure the rights of the tribes. Jackson refused to implement the judgment of the court, and he got away with it because his Indian removal policy was so popular. A statement often attributed to Jackson, but which is probably apocryphal, was that "John Marshall has made his decision; now let him enforce it."

FIGURE 11.7 - Elizabeth Brown Stephens, a Cherokee Indian who walked the Trail of Tears

In 1834, Congress established Indian Territory in present-day Oklahoma, and this eventually became the homeland of the "Five Civilized Tribes," known as such because of the adoption of many of the white cultural elements. These were the Cherokee, Choctaw, Chickasaw, Creek, and Seminole. The majority of Cherokee opposed moving to the Indian Territory, but in 1835, the leaders of a small group signed the Treaty of New Echota, agreeing to the relocation of the entire tribe. The Senate ratified the treaty by only one vote more than the required two-thirds majority. This led to a sorrowful chapter in removal but also to discord in the tribe that later had serious repercussions. In 1838, General Winfield Scott and 7,000 troops began the process of gathering the tribe together and housing them in makeshift forts. They then traveled mostly on foot the approximately 1,000 miles to their new home. Lack of food, cold weather, and the neglect of the soldiers resulted in the deaths of about 4,000 of the approximately 15,000 Cherokee. This became known as the "Trail of Tears" for the proud yet now-defeated tribe. Some of the Cherokee escaped the removal and settled in the hills of North Carolina. There were many critics of the removal policy, including Henry Clay and John Quincy Adams.

Other tribes also opposed forced removal, resulting in three major Indian uprisings. The Sac and Fox tribe, under Chief Black Hawk, moved west out of present-day Wisconsin in 1831. When they returned the next year, they were virtually annihilated in the Black Hawk War of June 1832, a tragedy that convinced other tribes in that part of the country to move west. The Creeks attacked parts of Georgia in 1836 but were defeated and forced west of the Mississippi River. Finally, the Seminoles in Florida fought the long Second Seminole War from November 1835 to August 14, 1843, before their defeat. They had used the numerous swamps of Florida to their advantage and cost the federal government approximately $20 million to win the eventual victory.

At War with the Bank of the United States

President Jackson developed his hostility toward the Bank of the United States in the 1820s. While he was suspicious of banks, he did not set out to destroy all banks—just the monster of monopoly. By 1830, 30 percent of all national bank deposits were in the national bank, and the bank made 20 percent of the nation's loans. The national debt from the War of 1812 led to the chartering of the Second Bank of the United States in 1816 during the presidency of James Madison. During a time of rest following a physical collapse in 1822, Andrew Jackson pondered the state of the nation with great trepidation, and his unease about the alarming conditions in the republic led to his acceptance from the Tennessee General Assembly of its nomination as a candidate to run for the presidency unanimously passed on July 20, 1822. Accounts of corruption of elected officials at all government levels, economic crisis, and banking scandals were stories that filled the daily newspapers. Writing in what Jackson called his "memorandums," he despaired that liberty was at risk from the many examples of corruption in government "and when the people call, the Citizen is bound to render the service required." Appalling to Jackson was the role the Second Bank of the United States played in the Panic of 1819. According to Jackson and his supporters, the bank was a threat to the republic because of its great economic power over the financial dealings in the nation. This was a central bank in private hands that were given special powers and privileges. It epitomized the fear of special interests and corrupt power that gripped Jackson. State banks believed that the bank had special consideration as well. Westerners and farmers perceived the national bank to be an agent for the special interests of the Northeast and its urban areas, as well as certain foreign interests.

In many ways, Jackson was wrong about the bank, but its symbol as a dangerous privileged elite triumphed over sound economic judgment, and the Jacksonians launched a crusade and war against the bank. The national bank was the principal depository for the funds of the United States government and controlled, to a large extent, the gold and silver of the nation, upon which rested general economic prosperity or ruin. Private banks issued paper notes, the paper currency at the time, but these lacked a stable value, connected to the stability of the issuing bank as they were. These paper notes also gave private bankers power over the national economy. The Bank of the United States added both credit and stability to the economy. The president, however, perceived this private institution as a tool of its elite private investors and undemocratic as well as unconstitutional, without any accountability to the American people.

Political maneuverings brought on the battle against the bank. In 1831, the National Republican Party began putting together its campaign to bring down President Jackson in the 1832 election. Henry Clay, the intellectual leader of the party, wished to be president. To accomplish this goal, Clay chose the renewal of the charter of the Second Bank of the United States as his main policy plank to defeat the incumbent president. He knew that Jackson would come out swinging on this issue and hoped to gain support from the many pro-bank Americans. The bank was not due for re-charter until 1836, but Clay and Daniel Webster convinced the bank president Nicolas Biddle to apply for renewal in 1832. The idea behind this early renewal request was the expectation that Congress would pass it, but President Jackson's veto would give Clay the issue of the national bank.

Indeed, in the summer of 1832, the Senate and the House voted to re-charter the Bank of the United States, firing the first shots in the battle. The New England and Mid-Atlantic states provided strong support for the bill, while strong opposition came from the South and West, and the Northwest and Southwest gave a divided reaction. As predicted, President Jackson vetoed the bill and sent his explanation to Congress on July 10, 1832. His reasons were unconstitutionality, special privilege, monopoly, and foreign ownership of stock in the bank. He challenged the judicial branch by claiming it was the province of Congress and the President as much as that of the Supreme Court to decide on the constitutionality of laws. The Supreme Court had previously ruled in the case *McCulloch v. Maryland* that the Congressional charter of the First National Bank was constitutional. Jackson was alluding to the balance of power that Americans accepted. He opened the door to strengthening the presidency through its role as the protector of liberty. There were many outraged critics of not only President Jackson's veto but of his intrusion into the powers of the other branches of government, particularly the legislative branch, which the Founding Fathers had established as the preeminent branch.

Congress was not accustomed to vetoes. All of the previous presidents together had only used the veto nine times. Daniel Webster, with his great intellect and oratorical genius, spoke against the president in the Senate and criticized the attempt of Jackson to usurp the power of the legislative branch. Henry Clay spoke against the president as well. On July 16, 1832, both houses of Congress adjourned without overriding the veto. It was left to the voters to decide if the national bank would have its charter renewed, just as Henry Clay politically desired.

The 1832 Presidential Election

The Candidates

Jackson's first term came to a close, and it was back to the business of deciding the national leader for the next four years. By this time, Jackson's party had dropped the "Republican" part of its name and was simply calling itself the Democratic Party. The first Democratic presidential convention met in May 1832. Their business was basically to choose a running mate for Jackson. The delegates from all the states, except Missouri, concurred on the nominations Jackson received from many states

Presidential Election Results in 1832		
CANDIDATES	**POPULAR VOTE**	**ELECTORAL VOTE**
Jackson	687,502	219
Clay	530,189	49

FIGURE 11.8 - Election of 1832

and then chose Martin Van Buren as his vice presidential running mate. There was no platform or address. A major issue for the two national parties was the future of the Second Bank of the United States.

The National Republicans met in Baltimore, Maryland in December 1831 for their nominating convention. Representatives from 18 states nominated Henry Clay for president and John Sergeant of Pennsylvania as his running mate.

The Campaign and Results

There were several firsts in the campaign of 1832. For example, the new Anti-Masonic Party became the first third party to nominate a candidate for president. This party opposed the influence and the secrecy of the Masons; Andrew Jackson was a Mason. The Anti-Masonic Party supported several issues of morality that appealed to evangelical Protestant Christian groups. Moreover, this election produced the first national nominating conventions.

In spite of the large war chest of the National Republicans, support from many newspaper editors, and the votes of New England, Jackson was the choice of the people, and he was reelected to a second term by an electoral landslide.

The Final Shots in the Bank War

Jackson's reelection convinced the president that the nation gave to him a mandate to bring down the Second Bank of the United States. The 1832 veto denied the bank its early re-charter, but renewal was still possible in 1836. Acting against advice by Congressional committees, several cabinet members, and two secretaries of the

treasury, Jackson's new Secretary of the Treasury, Roger Taney, agreed with the president that the federal funds would no longer stay in the national bank. Acting in the only constitutional way he could at the time, Jackson ordered the removal of nearly all the federal funds from the bank. By the end of 1833, the funds were in 23 state banks. Furthermore, Jackson restricted the state banks in which he deposited federal money to those banks that had supported him for reelection. This infuriated Jackson's critics, who called them Jackson's "pet banks."

The president of the Bank, Nicholas Biddle, hoped to convince politicians and the citizens of the nation that the Bank of the United States was necessary as a central bank to preserve the economy of the United States. In August 1833, Biddle began to engineer a financial crisis to prove his point. He presented state bank notes for redemption, called in loans, and contracted the credit controlled by the bank. The plan was not as effective as Biddle hoped, but existence of the bank became a matter of debate in Congress, the press, and the public. Although businessmen sent representatives to Washington, D.C. to persuade Jackson and Congress to continue the bank in its role as a central stabilizing force in banking, Jackson pointed out that the situation as forced by Biddle was an example of the corrupting influence of the bank. The charter was not renewed, and the Bank of the United States became a commercial bank and continued to operate until it failed in 1841. Jackson won the battles and the war against the Bank of the United States, but not without suffering certain economic consequences.

Economic Problems

With Congress adjourned in July 1836, Jackson and the Secretary of the Treasury issued the Specie Circular, prohibiting the use of paper money to purchase public land in order to control inflation in the economy. Speculation, or get-rich-quick schemes in the buying and selling of public land in the West and other parts of the nation, along with investment in canal building, roads, and railroads, drove an economic boom in the economy for the first half of the 1830s. But it was also a primary reason for a severe downturn in the economy beginning in 1837. The lack of economic policies of President Jackson following the war on the Bank of the United States led to public land sales of approximately 37 million acres purchased mostly on credit between 1834 and 1836. Funds were more easily available from the state banks, and borrowing was rampant because there were no effective controls by the Bank of the United States. But this problem led to greatly increased inflation. The Specie Circular indicated a no-confidence attitude on the part of Jackson in the bank notes of the state banks and set the stage for the Panic of 1837 and the depression that would follow during the presidency of Martin Van Buren.

Foreign Policy Matters

There were two major foreign policy issues that required the attention of President Andrew Jackson. First, the French government refused to repay the damages to American shipping during the Napoleonic Wars, as it agreed to do in 1831. When Jackson threatened to end diplomatic relations with France and to confiscate all French property in the United States, the French government finally paid the damages.

Second, the situation in Texas was a problem for several presidents, including Jackson. President John Quincy Adams attempted to purchase Texas, a province of Mexico to which many Americans were moving, for $1 million. The government of Mexico rejected the offer, as they did the offer of President Jackson of $5 million for the area. In 1836, the Americans in Texas declared independence, but it resulted in war with Mexico. When Mexico lost the war, the Republic of Texas was created. However, most American Texans viewed independence as the first step toward becoming part of the United States. But Jackson did not want war with Mexico, nor did he want to rekindle the slavery issue that the annexation of Texas as a slave

territory would certainly do. Therefore, he did nothing of substance except to officially recognize the Republic of Texas on his last day in office in early March 1837.

The Legacy of President Andrew Jackson

Andrew Jackson as president had many firsts. He was the first president from the West, the first born in a log cabin, the first married to a divorced woman, the first to ride on a railroad, and he faced the first assassination attempt on a president in 1835. While attending a funeral, a guest pulled out two pistols and attempted to shoot him. Both pistols failed to fire but were later found to be in perfect working order. The odds against two perfectly fine pistols misfiring were very high.

This larger-than-life man extended his presidential legacy far into the future. It was true that the force of his own personality was not duplicated for years to come, and much of the strength of his presidency came from him alone. He took democracy to a new level in the nation when he dedicated his administration to protecting and projecting the will of the "people." It was not that he increased democracy, but that he protected the gains made and became the symbol of democracy for eligible voters. His presidential style took the presidency away from that of primarily acting as the head of state or supporter of Congress to a leadership role. Jackson maintained that the president could impose his will on the federal government and should when it was in the best interests of the nation. He used the veto, which also expanded his influence over the legislative branch. The Jacksonian vision of democracy inspired a new party dedicated to expanding Jeffersonian republicanism to more properly accommodate the requirements of a changing nation. The Democrats began the second party system and remain as one half of the major party system today.

With regard to specific accomplishments as promised to the nation, his administration, according to recent studies, was one of the most honest and least corrupt. He saved the Union at the time with his actions against nullification. The government opened millions of acres of land, although this was at the expense of many Indian tribes, which was a mixed legacy. But he might have saved the tribes from extinction or harm with their removal to the West, at least according to his calculations. The tribes disagreed with his assessment. He brought economy to the government, and the country was prosperous and secure from foreign threats when he left office.

But his legacy was not entirely positive. His appointments were poor. His intentions in moving the tribes west might have contained some positive benefits in his mind, but he faced stiff criticism then and now for his actions. The horrible results of the trips west were particularly difficult to accept. He destroyed the national bank, and this impacted economic difficulties in the future because he had not planned for a suitable replacement.

According to Robert Remini, the accepted authority on Jackson, "Here, then was Jacksonian Democracy simply defined, here Jackson's legacy to the nation: the people are sovereign, their will is absolute; liberty survives only when defended by the virtuous." These are certainly words for presidents to abide by. His shadow extended over the presidents serving during his lifetime as he gave advice, as well as directly using his influence to bring about results he believed served the people of the nation.

The 1836 Presidential Election

The Democrats

The Democrats held their convention in Baltimore, Maryland, on May 20, 1835, to put forward their candidates for president and vice president. Jackson was too old and infirm to consider another term in office, but he hoped to keep his policies in place by influencing the selection of candidates. Vice President Martin Van Buren and Jackson were of a like mind on many issues, and Van Buren was the chosen successor. Although chosen by a unanimous vote, the Democrats were not wholeheartedly supportive of Van Buren. But he was the choice of Old Hickory, and using a lot of political clout, Jackson had his way. Nicknamed "the magician," Van Buren had a long tenure in politics even though it was his behind-the-scene stratagems that brought him political success, along with his nickname, rather than his own charisma or ideas resonating with the voters. He was one of the organizers of the Democratic Party and

of great assistance to Jackson in the 1828 presidential election. Richard M. Johnson of Kentucky was the vice presidential candidate, a man whose fame primarily stemmed from his claim that he had been the soldier who actually killed Tecumseh during the War of 1812, a claim that was never confirmed. A formal platform was not adopted. Instead, what amounted to a platform basically arose from Van Buren's letter of acceptance of the nomination, in which he stated he would "tread generally in the footsteps of President Jackson."

The Whigs

By 1834, the National Republican Party had died out, being replaced by the Whig Party. The Whigs were a weak coalition of the supporters of Henry Clay and his American System, those alienated by Jackson's war against the national bank, Southerners opposed to Jackson's vigorous stand against nullification and secession, and the few remaining by 1836 of the defunct Anti-Masonic Party. In other words, the only thing that just about every Whig had in common with each other was his hatred for Andrew Jackson, hardly a recipe for long-term growth and success.

Because the Whigs were not united in political philosophy, they gambled on an election strategy in 1836 that they hoped would deny any candidate a majority of the electoral votes and throw the election to the House of Representatives. Specifically, their strategy was to put forth several candidates nominated from various state legislatures rather than from a nominating convention, a tactic designed to divide the electoral votes among them and prevent any one of them from receiving a majority. The list of candidates consisted of Massachusetts Whig Senator Daniel Webster, Tennessee Senator Hugh L. White, William P. Mangum of North Carolina, and William Henry Harrison of Ohio, a national war hero. In this way, each major region of the country was represented by a Whig candidate for president.

The Anti-Masons

What was left of the Anti-Masonic Party met at Harrisburg, Pennsylvania, and also nominated William Henry Harrison for president and Francis Granger of New York for vice president.

Presidential Election Results in 1836		
CANDIDATES	POPULAR VOTE	ELECTORAL VOTE
Martin Van Buren	761,549	170
William Henry Harrison	549,567	73
Hugh L. White	145,396	26
Daniel Webster	41,287	14
William P. Mangum		11

FIGURE 11.9 - Election of 1836

The Results

The strategy backfired on the Whigs. By fragmenting the popular vote among the several states, Democrat Van Buren won an outright majority of the electoral votes to win the presidency. But in a twist of irony, none of the vice presidential candidates received a majority of the electoral votes, so the selection of the vice president fell to the U.S. Senate for the first time in history, as required by the Constitution. The Senate chose Richard M. Johnson, who had been Van Buren's running mate.

Introduction to the Van Buren Administration

The eighth president of the United States came into the White House with a great deal of political experience. He had successively served as a New York state senator, U.S. senator from New York, Governor of New York, Secretary of State, and Vice President of the United States. He was also Jackson's hand-picked successor, which brought him the presidency but not, unfortunately, the complete support of the party or the public. Along with a lack of support from many factions, Van Buren also inherited the former president's enemies and several problems in the making.

The Panic of 1837

A major problem for President Van Buren was an economic panic that resulted in a depression for the nation from 1837-1843. Economic boom and then recessions or depressions were not new to the United States, but the panic of 1837 led to the most severe depression yet. The economic policies of former President Jackson actually contributed to weakening the economy even though Van Buren coped with the blame for the depression. (See the section entitled "Economic Problems" for a brief discussion of the Specie Circular above.) Failure of wheat crops in the United States added to the distress of American farmers and consumers. Finally, the call from two failed British banks for a repayment of loans in the United States topped off the economic woes of the nation. On May 10, 1837, New York banks began to refuse to convert paper money into specie, and an economic panic began.

The nation toppled into a depression, and the suffering was deep and widespread. Out of 850 banks, 343 closed entirely, commodity prices dropped, public land sales decreased, imports dwindled, which in turn diminished customs revenues for the federal government, factories closed, and unemployment increased by the tens of thousands.

The solutions to the problem were few and not fully supported by either party. The Whigs supported the idea of a more active government in the economy of the country. They wanted an expansion of bank credit, increased tariffs, and more government-backed internal improvements. Van Buren continued to hold the Jackson course of distance between the government and the economy.

A central banking system might have alleviated some of the banking difficulties in the states, but Van Buren kept to his resolve of no banking regulation or central bank and advanced the idea of an independent treasury. He maintained that placing federal funds in private banks caused many of the current economic problems. Therefore, it was time to separate banking and the government completely. Government dollars would be withdrawn from private banks and deposited in vaults controlled by the Treasury Department in several of the large cities around the nation. This would also shrink available credit for many Americans and reduce inflation. The Independent Treasury Bill passed in 1840 in spite of mild support from the Democrats and outright condemnation from the Whigs. The Whigs hoped to keep the bill from passing in expectation of a revival of the Bank of the United States. There was a partial victory for the Whigs when they repealed the law in 1841, but the Democrats had the final say when the plan returned in 1846 and continued until the Federal Reserve System originated in 1913.

Van Buren's personal actions during the depression turned many against him. He redecorated the White House and posted guards to keep unwanted guests out of the president's residence. His detractors labeled him "Martin Van Ruin" and an aristocrat and blamed him for the depression. The problems of the depression dominated his administration.

Foreign Policy Problems

Van Buren, as did Jackson before him, opposed the annexation of Texas to the Union. An anti-slavery Democrat, he opposed bringing in a state that would add to the slave states another ally. There were also concerns about the reaction of Mexico with regard to the handling of the Texas issue. As explained in the next chapter, Texas would eventually be annexed by the John Tyler administration.

Another delicate foreign policy matter concerned the *Caroline* Affair. In 1837, William L. Mackenzie, a Canadian journalist, led a rebellion for more democratic government in what is now called Ontario. A group of sympathetic Americans used their own steamer, the *Caroline*, to deliver supplies to the rebels on Navy Island near Niagara Falls. During the night of

FIGURE 11.10 - Martin Van Buren

December 29, 1837, a small band of Canadians supporting the government set fire to the *Caroline* and set her adrift, resulting in the ship going over the falls. One American was killed in this episode, prompting President Van Buren to send General Winfield Scott to the region in order to prevent Americans from expressing their anti-British feelings through violent action. Although the *Caroline* Affair created tensions between the United States and Britain, the two nations avoided war.

The "Log Cabin and Hard Cider" Election of 1840

The Whigs

The campaign for president in 1840 was lively in a very modern sense. It was not usual for the candidates to actually run for office because it was viewed as greed for power. But that is what William Henry Harrison did.

The Whig Party's nominating convention met in Harrisburg, Pennsylvania on December 4, 1839 and decided to avoid the disastrous results of the 1836 run for the presidency and choose only one candidate. Henry Clay led on the first ballot. But he had gathered too many political enemies for his strong stands. Therefore, in the interests of "union and harmony," William Henry Harrison of Ohio won the nomination. John Tyler from Virginia, a states' rights advocate, was the choice for Harrison's running mate.

There was no formal platform adopted, and the party was still more of a coalition than a coherent party. Harrison said very little about the issues during the campaign, which prompted the Democrats to nickname him "General Mum." What the party lacked in substance, it made up for in campaign enthusiasm. A scathing article against Harrison in the Baltimore *Republican* gave the Whigs the images that the party promoted in the campaign, the log cabin and barrels of cider. The campaign was also full of placards, emblems, rallies, floats, transportable log cabins, and the slogans "Tippecanoe and Tyler too" and "Van, Van is a used-up man." They portrayed Harrison as a simple American man and Van Buren as an extravagant aristocrat. The opposite was actually the truth, but as the campaigning continued so did the evasions, misrepresentations, and irrelevant focus on personalities rather than important issues. As the campaign continued, more serious issues emerged. The country continued its economic depression. The Whigs believed that a strong national bank could alleviate some of the economic ills. They also supported higher tariffs and federal aid for interstate transportation. They won the support of many manufacturers, commercial farmers, and social reformers. Women were also allowed to participate in the campaign, although they could not vote.

William Henry Harrison was actually born into a wealthy and prominent Virginia family, contrary to campaign rhetoric. He obtained a commission in the army and was sent to the Northwest Territory and participated in the Battle of Fallen Timbers in 1794. It was his military success that brought him to national attention and the presidency. Following the division of the Northwest Territory, he accepted an appointment as the governor of Indiana Territory. As governor of the territory, he organized and led the militia in a campaign to destroy the tribal confederacy led by Shawnee brothers Tecumseh and Tenskwatawa. The battle at Tippecanoe

Creek was a victory for Harrison that assured him a place in history and a campaign slogan for president. He fought in the Battle of the Thames during the War of 1812 against the British in Canada, where Tecumseh was killed fighting for the British. Harrison moved his political aspirations to Ohio and supported Henry Clay in the 1824 presidential election. Clay made sure that Harrison was the choice as minister to Colombia. This was part of John Quincy Adams' and Clay's plans to improve relations with South America.

The Democrats

The Democratic Convention in Baltimore, Maryland nominated President Martin Van Buren as their candidate but could not agree upon a vice-presidential running mate. The Democrats ran with a platform consisting of opposition to Congressional interference with slavery, opposition to a national bank, opposition to internal improvements at the expense of the federal government, and a strict constructionist view for government. Van Buren and the Democrats continued much of the Jacksonian agenda. Government catering to special interests invited corruption and was not to be tolerated. However, Van Buren had little solid support in his second election, especially because of the economic depression. Even his home state of New York deserted him over the party's pro-southern policies.

Interesting Notes

One interesting legacy from the 1840 presidential campaign was the popularization of the expression "OK." First appearing in Boston's *Morning Post* newspaper in 1839 as a shortened symbol of "oll korrect" (oddball spellings were common then), the 1840 election campaign made "OK" a popular expression as representing Van Buren as "old Kinderhook," a reference to his Dutch-named hometown of Kinderhook, New York.

Another interesting note from this election: Abolitionists against slavery formed the Liberty Party in 1839 and ran their first presidential candidate, James G. Birney, an abolitionist from Kentucky who had fled that slave state and moved to Ohio for his own safety.

Presidential Election Results in 1840		
CANDIDATES	POPULAR VOTE	ELECTORAL VOTE
William Henry Harrison	1,275,017	234
Martin Van Buren	1,128,702	60
James G. Birney (Liberty Party)	7,059	

FIGURE 11.11 - Election of 1840

The Results

In November 1840, 78 percent of all eligible voters went to the polls in the highest percentage turnout in American history. Not only did Harrison win an electoral landslide victory, but the Whigs took control of both houses of Congress as well, handing the Democrats their worst defeat up to that time.

Barely a President

The campaign was interesting and invigorating, but the inauguration brought death to the newly elected president. The day of March 4, 1841 dawned cold, windy, and rainy in the nation's capital. Nearly 68 years of age, William Henry Harrison was the oldest elected president in American history until Ronald Reagan in 1980. The new president wished to show both his vigor and his intellectual qualities on this day and gave, without overcoat or top hat, the longest inaugural speech of any president. He made it clear to the country and Congress that the Executive branch expected to follow the lead of Congress.

Harrison chose a Cabinet and called Congress into special session to resolve the economic problems of the nation, but died of pneumonia on April 4, 1841, just 31 days after his inauguration. Harrison became the first American president to die in office of any cause. That made John Tyler the first vice president to take up residence in the White House following the death of a president in office, leading his critics to dub him, "His Accidency."

Introduction to the Tyler Administration

Following the death of President Harrison, there was a question about the position of the vice president under these circumstances as to whether he was an acting president or actually the next president. Tyler resolved the issue when he insisted he was President Tyler. Tyler, a slave-holding Virginian, was the vice presidential running mate for Harrison in order to balance the Whig ticket in 1840 with a Westerner and a Southerner. His anti-Jackson position was also a plus. As has often been the case, the party and the voters overlooked the vice president's suitability for the presidency. Tyler had difficulties governing from the beginning. A major problem was his disagreement with so many of the Whig positions on the issues. Tyler was at heart a southern Democrat, even though he left that party because of Jackson's stand against nullification. When he fell into the presidency, his Democratic beliefs came to the forefront in his policy-making.

Tyler retained the Harrison Cabinet, but when Congress began passing typically Whig, or anti-Democratic proposals, the president exercised the veto. Congress eliminated the subtreasury banking system. President Tyler then vetoed the next two bills that attempted to revive a national banking system. His cabinet resigned because of these actions, except for Secretary of State Daniel Webster. The Whigs retaliated by expelling Tyler from the Whig Party. Tyler filled a new Cabinet with conservative Democrats, but many resignations and new members were common throughout his administration. Amazingly, even former Vice President John C. Calhoun came back to Washington, D.C. as Secretary of State in March 1844, after Daniel Webster finally stepped down from that post. During the summer of 1842, Tyler vetoed two bills for higher tariffs. He did agree, however, to a higher tariff measure in August 1842 to replenish funds in an almost empty treasury. Without a national banking system, public funds were in the hands of the Secretary of the Treasury, and he deposited the funds in state banks, much as President Jackson had. Tyler continued to anger the Whigs in Congress, but a few supporters in the House of Representative were able to stop an impeachment attempt of the president.

Foreign Policy Issues

President Tyler had more success in foreign affairs than domestic. The border between Maine and New Brunswick, Canada had never been resolved, with both sides claiming the disputed territory that included the Aroostook River Valley. When Canadian lumbermen entered the valley in early 1839, Maine sent its militia to force them out. When New Brunswick responded by sending its own militia to the area, full-scale war seemed imminent. Indeed, there was a barroom brawl between American and British soldiers, but that was the extent of the so-called Aroostook War. General Winfield Scott arrived with an American force and negotiated the end of the crisis. During Tyler's administration, Daniel Webster and the president resolved the boundary dispute through the negotiation of the Webster-Ashburton Treaty, ratified by the Senate on August 20, 1842. The treaty fixed the boundary between Maine and New Brunswick along its present line, and extended the boundary westward to the Lake of the Woods, on the border with present-day Minnesota. The United States retained the large Mesabi iron deposits with this treaty.

In other foreign policy matters, the Tyler administration negotiated a treaty with China in 1844 that opened economic trade between the United States and China. But he would suffer one final defeat at the hands of Congress, when it voted to override a presidential veto for the first time in history on a bill that prohibited payment for naval ships that President Tyler had ordered without Congressional approval.

In 1844, Tyler organized his own party from which to run for the presidency. The Tyler Democrats focused their campaign on the annexation of Texas, knowing that Texas would eventually come into the Union as a slave state. As more fully explained in Chapter 13, Tyler signed the bill annexing Texas by the United States just before he left office in early 1845. However, Andrew Jackson urged Tyler to withdraw from the race in 1844 in favor of James K. Polk, his good friend from his own home state of Tennessee. The Democratic candidate also favored the annexation of Texas. In order to make certain the defeat of the Whigs and their candidate Henry Clay, Tyler withdrew from the race.

Concluding Thoughts

Although John Tyler was no Andrew Jackson, he embodied some of the leadership style of the former president. He was willing to stand for what he believed regardless of the results, and he was not afraid to use his power as president with the veto to achieve his policy goals. The shadow of Jackson was not quite finished. President Polk was a recipient of Jackson's support as well.

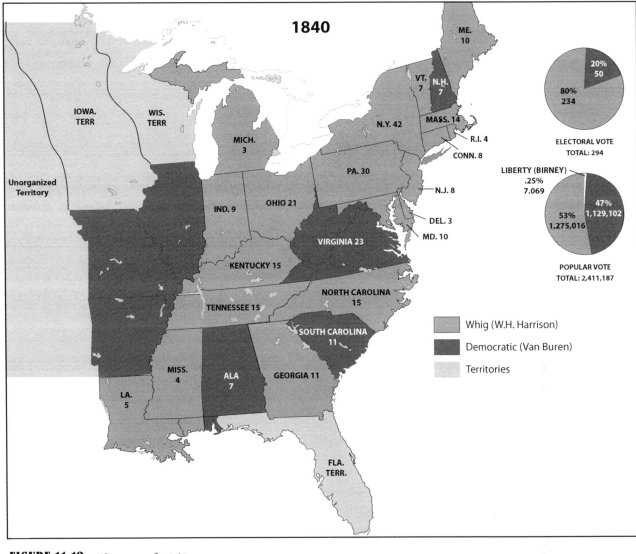

1840

ME. 10

VT. 7

N.H. 7

N.Y. 42

MASS. 14

R.I. 4

CONN. 8

PA. 30

N.J. 8

DEL. 3

MD. 10

IOWA. TERR

WIS. TERR

MICH. 3

IND. 9

OHIO 21

VIRGINIA 23

KENTUCKY 15

Unorganized Territory

NORTH CAROLINA 15

TENNESSEE 15

SOUTH CAROLINA 11

MISS. 4

ALA 7

GEORGIA 11

LA. 5

FLA. TERR.

ELECTORAL VOTE
TOTAL: 294

20%
50

80%
234

LIBERTY (BIRNEY)
.25%
7.069

47%
1,129,102

53%
1,275,016

POPULAR VOTE
TOTAL: 2,411,187

☐ Whig (W.H. Harrison)

■ Democratic (Van Buren)

☐ Territories

FIGURE 11.12 - Election of 1840

This vintage engraving depicts the portrait of Henry David Thoreau (1817-1862), the American author, poet, and naturalist. Engraved by an unknown artist, it was published in an 1882 biography of Thoreau and is now in the public domain. Digital restoration by Steven Wynn Photography. Copyright 2010 iStockphoto.

Chapter 12 Contents

CHAPTER TWELVE

American Culture and the Age of Social Reform

Major Events

Early 1800s	Romanticism flourished Second Great Awakening
1809	Washington Irving's *Knickerbocker's History of New York* published
1821	Emma Willard founded Troy (New York) Female Seminary
1825	New Harmony utopian community founded in Indiana by Robert Owen
1826	American Temperance Society founded James Fenimore Cooper published his *The Last of the Mohicans*
1830	Joseph Smith founded the Mormon Church
1830-60	Age of Social Reform
1837	Horace Mann became first leader of the Massachusetts Board of Education
1841	Brook Farm utopian community founded
1844	Great Disappointment for William Miller's movement
1848	Woman's Rights Convention began in Seneca Falls, New York Oneida Community established in New York
1849	Henry David Thoreau published his *On the Duty of Civil Disobedience*
1850	Nathaniel Hawthorne published *The Scarlet Letter*
1851	Maine became first state to pass Prohibition against alcohol Nathaniel Hawthorne published *The House of the Seven Gables* Herman Melville published his *Moby-Dick*
1855	Walt Whitman published his *Leaves of Grass*

Introduction

As described previously in Chapter 10, the United States was experiencing rapid changes in its development of the factory system, its Western expansion, and in a growing transportation network. These and other changes reinforced what had already become a tradition of optimism among Americans. The Age of Social Reform reflected this optimism for the future during part of the first half of the 19th century, specifically from 1830-1860. During this era, increasing numbers of Americans voluntarily formed or joined new movements to reform society in a variety of ways. These reform movements included the areas of health, temperance, women's rights, prison and mental health treatment, care for the poor, education, and an anti-slavery movement.

While historians usually date the Age of Social Reform from 1830-1860, the major influences that helped produce it extend back into the very late 18th century of post-Revolutionary War American society. The two most important influences were the rise of something called the Romanticist movement and a religious revival movement known as the Second Great Awakening.

Romanticism

The Enlightenment, with its mechanistic view of nature, inevitable progress, and perfectibility of man, had been the intellectual basis for the American Revolution. But by the 1790s, with the Revolution safely behind Americans, an intellectual shift occurred away from Enlightenment thinking to Romanticism. As was the norm before the 20th century, new movements such as this one began in Western Europe first and then migrated across the Atlantic to America. European writers who significantly contributed to this new spirit included men such as the German Johann von Goethe and Englishmen like Samuel Taylor Coleridge, William Wordsworth, and Thomas Carlyle.

Romanticism dominated American leaders after the Founding Fathers, and it was the intellectual basis for the political and social reforms, especially in the 1830s, '40s, and '50s. It had three fundamental principles, which perhaps can be better understood in contrast to the Enlightenment. First, each individual organism—including a person, institution, or society as a whole—has its own internal set of laws to govern it. By contrast, the Enlightenment had declared there is a body of natural law that governs every basic type of organism. Second, beliefs, behaviors, and institutions were fluid and expected to change or adapt to new conditions. This was in sharp contrast to the Enlightenment, which had taught that each organism should get in lockstep with the natural law that governs it. Third, Romanticism emphasized diversity, giving great value to differences of opinion and individual tastes. By contrast, the Enlightenment had stressed uniformity in accordance with mechanistic natural law. Indeed, one can say that Romanticism was internal and glorified the individual, while the Enlightenment had been external and glorified natural law. In other words, change, growth, feelings, emotions, and "worship" of the individual were of vital importance to Romanticist thinkers, while rigid conformance to objective natural law, reason, and intellect were more important to Enlightenment thinkers.

Yet in the midst of these contrasting positions, it is ironic that both Romanticism and the Enlightenment shared a common optimistic view of human nature and agreed that progress is inevitable and perfection is possible.

The Second Great Awakening

Backdrop to the Second Great Awakening

Religion has always played an important role in shaping American thought. Even the famous French nobleman, Alexis de Tocqueville, who toured the United States in the early 1830s, declared that "there is no country in the world where the Christian religion retains greater influence" than in the United States. Therefore, to ignore religion in American history is to deny a sufficient understanding of its culture. Until almost the 20th century, American religion was primarily defined as Protestant Christianity, although numerous denominations represented a rich mix of religious ideas within Protestantism.

By the close of the 18th century, the impact of the Enlightenment, with its Age of Reason, had been to partially erode traditional Christian belief. In New England, the well-established strict Puritan tradition had created fertile ground for a religious backlash, especially among intellectuals. In a primary sense, Deism was the religious outlook of Enlightenment thinkers on both sides of the Atlantic. Deists acknowledged the existence of God who had created the whole universe, but they insisted that God created natural law to run the universe. Then when God equipped mankind with a special intelligence based on his ability to reason, He gave man the responsibility to discover that natural law and to govern his life and institutions in harmony with it. This means that God intervenes very little, if at all, in the affairs of man. Therefore, Desists denied the divinity of Jesus and the Bible as the inspired Word of God. Instead, Jesus was viewed only as a great ethical teacher and the Bible as a fascinating collection of respected ancient literature. Reason and science replaced revelation and the Bible as the primary sources of knowledge about everything, including moral behavior. Many, but by no means all, of America's most influential Founding Fathers were Deists, including Benjamin Franklin and Thomas Jefferson.

The Deistic liberal challenge to traditional Christianity was followed near the end of the 18th century by Unitarianism, also more popular among New England intellectuals. Rejecting the divinity of Jesus like Deists meant that they also rejected the traditional Christian doctrine of the trinity, that one God exists within an eternal unity of the Father, the Son (Jesus), and the Holy Spirit. This belief accounts for their name, for the prefix *uni* refers to an absolute one, as in one Being called God. They emphasized the loving nature of God as Father, who, contrary to Deism, does interact with man in history. Unitarians also rejected the doctrine of original sin and believed in the essential goodness of man, a goodness that education could help develop in a person over a long, slow process of character building. For this reason, Unitarians criticized revivalism as being

FIGURE 12.1 -
Ralph Waldo Emerson.

merely a splashy show. Ralph Waldo Emerson, of great literary fame, was perhaps the most famous early American Unitarian. Although small in number, Unitarians attracted many wealthy and well-educated people, which meant that they were (and are today) more influential than their numbers would suggest.

The Actual Second Great Awakening

While Deism and Unitarianism had represented a liberal, rationalist, and humanistic reaction to the perceived excesses of the Puritan tradition, this reaction in turn fostered a religious reaction to it. Beginning about 1795 and extending to about 1830, Americans experienced a massive revival movement in many of their churches. It so rivaled the Great Awakening of the early 18th century that it became known as the Second Great Awakening. This new revivalism and religious fervor especially swept the Western frontier and the South, and it was the strongest among Methodists and Baptists, with a fair number of Presbyterians as well. By 1830, church attendance and belief in the literal interpretation of the Bible was so strong in the South that this region became known as the Bible Belt.

As with most Protestant revival movements, this one emphasized emotions and personal conversions. Many had ecstatic conversions and "got saved." Camp meetings were held in rural areas of the country, in which people came by the thousands to live temporarily in tents and listen to emotionally, fiery preachers exhorting them to repentance and a better moral life. The most famous camp meeting occurred in Cane Ridge, Kentucky in 1801, where 15,000 to 25,000 people attended the meetings that August. After the Erie Canal was completed in 1825, new canal towns sprang up in western New York state and brought more drinking and gambling as well as prosperity. Such fertile ground for revivals brought so many of them that western New York became nicknamed the "burned-over district" because of all the "fire and brimstone" preaching there.

Yale Professor of Divinity Nathaniel William Taylor and evangelists Charles G. Finney, James McGready, Peter Cartwright, and Barton Stone were some of the key leaders of the Second Great Awakening. Among them, Charles Grandison Finney (1792-1875) eventually became recognized as the most significant theologian, or scholar, of this revival movement. Finney was a lawyer who abandoned his law practice after a personal conversion experience in 1821. He had read some of the works of John Wesley, the British preacher whose theology had led to the founding of the Methodist Church. Finney was particularly impressed with the notion of the "second blessing." The idea is that all genuine Christian believers receive a portion of the Holy Spirit at their new birth, or conversion, which is the "first blessing" of the Holy Spirit. However, there is more power available to the Christian than is obtained at one's conversion. A believer can receive the "second blessing" of the Holy Spirit, in which He comes into full control of the person, thus bringing the gift of spiritual perfection. Second Great Awakening preachers divided over how a believer obtains this "second blessing," with some maintaining that it comes instantaneously through some ecstatic experience, and others insisting that it is a more gradual process of maturity until spiritual perfection has been attained.

No matter how the "second blessing" is achieved, most Second Great Awakening preachers taught that perfected American believers would help lead the way to the eventual establishment of the millennium, a Christian doctrine that most believers viewed as a reign of peace, prosperity, and goodwill on Earth, lasting anywhere from 1,000 years (literal meaning of the word *millennium*, derived from the Latin) to an indefinite long period of time. This view is also called post-millennialism because it teaches that Christ will return visibly to establish His literal kingdom on Earth after the millennium has ended.

An integral part of Finney's theology was man's free will, or power of choice, that one could choose to live a better life and reach perfection with the assistance of the Holy Spirit. Therefore, the Second Great Awakening placed more emphasis on free will, in contrast to the predestination of the original Great Awakening. Belief in the ability to attain spiritual perfection and push the

world toward the millennium provided a great incentive to engage in various social reform movements to speed up progress toward this goal. Reform movements of every kind flourished in this religious climate. On the religious front, the American Bible Society was organized in 1816 to greatly multiply the number of Bibles available for distribution. Sunday schools were promoted in churches to bring the blessings of Christianity within the easier reach of children and young people. Many sought to close most places of business and shut down postal mail delivery on Sundays, partly through a renewed campaign for Sunday blue laws. On other fronts, churches became more involved in reform movements like temperance, prison reform, and the anti-slavery cause, although the latter movement was ignored by most believers in the South, where slavery was flourishing as never before.

Women were especially energized as they more eagerly responded to the Second Great Awakening than men. They formed missionary societies, distributed millions of Bibles and other religious literature, and began a campaign to encourage Godly mothering within Christian homes. Moreover, many women took notice that they had little or no political rights and organized the first real women's rights movement in American history. In many other reform movements, women took major leadership roles in the effort to bring the millennium to the world.

Political Reform in the Midst of Social Reform

In the early days of the Republic, most Americans seemed to agree that the new government needed to be run by the upper classes, who in turn, should protect the equal rights and opportunities of all men—all except women, Indians, and blacks, of course. But Romanticism and the Second Great Awakening pushed many white Americans to demand more democratization for themselves. Also, an expanding western frontier, with its rugged individualism and rough equality, added fuel to the fires of political reform.

By the early 1820s, many appointed offices at the local and state levels of government became elected offices instead. Voting rights became liberalized during this period as both religious and property qualifications for white males faded away by the 1830s, and even sooner in some Western states. Written ballots gradually replaced the old "stand up" voice method of voting by the early 1820s. While less intimidating, it wasn't until the 20th century that the introduction of the secret ballot actually made voting a private process in America. Political reforms related to presidential elections were also undertaken in the early 19th century. The Constitution leaves to the states how to determine the selection of its presidential electors after every presidential vote. Originally, state legislatures selected the electors. However, in the spirit of democratic reform, by 1824 only six of 24 states still had their legislatures selecting electors for presidential elections. Instead, most of the states were then allowing their voters to directly elect a slate of electors for their state. This trend continued until by 1832, only South Carolina was left with the more undemocratic method. In fact, it was after the Civil War before South Carolina allowed its voters to elect presidential electors.

The old system of Congressional party caucuses nominating candidates for President and Vice President broke down in 1824. Under that old system, members of Congress would attend a caucus consisting only of their Congressional colleagues of the same political party, and their caucus would select the presidential and vice-presidential candidates for their party. Under the so-called Era of Good Feelings, when everyone called himself a Republican, there wasn't much point in attending the Congressional caucus. After the Anti-Masonic Party, the first nationwide third party in American history, introduced the concept of a nominating convention to nominate its presidential ticket in 1831 (the current President, Andrew Jackson, was a Freemason), the major parties began to follow suit. The National Republican Party held such a convention in late 1831, and the Democratic Party did so in May 1832.

These political reforms both reflected and caused the early 19th century to become the age of the "common man," at least for the white male. The percentage of white men voting rose sharply during this time. Of course, almost no state gave free black men the right to vote, and women were not allowed to vote either. Nevertheless, this limited but energetic democratic spirit gave further impetus to rising expectations among women especially,

and even to men also. It was, therefore, only natural that many Americans would turn to non-political reform organizations also, in order to further the cause of various reforms in society.

Political Parties and the Age of Social Reform

At the time the Age of Social Reform was just cranking up in the early 1830s, the two major political parties were the Whigs and the Democrats. Both of these parties, as organizations, tended to ignore the controversial social issues of the day, like slavery, women's rights, and temperance. Both parties had a pro-slavery Southern wing, which they did not wish to offend. Although the Whig Party ignored most of the social issues of the day, most social reformers were Whigs. The reason had more to do with the Democratic Party than with the Whig Party, however.

The Democratic Party was particularly dominated by its Southern wing, which because of its pro-slavery stance, encouraged the party as a whole to avoid the anti-slavery movement. The South also remained indifferent regarding public education, partly due to the plantation elite rejecting the idea that their property tax money should be used to educate other families' children since they could afford to send their children to private schools in the North or even abroad or hire private tutors, and partly because it was a more class-conscious society that was less upwardly mobile and thus needed little formal education. Moreover, the South held to certain aristocratic notions about the role of men and women in society, notions that militated against support for the expansion of women's rights. In the North, Democrats appealed to new immigrants and laborers, who were more likely to carry traditional European attitudes toward women and alcohol and to be hostile to free black Americans, whose competition with them for jobs was perceived to keep wages relatively low. For all these reasons, few Democrats were involved in any of the social reform movements of the era.

From a geographical perspective, the primary center of social reform was New England, New York, and areas of the Midwest (the old Northwest Territory), which had been heavily settled by New Englanders. Although the two major political parties were competitive in the North, especially outside New England, the facts presented earlier about the Democratic Party explain why more northern Whigs were sympathetic to social reform causes than most Democrats. However, the fact that neither political party as an organization wanted to touch most of the social issues of the day left Americans to pursue reforms largely outside the political arena. Thus, private voluntary organizations flourished and drove the cause of social reforms during the period from 1830-1860.

For the next several pages, this chapter examines the most important specific social reform movements of the era. The entire question of slavery and the anti-slavery movement, however, is addressed separately in Chapter 14.

Health Reform

The major obstacle to good health in the early 19th century was a lack of knowledge about proper nutrition, germ theory, and the need for sanitation. This led to poor dietary habits and the prevalence of harmful bacterium that brought frequent infections. Epidemics of smallpox and yellow fever killed thousands. The life expectancy was no more than about 40 years. At the same time, physicians still engaged in the practice of bleeding patients who were ill, on the grounds that the sickness must be in the blood. They also frequently treated patients with large doses of poisonous drugs and other substances, such as mercury. Most of these practices had been going on from the early colonial period, of course. Therefore, it was still true in the 19th century that the best thing a sick person could do to get well was to stay away from a physician.

It was little wonder, then, that physicians were widely distrusted. This situation created a vacuum that was filled by more popular health treatments prescribed by non-physicians. Some of them were effective and some mere quackery. Incidentally, the word "quack" as applied to pseudo-doctors originated in the early 20th century and was a shortened version of a longer term referring to the 19th century practice of prescribing mercury for various illnesses.

Probably the most popular alternative to traditional, medical practice was the use of hydropath treatments, often called the "water cure." The idea of alternately applying hot and cold water to the human body originated in Europe and came to the United States in the 1840s. Sanitariums offering hydropath treatments sprang up all over the country as places that Americans could go and receive rest, relaxation, and hot and cold treatments. Hydropath treatments, like all natural remedies, including herbs, take longer to work than modern medicines, but generally do improve health in the long run. We now understand, for example, that the use of alternate hot and cold water stimulates the bone marrow to produce more white blood cells, the body's natural antibodies.

The best-known health reformer of the period was Sylvester Graham, of Graham cracker fame. In the 1830s, Graham began advocating a vegetarian diet that included the regular consumption of vegetables, fruit, and whole wheat. He warned that eating red meat and foods containing refined flour promoted ill health. There were other health reformers saying essentially the same things about diet that Sylvester Graham did. The irony of this teaching is that nutrition science in the late 20th century largely confirms the healthfulness of Graham's diet, even though many Americans do not make those changes in their eating habits. What is so amazing is that Graham and other nutrition health reformers did not have the benefit of scientific studies to validate their claims.

On the quackery side of health reform, ordinary salesmen, claiming that their particular tonic could cure virtually any illness, peddled numerous patent medicines. Most of them contained rather generous amounts of alcohol. Then there was the so-called science of phrenology, which had originated with an Austrian doctor in the 1830s. In the 1840s, American brothers Orson and Lorenzo Fowler wrote and sold books on phrenology. The basic concept is that the shape of the human skull, with its bumps and depressions, could explain a person's development and thus his character. Supposedly, there were 37 distinct "organs" in the human brain. It became quite a fad for a while to draw phrenological charts on each other at parties. More than one wedding was called off when it was "discovered" that their heads were incompatible. On a more serious side, Adolf Hitler later combined the idea of phrenology with new racial theories in the 20th century. Heinrich Himmler, his S.S. leader, claimed to be an expert phrenologist, alleging that it proved the inferiority of the Jews and the superiority of the German race.

The Temperance Movement

Americans had experienced a serious alcohol problem from colonial times, but as more towns and cities arose, so did the alcohol-related problems of public drunkenness, fighting, and crime. Alcohol consumption had risen steadily, so that by 1830 annual per capita consumption of alcohol among those over the age of 13 was almost 40 gallons. At least two specific reasons for this high rate of consumption were the poor quality of drinking water in most American cities and the growth of the working-class population, who usually worked long, hard weeks of 60 hours or more. Even American military services and colleges served rum or ale with meals.

Women were often the victims of abuse at the hands of their intoxicated husbands, although some were drinkers too. Women who drank generally stayed in the privacy of their homes, for women who frequented saloons were perceived to be prostitutes. But men drank socially and often all day on Sunday, after six days of hard work. That's why Protestant ministers and women got involved in an anti-alcohol crusade known as the temperance movement. Many Protestant churches pushed for Sunday blue laws in various states, hoping that the closing down of business establishments, including taverns, would encourage more men to attend church on Sundays. Thus, the 19th century advocates of temperance often also worked for the passage of tougher Sunday laws, tying those two issues together.

Lyman Beecher, a Protestant minister from Connecticut and father of Harriet Beecher Stowe of *Uncle Tom's Cabin* fame, delivered a series of six lectures on the evils of "demon rum" in 1825. One year later, in 1826, he and other conservative Protestants helped create the American

Society for the Promotion of Temperance, better known as the American Temperance Society, in Boston. Within a few years, there were a few thousand local chapters of the ATS scattered across the nation. Then in 1836 the American Temperance Union was established. In the early years of the temperance movement, most of the temperance societies used the voluntary approach of trying to persuade Americans to sign temperance pledge cards, in which the signatory pledged total abstinence from alcoholic beverages. Even children were involved in the cause against alcohol, with thousands of them joining what was called the Cold Water Army.

Temperance reform was the most widely supported and successful of all the social reform movements of the period. It was particularly popular among Protestant churchgoers, although Roman Catholics were divided on the issue. More recent Catholic immigrants among the Irish and German working classes tended to oppose the movement. However, in 1840, working-class support increased when six reformed drunks in Baltimore formed the Washington Temperance Societies, deciding that after the 1837 economic depression, the economy needed more stable, sober workers in order to survive future economic crises. Of course, the fact that many employers began requiring their employees to take the temperance pledge did not hurt the movement either.

Despite its relative success, many temperance reformers decided that education and voluntary methods were insufficient. As a result, legal prohibition became a major goal by the end of the 1830s. The first and most successful statewide prohibition law came in Maine in 1851, as the result of Neal S. Dow's efforts. Dow was the mayor of Portland, Maine, and became known as the "Father of Prohibition." Before the end of the 1850s, a total of 13 of the 31 states had legally prohibited the manufacture, sale, and consumption of alcoholic beverages, all of them in the North. In the post-Civil War era, however, most of those states repealed such laws, or their state supreme courts ruled them unconstitutional. Nevertheless, the effect of the temperance movement was to reduce per capita consumption of alcohol by more than one-half in the 1840s of what it had been in the '20s. Of course, that gain faded quickly after the Civil War, and the temperance movement would rise again in the latter half of the 19th century.

The Women's Rights Movement

Influenced by British common law, most states held that women legally "disappeared" when they married. That is, the husband became the owner of his wife's property and income, if she had any. At the same time, however, the wife was still responsible for paying her own previous debts. Her husband could even legally beat her. Finally, jobs outside the home or family business were very limited for women, and they could not vote or hold public office either. Despite the introduction of liberal elements from the Enlightenment and the American Revolution, traditional conservative forces kept women from being part of the clause, "all men are created equal."

Feminist leaders, although they weren't called that then, originally limited their call to equal educational opportunity, trusting that it would eventually open doors to full gender equality. Even that was a struggle to achieve since men generally held women as inferior and believed a woman's place was in the home and that their minds were incapable of comprehending subjects like law, science, and philosophy. A mathematician named Emma Hart Willard first cracked the wall by founding the Troy Female Seminary in 1821 in Troy, New York. Others followed her lead. For example, Catherine Beecher, Lyman Beecher's daughter and Harriet Beecher Stowe's sister, established the Hartford Seminary in Hartford, Connecticut, in 1822. And in 1837, Mary Lyon founded a college for women called Mount Holyoke Seminary in South Hadley, Massachusetts. Nevertheless, progress in education for women was quite slow. On a less political note, this state of affairs also resulted in the intentional decision in the 1850s by about 10 percent of adult women to remain single, to be "spinsters" as they were usually called.

Eventually, experience in other reform efforts, like the temperance and abolitionist movements, led many women to work directly for the expansion of women's rights during the Age of Social Reform. In 1838, Sarah and Angelina Grimke, abolitionist sisters who fled the South and also became leading feminists, published their *Letters on the Equality of Sexes and the Condition of Women* (Sarah) and *Letters to Catherine E. Beecher* (Angelina), thus launching a more militant women's rights movement. Perhaps the most interesting woman feminist and abolitionist leader was Sojourner Truth, who began lecturing in the mid-1840s. In her most famous speech, delivered to the Ohio Women's Rights Convention in 1851, she emphatically declared that, "If the first woman God ever made was strong enough to turn the world upside down all alone, these women together ought to be able to turn it back, and get it right side up again!"

In 1840, two female activists in the abolitionist movement, Lucretia Mott, a Philadelphia Quaker, and Elizabeth Cady Stanton, were forced to sit in a separate screened-off area at the World's Anti-Slavery Convention in London. They were so incensed by their treatment there that both women abandoned the abolitionist movement altogether to devote their fulltime energies in a women's rights movement. In July 1848, Mott and Stanton joined forces with Lucy Stone, another former abolitionist, to organize the very first Woman's Rights Convention in Seneca Falls, New York (sometimes called the Seneca Falls Convention). A few hundred women and men assembled at that convention and passed a Declaration of Sentiments, which asserted that "all men and women are created equal."

The Seneca Falls Convention was the first of several conventions demanding equal education access, the right to vote, property rights, and other rights for American women. But women's rights came slowly, partly because the piecemeal gains obtained state by state satisfied many women (especially property rights) and partly because the women's rights movement was closely linked to the abolitionist cause, which was unpopular even among most who opposed slavery.

A few prominent men, including abolitionists Frederick Douglass and William Lloyd Garrison, actively supported the women's right to vote. But most men vehemently opposed the granting of women's suffrage (the right to vote) and also believed that women should be subservient to their husbands in all things. Nevertheless, 19th century feminists were undaunted in the fight for equal rights for women. Susan B. Anthony, a Quaker like Lucretia Mott, was an early abolitionist and women's rights advocate, especially for women's suffrage. After the Civil War, she and Elizabeth Cady Stanton organized the National Woman Suffrage Association in 1869. But it would not be until the 19th Amendment to the U.S. Constitution was ratified in 1920 that American women had the right to vote in all levels of government in every state in the Union.

Women showed their independent spirit in other ways during the early 19th century as well. For example, Lucy Stone, referred to above, was the earliest famous American woman to keep her maiden name after she married. Elizabeth Blackwell became the first woman doctor in the nation. Finally, Amelia Bloomer defied the conventional female dress for the times by replacing her long, street-sweeping skirt with a much shorter skirt and Turkish pants, an outfit that was quickly dubbed "bloomers." Actually, bloomers were much healthier than the long dresses that dragged that the ground and picked up dirt and bacterium from floors and streets.

Prisons, Asylums, and the Poor

In the 18th century, the threat of hanging, rather than prison, was deemed a better deterrent to crime. Jails and prisons were mostly for those awaiting trial or for debtors. But influenced by the changing standards of western European nations and the American optimism of the era that human nature can be reformed, most states in the 19th century reduced the number of crimes punishable by the death penalty. Instead, the idea emerged that a lack of parental discipline in childhood was the major cause of crime. Therefore, prisons were used as a kind of substitute for parental discipline, so that rehabilitation of criminals became as important as their punishment. This new thinking inspired the terms "penitentiaries" (from the word "penance"), "reformatories," and "houses of correction." Nevertheless, the methods used to rehabilitate prisoners were often cruel and very ineffective. The most extreme of these rehabilitation efforts were in Pennsylvania, whose state prisons' methods simply became known as the "Pennsylvania System." This prison system used solitary confinement in

FIGURE 12.2 - Susan B. Anthony.

an attempt to rehabilitate criminals, providing separate walled areas outside for exercise and permitting absolutely no mail and no visitors.

Imprisonment for debt especially plagued the poorer working classes, as people were sometimes even imprisoned for debts of less than one dollar. However, as democratic political reforms eliminated property qualifications for voting, the working class used its growing political clout to gradually get state legislatures to abolish debtors' prisons before the Civil War.

During most of America's early history, the mentally ill were either kept hidden at home or were sent to jails, mental asylums, or poorhouses. In jails and prisons, of course, the mentally ill were housed with the criminal element, in keeping with the prevailing view that the insane were willfully deranged. Even in mental asylums and poorhouses, those suffering from mental illness lived in horrendous and filthy conditions and often along with the sane in the poorhouses. All that began to change when Dorothea Dix, a New England teacher, taught a Sunday School class in a jail near Boston in 1841. There she found that insane people were kept in an unheated room. Over the decade of the 1840s, Dorothea Dix traveled all over the United States (and later in Europe), documenting from firsthand observations the horrible conditions in America's asylums and prisons. She then became a champion for prison and mental health reform. After convincing the Massachusetts state legislature to clean up the mess in that state, Dorothea Dix worked tirelessly to improve conditions elsewhere in the country. By 1860, 28 of the 33 states had established separate public institutions for the mentally ill and had removed such persons from living with criminals and the sane.

In colonial times, Americans viewed poverty as a permanent feature due to their negative perspective on human nature, which by the way, had been influenced by the Calvinistic Puritan theology of predestination (that God predestines some to be lost and others to be saved).

But the intellectual and religious environment of the early 19th century brought the great optimism to Americans that human nature itself could be changed. Therefore, the emphasis shifted to the causes of poverty, in the belief that studying them would lead to a cure. In colonial days, the poor were supported in a household, a concept called "outdoor relief." But in the 19th century, almshouses for the infirm poor and workhouses for the able-bodied poor, called "indoor relief," were built. The theory for "indoor relief" was that placing the poor in highly regimented institutions would make them virtuous, productive citizens. But poor results were obtained because of much overcrowding and the mixing of the sick, the insane, and unwed mothers with the healthy poor.

Education Reform

In the colonial period, colonies outside the South had established common schools. But parents were still required to pay tuition for their children to attend. In fact, a mixture of tuition, property taxes, fuel contributions to the schools (wood or coal), and the boarding of single teachers (usually women) in parents' homes on a rotating basis constituted the financing for these common schools. The majority of students were from poorer families, a fact that led many more prosperous families even in the North to oppose a strictly public education that was financed entirely by tax dollars because they could hire private tutors for their own children.

However, by the early 19th century, attitudes were changing. Many reasoned that uneducated children might grow up to become criminals. Therefore, it would be easier to pay taxes now to support public education than to add to the nation's crime burden later and to pay for more prisons. The result was the adoption of a free public education system in some northern states as early as the 1790s, followed by southern states in the 1820s and later. Historians generally regard North Carolina's public education system as the best in the South but as second-rate in contrast to any of the northern states' public schools.

Children in the early 19th century typically studied in a one-room schoolhouse with up to 20 or more students from the first eight grades, fewer students in rural areas.

Most schools only managed to teach the three R's of reading, writing, and arithmetic. While most unmarried teachers were women, most of the nation's public school teachers were, in fact, men at that time. Regardless of gender, however, many teachers were poorly trained and poorly paid.

Although girls were admitted to most public schools by the early 19th century, few of them had anywhere else to go to continue their education after graduating from primary, or common, school. Indeed, even boys had few opportunities to attend high schools because so few of them existed. The major growth in public high schools would have to wait for the late 19th century. Instead, a small number of boys attended private secondary schools called academies, while even fewer went on to one of a couple of dozen colleges in America at that time. Instead, most boys finished the eighth grade at the age of 14 and entered apprenticeships in specific skilled trades or sought employment as clerks in the booming urban areas of America cities.

This state of the nation's public education became an object of attention for social reformers. Not surprisingly, Massachusetts led the way in education reform. Remember that Massachusetts Bay Colony had been the first to begin establishing common schools as early as the 1630s. The most important education reformer of the entire 19th century, in fact, was Horace Mann, the first secretary of the newly created Massachusetts Board of Education in 1837. Throughout the late 1830s and the '40s, Mann and the Massachusetts Board of Education promoted several sweeping changes in that state. These included introducing the grading system to encourage student performance; thus the term "grade schools." Massachusetts also lengthened the school year from two to three months to as long as 10 months, standardized textbooks across the state, and made school attendance compulsory. In fact, Massachusetts adopted the first statewide compulsory attendance law in the United States in 1852.

In terms of curriculum reform, *McGuffey's Readers*, developed by a Protestant minister from Ohio named William McGuffey in the 1830s, were used for most of the 19th and even early 20th centuries to teach young students the moral lessons of honesty, industry, and patriotism by numerous references to various passages from the Bible. Noah Webster, from Connecticut, who published his famous American English dictionary in 1828, also wrote books for the teaching of reading in America's public schools. The latter accomplishment earned him the nickname "Schoolmaster of the Republic."

Manufacturers, who needed a disciplined work force, merchants, lawyers, and progressive farmers supported education reform, for all of these groups realized that education was increasingly being needed to help prepare young people for a changing industrial economy. Native-born Americans also saw public education as a kind of Americanization of immigrants' children that gave them a common culture through a standardized curriculum. So they tended to support education reform as well. Women supported education reform in large numbers, at least partly because they saw this as a way to open the teaching profession to them, especially as they believed they were better suited to handling children of different ages in a one-room classroom. Indeed, in 1800, most teachers were men, but by 1900 about 70 percent of American public schoolteachers were women.

There was also formidable opposition to education reform, and opponents came from a variety of areas. Less nationally-minded farmers insisted on keeping their sons home to work on the farms more, a fact that had traditionally restricted the typical school year to two or three months. Many working-class parents objected to compulsory attendance also because many needed their children to work in factories or elsewhere to produce more income for the family. Urban Catholics tended to oppose education reform because they complained about the Protestant bias in many textbooks. This Catholic complaint was often true. One textbook, for example, said that Catholic immigrants threatened to turn the United States into the "common sewer of Ireland." Rural, Protestant farmers and urban Catholics could not work together, however, and when some local workingmen's political parties began supporting education reform, the opponents were doomed to lose the struggle.

Higher education had been the exclusive domain of private religious groups in the colonial period, established to provide a classical education of Latin, Greek, mathematics, and philosophy and to train Protestant ministers. But public colleges and universities arose in the early years of the Republic, fueled by federal land grants given to the states for the very purpose of establishing public institutions of higher education. Ironically, the first of these were created in the South, specifically North Carolina in 1795. More famous was the University of Virginia, founded in 1819, mostly by the vigorous efforts of Founding Father and former President, Thomas Jefferson. Jefferson was a great believer in the power of education to open eyes and transform character. He regarded the establishment of the University of Virginia as the greatest achievement of his life. As noted in the earlier section entitled "The Women's Rights Movement," higher education for women was considered by most Americans of the day to be irrelevant and ill-advised. Review that section for a quick overview of some early pioneers in women's higher education.

For those adults already out of school, there were a variety of ways to increase their knowledge of the world around them. Libraries became a valuable source for acquiring additional knowledge. Most of the earliest American libraries were for-profit businesses that charged subscription fees. But free public libraries were growing in number throughout the 19th century. In 1825, the libraries of the five largest American cities had 20 times more books than the entire United States had in George Washington's day. Door-to-door salesmen, who sold books in many parts of the country, were another source of information. But what captured so much of the public attention in those days before radio, television, and the Internet were public lecturers. Josiah Holbrook, a Massachusetts educator, founded the American Lyceum of Science and the Arts in 1826. This organization was the first national agency of adult education in the country, and it sent out experts on the lecture circuit. Other lyceums were organized as Americans flocked to auditoriums, churches, and various public buildings to hear lectures about science, history, literature, and other parts of the world.

Utopian Communities

Belief in mankind's perfectibility led some Americans into the utopian community movement. Competition was replaced by cooperation in these communities because competition was deemed to be unnatural. Basically, they were communitarian in nature and represented something close to pure communism, unlike the communism taught by Karl Marx or the communism practiced in the Soviet Union and other communist nations of the 20th and 21st centuries. Since the generation of the 1960s, we might call the 19th century utopian societies communes. Their essential purpose seems to have been to try to create and model perfect societies as confirmation of America's optimism and to give hopeful encouragement for others' self-improvement goals.

Robert Owen, a Scottish textile-maker, founded one of the first known utopian communities in 1825 at what he called New Harmony in Indiana. Owen was attracted to America because of its cheap land and the American willingness to experiment. But New Harmony failed within two years, largely because of too many conflicts among the people living there.

Brook Farm

Beginning in the depression of 1837 and extending through the early 1840s, other idealists formed dozens of communities. The most famous of these was Brook Farm, established near Boston in 1841 by a Unitarian minister named George Ripley and dominated by transcendentalists. Transcendentalism arose to prominence among intellectuals in New England in the 1830s. Influenced by Romanticism and Eastern religious traditions, transcendentalists stressed the infinite spiritual and intellectual capacities of man, that man can transcend the ordinary human limitations and soar to new heights by using his own inner light to get in touch with God, sometimes referred to as the Over-Soul. Transcendentalism was much like Eastern religions and the modern New Age movement in its mystical practices of meditation or other techniques employed to reach one's own inner light. But it was also an extension of American freedom, individualism, self-reliance, and self-improvement that flourished to new heights during the Age of Social Reform. It is no coincidence, then, that leading transcendentalists were activists in the women's and anti-slavery abolitionist movements.

Novelist Nathaniel Hawthorne lived at Brook Farm for a while. Other influential transcendentalists included literary figures Ralph Waldo Emerson and Henry David Thoreau. More information about their personal backgrounds and/or literature is given in the section of this chapter entitled "American Literature." A devastating fire in 1846 led to its demise the following year.

Fourierism

Fourierism, named after the French socialist Charles Fourier, was another source of utopian communities in America, with at least 28 such communities established between 1841 and 1858. Fourierism called for dividing society into cooperative units called phalanxes, with each phalanx constituting a separate community of no more than 1,800 persons. However, most of these communities lasted no more than two or three years because most residents spent little time doing the work necessary to ensure their survival.

Shaker Communities

In addition to the secular and transcendentalist communities, Shakers and other religious groups established overtly religious communities. The Shakers had originated in England in 1736 by the movement's founder, Mother Ann Lee, and took their name from a religious dance they did. After a brief time in prison, she moved to America. The Shakers were separatists and anti-materialistic, so they established a series of at least 20 rural communities (or communes) scattered among several states, where a total of about 6,000 different members lived between 1820 and 1860. All of Ann Lee's children had died as babies, a tragedy she interpreted as punishment from God for the sin of having sex. Therefore, the Shakers were abstainers from both marriage and sex, which meant they survived only by obtaining new converts. They peaked in the second quarter of the 19th century at about 6,000 members, and they finally died out altogether by about 1940.

As suggested by the experience of the Shakers, religious separatist communities usually lasted longer than secular ones, probably because religion seems to provide greater incentives for people to try harder to make positive changes. In other words, religion is a kind of glue that bonds people together for a longer time.

The Oneida Community

Another of the more radical religious communities was the Oneida Community in upstate New York. It was founded by Yale Divinity School graduate John Humphrey Noyes in 1848 and lasted until 1881. Noyes took the perfectionist theology of the Second Great Awakening to its logical extreme conclusion by declaring that because he had attained spiritual perfection, he was incapable of sinning. It was for this view that he had previously been refused ordination to the ministry. Moreover, he taught that private property, including the view that the wife exclusively belonged to her husband, was the root cause for all sin and evil in the world. Therefore, all private property was abolished at Oneida, and a system of "complex marriage" replaced the traditional institution of marriage. Essentially, "complex marriage" was the idea that adults should not be limited to one sex partner, but that every adult man at Oneida could have sex with any adult woman there. In effect, every adult man was married to every adult woman and vice versa. Nevertheless, this was not quite the free love that critics charged because the community carefully controlled sexual activity. Most of the time, a man was encouraged to practice sex without ejaculation, unless he had been chosen to father a child. In cases where the community desired another child, the sex partners were pre-selected in an attempt to produce children with greater intelligence and other valuable character traits. The children were then raised in a communal nursery. As the leader, "Father Noyes" proclaimed himself the "first husband," which gave him the right of first sex with every new woman admitted into the community.

Neighbors outside the community scornfully regarded its inhabitants as adulterers. Such pressure, in addition to internal problems, led to the abandonment of "complex marriage" at Oneida in 1879. Two years later, the Oneida Community officially ended. It had lasted for just more than 32 years, partly because its production of silver plates and strong steel traps kept it financially afloat. Even today, Oneida, New York is famous for its silverware.

MORE SOCIAL HISTORY IN THE EARLY NINETEENTH CENTURY

Changes Brought by New Immigrants

In the early 19th century, the economic and social changes in the United States were accompanied, and sometimes produced, by the addition of new immigrants from Europe. Approximately 5 million new European immigrants arrived in the nation between 1815, at the end of the War of 1812, and 1860, on the eve of the Civil War. More than 80 percent of that number arrived between 1840 and 1860.

The Irish constituted the largest number of these new immigrants. Most Irish immigrants came to the United States from 1845 to the early 1850s as a result of the great potato famine in Ireland. They were poor, unskilled, and settled mostly in Eastern coastal towns not far from where they got off the docks. Their relative lack of specific job skills forced them into job competition with free blacks, which in turn, resulted in an anti-black and therefore anti-abolitionist attitude among many of them. This willingness to work for cheap wages also led to discrimination by labor unions. Finally, the fact that about 95 percent of the Irish immigrants were Roman Catholic gave many native-born Protestant Americans an excuse to distrust and hate them. In June 1844, the so-called "Bible Riots" broke out in Philadelphia when some Protestants reacted to the school board's decision to use the Catholic Douay version of the Bible for the Bible reading each morning in the city's public schools. Protestant mobs attacked Catholic neighborhoods and burned 30 buildings. At least 16 people were killed in the rioting before the state militia restored order.

German immigrants were a fairly close second to the Irish in terms of numbers of immigrants who arrived between 1815 and 1860. German immigrants were often political refugees from one of the democratic conflicts within the many independent German states in Europe. Like the Irish, most German immigrants settled in the North, both because of its climate being more like that of Europe's and the fact that most steamship lines terminated in the North. However, unlike the Irish, German immigrants tended to be hardworking farmers or highly skilled workers. Henry Steinway and Levi Strauss were the two most famous German immigrants of this period. Steinway immigrated to the United States as Heinrich Steinweg in 1851, but Americanized his name to Henry Steinway. Two years later, he established Steinway & Sons in New York City, which made some of the finest pianos in the world. Levi Strauss, who was born in Bavaria as Loeb Strauss in 1829, moved to New York City in 1847. In 1853, he moved to San Francisco, California, and opened a dry goods store there. Noticing that the clothes of gold miners did not last long in the work environment of mining, Levi Strauss first began making pants out of canvas, and later out of denim. Levi denim jeans eventually became the standard wear for many manual laborers and casual wearers.

Religiously, the German immigrants were a good mixture of Catholic and Protestant, the latter including Lutherans and some pietistic groups. What concerned native-born Americans more about these German immigrants was the fact that the latter tended to congregate together and maintain their use of the German language in their homes and in German-language newspapers. Because these immigrants came from a part of Europe not used to democracy, many other Americans feared that they might end up weakening American democracy. Those fears were unfounded, for the German immigrants adopted democratic principles quickly and eagerly.

The large majority of the 5 million new European immigrants between 1815 and 1860 settled in the North. The close proximity to them caused native-born Northerners to resent the immigrants for the reasons just discussed. However, many Southerners also objected to these immigrants, but for a different reason. Southerners resented the fact that new waves of immigrants living in the North resulted in increasing northern political representation in Congress and an increasing northern influence on the outcome of presidential elections. Nevertheless, despite native-born Americans' various fears and prejudices toward the recent immigrants in the early 19th century, these immigrants enriched American society through their cultural and religious diversity, a diversity that eventually helped Americans develop greater acceptance of different perspectives and an even deeper love for the freedom to be different.

Movement Toward Greater Religious Freedom

During the American Revolution and immediately after, states included in their state constitutions and in new laws provisions that guaranteed freedom of conscience in religious matters. At the same time, most states, but not all, began moving in the general direction of the principle of the separation of church and state. The most noticeable change was that states no longer funded any churches with tax money. Thomas Jefferson successfully pushed for the enactment of the Statute for Religious Freedom by the Virginia state legislature in 1786, which he declared as providing for the separation of church and state there.

Massachusetts, New Hampshire, and Connecticut were the major exceptions to this trend toward separation of church and state in the Revolutionary and post-Revolutionary period. Those states tended to be in the religious grip of the Congregationalist Puritan tradition. However, some religious qualifications for voting and/or holding public office remained in most states, which discriminated against Catholics, Jews, and even minority Protestant sects. However, in the wake of rising nationalism, with all its ethnic and religious diversity, Americans gradually moved toward a more complete adoption of the First Amendment principle of government neutrality in religion, and tax-supported churches, religious discrimination, and religious qualifications for voting and holding public office were all gone by the 1830s.

New American Christian Groups

The Mormons

Among the Christian groups originating in America during the early 19th century, none was as successful as the Mormons. Officially named the Church of Jesus Christ of Latter-day Saints, it was founded by Joseph Smith, of western New York, on the eve of the Age of Social Reform. In 1827, Smith claimed that an angel called Moroni handed him some inscribed gold plates along with a breastplate on which were two precious stones called the Urim and the Thummim that would enable him to translate the gold plates. Smith completed the translation and published it as the *Book of Mormon* in 1830, the same year that he established his new church. Mormon is considered to have been a prophet-historian of the fourth century A.D. who compiled an abridged history of God's dealings with the peoples of the Western Hemisphere originally written by many ancient prophets. Completed by his son Moroni, the plates purport to cover the period from 600 B.C. to A.D. 421. The highlight of the book is the personal ministry of Jesus among one of the great civilizations in the Western Hemisphere, where Jesus was said to have come soon after His resurrection. Moroni then hid the plates and the breastplate in what later became western New York until the prophesied day when they would be dug up and translated. After he died, Moroni then became an angel who lives in heaven.

His followers considered Joseph Smith to be a prophet, so they yielded allegiance to his leadership. Beginning in 1831, Smith and his new church moved to Ohio and then Missouri, in a quest to create a colony they called "New Jerusalem." But opposition to their rapid expansion and fear of their potential political power (Mormons tended to vote as a bloc) forced them out of those states, and they settled in Nauvoo, Illinois. Their new state gave them a self-governing city charter. However, after their political strength increased and Smith introduced polygamy into their community in 1841, his enemies got him charged with treason. In June 1844, a mob killed Smith and his brother after breaking into the jail in Carthage, Illinois.

Within two years after the murder of Joseph Smith, the Mormons left Illinois under the leadership of his successor and prophet, Brigham Young. Young took the Mormons out West to the Great Salt Lake area, which was then part of Mexico, for which he was often called Moses, in honor of the Biblical Moses who led the Israelites from a persecuted land in an exodus across a desert up toward the Promised Land. There, the Mormons had complete religious freedom and political autonomy. Moreover, under Young's leadership, an extensive irrigation system was built, and the Mormons prospered and multiplied.

The Mormons of the 19th century were most famous for practicing polygamy, the idea that a man could have more than one wife. However, federal anti-polygamy laws after the Civil War led to political tensions. When Congress insisted that the Utah Territory make polygamy illegal as a condition for becoming a state, Mormonism's prophet-leader at the time soon reported that God had shown him in vision that it was indeed time to abandon polygamy. Utah was granted statehood in 1896.

Despite ridicule of its practice of polygamy, Mormonism greatly expanded its numbers after settling down in the Great Salt Lake region. At least two major factors contributed to the growth of Mormonism. First, it put America at the center of its brand of Christianity, which appealed to the long-held tradition that God had blessed America to be a special Godly example to the world. Second, its *Book of Mormon* offered a kind of relief to some Americans, who were confused by so many interpretations of the Bible.

The Millerite Movement

The Millerites, also known as Adventists for their expectation that Jesus would soon return to the world in the Second Advent, were followers of William Miller, an upstate New York farmer-turned-Baptist preacher in 1831. Earlier in his life, Miller had been a Deist because of his association with Deist friends. Shortly after serving as an officer in the War of 1812, he returned to his boyhood town of Low Hampton, New York, and was converted in 1816, eventually becoming a Baptist Christian. Impressed by Biblical prophecies of the nearness of Christ's Second Advent, Miller rejected the post-millennialism that dominated most of Protestant Christianity in America in the early 19th century. Instead, his Bible study led him to insist that not even the Holy Spirit could produce spiritual perfection in man because of inherent sin. This meant, he declared, that only the sudden, cataclysmic divine intervention of the Second Advent could establish the perfect harmony of the millennium on Earth. Therefore, the subsequent religious movement that bore his name became the preeminent expression of pre-millennialism, the view that the Second Advent of Jesus precedes and begins the millennium. It was also the most significant exception to the popular notion concerning the perfectibility of human nature.

William Miller immersed himself in a study of the end-time prophecies of the Bible. He was particularly drawn to the prophetic book of Daniel in the Old Testament. Convinced that the Bible was its own best interpreter, he began a systematic study of Daniel 8:14, which refers to the "cleansing of the sanctuary" at the end of a period of 2,300 days. Miller understood the word *sanctuary* as referring to God's faithful people as the metaphorical temple, or sanctuary, spoken of in the New Testament. Thus, the cleansing of the sanctuary would be a complete spiritual cleansing of the church at the same time that Jesus returned to also cleanse the Earth by fire at His Second Advent. By comparing the Bible with itself and secular history, he concluded that the 2,300 days were literally 2,300 years and that they began with the 70 weeks of Daniel 9, sometime in the days of the Persian Empire. On the basis of his study and basic math, Miller was convinced that Jesus would return sometime during 1843 or 1844.

When William Miller began preaching his views in 1831, he quickly attracted great attention from many believers scattered among the many Protestant churches. Although it conflicted with the popular post-millennial view of the day, a number of Baptists, Methodists, Congregationalists, and others joined the ranks of the Millerite movement. As their fervor and zeal increased, however, pressure from other popular religious leaders forced the Millerites out of their respective church congregations. The irony, of course, was that Christian churches were disfellowshiping members who were expecting the soon Second Coming of Jesus, when that expectation had long been a traditional belief and hope among Christians throughout history.

Developments among other scholars in the Millerite movement eventually led William Miller to predict that Jesus would return on October 22, 1844, in association with the movement's conclusion that this was the true date for Yom Kippur that year. (The connection to Yom Kippur, literally Day of Atonement, was based on that day representing a kind of cleansing of the literal sanctuary in Old Testament Israel, according to Leviticus 16.) When Jesus did not return on that date, this became known as the Great Disappointment. Many of the Millerites returned to their former churches, which had previously expelled them. Others were so bitterly disappointed

that they gave up on God and Christianity altogether. A few continued to set subsequent dates for the Second Coming of Jesus. A relatively few re-examined Daniel 8:14's prophecy and concluded that William Miller had been right about the date but only wrong about the event. Instead, they reached the conclusion that the cleansing of the sanctuary was the beginning of a pre-Advent judgment in association with the sanctuary in heaven mentioned in the New Testament book of Hebrews. These believers formed the most significant Christian denomination to come out of the Millerite movement, the Seventh-day Adventist Church, in 1863. As their name implies, Seventh-day Adventist Christians observe the seventh-day Sabbath (Saturday) and proclaim the soon, but undated, Second Advent of Jesus.

Marriage, Family, and Morals

In the post-Revolutionary War era, expanding industry in the Northeast and agriculture in the West meant that young men did not need to wait so long to obtain sufficient money to marry. Furthermore, young women were nearly always in short supply on the frontier. These factors meant that both men and women tended to marry young. And while extramarital affairs were probably fewer here than they were in Europe, when "needed," divorce was generally easier to get in America.

American families were less tight-knit than in Europe, even though the family unit was still the foundation for American society. Parents tended to have more children than they do today, partly to offset the infant mortality rate and partly because many hands make light work on the family farm.

Even on the farm, children grew up fast and had more responsibilities than their counterparts in Europe. Boys could, and often did, find work in the cities at the age of 14, or even as young as 11 or 12, and girls often worked in the textile mills or as domestic servants or seamstresses at relatively young ages. This fact allowed young ladies to become independent regardless of their marital status, although single women usually did not fare as well financially as married ones did. Nevertheless, sons and daughters could usually expect to outdo their parents' generation in terms of their standard of living.

Food and Clothing

Overall, there was a greater variety of food in America than in Europe, and Americans tended to eat more, although only wealthier Americans could afford a significant variety and abundance in their diet. Habit and a lack of nutrition knowledge resulted in an ill-balanced and monotonous diet for the average American. On the frontier, the diet was typically limited to mush, molasses, beans, hominy, pork, and wild game, such as rabbits, squirrel, and deer. In the cities, the diet often consisted of bread and meat, usually salt pork, pickled beef, salt fish, and sausage. Neither rural nor urban Americans got much fresh vegetables or fruit, so scurvy and rickets were nearly epidemic, especially among the poor. After 1820, commercial canning (glass, then later, tin) and better iceboxes improved the situation somewhat, although it wouldn't be until the last two or three decades of the 19th century before great progress would be made.

Clothing fashions for both men and women came and went. Better spinning and looming machinery and the expansion of the textile industry made cloth cheaper. Nearly every American family had some factory-made clothing as a result. Ordinary clothing in the South consisted of cotton-flax combinations called fustian. In the North, a wool-cotton mixture called jeans tended to dominate the material until Levi denim jeans replaced them at some point after the Civil War.

Entertainment

The 19th century Americans, of course, did not experience the electronic age of radios, stereos, televisions, videos, DVDs, and computers, so families tended to do more things together. There was not much variety of things to do. However, Americans went back to the theater in big numbers after the end of the American Revolution; theaters had been ordered closed by the Continental Congress in 1774 as a frivolous waste of time during the crisis with Britain. Theater-building skyrocketed from 1790 to 1840 all over the country. The original plays were mostly British, but American plays soon multiplied. John Howard Payne's *Clari* (1823) introduced the song, "Home, Sweet Home" to Americans.

Only wealthier Americans could afford regular attendance at the theater in the early days. But popular demand lowered ticket prices, so that by 1820, seats in the gallery were at a low of 12½ cents, and box seats were at the high end of the scale at 75 cents each. Pageants, or spectacles, were also popular, as stage re-creations of historical events, such as "The Battle of Bunker Hill" (1793) and "The Last Days of Pompeii" (1830). During theatrical performances, the prime seats were reserved for white men; blacks and women sat in segregated sections. Wherever a ticket-holder sat, however, they were encouraged to interact with the actors by shouting, jeering, and stomping their approval or disapproval. In short, theaters were pretty wild places during evenings in the cities.

Other forms of entertainment included the circus, which began in the early19th century as animal shows with a few acrobats or puppeteers thrown in for good measure. Canvas walls later gave way to tents, with the Turner show probably being the first circus under "the big top" in 1826. Finally, lyceums began introducing Americans to lectures from traveling speakers on all kinds of topics, from history to science and literature.

American Literature

Several factors created a great demand for books and other literature of every kind in the early 19th century. The American population nearly doubled between 1790 and 1830. An emphasis on public education led to rising literacy rates. Steam-powered cylinder presses were perfected in the 1830s, making mass production of printed materials possible, thus reducing prices. Finally, a more efficient postal system gave rise to an explosion of magazines and newspapers that could be delivered in the mail. All of these factors resulted in a boom for dime novels and pamphlets, both of which offered mysteries and adventures of all types for young and older readers alike. Religious leaders and literary critics both took negative aim at the novel, but the novel flourished anyway. Historical romances, patterned after British author Sir Walter Scott, were the most popular.

The Knickerbocker Group

Washington Irving (1783-1859) led a group of New York writers called the Knickerbocker Group. In the 17th century, New York City was a Dutch settlement called New Amsterdam and part of the larger Dutch colony of New Netherlands. Descendants of those Dutch settlers became known as knickerbockers after Washington Irving used the fictional Dutch name of Diedrich Knickerbocker to author his *Knickerbocker's History of New York* in 1809. The Knickerbocker Group broke away from a European style to create a unique American style of literature.

Irving began his writing career by contributing to various newspapers and journals. However, it was his *Knickerbocker's History of New York* that first attracted the American public. After he published *The Sketch Book* in 1819-20, Irving became the first American writer to achieve fame in Europe. *The Sketch Book* included such favorite short stories as "Rip Van Winkle" and "The Legend of Sleepy Hollow." The first was about a man who awoke after having been asleep for 20 years, and the second concerned an encounter between a schoolmaster and a headless horseman. Irving also spent several years in Europe, living in places like Dresden (Germany), London, Paris, and Madrid. From 1842-45, Washington Irving was the American ambassador to Spain.

James Fenimore Cooper (1789-1851) was born in New Jersey, but a year later his family moved to New York state, where his father founded the city of Cooperstown, where the Baseball Hall of Fame is located today. Cooper became the first significant American novelist, writing more than 50 works. His best-known novels were part of a group called the *Leatherstocking Tales*, which are named for the nickname of his famous fictional frontier character Natty Bumppo. *The Pioneers* (1823) and *The Last of the Mohicans* (1826) are probably the two most famous novels within that group, which romanticizes both the frontier and American Indians.

Another major member of the Knickerbocker Group was William Cullen Bryant (1794-1878), a 19th century poet and newspaper editor. His earlier poems, such as "Thanatopsis," "To a Waterfowl," and "The Yellow Violet," reflected his great respect and love for nature.

Bryant practiced law in Massachusetts until he moved to New York City in 1825. There he was associated in different capacities with the New York *Evening Post* until his death in 1878. Largely through that newspaper, Bryant championed the abolition of slavery and other reforms. However, his love for poetry continued throughout his life, and he became the first American to speak about the theory of poetry.

The Transcendentalists

The quasi-religious ideas of transcendentalism were previously introduced under "Brook Farm" in the section entitled "Utopian Communities" in this chapter. The foremost spokesperson for transcendentalism was Ralph Waldo Emerson (1803-1882), who was known as the "Sage of Concord." The son of a Unitarian minister from Boston, Emerson himself attended Harvard Divinity School for a while, until tuberculosis forced him to leave New England for warmer climate. He returned to Boston in 1829, where he pastored the Second Unitarian Church in that city until his radical view that Jesus never intended to establish the Communion service led to his retirement in 1832. He then traveled in Europe for about two years, meeting some of the great literary figures there. In 1834, he returned home and settled in Concord, Massachusetts, from where he launched a career in writing and lecturing. His most famous work was entitled *Nature*, published in 1836, which outlined his transcendentalist views and for which he is sometimes classified as a naturalist.

Henry David Thoreau (1817-1862) was another famous naturalist and transcendentalist author. In fact, he grew up in Concord, Massachusetts, and he and Emerson eventually became good friends. Thoreau was an extreme individualist who railed against social conformity and the evils of materialism. He took his own views seriously, choosing to live in near isolation from the world in a cabin he built at Walden Pond near Concord for about two years, beginning in 1845. He kept a detailed journal of his activities and thoughts at Walden Pond, which he later used to write one of his classic works, *Walden: Or Life in the Woods*, in 1854. That book also outlined his transcendentalist views.

Perhaps more influential was Thoreau's essay entitled *On the Duty of Civil Disobedience* (1849), a product of a brief stay in jail for refusing to pay a special tax used to help finance the Mexican-American War (1846-48). Opposing that war on the grounds that it represented an attempt by the South to expand slavery, Thoreau insisted that unjust laws should not be obeyed. Thus, he refused to pay the special tax. In willingly accepting the consequence for his violation of the law, Thoreau helped establish the tradition of civil disobedience. Succinctly stated, civil disobedience is the intentional disobedience of a law or action considered to be unjust and the willingness to suffer the legal consequences in order to call public attention to its injustice. In the 20th century, Mahatma Ghandi in India and Dr. Martin Luther King, Jr. in the United States, each used civil disobedience as a non-violent way to change the status quo in their respective societies.

The Romantics

The Romantics were a group of writers who delved deeply into the human heart and mind, often exploring the themes of good and evil. Foremost among them was Edgar Allan Poe (1809-1849), an American poet and short-story writer. Poe lived a tragic life that began at the age of 3, when his parents died. Raised by his godfather after that, Poe attended schools in England and Scotland before returning to the United States to resume his education in Virginia. Unfortunately, gambling and alcohol plagued his life, resulting in his expulsion from the West Point Military Academy and later as editor of the *Southern Literary Messenger* in Richmond, Virginia. In 1849, he died tragically as the result of a drinking binge in Baltimore, Maryland.

His tragic life drew him to the darker themes of horror and death but ironically was probably responsible for his greatness as a writer. Edgar Allan Poe is called the "father" of the short story because he established the first guidelines that a good short story should have, among them brevity, intensity, and getting right into the story with a minimum of background information. He is also considered to be the "father" of the detective story. Many of his short stories were originally published in magazines and later collected and published in the book *Tales of the Grotesque and Arabesque* in 1840. In 1845, he achieved acclaim in both the United States and Europe for his

collection of poems entitled *The Raven and Other Poems*. Nathaniel Hawthorne (1804-1864) was also a Romantic novelist and short-story writer of the period. Born and raised in humble surroundings in New England, Hawthorne began serious writing after his college education. He is often remembered as a voice of conscience in pointing out what man ought to be in contrast to what he is. In *The Scarlet Letter*, published in 1850, Hawthorne explored the issues of evil and guilt in the context of 17th century Puritan New England. His other well-known novel was *The House of the Seven Gables* (1851), a story of romance revolving around characters involved with a house having a long, strange history. For about six months, Hawthorne lived in the transcendentalist community of Brook Farm, but he left because he did not share their optimism of mankind's potential. His good college friend, Franklin Pierce, appointed him as the American consul in Liverpool, England (1853-57), after Pierce became President of the United States. In 1864, Hawthorne died while visiting the White Mountains in New Hampshire with former President Franklin Pierce.

The third great Romantic writer of the period was Herman Melville (1819-1891). Despite being born into a poor family, Melville had some interesting life experiences. As a young adult, he and a friend escaped a whaling ship they were working on and were captured by cannibals, who actually treated them well. After their rescue from that episode, Melville spent about two years living in various South Pacific islands, including Tahiti, before returning home. These experiences on the high seas left a deep impression, which he wrote about in works such as *Typee: A Peep at Polynesian Life* (1846) and *Omoo: A Narrative of Adventures in the South Seas* (1847). Of course, Melville's most famous novel was *Moby-Dick*, published in 1851. Set as the story of a whaling captain's obsession to kill the great white whale (named Moby-Dick) that had torn his leg off, *Moby-Dick* was also an exploration of American prejudices regarding race and class distinctions. After the Civil War, Melville was sidetracked by financial problems and did not return to writing fiction until the last few years of his life. *Billy Budd*, whose manuscript was discovered for the first time in 1924, was a short novel about a doomed sailor, thought by some literary scholars to represent Melville's view of his own life of frequent literary rejection.

The Humanitarians

Another group of serious American writers were the Humanitarian poets, the most notable being Longfellow, Whittier, and Lowell. The designation of "Humanitarian" is given to them because of their support for various humanitarian causes, particularly the anti-slavery movement. Henry Wadsworth Longfellow (1807-1882) is often regarded as the first professional American poet and as the most popular American poet of the 19th century. Born into a prominent Portland, Maine family, Longfellow finished Bowdoin College (in Maine) and traveled extensively in Europe, where he learned several languages. He also served as an editor and translator, college professor and librarian at Bowdoin, and a professor of modern languages at Harvard. His best poems were long, narrative ones, such as *Evangeline* (1847), *The Song of Hiawatha* (1855), *The Courtship of Miles Standish* (1858), and *Tales of a Wayside Inn* (1863), the last of which made Paul Revere famous for his midnight ride on the eve of the American Revolution.

John Greenleaf Whittier (1807-1892) was a Quaker and New England poet from Massachusetts. Abolitionist editor William Lloyd Garrison published Whittier's first group of poems in the Newburyport *Free Press* in 1826. As a result, the two men became good friends for life. As an abolitionist himself, Whittier served one term in the Massachusetts state legislature, ran for the House of Representatives on the Liberty Party ticket in 1842, and was one of many founders of the modern Republican Party in the 1850s. One of his earlier poems was *Moll Pitcher* (1832), which extolled the virtues of the simple life in New England. However, his most famous poem was *Snow-Bound* (1866), which portrayed an idealistic view of his childhood home. Although not as well known today, Whittier also wrote almost 100 Christian hymns in addition to several secular ballads.

James Russell Lowell (1819-1891) was another New England poet and social critic of his day. Lowell was born into the same family of which the founder of Lowell, Massachusetts had been part. As a young man, Lowell left law practice to establish a literary magazine called the *Pioneer*. Although that magazine failed after only two issues, he persisted in his quest to contribute to American literature, getting *Poems*, *A Fable for Critics*, and *The Vision of Sir Launfal* published in the 1840s. However, it was *The Bigelow Papers* that really cemented his fame as a political satirist. The first series of *The Bigelow Papers* appeared in 1848 as a harsh but satirical commentary against the Mexican-American War, which Lowell, like other anti-slavery Americans of the time, viewed as an attempt by the South to expand slavery. The second series of *The Bigelow Papers*, published in 1867, lambasted the South and supported the Union in the Civil War.

From 1855 to 1876, Lowell was a professor of modern languages at Harvard. While there, he also served as editor of the *Atlantic Monthly* and then the *North American Review*. Then from 1877 to 1885, Lowell was the American ambassador to England, living in London. There he had a positive influence on European views of American culture. Some literary critics believe that his speeches in England, published in book form as *Democracy and Other Addresses* in 1887, may have well been his best work.

Other Important Literary Figures

Other important literary figures of the 19th century included Walt Whitman, Emily Dickinson, and Louisa May Alcott. Walt Whitman (1819-1892) is regarded by many literary scholars to have been the greatest American poet. As a young man, Whitman worked in the printing side of literature. Then after a brief stint as a teacher on Long Island, New York, he began a career of working as an editor for various newspapers and periodicals in the New York City area. In 1855, he published *Leaves of Grass*, a book of 12 of his poems that proclaimed the dignity of the individual and the virtues of democracy. *Leaves of Grass* attracted many critics, however, for some of its language in glorifying the human body and sexual love. Later editions of the same title were written and published, the last one in the same year of Whitman's death (1892). During the Civil War, Whitman volunteered as a hospital nurse in Washington, D.C. Right after the war, he published a group of Civil War poems in *Drum-Taps* (1865), which he personally regarded as his finest poems.

Emily Dickinson (1830-1886) was the most famous female poet in 19th century America. She was born in Amherst, Massachusetts, and spent almost all of her life there. Although she attended higher education institutions and lived a normal life for a while, Dickinson gradually became a recluse in her 30s, rarely leaving her home. The most popular theory explaining her withdrawal from society says that she suffered a severe disappointment in love, but that is only speculation. Only seven of her poems were published during her lifetime, but after her death, her sister discovered nearly 2,000 other poems in Dickinson's bureau. Her poems reveal a romantic person of deep attachment, but they also seem to reflect her struggle for spiritual peace of mind, as she could not accept the traditional Christian beliefs of her domineering father.

Louisa May Alcott (1832-1888) was born in Germantown, Pennsylvania, but largely grew up in Concord, Massachusetts, where she became friends with Ralph Waldo Emerson and Henry David Thoreau. In fact, her first book, *Flower Fables* (1854), contained a series of stories designed to entertain Emerson's daughter. Alcott served the Union cause as a nurse during the Civil War, an experience that led to her writing of *Hospital Sketches* in 1863. Among her many novels, perhaps the most

FIGURE 12.3 - Louisa May Alcott.

famous was *Little Women* (1868), an autobiographical account of adventures that Alcott and her three sisters experienced together as young people. *Good Wives* (1869), *Little Men* (1871), and *Jo's Boys* (1886) were sequels to *Little Women*. Louisa May Alcott was also an abolitionist and a feminist. In 1879, she became the first woman in Concord to register to vote in a school board election.

Alexis de Tocqueville

At the beginning of the Age of Social Reform, a French nobleman named Alexis de Tocqueville toured the United States for about nine months during 1831-32, officially to study our penal system. But de Tocqueville observed far more than our prisons. In 1835 and 1840, he wrote two volumes of his *Democracy in America*, which gave Americans a more objective look at themselves in the days before the Civil War. His evaluation was generally positive, even though he did express some concerns.

He wrote that the "general equality of condition among the people" was the source from which flowed most other American characteristics. He also noted that there was some inequality, and specifically warned that slavery and the race issue threatened "the future existence of the Union." Except for slavery, de Tocqueville praised the relative absence of class distinctions. He also praised the lack of great centralization of power and the unity of religion with freedom; in Europe, religious forces were generally opposed to movements for greater freedom. Perhaps most of all, de Tocqueville admired American optimism because he predicted it would lift Americans to new heights and even world influence. He was concerned, however, that the majority might someday become a "tyranny of the majority" that would trample on the rights of a minority. He also worried that the factory system, then relatively young, would create an American aristocracy based on wealth and economic power that might tend to undermine our democratic spirit and tradition.

Alexis de Tocqueville was uncannily accurate in his insights of American social development. America was a rising, struggling democracy, undergoing some serious growing pains. The slavery issue would indeed threaten "the future existence of the Union." And the "robber barons" of the late 19th century Industrial Revolution would alarm many Americans and alter the role of government in the 20th century. Finally, American optimism and ingenuity would produce the most influential economic, military, and political power on a global scale thus far in world history.

The front facade of Alamo, in San Antonio, Texas. Location: San Antonio, Texas, USA. Copyright 2010 iStockphoto.

Chapter 13 Contents

CHAPTER THIRTEEN

Manifest Destiny

Major Events

1822	Stephen F. Austin migrated to Texas
1829	Mexico attempted to outlaw slavery
1836	Tragedy at the Alamo Battle of San Jacinto Texas won its independence from Mexico
1840s	"Oregon Fever" and the Oregon Trail
1844	James K. Polk elected president
1845	U.S. annexed Texas under President John Tyler Texas became a large slave state in the U.S. Term "Manifest Destiny" coined by journalist John L. O'Sullivan
1846	Oregon dispute resolved peacefully with Britain
1846-47	Donner Party Tragedy in Sierra Mountains
1846-48	Mexican-American War
1848	Treaty of Guadalupe Hidalgo ended the Mexican-American War

The Ideology of Manifest Destiny

A growing population, a thirst for adventure, and even greater economic opportunity led Americans in large numbers to push the boundaries of the nation further west. This western expansion boomed in the 1840s, a decade in which the United States accumulated more than a million square miles, representing a larger addition to American soil than the previous acquisition of the Louisiana Territory in 1803. Except for a few adjustments to its borders, the United States achieved its continental status from the Atlantic to the Pacific before the end of that decade.

The inspiration for expansionist fervor was the ideology of Manifest Destiny. Although New York journalist John L. O'Sullivan coined the expression "manifest destiny" in 1845, the concept was much older. Indirectly, one can see it in the Puritan founders of Massachusetts Bay Colony in 1630, who spoke about their destiny to create a "city on a hill" that would produce a beacon of light to show the whole world how to form a superior, if not perfect, society. This feeling of moral superiority, which has ebbed and flowed throughout American history, was part of the foundation for later expansionism. In his day, Thomas Jefferson envisioned what he called an "empire of liberty," a concept that was partially completed with the Louisiana Purchase, which had approximately doubled the size of the United States without war. By the early 19th century, many Americans believed it was their destiny to shine from sea to sea.

This belief in American destiny accompanied the notion that God was its source. It was often argued that God had blessed Americans with a superior political system of representative democracy, a system that might eventually sweep the whole world with its emphasis on freedom and liberty. Therefore, spreading this system through American expansionism was not considered an act of selfishness, but rather an act of unselfishly bringing the ideals of freedom to others. Of course, those who stood in the way were also viewed as standing in God's way because He had bestowed this destiny. Indeed, it was believed that some would inevitably oppose this divine course because they were racially inferior and unable to adopt a democratic way of life. White Americans of northern and western European descent represented the superior "American race," an expression often heard in the 1840s. Manifest Destiny expressed both a religious and a racial bias as many Americans sought to heed what they believed was a divine command.

In addition to political and racial ideology, there were, of course, different specific concerns that motivated Americans to accept Manifest Destiny. White Southerners usually viewed western expansion as a means to expand slavery, although most doubted a profitable return on slave labor north of the 36° 30′ parallel. Others perceived acquiring the Far West as crucial in providing a much easier and inexpensive way to get American agricultural products to Asia, especially China. The only viable route available then was to sail around the southern tip of South America, a route that made the voyage far too long to be economical, because the Panama Canal was not built until the early 20th century. Many Americans shared Thomas Jefferson's ideal of an agricultural economy as the best chance to safeguard democracy and avoid the social stratification and class strife resulting from a heavily industrialized economy dominated by big business. Finally, many Americans supported Manifest Destiny from a fear that the British or other European nations might obtain a foothold in the Far West. This fear led to an intensified nationalistic effort to acquire it first.

Although it appears that a majority of Americans supported Manifest Destiny, not all did so. Many northern Whigs and a few northern Democrats were suspicious of a pro-slavery plot to expand slavery and feared that western expansion would reignite the slavery question and even threaten the unity of the nation, a fear that proved to be accurate. Others, mostly Whigs, were also concerned of the West's political tendency thus far to distrust the idea of a national bank. And, of course, there were also Americans who opposed any ideology based on religion and race. Despite some critics, however, Manifest Destiny enjoyed widespread support in the early 19th century and even more so in the 1840s.

Trouble in Texas

The North American continent west of the Louisiana Territory had once been part of the Spanish empire in the New World, the result of Spanish explorers who came to this hemisphere in the 16th century following Columbus' discoveries. But when Mexico won its independence from Spain in 1821, these lands then belonged to the Mexican Empire. By the 1840s, it was this territory that remained the major obstacle to the fulfillment of America's Manifest Destiny.

Texas was the province of Mexico that bordered the American South. The United States had originally claimed Texas as part of the Louisiana Purchase, but it had abandoned that claim in the 1819 Adams-Onis Treaty with Spain. However, an independent Mexico faced many problems and soon saw an advantage in encouraging immigration of Americans to Texas. Mexico's government wanted to strengthen its economy and needed an increased tax base that newcomers could provide. Americans living in Texas could also constitute a kind of buffer zone against hostile Indians to the north, especially the Apache, Comanche, and Kiowa. To give migration into Texas a boost, Mexico passed a law in 1824 that offered cheap land, at only 10 cents per acre, and an exemption from taxes for four years.

Among the first American immigrants was Stephen F. Austin, for whom the present capital of Texas is named. Austin migrated from Missouri to Texas and created the first American settlement there in 1822, even before the new Mexican law. Over the next several years, thousands of Americans moved to Texas, not only enticed by the cheap land, but also recruited by American agents who were given large land grants for doing so. By 1830, the American population in Texas was about 7,000, a little more than twice the number of Mexicans.

Before the end of the 1820s, however, several major differences between the ethnic groups resulted in a serious clash of American and Mexican cultures. One of these differences was religion. Americans were overwhelmingly Protestant in their Christianity, whereas Mexicans were Roman Catholic. And this was still the era when these two branches of Christianity showed little Christian charity for each other. Language was another barrier to peace and harmony. Americans spoke English and had no interest in learning Spanish. Finally, most Americans in Texas were Southerners, many of whom brought their slaves with them to help grow cotton.

Most Mexicans opposed slavery. The clash of cultures led to an unsuccessful revolt for independence as early as 1826 by a group seeking to establish a new country called Fredonia.

By 1829, Mexico realized it had made a serious mistake in encouraging American immigration to Texas. In that year, the government outlawed slavery, although American slave owners ignored the new law by calling their slaves servants instead. Then in 1830, Mexico passed a law prohibiting all new immigration from the United States. However, Mexico was too weak militarily to enforce either of these restrictions, and the American population in Texas doubled from about 7,000 in 1830 to more than 14,000 by 1834. Stephen Austin, who had worked for reconciliation rather than independence, persuaded the government to lift the immigration ban in 1833 since it was not working anyway. By 1835, there were more than 30,000 Americans living in Texas, including about 5,000 slaves, in contrast to fewer than 8,000 Mexicans.

Texas Wins Independence from Mexico

General Antonio Lopez de Santa Anna became the new Mexican president in 1833. Santa Anna crushed liberalism across Mexico and centralized government control by 1835, a move that Americans in Texas believed was especially aimed at them. In that same year, there were a few small skirmishes between the two sides. Finally, the conflict led Americans in Texas to outright rebellion, declaring their independence from Mexico on March 2, 1836. Stephen Austin, who had helped Mexico put down the smaller independence revolt of 1826, had definitely sided with his fellow American Texans by the end of 1835 and supported the 1836 revolt. General Sam Houston, for whom the city of Houston, Texas was named, agreed to command the Texas rebels. Houston had fought in the War of 1812 under Andrew Jackson. Later he served in Congress and then as governor of Tennessee before moving to Texas in 1832.

Santa Anna, with a sizeable army of several thousand, marched into Texas to crush the resistance. On March 6, 1836, just four days after the declaration of independence, the Mexican Army attacked a group of 187 men holding

FIGURE 13.1 - The Alamo as it looks today.

the Alamo, an old abandoned Catholic Spanish mission at San Antonio. Among the Americans at the Alamo were Colonel William Travis, their commander, Jim Bowie of Louisiana, and the famous frontiersman and former Tennessee Congressman Davy Crockett, who had several of his men from Tennessee with him. Several Mexicans from Texas, called Tejanos, were also among the forces occupying the Alamo. They put up a valiant fight, inflicting more than 1,500 casualties among the Mexican troops before every last man in the Alamo was killed.

On March 20, just two weeks after the defeat at the Alamo, American forces under James Walker Fannin surrendered their garrison of about 365 men at Goliad. After the surrender, most of the captured were executed on Santa Anna's orders. These tragedies at the Alamo and at Goliad disheartened the movement for independence and threatened to end it. But Sam Houston had managed to keep an army together under his direct command, and the battle cry, "Remember the Alamo!" became a rallying cry for Texans to continue the fight.

Just as the cause looked hopeless, the tide turned quickly when Sam Houston's army defeated the Mexicans in the Battle of San Jacinto, near present-day Houston, on April 21, 1836. Although outnumbered, the surprise attack by the Texans routed the Mexicans, resulting in more than 800 Mexican casualties and more than 700 captured, in contrast to about 30 Texan casualties. Santa Anna himself had initially escaped the

battlefield, wearing a private's uniform of one of his dead soldiers. But when General Houston ordered troops to pursue the fleeing Mexicans, Santa Anna was brought back. However, not until some of the captured prisoners automatically saluted Santa Anna when they recognized him did the Texans realize they had him. Although many of Houston's men wanted to execute the Mexican president, Houston chose to negotiate with him. At Velasco, Texas, Santa Anna and Interim President David G. Burnett signed the Treaty of Velasco on May 14 of that same year. Actually, there were two treaties signed at Velasco, but the more significant one granted Texas its independence. Later, of course, Santa Anna renounced the Treaty of Velasco, citing the fact that it had been signed under duress. The result was that the government of Mexico refused to ratify the treaty. Nevertheless, Mexico could not militarily undo the treaty. Texas had its independence. That fall, Sam Houston was elected as the first official president of the Republic of Texas.

Annexation of Texas

Most Texans viewed independence as only the first step toward becoming part of the United States. The Lone Star Republic, as it became known, soon sent official representatives to Washington, D.C. to

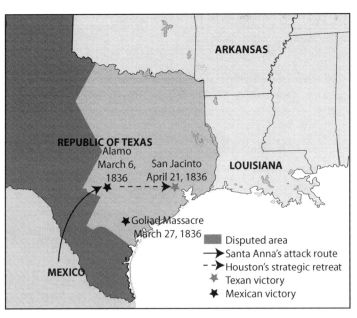

FIGURE 13.2 - The Texas Revolution, 1835-1836.

discuss the possibility of annexation. There certainly was enthusiastic support for this among southern Democrats, who saw the acquisition of Texas as a way to expand slavery within the nation. Many Westerners were also anxious for the country to move closer to achieving its alleged Manifest Destiny. However, there was also much opposition to the annexation. Most Northerners opposed slavery, and many of them viewed the annexation issue as a Southern attempt to expand that institution in the nation. Others were concerned about more direct economic issues that divided North and South and feared the increase in southern votes in Congress and electoral votes in presidential elections that would result from the annexation. Still others, including President Andrew Jackson, feared igniting a war with Mexico, which refused to recognize Texan independence since Santa Anna's return to Mexico City after his defeat at the Battle of San Jacinto. As a result, President Jackson opposed annexation and even delayed official American recognition of the Republic of Texas until his last day in office, in early March 1837.

Jackson's successor was Martin Van Buren, a Democrat from New York, who was elected president in November 1836. As a Northerner, Van Buren was philosophically opposed to slavery. Therefore, he rejected the annexation of Texas because it would eventually become another slave state, and he wanted to avoid the sectional conflict that the expansion of the slave system almost certainly would engender.

Meanwhile, Texas was forced to spend enormous sums for defense against a Mexican army that greatly outnumbered them, and this was taking a heavy toll on its economy. Therefore, having been rejected by the United States, the Republic of Texas was forced to seek other allies and other directions. Some Texans even dreamed of their own Manifest Destiny to expand their Republic all the way to the Pacific Ocean. By 1840, Britain, France, Holland, and Belgium recognized the new Republic and agreed to trade treaties. Britain was especially eager to see an independent Texas. British manufacturers regarded Texas as an important free-trade nation that would be a welcome relief from the protectionist trade policies of the United States. The British textile industry also viewed Texas as a major cotton producer and an alternative to their heavy reliance on American cotton. On the other hand, many anti-slavery Britons hoped to end slavery in the independent republic and use that as a base to inspire massive slave revolts in the American South. Finally, the British and French governments regarded this new nation as a possible wedge to wield influence in the New World against the growing size and influence of the United States.

After the death of President William Henry Harrison, the annexation of Texas finally had an ally in the White House. The new president, John Tyler, was really an old southern Democrat from Virginia, who had bolted from the Democrats over Andrew Jackson's vigorous opposition to nullification in the tariff dispute with South Carolina. As a Southerner, Tyler supported annexation, and he convinced Texas to make their request again in 1844, during his last full year in office. Tyler's fourth Secretary of State, John C. Calhoun, negotiated an annexation treaty with Texas that year. But a coalition of anti-slavery Whigs and Democrats from outside the South defeated the treaty's ratification in the Senate in June 1844. After Democratic victories in the 1844 fall elections, which President Tyler interpreted as a mandate to annex Texas, a resolution was passed by Congress in February 1845 and signed into law by President Tyler on March 1, 1845, just three days before James K. Polk became president. An annexation resolution required only a simple majority vote rather than a two-thirds vote to pass. At a special convention, the Lone Star Republic officially accepted annexation on July 4, 1845. Then on December 29, 1845, Texas became the 28th state in the Union, and the largest slave state.

The United States Claimed Oregon Territory

Another obstacle to achieving America's alleged Manifest Destiny was the Oregon Territory in the far Pacific Northwest of the continent just southwest of British Canada. Oregon was a vast territory of approximately a half million square miles extending from the northern border of Mexico, which was at the 42nd parallel, to the southern border of Alaska, at the 54o 40′ parallel. In relation to modern borders, Oregon included all of the present-day states of Washington, Oregon, and Idaho, and parts of Montana, Wyoming, and roughly half of British Columbia.

In the very early 19th century, Spain, Russia, Britain, and the United States all claimed Oregon as their territory. In the Adams-Onis Treaty of 1819, Spain abandoned its claim to Oregon at the same time it conceded Florida to the United States. Russia, which possessed Alaska at the time, had also claimed Oregon. However, in separate treaties with the United States and Britain, in 1824 and 1825 respectively, Russia gave up its claim south of the 54º 40′ parallel.

After 1825, only the British and the Americans claimed Oregon. The British claim was based on the explorations of one of its naval officers, George Vancouver, in the 1790s and on the subsequent fur trade of the Hudson Bay Company with local Indians. The American claim to Oregon rested largely on the explorations of Captain Robert Gray, a fur trader who apparently had been the first white man to discover the Columbia River in 1792. The claim was reinforced by the Lewis and Clark Expedition of 1804-06, which had made it all the way to the Pacific Ocean at what would later be the border between the states of Washington and Oregon. But until the 1830s, most of the white men in Oregon were either American or British fur traders.

In 1818, Secretary of State John Quincy Adams negotiated the Anglo-American Convention, also known as the Treaty of 1818, with Britain on behalf of President James Monroe. The treaty settled the boundary dispute between British Canada and the Louisiana Territory at the 49th parallel from the Lake of the Woods, bordering on present-day Minnesota, and the Rocky Mountains. Monroe and Adams pushed the British to establish the 49th parallel all the way to the Pacific Ocean, but failed because the British viewed the Columbia River as of equal importance to British Canada in the West as the St. Lawrence River was in the East. Instead, the agreement called for a joint occupation of Oregon Territory for 10 years, which was also renewable. This "joint occupation" arrangement was renewed in 1827 for an indefinite period of time, with the agreement that either nation could terminate it by giving one year's notice.

Even before 1830, American missionaries were inspired to go to Oregon to convert the Indians. This was partly motivated by the common Protestant desire to spread the Christian gospel and partly by concerns that Roman Catholic missionaries from Canada might make a later annexation by the United States impossible. This missionary zeal was enhanced by the arrival of a small group of Indians in St. Louis in 1831. There were four Indians, from the Nez Percé and Flathead tribes, who had apparently made the voyage from Oregon. Although all four died before anyone discovered the purpose of their visit, some Christians interpreted this as a divine call for more missionaries to go to Oregon. Among them were Marcus Whitman and his wife Narcissa, who founded a mission post among the Cayuse Indian tribe east of the Cascade Mountains in the 1830s near present-day Walla Walla, Washington, and became the most famous American missionaries in Oregon. They were killed in an attack by Cayuse Indians in 1847, when the tribe blamed Whitman for an epidemic of measles that had wiped out a major portion of its people.

Oregon Fever and the Oregon Trail

American missionary efforts were largely unsuccessful in converting the Indians in Oregon. However, their lack of success ironically increased the numbers of Americans streaming into Oregon, which in turn led to greater demands for the American government to end its joint occupation with Britain and claim all of the territory. The reason for these developments was that Indian resistance to the missionary efforts resulted in the widespread conclusion that the Indians no longer deserved the land. In other words, by rejecting God, the Indians had lost any sovereignty they previously may have had, and white Christian Americans were now entitled to take the land.

By 1841, "Oregon Fever" had hit Americans in a big way. Attracted to Oregon by the rich soil, abundant rainfall, cheap land, and a nationalistic motive of winning Oregon for the United States, thousands of Americans braved the cruel journey on the Oregon Trail, which extended roughly 2,000 miles from Independence, Missouri to near present-day Portland, Oregon. Oregon Fever was encouraged by a provisional government formed by Americans on their own authority in 1843-44.

Along the Oregon Trail, wagon trains consisting of Conestoga wagons, so-called because they were

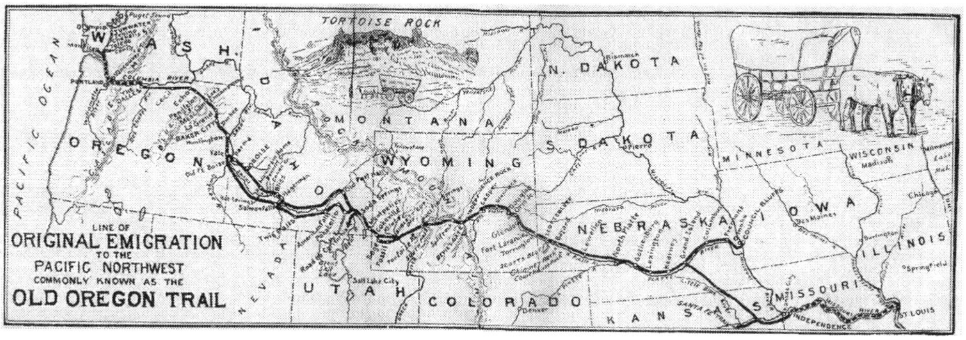

FIGURE 13.3 - Oregon Trail. Line of Original Emigration to the Pacific Northwest

manufactured in Conestoga, Pennsylvania, rolled slowly toward the Pacific Northwest. It was a very dangerous journey that usually lasted between five and six months because the average speed of the wagon trains was only between one and two miles an hour. Weather conditions limited most expeditions from May to November. Extreme temperatures and a lack of sufficient, good food and water led to disease. Accidents also added to the troubles. Tens of thousands of Americans died without reaching Oregon. The most tragic incident concerned the Donner party, a group led by George Donner. During the winter of 1846-47, the Donner party was stranded in the Sierra Mountains of northern California. Although a few relief parties managed to reach the group, their efforts were insufficient to keep all alive, and the survivors of the winter resorted to cannibalism.

Other Western Trails

In addition to the migration to Oregon, hundreds of thousands were on the move to other parts of the West between 1840 and 1860. The chief destination was California, which was a province of Mexico until the United States acquired the American Southwest in the Mexican-American War of 1846-48. One of the major trails into California was called the California Trail, which veered off the Mormon Trail just north of present-day Salt Lake City, Utah, and moved into southern present-day Idaho before heading across Nevada into northern California. Another major trail into California was the Old Spanish Trail, which extended from the Mormon Trail in Utah, went past present-day Las Vegas, Nevada, and ended in Los Angeles, California at the Pacific coast. New Mexico, established as a northern trading outpost

in Spanish Mexico back in the 16th century, was another destination of Americans, who often traveled along the Santa Fe Trail from Independence, Missouri to Santa Fe, New Mexico.

The major portions of all the western trails were rugged and primitive by modern standards. Like the earliest roads in colonial times, they were often little more than ruts or well-worn paths. These trails, including the miles over the mountains, were hazardous to wagons, which often broke down and delayed the travelers. To lighten the loads of the wagons, most walked their way across the West. Then after walking most of the day, the wagon train would stop for the evening, and the women would cook the suppers for their families. In contrast, the men usually drove the wagons, repaired them when they broke down, and then rested when the group stopped for the evening. Clearly, the average woman worked harder than the average man on these wagon trains.

Contrary to modern popular belief, Indians did not constitute a significant source of problems for American migrants to the West. In fact, historical estimates conclude that fewer than 400 Americans were killed in Indian conflicts, a figure which represents only about one-tenth of 1 percent of all migrants. Moreover, Indians often served as guides and traded with the migrants, usually involving food, clothing, and horses.

The 1844 Presidential Election

The Candidates

The major political issues on American minds in 1844 were Oregon and Texas. Oregon Fever had resulted in American citizens outnumbering British citizens in Oregon by a margin of about 5 to 1, and the clamor for total control of Oregon was heard far and wide among Americans. The nation was also divided over the Texas question. In effect, Manifest Destiny itself seemed to be on the ballot. In this charged atmosphere, the country prepared for another presidential election campaign.

Both political parties met in Baltimore, Maryland in the spring of 1844 to nominate their respective candidates. The Whig Party turned to its traditional, non-southern base and nominated Henry Clay of Kentucky, the "Great Compromiser." His vice-presidential running mate was Theodore Frelinghuysen, a prominent northern Presbyterian layman who espoused temperance and supported other social reforms. The leading Democrat for the nomination was former President Martin Van Buren of New York. However, Van Buren was opposed to slavery, and when he publicly announced his opposition to the annexation of Texas, the convention deadlocked between Van Buren and William Cass of Michigan. Finally, after several ballots, pro-Texas southern Democrats turned to a surprise candidate, James K. Polk of Tennessee, and Polk was nominated as the first so-called "dark horse" candidate of a major political party in American history.

While Polk may have been a "dark horse" candidate for president, he was hardly unknown to most Americans. He had served in the House of Representatives for 14 years,

FIGURE 13.4 - James K. Polk.

four of them as Speaker of the House, before serving two terms as governor of Tennessee. Although he had been out of political office for three years, his strong support for Manifest Destiny in general and the annexation of Texas in particular gave him the nomination after the convention had deadlocked. Polk was also aided by support from his friend and fellow Tennessean, former President Andrew Jackson. In fact, Democrats in 1844 began referring to Polk as "Young Hickory," an indirect reference to Jackson's nickname of "Old Hickory."

The abolitionist Liberty Party, having first appeared on the political scene in time for the 1840 presidential election, once again nominated James G. Birney of Ohio for president.

The Campaign

The Democrats enthusiastically endorsed Manifest Destiny. Specifically, the party platform demanded the annexation of Texas and insisted that Oregon become an American territory with its northern border at the 54º 40′ parallel. The campaign slogan became "All of Oregon or None." Although often confused with the 1844 election campaign, it appears that the more famous slogan, "54º 40′ or Fight," was not coined until 1846. Polk and the Democrats used the terms "reannexation" and "reoccupation," implicitly making the claim that it was America's right to repossess territories that somehow already belonged to them, a claim that had no accurate historical foundation. By linking Texas and Oregon, the Democrats tried to appeal to pro-slavery southern voters and anti-slavery northern expansionist voters at the same time.

Henry Clay and the Whigs tried to make tariffs the major issue in the campaign. But the Texas issue would not stay in the background. Clay hurt his chances for election when he equivocated on the annexation of Texas, saying that he would support it under certain circumstances. This weakened his support among anti-slavery voters without satisfying pro-slavery voters. With Polk unwavering in his commitment to annexation, Texas became the primary issue in the campaign. In the meantime, Clay alienated the Irish Catholic voters of New England over his support for several social reform movements and the support he received from anti-immigrant, or nativist, voters.

The Results

The election was relatively close, with Polk winning the popular vote with 1.34 million votes to Clay's 1.3 million votes and the electoral vote 170 to 105. Liberty Party candidate James G. Birney received an impressive 62,000 popular votes, but he received no electoral votes. However, Birney won almost 16,000 votes in mostly western New York, which cost Clay the state by only about 5,000 votes. That was enough to hand Polk the victory in the race for the White House. Furthermore, in a touch of irony, the Liberty Party, which opposed both slavery and the annexation of Texas, in helping to elect James K. Polk, prompted the annexation of Texas under John Tyler and the acquisition of the entire American Southwest under President Polk.

Introduction to the Polk Administration

James K. Polk was a man of strong will who usually got what he wanted, although no one accused him of being the smartest president in the White House. Nevertheless, Polk proved that hard work and an iron will were often more important to success than raw intelligence. These qualities enabled him to achieve the four main goals of his administration: a revival of the independent treasury, lower tariff rates, and the acquisition of both Oregon and California.

As a result of the economic panic of 1837 and subsequent depression, President Van Buren had finally convinced Congress to pass the Independent Treasury Bill in June 1840, to release the national government from dependence on the banks by putting federal funds in federal vaults under the control of the Treasury Department. Congress passed the measure in 1840 but eliminated it the next year. Now President Polk argued for the restoration of the independent treasury, and despite the outrage of the Whigs, the Democrats finally passed the president's proposal in 1846.

Once again the tariff was an issue. In 1846 Secretary of the Treasury Robert J. Walker pushed through Congress a measure that reduced the average tariff rate from about 32 percent to about 25 percent. By lowering tariffs, the Tariff Act of 1846 encouraged more imports, which resulted in greatly increased revenues for the federal government. A lower tariff proved to be a revenue tariff, a point long argued by advocates of lower rates.

The Oregon Dispute Resolved

During the 1844 presidential election, candidate James K. Polk had claimed all of Oregon up to the 54° 40′ parallel. But after his election, southern Democrats retreated from this election-year position because they realized that slavery would never be economically feasible in the Pacific Northwest. Polk, himself a southern Democrat, had no intention to push the 54° 40′ parallel as the northern boundary of Oregon. However, most Americans, especially in the West, were vocal in their enthusiastic demand for all of Oregon. Thus, Polk determined to resolve the long-standing dispute by using 54° 40′ as a bargaining tactic and then proposing to settle for the 49th parallel instead. After all, the Anglo-American Convention of 1818 had set a precedent for the 49th parallel as the border between the United States and Canada in the West. Polk was close to war with Mexico over Texas and the American Southwest, so he could ill afford to go to war with Britain over Oregon.

At first, the British rejected the American offer. This led to the popular cry in the United States of "54° 40′ or Fight!" in early 1846. The British recognized

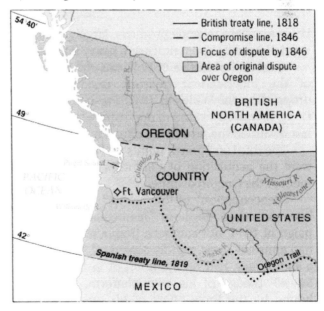

FIGURE 13.5 - The Oregon Controversy, 1846.

that Americans far outnumbered Canadians in most of Oregon, and not wanting a war, they finally agreed to settle the boundary dispute at the 49th parallel. The treaty, which yielded all of Vancouver Island to the British even though its southern end lies south of the 49th parallel, was ratified by the United States Senate on June 15, 1846. Most of the nation rejoiced in a wave of nationalistic pride and in the acknowledgment that Manifest Destiny had just taken another important step toward its full completion. More significantly, the Polk Administration had resolved a long-standing dispute without war, and in doing so, the entire U.S.-Canadian border was now firmly established.

Problems with Mexico

President Polk's last major goal was to acquire California from Mexico. Its rich valleys and the ideal port at San Francisco seemed to offer the greatest opportunity among Mexico's provinces for increasing America's wealth. Part of that dream was that San Francisco could become the gateway to economic trade with the Far East. Of course, California was also viewed as part of the Manifest Destiny. Moreover, President Polk knew that to ensure a more efficient access to California and to provide for the possibility of even further expansion of slavery, the United States needed to acquire New Mexico as well. Like Texas, Mexico had encouraged American citizens to migrate into New Mexico in the 1820s. And by the 1840s, New Mexico was more American than Mexican, both in its population and economy, with a flourishing economic trade along the Santa Fe Trail between Santa Fe, New Mexico and Independence, Missouri. Together, California and New Mexico occupied the present-day states of California, Nevada, Utah, most of Arizona and New Mexico, and even parts of Colorado and Wyoming.

The American presence in California originated with American maritime traders conducting business along the Pacific coast of the province. This resulted in American merchants and other businessmen establishing places of business. Finally, more Americans began arriving in the 1830s and 1840s via the California Trail and settling in the north, especially in the Sacramento Valley. President Polk revealed to some Americans in California that he would welcome an independence movement in that province.

By the 1840s, tensions between Mexicans and American citizens were rising in California and New Mexico. Meanwhile, trouble was brewing over Texas. Mexico had never accepted the loss of Texas in the Revolution of 1836, and it periodically threatened war to regain the former province. Therefore, after the United States annexed Texas, the Mexican government recalled its ambassador to the United States in the summer of 1845. After Texas was admitted as a state into the Union in December of the same year, Mexico officially ended all diplomatic relations with the United States. More trouble between the two nations ensued when Mexico claimed the Nueces River as the southwestern border of Texas, some 150 miles north of the Rio Grande, which the Texans had claimed as their border with Mexico.

The Mexican-American War

Polk Provokes War with Mexico

President James K. Polk, the most pro-Manifest Destiny president in American history, saw this diplomatic crisis as the perfect opportunity to provoke a war with Mexico and acquire land all the way to the Pacific Ocean at the same time. In June 1845, the president sent General Zachary Taylor with a 4,000-man force called the Army of the Occupation of Texas to the Nueces River area at Corpus Christi, allegedly as a defensive move. Then he made a last diplomatic offer to settle the dispute over Texas peacefully. In November of that same year, Louisiana politician John Slidell was sent to Mexico City to offer $25 million for all of New Mexico and California territories. The United States also offered to assume all Mexican debts owed to U.S. citizens, some $3 million which had resulted from damage to American citizens. In exchange, the United States asked for official Mexican recognition of the Rio Grande as the southwestern border of Texas.

Mexico called the American offer "insulting" and rejected it outright, eventually forcing Slidell to leave Mexico City in March 1846. Upon hearing the news of Mexico's rejection of the offer, President Polk ordered General Taylor and his army from the Nueces River south to the Rio Grande River on January 13, 1846. The president hoped to provoke an attack by placing American armed

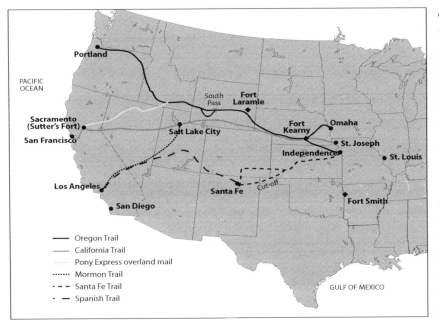

FIGURE 13.6 - Main routes West before the Civil War.

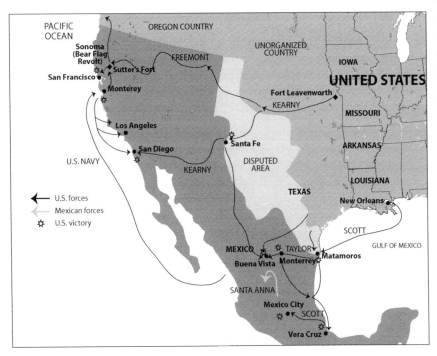

FIGURE 13.7 - Major campaigns of the Mexican-American War.

envoy, and refused to pay its debts to American citizens. Ironically, news reached Washington, D.C. later in the same day as the president's cabinet meeting that Mexican troops had crossed the Rio Grande and attacked Taylor's army on April 25, and killed or wounded 16 American soldiers.

Although there was some dispute about the facts of the skirmish, President Polk was in no mood for a time-consuming and careful evaluation of the facts. He had his excuse, and he took it to Congress and asked for a declaration of war against Mexico. Abraham Lincoln, a Whig member of the House of Representatives from Illinois, made numerous attempts to get Congress to pass a resolution requiring an official inquiry into the exact spot where the attacked had occurred. But the country was swept into a patriotic fever, and his efforts failed pitifully. Most Whigs were afraid that what had happened to the Federalist Party after its opposition to the War of 1812 would also happen to them. That memory, in addition to the popular support sweeping the nation following the news that Mexico had attacked Americans, melted most opposition away. The result was an overwhelming vote for the declaration of war on May 13, 1846, 174 to 14 in the House of Representatives and 40 to 2 in the Senate.

The War

forces in disputed territory. But when no news of an attack had come by May 9, the frustrated president called a cabinet meeting and stated his intention to ask for a declaration of war against Mexico on the grounds that it had rejected their offer, insulted his personal

At the start of the war, President Polk expected a quick and easy victory, with a major American battle victory or two resulting in Mexico's willingness to negotiate a settlement. That proved to be too optimistic and undoubtedly reflected an ethnic bias against what many Americans viewed as the "lazy" Mexicans. The Mexican Army far outnumbered the standing American army of less than 7,500 soldiers. And Mexico was fighting a defensive war for and on its own territory. Furthermore, Mexicans had felt insulted by the entire affair over Texas and the Slidell mission. The truth is that Mexican troops fought valiantly in the Mexican-American War. Nevertheless, better trained army officers, superior artillery and other military equipment, and eager troops, most of them volunteers who swelled the ranks of the American army, eventually won the war for the United States, although it took longer than most Americans expected it would take.

Despite the patriotism which swept the nation, resulting in more than 112,000 Americans, mostly volunteers, putting their lives on the line for the war, Americans were badly divided. While most Northerners had never been very enthusiastic for a war they suspected would lead to an expansion of slavery, a committed group of mostly northern Whigs argued vehemently against it. Several charged that the president had deliberately provoked war with Mexico, which the evidence certainly suggests was true. These opponents showed their contempt for the war by calling it "Mr. Polk's War," suggesting it was a southern plot to further promote slavery, and even attacking the president's intelligence. Nevertheless, President Polk remained undaunted, and he pursued victory with great tenacity and an iron will that had already made him famous.

In May 1846, General Zachary Taylor, or "Old Rough and Ready" as he was affectionately known, crossed the Rio Grande into northeast Mexico, where he won two quick victories that month, first at Palo Alto and then at Resaca de la Palma. Marching more deeply into Mexico, General Taylor's army captured the city of Monterrey in tough house-to-house fighting in late September of the same year. The pinnacle of Taylor's military success came at Buena Vista, where his army, outnumbered by about 20,000 to 5,000, forced Santa Anna to withdraw in February of 1847. Among the heavy American casualties at Buena Vista was Henry Clay, Jr., whose famous father had feared that the annexation of Texas would someday lead to war with Mexico.

Meanwhile, Colonel Stephen W. Kearny was sent from Missouri with 1,700 men to Santa Fe, which he captured without firing a shot on August 18, 1846. From there,

Colonel Kearny took a small force of only about 300 and proceeded to head for California. However, even before word reached California that the war had begun, Americans there revolted against Mexican rule. Aided by the famous explorers Captain John C. Fremont and Kit Carson, Americans had overthrown the Mexican government in California and then proclaimed the Bear Flag Republic in June 1846. By the time Kearny arrived in San Diego, California, it was the Mexicans who were fighting to overthrow the American rule of the California Republic. After victories at San Pasqual in December 1846 and at San Gabriel in January 1847, Kearny occupied Los Angeles, effectively securing California. Americans gladly gave up the idea of a separate republic, and California was added to the United States at the conclusion of the war.

Despite the capture of virtually all the territories in the Southwest that President Polk had sought, Mexico refused to surrender or to begin the process of negotiating a peace treaty. Instead, humiliated by previous American actions, the Mexicans stubbornly refused to yield in spite of the military predicament. Thus it became clear to Polk that only the capture of the capital of Mexico City would force an end to this war. While General Taylor was making solid inroads in northeastern Mexico, he was not the decisive military commander that President Polk believed was necessary to take the Mexican capital. Moreover, Taylor's popularity, which grew with each battle victory, was already producing talk of the presidency in 1848, and Polk was not eager to add to a potential political opponent's accolades. Therefore, he gave General Winfield Scott the assignment of pushing on toward Mexico City.

General Scott's troops had occupied Tampico on the Gulf coast of Mexico in November 1846. From there, they made their journey by sea south toward Veracruz, where a successful amphibious landing was made in late March 1847. The 8,600 American troops under Scott's command surrounded the city of Veracruz, which surrendered in less than a week. From Veracruz, Scott's army undertook the most dangerous and heroic effort of the war, traveling about 250 miles inland toward Mexico City. Not only would General Scott's soldiers face overwhelming Mexican forces desperate to defend Mexico City, but they would have to leave their supply base at Veracruz and carry everything they needed along a mountainous trail. After loading 9,300 wagons and 17,000 pack mules, Scott's troops set out in early April 1847. After beating back an attack from Santa Anna at a mountain pass called Cerro Gordo, General Scott lost about 3,000 troops whose one-year's enlistments had expired, and he was forced to wait for reinforcements before proceeding to Mexico City. In July, Scott resumed his march on Mexico City.

Having arrived at the outskirts of the Mexican capital in August, General Scott's forces began a bloody campaign to oust Santa Anna's army. Slowly, and at great cost to both sides, the Mexican army retreated and then evacuated the city. On September 14, 1847, General Winfield Scott entered Mexico City in triumph. Santa Anna's government collapsed, and the new government agreed to peace talks.

The Treaty of Guadalupe Hidalgo

With foresight, President Polk had sent Nicholas P. Trist, a State Department official, to travel with General Scott's army all the way to Mexico City. Although Polk became frustrated with Trist, and had recalled him to Washington, Trist refused to return. Instead, taking advantage of the chaos at the end of the war, Trist negotiated with the new Mexican government and signed what history records as the Treaty of Guadalupe Hidalgo on February 2, 1848.

In the Treaty of Guadalupe Hidalgo, Mexico ceded all of California and New Mexico to the United States and agreed to the Rio Grande as the border between Texas and Mexico. In exchange, the United States agreed to pay Mexico $15 million and to assume the Mexican debt owed to American citizens in the amount of $3.25 million.

Along with most Southerners, President Polk was not happy with the terms that Trist had negotiated in the peace treaty. The South wanted to know why the United States did not take over all of Mexico, given the fact that the Americans had taken its capital city and overthrown the Santa Anna government. But the Whigs had gained control of the House of Representatives as a result of the Congressional elections in the fall of 1846. Their opposition to the war had grown vicious and they had even threatened to cut off supplies for the troops if it did not end soon. Moreover, effective control and policing of all of Mexico would have proven to be an enormous headache, and it probably would have led to revolts in Mexico. Cooler heads prevailed, as typified by John C. Calhoun, the aging voice of the South, who argued that demands for all of Mexico would play into the hands of anti-slavery Northerners and might well lead to sectional division and civil war. In the end, Polk asked the Senate to ratify the treaty, which it did on March 10, 1848, by a vote of 38 to 14.

Legacy of the Mexican-American War

In many ways, the Mexican-American War had been a proving ground for the American Civil War that would come just 13 years later. Dozens of officers demonstrated the success of the West Point Military Academy, established in 1802, because the war provided excellent opportunities to sharpen their battlefield skills. Among them were Lieutenant Ulysses S. Grant of Illinois and Captain Robert E. Lee of Virginia. And the Marine Corps, established in 1798, would later include words about "the halls of Montezuma" in its moving anthem.

Militarily, the Mexican-American War resulted in the deaths of about 13,000 Americans and about 50,000 Mexicans, the large majority of them from disease. Americans had won its most difficult war to date in spite of very rough terrain, desert conditions, and long marches of soldiers, a fact that only deepened pride and self-confidence. More importantly, the acquisition of the northern half of Mexico had increased the size of the United States by almost one-third, and had accomplished the nationalistic dream of expanding to the Pacific. America's so-called Manifest Destiny to dominate the North American continent south of Canada from sea to shining sea was now a reality.

American supremacy on the continent did not come without a price, however. It certainly intensified the already-bitter resentment that Mexicans had toward the Yankees of the North. They were humiliated by the loss of one-half of their nation in just over 25 years after their independence from Spain. However, it was also true that this bitter resentment encouraged the rise of Mexican nationalism while Mexico was still in its infancy as an independent country. Perhaps most significantly, the war had, with the aid of the discovery of gold in California, heightened tensions within the United States over the slavery question, tensions that will be explored in some depth in the following chapters.

Vintage engraving of slaves working sugar on a plantation. Copyright 2010 iStockphoto.

Chapter 14 Contents

CHAPTER FOURTEEN

The Question of Slavery

Major Events

1775	Quakers created the first anti-slavery organization in American history
1776	Adam Smith published *The Wealth of Nations*
1793	Eli Whitney's improved cotton gin led to major spread of cotton production in South
1800	Gabriel Rebellion (slave revolt)
1816-17	American Colonization Society established
1830	Cotton had become "King Cotton" by this year
1831	William Lloyd Garrison's abolitionist newspaper, *The Liberator*, first published Nat Turner Slave Revolt
1833	American Anti-Slavery Society founded
1836	House of Representatives passed the so-called "Gag Rule"
1837	Pro-Slavery mob killed abolitionist editor Elijah Lovejoy in Alton, Illinois
1843-44	Baptist and Methodist churches each split over slavery
1845	Frederick Douglass published his *Narrative of the Life of Frederick Douglass*

Introduction

Among all the issues facing Americans in the early 19th century, the most vexing one was slavery. As noted in an earlier chapter, slavery had already begun to be entrenched in the South just before the dawn of the 18th century. The reliance on a relatively few staple, or cash, crops like tobacco, rice, indigo, and sugar had given rise to large-scale farms called plantations. These plantations required large numbers of backbreaking laborers, and the expanded use of black slaves, already present in all of the colonies, seemed to be the natural way to meet the labor shortage. By the time Americans won a hard-earned independence in the American Revolution, slavery was firmly planted in southern American soil, and there seemed to be no turning back for the South.

The same American Revolution, fueled by the liberal ideas of the Enlightenment, gave rise to an anti-slavery movement in the North, where slavery had already diminished in economic importance. In contrast to the South, the North had experienced economic diversification during most of the 18th century, resulting in greater economic opportunities, more immigration, and less need for slave labor. That different economic development also allowed most Americans there to see that fighting a war for freedom and independence was inconsistent with the notion that men could claim ownership of other people.

In this way, the nation was increasingly becoming divided between North and South over the slavery question and poised for conflict. Therefore, when Romanticism and the Second Great Awakening intensified traditional American optimism with a greater emphasis on free will, self-improvement, progress, and the possibility of perfection in the early 19th century, it was probably inevitable that the question of slavery would eventually envelop all other social reform movements during the Age of Social Reform (1830-1860). This chapter addresses the larger question of slavery, its economic and social impact, and the heated arguments on both sides.

The Expansion of Slavery

In the early days of the American Republic, however, a technological development spurred an even more rapid growth in the use of slave labor in the South and thereby contribute to a much stronger anti-slavery movement, whose showdown with slavery would threaten the very fabric of national unity. In 1793, just 10 years after Britain officially recognized the independent United States, Eli Whitney perfected the cotton gin; the word "gin" is short for "engine." This new and improved version of the cotton gin had long-range consequences far beyond anyone's imagination at the time.

The process of separating the seeds from the cotton lint had been so expensive that cotton cloth was costly and rare. However, the new cotton gin could quickly separate the seeds from the lint and turn out cotton much more efficiently and cheaply. The result was that cotton production spread like wildfire in the South during the early 19th century and surpassed all other crops as the chief staple crop and economic resource in the region. While cotton was eventually produced in virtually every southern state, it was particularly prominent in South Carolina, Georgia, Alabama, Mississippi, Louisiana, Arkansas, and Texas.

Cotton production became so dominant that Southerners began referring to "King Cotton." While it is difficult to assign a date to this effect, cotton was certainly king by the dawn of the Age of Social Reform in 1830. Indeed, from 1840-1860, cotton accounted for 50-60 percent of the value of all American exports, as the ever-increasing global demand for cotton textile products outpaced the supply. The American South supplied more than half of the world's cotton. The number one importer of American cotton was England, where the textile industry was the largest manufacturing sector in their economy. By 1850, England was obtaining about 75 percent of its cotton from the American South, and roughly 20 percent of its population received some kind of economic benefit from that industry. France was another major importer of American slave-produced cotton. What England and other countries did not buy, northern textile mills bought, as that industry grew in the United States as well.

FIGURE 14.1 - Cotton is king - A plantation scene, Georgia.

Meanwhile, the spread of cotton production westward in the South was accompanied by the expansion of slavery. Although it might superficially appear logical that the cotton gin would have reduced the need for slave labor to pick the cotton, the reverse was actually true. The cotton gin could not do all the work involved in processing cotton. Therefore, the continued "need" for slaves actually grew in the South as cotton production increased. In 1790, just three years before Whitney's technological breakthrough, there were a little more than 700,000 slaves in the United States. But by 1860, there were more than 3.9 million, more than a 550% increase.

Most of the growth in the use of slave labor came from increased birth rates among slave women because Congress had passed a measure in 1807 that made the African slave trade illegal as of January 1, 1808, the same time that England's law also took effect. The higher demand for slaves drove the slave prices up and fostered the continuation of the slave trade illegally, but it was at a much-reduced rate since slave traders were subject to the death penalty. Slave owners used a variety of ways to compensate for the relative lack of newly imported slaves. Most slave owners hired free laborers to do the more dangerous jobs around the plantation in order to keep the injury and death rates of their slaves down. Slaves were increasingly given more autonomy in their family and religious lives, with the result that many slave families had more children. Slave women were encouraged to bear large numbers of children, with some slave owners promising freedom after giving birth to 10 or more. Finally, the rape of female slaves by white masters increased during the 19th century, with the mulatto offspring usually being treated as lifetime slaves.

The Economics of Slavery

Much of the blame for slavery's expansion can be indirectly laid on the doorsteps of many Northerners, for it can be argued that ironically, the North received more economic benefits from slavery than did the South. Not only did northern textile mill owners and workers economically benefit from the expansion of cotton and slavery, but so

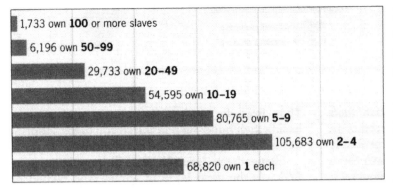

FIGURE 14.2 - Slave-owning families, 1850.

did a host of northern middlemen, who did most of the financing, selling, and transporting of cotton and other slave-produced commercial crops such as tobacco and rice. The resulting expansion of the American textile industry in New England also stimulated other manufacturing industries, all of which in turn increased consumer purchasing power and thus helped other businesses, both small and large, succeed in the region.

In contrast to its positive economic impact on many Northerners, the institution of slavery benefited very few Southerners. First, it should be noted that approximately 75 percent of all white Southerners never owned a single slave in their entire lives. The initial investment of purchasing slaves, whose price could run more than $1,000 each, and the continuing expenses of housing, feeding, clothing, and health care, prevented most Southerners from owning any slaves. Second, among the 25 percent who did own slaves, only about ½ of 1 percent owned 100 slaves or more, whereas more than 73 percent owned fewer than 10 slaves. Finally, when these percentages are placed in the context of the entire white southern population, those who owned 100 slaves or more only represented about one-tenth of 1 percent. These were the slave owners of the large plantations who obviously profited a great deal financially from the use of slave labor.

On the other hand, the 18½ percent of all white Southerners who owned fewer than 10 slaves did not profit very much from slavery. Most of those slave owners were small farmers whose incomes were fortunate enough to cover the expense of housing, feeding, and clothing their slaves in addition to their own family members. That left the 6½ percent of white Southerners, who owned

between 10 and 99 slaves, and the one-tenth of 1 percent who owned 100 or more slaves, as the modest to major recipients of slavery's financial benefits.

In other words, about 93½ percent of all white Southerners received virtually no economic benefits from slavery at all. Furthermore, they were denied economic opportunities that were available to most Northerners because the over-reliance on cotton production limited economic diversity. Therefore, most of that number scratched out an existence as subsistence farmers, growing corn and other vegetables and raising hogs or other animals for meat. Their lives were frequently plagued by malnutrition and other common maladies of the day. Thus, their economic lot in life left them out in the cold, and they failed to achieve the American dream.

Finally, it is obvious that slavery did not provide financial benefits to the slaves, although many slave-owners often argued that slaves benefited through receiving free housing, food, clothing, and medical care. For all the reasons discussed in this section, we safely conclude that slavery benefited more Northerners than it did Southerners.

The economic impact of "King Cotton" on the South was primarily the result of a conscious decision on the part of the wealthy planters not to industrialize their region. They used their great wealth, along with the pervasive white fear that freeing the slaves would lead to race wars, racial intermarriages, and the ultimate destruction of society, to dominate the region politically and culturally, as well as economically. Their opposition to economic diversification was founded on at least three fundamental points. First, reliance upon cotton was easy money. Growing worldwide consumer demand for cotton textiles meant rising cotton prices even at a time of increasing supply, a condition that is every agricultural owner's dream. Second, large industries in the South might attract Northerners to the South to work and live in its milder climate. Those transplanted northern workers would almost certainly not tolerate competition with free slave labor in the industrial sector. Finally, industrialization would create powerful industrialists and other economic allies like bankers. Moreover, an industrial elite would compete with the wealthy planter elite, and when the two economic cultures clashed, the industrial elite could not be counted on to look out for the interests of slave-owners.

Unique Characteristics of American Slavery

After the colonization of the New World in the wake of Christopher Columbus' re-discovery in 1492, the Western Hemisphere quickly became the number one market for black African slaves because of the extreme labor shortages there. Slaves were imported to Portuguese Brazil and the many Spanish colonies of Latin America, as well as to the English colonies of the Atlantic seaboard. But there were some important differences between the slavery practiced in the English colonies and that practiced in Latin America.

The two most important differences were the near equal population of males and females and a moderate ratio of slaves to non-slaves in the English colonies in contrast to an overwhelming number of males and a high ratio of slaves to non-slaves in Latin America.

English slave-owners almost from the beginning tended to emphasize family units much more than Latin Americans. Indeed, American slavery became virtually self-sustaining through high birth rates after the January 1808 ban on new slave imports entering the United States. This also helped provide a near equal population of males and females, which resulted in strong family ties among American slaves. Latin Americans, on the other hand, were forced to rely on a constant supply of new imports of slaves because they demanded an almost exclusive slave population of strong males.

In the English experience, there was also a moderate ratio of slaves to non-slaves. For example, slaves accounted for only about one-third of the American South's population overall throughout the antebellum (pre-Civil War) period. In Latin America, however, the slave population exceeded the non-slave population most of the time. This fairly modest ratio in the English-American experience was reflected in the fact that about 75 percent of the slaves lived in immediate areas that contained fewer than 50 slaves.

As a result of the male-female balance, with its accompanying family ties, and the moderate ratio of slaves to non-slaves in America, there were far fewer escapes here, and even fewer outright slave revolts, with just a little more than 200 documented revolts. But in Latin America, where slaves often outnumbered non-slaves, and there were far fewer family ties among them, slaves were much more likely to attempt escape, and much more likely to kill their white owners in the process.

The moderate ratio of slaves to non-slaves in America also resulted in slaves acquiring and adapting some key American cultural characteristics. In other words, they were becoming African-Americans. The most significant example of this is the fact that most slaves here adopted the Christian religion, albeit it was a Christianity altered by their experience as slaves. The slave naturally placed a heavy emphasis on liberation, and often compared their dream of emancipation from slavery to the deliverance of the Israelites from Egyptian bondage in the time of Moses. Christian hymns called Negro spirituals largely reflected this theme of deliverance. These spirituals laid the foundation for the later development of jazz and rhythm-and-blues music forms. In other words, they represented a kind of Africanization effect on the American music culture.

Life for the Slaves

Even among 21st century Americans, myths still exist regarding the days of slavery. One of those myths is that black African slaves were economically backward and completely lacking in the job skills required for living in freedom. This is sometimes said as if to justify, or at least excuse, American slavery. But this could not be further from the truth. Most African slaves imported to the English colonies and the later United States possessed skills equal to the ordinary Englishman of the time. Their agricultural tools were also about the same in diversity and quality as the English farmers' were.

Many slaves were, or quickly became, skilled in those areas required to run a successful plantation. Indeed, slaves did most of the skilled labor on the plantations, along with the unskilled labor. Several of the male slaves were craftsmen, such as blacksmiths, cobblers, carpenters, and coopers. Others were drivers and mill workers. Female slaves were mostly used as house servants and served as cooks, seamstresses, and even nurses. The irony was that although white slave-owners believed slaves to be sub-human, they often entrusted much of the childrearing of their own children to slave women. Male slaves were also sometimes used as house servants, chiefly as butlers. On large plantations, of course, most slaves were employed as field hands, especially on cotton and tobacco plantations. These field hands endured the most physical exhaustion in the hot sun, for they worked hard from sunup to sundown during the agricultural season, which was most of the year in the South.

The idea frequently espoused by supporters of slavery that the typical slave was contented is also a myth. The so-called "Sambo" image of the contented slave was only a front. The reality was very different. It is true that runaways were relatively few because of the strong family ties among slaves; men were afraid that women and children would slow them down and increase the likelihood of getting caught. As a result, approximately 80 percent of all escape attempts involved males, many of them single. On the other hand, slaves showed their contempt for slavery by often faking illnesses, working slowly, and breaking tools and other equipment. In return, most slave-owners employed a variety of methods to keep their slaves completely dependent upon them. These included the frequent use of the lash, or whip, as a form of punishment; stricter curfews for being inside their shacks at night; denying the acquisition of literacy skills; and the occasional intentional separation of families by selling family members to different buyers. This interaction of contempt and control between slaves and their masters took on aspects of a game, with each side carefully measuring how far they could go without doing more harm than good. After all, slaves did not enjoy severe beatings or other punishments, and slave-owners needed the slaves to do most of the work that was done on their property.

Slaves were usually given some level of autonomy in their own living quarters. They were allowed to conduct their own religious meetings, for example. But most owners, who sometimes conducted their own Bible readings in an attempt to persuade their slaves to be loyal to them and work hard, limited this autonomy. Slave-owners also periodically issued arbitrary rules designed to show their authority over their slaves.

Slave marriages had no legal status, but they were usually encouraged or at least tolerated most of the time as a stabilizing force among the slaves. Slave-owners realized that attempted escapes were fewer when family ties were stronger. Indeed, family ties were so strong among the slaves that the occasional breakup of a slave family resulted in the unofficial adoption of the remaining children by other slave families. The father of a slave family was the head of that family. It was after the Civil War, and especially after the Reconstruction Era (1865-1877), that began the long road to destroying many black families. At that time, southern states began requiring cash license fees for black Americans to use their job skills and adopting other forms of racial discrimination in a successful effort to force black families into a sharecropping life and its resulting cycle of poverty through complete dependence on their landlords. (See Chapter 17 for a more detailed discussion of this trend.)

White masters or their sons often forced sexual relations on female slaves, resulting in a rather large mulatto population. This was common knowledge even to the wives of the owners, who suffered in silence for the most part because they didn't have many legal rights either. White men even often defended the rape of slave women on the grounds that it protected the chastity of white women. In other words, white men who owned or worked with slaves could fool around sexually with women they knew they would never marry, thus making it more likely that they could marry virgins. Sexual activity, whether legitimate or illicit, gave rise to higher birth rates among slave women. However, a majority of slave babies died in their first year of life, which represented a mortality rate more than two times greater than for white babies of that day.

Religion was the glue that held the slaves' psyche together, giving them hope for a better future after their days of slavery ended. Bible stories and Negro spirituals celebrated the theme of freedom and liberation, as briefly discussed in the preceding section of this chapter.

The horrors of slave life and the very notion that certain human beings have the right to claim ownership of other human beings were patently at odds with the American penchant for freedom and rugged individualism. These inconsistencies led many to call slavery the "peculiar institution" and to demand its elimination through one method or another.

The Status of Free Blacks

By the dawn of the Civil War, there were about 500,000 free blacks in the United States, divided fairly equally between North and South. Most free blacks in the North were freed as a result of separate state actions to end slavery in the wake of the American Revolution. The situation in the South was, of course, quite different. Some owners, who had second thoughts about slavery, followed the example of George Washington, who freed all of his slaves in his will. In other cases, owners freed mulattoes that they had illegitimately fathered with slave women, either out of embarrassment or conscience. A few slaves were allowed to earn small amounts of money for work done outside of regular hours. They often saved this money until they could purchase their freedom. Ironically, a tiny few of these free blacks eventually bought slaves of their own, the most infamous being William T. Johnson, the "barber of Natchez" in Mississippi.

Life for most free black Americans was only a little less oppressive than it was for slaves. In the North, where racial prejudice and anti-slavery feelings usually ran high in the same whites, free blacks were often despised, beaten, and denied public education, decent housing, the better jobs, and the right to vote. In fact, racial prejudice was so strong in the North that several states there even passed laws denying the admission of free blacks into their state. In the South, free blacks were also harassed and denied public education and decent housing. They were also prohibited from entering certain occupations. Legally, they had no right to vote in any southern state and could not testify in a court of law against a white defendant. Moreover, free blacks in the South faced the additional ever-present danger of being forcibly, albeit illegally, taken and sold into bondage by agents working for wealthy planters.

A New Southern Attitude Toward Slavery

The conscience of the nation had been awakened during the American Revolution to the disturbing fact that it appeared incongruent to own slaves while fighting for one's own liberty. While the Revolution did harden the South's attitude toward slavery, it was more of a defensive posture. From the Revolution to the 1830s, most Southerners defended slavery on the grounds that it was allegedly preferable to race war and interracial marriages, which Southerners predicted would be the result if slavery were ever abolished. Basically, if a typical Southerner were pushed on the issue, he would defend slavery during that period as a "necessary evil." Interestingly, in 1827, there were more emancipation societies in the South than in the North: 106 societies, with about 5,150 members, in the South, and only 24 societies, with a total of about 1,475 members in the North. The largest number of these societies in the South was in the Upper South, most prominently in states like Maryland, Virginia, Kentucky, and Missouri. These emancipation societies urged voluntary emancipation by slave owners and no further spread of the "peculiar institution."

In the 1830s, however, with the arrival of cotton as "king," a dramatic shift in white southern opinion about slavery occurred. Rather than an almost apologetic defense of slavery as a "necessary evil," slavery became championed as an "absolute positive good." There are at least three important reasons for this change of attitude. First, "King Cotton" had ridden across the South on the backs of many hundreds of thousands of slaves, as explained earlier in this chapter. By 1830, cotton production was the very symbol of the southern economy and way of life, and slaves were deemed as an absolutely crucial factor in keeping it that way. In other words, slavery was so deeply entrenched in the southern economy and mindset that any perceived threat to slavery was regarded as an attempt to destroy the entire southern way of life.

Second, a few of the little more than 200 documented slave revolts were quite devastating in their effects on southern thinking. For example, a Virginia slave named Gabriel organized a massive revolt involving perhaps 1,000 slaves near the state capital of Richmond in 1800. Hoping to start a groundswell revolt among all Virginia slaves, the Gabriel Rebellion planned to burn the city of Richmond and kidnap Governor James Monroe in August of that year. When rain postponed the attack, this gave time for informers among the slaves to reveal the plot. Eventually, 26 slaves were hanged, including Gabriel himself. Then there was the case of Denmark Vesey, a former slave who had bought his freedom and lived in Charleston, South Carolina. Although historians debate whether a slave revolt conspiracy actually existed at all, Vesey and 36 others were convicted and executed for allegedly plotting one in 1822.

The most dramatic of all slave revolts was organized and carried out by a Virginia slave named Nat Turner in August 1831. The Nat Turner Slave Revolt became the largest slave revolt in American history. Approximately 60 whites of both genders and all ages were killed during this two-day revolt. Turner himself was eventually captured and hanged. Moreover, the revolt produced a wave of mostly random terror in the South by whites against black slaves in which perhaps as many as 200 were slaughtered. This slave revolt was so terrifying and left such a scar on the white southern mind that most Southerners were approaching a state of paranoia about the very survival of the "peculiar institution." The best-selling book *The Confessions of Nat Turner*, published very shortly after Turner was hanged, inflamed the paranoia. Turner and a lawyer named Thomas R. Gray had co-written it during the time that the former was in jail awaiting his execution. This biographical sketch of Turner's life portrayed him as a zealous but mystical man that made him both fascinating and frightening to southern whites.

In a surprise move, many members of the Virginia state legislature reacted to the Nat Turner Slave Revolt by proposing a plan that would have provided for gradual emancipation beginning in 1858. Under the proposal, newly freed slaves would be expelled from the state so that the ranks of the free blacks would not multiply. When this plan was defeated in the legislature, it marked the last time that whites in the South would seriously consider any plan to free the slaves. Instead, southern reaction was to tighten their grip on the slaves and to champion slavery as a positive institution.

The third factor that contributed to the new southern attitude toward slavery was the emergence of a noisy abolitionist movement by the 1830s. Based primarily in New England, this movement seemed to confirm the South's worst suspicions about northern interference with its economy and institutions. Abolitionists were the most extreme opponents of slavery, demanding its total abolition everywhere in the nation. As the 1830s extended into the '40s and '50s, more and more Southerners became absolutely convinced that most Northerners were abolitionists, bent on destroying their way of life. While that impression was completely untrue, it illustrates that it is not reality that counts in life, but one's perception of reality. If you believe something to be true, then that is what you will act on.

All three of the reasons for the new southern attitude toward slavery by about 1830 can be summarized as an illustration of a common reaction in human nature. Most people tend to cover up any doubts or pangs of conscience they may have about something they are doing when they perceive that they are being attacked in that area by defending their actions or attitudes as absolutely right or positively good. In other words, when people are backed up against the wall, most will try to come out fighting.

Southern Arguments for Slavery

Four major arguments were developed and/or expanded to champion slavery as an absolute positive good by or during the 1830s. They are briefly outlined in the next several paragraphs.

One of these was the historical argument. White Southerners often argued that human inequality was part of natural law. In support of that reality was the fact that all the great civilizations in world history, they maintained, were built on the foundation of slavery, like the Babylonians, Egyptians, Greeks, and Romans. While it is true that most great civilizations of the past used slave labor to create much of their wealth, the historical argument ignored the changing face of Western civilization. A spirit of individual achievement in economic, religious, political, and cultural areas of human life had eventually replaced the feudal system of the Early Middle Ages. This Renaissance spirit was creating more wealth for more people, thus allowing for the possibility of greater equality among people. Moreover, it is also interesting to note that while nearly all civilizations developed and practiced slavery, Western civilization became the first world civilization to also develop an internal anti-slavery movement strong enough to bring an end to slavery within its own civilization.

The religious argument was also used to champion slavery, which should not surprise us when we remember that the South was becoming known as the Bible Belt by the 1830s. The Biblical argument concluded that God must approve of slavery because He provided for its existence in Old Testament Israel by giving the nation certain laws governing slavery and that the apostle Paul counseled a slave to return to his Christian master in the New Testament book of Philemon. Therefore, if God approves of slavery, it means that slavery must be valid and positively good. Anti-slavery Christians countered this religious argument by declaring that God does not necessarily approve or require something just because He permits it. Sometimes, it was said, God takes people where they are, softens the evil results of their errors, and eventually leads them to abandon those errors altogether when they are better prepared to see the light.

There was also a racial argument. White Southerners argued that since blacks were (allegedly) inherently inferior to whites, slavery of blacks by whites actually did black people a favor. Black African slavery allowed white Christians to practice Christian charity and give them the basic necessities of life that they were incapable of obtaining for themselves if they were free. This argument appealed to a number of northern whites because racism was equally prevalent among them. Even though few white Northerners actually championed slavery, the fear of violence, crime, and vagrancy that they expected would run rampant if the slaves were freed led some of them to grudgingly defend slavery.

Finally, an economic argument was employed to champion slavery in the South. Specifically, this was the wage-slavery argument. Southerners alleged that northern capitalism enslaved factory and mine workers at low wages and poor working conditions. There were no provisions for ill health; there was periodic unemployment; and there was forced retirement without pay at the end of a worker's productive life. Southern slavery, it was argued, provided for lifetime care of the slaves, as it was in the best economic interest of the slave-owners to do so. Thus, slaves never experienced sick leave without pay, unemployment, or retirement without the benefits of housing, food, and clothing. In addition, slavery united almost all whites on the basis of race, so that there were few serious labor-management problems in the South. Therefore, the argument ran, both major regions of the country practiced slavery, but when you compare the North's wage-slavery system to the South's version, southern slavery was far more humane.

There were few white Southerners in the middle class because the institution of slavery as practiced in the South greatly restricted economic opportunities for most whites. Nevertheless, most poor whites seemed content that at least they were not slaves, and that someone else (the slave) would always exist at the very bottom of the socioeconomic ladder. Despite their resentment of the wealthy planter class, most white Southerners seemed psychologically comforted by the fact that someone else was at a lower class than they were. Apparently, this was the most important factor in causing non-slave-owning poor whites to often become more virulent and emotional in their support of slavery than middle and upper class slave-owners were.

Factors Contributing to the Rise of an Anti-Slavery Movement

An Inherent Contradiction

The high value most Americans had always placed on freedom and individualism from the earliest colonial times inevitably propelled the American journey toward a clash with slavery. This spirit of freedom reached a milestone in 1776, when Thomas Jefferson wrote in the Declaration of Independence that "all men are created equal." Of course, he did not really mean for his statement to apply literally to every human being, and certainly not to women, Indians, or blacks (at least not in his day). But was it only a "glittering generality," as John Adams had declared, a good rallying cry to fight for but rather vague and meaningless? Jefferson himself did not think so. In the same year that he wrote those words

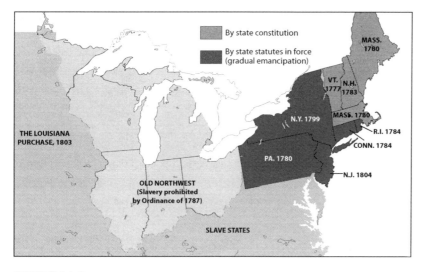

FIGURE 14.3 - Early emancipation in the North.

in the Declaration of Independence, Jefferson personally tried unsuccessfully to get an anti-slavery provision in Virginia's new state constitution.

Of course, the irony was that Jefferson himself was a slave-owner. For most of his adult life, he engaged in an inner struggle between gnawing feelings that the enslavement of other people was not right and his fear that blacks could not survive, let alone flourish, as a free and independent people. In his own personal struggle, Thomas Jefferson embodied the inherent contradiction between freedom and slavery that first afflicted colonial society and then the young independent nation. Sadly, he could never see his way clear to free his slaves, despite the fact that fellow Virginian and Founding Father George Washington had done so.

The American rendezvous with destiny to resolve this contradiction between freedom and slavery was slowed by conflicting racial theories. In the 18th century, it was widely believed that all human beings belonged to the same species, with races being classified as varieties of that one species. Some argued that racial differences had been caused by environmental differences on Earth, while others said that each race was a special creation by God. Some argued that education could result in racial equality, but others denied the possibility of racial equality, declaring that God had always intended for some races to rule others. Thomas Jefferson himself originally denied any possibility for racial equality, but in his later life he expressed the hope that this might actually happen some

day. Anthropologists in the 19th century, however, more and more rejected the idea of racial equality as a possibility. Instead, they classified races from the best to the worst, beginning with whites at the top and then moving down in descending order to yellow, brown (Malayans), red, and black.

Positive Factors

Despite these various racial theories, there were other powerful forces operating in America, and some in Western Europe too, which propelled Americans toward a showdown over the "peculiar institution." Among them were certain post-Reformation radical Protestant Christian groups. The most important by far of these was the Society of Friends, better known as the Quakers. Quakers emphasized the equality of all human beings before God, a belief that compelled them to take a stand against slavery. In fact, the Quakers were the first American group of any kind, religious or secular, to publicly call for an end to slavery, when they did so in 1760. Then in 1775, the year the American Revolution began, the Quakers organized the Pennsylvania Society for Promoting the Abolition of Slavery, the very first anti-slavery organization in American history.

Religion played a prominent role in the anti-slavery cause in another way. The First Great Awakening (1720s-1740s), before the American Revolution, emphasized that sin was a form of enslavement to Satan. This led some Christians to think that if sin were a form of slavery, then perhaps human slavery was a form of sin. Then after the Revolution, the Second Great Awakening (1795-1830) placed a major emphasis on man's free will, perfectionism, and hope for an earthly millennium of peace and prosperity, an emphasis that seemed incompatible with the existence of slavery.

On the intellectual front, the Enlightenment of the 18th century had assumed that the result of following natural law would be the greatest good for the greatest number. For obvious reasons, slavery seemed inconsistent with this expectation. Then at the close of the 18th century and in the early 19th century, Romanticism furthered the anti-slavery feeling with its emphasis on the individual, his feelings, and change. It was naturally asked by many how a society could glorify the individual and still enslave some individuals.

In 1776, a British economist named Adam Smith wrote a book with the abbreviated title, *The Wealth of Nations*. Smith was the first notable economics thinker of the Enlightenment. Among other economic ideas in his book, Smith argued that slavery was bad economics for two reasons. First, he said that it is inherently inefficient because there is absolutely no incentive for a slave to work harder or more efficiently since he will never share in the fruits of his labor. In fact, just the opposite is true in that he has a disincentive to work hard, and an incentive to work slowly, break equipment, and fake illness to get out of work as often as possible. Second, cheap slave labor is unfair job competition with free labor. For both of these reasons, Smith predicted that an industrial society would eventually be destroyed by the use of slave labor. The significance of Adam Smith is that his ideas were more influential on Americans than on any other people in the world.

Finally, Western civilization's Age of Democratic Revolution (1775-1848), that began with the American Revolution and ended with the unsuccessful democratic revolutions in the German states of central Europe, promoted the powerful idea that human slavery was inconsistent with the ideals of democracy and freedom. Moreover, this age of revolution resulted in the independence of most of the Latin American colonies from Spain and the subsequent abolition of slavery in most of those former colonies. But increasing cotton production in the American South, sugar production in Cuba, and coffee production in Brazil left slavery more entrenched in those places than ever before. At the same time, Britain, France, and Denmark ended slavery in their colonies around the world, thereby intensifying the irreversible trend of the abolition of slavery in the rest of Europe's colonies.

Major Anti-Slavery Views

The American experience and the powerful liberalizing forces within Western civilization as a whole combined to intensify anti-slavery feelings among Americans outside the South. But that did not mean that all anti-slavery Americans agreed on exactly how to respond to that institution. Indeed, there were some very different ideas that often sparked hostility as well as debate in the anti-slavery North. During the first half of the 19th century, three different major anti-slavery views emerged. But whatever their differences, by the time of the Age of Social Reform (1830-1860), the anti-slavery movement had become a potent force to be dealt with. And in the 1850s, events would propel it to the forefront of the social reforms being promulgated in the country. In fact, the anti-slavery movement would then eclipse and overwhelm all other movements to reform American society. The three major anti-slavery views are examined in this section.

The Colonization Movement

Widespread racism among white Americans, even in those opposed to slavery, became the basis for the notion that the slaves should be gradually emancipated and subsequently shipped out of the country, either to Africa or the Caribbean region, where the newly freed slaves would colonize—thus, the term "colonization movement." This approach seemed to promise an eventual end to slavery while avoiding the widely expected problems created by an enormous population of free blacks living in the United States. It was also believed that gradual emancipation would give the South plenty of time to diversify their regional economy.

A group of white Virginians created the American Colonization Society in Washington, D.C. in December 1816 and January 1817 to get the colonization movement off the ground. Their idea was to compensate slave-owners who were willing to free any of their slaves and then find a location to which they would literally ship those former slaves. Money was raised from private donations, the state legislatures of Virginia and Maryland, and even the United States Congress. Then in 1821, the Society purchased land on the west coast of Africa, and the first former slaves arrived there the next year. This territory was the basis for the nation of Liberia, which was given its independence in 1847. The very name Liberia is related to the word *liberty*, and its capital Monrovia was named after James Monroe, the American president at the time of the first African-American settlers to colonize the place. The colonization movement was supported by a number of famous Americans, including George Washington's nephew Bushrod Washington, Thomas Jefferson, James Madison, James Monroe, John Marshall, Henry Clay, Daniel Webster, and Abraham Lincoln (in his earlier years). However, the movement was ineffective for a variety of reasons. First, most slave-owners did not wish to free their slaves even if they were compensated for their losses. Slavery was simply too much a part of the southern way of life by the early 19th century. Second, colonization was never really a feasible solution. There were too many slaves, and more born every day, and never a sufficient amount of funds to realistically expect that slavery could be eliminated by this method. Finally, although some free blacks advocated colonization early on, the vast majority vigorously opposed the movement on the grounds that slaves of African descent in America were no more Africans than white Americans were Europeans. In other words, slaves and free blacks had become African-Americans, and because American slavery was an American problem, it required an American solution. By 1860, only about 15,000 slaves had gone to Liberia. The movement gradually died out as most of its supporters eventually recognized that it was an unrealistic solution.

The Free-Soilers

As public perception grew that colonization was not a viable solution to the question of slavery, a new anti-slavery position emerged on the political landscape. Spurred by the acquisition of the American Southwest from Mexico in the Mexican-American War (1846-48), which had been viewed by Southerners as a golden opportunity to spread slavery all the way to the West coast, a rapidly growing number of white Northerners adopted what was called the Free-Soil perspective on slavery.

Although some Free-Soilers opposed slavery on moral grounds, the movement emphasized its opposition to slavery primarily on economic grounds. In doing so, it adopted the views of Adam Smith in declaring that slavery was inherently an inefficient economic system whose spread would eventually ruin the entire nation (see "Factors Contributing to the Rise of an Anti-Slavery

Movement" above). At the same time, most Free-Soilers wanted to keep blacks in the South so that they would not become a source of unfair cheap labor competition for free workers in the North. Therefore, most were content to leave slavery intact in the South. This position can be summarized in two major points. First, it promised to leave slavery alone where it already existed in the South. Second, it drew a line in the proverbial sand and declared its emphatic opposition to the expansion of slavery anywhere else, period.

The Free-Soil movement attracted many adherents as the most popular departure from the earlier concern to maintain an even balance between the number of free states and slave states in the Union. Moreover, it was less radical than abolitionism (see "Abolitionism" below), so Northerners could distinguish themselves from radicals while still remaining anti-slavery. And it seemed like a practical way to avoid civil war. By 1850, the majority of white Northerners had adopted the Free-Soil position and made it the number one anti-slavery viewpoint in the nation. Abraham Lincoln was among them by that time period.

Politically, Free-Soilers began to challenge the two major parties outside the South as early as 1848, the year the Mexican-American War ended and a presidential election was held. That very year, the Free-Soil Party was formed out of the remnants of the old Liberty Party, with the addition of some northern anti-slavery Democrats as well. Former Democratic President Martin Van Buren, was its nominee for president that year. Later, in 1854, Free-Soilers joined northern Whigs and some additional northern Democrats to create the modern Republican Party.

Abolitionism

As its root word implies, abolitionists favored the total abolition of slavery in the United States. Unlike the Free-Soilers, the abolitionists' position was primarily based on moral grounds, on the deeply held belief that slavery was a moral evil. The Quakers became the first organized group calling for the abolition of slavery in America, a fact already noted above. It was only natural, of course, that free blacks also supported this cause before it caught on among many whites. Notable among free blacks was David Walker, who wrote a pamphlet entitled

Appeal ... to the Colored Citizens of the World in 1829. In his publication, Walker urged slaves to use violence in their revolt against the chains of slavery. It had little effect on slaves, however, because few slaves ever read it.

It was not until the 1830s, however, that the abolitionist movement began to receive greater attention and additional support from a small but vocal group of whites. In 1831, William Lloyd Garrison helped galvanize that support when he became the editor of a weekly abolitionist newspaper called *The Liberator*. Based in Boston, the newspaper's first issue was published on January 1 of that year. It also put Garrison in the spotlight and made him the most famous white abolitionist in American history.

Like many abolitionists, the Second Great Awakening and its call for repentance influenced Garrison. Thus, Garrison approached the abolitionist cause with the moral fervor of an evangelist who preaches his heart out. To him, as to most abolitionists, slavery was a sin against God and against humanity. His zeal was never in doubt, as illustrated in his most famous words that appeared in *The Liberator*: "I am in earnest—I will not equivocate—I will not excuse—I will not retreat a single inch AND I WILL BE HEARD!"

Also like an evangelist, Garrison hoped that slave-owners would be converted to the anti-slavery position and voluntarily free their slaves so that violence to end slavery would never come. Although his words were often violent and inflamed the passions of people on both sides of the slavery question, Garrison never actually advocated violence to overthrow slavery. Nevertheless, most white Northerners considered him to be a dangerous fanatic. Even some abolitionists, nicknamed "gradualists," avoided him because they perceived his hostile speech as making it more difficult to morally persuade and successfully use politics in the fight against slavery. By contrast, Garrison opposed the use of politics, claiming that the federal government and even the Constitution were all morally responsible for the evil of slavery. In 1843, he even demanded the secession of the free states from the Union if the slave states were not expelled. Garrison and other like-minded abolitionists were sometimes called "immediatists" because they demanded the immediate, no-compromise end to slavery.

Theodore Dwight Weld was another prominent white abolitionist. Weld had been converted to Christianity by the preaching of Charles G. Finney in upstate New York. He then adopted the abolitionist point of view against slavery and agitated for it wherever he went. In 1834, while studying to become a minister, he was expelled from a Protestant seminary for organizing an unauthorized debate on slavery at the school. His book, *American Slavery As It Is: Testimony of a Thousand Witnesses*, was published in 1839. Based on written testimonies of slave owners that had already appeared in numerous southern newspapers, it described the sometimes brutal treatment and punishment meted out to the slaves. It became second in influence only to Harriet Beecher Stowe's *Uncle Tom's Cabin*, which was partly based on Weld's pamphlet.

In 1833, the American Anti-Slavery Society was created through the efforts of men like William Lloyd Garrison and Theodore Dwight Weld. It became the most important national abolitionist organization in the entire country. By 1838, there were 1,350 chapters with more than 250,000 members. The society organized a lecture circuit for prominent abolitionists and used pamphlets, newspapers, and petition drives as weapons in the war against slavery.

Some early abolitionists, including Garrison, believed in equal rights for blacks and women, although the majority of abolitionists, as the movement gained followers, did not. Indeed, most white abolitionists were just as racist as most other Americans. Championing equal rights for women, William Lloyd Garrison and his followers were able to name a woman to the executive committee of the American Anti-Slavery Society in 1840. This resulted in a split with the anti-women's movement abolitionists. Charles G. Finney, along with a number of other religiously motivated Americans, left Garrison's organization, leaving the abolitionist movement a little weaker. At one time or another, Lucretia Mott, Lydia Maria Child, and Maria Chapman each served on the executive committee of the American Anti-Slavery Society.

Southern and Black Abolitionists

While most abolitionists were clearly from the North, the South also produced a few highly visible abolitionists. Among them were the Grimke sisters, Sarah and Angelina, who were daughters of a prominent slave-owning family from Charleston, South Carolina. After breaking with their parents over the question of slavery, the two sisters moved to the North and became active in the immediatist abolition cause, as well as the women's rights movement. They both eventually joined the Quakers, and in 1838, Angelina married Theodore Weld. She and her sister then edited the book *American Slavery As It Is: Testimony of a Thousand Witnesses*, published the next year, although only Theodore Weld was listed as the editor.

James G. Birney of Kentucky was another prominent southern white abolitionist. After experiencing some vandalism for his outspokenness against slavery in that slave state, Birney moved north to Ohio in the 1830s. There he helped create the Liberty Party in 1839-40 and was its first presidential candidate in the 1840 election, gaining only about 7,000 popular votes and no electoral votes. Four years later, in 1844, he received about 62,000 popular votes, but again, no electoral votes.

Black abolitionists welcomed the addition of whites to their cause and were emboldened to speak out more forcefully as a result. The most powerful black abolitionist of his day was Frederick Douglass, who had escaped slavery in Maryland as a young man in 1838 and fled to Massachusetts. Douglass was an impressive man and an eloquent speaker. After a fiery speech at an abolitionist meeting in New England in 1841, Douglass began lecturing in various northern cities. In 1845, he wrote a partial autobiography, *Narrative of the Life of Frederick Douglass*, using his own earlier experience as a slave to help make slavery better understood in terms of its very personal effects on human life. After lecturing in England for two years against the evils of slavery, he returned to the United States in 1847, bought his legal freedom from his slave owner in Maryland, and began the *North Star*, an abolitionist newspaper in Rochester, New York. After the Civil War, Frederick Douglass continued to champion the cause of civil rights just as fervently as he had the abolitionist cause. Much later in his life, this former slave served his country as the ambassador to Haiti.

Harriet "Moses" Tubman was another outstanding black abolitionist. Like Frederick Douglass, she too had escaped slavery in Maryland in 1849 and became a conductor in the Underground Railroad. She also led perhaps as many as 19 trips into the South to rescue about 300 slaves, including her parents and brother. For this, she earned the nickname "Moses," for it was Moses that the Biblical story says was the human leader who led the children of Israel out of Egyptian bondage in the exodus. Tubman later served as a nurse, cook, and spy for the Union army in the Civil War.

Then there was Isabella, who used a variety of last names, usually depending upon her most recent slave owner (e.g., Baumfree, Van Wagener). She was born a slave in New York state about 1797 and received her freedom there, probably when all remaining slaves in that state did in 1828. Isabella renamed herself Sojourner Truth in 1843 after a deep, mystical religious experience. At that time, she left New York City because she believed that God had told her "to travel up and down the land" preaching against the evil institution of slavery and the unjust treatment of women. She did just that all over the North throughout the 1840s and '50s.

FIGURE 14.4 - Harriet Tubman.

The Underground Railroad

Much has been written about the so-called Underground Railroad, a loose network of brave abolitionists who helped runaway slaves escape into the North or even to Canada. Their operators, both white and black, were called Underground Railroad "conductors" for hiding and feeding runaways in their root cellars, barns, and secret passageways, and then giving them directions for a safer flight further northward. Black conductors included names like Jacob Gibbs, John Parker, William Still, and David Ruggles. White conductors included Levi Coffin and John Byington, who later became the first president of the Seventh-day Adventist Church. Pro-southern neighbors, who were particularly hostile to abolitionism, surrounded many conductors living in the states bordering slave states, places like Pennsylvania, Ohio, Indiana, and Illinois. These hostile neighbors created a climate of fear for the safety of the Underground Railroad conductors should they be caught helping runaway slaves.

Though there is no denying the courage of many Underground Railroad conductors, the Underground Railroad was not nearly the organized, extensive secret network that legend has portrayed in almost romantic terms. Perhaps less than 30,000 slaves escaped to the North from 1830-1860, most of them in the 1850s. Nevertheless, it became a significant part of American anti-slavery history.

Even more important than the Underground Railroad in helping escaped slaves were the so-called Vigilance Committees in many northern cities. These were generally operated by free blacks, who temporarily housed, fed, and clothed escaped slaves and then assisted them in finding jobs and more permanent housing. They also protected runaways from slave agents seeking to capture and return them to slavery in the South.

Opposition to Abolitionism

Hostility to abolitionism was rampant in both the North and South. For example, in 1834, a mob in Philadelphia burned an abolitionist headquarters called the "Temple of Liberty" to the ground. In 1835, a group

FIGURE 14.5 - Sojourner Truth.

of businessmen and professionals forced the closing of New York state's Anti-Slavery Convention in Utica. In Boston during the same year, angry citizens kidnapped William Lloyd Garrison and would have hanged him if the authorities had not placed him in the Boston jail under protective custody. Sometimes the escalation of violence resulted in the actual murders of abolitionists, as when angry mobs killed 44 people in Louisiana and South Carolina in 1835. Pro-slavery mobs also murdered the Alton, Illinois abolitionist newspaper editor Elijah P. Lovejoy and destroyed his printing presses in late 1837. Ironically, Lovejoy had been forced to leave his home state of Missouri, a slave state, because of his anti-slavery agitation. Even in Illinois, his printing presses had been destroyed on three previous occasions. On the fourth occasion, he chose to remain in his office to defend them. But after the mob set fire to the building, Lovejoy was shot as he fled the scene.

In the 1830s, technological improvements in the printing industry allowed for the mass production of pamphlets.

Abolitionists seized on this new development, and the American Anti-Slavery Society published millions of pieces of anti-slavery literature and then mailed them especially to places all over the South. In 1835, after the local Charleston, South Carolina postmaster announced his refusal to deliver abolitionist literature, a local mob broke into the post office and destroyed several bags of it. President Andrew Jackson, himself a slave owner, tried but failed to get Congress to pass a law denying the use of the federal mail system for what he called "incendiary literature." However, in 1835, the Jackson administration bowed to southern pressure by ordering that southern postmasters actually destroy abolitionist literature rather than deliver it. While federal authorities did not enforce that order, the Postmaster General intentionally failed to do anything to enforce the lawful delivery of anti-slavery mail.

During the 1830s, abolitionists overwhelmed the House of Representatives with petitions to abolish both the slave trade and slavery in the District of Columbia, which was governed by Congress. Abolitionists targeted the House of Representatives because most House members were anti-slavery. However, most of them were not abolitionists. In 1836, the House passed what abolitionists called the "gag rule," which automatically tabled all such petitions, thereby prohibiting any discussion and debate on them. John Quincy Adams, who less than two years after leaving the presidency had been elected to the House of Representatives from his home state of Massachusetts in 1830, was a strong abolitionist. The so-called "gag rule" energized him far beyond his years, and he finally persuaded the House to repeal the "gag rule" in 1844.

Opposition to abolitionism only served to further promote the anti-slavery movement in general in two major ways. First, mob violence and the denying of freedom of speech to abolitionists only attracted sympathy for the movement, or at least for the abolitionists themselves. Second, the political efforts to cut off debate over anti-slavery petitions in Congress and to deny the use of the postal system to abolitionists offended the political sensibilities of many Northerners. The result, then, was to embolden all anti-slavery Americans and to increase the visibility of the entire anti-slavery movement, propelling it toward eventual

domination in the Age of Social Reform (1830-1860) and into the national political spotlight, a result hardly desired by pro-slavery Americans.

The *Amistad* Case

Nothing captured the attention of the entire nation and focused it on the question of slavery like the case of the *Amistad* passengers. In 1839, some Portuguese slave traders kidnapped a large number of Africans from Sierra Leone in complete violation of all the multilateral treaties that had forbidden the international slave trade. Two slave-owning Spanish planters purchased 53 of these Africans and sent them to Cuba on board a Cuban vessel called the *Amistad*. However, the Africans took over the ship on July 1, 1839, and put most of the crew onto a Caribbean island after killing two of them first. At that point, they attempted to sail the ship back to Africa. However, cloudy night travel obscured their true course, so the *Amistad* wound up off the coast of Long Island, New York, where an American naval vessel seized it on August 24 and arrested the Africans as pirates.

Most Americans, including President Martin Van Buren, favored sending the Africans to Cuba, which the Spanish government was demanding; Cuba was a Spanish colony at that time. But abolitionists opposed this sentiment, arguing that they should be freed on the grounds that the international slave trade was illegal and therefore they should never have been forcibly removed from Africa in the first place. When a federal court in Hartford, Connecticut ruled that the case was within American jurisdiction and put them on trial for murder in September 1839, abolitionists raised money to legally defend the Africans. The same federal court acquitted the defendants, agreeing with the abolitionists that the killing of the two crew members was justified on the basis that the Africans had been illegally placed on board the *Amistad*. The Van Buren administration's Justice Department appealed the decision to the U.S. Supreme Court, where former President John Quincy Adams, then a Massachusetts Congressman, argued on behalf of the Africans. In 1841, the Supreme Court agreed with Adams and upheld the lower court's acquittal. In doing so, the Supreme Court established the principle that all slaves who had been taken into slavery illegally and subsequently escaped to an American jurisdiction were to be legally considered free. Of the original 53 Africans on board the *Amistad*, some had died at sea before the American navy had seized the ship, and still others had died awaiting trial. But abolitionists paid for the return to Africa of the 32 remaining Africans.

Conclusion

While already entrenched in the South before independence from England, slavery expanded to monolithic proportions as an indirect result of Eli Whitney's perfection of the cotton gin in 1793. By the time cotton was "king" in 1830, slavery was so much a part of the southern psyche, as well as its economy, that any perceived threat to it was also perceived as a threat to the entire southern way of life.

This expansion of slavery and its elevation to virtual kingdom status had forced the South to reevaluate its defense of the "peculiar institution," with the result that white Southerners moved away from defending slavery as a "necessary evil" to championing it as an absolute

positive good institution. The rise of a better organized abolitionist movement in the North by about the same time only served to further polarize North and South, despite the fact that most Northerners hated abolitionism almost as much as most Southerners. In point of fact, the nature of the opposition to abolitionism simply served to strengthen the resolve of the abolitionists and even of Free-Soilers as well, further uniting Northerners against slavery, despite their different approaches to it.

The polarization not only affected American politics, as seen in the dispute over free speech and the use of the federal postal system, but also religion. In the 1843-44 period, differences over the slavery question caused a regional split within both the Baptist and Methodist churches, with the northern branches as anti-slavery and the southern branches as pro-slavery.

During the Age of Social Reform (1830-1860), it was evident that the nation was headed for a showdown over the question of slavery. The only specific questions to be decided concerned when the conflict would come and how severe it would be. In 1861, the wait would be over, as both of those questions were answered in the coming of the Civil War.

GOLD-WASHING IN CALIFORNIA.

Viintage engraving showing prospectors washing for gold in a river in California. Copyright 2010 iStockphoto.

Chapter 15 Contents

CHAPTER FIFTEEN

Countdown to Civil War

Major Events

1849	California Gold Rush
1850	Daniel Webster's "7th of March Speech" President Zachary Taylor died Great Compromise adopted
1852	Harriet Beecher Stowe's *Uncle Tom's Cabin* published in book form Franklin Pierce won the presidential election
1854	Japan opened its doors with Matthew Perry's show of force Kansas-Nebraska Act passed Republican Party created Gadsden Purchase ratified by U.S. Senate Ostend Manifesto
1856	"Bleeding Kansas" James Buchanan elected president
1857	*Dred Scott Case* Hinton R. Helper's *The Impending Crisis of the South* published
1858	Lincoln-Douglas Debates
1859	Harper's Ferry incident
1860	Abraham Lincoln became first Republican elected to the presidency South Carolina voted to secede from the Union
1861	Confederate States of America established Crittenden Compromise defeated in Congress Fort Sumter surrendered to the Confederates

Introduction

The Mexican-American War (see Chapter 13) opened up new, expansive areas of the West to permanent American settlement, territorial status, and eventual statehood. Although a patriotic fever spread throughout the nation, the war had also opened up old wounds over the slavery issue. A vigorous debate over slavery had been raging at least since the early 1830s, when the issue advanced to the forefront as part of the Age of Social Reform (1830-1860). At the same time, the political parties had avoided a national fight on the matter in Washington, D.C. since the Missouri Compromise of 1820. The war changed all of that, as the question of whether slavery would now be permitted to expand to the Far West became the burning issue of the day. Just after the war began in 1846, Pennsylvania Congressman David Wilmot sponsored an amendment to an appropriations bill called the Wilmot Proviso, which would have prohibited slavery in any territories acquired from Mexico in that war. Although the House of Representatives passed it on two different occasions, the Senate rejected it twice, so the Wilmot Proviso never became law. Unfortunately, the war and related subsequent events propelled the nation into a series of increasingly emotional crises over slavery until neither side had left any room for another compromise that might avert civil war. Indeed, by 1848, one can say that the countdown to civil war had already begun.

Popular Sovereignty

The Democrats and the Whigs both enjoyed broad support in all major sections of the country, and neither political party wished to take a strong stand on slavery because of the fear that it would create sectional parties to replace them, thus endangering the stability of the nation. It therefore seemed safer for the national parties to avoid the issue altogether.

Nevertheless, debate over the Wilmot Proviso during the Mexican-American War had already placed slavery as a hot topic in Washington, D.C. This fact led to a search for middle ground on the part of some politicians. The alleged middle ground was first proposed as squatter sovereignty by Michigan Democratic Senator Lewis Cass. The idea was that the people of each territory should decide whether or not to permit slavery.

This position quickly gained the support of many northern Democrats, most notably, Illinois Democratic Senator Stephen A. Douglas. Senator Douglas called it popular sovereignty, the name which became more common, and which would later thrust Douglas into the national spotlight. Popular sovereignty was an attempt to take the slavery issue out of the national debate altogether and thus diffuse tensions. It also had the advantage of appealing to the democratic impulses of many Americans. Most of its supporters assumed that if it were extended to the areas obtained from Mexico that slavery would not survive because of the dry, arid climate. Therefore, popular sovereignty gave a number of northern Democrats the opportunity to say they still opposed slavery and hopefully avoid splitting their party, since southern Democrats, led by Senator John C. Calhoun of South Carolina, were explicitly pro-slavery.

However, many Americans did not view it as the compromise position that the supporters professed. Congress had twice before in history restricted the expansion of slavery, once in the Northwest Ordinance of 1787, which prohibited slavery in the Northwest Territory, and in the Missouri Compromise of 1820, which had prohibited slavery north of the 36º 30′ parallel within the Louisiana Territory. These measures had, therefore, set precedents for Congress to curb the expansion of slavery. Thus, many Americans outside the South viewed popular sovereignty as a pro-southern position because it threatened to turn the clock back and take the issue out of Congress' hands and theoretically allow the wide-open expansion of slavery to the new territories.

The 1848 Presidential Election

The Democrats

President James K. Polk had never intended to run for a second term, and poor health guaranteed that he kept this commitment. This first presidential election after the Mexican-American War would be crucial for the country's future. The Democratic National Convention met in Baltimore and nominated Lewis Cass, the father of what became known as popular sovereignty and a former general during the War of 1812. The convention also nominated General William Butler of Kentucky for his vice-presidential running mate. Although Cass supported popular sovereignty, the party platform adopted at the convention skirted the issue altogether.

The Whigs

The Whigs rejected Henry Clay, the ideological leader of their party, because he was now 71 years old and had made a number of political enemies. Instead, the party nominated General Zachary Taylor of Louisiana, an old frontier Indian fighter and the hero of Buena Vista in the Mexican-American War. Nicknamed "Old Rough and Ready," Taylor was a major slave-owner who was enthusiastically cheered by Southerners as one of their own. Taylor was also the father-in-law of Jefferson Davis, who was destined to become the president of the Confederacy just before and during the Civil War. To balance the ticket, the convention nominated Representative Millard Fillmore of New York for vice president. And in an effort to avoid a party split, the Whig National Convention in Philadelphia that year adopted no political platform, just as it had done in 1840.

The Free-Soilers

Anger over the rejection of the Wilmot Proviso and the failure of both political parties to address slavery led to the formation of what Massachusetts Whig and abolitionist Senator Charles Sumner hoped would be "one grand Northern party of Freedom." In the summer of 1848, anti-slavery Whigs, called "Conscience Whigs" because they were tired of the influence of the "Cotton Whigs'" business ties with slave-produced southern cotton, and anti-slavery Democrats gathered in Buffalo, New York, and formed the Free-Soil Party. Joining them were activists from the Liberty Party, which had been organized in 1839 and had fielded presidential candidates in 1840 and 1844. In fact, this abolitionist party had already nominated John P. Hale of New Hampshire, but he withdrew after the formation of the Free-Soil Party that year.

The anti-slavery Democrats were led by the so-called "barnburners," former President Martin Van Buren's faction within the New York State Democratic Party, who obtained this nickname when the opposing faction accused them of a willingness to destroy the party to win control of it, like the farmer who burned his barn down to get rid of the rats. The Free-Soil Party nominated Van Buren for president and Charles F. Adams, a Massachusetts "Conscience Whig" and son of former President John Quincy Adams, for vice president.

The Free-Soil Party officially endorsed the Wilmot Proviso and opposed any further expansion of slavery. Their campaign slogan was "Free Soil, Free Speech, Free Labor, and Free Men." This Free-Soil position on slavery soon included the notion of leaving slavery alone where it already existed, a compromise to avoid civil war if possible. The two-fold Free-Soil position was based largely on British Enlightenment economic thinker Adam Smith's views on slavery, which he had articulated in his classic *The Wealth of Nations*, published interestingly enough in 1776 just as the Continental Congress was declaring independence from England. Smith's contention, adopted by the Free-Soilers, was that slavery was an inherently inefficient economic system because slaves had no incentive to work harder. Therefore, he had argued that slavery would eventually destroy any society's economy. Although many Free-Soilers also opposed slavery on moral grounds, it was the economic argument that they emphasized, arguing that slavery's expansion threatened jobs and other opportunities for free working men and thus undermined the middle class standard of living. This argument would soon prove persuasive, making the Free-Soil position on slavery the plurality, if not majority, viewpoint outside the South within just a year or two. As such, the Free-Soil Party paved the way for the emergence of the Republican Party in 1854, after more crises over slavery finally broke apart the Whig Party.

The Results

The Free-Soil Party attracted enough Democrats in New York to throw that state to Taylor, and enough Whigs in Ohio to give that state to Cass. Zachary Taylor won the election with 163 electoral votes, compared to 127 for Lewis Cass. Van Buren won no electoral votes, although his support in New York apparently handed the victory to Taylor. Taylor, the Whig, carried eight slave states and seven free states, while Cass, the Democrat, carried eight free states and seven slave states. The country had elected a man who had never held public office and had never voted in a presidential election.

The Compromise of 1850

The California Gold Rush

FIGURE 15.1 - California gold prospector 1849

Despite his lack of political experience, Zachary Taylor may have muddled through his presidency if it were not for the discovery of gold in early 1848 at a place called Sutter's Mill in northern California, well before his election. "Gold fever" swept many Americans to the area, creating the California Gold Rush of 1849. Conflicting claims, shortages of supplies, gambling, liquor, prostitution, and a woeful lack of whole family units led to violence and chaos before the end of 1849.

President Taylor assumed that the best way to maintain law and order was to expedite California's statehood. This would mandate additional courts and police, resulting in more families coming, bringing schools, churches, and other traditions of civilized society. In fact, such a move was already under way in 1849, when California's law-abiding citizens applied for statehood under a proposed constitution that outlawed slavery. In January 1850 President Taylor recommended to Congress that California and New Mexico eliminate the territorial steps of statehood and join the Union as soon as possible, California immediately and New Mexico as soon as it was ready to apply.

It was not lost on the South that California would eventually become a large and powerful state in the Union. Its admission as a free state seemed to spell doom for any meaningful expansion of slavery. As a result, the South denounced Taylor as a traitor to his region. Who could have guessed that the slave-owning Zachary Taylor would adopt what was essentially the Free-Soil position against the expansion of slavery? Meanwhile, by the end of 1849, Californians had created their own free state government without waiting for Congress; New Mexico would do so in June 1850. Both would still need to have the official sanction from Congress, of course, before actual admission to the Union.

The Great Debate

When Congress reconvened in December 1849, there was a sense of history in the air. Push was coming to shove, and Americans nervously awaited what became known as the Great Debate because they knew that the fate of the nation was at stake. After President Taylor formally recommended that California come into the Union immediately as a free state in January 1850, the Great Debate began in earnest.

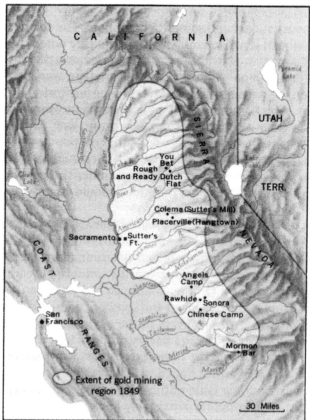

FIGURE 15.2 - California Gold Rush Country.

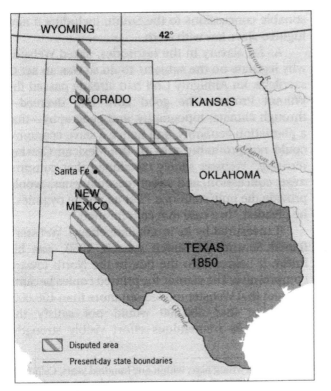

FIGURE 15.3 - Texas and the disputed area before the Compromise of 1850.

It was quite apparent that the only hope to save the Union was to take the path of compromise. So once again, in late January 1850, Senator Henry Clay, the Great Compromiser or Great Pacificator, rose to the occasion by offering a comprehensive package designed to pacify both sides of the slavery dispute. It was called an omnibus bill because it carried a number of "passengers" (or conditions), just as the literal horse-drawn omnibus of its day did. Clay's major proposals are summarized in the following points:

- California would come in as a free state.
- The New Mexico and Utah territories would be organized, allowing their own state constitutions to determine the status of slavery there.

- The Texas border would be adjusted in New Mexico's favor. (Texas had claimed a little more than the eastern half of present-day New Mexico.)
- The slave trade would be abolished across the boundaries of the District of Columbia, while permitting slavery to remain inside the District.
- A strong new Fugitive Slave Law would make it much easier for slave-owners to get their runaway slaves returned legally.

In speeches in early February, Clay appealed for national unity through his so-called Compromise of 1850. To win anti-slavery votes in Congress, he reminded those elected members that nature would prevent slavery from succeeding in the territories acquired from Mexico because it was simply too arid to grow staple, slave-produced crops. To pro-slavery Southerners, Clay warned that civil war would be the result of any secession attempt, and that secession, whether peaceful or not, would make it extremely difficult to get their runaway slaves returned to the South. Therefore, both sides of the slavery issue had no choice, in effect, but to accept his compromise.

Reaction to Clay's proposal was swift and vicious. Abolitionist members of Congress denounced it as an ill-founded compromise with the moral evil of slavery. Most Free-Soilers condemned it on principle for allowing the possibility of the expansion of slavery into the New Mexico and Utah territories. While Southerners agreed with Clay's assumption that the New Mexico and Utah territories were too arid for slavery to succeed there, California's potentially rich valleys held the promise of a prosperous slave economy. Adding to the trouble was President Taylor's opposition to Clay's compromise package. He threatened to veto any bill that included anything other than the immediate admission

Concessions to the North	Concessions to the South
California admitted as a free state	The remainder of the Mexican Cession area to be formed into the territories of New Mexico and Utah, without restriction on slavery, hence open to popular sovereignty
Territory disputed by Texas and New Mexico to be surrendered to New Mexico	Texas to receive $10 million from the federal government as compensation
Abolition of the slave trade (but not slavery) in the District of Columbia	A more stringent fugitive-slave law, going beyond that of 1793

FIGURE 15.4 - Compromise of 1850.

of California as a free state because he wanted to avoid stirring up the country's emotions over slavery. This was a great miscalculation, however, because the bottom line was that emotions were already too high for compromise to succeed easily.

The debate raged on for most of the year and was one of the most dramatic in the history of the Congress. It proved to be the last significant debate for the aging triumvirate of the Congress: Henry Clay, John C. Calhoun, and Daniel Webster. South Carolina Senator John C. Calhoun, then 68 years old and suffering from tuberculosis, was too weak to give his own speech. Instead, Virginia Senator James Mason gave it in early March. Calhoun warned that southern slave states would secede if California came in as a free state. This was to be the Great Nullifier's last stand, for he died later in the year before Congress reached any compromise. The future president of the Confederacy, Mississippi Democratic Senator Jefferson Davis, also opposed Clay's compromise package.

On the other side of the slavery issue was Senator William H. Seward, a Whig from New York and a close advisor to President Taylor. However, he also opposed Clay's bill and urged his Christian colleagues to vote against any compromise with slavery in obedience to God's law, which he called "a higher law than the Constitution." This kind of language only infuriated southern members of Congress and intensified the emotional furor in the country.

There were those who supported Clay's bill, of course. Prominent among them were Illinois Democratic Senator Stephen A. Douglas and Massachusetts Whig Senator Daniel Webster. It is often said that "politics make strange bedfellows," and that was certainly true in the Great Debate. Webster was a staunch opponent of slavery, but on March 7, he gave an eloquent speech

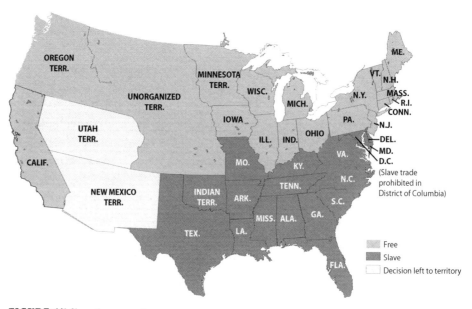

FIGURE 15.5 - Slavery After the Compromise of 1850.

in support of Clay's compromise. He opened his speech with the words, "I wish to speak today, not as a Massachusetts man, nor as a northern man, but as an American. I speak today for the preservation of the Union." Webster made two primary points in defense of the proposed compromise. First, to Northerners he said there was no point in arguing for the Wilmot Proviso because God Himself had already passed it by creating the geography and climate of the American Southwest that would make a slave-plantation economy impossible. Second, to Southerners he argued that secession would only result in war.

Northern reaction to Webster's "7th of March Speech," as it became known, was mixed. Many business interests applauded it because they feared great financial losses if secession occurred. However, abolitionists condemned Webster and called him a traitor to the anti-slavery movement and having sold out to the "devil." Four months later, he was rescued from the wrath of his constituents in Massachusetts when new President Millard Fillmore appointed him Secretary of State, a post he held until his death in late 1852. On balance, Webster's speech increased the mood for compromise in much of the North, although Southerners remained adamantly opposed because of the California issue. Despite some increased support for compromise, southern opposition and President Taylor's threat to veto Clay's proposal combined to defeat the bill that spring.

Taylor's Death and Final Passage of the Compromise

Meanwhile, President Taylor made it very clear that he would not tolerate secession. Like Andrew Jackson before him, Taylor was a southern slave-owner who was also a strong Unionist. But the president's unwillingness to compromise threatened to destroy his Whig Party and to risk civil war. However, circumstances intervened to end Taylor's influence. On July 4, 1850, soon after publicly supporting New Mexico's application for statehood in June, the president sat in the hot sun listening to patriotic speeches defending the Union. After returning to the White House, the president consumed large quantities of cold water, milk, and cherries, which led to extreme gastritis. Five days later, on July 9, President Zachary Taylor died.

President Taylor's death increased the chances for a successful compromise and may well have been responsible for delaying the Civil War for another decade. Vice President Millard Fillmore was sworn in as the new president and announced that he would support Clay's compromise, for he had been impressed by senators' speeches on behalf of saving the Union when he had chaired the Senate debate as vice president. Henry Clay was now quite ill and unable to attend the Senate, but his banner was taken up by Stephen A. Douglas. Borrowing a page from Clay's own strategy in successfully obtaining the Compromise of 1820, Senator Douglas proposed the same five provisions as separate bills in order to negotiate and build coalitions large enough to pass them all. It worked. On September 17, the last bill was passed, and President Fillmore signed it into law three days later.

The Compromise of 1850, what President Fillmore called the "final settlement," had finally passed. But many historians believe it was much less a compromise and more a temporary reprieve for the nation. Civil war had been averted for the moment, but the legislative successes by the forces of compromise had been achieved, not by conciliation and "give and take," but by very skillful coalition building for each separate measure. In any case, the reprieve did not last long because details of the new Fugitive Slave Law would quickly unite the North in angry opposition to any compromise involving slavery.

The Fugitive Slave Law (1850)

The Fugitive Slave Law was clearly the most controversial part of the Compromise of 1850 and the only real concession to the South in that compromise. Congress had enacted a federal fugitive slave law in 1793. In the 1830s many northern states had passed so-called "personal liberty" laws that slowed down enforcement of the federal law. At the same time, the Underground Railroad was also assisting escaped slaves, as were vigilance committees that found homes and jobs for them. By 1850, there were about 30,000 escaped slaves living in the North, a fact that galled the South.

Technically an amendment to the 1793 fugitive slave law, this 1850 version was much tougher. Nicknamed the "Bloodhound Bill," it significantly strengthened the ability of slave-owners to recover their runaway slaves by adopting the following major provisions:

- It allowed slave-owners to use the courts in their home states to declare an escaped slave legally a runaway. Armed with legal paperwork, including a personal description from the local court, an agent or United States marshal who captured a runaway only had to prove the identity of the captured person rather than that he was a slave.
- Jury trials were replaced by a system in which special commissioners were appointed to hear and decide alleged cases of runaway slaves.
- A commissioner received a $10 fee for ordering a person returned to a slave-owner but only a $5 fee for not doing so. This provision virtually invited commissioners to a bias and was widely denounced in the North as bribery.
- Accused runaways were denied the right to testify on their own behalf.
- Children born to an escaped slave were slaves also and could be taken into slavery as well.
- Whites could be forced to assist those catching escaped slaves.
- Harboring a fugitive slave was made a felony, with imprisonment up to six months and/or fines up to $1,000 for those convicted.

Reaction to the new Fugitive Slave Law was swift and furious in the North as Americans there rallied to the anti-slavery movement. Tougher personal liberty laws were passed in several northern states to try to prevent the kidnapping of free blacks and the return of escaped slaves. Although these were not effective, it was still true that during the 1850s, more slaves were helped by the strengthened Underground Railroad than were returned under the Fugitive Slave Law. Many pastors and rabbis urged their congregations to willfully disobey this unjust law if they found themselves in a position to help a runaway slave. It became one of the most widely ignored federal laws in American history, although a few black soldiers in the Union Army were returned to the South during the early part of the Civil War. The greatest effect of the Fugitive Slave Law was to increase the quantity and quality of resistance to slavery in the North, something that was hardly in the best interests of the South.

Anti-Slavery Literature Fuels the Fire

Uncle Tom's Cabin

One specific reaction to the Fugitive Slave Law that greatly irritated pro-southern Americans was the novel *Uncle Tom's Cabin* by abolitionist Harriet Beecher Stowe. It first appeared in serial form in a weekly anti-slavery newspaper in 1851 but was published in book form the next year. Mrs. Stowe was part of the prominent 19th century Beecher family. Her father was the famous Congregationalist preacher Lyman Beecher, who had been active in the temperance movement in 1830s Boston. Her sister Catherine was an activist in expanding educational opportunities for women, while her brother, Henry Ward Beecher, eventually became the pastor of the Brooklyn Congregational Church in New York City and the nation's best-known Protestant minister of the 19th century.

Uncle Tom's Cabin made an emotional appeal for the abolition of the institution of slavery by showing the impact of slavery on the family unit and making slavery seem real to people who had no experience with it. The nature of slavery, according to her main thesis, was that it eventually destroyed everything it touched. The book did not become an instant success because the national mood in 1852 longed for an end to bickering between North and South. But by the end of the decade, more than three million copies had been sold, many

of them in the South. It had a profound impact in the countdown to the Civil War, stirring up and hardening the anti-slavery attitudes of Northerners and convincing many Southerners that this must be part of a northern abolitionist plot to destroy the entire southern way of life. It so increased the emotional pitch over slavery that when President Abraham Lincoln later met Mrs. Stowe in 1862 during the Civil War, he purportedly exclaimed, "So you're the little woman who wrote the book that made this great war!" If Lincoln did say that, he certainly was being facetious, because he knew it was only one factor that affected the nation in the countdown to civil war. Perhaps its value lay in the fact that the novel was extremely popular in England and France, discouraging the governments there from intervening on behalf of the Confederacy once the American Civil War began.

The Impending Crisis of the South

In 1857, five years after *Uncle Tom's Cabin* made its book debut, a Southerner from North Carolina added his own contribution to the fire over slavery. Hinton R. Helper wrote *The Impending Crisis of the South*, which argued that non-slave-owning white Southerners were badly hurt by the institution of slavery, especially because it discouraged economic diversity and thus denied economic opportunities to them. Helper was forced to find a northern publisher for his book, which was banned and burned all over the South. Unfortunately for the anti-slavery movement, Helper's book did not reach many poor whites in the South, which were his primary targeted readers.

The 1852 Presidential Election

The Democrats

The Democrats managed somehow to hold their party together at their national convention in Baltimore in 1852, nominating Franklin Pierce of New Hampshire. Pierce, a likeable person, was a veteran of the Mexican-American War and a former senator. His appeal in the South was largely based on his southern political leanings, although his northern critics called him a "doughface," a term for northern Democrats with pro-southern tendencies.

Despite this fact, the old New York "barnburners" generally returned to the party after their flirtation with the Free Soil Party four years earlier. This hurt the Free Soil candidate, John P. Hale, who, like Pierce, was from New Hampshire.

The Whigs

The Whigs were unhappy with the dull Millard Fillmore and otherwise badly divided. Finally, on the 53rd ballot, the Whig convention turned to a patriotic approach by nominating Mexican-American War hero General Winfield Scott of Virginia. Scott, nicknamed "Old Fussin' Feathers," was an unstable man politically, not sure of what he believed. He did have an anti-slavery reputation, which endeared many northern Whigs to him. Yet he was a Southerner who had helped win the Mexican-American War, which the South had supported more strongly than the North.

The Results

Free-Soil candidate John P. Hale only received about half the votes that Martin Van Buren had received four years earlier. Although the popular vote was fairly close, Democrat Franklin Pierce won a landslide electoral victory over Winfield Scott, carrying 27 states and winning 254 electoral votes to Scott's four states and 42 electoral votes. Again, the Free-Soilers carried no states and received no electoral votes.

Foreign Policy

U. S.-Japanese Relations

With the completion of our so-called Manifest Destiny, Americans increasingly looked to the Far East as a potential gold mine for economic trade. China had opened its doors to American business interests, but Japan kept a closed door to the outside world, with the exception of a Dutch trade relationship operating from the port of Nagasaki. But Russia appeared to be a growing threat to Japan by the middle of the 19th century, prompting the Japanese to reluctantly open their country to more foreigners.

In July 1853, Commodore Matthew C. Perry, the brother of Oliver H. Perry, who had won the Battle of Lake Erie in 1813 during the War of 1812, entered what would later be known as Tokyo Bay with four large naval ships. Perry asked for the protection and return of shipwrecked American sailors and the opening of one or two ports to American trade. The Japanese had a policy of detaining all shipwrecked foreign sailors who washed up on their shores.

Perry's ships went back to China before returning in February 1854 with a larger fleet of vessels. With an intimidating show of force and much tact, Commodore Perry was able to persuade Japan to sign a treaty opening two Japanese ports to American trade in late March of that year. Although small, it was an important step in Japan's entrance into the world community of nations. Ironically, it contributed to the eventual industrialization and militarization of Japan, against which the United States would wage war in the next century.

Problems in Nicaragua

The expansion of the United States to the Pacific coast and the discovery of gold in California aroused the interest of Americans in building a canal across an isthmus in Central America. It would not only have the advantage of providing a sea route from one American coast to the other, but it also offered easier and cheaper access to the Far East.

The easiest path for building such a canal was across part of Nicaragua, but the British were wary of further American expansion in Mexico and Central America. As a result, Britain took control of Greytown on the Gulf of Mexico side of the proposed canal route to thwart the United States and send a diplomatic warning not to expand there. This British action was a violation of the Monroe Doctrine, and tensions quickly built between the two nations. War was averted, however, by the signing of the Clayton-Bulwer Treaty in 1850, in which both nations promised not to build or control a Central American canal. Although the agreement stopped the British and prevented war, it would later make it more difficult for the United States to build a canal.

Despite the uneasy relations with Britain over Nicaragua, Southerners viewed that small country as an ideal place to gain a foothold in Central America in order to expand slavery. In June 1855, an American filibusterer, William Walker, invaded Nicaragua with an army of mostly southern volunteers and at the invitation of a revolutionary faction within Nicaragua. He managed to take control of the country and announced in July 1856 that he was the president of Nicaragua. He also immediately legalized slavery. But Walker's experiment was short-lived because a coalition of other Central American nations overthrew his government in May 1857, with the aid of his former friend and railroad tycoon Cornelius Vanderbilt, whose company controlled Walker's supply lines. In 1860, he again attempted to gain a foothold in Central America, but he was forced to surrender to the British navy. The British then turned him over to authorities in Honduras, who executed him in September 1860.

The Gadsden Purchase

Completion of our so-called Manifest Destiny in the Mexican-American War also meant that the United States was geographically extended so that the Atlantic and Pacific coasts were somewhat isolated from each other. At this time, most Americans saw the usefulness of a transcontinental railroad linking the East Coast with the West Coast. But like nearly everything after the Mexican-American War, this popularly supported effort also divided the nation along sectional lines and kept the conflict over slavery very much alive. The reason for this was that four major cities in the middle of the nation were each proposed as the link to the West: Chicago, Illinois, St. Louis, Missouri, Memphis, Tennessee, and New Orleans, Louisiana. It was clear that whatever site was selected, that city and region would reap great financial rewards. Many in the Deep South favored New Orleans, but the easiest and least expensive route lay in what was then northern Mexico.

In 1853, encouraged by his Secretary of War, Jefferson Davis, President Pierce authorized James Gadsden, the American ambassador to Mexico and a railroad developer from South Carolina, to negotiate the purchase of

FIGURE 15.6 - Secretary Jefferson Davis 1853

about 250,000 square miles of northern Mexico, including Baja California, for up to $50 million. However, the Mexican dictator, Santa Anna, would not agree to the loss of that much territory. In late December 1853, a treaty was signed to purchase only about 39,000 square miles. The treaty angered many northern politicians, who feared that any additional territory acquired from Mexico might allow for the expansion of slavery. The result was that the Senate first defeated it. However, after 9,000 square miles

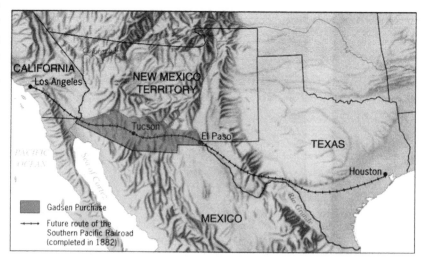

FIGURE 15.7 - The Gadsden Purchase, 1853.

were cut from the agreement, the Senate ratified what became known as the Gadsden Purchase in 1854. For $10 million, the United States acquired 30,000 square miles of land south of the Gila River and west of the Rio Grande, land which now forms the southern border of Arizona and the eastern one-third of New Mexico's southern border but which was initially part of the New Mexico Territory. Tucson, Arizona, is the most important city in the old Gadsden Purchase.

The land deal was so unpopular in Mexico that it helped oust Santa Anna from power, thus ending his long political career. For Americans, the greatest significance of the Gadsden Purchase was that it represented the last acquisition of territory in the contiguous United States. Ironically, the Southern Pacific Railroad was completed in 1882, long after the Civil War had ended slavery in the nation.

The Ostend Manifesto

Another conflict with slavery overtones concerned the South's agitation for obtaining Cuba. The Caribbean island was still a Spanish colony, and slavery thrived there. Furthermore, most of the sugar refined in the United States came from Cuba's sugar cane industry. If the United States could obtain it, Cuba could be divided into more than one slave state and help counter the growing Free-Soil movement in the North. President James K. Polk, himself from the slave state of Tennessee, had unsuccessfully attempted to buy Cuba from Spain in the 1840s. In 1850-1851, there were two different attempts by southern-supported American volunteers to take Cuba by force. Consisting of several hundred men each time, both were disastrous defeats. Such private wars were called "filibustering" expeditions because the Spanish word for "filibuster" means "pirate" or "freebooter."

In retaliation for these filibustering adventures, Spain captured an American vessel called the *Black Warrior* in 1854. As a "doughface," President Franklin Pierce supported the acquisition of Cuba and tried to use this crisis as a pretense for going to war with Spain. First, Pierre Soule, the American ambassador to Spain, offered Spain $130 million for Cuba as Secretary of State William Marcy instructed. After Spain rejected the offer, the president ordered a conference of three American diplomats to meet in Ostend, Belgium to make recommendations on how the United States could obtain Cuba. Soule met in Belgium with James Buchanan, ambassador to Britain, and John Mason, ambassador to France. All three diplomats were pro-slavery Democrats. The document they constructed in October 1854, labeled the Ostend Manifesto, called for the use of force to seize Cuba if Spain were still unwilling to sell her colony. However, when the press reported the story of the Ostend Manifesto, northerners were almost unanimously angered. The Ostend Manifesto, along with the previous filibustering adventures, had created great suspicion in the North that Southerners would stop at nothing in their quest to expand the institution of slavery, even to the point of endangering the country with war. The anti-slavery forces smelled a pro-slavery plot, and the Pierce administration backed away.

The Kansas-Nebraska Act

In 1854 Congress enacted a law that nearly tore the Union apart immediately. Ironically, it was designed to encourage the building of the transcontinental railroad with Chicago, Illinois, as the eastern link with the West. To do this, Senator Stephen A. Douglas, Democrat of Illinois, proposed a bill in January 1854 to organize the Nebraska Territory, which lay directly west of Missouri, Iowa, and the Minnesota Territory. Although this region was permanently reserved for American Indians in 1830, the Indians were facing the eventual loss of land to white settlers moving onto this rich farmland and benefiting from the transcontinental railroad traffic. That did not concern Stephen Douglas, especially considering the financial benefits to both himself and his home state if Chicago became the eastern link with the West Coast.

Pro-slavery southern members of Congress, who had mostly favored the route from New Orleans, insisted on the division of the proposed Nebraska Territory into two separate entities, Kansas in the south and Nebraska in the north. There was a reasonable chance for slavery to succeed in the southern portion but not in the northern sector. Of course, the Compromise of 1820 had prohibited slavery inside the Louisiana Territory north of the 36° 30′ parallel, and its repeal would ignite a firestorm of protest in the North. Douglas did not have

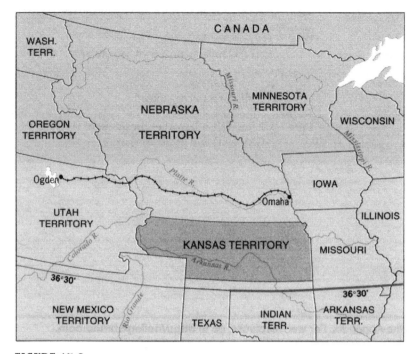

FIGURE 15.8 - Kansas and Nebraska, 1854.

strong feelings about slavery itself but was committed to popular sovereignty. Therefore, Douglas accepted the suggestions made to him by some prominent southern congressmen and included the division of the initial section into the Kansas Territory and the Nebraska Territory, allowing for popular sovereignty to rule on the issue of slavery in these territories.

Douglas underestimated the anger that his bill might generate from Northerners, but the "Little Giant" was perhaps the best of the scrappy debaters in the Senate at the time. With the support of President Franklin Pierce, a coalition of pro-slavery Southerners and about half of the northern Democrats in Congress passed the Kansas-Nebraska Act in May 1854.

Political Realignment

Stephen Douglas had grossly miscalculated the depths of emotions over the slavery issue prevailing in the nation by this time. His popular sovereignty had been designed to take the slavery issue out of the national spotlight and thus cool tensions. He was wrong. Most Northerners, who thought that the Missouri Compromise was permanent and who viewed it as a sacred trust, now felt betrayed and angry.

The first concrete result of the Kansas-Nebraska Act was the collapse of the Whig Party and the formation of the modern Republican Party. Most northern Whigs, some northern Democrats, Free-Soilers, and abolitionists created the Republican Party. The first organizational meeting of what would become the Republican Party was probably held in Ripon, Wisconsin, in 1854, although Jackson, Michigan contends that it hosted the first. These Republicans held different views about what to do about slavery, but they all shared a decidedly anti-slavery attitude. Economically, because of the types of Americans it attracted, the Republican Party as a whole was very much like the former northern Whigs, which meant they generally favored federal financing of internal improvements, high protective tariffs to encourage American industry, and conservative monetary policies.

For a good 20 years, the Whig and Democratic parties had managed to hold the Union together because they were national parties with strong northern and southern wings. But the beginning of the end of the Whig Party can be marked when President Zachary Taylor had so stubbornly insisted that California come into the Union as a free state back in 1850. Southern Whigs felt dismayed and even shocked at the political stance of one of their own. Meanwhile, the events of the early 1850s had diminished the number of "Cotton Whigs" in the North and given the anti-slavery "Conscience Whigs" a clear majority in the northern wing of their party. The result was that the Whigs did very poorly in the presidential election of 1852 and were ready to crumble. The Kansas-Nebraska Act of 1854 was the last straw that broke the proverbial camel's back. The Democrats' turn to break apart would come six years later in 1860.

Early Developments in Kansas

After the passage of the Kansas-Nebraska Act, Kansas Territory became the focus of the nation because both sides in the slavery debate realized that popular sovereignty would only work for them if they were more successful in getting Americans of their persuasion to move to Kansas than the other side was. Voters were obviously the key to winning a referendum on slavery in the territory. Even pro-slavery Americans realized that slavery would almost certainly not be viable as far north as Nebraska.

Eli Thayer, a Bostonian, organized the New England Emigrant Aid Company in the summer of 1854 for the purpose of encouraging and assisting Northerners to travel to Kansas. This effort hoped to create a free Kansas. Thayer's company compiled information on Kansas, advertised, and bought group-rate railroad tickets, which it then sold for a profit. Southerners accused Eli Thayer's company of actually paying people to go to Kansas, but that was not true. It was only natural that cheap land with good farm soil attracted many Americans seeking a new life on the frontier.

Northerners moving to Kansas by wagon were often harassed as they journeyed through Missouri, a slave state. As word of this spread, others went through Iowa and then hooked south into Kansas. Some western Missourians, who tended to be pro-slavery, also moved into the eastern one-third of Kansas, where they could grow hemp as easily as in western Missouri. Hemp is the raw material for making rope. But strangely, there was no organized effort by pro-slavery forces to help Southerners move to Kansas, although many came from Alabama.

Before the end of 1854, the majority of Kansans were anti-slavery Americans called free-staters. An election was set for the fall of 1854 to elect a territorial delegate to Washington, D.C. Although the majority of Kansans were anti-slavery, "border ruffians" from Missouri crossed the line, voted, and then went back home. Because of this, Kansas Territory sent a pro-slavery delegate to Washington. It may be important to note that there were none of the sophisticated means of proving residence as there are today.

In March 1855, the same illegal tactics were used by pro-slavery Missourians to elect a pro-slavery territorial legislature. When the results were made public, free-staters in Kansas by passed the territorial legislature and called for a constitutional convention to meet in Topeka. This convention met in October but was boycotted by the pro-slavery forces since the legislature had not authorized it. Therefore, the Topeka convention wrote a state constitution forbidding slavery in Kansas as well as excluding free blacks. But when they submitted it to Congress for approval and admission as a state, President Franklin Pierce used political pressure to block its admission. The political chaos increased when the anti-slavery Kansans elected their own territorial legislature and governor, which began to "function" by March 1856 in an attempt to force Congress to choose between the pro-slavery and the anti-slavery legislature. President Pierce and the majority of the Senate favored the pro-slavery legislature, whose capital was Lecompton. The majority of the House of Representatives, on the other hand, favored the Topeka-based anti-slavery legislature. Thus, the nation as a whole was just as divided over Kansas as the Kansans were, and the stalemate continued. In the meantime, both sides armed themselves. The anti-slavery Reverend Henry Ward Beecher sent rifles to Kansas, where they became known as "Beecher's Bibles."

"Bleeding Kansas"

As early as the spring of 1855, newspapers on both sides of the slavery issue were openly fomenting violent behavior as virtually all journalistic standards disappeared. Whole towns in Kansas grew up as centers of pro-slavery or anti-slavery sentiment. The highly charged atmosphere over the slavery controversy combined with numerous conflicting land claims to produce a violent year in 1856. So bad was the violence that Kansas earned the description of "Bleeding Kansas." People were murdering each other over the slavery issue primarily, although slavery was sometimes used as a cover for other motives.

Lawrence was the most radical free-state town in the Kansas Territory. On May 21, 1856, a large body of pro-slavery men raided Lawrence while searching for those who had earlier killed some of their people. The "sack of Lawrence" resulted in only one death, miraculously, as the raiders stole property and destroyed the town's anti-slavery newspaper press, a hotel, and several other buildings.

The increasing violence connected to the slavery issue manifested itself in Washington, D.C. as well. Days after the raid on Lawrence, word reached Kansas that

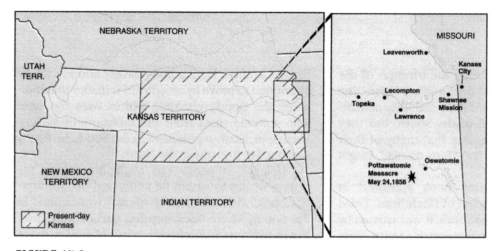

FIGURE 15.9 - Bleeding Kansas, 1854-1860.

Congressman Preston Brooks, of South Carolina, had nearly beaten abolitionist Senator Charles Sumner to death with a cane. Senator Sumner, a Massachusetts abolitionist, had delivered his "Crime against Kansas" speech on the floor of the Senate on May 20. In the speech, Sumner had insulted Representative Brooks' uncle, Senator A.P. Butler, also from South Carolina. Butler was elderly and in poor health, so Brooks came to his defense two days later in the Senate chamber after the day's session. Several witnesses did nothing as Brooks seized his cane and proceeded to gravely injure the senator. While awaiting trial, Brooks received scores of canes from fellow Southerners, with letters urging him to finish the job with their cane after he was released from jail.

Meanwhile, John Brown, a radical abolitionist from Osawatomie, Kansas, led several men to Pottawatomie Creek on the 24th of May, and murdered five pro-slavery men in cold blood in their own yards. This Pottawatomie Massacre touched off more rounds of violence across Kansas. Order was not restored until shortly before the presidential election in November of that year.

The 1856 Presidential Election

The Democrats

The negative reaction in the country to the Kansas-Nebraska Act and "Bleeding Kansas" drove the Democrats to find a candidate who was not well known and certainly not associated with the chaos in Kansas. Thus, when the Democrats met at their nominating convention in Cincinnati in 1856, they selected James Buchanan, a wealthy Pennsylvania lawyer who had been the United States ambassador to Britain during the Pierce administration. Although he had been out of the country during the debate and vote on the Kansas-Nebraska Act, Buchanan had been one of the trio of American ambassadors in Europe who had drafted the infamous Ostend Manifesto in 1854. Nicknamed "Old Buck," Buchanan was another "doughface" like Franklin Pierce, a Northerner with southern sympathies. Buchanan's running mate was John C. Breckinridge of Kentucky. The Democratic platform endorsed the Kansas-Nebraska Act and popular sovereignty despite its obvious failure in actual practice in Kansas.

FIGURE 15.10 - Image illustrating John Brown in Bleeding Kansas

The Republicans

The new Republican Party had its first opportunity to enter a presidential race in 1856. When the Whig Party had collapsed over the Kansas-Nebraska Act two years before, the great majority of southern Whigs joined the Democratic Party. Therefore, for the first time in American political history, the two major parties in 1856 were the Republicans and the Democrats.

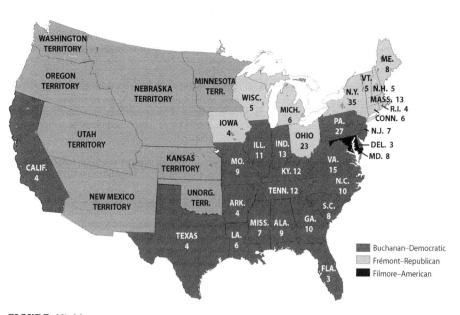

FIGURE 15.11 - Presidential election of 1856 (electoral vote by state).

The Republican convention convened in Philadelphia that year and nominated John C. Fremont, a young explorer from California who had taken part in the very brief Republic of California during the Mexican-American War. Fremont, the "Pathfinder of the West," lacked political experience, but at least he was not tarnished by the confusion in Kansas. He was married to a daughter of Missouri Senator Thomas Hart Benton.

The Republican platform condemned the Kansas-Nebraska Act and blamed the chaos in Kansas on the Democrats. Concerning slavery, the party adopted the Free-Soil position and campaigned on the slogan, "Free soil, free speech, and Fremont."

The Know-Nothings

For a short time, a political group known as the Know-Nothings competed as an alternative to the Democratic Party. The Know-Nothings were so named because the members of this secret organization would respond to questions about it by declaring, "I know nothing." Know-Nothings consisted of old-stock Protestant Christians who were alarmed at the growing number of Roman Catholic Irish and German immigrants coming into the United States from the mid-1840s to the mid-1850s. This anti-immigrant attitude, known as nativism, was also reflected in a variety of fraternal societies, chiefly the Order of the Star-Spangled Banner, which had been organized in 1849, although the first one was the Native American Association, established in 1837.

Officially, the Know-Nothings organized themselves in what they called the American Party and quickly took control of several state legislatures in all regions of the country in the early 1850s. They were the strongest in Massachusetts, where they even elected a governor. Although the American Party attracted both Whigs and Democrats, increasingly it attracted more Whigs, partly because most new immigrants tended to become Democrats and partly because the Whig Party was falling apart in the middle of the 1850s. Nevertheless, the anti-slavery fever sweeping the North eventually caused most northern Know-Nothings to join the Republican Party and most southern Know-Nothings to join the Democratic Party.

In the 1856 presidential contest, the American Party nominated former President Millard Fillmore of New York, an ex-Whig. Before doing so, however, the convention adopted a platform plank in support of the Kansas-Nebraska Act. This action led to a major walkout among Northerners at the convention and their subsequent affiliation with the Republican Party. It also meant the end of any chance for the American Party to become the major rival to the Democrats.

The Campaign and Results

The campaign in 1856 was a vicious one, with the Republican candidate receiving a disproportionate share of the mudslinging. Democrats made much of the fact that Fremont was an illegitimate child, born to a southern planter's wife who had left her family for a man of French descent. The accusation that Fremont was a Roman Catholic probably damaged him more. Apparently he was a former Catholic at the time, although he denied it, but the issue did hurt him among nativists and some others nonetheless. For their part, the Republicans denounced Buchanan for being a bachelor.

Democrat James Buchanan won the election with 174 electoral votes to Fremont's 114 and Fillmore's eight. However, it was clearly a sectional election. Buchanan carried every slave state except Maryland, which was the only state carried by Fillmore. And Fremont carried 11 free states. Buchanan's election was the first in American history that a president was elected without the majority of the vote in both major sections of the country, North and South. That did not bode well for the Union, which now was coming apart at its political seams. But the inexperienced and much-maligned Fremont had done remarkably well, signifying that the Republican Party had emerged as the major alternative to the Democrats.

The Dred Scott Case

On March 6, 1857, just two days after James Buchanan's inauguration, the United States Supreme Court issued a ruling in the *Dred Scott* Case that propelled the nation closer to the brink of civil war.

The case was complicated by residency in more than one state or territory. In 1834, Dr. John Emerson, an army surgeon, took his personal slave, Dred Scott, from his home in St. Louis, Missouri, to Fort Armstrong, Illinois, and from there to Fort Snelling in Wisconsin Territory (present-day Minnesota). Emerson returned to St. Louis in 1838 with Scott, who had married in the meantime. In 1846, three years after Emerson's death, Scott sued Mrs. Emerson for freedom on the basis that his time living in a free state and a free territory had made him a free man. Although he won in a local court, the Missouri

Supreme Court ruled against him. Meanwhile, Mrs. Emerson's brother, John Sanford, had been named the legal administrator of her property. Sanford personally opposed slavery and worked with Scott to take the case into the federal court system. Because Sanford's residence was in New York, a federal court agreed to hear the case on the grounds of interstate jurisdiction. But when that court ruled against Scott, the matter was appealed to the United States Supreme Court.

The Supreme Court consisted of five southern justices, including Chief Justice Roger B. Taney of Maryland, an appointee of President Andrew Jackson in 1836. On March 6, 1857, in *Dred Scott v. Sanford*, the Supreme Court ruled 6-3 against Scott; one of the northern justices concurred with part of the majority, leading some scholars to report the vote as 7-2. There is some evidence, although not conclusive, that President Buchanan may have pressured Justice Robert Grier, from the president's home state of Pennsylvania, to vote with the majority to make the decision look less sectional. In any case, Chief Justice Taney wrote the majority report, which reflected the most pro-slavery viewpoint possible. First, the court declared that Dred Scott was not a United States citizen, nor were any free blacks, and therefore he had no legal standing in the federal courts. Second, Mr. Scott was still a slave because residence in a free state or territory did not change his status. Finally, the court declared that Congress had no authority to prohibit slavery in the territories and specifically ruled that the Compromise of 1820 was unconstitutional despite the fact that the Kansas-Nebraska Act had already invalidated it.

Southern Democrats were jubilant upon hearing the decision of the court. The distinction between free and slave states and territories was now meaningless, for all slave owners had to do was to bring their slaves with them to a free state or territory, and that region could no longer prohibit slavery.

For the same reasons, Republicans were outraged and denounced the ruling for its defense of slavery everywhere in the country. They argued that once the court's majority had written that Dred Scott had no legal standing in the federal courts, there was no legal case on which to render an official verdict. Therefore, the entire ruling was simply an *obiter dictum*, dealing with non-essential elements, and not legally binding upon the nation. Even most northern Democrats were furious because popular sovereignty had been nullified by this decision just as much as the Free-Soil option had been. Stephen Douglas, the champion of popular sovereignty, was placed in a most difficult position, and it was now only a matter of time before the Democratic Party would split between its northern and southern wings.

Opposition to the court ruling was so rampant in the North that it could not be, and thus was not, enforced. When the South realized that it would not be enforced, that region felt betrayed and concluded that northern abolitionists had taken over the Republican Party, which was out to destroy the entire southern way of life. From that moment forward, pro-slavery Democrats demanded a federal slave code, a law that would explicitly declare what the Supreme Court had ruled so that there could be no question about the legality of protecting slavery wherever it went.

As for Dred Scott and his family, they were given their freedom in May 1857 by the son of the original owner, who had just bought them. Unfortunately, Dred Scott died a little more than a year later, in September 1858.

The Panic of 1857

Slavery was not the only issue that brought panic to anti-slavery Americans in 1857. A financial panic erupted in late August 1857, triggering a brief economic depression until its end in 1859. Gold from California had increased the nation's money supply too rapidly and inflated its currency. The end of the Crimean War (1854-56) resulted in a substantial decrease in the European demand for American grain, which by then was in over abundance. The fact that American manufacturing was generally oversupplying the domestic market with goods and that railroad and land speculation was rampant also led to the Panic of 1857.

The South was least affected by the depression, for although cotton prices fell slightly, they recovered quickly. The manufacturing-based North, however, was severely hurt, in both the manufacturing and farming sectors of the economy. This led Southerners to conclude that their economic system of slavery was superior to the wage-slavery system of the North. Pro-slavery southern arrogance was rising quickly in the late 1850s, and it was propelling them toward a willingness to secede from the Union by foolishly believing they could thrive without it.

The Lecompton Constitution

Although physical order had been restored in Kansas just prior to the November 1856 presidential election, the political crisis there had not been resolved. The two territorial legislatures were still competing with each other, leaving nothing but political chaos. In February 1857, the pro-slavery legislature, based at Lecompton, called for a constitutional convention. The great majority of anti-slavery Kansans boycotted the election of delegates, set for June of that year, because the special districts from which the convention delegates were to be elected were gerrymandered in favor of pro-slavery voters. As anticipated, the boycott assured that pro-slavery delegates would control the convention, scheduled to meet that fall. The convention wrote a state constitution that permitted slavery in Kansas and set the date of December 21, 1857, as the ratification election by popular vote. But the ratification election was also boycotted by anti-slavery voters, this time because the ballot allowed for only two choices: for the Lecompton Constitution "with slavery," or for the Lecompton Constitution "without slavery." There was no opportunity to vote against the entire constitution. Furthermore, "without slavery" only meant that the importing of new slaves would be prohibited, with the approximate 200 slaves already in Kansas, and their offspring, still legally regarded as slaves. Predictably, the Lecompton Constitution "with slavery" was ratified by a vote of 6,226 to 569.

Meanwhile, the territorial governor appointed by President Buchanan persuaded anti-slavery leaders to participate in an election of a new territorial legislature to replace the two competing ones. So in October 1857, the first completely open, fair election in Kansas was held. As expected in such an election, anti-slavery forces won and thus controlled the new territorial legislature.

On January 4, 1858, Kansas' voters overwhelmingly defeated the Lecompton Constitution: 10,226 against the entire document, 138 for it "with slavery," and 24 for it "without slavery."

Pro-slavery Kansans charged that the January ratification vote was fraudulent. Following their lead, President Buchanan then endorsed the Lecompton Constitution and immediate statehood for Kansas. Senator Stephen A. Douglas, chairman of the Senate Committee on Territories, could not afford to align himself with a pro-slavery position, so he led the opposition to Kansas' statehood in Congress on the grounds that the December 21 vote in Kansas had not been fair. Playing hardball politics, the president then fired all federal employees from Illinois who owed their jobs to Senator Douglas and got the Senate to vote for Kansas' statehood under the pro-slavery Lecompton Constitution. However, enough anti-slavery northern Democrats in the House added to the Republican members to not only defeat the measure there but also to next pass an amendment requiring a new ratification election in Kansas. President Buchanan and the Senate went along with that because they expected that the Lecompton Constitution would pass, since its defeat would delay statehood until the Kansas population reached the standard requirement of 90,000 citizens. The pro-slavery elements in Congress and the White House had miscalculated the level of anti-slavery feeling in Kansas, for on August 2, 1858, voters there rejected the Lecompton Constitution by the lopsided vote of 11,300 to 1,788. This last vote finally spelled the end of hope for pro-slavery forces. An anti-slavery constitution was later ratified, and Kansas came into the Union as the 34th state on January 29, 1861.

Harper's Ferry

Shortly after the Pottawatomie Massacre on May 24, 1856, John Brown left Kansas and began raising money among New England abolitionists for a violent strike at slavery in the South. His scheme was to establish a free black colony in the mountains of western Virginia, which he would use as a base to arm slaves and create a chain reaction that, he hoped, would end slavery by violence. Brown was confident of the righteousness of his cause because he believed God had raised him to end

FIGURE 15.12 - John Brown

the institution of slavery in America. He bought a farm in western Maryland and waited for his opportunity.

To launch his scheme, Brown needed more weapons, which the federal arsenal at nearby Harper's Ferry, Virginia (present-day West Virginia), could furnish. Therefore, on the night of October 16, 1859, Brown and 21 followers, including five blacks, crossed the Potomac River and took control of the arsenal by surprise. But poor planning led to a delay and a gun battle with townsmen, seven of whom were killed. Ten or more were injured. In the process, Brown took a few hostages as he was trapped in a building in town. Gunfire erupted the next morning, killing one of Brown's sons and another man who were carrying the white flag of truce. Eventually, the U.S. Marines commanded by Lieutenant Colonel Robert E. Lee arrived, and on the morning of October 18, they broke down the door and ended the siege. When the entire episode had ended, 10 of Brown's men were killed, including two sons, seven were captured, and five escaped. John Brown failed in his alleged divine mission.

John Brown was charged with treason against the state of Virginia and inciting an insurrection. By rejecting his defense attorneys' request to plead insanity, Brown was able to use the trial for publicizing the abolitionist cause. In truth, he probably was not insane, although insanity was in the family of his first wife. Among other things, John Brown uttered these stirring words at his trial: "If it is deemed necessary that I should forfeit my life for the furtherance of the ends of justice, and mingle my blood further with the blood of ... millions in this slave country whose rights are disregarded by wicked, cruel, and unjust enactments, I say, let it be done." He was convicted and sentenced to death by hanging, yet he remained calm and fatalistic to the very end, thereby making himself an almost mythical character. He calmly went to the gallows and was hanged on December 2, 1859. Just before his execution was carried out, Brown handed an official a note with these prophetic words: "I John Brown am now quite certain that the crimes of this guilty land will never be purged away, but with blood." Unfortunately, he was proven correct.

Many Republican leaders and other Northerners denounced John Brown for his violent attempt to end slavery. But there were others in the North to whom John Brown became a hero. The song "John Brown's Body" was a song about an earlier, different John Brown from Massachusetts. But it was adapted and applied to the most violent abolitionist of American history. Perhaps one may assume that it was easier to do that than to write a completely new song.

Southerners were unanimous in their denunciation of John Brown. The fact that he was dead did not seem to calm their fears of future attempts to end slavery by force. The South, in fact, incorrectly linked the Republican Party to John Brown's philosophy and methods. The incident at Harper's Ferry proved to be a major road marker on the way to our nation's self-destructive civil war.

The Rise of Abraham Lincoln

Before turning to the fateful presidential election of 1860, it is important to note the rise of a man whose principles and down-to-earth manner pushed him onto the stage of history at such a crucial time.

An Overview

Abraham Lincoln had been born of humble origins in a Kentucky log cabin in 1809 and raised on farms in Indiana and then Illinois. He basically taught himself how to read and write, held odd jobs, and served in the Black Hawk War of 1832, named after the Sac and Fox chief who resisted President Jackson's Indian removal policy to lands west of the Mississippi River. Although he lost his first election, Lincoln was elected to the Illinois legislature at the age of 25 in 1834 as a Whig. He read enough law books to pass the bar exam and began practicing law in 1836. Impressed with his passion for justice, his common sense, and his honesty, the people of his district elected "Honest Abe" to the U.S. House of Representatives in 1846, where he served just one term as a Whig. Disillusioned with politics, Lincoln retired from it after his term in early 1849. However, the

FIGURE 15.13 - Abraham Lincoln.

Kansas-Nebraska Act and its aftermath angered Lincoln enough to bring him back into the political arena as a Republican, where he became the major opponent of his home-state senator, Democrat Stephen A. Douglas.

The Lincoln-Douglas Debates

The Republicans selected Lincoln to run against Douglas as the latter sought reelection to a thrid term in 1858. Technically, the state senate elected the U.S. senators until the Seventeenth Amendment was ratified in 1913. But these two men campaigned in order to convince Illinois voters to elect state senators of their respective parties so that the state senate would then elect them to the U.S. Senate.

A series of seven debates between Lincoln and Douglas occurred from August 21 to October 15, 1858. The most famous of these debates was the second one, which took place in Freeport. Douglas tried to make Lincoln look like a racial extremist for his day by painting him as someone who favored racial equality. But Lincoln made it clear that he opposed "social and political equality" between the white and black races, declaring that such a state of equality was impossible. This was the opinion of the great majority of Americans, regardless of their views on slavery or the region they lived in. In retaliation, Lincoln put Douglas on the defensive when he asked the senator how he could reconcile his notion of popular sovereignty with the Dred Scott decision. Douglas' reply became known as the Freeport Doctrine, which was his statement that a territory could still exclude slavery simply by refusing to pass police regulations necessary to protect it. Douglas' answer was evasive and defensive, but he was obligated by conscience to give it because he held popular sovereignty to be the morally correct position on slavery.

Although the total number of Republican votes in the state senate contests were greater than the total number of Democratic votes, gerrymandering of the senate districts still gave the Democrats control of the Illinois senate, and Stephen Douglas was reelected to the U.S. Senate. Nevertheless, the 1858 Illinois senate race had given Abraham Lincoln the national exposure that would thrust him into the presidency just two years later.

The 1860 Presidential Election

There was a widespread belief in 1860 that the presidential election that year would decide the fate of the nation. The country had already polarized into two camps over the slavery question, and very little was required to push it into civil war.

The Republicans

The Republicans met in Chicago that year determined to elect a winning candidate for president. With the Democrats badly divided, the Republicans could smell victory in the air. New York Senator William H. Seward, the old former Whig, was finally a viable candidate for the nomination by a major party for president. Seward had made a number of enemies, however, and many Republicans wanted a fresh face. Abraham Lincoln had developed a national following since his debates with Stephen Douglas two years earlier. His dry wit and homespun wisdom, coupled with his adamant Free-Soil position on slavery, attracted people to him and also to the Republican Party. By the eve of the convention, Lincoln was nearly every delegate's second choice if he was not the first choice. Finally, the fact that the Republican Convention was held in Chicago, on Lincoln's home soil, was a further advantage for his cause. His campaign leaders master minded the convention by placing Lincoln delegates in strategic positions all over the convention floor, instructing them to yell and cheer every time Lincoln's name was even mentioned in passing by a convention speaker. This made it appear that his supporters were even more numerous than they were. On the third ballot, Abraham Lincoln won his party's nomination for president. Hannibal Hamlin, a former Democrat from Maine who joined the Republicans after the 1856 Democratic Convention endorsed the Kansas-Nebraska Act, was selected as Lincoln's vice-presidential running mate.

The Republican Party platform condemned the Kansas-Nebraska Act, endorsed a Free-Soil plank on the slavery question, favored higher, protective tariffs for manufacturers, supported federal assistance for a transcontinental railroad and other internal improvements, and promised free federal land for settlers

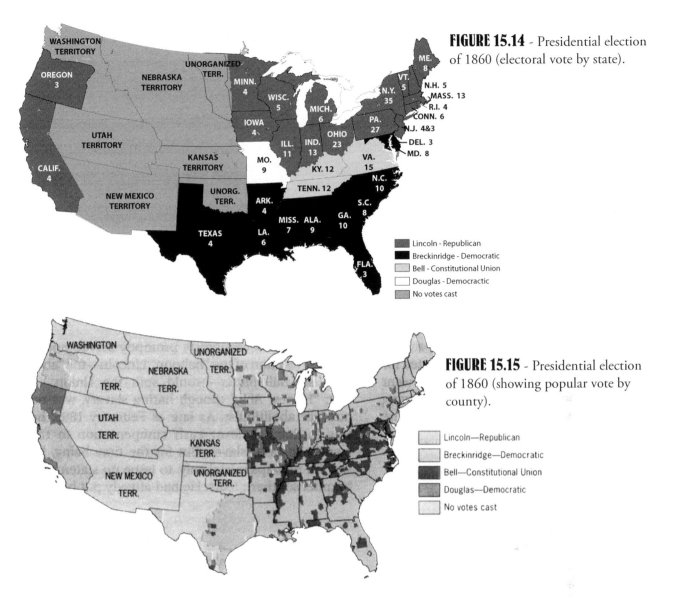

FIGURE 15.14 - Presidential election of 1860 (electoral vote by state).

Map legend:
- Lincoln - Republican
- Breckinridge - Democratic
- Bell - Constitutional Union
- Douglas - Democractic
- No votes cast

FIGURE 15.15 - Presidential election of 1860 (showing popular vote by county).

Map legend:
- Lincoln—Republican
- Breckinridge—Democratic
- Bell—Constitutional Union
- Douglas—Democratic
- No votes cast

moving west. Economically, then, it resembled the former Whig Party. Indeed, Henry Clay was Lincoln's political idol.

The Democrats

The Democratic Convention first met in April at Charleston, South Carolina. Democrats were badly split over the slavery question, which made Charleston a poor choice for their convention site because of its long history of support for secession. Pro-slavery southern Democrats insisted on a federal slave code plank in the party platform. Such a federal law would protect the property of slave-owners in all the territories and states. But most northern, or Douglas, Democrats favored a popular sovereignty plank instead. When the popular sovereignty plank won over the federal slave code plank,

many southern delegates walked out of the convention, led by delegates from Alabama. The remaining delegates could not muster the necessary two-thirds to nominate a candidate for president. The result was a decision to meet several weeks later in Baltimore in hopes that both time and a new location would give a chance for cooler heads to prevail. However, a fight over which delegates to officially seat at the June convention in Baltimore produced another, larger southern walkout after many Douglas delegates were seated from some southern states. The convention then proceeded to nominate Stephen A. Douglas for president and affirm the popular sovereignty plank in the platform.

The Democratic Party had finally succumbed to the slavery question and broke into a northern and a southern wing in 1860. The dissident southern delegates met first in Richmond, Virginia, but later moved their convention to Baltimore also. They nominated Vice President John C. Breckinridge of Kentucky, considered a moderate. But the delegates took a strong pro-slavery stand and adopted support for a federal slave code and the annexation of Cuba in their platform.

The Constitutional Union Party

Moderates, particularly from the border states, were unhappy with all three emerging choices for president in 1860. One accurate saying that described Americans by 1860 was that "attitude followed latitude." That is to say, the further south one lived, the more likely he was to be a strong defender of slavery, and the further north one lived, the more likely he was to be a strong opponent of slavery. This left Americans in the middle, or border states, more likely to adopt a moderate stance on the issue. Led by men like Kentucky Senator John J. Crittenden, these moderates formed the Constitutional Union Party that year. Many of them were diehard Whigs who had not joined either the Republicans or Democrats.

This Constitutional Union Party met in Baltimore and adopted only a simple resolution that declared a strong commitment to the Constitution and the preservation of the Union. It took no other official position on slavery or on any other topic of the day, for which it was nicknamed by critics as the "Do Nothing" party. Former Senator John Bell of Tennessee was the party's nominee for president.

The Campaign and Results

The actual campaign in 1860 looked more like two presidential campaigns, each with its own set of competing candidates. In the North, the contest was primarily between Lincoln and Douglas, while in the South, the contest was between Breckinridge and Bell. In fact, Lincoln was not even on the ballot in 10 of the 15 slave states, and Breckinridge was not on the ballot in three northern states.

Of all four candidates, only Stephen Douglas attempted to run a truly national campaign; the other three concentrated their efforts exclusively in their strongest regions. In fact, Douglas broke with tradition by becoming the first major party presidential candidate to personally campaign for himself. The various state elections coinciding with the presidential election year were not all held on the same day, but were often spread out over several weeks. In early October, when Douglas learned of convincing Republican victories in state elections in the traditionally Democratic states of Pennsylvania and Indiana, he concluded that Lincoln would win the presidency. Dejected and worn out, Senator Douglas declared, "Mr. Lincoln is the next President. We must try to save the Union. I will go South." He did so in a futile attempt to persuade Southerners to remain loyal to his beloved United States. He was in Mobile, Alabama, in early November when the results confirmed his prediction. Perhaps fortunately for him, Stephen Douglas died in June 1861 before the first real battle of the Civil War was fought.

Abraham Lincoln won the election with 180 electoral votes and nearly 1.9 million popular votes. He carried every free state and received all but three of New Jersey's seven electoral votes. Southern Democrat John C. Breckinridge came in a distant second electorally with 72 votes and a little more than 848,000 popular votes, carrying 11 of the 15 slave states. John Bell received 39 electoral votes and almost 593,000 popular votes, but carried only Kentucky, Tennessee, and Virginia. Finally, Stephen Douglas, the official Democratic candidate, won only a dismal 12 electoral votes, although he pulled nearly 1.4 million popular votes, second in that category to Lincoln. He lost his home state of Illinois to Lincoln and won only Missouri and three of New Jersey's seven electoral votes.

In the most sectional presidential election in the nation's history, Americans had elected, with just less than 40 percent of the popular vote, the first modern Republican president and the first anti-slavery candidate.

Southern Post-Election Viewpoints

Much, but not all, of the South reacted in horror to the election of Abraham Lincoln. Those who did so incorrectly believed he was an abolitionist who would destroy the southern way of life. Nevertheless, the news for the southern secessionists was actually not that good. Breckinridge had gone out of his way during the campaign to declare his support for keeping the Union together. Furthermore, slightly more than half of the Southerners who voted had cast votes for either Douglas or Bell, two candidates who strongly opposed secession. Thus, there was definitely no unanimity of viewpoint among Southerners, as three major groups emerged just after Lincoln's election, none of them representing an actual majority of opinion in the South.

The "immediate secessionists" were the hotheads in the lower South who favored immediate secession from the Union now that Lincoln had been elected president. Although a significant minority, the "immediate secessionists" probably were outnumbered by the "cooperationists," or "cooperatists," who perhaps held sway among 40 percent of Southerners and probably represented the single largest of the three viewpoints. Cooperatists emphasized the need for the slave states to cooperate or work together. Some of them favored giving the North an ultimatum to pass a federal slave code before proceeding to secede from the Union, assuming the ultimatum was not met. Other "cooperatists" were also labeled as "conditional Unionists" because they favored waiting for the North to attack before seceding from the Union.

The third, and smallest, southern viewpoint was represented by the term "unconditional Unionists." These Southerners, who tended to live in the upper South or border states, opposed the idea of secession altogether. One of these was Alexander Stephens, who ironically was elected vice president of the Confederacy just three months later. Stephens argued that extremist secessionists had created the current crisis and reminded the South that Lincoln had promised to leave slavery alone where it already existed. "Revolutions are much easier started than controlled." Stephens said, "I consider slavery much more secure in the Union than out of it." His words proved prophetic, for the coming civil war would end slavery in the United States.

Secession Begins

Although the South was divided among several specific viewpoints, one thing was clear: After the election of Lincoln, the majority of Southerners favored the step of secession at some point if their demands for a federal slave code were not met. It was the "immediate secessionists" who carried the day in the South because they were better organized and took decisive action. In the midst of the political confusion, as often happens, the most vocal and best organized group won the struggle for control by creating a political tide that swept the majority along with them. "He who hesitates is lost," is a familiar saying, and the "immediate secessionists" did not hesitate.

South Carolina, the home state of the late John C. Calhoun and long known for its radical states' rights views, led the way to secession. On December 6, 1860, exactly one month after Lincoln's victory, the South Carolina legislature called for an election of a special convention to consider the issue of secession. The convention met in Charleston on December 20 and voted to repeal South Carolina's ratification of the U.S. Constitution and declare its secession from the Union. This was done under the compact theory of the Constitution, a theory teaching that the Constitution was an agreement among the states rather than the people of the United States, therefore allowing any state

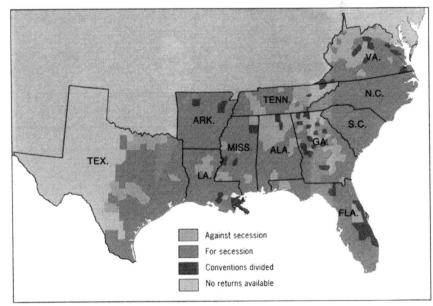

FIGURE 15.16 - Southern opposition to secession, 1860-1861 (showing vote by county).

to withdraw from that agreement whenever it wished to do so. The vote was 169-0 as South Carolina proved to be the only state whose secession vote was unanimous.

South Carolina next sent representatives to visit other slave states and persuade them to join in the secession movement. Unlike the Tariff of Abominations crisis 30 years earlier, this time South Carolina received promises of supportive action toward secession. By February 1, 1861, six other slave states voted to follow South Carolina's example and secede from the Union: Mississippi, Florida, Alabama, Georgia, Louisiana, and Texas, in that chronological order. Texas Governor Sam Houston was an old Jacksonian nationalist who refused to call the Texas legislature into special session to deal with the question of secession. Nevertheless, most of the legislators borrowed a page from the pre-Revolutionary War era by conducting an illegal meeting. Its recommendation for secession was submitted to the people of Texas in a referendum, making Texas the only state to use a popular referendum on the secession question. Governor Houston was powerless to prevent the referendum because of the overwhelming popularity for secession in his state. Indeed, the vote for secession in Texas was a large one, although ironically, the fact that the referendum itself was called illegally made it a violation of the state's own constitution. The average vote for secession in the first seven states to secede was 83 percent.

Formation of the Confederacy

The Confederacy Organizes

Six of the seven states that claimed to have seceded sent delegates to Montgomery, Alabama, where a constitutional convention began on February 4, 1861, to form the Confederate States of America (CSA), commonly called the Confederacy. The Texas referendum had been held too late to organize and send delegates. On February 7, just the fourth day of the convention, the delegates had written and adopted the Constitution of the Confederate States of America.

What the Founding Fathers of the United States had taken nearly four full months to do, the Confederates accomplished in four days. Of course, there was no need

to reinvent the wheel at Montgomery, so the Confederate constitution was quite similar to the U.S. Constitution. However, there were a few key differences between the two constitutions, reflecting strong southern feelings about some national issues. For example, a "general welfare" clause was omitted in order to prevent a national government from exercising too much authority over the Confederate states. The new constitution also explicitly guaranteed slavery in the states and territories. On the economic front, it prohibited all protective tariffs and federally financed internal improvements. Finally, the document provided for one six-year term for its president, who was also given the power to veto parts of specific legislation (called a line-item veto).

On February 9, the Montgomery Convention also elected a provisional president and vice president: Jefferson Davis, a wealthy slave-owning planter and former Democratic senator from Mississippi, and Alexander H. Stephens, a former Whig Representative from Georgia, respectively. The two leaders were inaugurated nine days later on the 18th, and more firmly sanctioned by an election in the Confederate states in November 1861. Meanwhile, delegates to the convention served as the provisional Congress until the same elections in November 1861. Montgomery served as the first national capital of the Confederacy.

Jefferson Davis

Jefferson Davis had been born in a Kentucky log cabin like Abraham Lincoln, but his family moved to Mississippi when he was just a boy. Davis graduated from West Point Military Academy in 1828, despite receiving several demerits for carousing, and joined the U.S. Army, where he fought in the Black Hawk War (1832) like Lincoln. He married the daughter of General Zachary Taylor in 1835, but she died about three months later. For the next 10 years he lived the life of a wealthy gentleman on his Mississippi plantation before marrying for the second time in 1845.

Politically, Davis served in the U.S. House of Representatives for a brief time in 1845 and 1846 before resigning to join the fight in the Mexican-American War, where he served valiantly but was injured on the right foot. He was appointed to the Senate to fill the remainder of the term but resigned in 1851 to run for governor of his home state, where he lost a close race. President Franklin Pierce appointed him as his Secretary of War in 1853 before he returned to the Senate four years later, where he served as an outspoken champion of slavery and its expansion, as well as states' rights.

Davis resigned from the Senate in January 1861, shortly after Mississippi voted to secede from the Union. He was then immediately given a military command in the Mississippi militia. Although he would have preferred military leadership during any civil war, Davis was elected to the presidency of the new Confederacy because he was considered a more neutral candidate. But he made a poor president by focusing on trivial things, making poor appointments to his cabinet, being an ineffective communicator, and generally not relating well to many people. He was also overly optimistic when caution was called for; and late in the Civil War, he interfered with his Confederate generals' military strategy. Most Southerners intensely disliked him by the end of the Civil War. Even Vice President Alexander Stephens thought Davis was too dictatorial. In the middle of the war, Stephens went back home to Georgia, and though he never resigned his political office, he often criticized President Davis publicly. Late in the war, Stephens even used his influence to get his home state of Georgia to place every able-bodied man in the state militia in order to prevent the Confederacy from drafting any additional Georgians.

FIGURE 15.17 - Proposed Crittenden Compromise, 1860.

Map legend:
- Slavery prohibited during territorial status, thereby virtually assuring free-soil states
- Slavery protected during territorial status; states might be either slave or free

The Failure of Compromise

During the four months between the election and the inauguration of Abraham Lincoln, President Buchanan issued no strong statements about the secession votes and the formation of the Confederacy. In his annual address to Congress on December 3, 1860, Buchanan simply announced that both secession and coercion to prevent secession were illegal. Therefore, he urged Congress to explore areas of compromise. This announcement prompted the *Cincinnati Enquirer* newspaper to declare in its editorial, "Seldom have we known so strong an argument come to so lame and impotent a conclusion."

In a partial defense of Buchanan, he was a conservative man in temperament and longed to find a way to avoid war. The U.S. Army was quite small, and most of the 15,000 or so troops were needed to control Indians in the West. Besides, Buchanan could find no justification for using force against the South in the Constitution. For his part, President-Elect Lincoln also said virtually nothing publicly about the growing separation of the country, apparently hoping that silence would at least not add to the state of agitation already existing.

Southern secessionists took advantage of the lack of leadership in the White House and declared control of federal military properties in the new Confederacy, such as arsenals and forts. While President Buchanan refused to take any offensive action, he did make the decision to hold on to a few island and harbor forts. One of these was Fort Sumter in Charleston Harbor, South Carolina. When South Carolina demanded the withdrawal of federal forces from Fort Sumter, Buchanan refused, and the attention of the entire nation became focused on that fort. The fort was running a bit short on supplies, so Buchanan ordered supplies delivered. But when the *Star of the West* arrived in Charleston Harbor on January 9, 1861, it was fired upon and then retreated. Still, there was no retaliation as the president was hoping for yet another political compromise to resolve the tensions.

Meanwhile, the lack of presidential leadership forced Congress to take the lead in crafting some kind of compromise. The Senate created the Senate "Committee of 13," chaired by Kentucky Senator John J. Crittenden, to help the nation find a last-minute compromise. Crittenden personally proposed that the significance of the 36° 30′ parallel of the Missouri Compromise be reinstated and extended all the way to California (but not running through that state) and that the federal government guarantee no interference with slavery where it existed. However, the "Committee of 13" could not agree on much of anything, and Republicans in Congress opposed any measure that would allow further expansion of slavery. In January, the House of Representatives defeated the so-called Crittenden Compromise by a vote of 113-80, and the Senate defeated it by the narrow margin of 20-19 in March. About the same time, the House of Representatives created a "Committee of 33," which also failed to agree on a compromise proposal. However, a number of proposals were sent to the floor of the Congress, without recommendation, for debate.

In the meantime, the Virginia state legislature called for a "peace convention" in early February to see if a body outside of Congress could be successful. Twenty-one states sent delegates to Washington, D.C., and former President John Tyler presided at the convention. The "peace convention" met for about three weeks in February and recommended a plan very similar to the Crittenden Compromise. But the only part of the proposals to pass Congress was a constitutional amendment to protect slavery where it already existed. Most Republicans, including President-Elect Lincoln, felt they could support that idea but nothing else. The amendment would have been the 13th Amendment to the U.S. Constitution, but subsequent events prevented its ratification. Ironically, the 13th Amendment which was later adopted abolished slavery altogether. The failure to find a compromise made the U.S. Civil War inevitable. All that was left was to wait and watch for the conflict that was now certain to come soon.

The Battle Lines Are Drawn

The Surrender of Fort Sumter

The four months from the election to the inauguration of the new president seemed like an eternity. Seven lower-South states had announced their secession, formed a new government, and occupied most of the federal military installations in their territory. Perhaps a strong word from either Buchanan or Lincoln could have forced the Confederate states to back down, but we will never know. At last, Abraham Lincoln was sworn in as the nation's 16th president at noon on March 4, 1861. In his inaugural address, the new president struck a conciliatory tone in announcing the following: "I have no purpose, directly or indirectly, to interfere with the institution of slavery in the States where it exists. I believe I have no lawful right to do so, and I have no inclination to do so." He did, however, declare that secession was wrong and illegal.

Nothing of any substance occurred during Lincoln's first month in office. By the end of March, Fort Sumter had nearly depleted its supplies. Major Robert Anderson commanded the garrison there with more than 80 men. Those troops and the fort they occupied became a symbol to both political sides. Who would flinch first? On April 6, President Lincoln sent word to the South Carolina governor that another attempt to resupply Fort Sumter was forthcoming, but that no arms, ammunition, or new troops would be part of the operation unless the federal forces were fired upon. He sent this message to the legally elected governor, thereby avoiding any tacit recognition of the Confederate States of America, which would have been the case had he sent the message to Jefferson Davis. Of course, he knew that Davis would hear of his decision to resupply the fort and would have to make a choice to challenge that effort or allow it to succeed.

Jefferson Davis made his fateful decision on April 9 not to permit the standoff to continue against the advice of some key advisors. Rather, the Confederacy would demand the surrender of Fort Sumter and militarily challenge any supply ships approaching the fort if it refused to surrender. Confederate General Pierre Gustave Toutant Beauregard, who ironically had studied artillery under Anderson at West Point, made the surrender demand on April 11. Although reduced to just a few days' worth of supplies, Major Anderson refused to surrender. With supply ships nearing, the Confederates began bombarding Fort Sumter at 4:30 a.m. on April 12, 1861. After his ammunition ran out about 34 hours

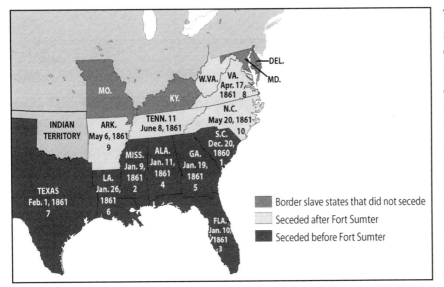

FIGURE 15.18 - Seceding states (with dates and order of secession).

later, Major Robert Anderson agreed to surrender. The formal surrender ceremony occurred at the fort on April 14. Although there had been no casualties in the bombardment, two federal soldiers were tragically killed when a cannon exploded during the final gun salute to the U.S. flag.

Lincoln Responds and the Crisis Deepens

The next day, April 15, President Abraham Lincoln issued a formal call for 75,000 volunteers to put down the rebellion. Four days later, the president announced that all southern ports would be blockaded. These measures were pitifully small, but they were taken with the conviction that any war would be fairly quick. Unfortunately, that would prove foolish thinking.

Within five weeks of the fall of Fort Sumter, four additional slave states voted to secede and join the Confederacy: Virginia on April 17, Arkansas on May 6, Tennessee on May 7, and North Carolina on May 20. Of the 11 states of the Confederacy, only Virginia was honest enough to officially refer to her secession as a "rebellion." In the mountainous areas of western Virginia and eastern Tennessee there were more Unionists than secessionists. Several counties broke away from Virginia and proclaimed a loyal government in western Virginia early in the war. Then on June 30, 1863, the state of West Virginia entered the Union as the 35th state.

That left four slave states which never voted to secede or join the Confederacy: Delaware, Maryland, Kentucky, and Missouri. Delaware's economy was too closely linked to Pennsylvania and New Jersey for that state to even think seriously about secession. Besides, her geographical location would have left her completely isolated from other Confederate forces.

Maryland's defection would have surrounded the U.S. capital with Confederate territory. Therefore, President Lincoln suspended the Constitutional *writ of habeas corpus* because Congress was not in session at the time and jailed all the known pro-Confederate leaders in the state as a preventative step. The *writ of habeas corpus* is a court order instructing an arresting officer or a corrections officer to bring a detained person to the court with a list of formal charges against the person. If that is not done, the detainee must be released. Its suspension meant that Americans could be and were jailed without being formally charged with a crime for an indefinite period of time. Article I, Section 9 of the U.S. Constitution says that this writ cannot be suspended except "in cases of rebellion or invasion" and then only by Congress and if public safety requires such action. Congress later gave specific authorization for the president's action.

The presence of federal troops in Kentucky and Missouri helped keep those states from declaring their secession, even though there was significant sympathy for the Confederate cause in both areas.

Thus, the political battle lines were all drawn before the end of May 1861. Shots had been fired at Fort Sumter. While both sides called for their volunteers, the nation waited to see what would happen next. Americans would not have long to wait, for the American Civil War would begin in earnest on a hot day in late July at a place called Manassas, Virginia.

Maryland, Antietam, President Lincoln and General McClellan at Antietam

Chapter 16 Contents

CHAPTER SIXTEEN

The Civil War

Major Events

1861	*Writ of Habeas Corpus* suspended First Battle of Bull Run
1862	Revenue Act created Bureau of Internal Revenue to collect income tax *Merrimack vs. Monitor* Battle of Shiloh New Orleans captured by David G. Farragut Peninsula Campaign in Virginia Battle of Antietam Creek President Lincoln issued the Emancipation Proclamation Battle of Fredericksburg
1863	Battle of Chancellorsville Battle of Gettysburg Battle of Vicksburg Fall of Port Hudson
1864	Battle of the Wilderness Battle of Spotsylvania Fighting at Cold Harbor Siege of Petersburg began Battle of Kennesaw Mountain Union victory at Atlanta Sherman's "March to the Sea"
1865	Lee surrendered to Grant at Appomattox Courthouse, Virginia

Introduction

Following the surrender of Fort Sumter to the Confederates on April 14, 1861, both President Abraham Lincoln and Jefferson Davis called upon volunteers to fight for their respective causes. Southerners who enlisted were confident in the righteousness of their cause. For most of the southern soldiers, this was a war for self-government, the right of a state to withdraw from the Union or legally sanction slavery. They were exercising this "right" of secession because they perceived that the North was on the verge of threatening the foundation of their way of life politically, economically, and socially. Since the Mexican-American War (1846-48), territorial expansion in the West seemed destined to bring more free states into the nation, along with their anti-slavery congressmen and senators. The South feared that an upset in the political balance between slave states and free states would embolden the anti-slavery forces to abolish slavery and make white Southerners economic slaves of the North. Most Northerners, by contrast, held that a compact among the people rather than the states created the United States under the Constitution, and they fought for the preservation of the Union, permanent and indissoluble. Of course, underlying the political theories was the issue of human beings enslaving other human beings. Although the Civil War was not officially fought to free the slaves until 1863, without the issue of slavery there would have been no Civil War.

Statements from Senators William H. Seward of New York and James Hammond of South Carolina revealed the fundamentally different views of the two regions. Seward claimed that the free labor system of the North brought about an educated, industrious, and democratic population. In contrast, a slave system created a region doomed to decay due to the control of a slave-holding aristocracy using its power to focus the major portion of government power on perpetuating a system and infrastructure that added to the plantation kingdoms. Hammond challenged this view by claiming that there must be, and had always been, a laboring class to perform the most menial of necessary tasks. The slaves were the laboring class performing the most menial tasks below the Mason-Dixon Line, but their lives were better than the white wage slaves in the North, an argument espoused by Hammond and probably a majority of Southerners to counter any criticisms of the slave system.

Causes of the Civil War

It was true that there were many similarities between the two regions. They spoke the same language, came from mostly the same European ancestry, believed in republican government, worshipped the Protestant religious creeds, fought for freedom from England, and created and lived under the regulation of the same Constitution. It was also true that there were differences between the North and the South regarding their history and development that often put them at odds with each other from the time of the writing of the Constitution they both shared. At the Constitutional Convention, James Madison declared that the states were separated by the "effects of their having or not having slaves." In the 1860s, the differences were more pronounced. For example, the differences in culture were apparent with 26 percent of the Northerners living in cities or towns and only approximately 10 percent of the Southerners living in cities or towns. Urban cultures were quite different from rural cultures.

The Civil War was one of the most important events in our nation's journey. Because of its significance, historians have scrutinized this war more carefully than most events. Many proposed and continue to offer theories as to the causes of the disintegration of ties between the regions that led to a civil war. In the previous chapter of this book, the steps taken or not taken by the nation in the last decade were carefully related. However, a deeper and more fundamental break compelled a war. After all, the states had compromised repeatedly from the time of the constitutional beginnings of the nation. What was different in 1861? With such divergent views on both sides, it was not surprising that there were those who could not see a peaceful coexistence for the North and South by 1860.

Perceived threats to slavery from the new Republican President Abraham Lincoln, westward movement, ideology, states' rights and the scope of the federal government, the breakdown of political party effectiveness, a different economic focus, and even a different sense of Southerners with regard to honor are just a few of the theories presented as the causes of the Civil War. Historian Eric Foner maintained that the ideology of the Republican Party and the election of their candidate was a primary cause of the Civil War. In his book *Free Soil, Free Labor, Free Men: The Ideology of the Republican Party Before the Civil War,* Foner claimed that the free labor ideology of this new party from which Lincoln came threatened the Southerners so greatly that they seceded from the United States.

The South believed that if the Republicans controlled the nation, slavery could not move into the western territories, and movement west was vital to the success of the South and its slave economy. Alexander H. Stephens, the Vice President of the Confederate States of America, defended the cause of states' rights in his book *A Constitutional View of the Late War Between the States.* He agreed with the position of South Carolina stated in the "Declaration of the Causes of Secession" that the North was usurping power in a manner that was unconstitutional and forcing the South to leave the Union or die. In *The Political Crisis of the 1850s,* Michael F. Holt agreed that the most important cause of the Civil War was political ideology, but of a different nature. Americans had always been nervous about any threat to their ideal of a republican society. The ideas of self-government, freedom, and equality for whites were sacrosanct and must be maintained even if the threat came from another region of the United States. The Whig and Democratic parties were able to keep the disagreements of the two regions under control in the normal functioning of the political party system. Holt maintained that when the Whig Party broke apart and the Democratic Party fractured, political compromise seemed hopeless and secession and war inevitable.

James M. McPherson recounted the widening economic differences of the two regions in *Ordeal by Fire: The Civil War And Reconstruction.* The modernization of the North with the use of technology increased the amount of manufacturing and changed the traditional methods of work in the factory. Even though agricultural production was important in both regions, the South remained traditional and committed to agriculture as its main economic focus and did not increase its manufacturing base. Bertram Wyatt Brown, in *Honor and Violence in the Old South,* took an unorthodox view of the differences between the North and South when he proposed that southern honor and a more violent nature brought the South to the battlefield rather than accept dishonor. All of the theories are based on sound research and are plausible. Which one was correct? Perhaps a combination of several of the theories advanced are correct, or perhaps none of the theories answer the question of why war began.

North and South Compared

The Civil War was not fought only by soldiers on battlefields. It was also fought on the home fronts. Population, economic strength, financial means, and citizen resolve were all vital aspects that determined the outcome of this war, as with most wars. This is especially true of civil wars, and the United States was no exception. What advantages and disadvantages did each side have? How did the Civil War affect civilians who never wore

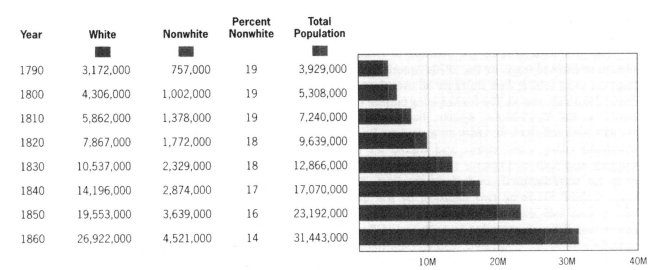

Year	White	Nonwhite	Percent Nonwhite	Total Population
1790	3,172,000	757,000	19	3,929,000
1800	4,306,000	1,002,000	19	5,308,000
1810	5,862,000	1,378,000	19	7,240,000
1820	7,867,000	1,772,000	18	9,639,000
1830	10,537,000	2,329,000	18	12,866,000
1840	14,196,000	2,874,000	17	17,070,000
1850	19,553,000	3,639,000	16	23,192,000
1860	26,922,000	4,521,000	14	31,443,000

FIGURE 16.1 - Population increase, including slaves and Indians, 1790-1860.

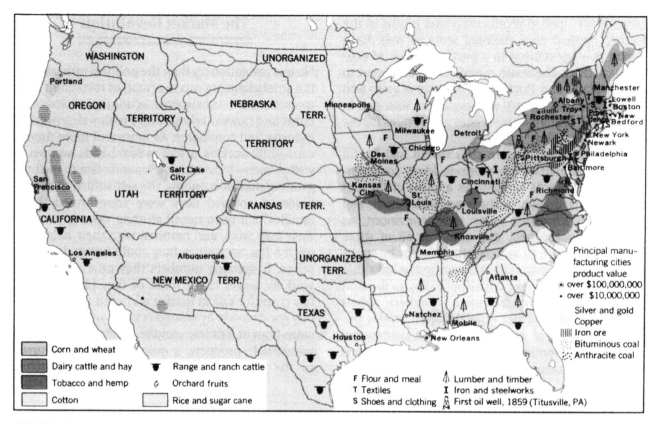

FIGURE 16.2 - Industry and agriculture, 1860.

Population

On the eve of the Civil War, there were 23 states in the North (defined as any state outside the Confederacy) with a total population of about 22 million. The Confederacy had 11 states and a total population of about 9.1 million, although about 3.6 million of those were slaves. Thus, the North had a vastly larger population from which to draw more military recruits. Its population advantage also meant greater production capabilities to supply the United States Army with all the materials it needed.

The Confederacy was at a distinct disadvantage with its smaller population. However, Southerners believed their tradition of hunting and general familiarity with guns would outweigh the numerical advantage of the northern shopkeepers who would fill the Union ranks as soldiers. A distinct advantage held by the Southerners was their knowledge of the land they expected to defend from invasion. A more objective analysis would have reached the conclusion that the overwhelming numerical superiority of the North would overcome in a long war any advantage that superior skills with weapons and intimate knowledge of the physical layout of the land brought. If the war had been shorter in duration, the Confederate soldiers' original advantages might indeed have continued to create southern victories. The great majority of Americans on both sides predicted a relatively easy and quick victory. They were wrong.

Industry

The North was the center of American manufacturing. Because of this industrialization, most of the country's largest cities were also in the North. Out of the 25 largest cities, only three were in the South: Charleston, South Carolina; Richmond, Virginia; and New Orleans, Louisiana. In a long war, northern industrial capacity could turn out weapons and ammunition in an overwhelming flood, thus assuring that the Union Army would never run out of the materials necessary to win the war.

The South, on the other hand, made a conscious decision not to industrialize. Compared with the North, it had a very small manufacturing capacity. Therefore, the Confederacy had just two alternatives to supply war and other materials. It could purchase war supplies from outside the country, thus increasing its debt, or attempt to build factories quickly under wartime conditions and without much experience. The southern reliance on growing "King Cotton" left them unprepared for a quick conversion to manufacturing. There was almost no way, short of British intervention on their behalf, that the Confederacy could match the North's wartime production capabilities. When the war came, the Union naval blockade and poor Confederate finances forced the South to rely increasingly on its own meager resources. "King Cotton" proved disastrous for the southern war effort, as the North's industrial power became a decisive advantage.

Money

Wall Street, in New York City, was the financial center of the country. Manufacturing and a multitude of related businesses needed more capital than the South had to stay healthy. The South was almost entirely agricultural, so it did not create the demand for as much capital or currency circulation. The South only had one mint, which meant that specie (hard, coin money) was in very short supply once the Confederacy broke with the United States. More money and a strong manufacturing base were great financial advantages possessed by the North.

The Confederacy suffered serious hyperinflation during the war as a result of its desperate financial condition.

Transportation

Approximately 25,000 miles of railroad track crisscrossed the North on the eve of the Civil War. The 11 Confederate states possessed only about 10,000 miles of railroad track, and many of their railroad tracks did not connect more than a few locations. Poor planning and many year-round navigable rivers had produced an ad hoc rail system. The transportation advantage was crucial for the North in its invasion of the South. It enabled Union military supplies, and sometimes troops, to get where they were needed in a timely fashion. In contrast, the Confederacy's rail system left it with major logistical problems. With an already poor manufacturing base, this was devastating.

Organization of the Union Army

Before President Lincoln's first call for volunteers to put down the rebellion, there were approximately 16,400 federal troops in the professional army. Most of these soldiers were in the West to keep the peace between settlers and Indians. Lincoln called for 75,000 volunteers on April 15, 1861 for 90 days' service. On May 3, the president asked for 45,000 men to enlist for three years. Needing more men, Congress on July 4 asked for 500,000 volunteers. Few young men had experienced war firsthand, so they glorified war and enlisted beyond the quotas that the states were given. The earliest volunteers

Section	Number of Establishments	Capital Invested	Average Number of Laborers	Annual Value of Products	Percentage of Total Value
New England	20,671	$257,477,783	391,836	$468,599,287	24
Middle states	53,387	$435,061,964	546,243	802,338,392	42
Western states	36,785	$194,212,543	209,909	384,606,530	20
Southern states	20,631	$95,975,185	110,721	155,531,281	8
Pacific states	8,777	$23,380,334	50,204	71,229,989	3
Territories	282	$3,747,906	2,333	3,556,197	1
TOTAL	140,533	$1,990,855,715	1,311,246	$1,885,861,676	

FIGURE 16.3 - Manufacturing by Sections, 1860.

FIGURE 16.4 - The men in this picture are from Company E, 4th United States Colored Infantry.

saw no action because their enlistment expired before the first combat of the Civil War.

After the first Battle of Bull Run on July 21, 1861, Congress issued another call for an additional 500,000 volunteers as it became apparent that this would not be a short war. As the war proceeded, many young men learned about the real horrors of war: disease, poor medical care, food, and gruesome combat. The result was a significant reduction in the number of volunteers. Therefore, in March 1863, Congress was compelled to enact a military draft. The draft also applied to territories like the Oregon Territory. There were few exemptions allowed by the law. State and federally elected officials and the medically unfit were exempted, however. Also, men were permitted to hire their own substitutes or pay a $300 commutation fee and thus avoid military service. Late in the war, in February 1864, religious objectors were allowed to go into the medical corps. The military draft proved to be a great stimulus to volunteering. Only about 46,000 northern men were actually drafted and another 118,000 hired substitutes. This total only represented between 7–8 percent of the total number of Union soldiers who served

in the war, which was between 2.1–2.3 million men; sources vary because available records are not precisely accurate. The main reasons for the high percentage of volunteers included the fact that volunteers received a bounty, or bonus, given to enlistees. Volunteers could also avoid the ridicule of forced enlistment; peer pressure led many men to volunteer rather than face the draft.

Free blacks in the North were initially rejected as volunteers because of racial prejudice. However, there were a few attempts to recruit blacks by men like David Hunter and John C. Fremont. In August 1862, the War Department sanctioned the use of black volunteers. The Emancipation Proclamation, effective January 1, 1863, provided the impetus for the actual acceptance of black volunteers in the United States armed forces. A total of 178,895 black Americans served the Union. They generally served in non-combat roles, such as digging trenches, building fortresses, and cooking meals. The army segregated the black units, but their officers were white. There were pay differences between the two groups, but in March 1865, Congress eliminated this difference with raises and retroactive pay to the underpaid black soldiers.

Draft Riots

The military draft was something foreign to Americans, and there were those who protested this, even violently. The most infamous of the draft riots occurred in New York City in July 1863. Lasting about one week, the draft riots left 120 people dead and about $2 million worth of property damage. Racial tensions were also part of the reason for the draft riots. Immigrants, mostly Irish-Americans, attacked free blacks in the streets because the Irish worried that their jobs would be taken by black Americans while the Irish served in the army.

FIGURE 16.5 - Robert E. Lee.

Organization of the Confederate Army

Almost one-third of the nation's army officers left the United States Army in order to join the Confederacy. Chief among them was Robert E. Lee, who was destined to lead the Army of Northern Virginia throughout the war and to become the supreme Confederate military commander near its end. Lee personally opposed slavery and had serious doubts about the legality of secession. However, like many Americans, Lee felt an obligation to remain loyal to his home state, which was Virginia.

President Jefferson Davis on March 6, 1861, called for 100,000 volunteers to enlist for a 12-month period. Then in May of the same year, the Confederate Congress authorized an additional 400,000 volunteers. Some British nationals, like Frances Dawson, volunteered, mostly for the Confederacy. Although southern men did respond to the calls, it became clear after less than a year that the South needed a military draft.

On April 16, 1862, the Confederate Congress passed the first military conscription law in American history.

It drafted white men between the ages of 18 and 35 for a three-year period. However, there were a larger number of exemptions in the Confederate draft compared to the Union draft. Newspaper editors, state militia personnel, certain political officials, teachers with 20 or more students, and one white man on plantations with 20 or more slaves were all exempted. Southerners could also hire their own substitutes from those not of draft age or pay a $500 commutation fee to avoid military service. This led to cries that this was "a rich man's war but a poor man's fight." Eventually, the Confederacy dropped the substitute provision from its draft. In February 1864, the Confederate Congress amended the conscription law to include white men from ages 17 to 50, although 17-year-olds and those over 45 were reserved for defense of their states.

Between 800,000 and 900,000 men served in the Confederate armed forces during the Civil War. Patrick Cleburne, from eastern Arkansas, had proposed the drafting of slaves early in the war, but this idea was rejected on the grounds that slaves would be most unreliable as Confederate soldiers. However, the number of desertions and the desperate military situation late in the war forced the Confederacy to draft about 350,000 slaves in February 1865. These slaves saw no military action because the war ended too soon. Nevertheless, slaves were used by the South to dig trenches and carry out other manual tasks.

Army Desertions

The unpopularity of the draft resulted in at least 200,000 men deserting their Union brothers in arms and at least 100,000 from the Confederacy. The percentage of Confederate desertions was higher because the conscription law from a central government authority seemed incompatible with the southern view of states' rights above federal authority.

Soldiers who deserted on both sides did so for most of the same reasons. Highly individualistic Americans had no conception of military order and discipline. Family hardships "required" some soldiers to desert in order to return to the family farm. Some deserted repeatedly as a way to collect enlistment bonuses; these men were called "bounty jumpers." The very young often deserted because they were simply too scared to fight. Southern and border state draftees in the Confederate Army especially tended to desert late in the war, not wanting to be on the losing side. Deserters on both sides who were caught were usually shot, although some were pardoned, particularly if they were quite young.

Women in the Civil War

Although the Civil War did not revolutionize the role of women in American society, it increased the scope of activity of many women on both sides of the conflict. Women joined sewing circles to make clothing, socks, and other everyday items for the soldiers. Others sent baked items or vegetables and dried fruit to the troops to supplement army rations. And still others spent their time raising funds or gathering special items for the soldiers. Northern women sent so many gifts that the United States Sanitary Commission was created in order to centralize distribution of these "extras" for Union troops at the front. In contrast, the South had no centralized system for distributing donated materials.

Dorothea Dix, a mental health reformer, became the Superintendent of Nurses for the Sanitary Commission. Ms. Dix also raised morale by organizing the writing of letters. Army hospitals desperately needed nurses behind the lines or at the front, and many women volunteered without formal training. About 3,000 women served as nurses in the Union Army, including the famous novelist Louisa May Alcott, the author of *Little Women*, and the black abolitionist Harriet Tubman. The most famous Union nurse, however, was Clara Barton, whose valor on the actual battlefield earned for her the nickname

of "Angel of the Battlefield." Florence Nightingale, who had been a nurse during the Crimean War (1854-56) in Europe, led the fight for increased sanitation in the Union Army. Certainly, the nurses themselves also brought an added measure of cleanliness to military hospitals. A Confederate nurse from Richmond, Virginia ran a private hospital in that city during the war. She and her small crew heroically saved the lives of 1,260 out of a total of 1,333 wounded Confederate soldiers who came under her care.

Job opportunities expanded for women in the several arms plants and in government clerk positions. And many women on both sides of the war were forced to take over the family business or farm until, or if, the husband and/or sons returned home from the war. It was the Civil War that led to female domination in the fields of retail sales and elementary education.

Women in Uniform

Although soldiering was in the male sphere, at least 400 women, with numbers perhaps as high as 750, enlisted disguised as men. These rebellious women strayed far from their accepted role during this time. Their reasons for enlisting and fighting in the Civil War included staying with loved ones, receiving a bounty or paycheck, living for excitement, and acting upon their own patriotism. Both sides forbade the enlistment of women. However, military service records for both sides provide documented records of female soldiers. While some were discovered accidentally by their fellow soldiers and forced out of the army, many kept their gender secret. Discovery generally came from injury or capture during the war, or it came from the details of their lives written in obituaries and books years after the war. Some received pensions as rewards for their service, but most had to settle for the fulfillment of personal goals as payment.

Women as Spies

Perhaps the most glamorous role of women during the Civil War was that of the spy. Dozens of women served as spies because they had the advantage of not being as suspect as a man. Also, the long and often baggy female clothing style made smuggling of documents relatively easy. Some used their feminine wiles to accomplish their mission. Elizabeth Van Leu helped several Union POWs (Prisoners of War) escape from Libby Prison in Richmond, Virginia. The guards ignored her in her role as an eccentric woman.

Rose Greenhow was a Washington, D.C. widow with openly pro-Confederate sympathies who often socialized with U.S. government and military officials. She became so careless in collecting and passing on military secrets to the Confederates that she was finally arrested, taken to a military prison for a time, and then banished to the South. President Jefferson Davis later sent her to Europe on a diplomatic mission, but she drowned in a shipwreck on her return voyage.

The infamous Belle Boyd was initially a 15-year old western Virginia spy for the Confederate General "Stonewall" Jackson. During the war, she was sent to Europe on a Confederate mission. On the return voyage a Union ship captured the vessel. Nothing to fear; she promptly seduced and married the captain and lived until the 1880s.

POW Camps

Neither side expected to take many prisoners of war. The Confederacy took about 211,000 Union POWs, while the Union took about 462,000 Confederates. The numbers would have been higher, but prisoners were paroled on the battlefield because of the inability to handle them. This was especially true of prisoners captured by cavalry units. They would usually have their weapons confiscated and had to promise to leave the other's territory. Of the 211,000 prisoners taken by the Confederates, about 16,000 were paroled. And of the 462,000 prisoners taken by the Union, about 247,000 were paroled. This meant that there were about 195,000 Union prisoners actually held in Confederate POW camps and about 215,000 Confederate prisoners held in Union POW camps. These are total numbers, not the numbers actually held at any one time. Tragically, about 30,000 Union POWs died in Confederate camps, which is a death rate of about 15 percent. About 26,000 Confederate POWs, or about 12 percent, died in Union camps.

It became an accepted practice for the two sides to exchange prisoners. In general, prisoner exchanges hurt the Union more than the Confederacy since the South needed every man it could get. Prisoner exchanges were made on an equal basis per officers and enlisted men. There were two interruptions in this practice during the war. The first one occurred in December 1862, when the Confederates halted further exchanges for a while to protest General Benjamin F. Butler's execution of a pro-Confederate citizen in New Orleans, Louisiana. Butler had been the occupation governor in the city since its capture at the end of April 1862. Then in April 1864, the Union halted further exchanges until the Confederates agreed to exchange black prisoners on an equal basis with whites.

POW camps on both sides housed up to three different types of prisoners. Each side held political prisoners, such as spies, officers, and enlisted men. Some camps contained only enlisted men. A few held only officers, some held both officers and enlisted men, and a few held all three types of prisoners. Generally, the officers received better treatment by both sides.

Whatever the type of prisoner or prisoners held by a POW camp, the camp was very likely to suffer from poor sanitation and inadequate food, clothing, and shelter. That's why disease killed the vast majority of POWs who did die in the camps. Both sides also tended to appoint as POW camp commandants men who were unfit for combat. In addition, neither side made POW camps a top priority on their agenda, which is a real understatement. Neither the Union nor the Confederacy could brag about its POW camps, although the worst camp of all was a Confederate camp. A brief look at the two worst camps follows in the next two paragraphs.

Elmira and Andersonville Camps

Elmira Camp, located in Elmira, New York, was the home for this Union-operated POW camp. It opened late in the war, in May 1864, prepared to hold 5,000 Confederates. It eventually contained more than 12,000. Inadequate food and sanitation resulted in scurvy, smallpox, and pneumonia epidemics. The conditions inside the camp were intolerable, and if this were not enough, the town built an observation tower from which the citizens were encouraged to gawk and shout at the prisoners. Out of the total of 12,123 Confederate POWs at the Elmira Camp, 2,963 of them died. This was about 24 percent, the largest death rate among the Union POW camps. There were only four attempts to escape at Elmira.

Andersonville Camp, the largest and worst Confederate POW camp and the worst overall of any of the camps, was located in Andersonville, Georgia. This camp held mostly enlisted men. Enclosed by a large pine tree stockade fence, twelve feet inside the fence was the so-called "dead line." Prisoners who crossed that line were shot without question. There were no shelters unless built by the Union prisoners. Therefore, most POWs lived and slept in the open, including during the very rainy season as well. Sanitation problems were enormous, due to a tiny creek running through the camp, which first ran through the guards' area. This creek was used both for bathing and as a latrine, contributing to the disease epidemics there. Once, after a storm blew away debris, it revealed a spring, which the POWs dubbed "Providence Spring" because they gave God the credit for revealing it to them. The odds at Andersonville were fairly good that if you did not escape, you would die from disease or a bullet. There were 329 successful escapes through underground tunnels that would be dug, usually as a result of digging for water wells. About 13,000 Union POWs died at Andersonville Camp, mostly from disease, out of a total of about 32,000 prisoners. That was a record high death rate of about 40 percent.

War Time Scoundrels

There were three well-known scoundrels connected with POW camps. Major Henry Wirz was the Confederate commandant of the infamous Andersonville POW camp. He was responsible for "shoot to kill" orders aimed at prisoners crossing the so-called "dead line." He was tried and then hanged for war crimes after the war, the only person executed in conjunction for wartime decisions after the end of the war. Some believed that he was more of a scapegoat for all of the anger that was left unresolved at the end of the war. Regardless of the merits of Wirz's execution, Andersonville was indeed a grim camp, although with no resources it was not possible to do much more for the prisoners.

General Neal Dow was the only general held in any POW camp during the entire Civil War. He was held at Libby Prison in Richmond, Virginia. When Dow was released by the Confederates, he took a few trunks full of blankets with him instead of leaving them for his fellow POWs that he left behind.

E.W. Gantt had been an Arkansan hothead for secession before the Civil War began. But when he failed to advance from the rank of Colonel to Brigadier General, Gantt maneuvered his capture by Union forces. He then proceeded to change sides, like Benedict Arnold, in order to receive some of the spoils of war. He received several different positions in the post-war Arkansas Reconstruction government, although few on either side of the conflict respected him.

The Home Front

In most places outside the Confederacy, people were not unduly affected by the war in terms of physical necessities and comforts. There was less alcohol because of the need to use more of the grains for food. Of course, there was some social virtue in that fact. Only family farms and businesses which had been marginal before the war really did badly.

People in the Confederate states were not so fortunate, however. Southerners, because of a lack of manufacturing, depended on the northern states or foreign nations for many of their manufactured items. With all available manufacturing in the South diverted to the war effort, the loss of northern products and the Union naval blockade stopping most of the foreign goods from entering the South, times quickly became difficult. The Confederacy hoped that Great Britain would become an ally, but Britain stayed officially neutral in the war, and because of a long history of using naval blockades, increasingly honored the Union blockade. This cut off the Confederacy from not only imported goods, but also from raw materials that might have been used to produce war materials. Shortages, along with an inherently weak financial base, produced a staggering inflation rate. From the beginning of the Civil War in 1861 to the end in 1865, the aggregate (total) inflation in the Confederacy was 9200 percent.

Among consumer items deemed necessary, food, coffee, and tea were in critically short supply. The coffee shortage especially was irksome to Southerners. There were many attempts at producing coffee substitutes, but most people did not like them. Food shortages especially led to a number of alternative means to get around them. Bartering increased, with people trading goods they already had in order to "buy" other goods or food. An increase in home gardening occurred, but thefts of garden produce and farm animals also increased. Mass hunting parties and the movement of large armies drove the deer and other game away, so hunting was not much of a solution. Besides, most wagons were taken by armies, which meant people could not carry a kill very far. Of all the Confederate states, Texas was least affected by the naval blockade or by the entire war.

Northern Opposition to the War

There was more division in the North with regard to rationale for going to war. Most supported the prosecution of the war against the Confederacy in order to end the idea of secession and therefore keep the country united. In many ways, however, the nation had always had North-South differences. Relatively few saw the war as a means of ending slavery. A radical wing of the northern Democratic Party was against war with the South. These Peace Democrats, known also as Copperheads, were most active from eastern Illinois to western Ohio, as these were areas of citizens with southern roots. They created secret societies whose sentiments and activities sometimes crossed the line from loyal opposition to treason. For example, some of them cut telegraph lines and encouraged draft resistance and desertions. Others simply engaged in anti-war propaganda.

President Abraham Lincoln had already assumed the authority to suspend the *writ of habeas corpus* in the spring of 1861 in order to deal with some trouble in Maryland. Throughout most of the Civil War, President Lincoln used this suspension to arrest and jail Northerners who were even vaguely suspected of disloyalty. Congress argued that since authority to suspend the writ was located in Article I of the United States Constitution, the article outlining Congress' authority, only Congress had the constitutional right to suspend it. Thus, in March 1863, Congress passed the Habeas Corpus Act, which gave the president the authority to do what he was already doing, but it did impose certain limitations. For example, the names of all arrested persons must be given to the nearest district court. If the local grand jury did not indict the arrested person, and if the person took an oath of allegiance to the United States, then he must be released.

More than 14,000 Americans during the Civil War were arrested with no *writ of habeas corpus* required. The most famous case was the arrest of Dayton, Ohio newspaper editor Clement L. Vallandigham, who was the leading Copperhead in the state. He had publicly criticized President Lincoln's policy of having persons arrested without charging them with a specific crime. For this criticism, Vallandigham was himself arrested in April 1863 and found guilty by a military court for damaging the war effort. He was sentenced to jail for the duration of the Civil War. However, President Lincoln did not want to create a hero, so he commuted his sentence by sending him into the Confederacy, an action also taken on highly questionable authority. Vallandigham eventually escaped to Cuba, went to Canada, and returned to Ohio in 1864. At that time Lincoln decided it would be too much of an embarrassment to further harass Vallandigham, so he left him alone.

Southern Opposition to the War

During the middle of the war, Confederate Vice President Alexander Stephens went home to Georgia in protest of what he regarded as President Davis' dictatorial nature. From his home base, although still the Confederate vice president, Stephens continued to snipe at Jefferson Davis for the remainder of the war. Naturally, and yet ironically also, southern opposition to the war centered on Stephens, the second highest political official in the Confederacy.

Southerners resented military conscription and other sacrifices that were necessary if the South had any hope of winning the war. The bottom line was that most Southerners simply were unwilling to change their lifestyles in order to win. Added to that was the fact that radical secessionists used states' rights as vigorously against the Confederate States of America as they had earlier against the United States. One of the very principles the South was fighting for was largely responsible for the near disintegration of the Confederacy even before the war had ended. A key illustration of this fact was that Georgia Governor Joseph Brown, once a strong advocate of the Confederacy, placed all able-bodied white men in the state militia near the end of the war in order to prevent any of them from being subjected again to the Confederate draft.

Beginning in the border states, opponents of the war joined "peace societies." Like Copperheads in the North, these anti-war Southerners had secret codes, passwords, and meetings in which their sympathies and loyalties were expressed. The difference was that northern Copperheads expressed sympathies for the South, and the southern "peace society" members expressed sympathies for the Union. Late in the war, these "peace societies" seemed to appear in all the southern states.

President Jefferson Davis was not a gifted leader and was therefore incapable of keeping the Confederate states united in any meaningful sense of the word. Although he held grudges and strongly disliked many people, President Davis did not suspend the Confederacy's constitutional guarantee of the *writ of habeas corpus* until the Confederate Congress gave him authority to do so on February 27, 1862. Even with growing opposition and a crumbling Confederacy, Davis rarely exercised that emergency authority.

Financing the War

Union Financing

The Union, as well as the Confederacy, used a combination of three different mechanisms for financing its Civil War effort. It printed paper money, which accounted for about 13 percent of its direct war costs. It also raised taxes, which accounted for about 21 percent. Finally, it borrowed money through the issuing of government bonds, which accounted for the remaining 66 percent.

The Legal Tender Act, passed in February 1862, authorized the Treasury Department to print a new kind of paper money called greenbacks, thus nicknamed because of the green color. During the life of the Civil War, about $447 million in greenbacks were placed into circulation via four separate issues. Unlike earlier paper money issued by the national bank system—a system killed by the Andrew Jackson administration in 1836, when the charter for the Second Bank of the United States expired—these greenbacks were not backed by hard money (i.e., gold and silver) but by faith in the United States government. Greenbacks accounted for about 13 percent of the Union's total costs of the war.

In August of 1861, the first personal income tax in American history was enacted. The great percentage of federal revenues during most of our history before the mid-20th century came from tariffs and the sale of federal lands. Although this first income tax applied to incomes over $800 per year at a 3 percent rate, it was never collected. Only when Congress passed the Revenue Act of 1862, effective July of that year, creating the Bureau of Internal Revenue, did the federal government collect any income taxes. Its major provisions included a personal income tax of 3 percent for annual incomes between $600 and $10,000 and a rate of 5 percent on incomes over $10,000, revised in 1864 to 5 percent on incomes between $600 and $10,000 and 10 percent on incomes over $10,000. It also imposed a series of excise taxes on alcohol, tobacco, and a number of other manufactured goods and on most professional services. Finally, the Revenue Act raised the average tariff rates on foreign goods to between 47 percent and 50 percent. The tariff increase was partially designed to protect American industries from foreign competition, which would naturally increase during the war since war production needs meant that Americans would tend to buy more foreign products. It also would give American industries some relief from the heavy excise taxes. All these sources of tax revenues raised about $667 million for the war effort, financing about 21 percent of the war. The federal income tax was phased out by 1872.

The greatest source of financing for the Union's prosecution of the Civil War was borrowing money by the sale of federal government bonds. As with all bonds, government and corporate, the issuing institution receives payments to help its cash flow problems in return for promising to pay the principal and interest at a specified future time. The funds raised by the sale of government bonds totaled about $2.2 billion, which was about 66 percent of the total costs of the war.

Because a large sum of new paper money was placed in circulation during a brief period, and war production reduced the supply of consumer goods, inflation resulted. Average consumer prices in the North rose about 80 percent during the Civil War. However, because tax revenues were greater than the extra money supply, and Northerners gained new confidence in their future victory in the war, inflation in the North was not nearly the disaster it was in the Confederacy. At the same time, though, interest on the national debt created by the large number of government bonds sold continued to plague the nation well after the end of the Civil War. Even in the 1880s, interest on the debt equaled about 40 percent of the entire federal budget, while another approximately 20 percent of the budget went for Union veterans' pensions.

Since the demise of the Second Bank of the United States in 1836, the monetary system of the nation had been unstable. Without real national control of the money supply, the numerous state banks had been printing their own separate state bank notes (paper money). This confusion threatened Union finances during the Civil War. Therefore, Congress passed the National Bank Act in February 1863, offering national charters to state banks, making them national banks, in effect. These national banks could issue national bank notes for up to 90 percent of the value of the federal government bonds it owned. By the end of 1864, there were almost 500 national banks, with more than 1,000 state banks operating in the United States. When a March 1865 federal law placed a 10 percent tax on all state bank notes, the latter were gradually forced out of circulation by 1873. State banks remained, but they no longer issued their own bank notes.

Confederate Financing

The Confederacy also used the same three means to raise funds for their war effort. The key difference was that the Confederacy relied mostly upon the printing of paper money, which accounted for about 60 percent of its finances. Government borrowing via war bonds paid

somewhere between 35 percent and 40 percent of the war, and tax increases pulled up the rear with less than 5 percent.

Beginning in February 1861, the Confederacy printed paper money to help finance its war costs. Cities, states, and some private businesses, such as insurance companies, also issued their own paper currency. The Confederate government alone issued a total of over $1.5 billion during its existence. By 1863, the exorbitant supply of money in the southern economy had created huge price increases. More money in circulation provides suppliers of goods with the incentive to increase production in order to make more money. But when the money supply rises much faster than production can, the suppliers know they can charge higher prices because consumers are demanding their products.

Confederate war bonds were first issued in 1861. In that year, nearly all the gold owned by Southerners was soaked up by the Confederacy as people purchased the bonds with gold. With prices skyrocketing because of the excessive paper moneys in circulation, the interest rate promised on the Confederate bonds could not come close to keeping up with inflation. Thus, fewer persons bought bonds. In addition, fewer Southerners purchased bonds because they had little or no confidence that the institution issuing them would survive long enough to pay them off. And the longer the war continued, the more even Southerners admitted to themselves that it was lost. More than $880 million in bonds were issued by the Confederate government to finance 35-40 percent of the war effort.

In August 1861, the Confederate government had instituted a .5 percent (½ of 1 percent) tax on property, including slaves. That measure would have raised a huge amount for the government, but the government allowed the states to collect the tax and gave them a 10 percent rebate on what they collected. Only South Carolina, Mississippi, and Texas actually collected the property taxes. Issuing more state bonds was an easier action to take politically, given the traditional resentment toward taxes. However, it only contributed to a growing inflation rate in the South, making the money collected worth that much less. Therefore, despite the American tradition of resisting taxation, new taxes were enacted in

April 1863 in order to soak up excess consumer demand. The new Confederate law imposed a personal income tax of 1 percent on incomes ranging between $1,000 and $1,500 per year and up to 15 percent on incomes over $10,000. It also slapped an 8 percent sales tax on consumer goods, a license tax on many occupations, and excise taxes on nearly everything. Furthermore, the April 1863 law instituted a "tax in kind," a 10 percent tax on farm produce after a family's own food needs were met, in order to help feed the Confederate troops. This latter provision was especially resented by farmers. Despite all these measures, the Confederacy's enforcement provisions were almost nonexistent, resulting in only about $119 million, or less than 5 percent of the total Confederate war costs, actually being collected from tax revenues.

Legal Approaches to Abolishing Slavery

Most Americans outside the South were initially willing to reunite the nation on a half-slave and half-free basis, a return to the pre-Civil War status quo, in other words. President Abraham Lincoln also shared this view in the very early stages of the war. But abolitionists saw the war as an opportunity—indeed, as the means—to end slavery once and for all.

Abolitionists grew in numbers and voice as the war proceeded. Early in the war, however, they were successful only in getting passage of a limited anti-slavery bill. In August 1861, Congress passed the First Confiscation Act, declaring that property, including slaves, used in the Confederate war effort would be confiscated; such slaves would then be given their freedom. During the early part of the war, this law affected very few slaves because proof of use by the Confederate war cause was necessary to give slaves their freedom.

Slavery was abolished in the District of Columbia and in the territories in the spring of 1862. This did not have a great impact on United States territories because relatively few slaves were living in most of those western areas. However, this federal action did reflect the fact that more Americans were beginning to see the war as an opportunity to abolish slavery. Even Lincoln was beginning to understand that the nation could not remain half-free and half-slave, although he avoided explicitly making the abolition of slavery an official war aim in the early days of the war. Instead, Lincoln played politics with the slavery issue.

Congress passed the Second Confiscation Act in July 1862, replacing the first one. Property would be confiscated and slaves freed of those Southerners who actually participated in the Confederate cause as punishment for their treason. Again, it was unclear exactly how actual participation was to be determined. Despite this vagueness, President Lincoln was still unhappy about the bill, and he forced Congress to pass a resolution stating that heirs of traitors would not have their property, including slaves, confiscated. This would have meant that treasonous slave owners could simply transfer their slaves to their children, which in effect, meant that they did not lose them. After the war, most Southerners convicted of treason were given presidential pardons or blanket amnesty, so very little property was ever confiscated from the former Confederate citizens.

While the Civil War was still in its first half, President Lincoln showed his hesitance to openly make the war a means of abolishing slavery. When John C. Fremont, the 1856 Republican Party candidate for president, and David Hunter had recruited slaves in the South and proclaimed slavery abolished, President Lincoln countermanded their orders.

Then on September 22, 1862, just five days after the Union victory at Antietam Creek, President Lincoln issued a preliminary Emancipation Proclamation. Effective January 1, 1863, all slaves in rebelling states would be free. However, slaves in the loyal slave states of Delaware, Maryland, Kentucky, and Missouri, and in areas under Union Army control were not affected by this proclamation. Of course, slaves still under Confederate control could not easily make their freedom effective. The President purposely limited the impact of his Emancipation Proclamation for political reasons. He wanted to win and maintain the loyalty of Southerners in those areas that his armies controlled, which was most of Tennessee and virtually all of Arkansas and Louisiana. Nevertheless, the significance of the Emancipation Proclamation was that it made the abolition of slavery another official reason the United States was at war.

President Lincoln still dreamed that gradual emancipation in the loyal states, combined with colonization in Africa or Haiti with freed slaves, might be the ultimate solution to the slavery question. But efforts to revive the colonization effort failed. Then, and only then, did Lincoln see the need for a constitutional amendment to abolish slavery in the United States. The 13th Amendment to the Constitution, making slavery unconstitutional, was proposed while Lincoln was still president. It was ratified in December 1865, eight months after his assassination. Slavery was officially ended before 1866 saw the light of day.

War Diplomacy

The Confederate States of America (CSA) counted on "Cotton Diplomacy" to bring Britain, and hopefully France, into the war on their side. Britain was obtaining about 80 percent of its cotton for its textile industry from the American South before the war. However, the British had about a 700,000-barrel surplus of cotton as the Civil War began because of bumper crops in the South in 1859 and 1860. Other European textile manufacturers also had surpluses of cotton. As the Civil War continued, Britain was able to eventually replace its source of cotton from Egypt, India, and elsewhere. Nevertheless, France, under Napoleon III, announced in the spring of 1861 that it would officially recognize the Confederate States of America if England did so first. However, on May 13, 1861, the British declared their neutrality, so France never officially recognized the Confederate government.

In November 1861, a British mail ship, the *Trent*, was stopped in international waters by an American vessel captained by Charles Wilkes. Two Confederate commissioners traveling from Havana, Cuba to Europe, James Mason and John Slidell, were taken prisoners. The British protested the violation of international law since this occurred without a state of war between Britain and the United States and was in international waters, and the two men were released without apology, ending the crisis. Actually, the Confederacy would have had a better chance to get Britain into the war if the United States had kept the commissioners in a POW camp, making martyrs out of them. But that is precisely why President Lincoln decided to release them.

International law forbids neutral countries from shipping arms to belligerents on either side during a war. However, a major British shipbuilder supplied the Confederacy with a total of 18 raiding warships during the Civil War anyway. Those 18 warships sunk hundreds of undefended United States commercial ships in the Atlantic, Pacific, and even Indian oceans. The *Alabama* and the *Florida* were the two most famous Confederate ships, accounting for 102 naval victories together. Late in the war, in October 1864, the *Shenandoah* sneaked out of Britain to engage in a series of raids. A British ship met it in the Bering Sea in July 1865 and had to tell the crew that the Civil War was over.

During the Civil War, France, Britain, and Spain took advantage of our preoccupation with the war by sending ships and troops to Mexico, which was in debt to these countries. The British and Spanish left, but the French overthrew Juarez and replaced him with Maximillian, an Austrian named as Mexico's emperor. Despite this crisis, the "new" Mexico did not officially recognize the Confederacy.

Most British citizens were sympathetic to the Union during the war despite the fact that the upper class was more sympathetic to the Confederacy. When President Lincoln issued the full Emancipation Proclamation, effective January 1, 1863, making slavery an official reason for continuing the war effort, any remaining chances that Britain would join the Confederate cause was destroyed because popular opinion would never have allowed it.

General War Strategies

When Fort Sumter fell in April 1861, General Winfield Scott was the highest-ranking general in the Union Army. However, at the age of 75, he was too old for a battle command. As the ranking officer, General Scott proposed strategy recommendations for how the Union should prosecute and win the war. Known as the Anaconda Plan, after the South American snake that suffocates its victims to death, his plan called for a naval blockade of the Confederate coastline, the control of key North-South rivers, such as the Mississippi, Tennessee, and Cumberland rivers, and a gradual constriction by ground troops to squeeze the Confederacy into surrender. President Lincoln announced a naval blockade on April 19, 1861, although it wasn't very effective until the summer of 1863. Newspaper editorials and public figures in the North scoffed at Scott's Anaconda Plan as being far too slow. Nevertheless, that was ultimately the way in which the war was prosecuted and won.

On May 21, 1861, the Confederate Congress accepted Virginia's invitation to move the Confederate capital from Montgomery, Alabama to Richmond, Virginia, where it remained for the duration of the Civil War. Although the South counted on a fairly quick and easy victory, a contingent strategy developed after hope for a quick resolution was shattered. The Confederate war strategy was essentially two-fold. First, fight a defensive war so that the world would view the Confederacy as the innocent victim and hope for a stalemate until the North gave up. Second, pray that "Cotton Diplomacy" would bring foreign intervention on its behalf, especially Britain and/or France in order to protect their supply of cotton for their textile industries. There was indeed stalemate in many areas for the first half or more of the war. However, foreign intervention never came to fruition.

town, while the Union named them after significant geographical features whenever possible. Thus, the Confederates called this the Battle of Manassas.

Many of the politicians and socialites of Washington, D.C. literally came out to the expected battle site with picnic baskets in their buggies. Excitement was in the air because this represented an unprecedented opportunity to see history made before their very eyes. Anticipation was high that this first real battle would win the war in one stroke for the Union.

McDowell attacked without detailed maps of the area, but for a while the Union appeared headed for victory. But late in the day, Confederate reinforcements under General Joseph E. Johnston arrived. Although there is much controversy surrounding what happened next, Union troops suddenly began to retreat and then panic, with civilian onlookers scrambling to get out of the way. Northern newspapers called it "the great skedaddle." Some northern Christians concluded that God must have sent angels disguised as Confederate troops in order to prevent a quick Union victory in the war and punish the North for having so long tolerated slavery. Whatever the reason, it was a humiliating Union defeat. This Confederate victory left almost 2,000 total Confederate

The First Battle of Bull Run

General Pierre G.T. Beauregard commanded a large number of Confederate troops in northern Virginia, about 25 miles southwest of Washington, D.C. President Lincoln wanted to defeat his army and capture the Confederate capital of Richmond to end the war quickly. In fact, the Union goal in the East remained the capture of Richmond throughout the war. Lincoln ordered General Irvin McDowell to take the Union offensive against Beauregard's main force at Manassas, Virginia, about 100 miles north of Richmond, near a creek called Bull Run on July 21, 1861. The Confederates tended to name battles after the nearest

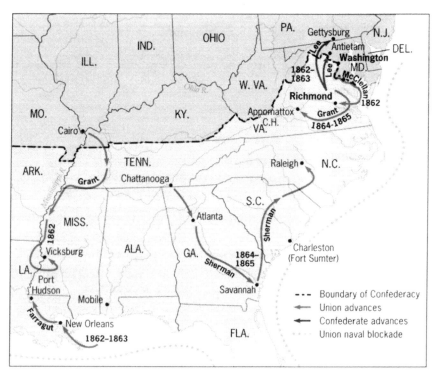

FIGURE 16.6 - Main Thrusts, 1861-1865.

casualties (killed, wounded, and missing) and about 2,700 total Union casualties. The defeat of the Union in the First Battle of Bull Run led many Northerners to believe that the war would be a long one after all.

During the battle, Confederate General Thomas J. Jackson, of Virginia, earned the nickname "Stonewall" after another Confederate officer rallied his own men by pointing to Jackson, saying, "Look, there is Jackson standing like a stone wall!" On the other side, General Irvin McDowell was demoted and the newly named Army of the Potomac was placed under the military command of General George B. McClellan. McClellan had been in charge of keeping Union control of the Baltimore and Ohio (B&O) Railroad line in northern and western Virginia, west of the Allegheny Mountains, and in controlling most of western Virginia. Fighting there had actually begun in May 1861 and had subsided about mid-July. But the First Battle of Bull Run had been the first significant battle of the Civil War. After Bull Run, General Robert E. Lee went to western Virginia to regain control, but he clearly had failed to do so by late October 1861. McClellan replaced General Winfield Scott as general-in-chief on November 1, 1861.

FIGURE 16.7 - General Stonewall Jackson

1862: War in the East

After the First Battle of Bull Run, the feeling that this civil war would be a longer war than most people had originally thought spread rapidly. Additional troops, military training, supplies, and strategic planning would be necessary, and these would take time. While the Union was engaged in these activities, the South continued its defensive posture. For these reasons, little fighting occurred for the remainder of 1861. But the next year would see sufficient battle action to satisfy any war hawk.

FIGURE 16.8 - Merrimack vs. Monitor.

The *Merrimack* vs. *Monitor*

Iron-plated ships, usually called ironclads, were developed early in the Civil War by the Union Navy and used in the western theater of the war. In an attempt to completely break the Union naval blockade of the East Coast, the Confederates raised the *Merrimack* at the Portsmouth, Virginia naval station, which they had occupied during 1861, and converted it into an ironclad ship. Although they renamed it the *Virginia*, the original name has stuck in history. On March 8, 1862, the *Merrimack* began wiping out wooden Union ships at the entrance to the Chesapeake Bay. Meanwhile, in October 1861, the Union Navy had contracted with a private company to build a super ironclad ship that would be superior to the *Merrimack*. This new ship, the *Monitor*, was completed just in time. On March 9, the famous battle between the *Merrimack* and the *Monitor* took place. Militarily, it was essentially a draw. In one sense, however, it was a strategic victory for the Union, which had successfully challenged the Confederate ironclad before the entire Union Navy in the East could be decimated.

Ironically, neither of these two famous ships survived the Civil War. The Confederates sank the *Merrimack* in May 1862 in order to avoid having it fall into Union hands at the time of the fall of Norfolk, Virginia. And the *Monitor* sank near the end of the war in bad weather off the coast of Cape Hatteras, North Carolina.

The Peninsula Campaign

In late January 1862, President Lincoln issued orders for General George McClellan to advance on Richmond by February 22, George Washington's birthday. However, McClellan persuaded the president that a peninsula campaign coming up from Richmond's southeast would be part of the best strategy for taking Richmond. The idea was for McClellan to move by ship from the Washington, D.C. area along the Chesapeake Bay to the tip of the Virginia peninsula. At the same time, General McDowell would move from Fredericksburg, Virginia, south toward Richmond.

General Stonewall Jackson's brilliant tactics in the Shenandoah Valley included a Confederate attack at Kernstown, a village just south of Winchester, Virginia, on March 23. While Jackson was rebuffed at Kernstown, President Lincoln was persuaded that the Confederacy had more troops west of the Fredericksburg-Richmond area than it actually had. Therefore, he ordered McDowell to stay at Fredericksburg in order to better protect the national capital, only 50 miles away.

Meanwhile, Confederate General John B. Magruder borrowed a page from Stonewall Jackson and moved troops and artillery around and faked McClellan into thinking he had more troops than he actually did on the peninsula. The result was that McClellan lay siege to Yorktown, Virginia, site of the decisive Revolutionary War battle, from April 5 through May 4. By then, Confederate General Joseph E. Johnston had moved the bulk of his army to the peninsula. By early May, the Confederates retreated in front of Richmond just as McClellan got his big siege guns in full place. McClellan was an excellent organizer and trainer of troops, but he was very cautious in battle. Lincoln came to say that he

FIGURE 16.9 - Peninsula Campaign, 1862.

had the "slows," and McClellan's moves in the peninsula seemed to demonstrate the veracity of that assessment.

Stonewall Jackson continued his diversionary moves from March 23 through June 9, so that Lincoln again had to suspend further plans to send McDowell toward Richmond. Thus, the real battles occurred in the peninsula during the first half of the year. Johnston attacked Union troops on the south side of the Chickahominy River, in what became known as the Battle of Seven Pines (the Confederates called it Fair Oaks) on May 31 and June 1, about five miles east of Richmond. The Confederates suffered about 6,000 casualties and the Union about 5,000. But the battle made McClellan even more cautious, while it emboldened the Confederates.

General Robert E. Lee replaced the wounded Johnston after the Battle of Seven Pines as commander of the newly named Army of Northern Virginia. Lee commenced to plan an attack on the north side of the river. On June 25, McClellan finally made his move with a large reconnaissance force. The next day Lee launched his attack, which finally ended in heavy Confederate losses from Union artillery and gunboats in the James River at

Malvern Hill on July 1. Thus, the maneuvers and fighting from June 25 through July 1 led to the battle being known as the Seven Days' Battle. The Confederates took almost 20,000 casualties and the Union about 16,500 casualties in that action.

While some of his generals wanted to pursue the weary Confederates and take Richmond, McClellan ordered a retreat to Harrison's Landing, near Petersburg. While there, "Taps" was written. On July 11, Lincoln brought General Henry Halleck from the western theater of the war and made him his new general-in-chief, replacing McClellan. In early August, General Halleck ordered McClellan and his men out of the Virginia peninsula.

Second Battle of Bull Run

General Henry Halleck ordered General John Pope, recently arrived from the western theater also, and McClellan to advance toward Richmond from the D.C. area. While moving into place, Pope was continuously teased by Stonewall Jackson. Pope attacked Jackson after he finally found him, on August 29. Before McClellan could arrive to reinforce Pope, Robert E. Lee ordered a counterattack against Pope's Union forces. The Confederate attack came on August 30, 1862, on Pope's flank, on almost exactly the same spot that the First Battle of Bull Run had been fought more than 13 months earlier. Like First Bull Run, this one was also a smashing Confederate victory. The Confederates suffered about 9,200 casualties while the Union suffered about 16,000. Union troops retreated to Washington, D.C., and John Pope was removed, with McClellan put in charge of actual operations in the eastern theater of the war, though Halleck was still the general-in-chief.

Antietam Creek

After the major Confederate victory in the Second Battle of Bull Run, General Robert E. Lee crossed the Potomac River in search of a great victory in Union territory, a victory which might get Britain and/or France to join the war on the Confederacy's side. However, Lee divided his forces temporarily, sending Stonewall Jackson to attack first at Harper's Ferry, Virginia. McClellan found out that Lee had divided his forces, but by the time he attacked the Confederates, Jackson had rejoined

Lee. The Union attack came on September 17 along Antietam Creek near Sharpsburg, Maryland. The Union had more than a two-to-one advantage with 75,000 men to Lee's more than 30,000 troops. But the Union took a greater number of casualties, more than 12,000 in contrast to Lee's approximately 11,000. In fact, this battle was the bloodiest single day of the Civil War, with the creek literally flowing blood-red by the end of the day. There were other battles in which a larger number of casualties were inflicted, but none of them was a one-day battle as Antietam Creek was. Despite heavier total casualties, Antietam was a strategic victory for the Union because Lee was forced to retreat south back into Virginia without a decisive win on Union soil.

The Union army was exhausted after the Battle of Antietam, and therefore McClellan did not pursue Lee to destroy his army. President Lincoln was constantly unhappy about the Union army's lack of pursuit after a battle, and while he was right about McClellan having the "slows," many historians believe he failed to understand how devastating this victory was. Nevertheless, after Antietam, Lincoln had McClellan reassigned to recruiting duties in New Jersey, never to fight again.

Fredericksburg

General Ambrose Burnside replaced McClellan as the commander of the Army of the Potomac in late 1862. Then Union troops under Burnside crossed the Rappahannock River in early December 1862 in order to attack Lee at Fredericksburg, Virginia. The Battle of Fredericksburg occurred on December 13, when Burnside attacked Lee. Although the Union army far outnumbered the Confederates at Fredericksburg, about 113,000 to 74,000, Lee's troops were well entrenched on a major hill on the western edge of the city, a place called Marye's Heights. The resulting battle forced the Union army to take about 12,500 total casualties as opposed to the Confederates' approximate 5,000. Fredericksburg was clearly a defensive victory for the Confederacy, forcing Union troops back across the Rappahannock River. During the rest of the winter of 1862-63, there was much fraternization between the two armies, trading supplies and singing songs across the river from each other. Traditionally, armies did not usually fight during the winter months.

Lee's victory at Fredericksburg illustrated how brilliant he was at fighting defensive battles. However, defensive victories do not really change anything, and unfortunately for the Confederates, Lee was not as adept at engaging in offensive military actions.

1862: War in the West

Shiloh

Kentucky state elections in the fall of 1861 were a victory for the Union side and gave it an opportunity to gain control of the Tennessee and Cumberland Rivers. General Albert Sidney Johnston took over command of Confederate forces in Kentucky, their entire Western Department, in fact, in 1861, with his headquarters at Bowling Green, Kentucky. Union forces in the state were under the command of General Don Carlos Buell. On September 6, 1861, General Ulysses S. Grant crossed the Ohio River from Illinois and occupied Paducah and Southland, Kentucky, at the mouths of the Tennessee and Cumberland Rivers. This action set the stage for Grant's campaign early in 1862 to drive the Confederates out of Kentucky and Tennessee.

Union forces under Grant captured Fort Henry on February 6, just south of the Kentucky-Tennessee border in Tennessee. Actually, gunboats on the Tennessee River, under the command of Flag Officer Andrew H. Foote, really caused the surrender. About 12 miles away lay Fort Donelson on the Cumberland River. Action to take that fort continued from February 13-16 by Generals Henry Halleck and Grant. On February 16, Fort Donelson fell to the Union. Halleck received the credit because he outranked Grant and was better at public relations than Grant. The capture of both these forts forced General Albert Sidney Johnston to abandon Kentucky and Tennessee and move into northern Mississippi at the railroad junction of Corinth. In the process of retreating south, Nashville, Tennessee surrendered to General Buell on February 25, the first Confederate state capital to surrender to the Union.

Grant pursued the Confederates south, but in March he regrouped and waited for Buell and others to reinforce

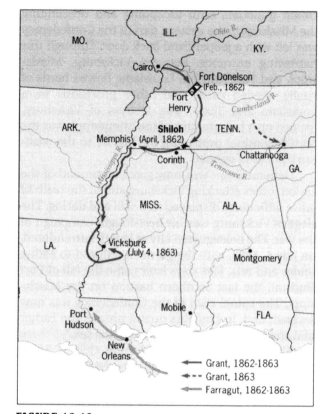

FIGURE 16.10 - The Mississippi River and Tennessee, 1862-1863.

him at Pittsburgh Landing, a steamboat landing on the Tennessee River, only 20 miles from Corinth, Mississippi. Johnston, however, refusing to wait until Grant was reinforced, moved north in early April to attack Grant's forces. The bulk of the Union army was camped in a large field called Shiloh, named after the little country Shiloh Methodist Church in it. Ironically, Shiloh is derived from a Hebrew word and essentially means "place of peace."

On April 6, the Confederates surprised the unprepared Union army before Buell had arrived. General Albert Sidney Johnston, however, died from a gunshot wound in his foot; he bled to death when he refused to leave the battlefield for the sake of his men's morale. General P.G.T. Beauregard took Johnston's place in the battle command. During the night of April 6, three of Buell's divisions arrived, and the next day Grant took the offensive. The Battle of Shiloh, April 6-7, was the worst bloodbath in United States history up to that time. Union casualties totaled between 13,000 and 14,000 men, while Confederate casualties totaled between 10,000 and 11,000 men. The total dead and injured at Shiloh exceeded all American casualties in the American

Revolution, the War of 1812, and the Mexican-American War combined. Yet by the end of the Civil War, Shiloh ranked only seventh in United States history in terms of battlefield casualties.

When the smoke from the rifles and cannons had cleared, Shiloh was a serious disaster for the Confederacy. General Halleck took Grant's place as field commander and drove the Confederates further into Mississippi after forcing them to abandon Corinth on May 30.

New Orleans

In April 1862, United States Flag Officer David G. Farragut went up the Mississippi River from the Gulf of Mexico heading for New Orleans. This was part of the Union Anaconda Plan to control the Mississippi River and help squeeze the Confederacy. After narrowly getting past two forts south of the city, one on either side of the river, Farragut arrived at New Orleans. The city was protected by only 3,000 Confederate militiamen because the Confederacy had not expected an assault from the south and had sent the bulk of Confederate forces north to fight at Shiloh. Therefore, New Orleans surrendered to Farragut on April 27 without firing a single shot, whereupon General Benjamin F. Butler brought troops into the city and occupied it. Thus the South's largest city and most important port was captured.

Farragut then sent a small fleet of Union gunboats further up the Mississippi River, capturing Baton Rouge, Louisiana, and then Natchez, Mississippi. Baton Rouge was the second Confederate state capital to fall to the Union. By the end of July, he had failed to take Vicksburg, Mississippi, however, because of its location on high bluffs. Meanwhile, the Union navy further north along the same river captured Memphis on June 6. After July, the Confederates reinforced the river valley for 200 miles from Vicksburg south to Port Hudson, Louisiana.

1862 Summarized

In the eastern theater of the war, centered in Virginia, the picture at the end of 1862 was a picture of stalemate. Neither side seemed capable of winning significant offensive battles. In contrast to the East, the western theater by the end of 1862 was far more successful for the

Union, which had gained control of Kentucky, western Tennessee, and most of Arkansas and Louisiana. Texas was basically isolated from the war, and all but 200 miles of the Mississippi River, from Vicksburg, Mississippi to Port Hudson, Louisiana, was in Union hands. On balance, then, the Union had been more successful in the West than in the East. The Confederacy's "success" by the end of 1862 must be confined to the statement that it had survived the year.

1863: War in the East

Chancellorsville

In late January 1863, General Joseph Hooker, nicknamed "Fighting Joe," replaced General Ambrose Burnside as commander of the Army of the Potomac. In late April, Hooker took about 70,000 of his Union troops far up the Rappahannock River, crossed it, and brought them southward and eastward to a position of eight to 10 miles east of Lee's Confederates near Fredericksburg, Virginia, at a place called Chancellorsville. In the meantime, about 40,000 Union troops remained across the river facing the 60,000-man Confederate Army of Northern Virginia. Lee recognized his predicament but gambled by dividing his forces. Leaving only about 10,000 men to defend Fredericksburg, Lee, along with Stonewall Jackson, moved the bulk of the Confederate forces west toward the larger Union force at Chancellorsville.

On May 1, about the same time that Lee was moving to meet him, Hooker moved his troops east about 2 miles into open country; the town of Chancellorsville was in the middle of a thick-growth area called the Wilderness. However, that same day, after advance Confederate units clashed with the Union troops, Hooker suddenly ordered a defensive retreat back to Chancellorsville inside the Wilderness. This was a terrible mistake because the heavy Union artillery and numerical advantage would be neutralized in the dense forest. No one knows for certain why Hooker ordered the retreat, but apparently he simply lost his nerve in the face of Lee's bold move. Then on May 2, Lee took an even larger gamble by dividing his forces again, this time sending most of them with Stonewall Jackson around Hooker's right flank about three miles west of Chancellorsville. If Hooker had discovered this move in time, the Union army could have easily blasted Lee out of the battle. But by the time he realized it was a serious Confederate maneuver, it was too late. Jackson attacked the evening of May 2, driving the Union forces further back by nightfall.

The next day, May 3, the numerically superior Union forces at Fredericksburg overran the Confederate forces there and threatened Lee from behind. Lee once again divided his force at Chancellorsville and turned approximately half of them around to face the enemy from the east. On May 3-4, the Confederates drove the Union troops across the Rappahannock River while Hooker, on Lee's west, did nothing despite his then overwhelming numerical superiority over the Confederate troops still left facing him. By May 6, when Lee was able to turn west and attack Hooker again, the Union army had actually retreated across the river.

In a series of daring moves, Lee's Confederate Army of Northern Virginia was able to defeat what had begun as an almost 2-1 numerical advantage for the Union army. Without General Hooker's incompetent actions, however, the Confederates would not have won the Battle of Chancellorsville. Union casualties were about 17,000 compared to about 13,000 Confederate casualties. A major blow to the South was the loss of Stonewall Jackson, who was accidentally wounded by his own forces the night of May 2 while he was riding his horse. His left arm was amputated, and he died of pneumonia on May 10. When he learned of Jackson's death, Lee said, "I have lost my right arm."

Gettysburg

Despite the Confederate victory at Chancellorsville, the Confederacy was still losing the war in the western theater and holding to a stalemate in the East. Also, despite the loss at Antietam Creek in September 1862, General Robert E. Lee persuaded Confederate President Jefferson Davis that only a successful major victory on northern soil could relieve the pressure in the West, especially at Vicksburg, where Grant had been building up forces since the fall of 1862. A major victory in the North could also possibly bring foreign intervention on behalf of the Confederacy. Lee's proposal to move north toward Harrisburg, Pennsylvania, was approved, and

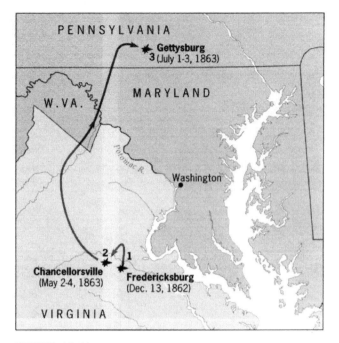

FIGURE 16.11 - The Road to Gettysburg, December 1862-July 1863.

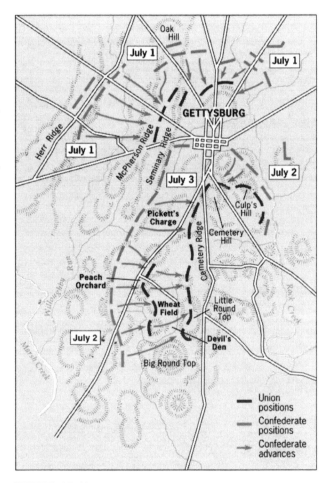

FIGURE 16.12 - The Battle of Gettysburg, 1863.

in early June, most of Lee's Army of Northern Virginia began to move. The Confederacy's most colorful cavalry leader, General James E.B. (Jeb) Stuart, spread his cavalry out in a maneuver designed to screen Lee's movements. On June 9, 1863, Union cavalry crossed the Rappahannock River and began the largest cavalry battle of the entire war at Brandy Station, near Culpepper, Virginia. Although surprised at Brandy Station, the Confederates did eventually win the battle, and Union cavalry forces moved back across the river. Meanwhile, Lee's Army of Northern Virginia moved west into the Shenandoah Valley, crossed the Potomac River, and moved into southern Pennsylvania.

In the meantime, General Joseph Hooker resigned and was replaced by General George G. Meade on June 28, 1863. Meade was nicknamed "Old Snapping Turtle" because of his infamous temper. Three days after assuming command of the Army of the Potomac, Meade fought the most decisive battle of the Civil War.

Lee's army moved into Pennsylvania and scattered out in the southern part of the state, foraging for food, shoes, and other supplies. For a time, neither Meade nor Lee knew with any degree of accuracy where the other one was, although Meade used his cavalry units more effectively and finally obtained better information than Lee did. On June 30, Confederate soldiers looking for shoes in the little town of Gettysburg, population about 2,400, spotted some Union cavalry units. The next day (July 1), when the Confederates returned to seize the shoes, the two sides clashed. Because Gettysburg was a town where about a dozen roads converged, Meade's cavalry officer there recognized its significance. Both sides immediately called for reinforcements, Lee's scattered army reunited, and the Battle of Gettysburg ensued.

On the first day of fighting (July 1), the Confederates forced the Union troops out of the town, where the latter eventually moved south and occupied the high ground on Cemetery Hill. Ironically, a sign posted on the cemetery gate read: "All persons found using firearms in these grounds will be prosecuted with the utmost rigor of the law." Meade now had the better defensive position amid the rocks and trees. On July 2, General James P. Longstreet advised Lee to move south of the Union troops and occupy a choice defensive spot between Gettysburg and Washington, D.C., thereby forcing Meade to attack them. Instead, Lee ordered attacks on both the Union army's left and right flanks, but both assaults had failed by the end of the day.

On July 3, the third day of the battle, Lee miscalculated badly and ignored Longstreet's protests to the contrary. Believing Union morale to be low from heavy losses the previous day and that Meade had weakened his center in order to fortify his flanks, Lee ordered General George E. Pickett's division to make a frontal assault at the center of Cemetery Ridge, straight across the open field that lay due west of the Union positions. The truth was that Union morale was quite high, and some of the best Union troops in the Eastern theater of the war were positioned in Meade's center ranks. The result was that Pickett's Charge was a total disaster, wiping out almost his entire division of 15,000 men. When General Lee asked Pickett to regroup his division after the failed attack, Pickett replied, "Sir, I have no division." Both men survived the Civil War, but even then Pickett never did forgive Lee for ordering the frontal assault at Gettysburg. The next day was the 4th of July, and Robert E. Lee's Army of Northern Virginia was retreating southward back to Virginia in the pouring rain. President Lincoln was unhappy about the fact that Meade did not chase Lee and finish him off, but after three days of fierce fighting, that may have been impossible anyway. Unlike his decision to fire McClellan after the latter had not pursued Lee's army after Antietam Creek the year before, Lincoln did not fire Meade.

Union casualties at Gettysburg were about 23,000 out of about 86,000 total troops, while Confederate casualties consisted of nearly 28,000 men out of an original force of about 75,000. The Battle of Gettysburg was the turning point in the Civil War. The Confederate defeat there killed any chance for foreign intervention helping to bail out the Confederacy, and after this, it would especially have great difficulty in replacing killed and wounded soldiers. Total Union victory in the war was now just a matter of time.

1863: War in the West

Vicksburg

After repeated failures to take Vicksburg during the winter of 1862-63, General Ulysses S. Grant persisted in his endeavor. Because efforts to go around Vicksburg and get to its south with sufficient supplies had failed, Grant decided to run his gunboats and supply boats right past the city. At the same time, he would march his troops on the west bank opposite from the city, and both troops and supplies would reunite south of Vicksburg. About mid-April 1863, Grant succeeded with minimum casualties in getting his Union army and supplies about 35 miles south of the city and then on the east side of the Mississippi River at Bruinsburg.

After Grant defeated a Confederate force at nearby Port Gibson on May 1, he changed his approach and ordered his men to carry as many supplies as they could because they were going to thereafter live off the land. Meanwhile, General William Tecumseh Sherman and Cavalry Colonel Benjamin Grierson hit the Confederates from the north and to the east of Vicksburg and Jackson, tearing up several miles of railroad track east of Jackson. Grant further confused the enemy by heading east for Jackson himself. After defeating the Confederates there and thus cutting off Vicksburg's supply line, the main Union force under Grant headed back west toward Vicksburg, the original target and the place where the major Confederate army was. By May 18, Vicksburg was surrounded on land and cut off on the Mississippi River side as well. General John C. Pemberton, a native Pennsylvanian who had sided with his wife's Virginia relatives, commanded about 30,000 Confederate troops inside the city.

Two land assaults against the very heavy defensive fortifications around the city, on May 19 and 22 respectively, resulted in heavy Union casualties. Grant then decided they would have to lay siege to Vicksburg, bombarding them from gunboats, and starving them into surrender. Thus began about a six-week siege of Vicksburg. Near the end, civilians were living in caves due to the many fires from the bombardment of the city. Soldiers and civilians alike were reduced to eating shoe leather, mules, and rats in order to survive. Near total starvation and exhaustion, General Pemberton formally

FIGURE 16.13 - Ulysses S. Grant.

surrendered the city on July 4, 1863, the day after Lee's defeat at Gettysburg. When President Lincoln heard the news of Vicksburg's surrender, he said, "Grant is my man and I am his the rest of the war."

Port Hudson

About 200 miles south of Vicksburg, Union General Nathaniel P. Banks began a siege of Port Hudson, Louisiana, on May 23, 1863, the day after Grant settled into a siege of Vicksburg. General Banks made two failed attempts to assault the city, one on May 27 and the other on June 14, and after that he simply waited for the siege to work. When Vicksburg surrendered on the 4th of July, the Confederates at Port Hudson had no choice but to also surrender, which they did on July 8. As of that date, with the occasional exception of snipers on the riverbanks, the Mississippi River was an unobstructed Union highway. This completed another major step in Winfield Scott's Anaconda Plan.

1863 Summarized

In the western theater before the summer of 1863 was over, the Union controlled the entire Mississippi River. In fact, for all practical purposes, the Union controlled the western theater of the war. In areas they did not control, they had managed to isolate Confederates from their comrades. Due to fighting in the eastern theater, by the end of 1863, the last hope of the Confederacy for foreign intervention had died. The remaining major battles, with the exception of Nashville, were largely confined to Georgia and Virginia.

The War in 1864

Because of General Grant's success at Chattanooga in November 1863, he was named general-in-chief of the entire Union Army on March 9, 1864. Grant headquartered with General George G. Meade, whose Army of the Potomac had won decisively at Gettysburg the previous year. Union strategy in 1864 basically focused on destroying the Confederate Army of Tennessee and Robert E. Lee's Army of Northern Virginia. General Joseph E. Johnston had replaced Braxton Bragg as commander of the Army of Tennessee after the Confederate defeat at Chattanooga. Grant ordered General William Tecumseh Sherman to pursue Johnston, while he used Meade's Army of the Potomac to pursue Lee. It has often been said that both Grant and Sherman designed a new strategy of attrition in 1864 by a policy of attacking, moving off, and attacking again. Actually, however, these tactics developed naturally as the result of Confederate defensive trenches and movements.

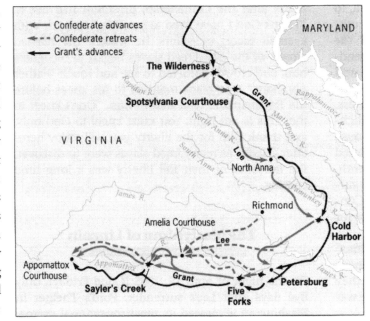

FIGURE 16.14 - Grant's Virginia Campaign, 1864-1865.

Battle of the Wilderness

Grant and Meade moved south and crossed the Rappahannock River in early May 1864 in yet another attempt to take the Confederate capital of Richmond. There in the Wilderness, west of Fredericksburg, Virginia, where the Battle of Chancellorsville had taken place just one year earlier, Grant and Lee met. The Battle of the Wilderness occurred on May 5-6 amid the forest, where repeated muzzle flashes set the underbrush on fire and hundreds of wounded soldiers died from smoke inhalation or fire. Grant's Union forces suffered more casualties than Lee's Confederates, but Grant kept up the pursuit. In the end, Union casualties in the Wilderness totaled more than 17,000 in contrast to about 11,000 Confederate casualties. Nevertheless, the Battle of the Wilderness had basically been a strategic draw.

Spotsylvania

Grant demonstrated President Lincoln's confidence in him by refusing to retreat after the military draw, as all previous Union commanders had done. Instead, after the Wilderness battle, he rested his men on May 7, and pursued Lee south toward Spotsylvania Courthouse, a few miles southeast of the Wilderness. Lee retreated through the Wilderness and arrived at Spotsylvania from the west; Grant's movement was to the east of Lee. By this move, Grant was attempting to get between Lee's army and Richmond, and force Lee to fight on ground of Grant's choosing. But an advance guard sent by Lee made it to Spotsylvania first and set up defenses there. From May 8-12, Grant repeatedly assaulted the Confederate defenses at Spotsylvania. Jeb Stuart, the Confederate cavalry hero, had once said, "All I ask of fate is that I may be killed leading a cavalry charge." He got his wish at Yellow Tavern, about five miles from Richmond, on May 12. But Grant failed to force the Confederates out as both sides suffered approximately 7,000 casualties in those five days of fighting. Another week of trying to maneuver around the Confederates brought the total casualties at and near Spotsylvania to about 18,000 for the Union and about 11,000 for the Confederates. Spotsylvania was a defensive victory for the Confederacy.

Cold Harbor

After failing to force Lee out of Spotsylvania, Grant next moved east and then south again. Lee now correctly guessed that Grant was attempting to get between him and Richmond, so the Confederates met the Union army at a crossroads called Cold Harbor, less than 10 miles northeast of Richmond, so named because the tavern there served only cold drinks and cold food. Fighting around Cold Harbor continued from June 1-3. In anticipation of battle the next morning, many Union soldiers pinned pieces of paper with their names and addresses onto their uniforms on the night of June 2, in order to help identify their bodies more quickly. One soldier wrote in his diary, "June 3. Cold Harbor. I was killed." When the Union assault began the next morning, fighting was as brutal as the soldiers expected. During the first 20 minutes of the Union assault on June 3, there were 7,000 Union casualties, in contrast to only 1,500 Confederate ones. Despite the numerical superiority of 50,000 to 30,000 for the Union, strong Confederate entrenchments outweighed it, and Grant was forced to move off yet again.

After Cold Harbor, Robert E. Lee sent General Jubal A. Early to raid the Shenandoah Valley in western Virginia, which had long been a source of food for the Confederates. But Grant ordered cavalry General Philip Sheridan to enter the valley from the north and stop the Confederates. In September 1864, Sheridan defeated Early and the Confederates at Winchester, Virginia. After that, the Shenandoah Valley was largely under Union control.

Petersburg

Grant's failure at Cold Harbor forced him to alter his strategy. He would have to head south and cut Richmond's railroad supply line at Petersburg before he could take the Confederate capital. Therefore, on the night of June 12, 1864, Union forces moved south toward Petersburg. For a while, Lee did not know where Grant was, a fact that gave Union engineers time to build a pontoon bridge across the James River east of Petersburg. By June 15, Union soldiers were crossing to the south side of the river, the Petersburg side, while Lee's Confederates were entirely north of the river.

Petersburg was defended by only 2,500 Confederates under General Beauregard's command and should have been taken before Lee could send reinforcements. However, Grant left the actual tactics against Petersburg to General George Meade. Meade bungled the job with poor communications. Low morale resulting from the battle at Cold Harbor was also part of the sluggishness in moving troops against Beauregard. In four days of

fighting (June 15-18), the Union army suffered about 11,000 casualties. By June 18, Lee had arrived (June 18) to heavily reinforce Petersburg, and both Grant and Lee began digging in along about a 25 mile line running north and south on the east side of the city.

One of the Pennsylvania coal miners in the Union army immediately facing Petersburg was heard to declare that they could blow a hole in the Confederate lines by digging a tunnel and planting a massive amount of explosives in it. The idea appealed to Grant, and he authorized the project. The soldiers in that area dug a tunnel about 511 feet, long enough to reach under the Confederate lines. It was then packed with four tons of gunpowder. About 4:40 a.m. on July 30, the powder was exploded, making a hole 170 feet long, 60 feet wide, and 30 feet deep. Confederates were blown into the air, and others in the area were stunned for a time. But confusion ensued, with many Union troops entering the area stopping to admire the engineering feat, which then gave time for the Confederate troops to regroup. This Battle of the Crater was a great opportunity to roll the Confederate lines and enter the city, but it was lost by sheer stupidity. Thereafter, Grant was forced to resume what turned out to be a nine-month siege of Petersburg, lasting from June 1864 to March 1865.

Sherman's March to Atlanta

About the same time that Grant was moving south to attack Lee's Army of Northern Virginia (May 1864), General Sherman began his march against Johnston's Confederate Army of Tennessee. Unlike Grant, Sherman was able to make a series of flanking moves that threatened the Confederate communications and supply lines. In this way, Joe Johnston was continuously forced to move south to protect those lines. Sherman's troops made a frontal assault on Johnston's Confederates at Kennesaw Mountain, in Georgia to the north of Atlanta, on June 27. When Sherman took about five times more casualties than Johnston did, he was forced to resume his flanking maneuvers.

Despite the Confederate defensive victory at Kennesaw Mountain, General Joseph E. Johnston came under increasing fire for his failure to take the offensive. His Confederate Army of Tennessee was outnumbered by

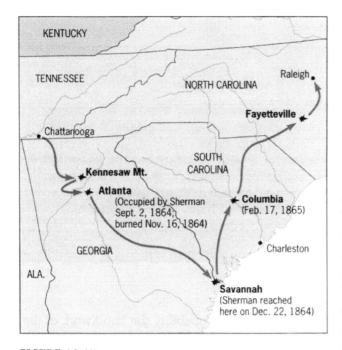

FIGURE 16.15 - Sherman's March, 1864-1865.

Sherman's roughly 90,000 to 60,000. Nevertheless, his avoidance of open battle became Confederate President Jefferson Davis' excuse to replace him with General John B. Hood on July 17. Davis had issues with Johnston from the beginning of the war.

With Union armies close to Atlanta, the capture of that city took on greater importance than simply smashing the Confederate army. Atlanta was a major railroad and manufacturing center in the South and would be a major prize and morale booster when taken. Sherman moved away from Kennesaw Mountain and toward Atlanta. On July 20, Hood attacked the flank of General George Thomas' Army of the Cumberland, which was present in support of Sherman, but failed to roll it up. That night, Hood retreated into the outer defenses of Atlanta. During most of August 1864, Sherman barraged Atlanta with artillery fire while laying plans to cut the railroad line south of the city. On August 25, Sherman outwitted Hood into thinking that Union forces were falling back. In reality, Sherman sent much of his own right flank in a counterclockwise direction around the city's south toward the rail lines there. While Union soldiers were destroying the rail lines south of Atlanta, Hood realized the danger of being surrounded and made his last attack on the 31st, at Jonesboro. When this Confederate assault failed, Hood's troops burned anything of military value in the

city and evacuated it on the night of September 1. The next day, September 2, Sherman marched into Atlanta and took the city. The fall of Atlanta greatly encouraged the Union armies and the northern population, while devastating the Confederacy.

The 1864 Presidential Election

Meanwhile, despite the war, 1864 was a presidential election year. Lincoln's Secretary of the Treasury, Salmon P. Chase of Ohio, wanted to be president of the United States. But Abraham Lincoln's popularity, fueled by Sherman's capture of Atlanta, destroyed any serious Republican opposition to Lincoln's reelection bid. Later, President Lincoln would appoint Chase as Chief Justice of the United States Supreme Court. The Republicans nominated the president, who selected the current military governor of Tennessee, former Tennessee Democratic Senator Andrew Johnson, as his running mate. Lincoln hoped to appeal to Democratic voters in the North and help prepare for a smooth reconstruction period once the Civil War was over. The Republican ballot labeled these men as candidates of the National Union Party in another attempt at influencing Democratic voters. But it was really only a cosmetic change.

The Democrats nominated General George B. McClellan, the former commander of the Army of the Potomac, whom Lincoln had fired after Antietam in 1862. McClellan expressed contempt for Lincoln even while commander of the Union forces. Although pro-Union, McClellan was a pro-slavery man who had opposed Lincoln's Emancipation Proclamation.

The Republicans campaigned against Democrats as traitors, telling voters that the Confederacy was hoping for a Democratic victory in order to negotiate a peace that would allow its permanent existence. In truth, Confederate leaders were hoping for just such a development. For their part, Democrats tried to play the race issue, accusing Republicans of fighting a war in order to mix the racial blood of the nation. Even vicious personal attacks on Lincoln were made, calling him an imbecile and an animal. And modern Americans think that politics has only recently gotten so nasty! But the Democrats never really caught on. The fall of Atlanta carried Lincoln to a landslide electoral victory, 212 to 21 electoral votes. Incidentally, some states allowed soldiers to vote by absentee ballot, although by no means all did. Also, Confederate states under Union control, such as Tennessee and Louisiana, were allowed to vote in the 1864 election.

Sherman's March to the Sea

After Hood's Confederates retreated from Atlanta, he moved north across northern Alabama into Tennessee, hoping to force Sherman to pursue him. But Grant persuaded Sherman not to chase Hood. However, Sherman did send General George Thomas back to Tennessee with about 30,000 troops, which defeated the Confederates at Franklin, Tennessee, and finally destroyed what was left of Hood's army in the Battle of Nashville on December 15-16.

Once Atlanta was captured, General Sherman issued an evacuation order to all its citizens. Although criticized by the city mayor and others, Sherman declared that he did not want to waste so many troops to guard against a hostile population. Sherman also was quite articulate about his view of war. "War is hell," he said. Furthermore, the Confederacy would have to learn that lesson if civil war were to be avoided in the nation's future. Therefore, Sherman advocated psychological warfare, the bringing of the war to the civilian population and cutting off their support from the Confederacy's military machine. Sherman asked Grant for permission to leave a group to guard Atlanta and then take the bulk of his army, live off the land, and attack so that he could "make Georgia howl!" With Hood's army and Confederate cavalry to Sherman's rear, Grant was skeptical of the proposal. So were President Lincoln's advisors, who also discussed the Sherman proposal. However, Grant already trusted Sherman, and the latter was very articulate. In the end, both Grant and the president gave their permission for Sherman's psychological warfare.

After burning about one-third of the city of Atlanta, General William Tecumseh Sherman left it on November 15 with about 62,000 troops, and began his 285-mile trek to Savannah, Georgia on the Atlantic coast. Sherman's men left a path of utter destruction averaging about 50 miles wide from Atlanta to Savannah. Averaging just over 10 miles per day, Sherman's troops burned the crops that they could not eat, houses, barns, and bridges.

They even tore up railroad track, heated them in large bonfires, and wrapped them around trees, for which they were quickly dubbed "Sherman's neckties." Only a few thousand Confederate cavalry and the Georgia militia could be mustered to harass Sherman, and they destroyed some of their own countryside in an attempt to prevent Sherman from living off the land. The Confederates were too few in number, however, to be anything more than a nuisance. Sherman's own estimate of damage inflicted on his March to the Sea was $100 million.

Sherman's army arrived at Savannah on December 10. Finding the fortifications heavy, Sherman sent a division south of the city to capture Fort McAlister on the Ogeechee River. Then the Union army began to close in on the city itself. The Confederates evacuated Savannah on December 21, before being trapped and seeing the proud city destroyed. The next day, December 22, General Sherman sent President Lincoln a telegram: "I beg to present you, as a Christmas gift, the city of Savannah."

1864 Summarized

By the end of 1864, it was obvious to nearly everyone that the Civil War was virtually over. Besides scattered and isolated troops in northern Louisiana and southern Arkansas and roaming cavalry units, only Robert E. Lee's Army of Northern Virginia remained. Nevertheless, despite 3½ years of fighting in Virginia, the capital of Richmond remained in Confederate hands.

The War in 1865

Sherman Marches into the Carolinas

In February 1865, General Sherman resumed his policy of widespread destruction by crossing the Savannah River and pushing north into South Carolina. He hoped to move all the way into Virginia and squeeze Lee's Army of Northern Virginia in between his own army and Grant's forces. On the way, Sherman's men burned more than a dozen towns. Georgia had indeed howled, but South Carolina would pay dearly for being the political instigator of secession and civil war. Destruction in that state was even worse than in Georgia. Columbia, South Carolina surrendered on February 17, and by nightfall it was in flames. Southerners accused Sherman's troops of setting fire to the city, while Sherman blamed retreating Confederates. Others have mentioned Wade Hampton, a South Carolina and Confederate cavalry officer (and politician after the war), as the culprit. The most likely explanation is that a combination of criminal elements, Confederate cavalry, and drunken Union soldiers was responsible for the blaze. Sober Union troops tried to put it out, and only a shift in the wind prevented the entire city from being engulfed. The next day, the city of Charleston, the Queen city of the South, which had been besieged by the Union Navy for almost two years now, finally surrendered.

From Charleston, Sherman took his army north into North Carolina. Since February 6, General Lee was general-in-chief of all Confederate armies. He promptly restored General Joseph E. Johnston to command and assigned him the impossible task of stopping Sherman from getting to Virginia. Johnston only had about 22,000 troops, while Sherman was soon to add another 30,000 from the North Carolina coast, giving him an even greater advantage over Johnston. The best hope lay in Johnston attacking Sherman before the latter was reinforced further. On March 19, 1865, Johnston attacked the Union army at Bentonville, near Raleigh. When Union troops dug in, the Confederates retreated north the next day. Sherman's army then moved east to Goldsboro for a much needed rest.

From Atlanta to Savannah (285 miles) and then from Savannah to Goldsboro (425 miles), Sherman's marches had left a broad path of almost complete destruction totaling about 710 miles long.

The Fall of Petersburg and Richmond

After nine long months of siege warfare along a stretch of some 25 miles or so east of Petersburg, the stalemate finally ended. Lee was anxious to try to join Joseph Johnston in North Carolina and combine their armies into one larger, more effective fighting force. Also, repeated Union cavalry raids by General Philip Sheridan in the Shenandoah Valley had already led to a severe shortage of food for Lee's men. He knew it was a gamble, but he also knew that defeat was certain if Sherman arrived to break the siege at Petersburg. To make his escape less risky, Lee attacked Grant's north flank on March 25. By this move, he expected Grant would send troops from his south flank to reinforce troops to the north, thus thinning the Union forces to the south of the city. But the Confederates were driven back without weakening the Union's left flank, and Grant then took the offensive. On April 1, 1865, Grant attacked the Confederates east of Petersburg at the Five Forks junction. The Confederates suffered 5,000 casualties in contrast to only about 1,000 Union losses. As a result of that defeat, Lee abandoned Petersburg and Richmond during the night of April 2. Leaving Richmond in flames, Lee's army made a desperate run for North Carolina.

Surrender at Appomattox

When the Confederates evacuated Petersburg and Richmond, they moved west toward the north-south railroad at Lynchburg about 100 miles away. On April 6, at Sayler's Creek, near Farmville, about 50 miles west of Petersburg and Richmond, 7,000 Confederates were cut off from their comrades and captured. Grant's army was in the process of encircling Lee's forces. General Philip H. Sheridan, the Union's best cavalry officer, moved his cavalry in front (west) of the Confederates on April 8. Lee made a final attempt to break through the surrounding enemy circle on the morning of the 9th. By then, however, he saw that the situation was hopeless. Rejecting suggestions from some of his subordinates to scatter and continue the war via guerilla warfare, Lee decided to surrender. Even Confederate President Jefferson Davis favored guerilla war rather than surrender. But on April 9, 1865, Lee arranged a surrender to Grant at Appomattox Court House, Virginia, about 30 miles west of Sayler's Creek. Interestingly, April 9 was Palm Sunday. The two men met in the home of Wilmer McLean. Ironically, McLean had lived in a house used as the Confederate headquarters during the First Battle of Bull Run in July 1861. After that battle, he had left northern Virginia in an attempt to get away from the clamor and violence of war. After Lee surrendered to Grant in his living room in Appomattox Court House, McLean allegedly declared that "the war began in my front parlor and ended in my living room." Indeed it had!

Grant offered generous terms to Lee's army, allowing his men to keep their sidearms, swords, and horses or mules. Only their rifle-muskets were confiscated. Then they were paroled, allowed to return to their homes on the promise that they would not take up arms against the United States. As Robert E. Lee mounted his famous horse Traveler, Union

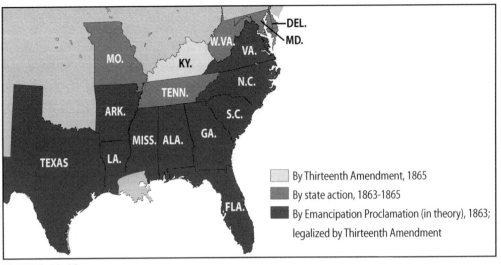

FIGURE 16.16 - Emancipation in the South.

troops started to cheer. Grant immediately stopped them with the words, "The war is over; the rebels are our countrymen again."

The End of the War

On April 18, 1865, General Joseph E. Johnston surrendered to Sherman in North Carolina, near present-day Durham. General Richard Taylor surrendered the remaining Confederate troops east of the Mississippi on May 4 in Alabama. Finally, the Army of Trans-Mississippi, headquartered at Shreveport, Louisiana, commanded by General Edmund Kirby Smith, surrendered on May 26. Nevertheless, Lee's surrender of his Army of Northern Virginia is considered the official end of the American Civil War because he was the Confederate general-in-chief at that time.

When Lee abandoned Richmond on the night of April 2, President Jefferson Davis had fled also, hoping to make his way to Mexico. However, he was captured in Georgia on May 10 and imprisoned for two years at Fort Monroe, Virginia, as federal officials contemplated whether to try him for treason or not. Finally, he was released without being charged in May 1867. After traveling abroad for about two years, Davis and his family returned to the United States. He worked for an insurance company in Memphis, Tennessee, which then went bankrupt. Even Davis' own history of the Confederacy did not sell many copies, and he was forced to rely on friends and relatives

in order to live out his remaining years. He never took an oath of allegiance to the United States, which would have given him his United States citizenship back. However, Congress later restored it to him posthumously in 1978. Jefferson Davis died penniless in 1899, broken in spirit as well as in pocketbook.

The Legacy of the Civil War

What were the major costs of the American Civil War? What was its impact? What legacy has it left Americans? Surely, these are the most difficult questions to answer about the war. The Civil War certainly was one of the intense experiences that defined us in so many different ways. One cannot adequately measure the legacy of war, particularly this one. Statistics simply will not do. Yet we are reduced to statistics and a few statements of general facts. The following sections represent a brief attempt to highlight the major legacy of the Civil War.

Militarily

Approximately 618,000 people died in the U.S. Civil War, out of probably a little more than 4 million men who served in some capacity at some time during the war. This death total was more than in all the American wars combined before the Vietnam War. Disease killed about 400,000 men, approximately twice as many men as actual combat. In addition, more than 400,000 wounded survived the war. The seven worst diseases were diarrhea or dysentery, pneumonia, malaria, typhoid-type fevers, measles, scurvy, and smallpox. There were two major underlying reasons that explain the high disease rate. First, a lack of knowledge about hygiene and how to treat specific diseases led to many disease deaths. The development of germ theory was just beginning in Europe in the 1860s. The science of bacteriology was still young, and its contribution to the identification of specific organisms that caused certain diseases was, for the most part, a couple of decades away. Of course, the development and use of antibiotics would have to wait until the 1930s and 1940s. A second major factor in the high disease death rate was an inefficient application of the medical knowledge that they did possess. Crowded camps, both for prisoners and for combat units, made it difficult to appropriately apply medical knowledge. Soldiers were often cramped in swampy areas infested with flies and mosquitoes, infecting the food and water supplies.

Economically

Many Northern-manufacturing companies earned extensive profits as a result of wartime production. These excess profits were largely available for new capital expansion in the post-Civil War period, which we call the American Industrial Revolution. The South's economy, on the other hand, was retarded for decades as a result of so much infrastructure damage and economic, political, and social chaos caused by the war.

The effect of the Civil War on the federal budget was also enormous. Even in the 1880s, about 40 percent of the budget was needed to pay the interest on the war debt. Another approximate 20 percent went to pay for Union veterans' pensions and bonuses. The Civil War's total cost perhaps exceeded $20 billion, about five times the total federal spending from the creation of the federal government through 1860.

Politically

Politically, the Union veterans became solidly Republican, and their organization, the Grand Army of the Republic (G.A.R.), the most influential wing of the Republican Party until near the end of the 19th century. Although the trend had begun the decade before the war, the Civil War helped cement the Solid South for the Democratic Party until the 1968 presidential election, with the exception of Dwight Eisenhower's two Republican victories in 1952 and 1956.

Socially

The Civil War helped breed deep resentment and hatred among many Deep South whites toward Yankees and black Americans. However, the effects of the modern civil rights movement, as well as an economic shift toward the South since the 1970s, have created a New South, with more moderate racial views. Old attitudes die hard, but they are finally dying, more than a century and a quarter after the Civil War.

Legally

The Civil War settled the question of whether or not a state could secede from the Union by clearly answering "No." The war also put an end, in effect, to the institution of slavery, which the 13th Amendment to the Constitution legally ratified in December 1865.

Perhaps the best tribute that could be paid to the brave men who fought on both sides of this great conflict was given by President Abraham Lincoln. On November 19, 1863, a new cemetery to honor the dead at Gettysburg, Pennsylvania was dedicated. Although Lincoln's words were specifically applied to those who died in the Battle of Gettysburg 4½ months earlier, they seem entirely appropriate to the war as a whole. The president incorrectly stated in his very short speech that "The world will little note nor long remember what we say here, but it can never forget what they did here." He closed his speech with the following words: "It is rather for us to be here dedicated to the great task remaining before us—that from these honored dead we take increased devotion to that cause for which they gave the last full measure of devotion; that we here highly resolve that these dead shall not have died in vain; that this nation, under God, shall have a new birth of freedom; and that government of the people, by the people, for the people, shall not perish from the earth."

Battle of Antietam, 1862; Confederate dead at Bloody Lane

Chapter 17 Contents

CHAPTER SEVENTEEN

Reconstruction: 1865-1877

Major Events

1865	Abraham Lincoln Assassinated
	Andrew Johnson began Presidential Reconstruction
	Thirteenth Amendment ratified
	Freedmen's Codes enacted in southern states
1866	Congress approved 14th Amendment
	Civil Rights Acts passed
	Ku Klux Klan founded
1867	Reconstruction Acts passed over President Johnson's vetoes
	Congressional Reconstruction
	Tenure of Office Act
	Southern states called constitutional conventions
1868	President Johnson impeached by the House, but acquitted in Senate trial
	14th Amendment ratified
	Most southern states readmitted to Union
	Ulysses S. Grant elected president
1869	Congress approved 15th Amendment
	National Woman Suffrage Association founded
1870	Ratification of 15th Amendment
1871	Ku Klux Klan Act passed
1876	Disputed election between Samuel Tilden and Rutherford Hayes
1877	Electoral Commission elected Hayes president
	Reconstruction officially ended

Introduction

On April 9, 1865, General Robert E. Lee, general-in-chief of all Confederate armies, surrendered to General Ulysses. S. Grant, general-in-chief of all Union armies. This surrender was the first of many that brought to a close four years of war. The Civil War, which had divided this country into North and South, was over, but the process of bringing unity to this country once again was just beginning. The process of reestablishing the correct and proper relationship between North and South was known as Reconstruction and included the following elements: politically bringing the South back into its proper place in the Union, physically rebuilding the South, and restructuring the South socially and economically to go forward without a slave system.

There were major stumbling blocks in the formulation of Reconstruction policies. First, the four years of bloody civil war—with approximately 618,000 killed and in excess of 400,000 wounded—left deep scars on the survivors of both sides. Second, the officials in control of the process did not have any precedents to follow. The United States had experienced neither civil war nor reconstruction before. Third, there was not a consensus in the nation or in the government on the future role of the freed slaves in American society. Finally, opinion was divided within the government and the public concerning how Reconstruction should proceed. Should the president or Congress control Reconstruction? Should the South be punished for attempting to secede from the Union? What rights should the former slaves have? Should some Confederate officials face execution? These questions required answers, but a consensus among the leaders of the nation was difficult to reach.

Democrats favored a quick and easy Reconstruction because the South was their base of support. Thus, they pressed for quick restoration of the rights of southern citizens and states without punishment.

The Radical Republican faction in Congress, led by Senator Charles Sumner of Massachusetts, Senator Benjamin Wade of Ohio, and Representative Thaddeus Stevens of Pennsylvania, favored a long and harsh Reconstruction to punish the South for its rebellion.

The Radicals believed the South should be treated as a conquered territory until the freedmen were protected from their former masters and the Republican Party controlled the politics of the South. Their programs to bring about radical changes in the South would take time.

The moderate Republicans, led by President Abraham Lincoln, favored a mild Reconstruction policy. They did not believe the South had left the Union. Because Lincoln and the moderates determined that secession had not occurred, the consequences for the South's actions should be mild. Lincoln's moderate views were hampered by ineffective moderate leadership in Congress.

This country faced serious problems immediately after the war. Although Union troops served as an occupation force in the South to protect the freed slaves and maintain law and order, thousands of Union soldiers had to be mustered out of the army. The federal government had to feed both whites and blacks in the South. The economy had to be placed on a peacetime footing as quickly as possible. Despite the immediate problems facing Congress, political reconstruction of the South was still a priority. Political rights for the Southerners and their state governments were invalidated at the end of the war. Government needed to exist in the South before social or economic reconstruction could begin. Deciding which branch of government would control Reconstruction became the next battlefield. President Lincoln, President Johnson, and Congress all wrote and attempted to implement a Reconstruction plan for the South.

President Lincoln's Plan

Reconstruction plans began before the end of the war. As the southern states were defeated by the Union armies, President Lincoln wanted to have a plan established so the states could take their proper place in the Union with speed and without punishment. Lincoln did not accept the notion that the southern states had seceded legally because he believed that secession was not constitutionally possible. With this premise in mind, he could afford to offer leniency to these wayward citizens.

On December 8, 1863, President Lincoln issued a Proclamation of Amnesty and Reconstruction. Any rebel state could form a government and take its rightful place with the other states once it had met the conditions of Lincoln's 10 percent plan.

The Conditions of the 10-Percent Plan

There was a general amnesty and restoration of property to all who took an oath of future loyalty to the Constitution and the Union. Some groups were exempt from the general amnesty, such as senior Confederate officers, civilian and diplomatic officers, and judges and congressmen who had formerly served the Union. Those individuals among the exempt groups had to apply to the president directly for a pardon.

When the number of those taking the oath reached 10 percent of the number of those who had voted in the 1860 elections in that particular state, this ten percent group could establish a state government. Lincoln believed that the loyalty of at least 10 percent of a state population was enough to begin reconstruction of a state.

State constitutional conventions would be called, delegates would be elected to the conventions, constitutions would be written, state governments would be established, and representatives would be elected to the national Congress. The new state constitutions would be required to abolish slavery.

By 1864, Tennessee, Arkansas, and Louisiana were under federal control and accepted the conditions of the 10 percent plan. These states organized new governments and elected representatives to the national Congress, but Congress refused to seat the members from the former Confederate states. President Lincoln strongly believed that his constitutional power to pardon gave him the authority to carry out his Reconstruction plan. But many in Congress, particularly the Radical Republicans, were resentful of the president's increased powers during the war and hostile to the southern states, so they refused to seat the members from the newly reconstructed states. It was believed that the 10 percent plan was too lenient, considering the enormity of the South's transgressions.

The Wade-Davis Bill

The Wade-Davis Bill was passed by Congress on July 8, 1864 as the Radical Republican effort to replace the president's plan. The battle then commenced between the executive branch and the legislative branch to control the reconstruction conditions for the southern states. The Wade-Davis Bill provided that (1) Congress, not the president, would administer Reconstruction; (2) a majority of a state's population must take an oath of future loyalty to the United States before a state government could be established; (3) a second oath, an "ironclad" oath, was required from southern males in order to vote or become a delegate to a state constitutional convention; this "iron clad" oath was a vow that the person had not voluntarily supported the Confederate side in the war; (4) important Confederate officials and military leaders were disenfranchised and could only be restored with a Congressional pardon; (5) slavery was abolished in the southern states; and (6) all Confederate debts were repudiated on the grounds that it was not fair for Southerners who had been loyal to the Union to help pay for the cost of a war which they had opposed. Lincoln pocket-vetoed the Wade-Davis Bill so that it did not become law.

Congressional opposition to President Lincoln's plans was based on a variety of motivating factors. Behind much of the opposition lay the fact that if the former slaves were now citizens to be counted as whole persons rather than three-fifths of a person (as the original U.S. Constitution had mandated for slaves), the population of each southern state would increase, and their representation in Congress would increase also. This meant the Southerners could control the political and economic life of the nation. The Republicans could not allow this.

Before the battle between Congress and Lincoln could be joined in earnest, Lincoln was assassinated on April 14, 1865, while attending a play at Ford's Theatre in Washington D.C. John Wilkes Booth, an actor who sympathized with the South, shot and killed the president. Lincoln's strong desire to see his country reunited could possibly have made the peace after the war easier. His words held such promise:

"With malice toward none; with charity for all; with firmness in the right, as God gives us to see the right, let us strive on to finish the work we are in; to bind up the nation's wounds; to care for him who shall have borne the battle, and for his widow, and his orphans, to do all which may achieve and cherish a just and a lasting peace, among ourselves, and with all nations." (Lincoln's Second Inaugural Address, March 1865)

Andrew Johnson Becomes President

Vice President Andrew Johnson became President with Lincoln's assassination. A skillful politician in his home state of Tennessee, Johnson did not have the political skills or power at the national level to carry out his own plan of Reconstruction, which closely resembled Lincoln's plan and defied the wishes of the powerful Radical Republican faction in Congress.

When Tennessee seceded from the Union, Andrew Johnson was serving in the United States Senate. Johnson did not believe that secession was constitutional and had stayed loyal to the Union, even though he was a Democrat from a southern state. Lincoln later appointed him military governor of Tennessee, once most of that state was in the hands of the Union army. In the 1864 election, Lincoln placed Johnson, a southern Democrat, on the Republican ticket as his vice-presidential running mate. Technically, the Lincoln-Johnson ticket had been labeled the National Union Party, but that name and Johnson's association with Lincoln was clearly an attempt to appeal to national unity and win Democratic votes.

Party leaders in 1864 did not truly consider what sort of president Johnson might make because Lincoln was in such good health. Andrew Johnson had many excellent political attributes, and under usual political circumstances, he probably would have been considered a fair president. After the Civil War, however, politics was not usual in Washington, D.C., and Johnson's political and personal failings soon came to overshadow his attributes. Johnson was a self-educated, intelligent man, devoted to duty and country. He was a good political speaker, but his style was suited to the politics of a rural state such as Tennessee.

FIGURE 17.1 - Andrew Johnson

Immediately after his ascendancy to the presidency, the Radicals in Congress believed Andrew Johnson was a new ally in their desire to delay Reconstruction in the South until the South was contrite for the war, the freed slaves were protected, and the Republican Party had gained more control of the South. Johnson talked of the Southerners as traitors, and traitors must be punished. Within a few weeks of becoming president, he changed his mind and pushed for a quick and non-punishing Reconstruction policy. He did not have the political or personal finesse to maneuver Congress to agree with his ideas on Reconstruction. He referred to Reconstruction as restoration. Johnson was inflexible, a man to hold grudges, frequently petty, and he used colorful language publicly to describe all of his political opponents. He was his own worst enemy; the more he spoke about Reconstruction, the more supporters he pushed to the side of the Radical Republicans.

Few presidents have been in as difficult a position as Johnson. He had to pull the country together after a war in which Americans had killed each other, instead of a common foe. Johnson governed in the shadow of a president who quickly took on the larger-than-life characteristics of a martyred leader. He did not have a political following in either the North or the South. Johnson had broken with the Democratic Party and was not accepted by the Republican Party. He was also a strict constitutionalist, which did not allow him much flexibility in his thoughts or plans. These difficulties do not excuse the president's poor judgement and failure to rise above his own personal failings. They merely are factors in understanding the whole story of the Johnson presidency.

President Johnson's Reconstruction Plan

Johnson put together his own plan based upon the moderate plan of Lincoln, with some modifications. Underlying Johnson's moderate plan was the theory that the southern states had never been legally out of the Union, so constitutionally, their relationship to the federal government was intact. Federal control of each state would last until loyal governments were established in each state. In the meantime, the decision was made that there would be no trials for treason of former Confederate leaders. And provisional civilian governors were appointed, except in Louisiana, Arkansas, and Tennessee. Johnson considered these states to be reconstructed already, just as Lincoln had announced earlier.

Among other provisions of President Johnson's plans were his proposals on how to deal with individuals who had rebelled during the war. On May 29, 1865, Johnson proclaimed a general amnesty for all Southerners who took the oath of allegiance to the country and the Constitution. Their political rights would thus be restored. However, there were 14 groups excluded from the general amnesty and required to request pardon from the president.

Those who must ask for pardons included civil and diplomatic officers of the Confederacy, state governors, general officers of the Confederate Army, former U.S. army and naval officers, former U.S. Congressmen and judges who went to the Confederate side, those who fled to Mexico, and Confederates whose taxable wealth in 1860 was $20,000 or more. This was Johnson's punishment for the rich aristocrats, whom he blamed for causing the war. Eventually, all Southerners who had held federal office before 1861 and who had afterward entered the Confederate service or gave aid and comfort to the rebellion were added to the groups that must ask for a pardon to have their political rights restored.

The eight states which Johnson did not consider reconstructed needed to elect members to conventions for the purpose of writing new state constitutions. The constitutional conventions had to invalidate their ordinances of secession, repudiate their state war debts, and declare slavery abolished by ratifying the proposed 13th Amendment. The 13th Amendment to the Constitution of the United States abolished slavery nationally upon its ratification on December 18, 1865. As to the issue of Confederate and state war debts, Johnson believed it would be unfair to use tax moneys from loyal Southerners to help pay debts accumulated by rebel governments which they had not supported. Specifically, this meant that war bonds issued to help finance the Confederate war cause would never be paid off; the loans to these governments would, in effect, become donations.

Elections were held in the southern states after the conditions of the president's Reconstruction plan were basically met. By the fall of 1865, civil governments were functioning across the South, except in Texas, and congressmen and senators were elected to take their places in Washington, D.C.

Many in the North criticized Johnson's mild Reconstruction plans because many believed that political Reconstruction should not occur until all problems between the North and the South had been resolved; the South was not remorseful nor reconciled to defeat; and the South still contained the spirit of rebellion.

President Johnson sent observers into the South to determine if the above northern objections were justified. He also received reports from Union military officers in the occupied South concerning the attitudes of the people. General Ulysses S. Grant, the Civil War hero for the Union, wrote these words to Johnson: "I am satisfied that the mass of thinking people in the South accept the situation of affairs in good faith." Other observers did not believe that the Southerners were repentant or that they had accepted defeat. But Johnson accepted the reports of those who believed the South was contrite and eager to resume their old position in the Union.

Congress Reacts

Congress met on December 4, 1865 for the year's session. Representatives and senators from the southern states were not officially recognized. Congress claimed that the status of these states was not yet decided because they had not been properly informed by the president of his plans nor had they approved their implementation. Therefore, the members from the southern states could not take their seats. A Joint Committee of Fifteen was formed to determine the Congressional position on Reconstruction. The Committee decided that the southern states had forfeited all rights due them under the Constitution and that their rights could only be restored by Congress. The states were intact, but their governments were not recognized as legitimate. Congress did not believe that the South was repentant; in fact, it seemed defiant.

Two situations in the South were particularly disturbing, and they were seen as signs that the war had not changed the attitudes in the South. Southern states had adopted Black Codes to control the freedmen, and many of the laws in the Codes seemed too much like a type of slavery. (See "Life in the South" in this chapter.) Also, Southerners sent former Confederate leaders as their representatives to Congress, including former Vice President of the Confederate States of America, Alexander Stephens, from the state of Georgia. But it was the Black Codes that were the final straw that led Congress to attempt to take over Reconstruction policy.

Thus, the battle lines were now clearly drawn between Congress and the president. Both branches claimed the right to write and implement Reconstruction in the South. One of the spoils of the battle was control over southern Reconstruction. The president made the first move with his 1865 Reconstruction plan. The radicals in Congress dismantled the presidential Reconstruction plan while also adopting measures to protect the freedmen in the South. Congressional Reconstruction would triumph over presidential Reconstruction, for better or for worse.

Congressional Reconstruction Policies

A series of confrontations between Congress and President Johnson began in early 1866. The confrontations dealt with the protection of the freed slaves in the South and political Reconstruction of the South.

Protection of the Former Slaves

Congress had originally created the Freedman's Bureau in March 1865 to help former slaves in their movement from slavery to freedom. The Bureau fed the hungry, built schools for the uneducated freedmen, and stepped in to protect their new rights. Congress passed a bill in February 1866 to extend the life of the Freedmen's Bureau beyond the first year, but Johnson vetoed it. This veto was one of Johnson's last victories over Congress. The Radical Republicans would soon possess the power to override all of Johnson's vetoes. Indeed, Congress passed another Freedmen's Bureau Bill on July 16, 1866. When Johnson vetoed this one, Congress quickly passed it over his veto.

The Civil Rights Act of 1866 declared African-Americans to be United States citizens and, as such, were entitled to "equality before the law." Johnson vetoed this bill too, but Congress overrode the veto on April 9, 1866. This was the first time in American history a major federal law had been passed over a presidential veto.

In June 1866, Congress passed the 14th Amendment on to the states for ratification. Congress decided a new constitutional amendment was needed to protect the rights of freedmen in the South. Congressional acts can be overturned by the Supreme Court as unconstitutional, and it was a real possibility that this might occur to the Civil Rights Act of 1866. The major provisions of the 14th Amendment are discussed in the next three paragraphs.

All persons born or naturalized in the United States were citizens with full rights. States cannot deny anyone life, liberty, or property without due process of law. States must give everyone equal protection under the law. This provision, of course, also applied to the freedmen.

If the right to vote was not granted to all males over the age of 21 (except for Indian males), that state would have its congressional representation reduced according to the percentage of potential voters who were denied their suffrage. In other words, if a state denied its African-American adult male population the right to vote, and African-American males made up 20 percent of that state's population, that state would lose 20 percent of its representation in the House of Representatives. It would also lose 20 percent of its electoral votes for presidential elections.

In other provisions of the amendment, anyone who had taken an oath to support the Constitution, and then supported the southern rebellion, could not hold a political office until pardoned by Congress. Also, southern states must cancel their war debts. And, of course, Congress could enforce this amendment with appropriate legislation.

President Johnson disagreed with the principles of the 14th Amendment and worked against the ratification of the amendment by urging the southern states not to ratify it. Ironically, Johnson's home state of Tennessee became the first state to ratify the amendment in July 1866, and it was readmitted to full standing in the Union. The ratification of the 14th Amendment by Tennessee, Johnson's home state, was another blow to the president's ability to persuade and thereby govern effectively. The 10 other former Confederate states refused to ratify the amendment, so Congress later made ratification of the 14th Amendment a condition for readmittance into Congress. The Radical Republicans were gaining support for a harsher Reconstruction, but they did not have enough votes from the other factions in Congress, particularly the moderate Republicans. The moderates still hoped to come to a compromise with Johnson, but the events of the summer and fall of 1866 made compromise impossible.

The 1866 Congressional Elections

As the Congressional campaigns began in the summer of 1866, it was clear that Reconstruction would be a major issue for the Republican and Democratic parties. A small group of conservative Democrats and Republicans hoped to support Johnson with the founding of a new political party, the National Union Party. A convention was called to meet in Philadelphia in August 1866. Johnson hoped the new party would bring northern support for his policies and neutralize the power of Congress in areas of disagreement between the executive and legislative branches. It did not. Events came together in the summer of 1866 that put a stamp of approval on the Radical Republican Reconstruction program and disputed Johnson's claims that all was well in the South. The result was that Northerners sent Republicans to Congress with a 3-to-1 majority over the Democrats.

Among the crucial events in the middle of 1866 that helped the Radical Republican cause was rioting by whites in the South. In May 1866, a quarrel in Memphis, Tennessee between whites and demobilized African-American soldiers broke into a general riot. White mobs moved into black sections, and at least 46 people were killed before it was over, with many white policemen joining the mob. In New Orleans, Louisiana, in July 1866, a white mob moved against delegates to an African-American suffrage convention. Johnson had approved an order by the mayor of New Orleans to stop the delegates from meeting, but the commander of the Union forces decided the convention should meet and had sent troops to protect the delegates. When the troops arrived, the mob had already killed 37 blacks. Both of these events were used by Radical Republicans as examples of the failure of Johnson's policies.

At the same time, the institution of the Black Codes in most of the former Confederate states (see "Life in the South"), seemed too much like slavery. Furthermore, the repudiation of the 14th Amendment by the southern states was another indication that the South was not accepting a new place for the freedmen in southern society. This was defiance of Congress that could not be tolerated. Were the Southerners defeated and willing to accept the freedmen as really free in their society? If nothing had changed in the South, then what had been the purpose of the war?

The actions of Andrew Johnson himself pushed people away from his policies. He campaigned against Republican candidates in his "swing around the circle," but his campaign tactics worked against him and his candidates and for those he opposed. He participated in shouting matches with hecklers; he traded insults with the crowds; he called the Radical Republicans traitors and other names. Thus, he threw away his chances to convince the northern Republicans he was right and Congress was wrong.

Congressional Political Reconstruction

The Radical Republicans gained the power to completely control Reconstruction with the Congressional elections of 1866. Thereafter, President Johnson's vetoes were simply overridden, as all hope of compromise between the two branches of government was gone. In terms of political Reconstruction, the Radical Republicans pushed through three significant Reconstruction Acts, each over the president's veto, and passed on the 15th Amendment to the states for ratification.

On March 2, 1867, Congress passed the First Recon-struction Act, also known as the Military Reconstruction Act, on its way to dominating Reconstruction policy after the congressional elections. The law dismantled Johnson's Reconstruction plan and substituted a congressional one in its place. While Tennessee was officially recognized as fully reconstructed, the other 10 ex-Confederate states were not. Those 10 states were to be divided into five military districts in order to protect all citizens and their property. A Union general was appointed to maintain law and order in each district, along with Union troops. The 14th Amendment, granting suffrage to African-American males and other rights to all freedmen, needed to be ratified by a state before its full readmittance into the Union. Eligible voters in each occupied state had to elect delegates to a constitutional convention to rewrite that state's constitution; this new constitution was required to include black suffrage. The constitution would then go to a direct vote of the people and for final approval to Congress. Eligible voters included all adult males who were not banned by the 14th Amendment. Only eligible voters could also serve as delegates to a state's constitutional convention, of course.

On March 23, 1867, Congress passed the Second Reconstruction Act, which ordered the five military governors to initiate voter registration and initiate the proceedings for the constitutional conventions. Then on July 19, 1867, with the Third Reconstruction Act, Congress declared that a majority of the votes cast, not a majority of the registered voting population, would be sufficient to bring about ratification of the 14th Amendment and readmission to the Union.

The 14th Amendment was ratified nationally in July 1868, in time for the presidential election. Four ex-Confederate states still refused to ratify the amendment— Texas, Virginia, Mississippi, and Georgia. The final four southern states delayed ratification long enough to have to ratify the new 15th Amendment along with the 14th in order to come back into their proper place in the Union. Georgia, the last state to ratify the 14th Amendment, did so in July 1870.

In a final action to support Reconstruction policy, Congress passed the 15th Amendment on to the states for ratification in February 1869. This amendment stated that states could not deny any adult male the right to vote because of race, color, or previous condition of servitude. Congress proposed the 15th Amendment to the Constitution because it wanted to make sure that the vote was not denied to the freedmen at a future time. The Republicans also needed the freedmen's votes for the development of a national party, and the freedmen needed their right to vote guaranteed to protect their rights against white infringement once the South was returned to southern rule. Congress also wanted to enfranchise northern African-Americans, who were not brought the right to vote by the 14th Amendment or the First Reconstruction Act of 1867. At the end of the Civil War, African-American men could vote in only five New England states. They could also vote in the state of New York, but only if they owned property. The 15th Amendment was ratified in March 1870. After that, white Southerners began using poll taxes and literacy tests in an attempt to prevent African-American voters from exercising their suffrage rights (See Chapter Five in volume 2 of *The American Journey*).

Andrew Johnson's Impeachment

Congress was successful in checking presidential power in the area of Reconstruction. With these successes

Congress decided to expand its power even further by taking away other rights of the president. In January 1867 there was an impeachment investigation of the president. The moderates on the investigating committee established there was no evidence of treason, bribery, or other high crimes and misdemeanors required by Article II of the Constitution for the impeachment of a president. So on March 2, 1867, Congress took further actions which they knew the president could not accept quietly. A rider was added to an army appropriations bill requiring the president to issue all orders through the general of the army. General Ulysses S. Grant was the general of the army at the time, and he also disagreed with the president's reconstruction policy. On the same day Congress also passed the Tenure of Office Act, which required the president to receive consent from the Senate to fire any government official the Senate had previously confirmed.

On August 12, 1867, the president suspended Secretary of War Edwin Stanton. Stanton was in agreement with the Radical Republicans on the issue of Reconstruction, and Johnson decided he could no longer tolerate this "traitor" on his cabinet. In response to the firing of Stanton without Senate approval, the House of Representatives in February 1868 established a committee to decide the charges to be brought against the president. Eight of the 11 impeachment charges made by the committee dealt with Johnson's violation of the Tenure of Office Act, an act that many doubt was constitutional in the first place. The full House of Representatives voted to impeach the president on February 24, 1868, by a vote of 126 to 47.

Impeachment, of course, is simply the bringing of formal charges against a political official; it is the political equivalent to the indictment in criminal proceedings. Impeachment, then, does not make anyone legally guilty. The Constitution provides that the House of Representatives may impeach a federal official like the president, but that the Senate must serve as the jury, with the Chief Justice of the United States Supreme Court acting as the presiding judge during the trial. The Senate began the trial of President Johnson on March 4, 1868, with Chief Justice Samuel P. Chase presiding. The trial lasted for almost 12 weeks before the final vote came. The Senate voted 35 to 19 for conviction, but

that was one single vote short of the two-thirds majority that the Constitution requires for conviction. Andrew Johnson was therefore not removed from office, but he did become the first United States president to be impeached.

One factor which may have played an important role in the legal acquittal of President Johnson concerned a personal feud between Chief Justice Chase and Senator Benjamin Wade. Both men were Ohio Republicans who had gotten in each other's way as they had climbed to power. Even former President Lincoln's appointment of Chase to the Supreme Court in 1864 did not lessen the hatred these two rivals had for each other. Under the laws then governing presidential succession in the event of the president's death, after the vice president came the president pro tempore of the United States Senate. But after Johnson had ascended to the presidency upon the assassination of Lincoln, the office of vice president remained vacant. Because Senator Benjamin Wade was the president pro tempore of the United States Senate in 1868, the conviction and removal of Andrew Johnson from the presidency would have automatically resulted in Benjamin Wade being sworn in as the next president of the United States. Chief Justice Chase could not tolerate this possibility. Therefore, Chase did everything he could in his statements and judicial rulings as the presiding judge in the trial of Andrew Johnson to place the president in the best light possible.

The story of Johnson's impeachment and trial illustrates human behavior on a collective scale. By 1868, the Radical Republican-dominated Congress was so angry with the president over what they perceived as obstructionism against their Reconstruction policies that the House of Representatives was determined to remove him from office. In all probability, the Tenure of Office Act was unconstitutional. Yet when Johnson fired Stanton because the latter supported Congressional Reconstruction, the House took its opportunity. They wanted a fight, and now they were going to force one. There are some historians who believe that President Johnson did not faithfully execute all aspects of Reconstruction law, which if true, might have been an impeachable offense. These historians believe that if the House had impeached him on these clearer constitutional grounds, Johnson may well have been convicted and removed from office. Of course, we will never know what the outcome would have been if different charges had been levied against the president.

What was left of President Johnson's influence was broken by his impeachment. He did not seek a place on the Republican ticket in the 1868 presidential election. The Republican Party searched for a different candidate and settled upon General Ulysses S. Grant. He was a leader of men and a war hero. What more could you ask for? General Grant won the election with the help of the votes of the freedmen. He was a great general, but he was not a great president. His administration became known for its scandals. (See Chapter Four in volume 2 of *The American Journey* for a discussion of President Grant's administration.) However, he did get along well with Congress on the issue of Reconstruction. Radical Reconstruction was carried out by Congress during Grant's two terms.

While it may be hard to understand why an impeached president would want to retain the presidency, Andrew Johnson hoped for the Democratic nomination in the election of 1868. The Democrats were not that ignorant of recent events, however. When Johnson failed to get the nomination, he returned home to Tennessee. There he unsuccessfully ran for Congress in 1869 and again in 1872. Persistence paid off, though, when the state legislature returned him to his old seat in the United States Senate in 1874. When he returned to Washington for the opening of the Congressional session in early 1875, Democrats controlled the House of Representatives for the first time since the Civil War. Johnson's feelings of personal vindication did not last long, for he died of a stroke on July 31, 1875.

Life in the South

The Civil War turned life in the South upside down for most Southerners. The African-American man and woman had to learn what freedom meant, and the southern white man and woman had to learn how to adapt to a society without slaves and a society of temporary northern dominance.

FIGURE 17.2 - Ulysses S. Grant.

Freedom for the Slaves

Approximately 1 million slaves were freed as the Union armies defeated the individual southern states. Then at the end of the war all were freed—approximately 3 million at this time. The 13th Amendment to the Constitution legally and constitutionally ended all slavery in the United States in December 1865. In the first months after the war, many of the freed slaves were not sure what to do with this gift of freedom, and their reactions to their new status were varied. Some stayed on with their old masters; some just took to the roads to sample life without dominance or to search for their families; and many moved to the cities. Black populations in many southern cities doubled or tripled.

It was a time of instability and unrest. The former slaves, now known as freedmen, suffered in this unorganized manumission. Deaths occurred from starvation, disease, and violence. Frederick Douglass, an African-American leader, criticized the manner in which the government set the slaves free when he said that "the freedmen were free from the individual master but a slave of society.

He had neither money, property, nor friends. He was free from the old plantation, but he had nothing but the dusty road under his feet. He was free from the old quarter that once gave him shelter, but a slave to the rains of summer and the frosts of winter. He was turned loose naked, hungry, and destitute to the open sky."

Movement of African-Americans to the cities brought concerns of increased crime and unemployment in southern cities and a labor shortage in the rural areas. The South was strongly agricultural, and the freedmen were needed to plant the crops and repair the damage from the war. Many were not working but were instead dependant on the Freedmen's Bureau to supply their needs while they waited for their "40 acres and a mule" from the government.

In 1865-1866, in order to retain control over the former slaves and to insure a labor supply to plant the barren fields of the South, Black Codes were passed by the former Confederate States. These state laws legislated what the freedmen could and could not do in the South. The following are a few examples of the various codes in the states: (1) they could sue and be sued; (2) they could own and inherit property; (3) they could testify in a court of law; (4) they could not vote; (5) they could not serve on juries; (6) they had to have permission to meet after sundown; and (7) they had to work, and many had to sign employment contracts. If an African-American man could not show he was employed, he could be arrested as a vagrant and his labor sold to whomever could pay his fine. These vagrancy clauses in the Black Codes amounted to an attempt to reimpose a type of slavery on the former slaves.

The codes were dismantled by Congress and the Freedmen's Bureau. Southerners did not believe the freedmen would work unless forced to work. Whites saw the fact that many freedmen were not working immediately after the war as confirmation of this long-held belief. Nor did they believe that African-American men had the intellectual capacity to make decisions without white control. Many in the South could not accept the sudden and complete freedom of those who had called them master a short time earlier. They would be forced to accept, for the time of occupation at least, many new roles for the freedmen.

To begin their new lives in the South, the freedmen knew they needed education and their own land. The Freedman's Bureau helped to a certain degree with both, but it had greater success in the area of education.

The Freedmen's Bureau

Officially titled the Bureau of Refugees, Freedmen, and Abandoned Lands, the Freedmen's Bureau was established on March 3, 1865. It was a bridge between slavery and freedom, and it provided many vital services. The Bureau officially functioned until 1869, but its educational activities continued until 1872. The Bureau's services included the following: (1) feeding refugees from both races; (2) drafting and enforcing labor contracts; (3) settling thousands of freedmen on abandoned lands; (4) settling points of law between freedmen and white Southerners; (5) establishing hospitals; and (6) establishing schools.

The Commissioner of the Freedmen's Bureau was General Oliver O. Howard. An assistant commissioner was appointed for each former slave state, and 550 local agents were appointed to carry out the mission of the Bureau. Most of the local agents were junior army officers. However, civilian agents were appointed, and some of these agents were former slaves. The dollars to support the Bureau's assistance to the freedmen were supplied by a tax on cotton. By 1869, the cotton tax brought in $68 million.

When the South resisted dealing fairly with the freedmen, especially in the judicial system, General Howard asked Congress for permission to establish special courts. The Freedmen's Bureau Bill of July 1866 gave the Bureau the power to establish military tribunals until the southern states were once again functioning in their proper roles. The courts functioned until 1868. Although southern whites criticized the Bureau for its interference in their daily lives, it brought assistance to the freedmen and helped stabilize them as a much-needed workforce. The Bureau later fell into disrepute through corruption and its political activities in using the former slaves to build the Republican Party in the South.

Education for the Freedmen

Freedmen's aid societies were organized during the war to assist the newly freed slaves in a variety of ways as southern states were defeated and then occupied by Union troops. One of their most important contributions was to begin a system of education for the African-American segment of southern society. An estimated 200,000 African-Americans were taught at the freedmen's schools during the war.

The Freedmen's Bureau worked with these societies to promote education for the former slaves after the war was over. The Bureau built schools and brought teachers to the South. The teachers included both white Americans and African-Americans. It is estimated that up to 20 percent of the 4,000 teachers were African-American. One-third of the Bureau budget from 1865 to 1870 was spent on education. Young and old alike went to school. Some schools even had to turn away those who wanted to learn to read and write. Education had been denied to slaves, and the freedmen knew it took education for them and their children to function in a free world. Schools were so important that the freedmen would use their own limited resources to build and support schools in areas where other agencies did not.

Institutions of higher education were founded also. Howard, Atlanta, and Fisk universities opened their doors in 1866-1867. Despite the promising advances in building schools, education for African-Americans lagged behind that of the whites. At the end of Reconstruction, at least 80 percent of the African-American population was still illiterate.

Land for the Freedmen

Most freedmen felt they must own title to their own land in order to achieve true freedom. There were those in the government, freedmen's aid societies, and the military who agreed. Several plans were formulated and a few implemented, but very little land was obtained by the freedmen.

The Confiscation Act of 1862, passed in July of that year, stated that those who actually participated in helping the Confederate cause would have their property confiscated.

Such confiscated land was to be given to freed slaves. However, at President Lincoln's insistence, Congress later passed a resolution declaring that any surviving heirs would not have their property confiscated. Therefore, the land was only the freedmen's until the heirs of the offender could claim it. Lincoln's amnesty proclamation of 1863 restored what relatively little land had been confiscated back to Confederate owners who took an oath of allegiance to the United States.

In 1865, Indiana Representative George W. Julian and Senator Charles Sumner proposed to give the freedmen 40 acres and a mule to begin careers as free farmers. The land would come from Confederate land taken under the Confiscation Act of 1862. However, their proposal was discarded for a system of rental property when the decision was made that heirs of Confederates could claim confiscated land. Confusion reigned about the alleged promise of 40 acres and a mule, and when the war was over, many former slaves refused to work for others because they were waiting for their 40 acres and a mule.

The Freedmen's Bureau was in control of some abandoned land on which some freedmen were settled. During the war, abandoned land had been seized, and land that southern owners had not paid their taxes on under the Direct Tax Act of 1861 was also confiscated. Land confiscated in the South Carolina Sea area was sold to freedmen, but this was the exception rather than the rule.

General William T. Sherman's Order No. 15 gave land along the coastal rivers in Georgia and South Carolina to freedmen, many of whom the Freedmen's Bureau had already placed upon the land. But President Johnson ordered the return of the land.

The Southern Homestead Act of 1866 was another attempt to give the freedmen the land that they so desperately needed. Forty-four million acres were set aside with the possibility to provide for individual grants of 80 acres to those who wanted them. Few took advantage of this program. Most of the land was of poor quality, and most freedmen did not have the capital to come to the areas and begin farms. Fewer than 7,000 used the Homestead Act, and only 1,000 completed the terms for ownership.

Too few in government were really committed to land ownership for the freedmen. Most were willing to give them political and constitutional rights, but when it came to giving land with which they might make their freedom viable, the politicians could not support it. This failure tied most of the freedmen, who knew nothing other than farming, to the land in another system called sharecropping. At the end of the war, there were thousands of whites with land and no one to work it, and thousands of freedmen who knew nothing other than agricultural work but had no money to buy land.

A variety of schemes were developed to provide workers for the land. There were some plantation owners who paid wages, but many wanted the freedmen to work in gangs under a boss. This was too much like their former work conditions under slavery and was therefore unacceptable. Some plantation owners paid cash for farm work, but there was not much cash in the South. Some freedmen did rent land from plantation owners, but too few had money. Therefore, a system of sharing tenancy was eventually worked out in the South. Share renting and sharecropping were eventually the most commonly used methods to get land to those who wanted to farm and workers for those who owned farmland. With share renting, the landowner usually provided the land and house only, and the share tenant usually paid out one-fourth of the crop as rent. With sharecropping, the tenant provided only his own labor and usually paid the landowner one-half of the crop in rent.

This system seemed to work out the problems of the agricultural South and get it back on its feet until cash and economic stability could be established. For a while, it did work. But the price of cotton dropped in the 1870s from the overproduction of this cash crop, and the country also went into an economic depression, produced by a number of other causes. This drove more farm workers, both freedmen and white, into sharecropping in order to make a living. By 1880, up to 80 percent of the land planted with cotton was farmed mostly by sharecroppers.

The rural South was also becoming a crop lien society, which increased the problems of the sharecroppers. Tenant farmers and sharecroppers placed liens on their crops to purchase necessary items from a local merchant until their crops were sold. The interest rate charged for the liens could run as high as 50 percent. Price gouging was also common. In the highly unlikely event that crops could be sold at a profit, the sharecropper had money left over after he paid the landowner and the local merchant (sometimes they were the same person) to save for his own small plot of land. If the crops could not be sold at a good profit, which was by far more common, the sharecropper owed more than he made. For many sharecroppers, farming became a cycle of debt and poverty from which they could not escape. (See Chapter Five in volume 2 of *The American Journey* for more information on the state of African-Americans after slavery.)

Government in the Southern States

Governments in the southern states during Congressional Reconstruction were originally controlled by the Republican Party. As the ex-Confederate Democrats regained their civil and political rights, they challenged and won control of state governments in the South again.

Republican Governments

Republican government in the South consisted of groups of carpetbaggers, scalawags, and freedmen. Carpetbaggers were Northerners who came to the South to live. The reasons the Northerners moved to the South were varied. Some came to buy inexpensive land or businesses and saw the South as a frontier, much as other Americans viewed the West. Union soldiers who had seen mild winters there during the war and the beautiful countryside came to live in a hospitable physical environment. Many others came to assist or teach the freedmen. And some did come to see what could be gained as a Northerner in a South dominated by Reconstruction governments. Southerners gave most of these northern immigrants the unflattering nickname of "carpetbaggers" because some came with so few belongings that everything they owned could fit into a carpetbag (cloth suitcase). Northerners were particularly considered carpetbaggers if they became involved in politics or the advancement of the freedmen. Whatever the motives were for these Northerners to journey south, they made new lives for themselves and began to participate in the government of their new communities. One out of every three offices in southern Reconstruction governments was held by a carpetbagger.

Scalawags were white Southerners who approved of and participated in Republican governments in the South during Reconstruction. Scalawags were considered traitors by southern white Democrats. However, scalawags also had a variety of reasons for rejecting the Democratic Party and supporting the Republicans. Some had favored the Union cause throughout the war and continued to support the party that demanded the Union stay intact. Others were opportunists who saw a chance for personal gain through political office. Working within the party in control of Reconstruction was a way for others to control some aspects of Republican rule in the South. The character and the motives of both scalawags and carpetbaggers were frequently, although not always, misjudged.

Freedmen made up the remaining constituency of Republican governments in the South. The motives of the freedmen for supporting the Republican Party were not as multifaceted as the carpetbaggers and the scalawags. They supported the government and the party that had given them freedom and continued to support their advancement in southern society. Freedmen were the backbone of the Republican votes in southern elections, supplying about 80 percent of the party's votes. Freedmen participated in the southern constitutional conventions, often called "Black and Tan" conventions because they were dominated by freedmen and what the more aristocratic Southerners called lower-class whites— small farmers who spent long hours in the hot sun and had developed significant tans. At one point, freedmen held almost 20 percent of the offices in southern governments. They were elected to state legislatures and sent 14 African-American congressmen and two African-American senators to the national Congress. Participation by African-Americans in the political process was an anathema to most white Southerners and was seen as dominance by many. In actuality, whites dominated the Reconstruction governments. Carpetbaggers made up approximately 30 percent of the officeholders, with the scalawags providing the remaining 50 percent. Only in South Carolina did African-Americans have a majority in a state legislature.

It was devastating for the South to have to accept Congressional Reconstruction when it thought it would have the easy restoration of President Johnson. When conditions to regain their proper place in the Union were stiffened, and Republican rule was the result of southern white disfranchisement, southern Democrats would not rest until their states were redeemed from what they called the "interlopers."

Redemption of the South by the Democratic Party

Most white Southerners wanted to redeem their states from the clutches of the Republicans inside and outside of southern governments. In order for redemption to occur—without another war, that is—the Democratic Party had to regain power in the South and then in the Congress of the United States. The Republicans dominated the present state of affairs in the nation, and without a rebuilding of the Democratic Party, there could be no challenge at the ballot box, which is the source of political power in a democratic republic. The ballot was the best hope for Southerners who wanted to resume controlling southern destiny. Ex-confederate leaders regained their political rights with individual presidential and congressional pardons and with mass amnesty acts. In May 1872, the Amnesty Act of 1872 restored political rights to approximately 150,000 former Confederate officials and left no more than 500 white southern men still unable to vote or hold political office.

Once the right to vote was restored to virtually all white Southerners, these Democrats began challenging the Republicans. In 1869, three years before the Amnesty Act of 1872, the Democrats were once again in control of Virginia and Tennessee. In areas with white-voter majorities, legal methods were sufficient to overthrow Republican rule in state after state. In areas with majorities of African-American voters, the Republican Party was not easy to oust from control, and white Southerners turned to illegal methods of intimidation, terror tactics, and in many instances, beatings or murder, to eliminate Republican support by both races at the ballot box.

The Ku Klux Klan

The Ku Klux Klan, which later spread terror to achieve its goal of white supremacy in the South, began very quietly as a social club in Pulaski, Tennessee in 1866. Six young ex-Confederate veterans were bored and decided they needed to form a small club to bring some amusement to their lives. They met, decided upon a name derived from the Greek word for circle (Kyklos), added Klan for alliteration, and ran around the house in sheets that inspired their later white-robed uniforms. At night, they began prowling the area near their homes, pulling pranks, and frightening anyone that happened to cross their path. Word of the antics of their group spread to other areas, and the club caught on. These clubs spread across the South under various names, including the Palefaces and the Knights of the White Camelia. Eventually the Klan had an organization that spread across the South, and the organized network became known as the "Invisible Empire."

The original group of young organizers tired quickly of aimless pranks and antics, and they began to find the intimidation of members of the African-American community particularly satisfying. The activities of the freedmen, such as owning land, going to school, voting, and running for office—in other words, attempting to gain true equality—were not to be tolerated. Vigilante groups rode at night to take back control of the South. They rode up to the cabins of freedmen in their ghostly white robes, maintaining that they were spirits of the dead. Some even cloaked their horses in white. Very few of the African-Americans believed these were visitors from the spirit world, but most were too afraid to let their intimidators know it.

Frightening African-Americans moved out of the realm of "fun" and into the realm of intimidation with a purpose by 1868. By this time, the former slaves were seen as a threat to the white supremacy of the South, and most southern white males could not accept that the freedmen were out of their "proper" place. Freedmen and the white Republicans, particularly the Union League, who promoted racial equality, taught the freemen to read, and pushed them to vote and run for public office, became the targets of the night-riding vigilante groups. Congress had dictated that the former slaves would have political

and civil rights in the South, and the occupation forces were there to make sure that this policy was carried out. The Klan, on the other hand, was intent on making sure that the Radical Republican plans for the South failed. Thousands of sympathizers of Reconstruction policy, people of both races, were beaten, mutilated, lynched, or murdered in other vicious ways by the Klan and other groups to stop Republican victories at the polls and to put the African-American man and woman back into their "proper" place in the South. That place was as a second-class citizen in subjugation to the white race.

The situation in the South became desperate. The activities of the Klan became so vicious that the leaders themselves attempted to disband the group in 1869. Republicans in the South begged the federal government to intervene and stop the night riders. President Grant pushed Congress to pass the Enforcement Acts to curb the vigilante groups, particularly the Ku Klux Klan, since it was so strong. Using the power given to them to enforce the 14th and 15th Amendments, Congress passed the first Enforcement Act on May 31, 1870. The act stated that interference with anyone's voting rights was a federal offense. The second Enforcement Act, passed on February 28, 1871, established that the federal government could organize supervision of registration and voting. The third Enforcement Act was passed on April 20, 1871, and was generally called the Ku Klux Klan Act. This third act gave the president the power to use the army to protect the civil rights of freedmen in the South, and to suspend the writ of habeas corpus where laws were not obeyed. With the Enforcement Acts, government infiltrators, and trials under federal jurisdiction, the federal government finally broke the organized power of the Klan, which disappeared "underground" until reemergence in the early 20th century.

President Grant was reelected in 1872 with a decisive victory over his Democratic opponent, Horace Greeley. (See Chapter Four in volume 2 of *The American Journey*.) His firm commitment to Reconstruction, even to the point of continuing the use of bayonet rule to carry out the dictates of Congress, was a positive factor in his campaign. Despite this fact, the importance of Reconstruction was already dwindling in the minds of many outside the South. By 1873, the country was moving into an economic depression. There were also problems in the West with the American Indian tribes, and many felt it was time to move on and let the freedmen take care of themselves. Most in the North felt they had done all they could do to guarantee the freedom of the former slaves. It was now up to them to find their own path in a new South. Most Americans were weary of the ongoing controversy and chose to escape by proverbially burying their head in the sand.

The Supreme Court and Reconstruction

The United States Supreme Court played an important role in the unraveling of Reconstruction. In its 1866 *Ex parte Milligan* decision, the Supreme Court ruled that military commissions could not try civilians in most places where civil courts existed. This ended the early practice of using military courts to enforce the Freedmen's Bureau Act. It also raised the question as to the legality of the entire Radical Reconstruction program. But in 1869, the Supreme Court, in *Texas v. White*, ruled that secession was impossible and that the Union had never been dissolved. The same decision, however, also stated that Reconstruction was constitutional because Congress had the power to protect the representative form of government in every state and to certify the legitimacy of any state government.

After the *White* decision, however, Supreme Court decisions in the 1870s contributed to the breakdown of Reconstruction by weakening the ability of the federal government to enforce 14th Amendment "due process" rights and the 15th Amendment's voting rights guarantees. (See Chapter Five in volume 2 of *The American Journey* for a more complete discussion of this process.)

An Assessment of Reconstruction: Historians Debate the Times and the Legacies

As time stretches forward from events of the past, historians develop varying interpretations of what happened and why. Known as schools of thought, experts develop a shared perspective of the past. Most historical viewpoints can be placed into Traditionalist and Revisionist schools of thought. Reconstruction is a case in point. The Traditionalists dominated the scholarly interpretation of Reconstruction well into the 20th century with their view of Reconstruction as a time of vindictive punishment from the North on a vanquished South. It was their contention that the North gained much from a humiliated South by plundering the region politically, economically, and socially. This is the basic assumption in the popular classic novel and film *Gone with the Wind*.

Writing in the mid-1900s, Revisionists developed a new perspective on the issue of Reconstruction. The Revisionists, labeled as such because they revised the older Traditionalist perspective, were able to distance themselves from the passions of the earlier writers on the issue and write without many of the biases and judgments of the earlier school. This is not to say that they did not have biases as well. But this new school of thought presented a more balanced view of Reconstruction. It was a time of struggle for both sides to work through the bitter feelings remaining from the most destructive of American wars, restore the political links of the nation, and build a new South with a place for the freed slaves. In the study of specific issues in the South from 1865-1877, the Revisionists challenged the assessments of the Traditionalists.

The Traditionalists laid the blame for higher state taxes and spending at the door of the Congress dominated by northern Republicans and the carpetbaggers and scalawags in the southern governments. This was supposedly an attempt to place the South in a permanent role of poverty and therefore submission. Revisionists countered that charge with the fact that, although taxes increased drastically after the war, in some cases up to six times higher, the physical damage to railroads, bridges, and public buildings warranted the increases. There were also new region wide public school systems needing funds. State taxes were, and remain, a primary source of revenue for these types of expenses. It was true that there were cases of corruption in Reconstruction governments and that several million dollars of taxpayer money was wasted. This corruption was overblown by critics, however, and there was certainly not a plot to keep the South economically dependent. That is apparent in the insistence of the northern-dominated Congress for the southern states to fund their own rebuilding and education programs.

One of the positive legacies of Reconstruction was the provision in the new southern state constitutions mandating universal education for all children of both races. Schools were expensive propositions. Before the war, only North Carolina had a real public education system, and it was judged second-best when compared to the systems of the northern states. Overall, education in the South lagged behind for several reasons. The pre-war South was dominated by the aristocrats who owned plantations, banks, and businesses and could afford private tutors or schools for their children. They saw no need to raise their property taxes to educate the children of the lower classes. The children of the slaves were forbidden an education by law. Education often leads to a middle class, which in turn might eventually threaten the political and economic power of this extremely powerful class. The wealthy elite had no wish to fund anything that they did not see as necessary or beneficial to their position.

Another difference between the two interpretations was their views toward the behavior of northern occupation troops and commanders. Traditionalists charged that the northern troops, with the support of the Republican Congress, treated the bowed and repentant Southerners with cruel contempt and maliciousness. Revisionists counter with the point that historically, occupation troops were not compassionate toward a former enemy. It was not uncommon in the past for conquerors to execute a majority of the remaining forces and confiscate whatever wealth the defeated possessed. The northern troops recently fighting in the field against many of these Southerners were generous, if not always kind, in their dealings with the former enemy. Only one southern officer was executed after the war for behavior during the conflict. Major Henry Wirz, commander of the infamous Andersonville (Georgia) prisoner of war camp, was hanged for war crimes; his camp was the worst of all of the POW camps, all of which were breeding grounds for despair, disease, and death on both sides. It was also a credit to American tolerance that the courts and the governments operating during northern military rule of the South appear to have usually dispensed justice fairly.

The Traditionalists alleged that Reconstruction forced political corruption upon the South, that freedmen controlled the governments of the South, and that Reconstruction legislatures accomplished nothing of lasting value. Revisionists agreed that corruption existed but maintained that corruption was the rule rather than the exception nationwide at the time, and historically the South was known for its political corruption from colonial times. The facts do not support the Traditionalist claim that the freedmen controlled the governments of the South. They did not serve in the office of governor in any state and held a majority only in the South Carolina legislature. A positive aspect of the legislatures of the time was passing laws that brought more equality to the South for all classes of whites as well as limiting the power of the aristocrats. These laws divided the tax burdens more equitably, provided for free public education, instituted charitable institutions, and advanced democracy. These reforms must have had value because when the Democrats regained control of the state governments, they were not overturned. On the national level, the most positive lasting contributions of Reconstruction were the 13th, 14th, and 15th Amendments.

Despite their many differences concerning the times, both groups classified Reconstruction as a general failure, although for very different reasons. Traditionalists stated it was a failure for what it allegedly did—plundering without mercy the assets of the South politically, economically, and socially. Revisionists maintained it was a failure because of what it did not do—failing to secure equality for the freed slaves or a protected environment for their freedom to take root and provide them with the claimed right of all Americans: "Life, Liberty, and the pursuit of Happiness."

The End of Reconstruction

By 1875, only Mississippi, Louisiana, Florida, and South Carolina were under Republican rule. In the off-year elections of 1875, Mississippi Democrats adopted the Mississippi Plan to take back that state. In the Mississippi Plan, physical intimidation—men with guns at polling places—and economic intimidation—the threat of the loss of jobs, especially for freedmen who voted Republican—placed the Democrats back in control of Mississippi that year. By the 1876 presidential election, Florida, South Carolina, and Louisiana were the only southern states still under Republican control.

In 1876, the Republican Party nominated Rutherford B. Hayes, the governor of Ohio. It was believed that the honest and upstanding Hayes would be the perfect candidate to counter the scandals of the Grant administration. The Democratic Party nominated Samuel J. Tilden, the reform governor of New York. When the votes were counted in November of 1876, Samuel Tilden claimed victory. However, there were disputes in the states of Louisiana, Florida, and South Carolina, with both parties claiming victory in these states. In those states, Democrats had adopted the tactics of the Mississippi Plan to attempt to win them, so the Republican-controlled election returning boards compensated by adjusting the vote count. Both parties obviously interfered with the election process in these southern states, casting doubt on Tilden's claim to victory and the will of the people of these states in the 1876 presidential election. Historians generally agree that if the black voters had not faced intimidation from Democrats, the Republicans would probably have carried each state. At the same time, if the Republican election boards had counted every vote cast for the Democratic candidate, that party could have clearly claimed victory in those states. There was also a dispute in the state of Oregon concerning the legality of one of that state's electors. A local postmaster was chosen an elector, although it was illegal for a federal employee to serve in that capacity. When that situation was made public in Oregon, the Democratic governor appointed a replacement; the other two electors, however, insisted that they had the legal right to name the third elector under those conditions. Altogether, the disposition of 20 electoral votes was at stake in the election—Louisiana (8), South Carolina (7), Florida (4), and Oregon (1 of its 3). Excluding these 20 disputed electoral votes, Tilden possessed 184 electoral votes, one short of winning the White House. Hayes' total of 165 votes left him 20 short of victory.

Article II of the United States Constitution states that Congress shall count the electoral votes and declare the winner in a presidential race. But the House of Representatives was controlled by the Democrats, the Senate was under Republican control, and the whole country was extremely tense about the delicate situation. Rumors of violence, and even a return to civil war, circulated throughout the nation. Under these conditions, Congress attempted to cool the crisis by passing the Electoral Count Act in very early 1877. This law created the Electoral Commission to determine how to allocate the 20 disputed electoral votes. The Electoral Commission was to consist of 15 members: five from the House of Representatives (three Democrats and two Republicans), five from the Senate (three Republicans and two Democrats), and five Supreme Court justices. In the latter category, four justices were specifically named in the law; and these four would choose a fifth member among the court—one who was fairly independent politically. They chose Justice David Davis. This selection meant that there were seven Democrats, seven Republicans, and one independent on the commission, which, of course, would have given Davis the deciding vote if the others voted on a strictly partisan basis.

Then an interesting twist of fate occurred. Davis wanted to be president of the United States. Unfortunately, the Supreme Court is not a place from which potential American presidents usually come. Therefore, David Davis resigned from the Supreme Court, and thus the Electoral Commission, in order to accept a seat in the United States Senate offered by his home state's legislature in Illinois. With little choice left, the four justices on the commission appointed Joseph B. Bradley, a partisan Republican from New Jersey.

When the Electoral Commission finally got down to business, it gave all 20 of the disputed electoral votes to Republican Rutherford B. Hayes on a partisan 8-7 vote. This gave Hayes the presidency by the closest of all electoral margins, 185 to 184. It also resulted in the collapse of the Republican governments in the three southern states with disputed electoral votes; there had briefly been great confusion there because each of two competing state governments attempted to claim it was the legitimate government. The Electoral Count Act stated that unless both houses of Congress overrode the Electoral Commission's decision, its verdict would prevail. By 4:00 a.m. on March 2, just two days before the presidential inauguration, Congress refused to vote to override.

Leaders of both parties wanted to avoid anything approaching civil war over this election. That proved to be the motivator for what history has termed the Compromise of 1877. Although many modern historians downplay the significance of this compromise, there was a behind-the-scenes agreement between Republican and southern Democratic leaders. This so-called Compromise of 1877 consisted of agreements on the part of President Hayes to give land grants and loans to build railroads across the South, federal subsidies to make improvements in the South, a cabinet member appointed from the South, and a presidential promise to withdraw all federal troops from the South.

During President Hayes' administration, few of the agreements were effectively implemented. However, Hayes had even promised during the presidential campaign that he would withdraw all federal troops from the South and end Reconstruction. (In this, Hayes and Tilden both agreed, so Reconstruction had not been a major issue in the campaign.) And this promise was kept by President Hayes when he ordered the withdrawal of the remaining few thousand troops in the South in April 1877, one month after his inauguration. Reconstruction was officially over for the South, although many of the problems of the era were not resolved.

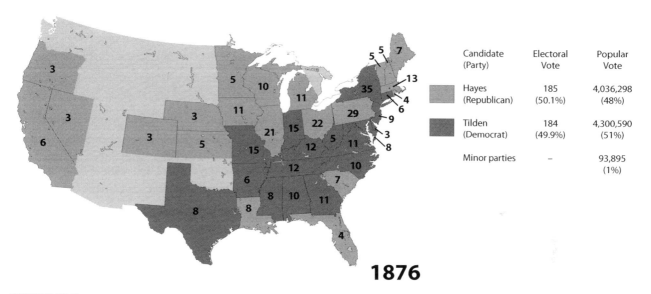

Candidate (Party)	Electoral Vote	Popular Vote
Hayes (Republican)	185 (50.1%)	4,036,298 (48%)
Tilden (Democrat)	184 (49.9%)	4,300,590 (51%)
Minor parties	–	93,895 (1%)

1876

FIGURE 17.3 - 1876 Presidential Election.

IN CONGRESS, July 4, 1776.

The unanimous Declaration of the thirteen united States of America.

The Declaration of Independence: A Transcription

IN CONGRESS, July 4, 1776.

The unanimous Declaration of the thirteen united States of America,

When in the Course of human events, it becomes necessary for one people to dissolve the political bands which have connected them with another, and to assume among the powers of the earth, the separate and equal station to which the Laws of Nature and of Nature's God entitle them, a decent respect to the opinions of mankind requires that they should declare the causes which impel them to the separation.

We hold these truths to be self-evident, that all men are created equal, that they are endowed by their Creator with certain unalienable Rights, that among these are Life, Liberty and the pursuit of Happiness.--That to secure these rights, Governments are instituted among Men, deriving their just powers from the consent of the governed, --That whenever any Form of Government becomes destructive of these ends, it is the Right of the People to alter or to abolish it, and to institute new Government, laying its foundation on such principles and organizing its powers in such form, as to them shall seem most likely to effect their Safety and Happiness. Prudence, indeed, will dictate that Governments long established should not be changed for light and transient causes; and accordingly all experience hath shewn, that mankind are more disposed to suffer, while evils are sufferable, than to right themselves by abolishing the forms to which they are accustomed. But when a long train of abuses and usurpations, pursuing invariably the same Object evinces a design to reduce them under absolute Despotism, it is their right, it is their duty, to throw off such Government, and to provide new Guards for their future security.--Such has been the patient sufferance of these Colonies; and such is now the necessity which constrains them to alter their former Systems of Government. The history of the present King of Great Britain is a history of repeated injuries and usurpations, all having in direct object the establishment of an absolute Tyranny over these States. To prove this, let Facts be submitted to a candid world.

He has refused his Assent to Laws, the most wholesome and necessary for the public good.

He has forbidden his Governors to pass Laws of immediate and pressing importance, unless suspended in their operation till his Assent should be obtained; and when so suspended, he has utterly neglected to attend to them.

He has refused to pass other Laws for the accommodation of large districts of people, unless those people would relinquish the right of Representation in the Legislature, a right inestimable to them and formidable to tyrants only.

He has called together legislative bodies at places unusual, uncomfortable, and distant from the depository of their public Records, for the sole purpose of fatiguing them into compliance with his measures.

He has dissolved Representative Houses repeatedly, for opposing with manly firmness his invasions on the rights of the people.

He has refused for a long time, after such dissolutions, to cause others to be elected; whereby the Legislative powers, incapable of Annihilation, have returned to the People at large for their exercise; the State remaining in the mean time exposed to all the dangers of invasion from without, and convulsions within.

He has endeavoured to prevent the population of these States; for that purpose obstructing the Laws for Naturalization of Foreigners; refusing to pass others to encourage their migrations hither, and raising the conditions of new Appropriations of Lands.

He has obstructed the Administration of Justice, by refusing his Assent to Laws for establishing Judiciary powers.

He has made Judges dependent on his Will alone, for the tenure of their offices, and the amount and payment of their salaries.

He has erected a multitude of New Offices, and sent hither swarms of Officers to harrass our people, and eat out their substance.

He has kept among us, in times of peace, Standing Armies without the Consent of our legislatures.

He has affected to render the Military independent of and superior to the Civil power.

He has combined with others to subject us to a jurisdiction foreign to our constitution, and unacknowledged by our laws; giving his Assent to their Acts of pretended Legislation:

For Quartering large bodies of armed troops among us:

For protecting them, by a mock Trial, from punishment for any Murders which they should commit on the Inhabitants of these States:

For cutting off our Trade with all parts of the world:

For imposing Taxes on us without our Consent:

For depriving us in many cases, of the benefits of Trial by Jury:

For transporting us beyond Seas to be tried for pretended offences

For abolishing the free System of English Laws in a neighbouring Province, establishing therein an Arbitrary government, and enlarging its Boundaries so as to render it at once an example and fit instrument for introducing the same absolute rule into these Colonies:

For taking away our Charters, abolishing our most valuable Laws, and altering fundamentally the Forms of our Governments:

For suspending our own Legislatures, and declaring themselves invested with power to legislate for us in all cases whatsoever.

He has abdicated Government here, by declaring us out of his Protection and waging War against us.

He has plundered our seas, ravaged our Coasts, burnt our towns, and destroyed the lives of our people.

He is at this time transporting large Armies of foreign Mercenaries to compleat the works of death, desolation and tyranny, already begun with circumstances of Cruelty & perfidy scarcely paralleled in the most barbarous ages, and totally unworthy the Head of a civilized nation.

He has constrained our fellow Citizens taken Captive on the high Seas to bear Arms against their Country, to become the executioners of their friends and Brethren, or to fall themselves by their Hands.

He has excited domestic insurrections amongst us, and has endeavoured to bring on the inhabitants of our frontiers, the merciless Indian Savages, whose known rule of warfare, is an undistinguished destruction of all ages, sexes and conditions.

In every stage of these Oppressions We have Petitioned for Redress in the most humble terms: Our repeated Petitions have been answered only by repeated injury. A Prince whose character is thus marked by every act which may define a Tyrant, is unfit to be the ruler of a free people.

Nor have We been wanting in attentions to our Brittish brethren. We have warned them from time to time of attempts by their legislature to extend an unwarrantable jurisdiction over us. We have reminded them of the circumstances of our emigration and settlement here. We have appealed to their native justice and magnanimity, and we have conjured them by the ties of our common kindred to disavow these usurpations, which, would inevitably interrupt our connections and correspondence. They too have been deaf to the voice of justice and of consanguinity. We must, therefore, acquiesce in the necessity, which denounces our Separation, and hold them, as we hold the rest of mankind, Enemies in War, in Peace Friends.

We, therefore, the Representatives of the united States of America, in General Congress, Assembled, appealing to the Supreme Judge of the world for the rectitude of our intentions, do, in the Name, and by Authority of the good People of these Colonies, solemnly publish and declare, That these United Colonies are, and of Right ought to be Free and Independent States; that they are Absolved from all Allegiance to the British Crown, and that all political connection between them and the State of Great Britain, is and ought to be totally dissolved; and that as Free and Independent States, they have full Power to levy War, conclude Peace, contract Alliances, establish Commerce, and to do all other Acts and Things which Independent States may of right do. And for the support of this Declaration, with a firm reliance on the protection of divine Providence, we mutually pledge to each other our Lives, our Fortunes and our sacred Honor.

The 56 signatures on the Declaration appear in the positions indicated:

Column 1
Georgia:
Button Gwinnett
Lyman Hall
George Walton

Column 2
North Carolina:
William Hooper
Joseph Hewes
John Penn
South Carolina:
Edward Rutledge
Thomas Heyward, Jr.
Thomas Lynch, Jr.
Arthur Middleton

Column 3
Massachusetts:
John Hancock
Maryland:
Samuel Chase
William Paca
Thomas Stone
Charles Carroll of Carrollton
Virginia:
George Wythe
Richard Henry Lee
Thomas Jefferson
Benjamin Harrison
Thomas Nelson, Jr.
Francis Lightfoot Lee
Carter Braxton

Column 4
Pennsylvania:
Robert Morris
Benjamin Rush
Benjamin Franklin
John Morton
George Clymer
James Smith
George Taylor
James Wilson
George Ross
Delaware:
Caesar Rodney
George Read
Thomas McKean

Column 5
New York:
William Floyd
Philip Livingston
Francis Lewis
Lewis Morris
New Jersey:
Richard Stockton
John Witherspoon
Francis Hopkinson
John Hart
Abraham Clark

Column 6
New Hampshire:
Josiah Bartlett
William Whipple
Massachusetts:
Samuel Adams
John Adams
Robert Treat Paine
Elbridge Gerry
Rhode Island:
Stephen Hopkins
William Ellery
Connecticut:
Roger Sherman
Samuel Huntington
William Williams
Oliver Wolcott
New Hampshire:
Matthew Thornton

The United States in Congress assembled shall also have the sole and exclusive right and power of regulating the alloy and value of coin struck by their own authority, or by that of the respective States — fixing the standards of weights and measures throughout the United States — regulating the trade and managing all affairs with the Indians, not members of any of the States, provided that the legislative right of any State within its own limits be not infringed or violated — establishing or regulating post offices from one State to another, throughout all the United States, and exacting such postage on the papers passing through the same as may be requisite to defray the expenses of the said office — appointing all officers of the land forces, in the service of the United States, excepting regimental officers — appointing all the officers of the naval forces, and commissioning all officers whatever in the service of the United States — making rules for the government and regulation of the said land and naval forces, and directing their operations.

The United States in Congress assembled shall have authority to appoint a committee, to sit in the recess of Congress, to be denominated 'A Committee of the States', and to consist of one delegate from each State; and to appoint such other committees and civil officers as may be necessary for managing the general affairs of the United States under their direction — to appoint one of their members to preside, provided that no person be allowed to serve in the office of president more than one year in any term of three years; to ascertain the necessary sums of money to be raised for the service of the United States, and to appropriate and apply the same for defraying the public expenses — to borrow money, or emit bills on the credit of the United States, transmitting every half-year to the respective States an account of the sums of money so borrowed or emitted — to build and equip a navy — to agree upon the number of land forces, and to make requisitions from each State for its quota, in proportion to the number of white inhabitants in such State; which requisition shall be binding, and thereupon the legislature of each State shall appoint the regimental officers, raise the men and cloath, arm and equip them in a solid- like manner, at the expense of the United States; and the officers and men so cloathed, armed and equipped shall march to the place appointed, and within the time agreed on by the United States in Congress assembled. But if the United States in Congress assembled shall, on consideration of circumstances judge proper that any State should not raise men, or should raise a smaller number of men than the quota thereof, such extra number shall be raised, officered, cloathed, armed and equipped in the same manner as the quota of each State, unless the legislature of such State shall judge that such extra number cannot be safely spread out in the same, in which case they shall raise, officer, cloath, arm and equip as many of such extra number as they judge can be safely spared. And the officers and men so cloathed, armed, and equipped, shall march to the place appointed, and within the time agreed on by the united States in congress assembled.

The united States in congress assembled shall never engage in a war, nor grant letters of marque or reprisal in time of peace, nor enter into any treaties or alliances, nor coin money, nor regulate the value thereof, nor ascertain the sums and expenses necessary for the defense and welfare of the United States, or any of them, nor emit bills, nor borrow money on the credit of the united States, nor appropriate money, nor agree upon the number of vessels of war, to be built or purchased, or the number of land or sea forces to be raised, nor appoint a commander in chief of the army or navy, unless nine States assent to the same: nor shall a question on any other point, except for adjourning from day to day be determined, unless by the votes of the majority of the united States in congress assembled.

The congress of the united States shall have power to adjourn to any time within the year, and to any place within the united States, so that no period of adjournment be for a longer duration than the space of six months, and shall publish the journal of their proceedings monthly, except such parts thereof relating to treaties, alliances or military operations, as in their judgement require secrecy; and the yeas and nays of the delegates of each State on any question shall be entered on the journal, when it is desired by any delegates of a State, or any of them, at his or their request shall be furnished with a transcript of the said journal, except such parts as are above excepted, to lay before the legislatures of the several States.

Article X. The committee of the States, or any nine of them, shall be authorized to execute, in the recess of congress, such of the powers of congress as the united States in congress assembled, by the consent of the nine States, shall from time to time think expedient to vest them with; provided that no power be delegated to the said Committee, for the exercise of which, by the articles of confederation, the voice of nine States in the Congress of the United States assembled be requisite.

Article XI. Canada acceding to this confederation, and adjoining in the measures of the united States, shall be admitted into, and entitled to all the advantages of this union; but no other colony shall be admitted into the same, unless such admission be agreed to by nine States.

Article XII. All bills of credit emitted, monies borrowed, and debts contracted by, or under the authority of congress, before the assembling of the united States, in pursuance of the present confederation, shall be deemed and considered as a charge against the United States, for payment and satisfaction whereof the said united States, and the public faith are hereby solemnly pledged.

Article XIII. Every State shall abide by the determination of the united States in congress assembled, on all questions which by this confederation are submitted to them. And the Articles of this confederation shall be inviolably observed by every State, and the union shall be perpetual; nor shall any alteration at any time hereafter be made in any of them; unless such alteration be agreed to in a congress of the united States, and be afterwards confirmed by the legislatures of every State.

And Whereas it hath pleased the Great Governor of the World to incline the hearts of the legislatures we respectively represent in Congress, to approve of, and to authorize us to ratify the said articles of confederation and perpetual union. Know Ye that we the undersigned delegates, by virtue of the power and authority to us given for that purpose, do by these presents, in the name and in behalf of our respective constituents, fully and entirely ratify and confirm each and every of the said articles of confederation and perpetual union, and all and singular the matters and things therein contained: And we do further solemnly plight and engage the faith of our respective constituents, that they shall abide by the determinations of the united States in congress assembled, on all questions, which by the said confederation are submitted to them. And that the articles thereof shall be inviolably observed by the States we respectively represent, and that the union shall be perpetual.

In Witness whereof we have hereunto set our hands in Congress. Done at Philadelphia in the State of Pennsylvania the ninth Day of July in the Year of our Lord one thousand seven Hundred and Seventy-eight, and in the Third Year of the independence of America.

On the part and behalf of the State of New Hampshire:
Josiah Bartlett
John Wentworth Junr. August 8th 1778

On the part and behalf of The State of Massachusetts Bay:
John Hancock
Samuel Adams
Elbridge Gerry
Francis Dana
James Lovell
Samuel Holten

On the part and behalf of the State of Rhode Island and Providence Plantations:
William Ellery
Henry Marchant
John Collins

On the part and behalf of the State of Connecticut:
Roger Sherman
Samuel Huntington
Oliver Wolcott
Titus Hosmer
Andrew Adams

On the Part and Behalf of the State of New York:
James Duane
Francis Lewis
Wm Duer
Gouv Morris

On the Part and in Behalf of the State of New Jersey, November 26, 1778.
Jno Witherspoon
Nath. Scudder

On the part and behalf of the State of Pennsylvania:
Robt Morris
Daniel Roberdeau
John Bayard Smith
William Clingan
Joseph Reed 22nd July 1778

On the part and behalf of the State of Delaware:
Tho Mckean February 12, 1779
John Dickinson May 5th 1779
Nicholas Van Dyke

On the part and behalf of the State of Maryland:
John Hanson March 1 1781
Daniel Carroll

On the Part and Behalf of the State of Virginia:
Richard Henry Lee

John Banister
Thomas Adams
Jno Harvie
Francis Lightfoot Lee

On the part and Behalf of the State of No Carolina:
John Penn July 21st 1778
Corns Harnett
Jno Williams

On the part and behalf of the State of South Carolina:
Henry Laurens
William Henry Drayton
Jno Mathews
Richd Hutson
Thos Heyward Junr

On the part and behalf of the State of Georgia:
Jno Walton 24th July 1778
Edwd Telfair
Edwd Langworthy

U.S. CONSTITUTION

We the People of the United States, in Order to form a more perfect Union, establish Justice, insure domestic Tranquility, provide for the common defence, promote the general Welfare, and secure the Blessings of Liberty to ourselves and our Posterity, do ordain and establish this Constitution for the United States of America.

Article. I

Section. 1. All legislative Powers herein granted shall be vested in a Congress of the United States, which shall consist of a Senate and House of Representatives.

Article. II.

Article III.

Article IV.

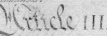

The Constitution of the United States: A Transcription

Note: *The following text is a transcription of the Constitution in its **original** form.*
Items that are hyperlinked have since been amended or superseded.

We the People of the United States, in Order to form a more perfect Union, establish Justice, insure domestic Tranquility, provide for the common defence, promote the general Welfare, and secure the Blessings of Liberty to ourselves and our Posterity, do ordain and establish this Constitution for the United States of America.

Article. I.

Section. 1.

All legislative Powers herein granted shall be vested in a Congress of the United States, which shall consist of a Senate and House of Representatives.

Section. 2.

The House of Representatives shall be composed of Members chosen every second Year by the People of the several States, and the Electors in each State shall have the Qualifications requisite for Electors of the most numerous Branch of the State Legislature.

No Person shall be a Representative who shall not have attained to the Age of twenty five Years, and been seven Years a Citizen of the United States, and who shall not, when elected, be an Inhabitant of that State in which he shall be chosen.

Representatives and direct Taxes shall be apportioned among the several States which may be included within this Union, according to their respective Numbers, which shall be determined by adding to the whole Number of free Persons, including those bound to Service for a Term of Years, and excluding Indians not taxed, three fifths of all other Persons. The actual Enumeration shall be made within three Years after the first Meeting of the Congress of the United States, and within every subsequent Term of ten Years, in such Manner as they shall by Law direct. The Number of Representatives shall not exceed one for every thirty Thousand, but each State shall have at Least one Representative; and until such enumeration shall be made, the State of New Hampshire shall be entitled to chuse three, Massachusetts eight, Rhode-Island and Providence Plantations one, Connecticut five, New-York six, New Jersey four, Pennsylvania eight, Delaware one, Maryland six, Virginia ten, North Carolina five, South Carolina five, and Georgia three.

When vacancies happen in the Representation from any State, the Executive Authority thereof shall issue Writs of Election to fill such Vacancies.

The House of Representatives shall chuse their Speaker and other Officers; and shall have the sole Power of Impeachment.

Section. 3.

The Senate of the United States shall be composed of two Senators from each State, chosen by the Legislature thereof for six Years; and each Senator shall have one Vote.

Immediately after they shall be assembled in Consequence of the first Election, they shall be divided as equally as may be into three Classes. The Seats of the Senators of the first Class shall be vacated at the Expiration of the second Year, of the second Class at the Expiration of the fourth Year, and of the third Class at the Expiration of the sixth Year, so that one third may be chosen every second Year; and if Vacancies happen by Resignation, or otherwise, during the Recess of the Legislature of any State, the Executive thereof may make temporary Appointments until the next Meeting of the Legislature, which shall then fill such Vacancies.

No Person shall be a Senator who shall not have attained to the Age of thirty Years, and been nine Years a Citizen of the United States, and who shall not, when elected, be an Inhabitant of that State for which he shall be chosen.

The Vice President of the United States shall be President of the Senate, but shall have no Vote, unless they be equally divided.

The Senate shall chuse their other Officers, and also a President pro tempore, in the Absence of the Vice President, or when he shall exercise the Office of President of the United States.

The Senate shall have the sole Power to try all Impeachments. When sitting for that Purpose, they shall be on Oath or Affirmation. When the President of the United States is tried, the Chief Justice shall preside: And no Person shall be convicted without the Concurrence of two thirds of the Members present.

Judgment in Cases of Impeachment shall not extend further than to removal from Office, and disqualification to hold and enjoy any Office of honor, Trust or Profit under the United States: but the Party convicted shall nevertheless be liable and subject to Indictment, Trial, Judgment and Punishment, according to Law.

Section. 4.

The Times, Places and Manner of holding Elections for Senators and Representatives, shall be prescribed in each State by the Legislature thereof; but the Congress may at any time by Law make or alter such Regulations, except as to the Places of chusing Senators.

The Congress shall assemble at least once in every Year, and such Meeting shall be on the first Monday in December, unless they shall by Law appoint a different Day.

Section. 5.

Each House shall be the Judge of the Elections, Returns and Qualifications of its own Members, and a Majority of each shall constitute a Quorum to do Business; but a smaller Number may adjourn from day to day, and may be authorized to compel the Attendance of absent Members, in such Manner, and under such Penalties as each House may provide.

Each House may determine the Rules of its Proceedings, punish its Members for disorderly Behaviour, and, with the Concurrence of two thirds, expel a Member.

Each House shall keep a Journal of its Proceedings, and from time to time publish the same, excepting such Parts as may in their Judgment require Secrecy; and the Yeas and Nays of the Members of either House on any question shall, at the Desire of one fifth of those Present, be entered on the Journal.

Neither House, during the Session of Congress, shall, without the Consent of the other, adjourn for more than three days, nor to any other Place than that in which the two Houses shall be sitting.

Section. 6.

The Senators and Representatives shall receive a Compensation for their Services, to be ascertained by Law, and paid out of the Treasury of the United States. They shall in all Cases, except Treason, Felony and Breach of the Peace, be privileged from Arrest during their Attendance at the Session of their respective Houses, and in going to and returning from the same; and for any Speech or Debate in either House, they shall not be questioned in any other Place.

No Senator or Representative shall, during the Time for which he was elected, be appointed to any civil Office under the Authority of the United States, which shall have been created, or the Emoluments whereof shall have been encreased during such time; and no Person holding any Office under the United States, shall be a Member of either House during his Continuance in Office.

Section. 7.

All Bills for raising Revenue shall originate in the House of Representatives; but the Senate may propose or concur with Amendments as on other Bills.

Every Bill which shall have passed the House of Representatives and the Senate, shall, before it become a Law, be presented to the President of the United States: If he approve he shall sign it, but if not he shall return it, with his Objections to that House in which it shall have originated, who shall enter the Objections at large on their Journal, and proceed to reconsider it. If after such Reconsideration two thirds of that House shall agree to pass the Bill, it shall be sent, together with the Objections, to the other House, by which it shall likewise be reconsidered, and if approved by two thirds of that House, it shall become a Law. But in all such Cases the Votes of both Houses shall be determined by yeas and Nays, and the Names of the Persons voting for and against the Bill shall be entered on the Journal of each House respectively. If any Bill shall not be returned by the President within ten Days (Sundays excepted) after it shall have been presented to him, the Same shall be a Law, in like Manner as if he had signed it, unless the Congress by their Adjournment prevent its Return, in which Case it shall not be a Law.

Every Order, Resolution, or Vote to which the Concurrence of the Senate and House of Representatives may be necessary (except on a question of Adjournment) shall be presented to the President of the United States; and before the Same shall take Effect, shall be approved by him, or being disapproved by him, shall be repassed by two thirds of the Senate and House of Representatives, according to the Rules and Limitations prescribed in the Case of a Bill.

Section. 8.

The Congress shall have Power To lay and collect Taxes, Duties, Imposts and Excises, to pay the Debts and provide for the common Defence and general Welfare of the United States; but all Duties, Imposts and Excises shall be uniform throughout the United States;

To borrow Money on the credit of the United States;

To regulate Commerce with foreign Nations, and among the several States, and with the Indian Tribes;

To establish an uniform Rule of Naturalization, and uniform Laws on the subject of Bankruptcies throughout the United States;

To coin Money, regulate the Value thereof, and of foreign Coin, and fix the Standard of Weights and Measures;

To provide for the Punishment of counterfeiting the Securities and current Coin of the United States;

To establish Post Offices and post Roads;

To promote the Progress of Science and useful Arts, by securing for limited Times to Authors and Inventors the exclusive Right to their respective Writings and Discoveries;

To constitute Tribunals inferior to the supreme Court;

To define and punish Piracies and Felonies committed on the high Seas, and Offences against the Law of Nations;

To declare War, grant Letters of Marque and Reprisal, and make Rules concerning Captures on Land and Water;

To raise and support Armies, but no Appropriation of Money to that Use shall be for a longer Term than two Years;

To provide and maintain a Navy;

To make Rules for the Government and Regulation of the land and naval Forces;

To provide for calling forth the Militia to execute the Laws of the Union, suppress Insurrections and repel Invasions;

To provide for organizing, arming, and disciplining, the Militia, and for governing such Part of them as may be employed in the Service of the United States, reserving to the States respectively, the Appointment of the Officers, and the Authority of training the Militia according to the discipline prescribed by Congress;

To exercise exclusive Legislation in all Cases whatsoever, over such District (not exceeding ten Miles square) as may, by Cession of particular States, and the Acceptance of Congress, become the Seat of the Government of the United States, and to exercise like Authority over all Places purchased by the Consent of the Legislature of the State in which the Same shall be, for the Erection of Forts, Magazines, Arsenals, dock-Yards, and other needful Buildings;--And

To make all Laws which shall be necessary and proper for carrying into Execution the foregoing Powers, and all other Powers vested by this Constitution in the Government of the United States, or in any Department or Officer thereof.

Section. 9.

The Migration or Importation of such Persons as any of the States now existing shall think proper to admit, shall not be prohibited by the Congress prior to the Year one thousand eight hundred and eight, but a Tax or duty may be imposed on such Importation, not exceeding ten dollars for each Person.

The Privilege of the Writ of Habeas Corpus shall not be suspended, unless when in Cases of Rebellion or Invasion the public Safety may require it.

No Bill of Attainder or ex post facto Law shall be passed.

No Capitation, or other direct, Tax shall be laid, unless in Proportion to the Census or enumeration herein before directed to be taken.

No Tax or Duty shall be laid on Articles exported from any State.

No Preference shall be given by any Regulation of Commerce or Revenue to the Ports of one State over those of another; nor shall Vessels bound to, or from, one State, be obliged to enter, clear, or pay Duties in another.

No Money shall be drawn from the Treasury, but in Consequence of Appropriations made by Law; and a regular Statement and Account of the Receipts and Expenditures of all public Money shall be published from time to time.

No Title of Nobility shall be granted by the United States: And no Person holding any Office of Profit or Trust under them, shall, without the Consent of the Congress, accept of any present, Emolument, Office, or Title, of any kind whatever, from any King, Prince, or foreign State.

Section. 10.

No State shall enter into any Treaty, Alliance, or Confederation; grant Letters of Marque and Reprisal; coin Money; emit Bills of Credit; make any Thing but gold and silver Coin a Tender in Payment of Debts; pass any Bill of Attainder, ex post facto Law, or Law impairing the Obligation of Contracts, or grant any Title of Nobility.

No State shall, without the Consent of the Congress, lay any Imposts or Duties on Imports or Exports, except what may be absolutely necessary for executing it's inspection Laws: and the net Produce of all Duties and Imposts, laid by any State on Imports or Exports, shall be for the Use of the Treasury of the United States; and all such Laws shall be subject to the Revision and Controul of the Congress.

No State shall, without the Consent of Congress, lay any Duty of Tonnage, keep Troops, or Ships of War in time of Peace, enter into any Agreement or Compact with another State, or with a foreign Power, or engage in War, unless actually invaded, or in such imminent Danger as will not admit of delay.

Article. II.

Section. 1.

The executive Power shall be vested in a President of the United States of America. He shall hold his Office during the Term of four Years, and, together with the Vice President, chosen for the same Term, be elected, as follows:

Each State shall appoint, in such Manner as the Legislature thereof may direct, a Number of Electors, equal to the whole Number of Senators and Representatives to which the State may be entitled in the Congress: but no Senator or Representative, or Person holding an Office of Trust or Profit under the United States, shall be appointed an Elector.

The Electors shall meet in their respective States, and vote by Ballot for two Persons, of whom one at least shall not be an Inhabitant of the same State with themselves. And they shall make a List of all the Persons voted for, and of the Number of Votes for each; which List they shall sign and certify, and transmit sealed to the Seat of the Government of the United States, directed to the President of the Senate. The President of the Senate shall, in the Presence of the Senate and House of Representatives, open all the Certificates, and the Votes shall then be counted. The Person having the greatest Number of Votes shall be the President, if such Number be a Majority of the whole Number of Electors appointed; and if there be more than one who have such Majority, and have an equal Number of Votes, then the House of Representatives shall immediately chuse by Ballot one of them for President; and if no Person have a Majority, then from the five highest on the List the said House shall in like Manner chuse the President. But in chusing the President, the Votes shall be taken by States, the Representation from each State having one Vote; A quorum for this purpose shall consist of a Member or Members from two thirds of the States, and a Majority of all the States shall be necessary to a Choice. In every Case, after the Choice of the President, the Person having the greatest Number of Votes of the Electors shall be the Vice President. But if there should remain two or more who have equal Votes, the Senate shall chuse from them by Ballot the Vice President.

The Congress may determine the Time of chusing the Electors, and the Day on which they shall give their Votes; which Day shall be the same throughout the United States.

No Person except a natural born Citizen, or a Citizen of the United States, at the time of the Adoption of this Constitution, shall be eligible to the Office of President; neither shall any Person be eligible to that Office who shall not have attained to the Age of thirty five Years, and been fourteen Years a Resident within the United States.

In Case of the Removal of the President from Office, or of his Death, Resignation, or Inability to discharge the Powers and Duties of the said Office, the Same shall devolve on the Vice President, and the Congress may by Law provide for the Case of Removal, Death, Resignation or Inability, both of the President and Vice President, declaring what Officer shall then act as President, and such Officer shall act accordingly, until the Disability be removed, or a President shall be elected.

The President shall, at stated Times, receive for his Services, a Compensation, which shall neither be increased nor diminished during the Period for which he shall have been elected, and he shall not receive within that Period any other Emolument from the United States, or any of them.

Before he enter on the Execution of his Office, he shall take the following Oath or Affirmation:--"I do solemnly swear (or affirm) that I will faithfully execute the Office of President of the United States, and will to the best of my Ability, preserve, protect and defend the Constitution of the United States."

Section. 2.

The President shall be Commander in Chief of the Army and Navy of the United States, and of the Militia of the several States, when called into the actual Service of the United States; he may require the Opinion, in writing, of the principal Officer in each of the executive Departments, upon any Subject relating to the Duties of their respective Offices, and he shall have Power to grant Reprieves and Pardons for Offences against the United States, except in Cases of Impeachment.

He shall have Power, by and with the Advice and Consent of the Senate, to make Treaties, provided two thirds of the Senators present concur; and he shall nominate, and by and with the Advice and Consent of the Senate, shall appoint Ambassadors, other public Ministers and Consuls, Judges of the supreme Court, and all other Officers of the United States, whose Appointments are not herein otherwise provided for, and which shall be established by Law: but the Congress may by Law vest the Appointment of such inferior Officers, as they think proper, in the President alone, in the Courts of Law, or in the Heads of Departments.

The President shall have Power to fill up all Vacancies that may happen during the Recess of the Senate, by granting Commissions which shall expire at the End of their next Session.

Section. 3.

He shall from time to time give to the Congress Information of the State of the Union, and recommend to their Consideration such Measures as he shall judge necessary and expedient; he may, on extraordinary Occasions, convene both Houses, or either of them, and in Case of Disagreement between them, with Respect to the Time of Adjournment, he may adjourn them to such Time as he shall think proper; he shall receive Ambassadors and other public Ministers; he shall take Care that the Laws be faithfully executed, and shall Commission all the Officers of the United States.

Section. 4.

The President, Vice President and all civil Officers of the United States, shall be removed from Office on Impeachment for, and Conviction of, Treason, Bribery, or other high Crimes and Misdemeanors.

Article III.

Section. 1.

The judicial Power of the United States shall be vested in one supreme Court, and in such inferior Courts as the Congress may from time to time ordain and establish. The Judges, both of the supreme and inferior Courts, shall hold their Offices during good Behaviour, and shall, at stated Times, receive for their Services a Compensation, which shall not be diminished during their Continuance in Office.

Section. 2.

The judicial Power shall extend to all Cases, in Law and Equity, arising under this Constitution, the Laws of the United States, and Treaties made, or which shall be made, under their Authority;--to all Cases affecting Ambassadors, other public Ministers and Consuls;--to all Cases of admiralty and maritime Jurisdiction;--to Controversies to which the United States shall be a Party;--to Controversies between two or more States;-- between a State and Citizens of another State,--between Citizens of different States,--between Citizens of the same State claiming Lands under Grants of different States, and between a State, or the Citizens thereof, and foreign States, Citizens or Subjects.

In all Cases affecting Ambassadors, other public Ministers and Consuls, and those in which a State shall be Party, the supreme Court shall have original Jurisdiction. In all the other Cases before mentioned, the supreme Court shall have appellate Jurisdiction, both as to Law and Fact, with such Exceptions, and under such Regulations as the Congress shall make.

The Trial of all Crimes, except in Cases of Impeachment, shall be by Jury; and such Trial shall be held in the State where the said Crimes shall have been committed; but when not committed within any State, the Trial shall be at such Place or Places as the Congress may by Law have directed.

Section. 3.

Treason against the United States, shall consist only in levying War against them, or in adhering to their Enemies, giving them Aid and Comfort. No Person shall be convicted of Treason unless on the Testimony of two Witnesses to the same overt Act, or on Confession in open Court.

The Congress shall have Power to declare the Punishment of Treason, but no Attainder of Treason shall work Corruption of Blood, or Forfeiture except during the Life of the Person attainted.

Article. IV.

Section. 1.

Full Faith and Credit shall be given in each State to the public Acts, Records, and judicial Proceedings of every other State. And the Congress may by general Laws prescribe the Manner in which such Acts, Records and Proceedings shall be proved, and the Effect thereof.

Section. 2.

The Citizens of each State shall be entitled to all Privileges and Immunities of Citizens in the several States.

A Person charged in any State with Treason, Felony, or other Crime, who shall flee from Justice, and be found in another State, shall on Demand of the executive Authority of the State from which he fled, be delivered up, to be removed to the State having Jurisdiction of the Crime.

No Person held to Service or Labour in one State, under the Laws thereof, escaping into another, shall, in Consequence of any Law or Regulation therein, be discharged from such Service or Labour, but shall be delivered up on Claim of the Party to whom such Service or Labour may be due.

Section. 3.

New States may be admitted by the Congress into this Union; but no new State shall be formed or erected within the Jurisdiction of any other State; nor any State be formed by the Junction of two or more States, or Parts of States, without the Consent of the Legislatures of the States concerned as well as of the Congress.

The Congress shall have Power to dispose of and make all needful Rules and Regulations respecting the Territory or other Property belonging to the United States; and nothing in this Constitution shall be so construed as to Prejudice any Claims of the United States, or of any particular State.

Section. 4.

The United States shall guarantee to every State in this Union a Republican Form of Government, and shall protect each of them against Invasion; and on Application of the Legislature, or of the Executive (when the Legislature cannot be convened), against domestic Violence.

Article. V.

The Congress, whenever two thirds of both Houses shall deem it necessary, shall propose Amendments to this Constitution, or, on the Application of the Legislatures of two thirds of the several States, shall call a Convention for proposing Amendments, which, in either Case, shall be valid to all Intents and Purposes, as Part of this Constitution, when ratified by the Legislatures of three fourths of the several States, or by Conventions in three fourths thereof, as the one or the other Mode of Ratification may be proposed by the Congress; Provided that no Amendment which may be made prior to the Year One thousand eight hundred and eight shall in any Manner affect the first and fourth Clauses in the Ninth Section of the first Article; and that no State, without its Consent, shall be deprived of its equal Suffrage in the Senate.

Article. VI.

All Debts contracted and Engagements entered into, before the Adoption of this Constitution, shall be as valid against the United States under this Constitution, as under the Confederation.

This Constitution, and the Laws of the United States which shall be made in Pursuance thereof; and all Treaties made, or which shall be made, under the Authority of the United States, shall be the supreme Law of the Land; and the Judges in every State shall be bound thereby, any Thing in the Constitution or Laws of any State to the Contrary notwithstanding.

The Senators and Representatives before mentioned, and the Members of the several State Legislatures, and all executive and judicial Officers, both of the United States and of the several States, shall be bound by Oath or Affirmation, to support this Constitution; but no religious Test shall ever be required as a Qualification to any Office or public Trust under the United States.

Article. VII.

The Ratification of the Conventions of nine States, shall be sufficient for the Establishment of this Constitution between the States so ratifying the Same.

The Word, "the," being interlined between the seventh and eighth Lines of the first Page, the Word "Thirty" being partly written on an Erazure in the fifteenth Line of the first Page, The Words "is tried" being interlined between the thirty second and thirty third Lines of the first Page and the Word "the" being interlined between the forty third and forty fourth Lines of the second Page.

Attest William Jackson Secretary

done in Convention by the Unanimous Consent of the States present the Seventeenth Day of September in the Year of our Lord one thousand seven hundred and Eighty seven and of the Independance of the United States of America the Twelfth In witness whereof We have hereunto subscribed our Names,

G°. Washington
Presidt and deputy from Virginia

Delaware
Geo: Read
Gunning Bedford jun
John Dickinson
Richard Bassett
Jaco: Broom

Maryland
James McHenry
Dan of St Thos. Jenifer
Danl. Carroll

Virginia
John Blair
James Madison Jr.

North Carolina
Wm. Blount
Richd. Dobbs Spaight
Hu Williamson

South Carolina
J. Rutledge
Charles Cotesworth Pinckney
Charles Pinckney
Pierce Butler

Georgia
William Few
Abr Baldwin

New Hampshire
John Langdon
Nicholas Gilman

Massachusetts
Nathaniel Gorham
Rufus King

Connecticut
Wm. Saml. Johnson
Roger Sherman

New York
Alexander Hamilton

New Jersey
Wil: Livingston
David Brearley
Wm. Paterson
Jona: Dayton

Pennsylvania
B Franklin
Thomas Mifflin
Robt. Morris
Geo. Clymer
Thos. FitzSimons
Jared Ingersoll
James Wilson
Gouv Morris

The Bill of Rights: A Transcription

The Preamble to The Bill of Rights

Congress of the United States begun and held at the City of New-York, on Wednesday the fourth of March, one thousand seven hundred and eighty nine.

THE Conventions of a number of the States, having at the time of their adopting the Constitution, expressed a desire, in order to prevent misconstruction or abuse of its powers, that further declaratory and restrictive clauses should be added: And as extending the ground of public confidence in the Government, will best ensure the beneficent ends of its institution.

RESOLVED by the Senate and House of Representatives of the United States of America, in Congress assembled, two thirds of both Houses concurring, that the following Articles be proposed to the Legislatures of the several States, as amendments to the Constitution of the United States, all, or any of which Articles, when ratified by three fourths of the said Legislatures, to be valid to all intents and purposes, as part of the said Constitution; viz.

ARTICLES in addition to, and Amendment of the Constitution of the United States of America, proposed by Congress, and ratified by the Legislatures of the several States, pursuant to the fifth Article of the original Constitution.

Note: The following text is a transcription of the first ten amendments to the Constitution in their original form. These amendments were ratified December 15, 1791, and form what is known as the "Bill of Rights."

Amendment I

Congress shall make no law respecting an establishment of religion, or prohibiting the free exercise thereof; or abridging the freedom of speech, or of the press; or the right of the people peaceably to assemble, and to petition the Government for a redress of grievances.

Amendment II

A well regulated Militia, being necessary to the security of a free State, the right of the people to keep and bear Arms, shall not be infringed.

Amendment III

No Soldier shall, in time of peace be quartered in any house, without the consent of the Owner, nor in time of war, but in a manner to be prescribed by law.

Amendment IV

The right of the people to be secure in their persons, houses, papers, and effects, against unreasonable searches and seizures, shall not be violated, and no Warrants shall issue, but upon probable cause, supported by Oath or affirmation, and particularly describing the place to be searched, and the persons or things to be seized.

Amendment V

No person shall be held to answer for a capital, or otherwise infamous crime, unless on a presentment or indictment of a Grand Jury, except in cases arising in the land or naval forces, or in the Militia, when in actual service in time of War or public danger; nor shall any person be subject for the same offence to be twice put in jeopardy of life or limb; nor shall be compelled in any criminal case to be a witness against himself, nor be deprived of life, liberty, or property, without due process of law; nor shall private property be taken for public use, without just compensation.

Amendment VI

In all criminal prosecutions, the accused shall enjoy the right to a speedy and public trial, by an impartial jury of the State and district wherein the crime shall have been committed, which district shall have been previously ascertained by law, and to be informed of the nature and cause of the accusation; to be confronted with the witnesses against him; to have compulsory process for obtaining witnesses in his favor, and to have the Assistance of Counsel for his defence.

Amendment VII

In Suits at common law, where the value in controversy shall exceed twenty dollars, the right of trial by jury shall be preserved, and no fact tried by a jury, shall be otherwise re-examined in any Court of the United States, than according to the rules of the common law.

Amendment VIII

Excessive bail shall not be required, nor excessive fines imposed, nor cruel and unusual punishments inflicted.

Amendment IX

The enumeration in the Constitution, of certain rights, shall not be construed to deny or disparage others retained by the people.

Amendment X

The powers not delegated to the United States by the Constitution, nor prohibited by it to the States, are reserved to the States respectively, or to the people.

The Constitution: Amendments 11-15

Constitutional Amendments 1-10 make up what is known as The Bill of Rights.

Amendments 11-15 are listed below.

AMENDMENT XI

Passed by Congress March 4, 1794. Ratified February 7, 1795.

Note: Article III, section 2, of the Constitution was modified by amendment 11.

The Judicial power of the United States shall not be construed to extend to any suit in law or equity, commenced or prosecuted against one of the United States by Citizens of another State, or by Citizens or Subjects of any Foreign State.

AMENDMENT XII

Passed by Congress December 9, 1803. Ratified June 15, 1804.

Note: A portion of Article II, section 1 of the Constitution was superseded by the 12th amendment.

The Electors shall meet in their respective states and vote by ballot for President and Vice-President, one of whom, at least, shall not be an inhabitant of the same state with themselves; they shall name in their ballots the person voted for as President, and in distinct ballots the person voted for as Vice-President, and they shall make distinct lists of all persons voted for as President, and of all persons voted for as Vice-President, and of the number of votes for each, which lists they shall sign and certify, and transmit sealed to the seat of the government of the United States, directed to the President of the Senate; -- the President of the Senate shall, in the presence of the Senate and House of Representatives, open all the certificates and the votes shall then be counted; -- The person having the greatest number of votes for President, shall be the President, if such number be a majority of the whole number of Electors appointed; and if no person have such majority, then from the persons having the highest numbers not exceeding three on the list of those voted for as President, the House of Representatives shall choose immediately, by ballot, the President. But in choosing the President, the votes shall be taken by states, the representation from each state having one vote; a quorum for this purpose shall consist of a member or members from two-thirds of the states, and a majority of all the states shall be necessary to a choice. [And if the House of Representatives shall not choose a President whenever the right of choice shall devolve upon them, before the fourth day of March next following, then the Vice-President shall act as President, as in case of the death or other constitutional disability of the President. --]* The person having the greatest number of votes as Vice-President, shall be the Vice-President, if such number be a majority of the whole number of Electors appointed, and if no person have a majority, then from the two highest numbers on the list, the Senate shall choose the Vice-President; a quorum for the purpose shall consist of two-thirds of the whole number of Senators, and a majority of the whole number shall be necessary to a choice. But no person constitutionally ineligible to the office of President shall be eligible to that of Vice-President of the United States.

*Superseded by section 3 of the 20th amendment.

AMENDMENT XIII

Passed by Congress January 31, 1865. Ratified December 6, 1865.

Note: A portion of Article IV, section 2, of the Constitution was superseded by the 13th amendment.

Section 1.
Neither slavery nor involuntary servitude, except as a punishment for crime whereof the party shall have been duly convicted, shall exist within the United States, or any place subject to their jurisdiction.

Section 2.
Congress shall have power to enforce this article by appropriate legislation.

AMENDMENT XIV

Passed by Congress June 13, 1866. Ratified July 9, 1868.

Note: Article I, section 2, of the Constitution was modified by section 2 of the 14th amendment.

Section 1.

All persons born or naturalized in the United States, and subject to the jurisdiction thereof, are citizens of the United States and of the State wherein they reside. No State shall make or enforce any law which shall abridge the privileges or immunities of citizens of the United States; nor shall any State deprive any person of life, liberty, or property, without due process of law; nor deny to any person within its jurisdiction the equal protection of the laws.

Section 2.

Representatives shall be apportioned among the several States according to their respective numbers, counting the whole number of persons in each State, excluding Indians not taxed. But when the right to vote at any election for the choice of electors for President and Vice-President of the United States, Representatives in Congress, the Executive and Judicial officers of a State, or the members of the Legislature thereof, is denied to any of the male inhabitants of such State, being twenty-one years of age,* and citizens of the United States, or in any way abridged, except for participation in rebellion, or other crime, the basis of representation therein shall be reduced in the proportion which the number of such male citizens shall bear to the whole number of male citizens twenty-one years of age in such State.

Section 3.

No person shall be a Senator or Representative in Congress, or elector of President and Vice-President, or hold any office, civil or military, under the United States, or under any State, who, having previously taken an oath, as a member of Congress, or as an officer of the United States, or as a member of any State legislature, or as an executive or judicial officer of any State, to support the Constitution of the United States, shall have engaged in insurrection or rebellion against the same, or given aid or comfort to the enemies thereof. But Congress may by a vote of two-thirds of each House, remove such disability.

Section 4.

The validity of the public debt of the United States, authorized by law, including debts incurred for payment of pensions and bounties for services in suppressing insurrection or rebellion, shall not be questioned. But neither the United States nor any State shall assume or pay any debt or obligation incurred in aid of insurrection or rebellion against the United States, or any claim for the loss or emancipation of any slave; but all such debts, obligations and claims shall be held illegal and void.

Section 5.

The Congress shall have the power to enforce, by appropriate legislation, the provisions of this article.

Changed by section 1 of the 26th amendment.

AMENDMENT XV

Passed by Congress February 26, 1869. Ratified February 3, 1870.

Section 1.

The right of citizens of the United States to vote shall not be denied or abridged by the United States or by any State on account of race, color, or previous condition of servitude--

Section 2.

The Congress shall have the power to enforce this article by appropriate legislation.

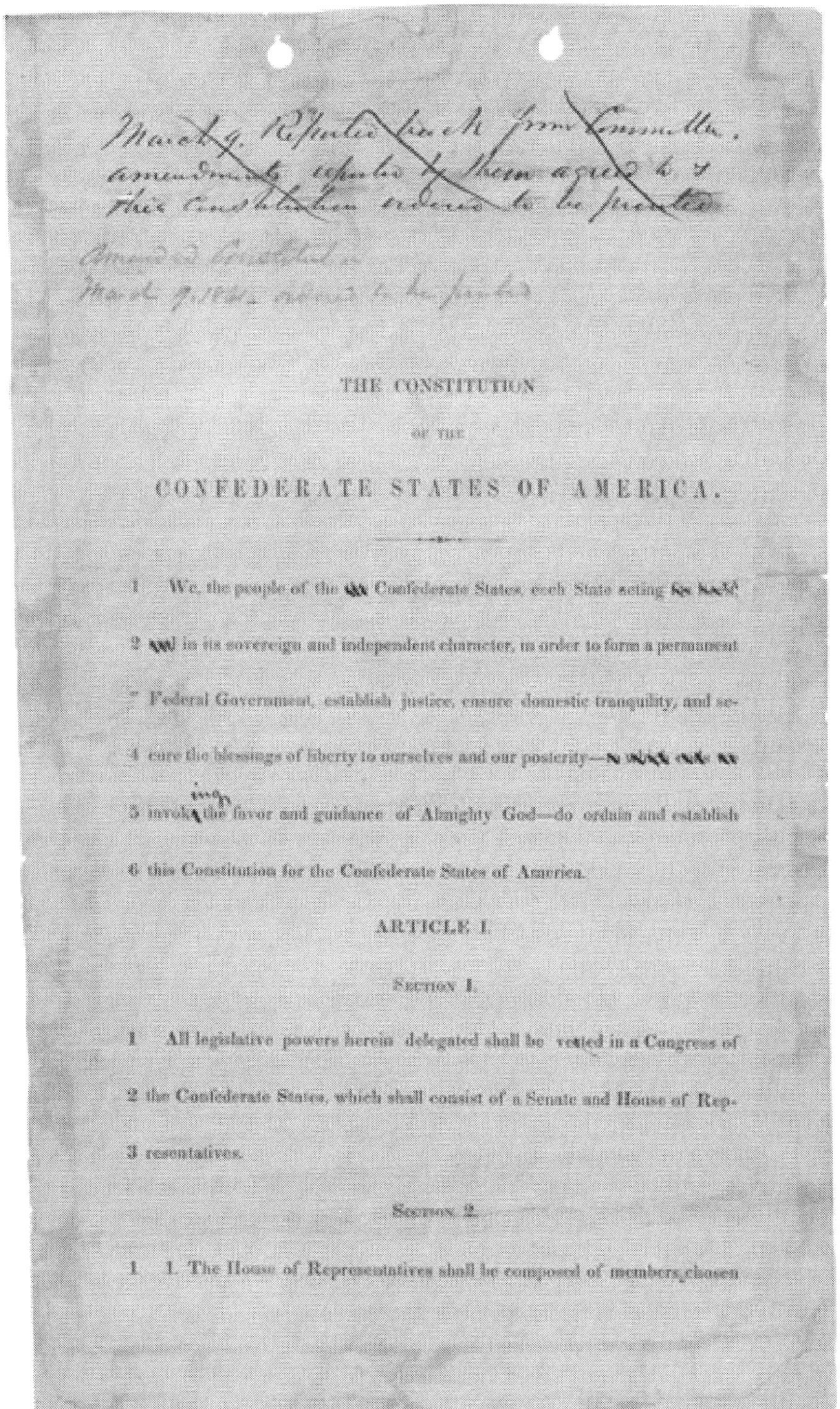

THE CONSTITUTION

OF THE

CONFEDERATE STATES OF AMERICA.

We, the people of the Confederate States, each State acting in its sovereign and independent character, in order to form a permanent Federal Government, establish justice, ensure domestic tranquility, and secure the blessings of liberty to ourselves and our posterity— invoking the favor and guidance of Almighty God—do ordain and establish this Constitution for the Confederate States of America.

ARTICLE I.

SECTION 1.

All legislative powers herein delegated shall be vested in a Congress of the Confederate States, which shall consist of a Senate and House of Representatives.

SECTION 2.

1. The House of Representatives shall be composed of members chosen

Constitution of the Confederate States of America

Preamble

We, the people of the Confederate States, each State acting in its sovereign and independent character, in order to form a permanent federal government, establish justice, insure domestic tranquillity, and secure the blessings of liberty to ourselves and our posterity — invoking the favor and guidance of Almighty God — do ordain and establish this Constitution for the Confederate States of America.

Article 1. - The Legislative Branch

Section 1 - The Legislature

1. All legislative powers herein delegated shall be vested in a Congress of the Confederate States, which shall consist of a Senate and House of Representatives.

Section 2 - The House

1. The House of Representatives shall be composed of members chosen every second year by the people of the several States; and the electors in each State shall be citizens of the Confederate States, and have the qualifications requisite for electors of the most numerous branch of the State Legislature; but no person of foreign birth, not a citizen of the Confederate States, shall be allowed to vote for any officer, civil or political, State or Federal.

2. No person shall be a Representative who shall not have attained the age of twenty-five years, and be a citizen of the Confederate States, and who shall not when elected, be an inhabitant of that State in which he shall be chosen.

3. Representatives and direct taxes shall be apportioned among the several States, which may be included within this Confederacy, according to their respective numbers, which shall be determined by adding to the whole number of free persons, including those bound to service for a term of years, and excluding Indians not taxed, three-fifths of all slaves. The actual enumeration shall be made within three years after the first meeting of the Congress of the Confederate States, and within every subsequent term of ten years, in such manner as they shall by law direct. The number of Representatives shall not exceed one for every fifty thousand, but each State shall have at least one Representative; and until such enumeration shall be made, the State of South Carolina shall be entitled to choose six; the State of Georgia ten; the State of Alabama nine; the State of Florida two; the State of Mississippi seven; the State of Louisiana six; and the State of Texas six.

4. When vacancies happen in the representation from any State the executive authority thereof shall issue writs of election to fill such vacancies.

5. The House of Representatives shall choose their Speaker and other officers; and shall have the sole power of impeachment; except that any judicial or other Federal officer, resident and acting solely within the limits of any State, may be impeached by a vote of two-thirds of both branches of the Legislature thereof.

Section 3 - The Senate

1. The Senate of the Confederate States shall be composed of two Senators from each State, chosen for six years by the Legislature thereof, at the regular session next immediately preceding the commencement of the term of service; and each Senator shall have one vote.

2. Immediately after they shall be assembled, in consequence of the first election, they shall be divided as equally as may be into three classes. The seats of the Senators of the first class shall be vacated at the expiration of the second

year; of the second class at the expiration of the fourth year; and of the third class at the expiration of the sixth year; so that one-third may be chosen every second year; and if vacancies happen by resignation, or other wise, during the recess of the Legislature of any State, the Executive thereof may make temporary appointments until the next meeting of the Legislature, which shall then fill such vacancies.

3. No person shall be a Senator who shall not have attained the age of thirty years, and be a citizen of the Confederate States; and who shall not, then elected, be an inhabitant of the State for which he shall be chosen.

4. The Vice President of the Confederate States shall be president of the Senate, but shall have no vote unless they be equally divided.

5. The Senate shall choose their other officers; and also a president pro tempore in the absence of the Vice President, or when he shall exercise the office of President of the Confederate states.

6. The Senate shall have the sole power to try all impeachments. When sitting for that purpose, they shall be on oath or affirmation. When the President of the Confederate States is tried, the Chief Justice shall preside; and no person shall be convicted without the concurrence of two-thirds of the members present.

7. Judgment in cases of impeachment shall not extend further than to removal from office, and disqualification to hold any office of honor, trust, or profit under the Confederate States; but the party convicted shall, nevertheless, be liable and subject to indictment, trial, judgment, and punishment according to law.

Section 4 - Elections, Meetings

1. The times, places, and manner of holding elections for Senators and Representatives shall be prescribed in each State by the Legislature thereof, subject to the provisions of this Constitution; but the Congress may, at any time, by law, make or alter such regulations, except as to the times and places of choosing Senators.

2. The Congress shall assemble at least once in every year; and such meeting shall be on the first Monday in December, unless they shall, by law, appoint a different day.

Section 5 - Membership, Rules, Journals, Adjournment

1. Each House shall be the judge of the elections, returns, and qualifications of its own members, and a majority of each shall constitute a quorum to do business; but a smaller number may adjourn from day to day, and may be authorized to compel the attendance of absent members, in such manner and under such penalties as each House may provide.

2. Each House may determine the rules of its proceedings, punish its members for disorderly behavior, and, with the concurrence of two-thirds of the whole number, expel a member.

3. Each House shall keep a journal of its proceedings, and from time to time publish the same, excepting such parts as may in their judgment require secrecy; and the yeas and nays of the members of either House, on any question, shall, at the desire of one-fifth of those present, be entered on the journal.

4. Neither House, during the session of Congress, shall, without the consent of the other, adjourn for more than three days, nor to any other place than that in which the two Houses shall be sitting.

Section 6 - Compensation

1. The Senators and Representatives shall receive a compensation for their services, to be ascertained by law, and paid out of the Treasury of the Confederate States. They shall, in all cases, except treason, felony, and breach of the

peace, be privileged from arrest during their attendance at the session of their respective Houses, and in going to and returning from the same; and for any speech or debate in either House, they shall not be questioned in any other place. No Senator or Representative shall, during the time for which he was elected, be appointed to any civil office under the authority of the Confederate States, which shall have been created, or the emoluments whereof shall have been increased during such time; and no person holding any office under the Confederate States shall be a member of either House during his continuance in office. But Congress may, by law, grant to the principal officer in each of the Executive Departments a seat upon the floor of either House, with the privilege of discussing any measures appertaining to his department.

Section 7 - Revenue Bills, Legislative Process, Presidential Veto

1. All bills for raising revenue shall originate in the House of Representatives; but the Senate may propose or concur with amendments, as on other bills.

2. Every bill which shall have passed both Houses, shall, before it becomes a law, be presented to the President of the Confederate States; if he approve, he shall sign it; but if not, he shall return it, with his objections, to that House in which it shall have originated, who shall enter the objections at large on their journal, and proceed to reconsider it. If, after such reconsideration, two-thirds of that House shall agree to pass the bill, it shall be sent, together with the objections, to the other House, by which it shall likewise be reconsidered, and if approved by two-thirds of that House, it shall become a law. But in all such cases, the votes of both Houses shall be determined by yeas and nays, and the names of the persons voting for and against the bill shall be entered on the journal of each House respectively. If any bill shall not be returned by the President within ten days (Sundays excepted) after it shall have been presented to him, the same shall be a law, in like manner as if he had signed it, unless the Congress, by their adjournment, prevent its return; in which case it shall not be a law. The President may approve any appropriation and disapprove any other appropriation in the same bill. In such case he shall, in signing the bill, designate the appropriations disapproved; and shall return a copy of such appropriations, with his objections, to the House in which the bill shall have originated; and the same proceedings shall then be had as in case of other bills disapproved by the President.

3. Every order, resolution, or vote, to which the concurrence of both Houses may be necessary (except on a question of adjournment) shall be presented to the President of the Confederate States; and before the same shall take effect, shall be approved by him; or, being disapproved by him, shall be repassed by two-thirds of both Houses, according to the rules and limitations prescribed in case of a bill.

Section 8 - Powers of Congress

The Congress shall have power -

1. To lay and collect taxes, duties, imposts, and excises for revenue, necessary to pay the debts, provide for the common defense, and carry on the Government of the Confederate States; but no bounties shall be granted from the Treasury; nor shall any duties or taxes on importations from foreign nations be laid to promote or foster any branch of industry; and all duties, imposts, and excises shall be uniform throughout the Confederate States.

2. To borrow money on the credit of the Confederate States.

3. To regulate commerce with foreign nations, and among the several States, and with the Indian tribes; but neither this, nor any other clause contained in the Constitution, shall ever be construed to delegate the power to Congress to appropriate money for any internal improvement intended to facilitate commerce; except for the purpose of furnishing lights, beacons, and buoys, and other aids to navigation upon the coasts, and the improvement of harbors and the removing of obstructions in river navigation; in all which cases such duties shall be laid on the navigation facilitated thereby as may be necessary to pay the costs and expenses thereof.

4. To establish uniform laws of naturalization, and uniform laws on the subject of bankruptcies, throughout the Confederate States; but no law of Congress shall discharge any debt contracted before the passage of the same.

5. To coin money, regulate the value thereof, and of foreign coin, and fix the standard of weights and measures.

6. To provide for the punishment of counterfeiting the securities and current coin of the Confederate States.

7. To establish post offices and post routes; but the expenses of the Post Office Department, after the 1st day of March in the year of our Lord eighteen hundred and sixty-three, shall be paid out of its own revenues.

8. To promote the progress of science and useful arts, by securing for limited times to authors and inventors the exclusive right to their respective writings and discoveries.

9. To constitute tribunals inferior to the Supreme Court.

10. To define and punish piracies and felonies committed on the high seas, and offenses against the law of nations.

11. To declare war, grant letters of marque and reprisal, and make rules concerning captures on land and water.

12. To raise and support armies; but no appropriation of money to that use shall be for a longer term than two years.

13. To provide and maintain a navy.

14. To make rules for the government and regulation of the land and naval forces.

15. To provide for calling forth the militia to execute the laws of the Confederate States, suppress insurrections, and repel invasions.

16. To provide for organizing, arming, and disciplining the militia, and for governing such part of them as may be employed in the service of the Confederate States; reserving to the States, respectively, the appointment of the officers, and the authority of training the militia according to the discipline prescribed by Congress.

17. To exercise exclusive legislation, in all cases whatsoever, over such district (not exceeding ten miles square) as may, by cession of one or more States and the acceptance of Congress, become the seat of the Government of the Confederate States; and to exercise like authority over all places purchased by the consent of the Legislature of the State in which the same shall be, for the erection of forts, magazines, arsenals, dockyards, and other needful buildings; and

18. To make all laws which shall be necessary and proper for carrying into execution the foregoing powers, and all other powers vested by this Constitution in the Government of the Confederate States, or in any department or officer thereof.

Section 9 - Limits on Congress, Bill of Rights

1. The importation of negroes of the African race from any foreign country other than the slaveholding States or Territories of the United States of America, is hereby forbidden; and Congress is required to pass such laws as shall effectually prevent the same.

2. Congress shall also have power to prohibit the introduction of slaves from any State not a member of, or Territory not belonging to, this Confederacy.

3. The privilege of the writ of habeas corpus shall not be suspended, unless when in cases of rebellion or invasion the public safety may require it.

4. No bill of attainder, ex post facto law, or law denying or impairing the right of property in negro slaves shall be passed.

5. No capitation or other direct tax shall be laid, unless in proportion to the census or enumeration hereinbefore directed to be taken.

6. No tax or duty shall be laid on articles exported from any State, except by a vote of two-thirds of both Houses.

7. No preference shall be given by any regulation of commerce or revenue to the ports of one State over those of another.

8. No money shall be drawn from the Treasury, but in consequence of appropriations made by law; and a regular statement and account of the receipts and expenditures of all public money shall be published from time to time.

9. Congress shall appropriate no money from the Treasury except by a vote of two-thirds of both Houses, taken by yeas and nays, unless it be asked and estimated for by some one of the heads of departments and submitted to Congress by the President; or for the purpose of paying its own expenses and contingencies; or for the payment of claims against the Confederate States, the justice of which shall have been judicially declared by a tribunal for the investigation of claims against the Government, which it is hereby made the duty of Congress to establish.

10. All bills appropriating money shall specify in Federal currency the exact amount of each appropriation and the purposes for which it is made; and Congress shall grant no extra compensation to any public contractor, officer, agent, or servant, after such contract shall have been made or such service rendered.

11. No title of nobility shall be granted by the Confederate States; and no person holding any office of profit or trust under them shall, without the consent of the Congress, accept of any present, emolument, office, or title of any kind whatever, from any king, prince, or foreign state.

12. Congress shall make no law respecting an establishment of religion, or prohibiting the free exercise thereof; or abridging the freedom of speech, or of the press; or the right of the people peaceably to assemble and petition the Government for a redress of grievances.

13. A well-regulated militia being necessary to the security of a free State, the right of the people to keep and bear arms shall not be infringed.

14. No soldier shall, in time of peace, be quartered in any house without the consent of the owner; nor in time of war, but in a manner to be prescribed by law.

15. The right of the people to be secure in their persons, houses, papers, and effects, against unreasonable searches and seizures, shall not be violated; and no warrants shall issue but upon probable cause, supported by oath or affirmation, and particularly describing the place to be searched and the persons or things to be seized.

16. No person shall be held to answer for a capital or otherwise infamous crime, unless on a presentment or indictment of a grand jury, except in cases arising in the land or naval forces, or in the militia, when in actual service in time of war or public danger; nor shall any person be subject for the same offense to be twice put in jeopardy of life or limb; nor be compelled, in any criminal case, to be a witness against himself; nor be deprived of life, liberty, or property without due process of law; nor shall private property be taken for public use, without just compensation.

17. In all criminal prosecutions the accused shall enjoy the right to a speedy and public trial, by an impartial jury of the State and district wherein the crime shall have been committed, which district shall have been previously ascertained by law, and to be informed of the nature and cause of the accusation; to be confronted with the witnesses

against him; to have compulsory process for obtaining witnesses in his favor; and to have the assistance of counsel for his defense.

18. In suits at common law, where the value in controversy shall exceed twenty dollars, the right of trial by jury shall be preserved; and no fact so tried by a jury shall be otherwise reexamined in any court of the Confederacy, than according to the rules of common law.

19. Excessive bail shall not be required, nor excessive fines imposed, nor cruel and unusual punishments inflicted.

20. Every law, or resolution having the force of law, shall relate to but one subject, and that shall be expressed in the title.

Section 10 - Powers prohibited of States

1. No State shall enter into any treaty, alliance, or confederation; grant letters of marque and reprisal; coin money; make anything but gold and silver coin a tender in payment of debts; pass any bill of attainder, or ex post facto law, or law impairing the obligation of contracts; or grant any title of nobility.

2. No State shall, without the consent of the Congress, lay any imposts or duties on imports or exports, except what may be absolutely necessary for executing its inspection laws; and the net produce of all duties and imposts, laid by any State on imports, or exports, shall be for the use of the Treasury of the Confederate States; and all such laws shall be subject to the revision and control of Congress.

3. No State shall, without the consent of Congress, lay any duty on tonnage, except on seagoing vessels, for the improvement of its rivers and harbors navigated by the said vessels; but such duties shall not conflict with any treaties of the Confederate States with foreign nations; and any surplus revenue thus derived shall, after making such improvement, be paid into the common treasury. Nor shall any State keep troops or ships of war in time of peace, enter into any agreement or compact with another State, or with a foreign power, or engage in war, unless actually invaded, or in such imminent danger as will not admit of delay. But when any river divides or flows through two or more States they may enter into compacts with each other to improve the navigation thereof.

Article 2. - The Executive Branch

Section 1 - The President

1. The executive power shall be vested in a President of the Confederate States of America. He and the Vice President shall hold their offices for the term of six years; but the President shall not be reeligible. The President and Vice President shall be elected as follows:

2. Each State shall appoint, in such manner as the Legislature thereof may direct, a number of electors equal to the whole number of Senators and Representatives to which the State may be entitled in the Congress; but no Senator or Representative or person holding an office of trust or profit under the Confederate States shall be appointed an elector.

3. The electors shall meet in their respective States and vote by ballot for President and Vice President, one of whom, at least, shall not be an inhabitant of the same State with themselves; they shall name in their ballots the person voted for as President, and in distinct ballots the person voted for as Vice President, and they shall make distinct lists of all persons voted for as President, and of all persons voted for as Vice President, and of the number of votes for each, which lists they shall sign and certify, and transmit, sealed, to the seat of the Government of. the Confederate States, directed to the President of the Senate; the President of the Senate shall,in the presence of the Senate and House of

Representatives, open all the certificates, and the votes shall then be counted; the person having the greatest number of votes for President shall be the President, if such number be a majority of the whole number of electors appointed; and if no person have such majority, then from the persons having the highest numbers, not exceeding three, on the list of those voted for as President, the House of Representatives shall choose immediately, by ballot, the President. But in choosing the President the votes shall be taken by States ~ the representation from each State having one vote; a quorum for this purpose shall consist of a member or members from two-thirds of the States, and a majority of all the States shall be necessary to a choice. And if the House of Representatives shall not choose a President, whenever the right of choice shall devolve upon them, before the 4th day of March next following, then the Vice President shall act as President, as in case of the death, or other constitutional disability of the President.

4. The person having the greatest number of votes as Vice President shall be the Vice President, if such number be a majority of the whole number of electors appointed; and if no person have a majority, then, from the two highest numbers on the list, the Senate shall choose the Vice President; a quorum for the purpose shall consist of two-thirds of the whole number of Senators, and a majority of the whole number shall be necessary to a choice.

5. But no person constitutionally ineligible to the office of President shall be eligible to that of Vice President of the Confederate States.

6. The Congress may determine the time of choosing the electors, and the day on which they shall give their votes; which day shall be the same throughout the Confederate States.

7. No person except a natural-born citizen of the Confederate; States, or a citizen thereof at the time of the adoption of this Constitution, or a citizen thereof born in the United States prior to the 20th of December, 1860, shall be eligible to the office of President; neither shall any person be eligible to that office who shall not have attained the age of thirty-five years, and been fourteen years a resident within the limits of the Confederate States, as they may exist at the time of his election.

8. In case of the removal of the President from office, or of his death, resignation, or inability to discharge the powers and duties of said office, the same shall devolve on the Vice President; and the Congress may, by law, provide for the case of removal, death, resignation, or inability, both of the President and Vice President, declaring what officer shall then act as President; and such officer shall act accordingly until the disability be removed or a President shall be elected.

9. The President shall, at stated times, receive for his services a compensation, which shall neither be increased nor diminished during the period for which he shall have been elected; and he shall not receive within that period any other emolument from the Confederate States, or any of them.

10. Before he enters on the execution of his office he shall take the following oath or affirmation: "I do solemnly swear (or affirm) that I will faithfully execute the office of President of the Confederate States, and will, to the best of my ability, preserve, protect, and defend the Constitution thereof."

Section 2 - Civilian Power over Military, Cabinet, Pardon Power, Appointments

1. The President shall be Commander-in-Chief of the Army and Navy of the Confederate States, and of the militia of the several States, when called into the actual service of the Confederate States; he may require the opinion, in writing, of the principal officer in each of the Executive Departments, upon any subject relating to the duties of their respective offices; and he shall have power to grant reprieves and pardons for offenses against the Confederate States, except in cases of impeachment.

2. He shall have power, by and with the advice and consent of the Senate, to make treaties; provided two-thirds of the Senators present concur; and he shall nominate, and by and with the advice and consent of the Senate shall appoint, ambassadors, other public ministers and consuls, judges of the Supreme Court, and all other officers of the Confederate States whose appointments are not herein otherwise provided for, and which shall be established by law; but the Congress may, by law, vest the appointment of such inferior officers, as they think proper, in the President alone, in the courts of law, or in the heads of departments.

3. The principal officer in each of the Executive Departments, and all persons connected with the diplomatic service, may be removed from office at the pleasure of the President. All other civil officers of the Executive Departments may be removed at any time by the President, or other appointing power, when their services are unnecessary, or for dishonesty, incapacity. inefficiency, misconduct, or neglect of duty; and when so removed, the removal shall be reported to the Senate, together with the reasons therefor.

4. The President shall have power to fill all vacancies that may happen during the recess of the Senate, by granting commissions which shall expire at the end of their next session; but no person rejected by the Senate shall be reappointed to the same office during their ensuing recess.

Section 3 - State of the Union, Convening Congress

1. The President shall, from time to time, give to the Congress information of the state of the Confederacy, and recommend to their consideration such measures as he shall judge necessary and expedient; he may, on extraordinary occasions, convene both Houses, or either of them; and in case of disagreement between them, with respect to the time of adjournment, he may adjourn them to such time as he shall think proper; he shall receive ambassadors and other public ministers; he shall take care that the laws be faithfully executed, and shall commission all the officers of the Confederate States.

Section 4 - Disqualification

1. The President, Vice President, and all civil officers of the Confederate States, shall be removed from office on impeachment for and conviction of treason, bribery, or other high crimes and misdemeanors.

Article 3. - The Judicial Branch

Section 1 - Judicial powers

1. The judicial power of the Confederate States shall be vested in one Supreme Court, and in such inferior courts as the Congress may, from time to time, ordain and establish. The judges, both of the Supreme and inferior courts, shall hold their offices during good behavior, and shall, at stated times, receive for their services a compensation which shall not be diminished during their continuance in office.

Section 2 - Trial by Jury, Original Jurisdiction, Jury Trials

1. The judicial power shall extend to all cases arising under this Constitution, the laws of the Confederate States, and treaties made, or which shall be made, under their authority; to all cases affecting ambassadors, other public ministers and consuls; to all cases of admiralty and maritime jurisdiction; to controversies to which the Confederate States shall be a party; to controversies between two or more States; between a State and citizens of another State, where the State is plaintiff; between citizens claiming lands under grants of different States; and between a State or the citizens thereof, and foreign states, citizens, or subjects; but no State shall be sued by a citizen or subject of any foreign state.

2. In all cases affecting ambassadors, other public ministers and consuls, and those in which a State shall be a party, the Supreme Court shall have original jurisdiction. In all the other cases before mentioned, the Supreme Court shall have appellate jurisdiction both as to law and fact, with such exceptions and under such regulations as the Congress shall make.

3. The trial of all crimes, except in cases of impeachment, shall be by jury, and such trial shall be held in the State where the said crimes shall have been committed; but when not committed within any State, the trial shall be at such place or places as the Congress may by law have directed.

Section 3 - Treason

1. Treason against the Confederate States shall consist only in levying war against them, or in adhering to their enemies, giving them aid and comfort. No person shall be convicted of treason unless on the testimony of two witnesses to the same overt act, or on confession in open court.

2. The Congress shall have power to declare the punishment of treason; but no attainder of treason shall work corruption of blood, or forfeiture, except during the life of the person attainted.

Article 4. - The States

Section 1 - Each State to Honor all others

1. Full faith and credit shall be given in each State to the public acts, records, and judicial proceedings of every other State; and the Congress may, by general laws, prescribe the manner in which such acts, records, and proceedings shall be proved, and the effect thereof.

Section 2 - State citizens, Extradition

1. The citizens of each State shall be entitled to all the privileges and immunities of citizens in the several States; and shall have the right of transit and sojourn in any State of this Confederacy, with their slaves and other property; and the right of property in said slaves shall not be thereby impaired.

2. A person charged in any State with treason, felony, or other crime against the laws of such State, who shall flee from justice, and be found in another State, shall, on demand of the executive authority of the State from which he fled, be delivered up, to be removed to the State having jurisdiction of the crime.

3. No slave or other person held to service or labor in any State or Territory of the Confederate States, under the laws thereof, escaping or lawfully carried into another, shall, in consequence of any law or regulation therein, be discharged from such service or labor; but shall be delivered up on claim of the party to whom such slave belongs; or to whom such service or labor may be due.

Section 3 - New States

1. Other States may be admitted into this Confederacy by a vote of two- thirds of the whole House of Representatives and two-thirds of the Senate, the Senate voting by States; but no new State shall be formed or erected within the jurisdiction of any other State, nor any State be formed by the junction of two or more States, or parts of States, without the consent of the Legislatures of the States concerned, as well as of the Congress.

2. The Congress shall have power to dispose of and make all needful rules and regulations concerning the property of the Confederate States, including the lands thereof.

3. The Confederate States may acquire new territory; and Congress shall have power to legislate and provide governments for the inhabitants of all territory belonging to the Confederate States, lying without the limits of the several Sates; and may permit them, at such times, and in such manner as it may by law provide, to form States to be admitted into the Confederacy. In all such territory the institution of negro slavery, as it now exists in the Confederate States, shall be recognized and protected by Congress and by the Territorial government; and the inhabitants of the several Confederate States and Territories shall have the right to take to such Territory any slaves lawfully held by them in any of the States or Territories of the Confederate States.

4. The Confederate States shall guarantee to every State that now is, or hereafter may become, a member of this Confederacy, a republican form of government; and shall protect each of them against invasion; and on application of the Legislature or of the Executive when the Legislature is not in session) against domestic violence.

Article 5. - Amendment

1. Upon the demand of any three States, legally assembled in their several conventions, the Congress shall summon a convention of all the States, to take into consideration such amendments to the Constitution as the said States shall concur in suggesting at the time when the said demand is made; and should any of the proposed amendments to the Constitution be agreed on by the said convention ~ voting by States ~ and the same be ratified by the Legislatures of two-thirds of the several States, or by conventions in two-thirds thereof ~ as the one or the other mode of ratification may be proposed by the general convention ~ they shall thenceforward form a part of this Constitution. But no State shall, without its consent, be deprived of its equal representation in the Senate.

Article 6. - The Confederacy

Section 1 - Transition from the Provisional Government

1. The Government established by this Constitution is the successor of the Provisional Government of the Confederate States of America, and all the laws passed by the latter shall continue in force until the same shall be repealed or modified; and all the officers appointed by the same shall remain in office until their successors are appointed and qualified, or the offices abolished.

Section 2 - Debts of the Provisional Government

2. All debts contracted and engagements entered into before the adoption of this Constitution shall be as valid against the Confederate States under this Constitution, as under the Provisional Government.

Section 3 - Supremacy of the Constitution

3. This Constitution, and the laws of the Confederate States made in pursuance thereof, and all treaties made, or which shall be made, under the authority of the Confederate States, shall be the supreme law of the land; and the judges in every State shall be bound thereby, anything in the constitution or laws of any State to the contrary notwithstanding.

Section 4 - Oaths of Office

4. The Senators and Representatives before mentioned, and the members of the several State Legislatures, and all executive and judicial officers, both of the Confederate States and of the several States, shall be bound by oath or affirmation to support this Constitution; but no religious test shall ever be required as a qualification to any office or public trust under the Confederate States.

Section 5 - Reservation of unenumerated rights

5. The enumeration, in the Constitution, of certain rights shall not be construed to deny or disparage others retained by the people of the several States.

Section 6 - State powers

6. The powers not delegated to the Confederate States by the Constitution, nor prohibited by it to the States, are reserved to the States, respectively, or to the people thereof.

Article 7. - Ratification

1. The ratification of the conventions of five States shall be sufficient for the establishment of this Constitution between the States so ratifying the same.

2. When five States shall have ratified this Constitution, in the manner before specified, the Congress under the Provisional Constitution shall prescribe the time for holding the election of President and Vice President; and for the meeting of the Electoral College; and for counting the votes, and inaugurating the President. They shall, also, prescribe the time for holding the first election of members of Congress under this Constitution, and the time for assembling the same. Until the assembling of such Congress, the Congress under the Provisional Constitution shall continue to exercise the legislative powers granted them; not extending beyond the time limited by the Constitution of the Provisional Government.

Adopted unanimously by the Congress of the Confederate States of South Carolina, Georgia, Florida, Alabama, Mississippi, Louisiana, and Texas, sitting in Convention at the capitol, in the city of Montgomery, Alabama, on the Eleventh day of March, in the year Eighteen Hundred and Sixty-One.

HOWELL COBB,
President of the Congress.

1. South Carolina: R. Barnwell Rhett, C. G. Memminger, Wm. Porcher Miles, James Chesnut, Jr., R. W. Barnwell, William W. Boyce, Lawrence M. Keitt, T. J. Withers.

2. Georgia: Francis S. Bartow, Martin J. Crawford, Benjamin H. Hill, Thos. R. R. Cobb.

3. Florida: Jackson Morton, J. Patton Anderson, Jas. B. Owens.

4. Alabama: Richard W. Walker, Robt. H. Smith, Colin J. McRae, William P. Chilton, Stephen F. Hale, David P. Lewis, Tho. Fearn, Jno. Gill Shorter, J. L. M. Curry.

5. Mississippi: Alex. M. Clayton, James T. Harrison, William S. Barry, W. S. Wilson, Walker Brooke, W. P. Harris, J. A. P. Campbell.

6. Louisiana: Alex. de Clouet, C. M. Conrad, Duncan F. Kenner, Henry Marshall.

7. Texas: John Hemphill, Thomas N. Waul, John H. Reagan, Williamson S. Oldham, Louis T. Wigfall, John Gregg, William Beck Ochiltree

PRESIDENT	PARTY	TERM AS PRESIDENT	VICE-PRESIDENT
1. George Washington (1732-1799)	None, Federalist	1789-1797	John Adams
2. John Adams (1735-1826)	Federalist	1797-1801	Thomas Jefferson
3. Thomas Jefferson (1743-1826)	Democratic-Republican	1801-1809	Aaron Burr, George Clinton
4. James Madison (1751-1836)	Democratic-Republican	1809-1817	George Clinton, Elbridge Gerry
5. James Monroe (1758-1831)	Democratic-Republican	1817-1825	Daniel Tompkins
6. John Quincy Adams (1767-1848)	National Republican	1825-1829	John Calhoun
7. Andrew Jackson (1767-1845)	Democrat	1829-1837	John Calhoun, Martin van Buren
8. Martin van Buren (1782-1862)	Democrat	1837-1841	Richard Johnson
9. William H. Harrison (1773-1841)	Whig	1841	John Tyler
10. John Tyler (1790-1862)	Whig	1841-1845	.
11. James K. Polk (1795-1849)	Democrat	1845-1849	George Dallas
12. Zachary Taylor (1784-1850)	Whig	1849-1850	Millard Fillmore
13. Millard Fillmore (1800-1874)	Whig	1850-1853	.
14. Franklin Pierce (1804-1869)	Democrat	1853-1857	William King
15. James Buchanan (1791-1868)	Democrat	1857-1861	John Breckinridge
16. Abraham Lincoln (1809-1865)	Republican	1861-1865	Hannibal Hamlin, Andrew Johnson
17. Andrew Johnson (1808-1875)	National Union	1865-1869	.
18. Ulysses S. Grant (1822-1885)	Republican	1869-1877	Schuyler Colfax

INDEX